PIMLICO

96

THE AGE OF BATTLES

Russell F. Weigley has taught history at the University of Pennsylvania, Drexel Institute of Technology, Haverford College and Temple University, where he is now the Distinguished University Professor. He has also lectured at all the American military service academies and war colleges. In 1989 he was awarded the Samuel Eliot Morison Prize of the American Military Institute for his contribution to military history. In 1992 *The Ages of Battles* received a Distinguished Book Award from the Society for Military History. Professor Weigley's other books include *History of the United States Army, The American Way of War* and *Eisenhower's Lieutenants: The Campaign of France and Germany, 1944-1945*.

THE AGE OF BATTLES

BATTLES

The Quest for Decisive Warfare from
Breitenfeld to Waterloo

RUSSELL F. WEIGLEY

PIMLICO

PIMLICO

An imprint of Random House
20 Vauxhall Bridge Road, London SW1V 2SA

Random House Australia (Pty) Ltd
20 Alfred Street, Milsons Point, Sydney
New South Wales 2061, Australia

Random House New Zealand Ltd
18 Poland Road, Glenfield
Auckland 10, New Zealand

Random House South Africa (Pty) Ltd
PO Box 337, Bergvlei, South Africa

Random House UK Ltd Reg. No. 954009

First published in the U.S.A. by
Indiana University Press, 1991
First published in Great Britain by Pimlico, 1993

1 3 5 7 9 10 8 6 4 2

Printed and bound in Great Britain by
Mackays of Chatham PLC, Chatham, Kent

ISBN 0-7126-5856-4

CONTENTS

Part Two   THE EIGHTEENTH CENTURY: THE CLASSICAL EPOCH OF MODERN WAR

Part Three THUNDERSTROKES OF BATTLE: THE FRENCH REVOLUTIONARY AND NAPOLEONIC WARS

MAPS

INTRODUCTION

The grand-scale battle, with tens of thousands of soldiers fighting, cursing, trembling, falling, screaming in agony, dying, all in a spectacle covering an amphitheater-like field—this dramatic epitome of war is the chief source of the enduring fascination of military history. The thirst to experience vicariously the intense emotions of battle goes far to explain why books of military history are written and read, however much their authors and readers may profess higher concerns about removing or at least palliating the scourge of war.

In the history of the Western world, the era from Breitenfeld to Waterloo was quintessentially the age of battles: from the triumph gained by Sweden's disciplined infantry brigades and cavalry regiments in the Thirty Years War because those units embodied a new kind of tactical proficiency in both firepower and maneuver, to the downfall of Napoleon when the Emperor's Old Guard, proclaiming it would not surrender, nevertheless died. Following the desultory raiding expeditions and siegecraft that shaped medieval war, and before the nightmare of endless grappling in sodden trenches of the 1864–1865 campaigns of the American Civil War and then of the First World War, the epoch from Breitenfeld in 1631 to Waterloo in 1815 saw the grand-scale battle as the principal instrument of the military strategist, the focus of all his efforts to attain decision in war. And battle in the age from Breitenfeld to Waterloo was perhaps more than in any other era the theatrical spectacle that lends the very word its resonance. Battalions still marched against each other in paradeground formations, brave in bright red or blue or white uniforms trimmed in gold, flags flying, drums rolling, fifes squealing, pipes skirling, bayonets and sabers flashing, horses neighing, the somberly gleaming guns responding with volcanic eruptions of fire from the elaborate ritual dance performed by the artillerists in obeisance to them.

Battles and Decisiveness in War

As the battle is the distillation of the essence of war, however, so the history of the Breitenfeld-to-Waterloo age of battles distills much of the entire human experience of war, to provide us with that instruction in possibilities for taming the scourge of war which ought to accompany indulgence of our fascination with the high drama of battle.

War between 1631 and 1815 revolved around grand-scale battles because, in that age more than any other, the economic, social, and technological circumstances of war permitted the massing of tens of thousands of soldiers on a single field for the test of battle, while at the same time military strategists hoped by means of battle to secure decisions in war, and thereby to secure the objects for which men went to war, with a quickness and dispatch that would keep the costs of war reasonably proportionate to the purposes attained. Earlier, in the Middle Ages, the political, economic, and social context of war had in various ways inhibited the raising and risking of large numbers of men for and in battle, to make the phenomenon of large-scale battle relatively rare. In the nineteenth and twentieth centuries after Waterloo, yet another, different context for war caused the episodes of battle lasting through one or a few days to give way to continuous, unbroken combat over months and years. As long as the grand-scale battle could readily occur, however, strategists focused on it to achieve decision in war. If in a successful battle the enemy army could be substantially destroyed—an outcome not only conceivable but occasionally taking place—then the whole course of a war might be resolved in a single day, and wars thereby might be won at relatively low costs, by avoiding the prolonged expenditure of resources and lives.

Yet the age of battles nevertheless proved to be an age of prolonged, indecisive wars, wars sufficiently interminable that again and again the toll in lives, not to mention the costs in material resources, rose grotesquely out of proportion to anything their authors could hope to gain from them.

The Elusiveness of Decision

One of the most admirable of American military historians was Walter Millis, a founder of the "new" military history that sought to examine war and military institutions not in isolation from other historical phenomena, as earlier military historians too often had done, but as part of the seamless fabric of all history. Millis was admirable particularly because he was also a military historian who took seriously the idea that the historian specializing in war studies bears a special obligation to confront the problem of terminating or at least mitigating war.

Probably Millis's most important book, to this day the best one-volume overview of the military history of the United States, is *Arms and Men: A Study in American Military History*. As part of his effort to grapple with the problem of war, Millis reflected in that book on the age of battles that ended in 1815 with Waterloo. "Waterloo was the final and most decisive of these grim dramas," he said. "It was not often to be repeated [thereafter]. War was beginning to lose its one virtue—its power of decision."[1]

Although he thus commented on pre–1815 war, Millis was concerned primarily with more recent wars. He can be excused therefore for a misjudgment in his

1. Walter Millis, *Arms and Men: A Study in American Military History* (New York: G. P. Putnam's Sons, 1956), p. 78.

quoted remark—and excusing him is imperative because of the general excellence of his military history and the uncommon dedication to remedying the problem of war that he saw as his obligation as a military historian. The misjudgment is his perception of warfare as possessing a power of decision before Waterloo. In fact, war in the age of battles was redeemed by no appreciably greater capacity to produce decisive results at a not-exorbitant cost than in the more recent era or in any other age. Its indecisiveness took different forms than in the trenches of World War I or the guerrilla raids and counterraids of Vietnam, and the drama intrinsic to great battles often diverted attention from indecisiveness; but recalcitrant, intractable indecision nevertheless persisted.

If "its power of decision" was the "one virtue" that war had ever had, then war never had any virtue. If in the age of battles, when the possibility of waging a grand, climactic battle provided at least a hope of deciding the outcome of war promptly and at a cost that might not appear exorbitant, nevertheless that hope could not be realized in the aftermath of battle, then war never possessed a satisfactory power of decision.

To this grim conclusion a history of the age of battles must lead. The best opportunity ever presented for war to offer the virtue of decision at reasonable cost was at a time when its context made possible battles that might conceivably resolve a war in an afternoon. If wars remained incapable of producing decisions at costs proportionate to their objects even then, consequently the whole history of war must be regarded as a history of almost unbroken futility. So it has been.

Further Themes of This Book

Nevertheless, humankind is unlikely to forgo wars in the foreseeable future. And indeed there may be occasions when war, though incapable of yielding positive rewards at reasonable costs, may be the only recourse in defense of some value not to be measured in terms of everyday reasonableness or of cost-effectiveness. These things being true, the study of past wars in general and of the age of battles in particular may retain a certain value beyond the demonstration of war's customary futility. To that end, this book develops certain ongoing themes.

First, it examines the rise of a profession of military officership. In the generation just before the battle of Breitenfeld, appointment to and advancement in officership began to depart from the criteria of socioeconomic class that had governed them in the medieval age of knighthood. Instead, they began to be based sufficiently on talent, and on an expertise developed through a specialized education in the management of war, to make officership less a social perquisite and in its exercise less merely a craft than ever before. Officership became rather a profession in the larger modern meaning of the word. Officership came increasingly to be based on standards of education and social responsibility, to make it also not simply a career but a profession in the sense in which medicine and law are professions.

The essentials of military professionalism had developed by the beginning of the age of battles. The presence of officer professionalism distinguished this age in the history of warfare from the preceding medieval age. Officer professionalism also helped shape the period 1631–1815 as the age of battles, because in the circumstances of the time the pursuit of the climactic battle of annihilation against the enemy army was the most rational means of seeking a rapid, cost-effective decision in war. The preeminence of battle was, under the conditions of the time, an expression of that rationality in military strategy which was to be expected from the rise of professional education as the foundation for command in war.

Second, the book concerns itself with the means available to the newly professional military officer for exercising that management of war which was his field of professional expertise. It concerns itself with command and control in war, especially on the battlefield. Before the invention of wireless electrical communication, the impediments to effective command and control over battle were so immense that translating a strategic design for the destruction of an enemy armed force in battle and the winning of a war into the tactical realities of the battlefield was difficult in the extreme. The value of professional education was severely compromised by the difficulties of applying the education to battlefield situations. Even with the advantages of twentieth-century communications, attaining decision in war remains elusive—and modern communications display an exasperating tendency to fail to function as advertised when they are subjected to the stresses of combat. The graver difficulties of command, control, and communication in early modern war did much to reduce still further the potential for battle to achieve its strategic purposes, the destruction of the enemy forces and the rapid winning of wars. These difficulties, we shall see, were more insuperable still in naval than in land war.

A third theme concerns the means of achieving tactical decisiveness in battle. In the age of battles, the possibility of tactical decisiveness usually hinged upon the effective use of the most mobile combat arm, the cavalry. The mobile arm could most readily maneuver and strike against the enemy's relatively vulnerable flanks and rear. Direct shock action might also be enhanced, under the right circumstances, by the mobility of the cavalry. Infantry had to form the heart of any effective army, to give the army tactical solidity and sustained power. In the age of battles, however, whenever infantry almost completely predominated over cavalry, tactical indecisiveness tended to compound the problem of attaining strategic decisiveness. Whenever an army developed an effective cavalry, that army became capable of winning the tactical decisions of the battlefield by margins in favorable casualty rates and psychological advantage wide enough to create at least a possibility that strategic decisiveness might follow as well.

These generalizations about a mobile arm apply also to warfare after Waterloo. Wars fought predominately by infantry tend to be cursed even more devastatingly by the plague of indecision than do other wars. World War I offers an appalling example. While infantry can conduct a form of shock action in the infantry assault, more mobile forces possess an added power of shock action that in combination with the greater power of the mobile arm to seek out the enemy's vulnerabilities can to some degree redeem warfare from the tactical phase of indecision. The contrast between World War I and the impact of the new mobile arm, mechanized forces, upon World War II illustrates the point. The military commander in quest of decisiveness needs an effective arm of mobile war.

Note, however, that this discussion of the importance of a mobile force has not thus far touched on one of the principal theoretical roles of cavalry, exploitation and pursuit. The reason is that pursuit of a defeated enemy after a victorious battle has always been much more an ideal of the military theorist than a reality. Even the greatest generals have rarely followed up triumphant battles with devastating pursuit. Major battles have consistently damaged both contending armies so severely that the victor has not retained the ability to pursue the vanquished effectively. If he has taken a good mobile arm into the battle, its ability to exploit and pursue will almost certainly prove sadly depleted by the time the battle ends.

Fourth, there is the matter of limitations upon the violence of war through the restraints of international law and custom. If it is true that war will almost certainly continue to plague our children and our children's children, that in spite of its futility its elimination in the foreseeable future is unlikely, then at least we might be able to reinvigorate the international war convention, which from the time with which this book begins until the early twentieth century appeared to be gradually curbing the violence of war—exceedingly gradually and with considerable periodic backsliding, but still with measurable progress.

In particular, the principle of noncombatant immunity within the war convention had by the early twentieth century largely come to protect the lives and even the private property of noncombatants from the violence of war, by confining legitimate violence to combatants who could possess some capacity to protect themselves and to retaliate. Then came unrestricted submarine warfare, a foot in that door which had been closed against violence toward noncombatants, and, far worse, aerial bombing of civilian targets culminating in the atomic bombing of Hiroshima and Nagasaki on August 6 and 9, 1945. By jettisoning the principle of noncombatant immunity as the central principle of the war convention, our own century has threatened to make war so all-consuming in its destructiveness that it imperils civilization and all of human life.

Perhaps airplanes, intermediate-range and intercontinental ballistic missiles, cruise missiles, and nuclear weapons make the restoration of the principle of noncombatant immunity altogether hopeless. In any event, the very concept of the noncombatant may well appear meaningless in a time of total war; it can be persuasively argued that the factory worker manufacturing munitions is as much a combatant as the soldier who shoots off the munitions in the direction of the enemy. Yet however arbitrary it may be, the principle of noncombatant immunity offered a generally recognizable dividing line between the legitimate and the illegitimate targets of warfare. There is much to be said for attempting to restore that dividing line, if we are to prevent war from killing everybody. And late-twentieth-century weaponry notwithstanding, the progress however halting during the age of battles, and for a hundred years after 1815, toward general acceptance of the international war convention, and of the principle of noncombatant immunity in particular, gives the lie to the notions that war must always be unrestrained, that all weapons that can be used will be used, and that any limitations upon the violence of war must fail. Instead, the history of war in the early modern era shows that it has been possible for nation-states to restrain themselves, recognizing that curbing the violence of war can be to everyone's benefit.

Yet armed forces are brutal instruments, and the international convention limiting the violence of war was always a weak reed on which to lean. We cannot afford to reject out of hand the idea of restoring it, but it would be better to acknowledge that the indecisiveness of war has made it a generally futile instrument for achieving the goals of policy, and therefore to abandon war.

Reference to the weaponry of the late twentieth century calls attention to a final theme of the book, or rather to a theme that the reader might expect to find but that is mostly conspicuous by its absence. We have grown accustomed to dazzlingly rapid advances in the technology of war, such that weapons are likely to be obsolescent before the time the first production models go into service. There was no such rapid pace of technological change in the epoch from Breitenfeld to Waterloo. The hardware of war was essentially the same in 1815 as in 1631. In the interval, the introduction of the socket bayonet wrought important changes in infantry organization and tactics by erasing the division of infantry units into musketeers and pikemen; with the bayonet, every musketeer became in effect his own pikeman. Cannon made impressive advances in mobility in proportion to the weight of guns, carriages, and projectiles, thanks to improvements in the technology of metallurgy and gun-founding and better designs of carriages. But technological change was decidedly incremental. To the extent that professional military men developed a reputation for technological conservatism that clung to them well into the twentieth century, it was largely because the early modern era brought few technological advances worth destabilizing existing tactics to accept. Military technology in the age of battles was essentially stable.

The size of armies changed little more during the age. Numerical growth in total numbers within any nation's armed forces and in the size of field armies was for the most part gradual. Even the change brought about by the democratization and nationalization of war in the era of the French Revolution and Napoleon was less dramatic than we have often assumed; considerations of logistics and of command and control prevented field armies from growing as much beyond the size of their eighteenth-century counterparts as the principle of the nation in arms might imply. When, departing from this generalization, the Emperor Napoleon left behind the field armies of not much over 100,000 of his earlier campaigns to lead into Russia in 1812 a *Grande Armée* that along with auxiliary troops comprised about 600,000, the effect was an overstraining of his ability to command and control and of his logistics that did much to assure the catastrophe he suffered in the East.

The technology of war in the early modern era was not only stable but relatively inexpensive. Consequently the military strengths of the European powers were by no means directly proportionate to their wealth and resources. Medium-sized states like Sweden and Prussia—medium in economic strength, territorial extent, and population—could by virtue of concentrating finances and energy upon military preparations join the exclusive club comprising the great powers. To be sure, the limitations of Sweden's resources helped restrict its membership in the club to a relatively brief period; but complex political and social factors at home as well as economic stringencies contributed to the early ending of its great-power status. Prussia, with little more economic potential than Sweden, remained a great power continuously from the early eighteenth century throughout the age of battles, except for a very short time after 1806.

Nor was military strength directly proportionate to any particular political or social arrangements. Rather, the military power of a state was much more independent of the other aspects of the life of the state than historians have often believed. This autonomy of military power during the age of battles partly reflected the relative cheapness of the weaponry of the day and the relative absence of complexity in military organization and administration. In truth, however, even in the post–1815 era, military strength has remained remarkably independent of the other elements of national life. Armies are often thought of as mirrors of the polities, economies, and societies they serve, but in fact the military history of the Western world since Breitenfeld presents numerous examples of armed forces much more formidable than a study of the societies they have served would lead the historian or military critic to predict. Sweden in the seventeenth century, Prussia in the eighteenth, the Confederate States of America in the nineteenth, Russia and Austria in the First World War, and the Soviet Union today all offer examples of impressive and resilient military strength in spite of grave economic weaknesses and sometimes even political decrepitude. In such states as the Southern Confederacy and the Soviet Union, almost nothing has functioned well except the military, but these states nevertheless have mustered impressive military power. For these reasons this book treats armed forces and war as institutions and endeavors that are in large measures autonomous, functioning and therefore capable of being studied without extensive reference to their political, economic, and social contexts.

An Overview

If military technology, tactics, and organization remained essentially stable from Breitenfeld to Waterloo, the killing power of early modern armies and weaponry nevertheless proved more than ample to make warfare destructive of lives and property well beyond any reasonable calculations of the price that would have made war cost-effective. Stable weapons technology did not prevent the slaughter of the typical eighteenth-century battlefield, where casualties approaching one-fifth of the troops engaged were not unusual. Such shambles mocked the idea that the age was one of limited war; it would be ill advised to prattle about limited war to any ghosts of eighteenth-century field soldiers we might chance to meet.

So we turn to the history of that chapter in the chronicles of war that was quintessentially the age of battles: romantic, even glorious in their spectacles of brightly colored uniforms, glittering sabers and bayonets, blaring musical battle-calls, charging men and horses; inspiring in their instances of courage and devotion to duty; horrible beyond imagination in the wreckage of crushed and mutilated bodies they left behind; futile in their habitual failure to achieve that complete destruction of the enemy army through which they might have justified themselves by bringing quick decisiveness to war. The swift decisions almost never came. If war's one virtue was its capacity to produce decisions at a tolerable cost, it had lost its virtue before the age of battles commenced.

NOTE ON DATES

In March 1582 Pope Gregory XIII (Ugo Buoncompagno) introduced a reform of the calendar. Under the Gregorian calendar (New Style) the day following October 4, 1582, became October 15, 1582, in the Papal States, various other parts of Italy, Spain, and Portugal. France adopted the reform the following December, and it went into effect within two years in most of the Catholic parts of Germany, the Low Countries, and Switzerland. Hungary accepted the change in 1587. The northern European Protestant states generally adopted it in 1699 to take effect in 1700, although the German Protestants retained the former calculations of the dates of movable feasts until 1776. In Great Britain, however, the Old Style or Julian calendar (named for *Dictator* Gaius Julius Caesar) remained in effect until the day following September 2, 1752, became September 14. Moreover, in England and the colonies the legal date of the beginning of the new year was March 25 through 1751, although in Scotland the new year was dated from January 1 from 1600. In Russia the Old Style was retained until the day after January 31, 1918, became February 14, 1918. In the present volume, both Old Style and New Style dates are given for events involving states that used the two calendars.

MAP SYMBOLS USED

XXXX
☐ Army

XXX
☐ Cavalry Corps

XXX
☐ Corps

XX
☐ Cavalry Division

XX
⊠ Infantry Division

X
☐ Cavalry Brigade

X
⊠ Infantry Brigade

III
☐ Cavalry Regiment

III
⊠ Infantry Regiment

II
☐ Cavalry Squadron

II
⊠ Infantry Battalion

■ Buildings

◉ City/Town Location

⌒⌒ Fortress Walls

✕ Battle Location

On maps depicting events of the seventeenth and eighteenth centuries, before the higher forms of military organization had crystallized, the symbols for divisions and brigades largely represent the equivalents thereof rather than formal organizations.

All maps were produced on Apple Macintosh computers by Stephen B. Shore at Temple University Carographic Lab, Philadelphia, Pa.

Part One

THE PROFESSION OF OFFICERSHIP AND THE BIRTH OF MODERN WAR

THE RETURN OF THE LEGIONS: GUSTAVUS ADOLPHUS AND BREITENFELD

The battle began in the low-lying haze of an early autumn morning. The attacking troops displayed at first sight surprisingly little martial panoply to frighten the larks that chirped among the green fields and fruitful orchards around the village of Breitenfeld just north of the city of Leipzig. The soldiers wore almost none of the shining armor so recently in vogue; plate metal had always been stifling in these waning days of warm weather, and it gave too little protection against firearms to be worth its expense and discomfort. To distinguish themselves from the enemy, some of the advancing troops decorated their hats with sprigs of green.

The relative absence of fierce array was deceptive. The thirty-five-year-old King Gustavus II Adolphus (Gustav II Adolf to his own countrymen of Sweden) was leading forward that September 7/17, 1631, the first disciplined fighting force in Europe since the Roman legions to be able to combine all available combat arms in cohesive action either offensively or defensively: the first of modern armies.

The rank and file were bound together by loyalty to their tall, broad-shouldered, coolly reserved but respected sovereign and to their nascent nation-state. The commissioned officers had acquired an expertise in the management and maneuvering of troops that ought to qualify them to be called, in the terminology of later centuries, professional officers. The pioneer sociologist Max Weber would one day see in such expert military functionaries the prototypes of all modern public-service bureaucrats.[1] The sociologist of military institutions Jacques van Doorn perceives in the rational division of labor among the various combat arms the anticipation of Frederick W. Taylor and of all modern rationalization of industrial tasks.[2]

Not many years before, the feudal hosts that jostled each other in medieval battles had been little better in discipline and maneuver than armed mobs. Now Gustavus Adolphus marshaled his men in compact battalions or squadrons of 400 to 500 soldiers each, four companies to a battalion or squadron. The basic maneuver units, the squadrons, could be utilized also in regiments of two squadrons each and in brigades of two regiments. Aligned in brigades as they were this day at Breitenfeld, the Swedish squadrons advanced as virtual mobile castles. Gustavus Adolphus's prescription for victory in battle was to blend the precise maneuver of his battalions or squadrons with unprecedented firepower, to produce an amalgam of missile and shock tactics unknown in Europe since the legions.

In each squadron, pikemen guarded the flanks against marauding enemy cavalry, while the initial weight of the attack was delivered by musketeers in the squadron's center. The musketeers filed between the pikemen in such a way that three musket lines could fire at once: one line kneeling, the second stooping forward, the third standing erect. Their missiles unloosed, the musketeers would retire to reload behind the glistening shelter of the pikes.

As a general seeking to combine fire and maneuver, missile and shock, Gustavus Adolphus led also onto the battlefield the first system of battalion or squadron artillery, whereby he supplemented his heavier siege and field cannon—which were of standardized calibers for the first time in history—with two three-pounder (1.36-kilogram) guns[3] per squadron, each weighing some 600 pounds (272 kilograms); this weight was not too much to be moved around on the battlefield by four men or one or two horses.

After the firepower of muskets and artillery had bruised and demoralized the enemy, Gustavus Adolphus would turn to shock tactics for his climactic blows—the shocks to be delivered by the bristling pikes of his mobile infantry castles, and still more by the charge of the best trained and best disciplined cavalry in western Europe.

The deceptive tranquility of the September morning ended abruptly after the Swedish army had reached its jumping-off positions and completed its Prot-

1. Max Weber, "The Origins of Discipline in War," in *Economy and Society: An Outline of Interpretive Sociology*, edited by Guenther Roth and Claus Wittich, Translation: Ephraim Tirchoff, Hans Gerth, Arthur M. Henderson, Ferdinand Kolegar, Charles Wright Mills, Talcott Parsons, Max Rheenstein, Guenther Roth, Edward Shils, Claus Wittich (3 vols., New York: Bedminster Press, 1968), III, 1150–1155.

2. Jacques [Jacobus Adrianus Antonicus] van Doorn, *The Soldier and Social Change: Comparative Studies in the History and Sociology of the Military* (Beverly Hills/London: SAGE Publishers, 1975), p. 10.

3. By 1764 British standards, a 3-pounder brass or iron gun had a caliber of 2.91 inches (73.914mm.); Swedish guns would have been similar in bore. See table, "Dimensions of All Sorts of Cannon; as Established by the [British] Board of Ordnance in 1764," in Harold L. Peterson, *Round Shot and Rammers* (Harrisburg, Pennsylvania: Stackpole Books, 1969), pp. 41 (brass guns)–42 (iron guns). These equivalents are used throughout the present work.

estant prayers. Then the clamor of trumpets and the rattle of drums tore through the mist, and Gustavus deployed his infantry into a first line of four brigades, with two additional brigades and a cavalry regiment in support, followed by a reserve line of three brigades supported by another cavalry regiment. Cavalry also formed up to both the right and the left of the infantry, and on the far left there mustered the allied troops of the Elector and Duke John George (Kurfürst and Herzog Johann Georg) of Saxe-Weimar, ruler of Saxony. The latter, unfortunately for Gustavus, was a less than energetic military chieftain and a reluctant partner in whose forces the Swedish King could hardly repose full confidence.

The battle line paralleled the campfires of the enemy, the army of Ferdinand II, the Holy Roman Emperor of the German Nation, commanded by Johann Tzerclaes Reichsgraff (Imperial Count) von Tilly. Tilly had a well-earned formidable military reputation gained at die Schlacht auf Weissen Berg (the battle of White Mountain) just north of Prague on October 29/November 8, 1620, the first great clash of arms in a long, harsh war, and he had carried many sanguinary fields since then. The Imperial army numbered some 32,000, against whom Gustavus Adolphus opposed about 22,000 Swedes and 15,000 Saxons.

The Army of Gustavus Adolphus and the Rise of the Military Profession

Modern armies are made up of soldiers professional in two senses. These armies have shaped modern war in various ways because of the dual nature of their professionalism, which sets their members apart from civilian society and nurtures in them distinctive ethics and values. The Swedish Army whose principal field force Gustavus Adolphus led to the battleground of Breitenfeld in the linked causes of Protestantism and Swedish national security and aggrandizement ranks as the first modern army because of the measure of professionalism it attained in both senses.

First, its soldiers made military service their principal career; they were professionals in the sense that they were careerists. The basis upon which Gustavus Adolphus built his professional army was a national conscript force. Like nearly all the emerging European nation-states, Sweden had inherited a *levée en masse* from the medieval past. To enforce the levy, the united kingdom of Sweden and Finland was divided into cantons each obligated to provide a quota of soldiers for the defense of the state. In Sweden, unlike most of the other emergent European states, the militia obligation had been transformed into a recruiting device for a standing army. In the far north of Europe, Sweden was a relatively impoverished country with an only slowly developing economy; but the very backwardness of the economy permitted the transformation of the medieval militia system by making military service a comparatively attractive prospect.

Sweden's population was 95 percent rural, in an economy that in large part rose little above subsistence-level agriculture. Subsistence indeed was so meager that during the long winters barley meal had to be eked out with additional bulk provided by an admixture of tree bark and a variety of other substances, not excluding horse droppings. It was often difficult to get through the winter without slaughtering all the livestock, including the breeding stock. (Nevertheless, farmers strove to keep cattle and pigs. The familiar routine of slaughtering farm animals may have contributed no small measure to inuring the Swedes like other northern Europeans to the killing and maiming to be found also in war.)

In spite of a limited economy, however, the Reformation had enriched the Swedish monarchy with confiscated church lands, and the King could therefore attract men from the bleak farms to a soldier's life with the assurance of reasonably regular pay. The backwardness of the economy also made it acceptable for a soldier's pay to be delivered partly in land and partly in goods.

The total population of Sweden and Finland was only about one and a half million. To draw too many of those limited numbers into the army would obviously ruin such economic development as was occurring, especially in the growing commerce of the towns in the south. Gustavus Adolphus began by transforming a portion of the national militia into a long-service army that he intended to remain very much a national, Swedish and Protestant, force; but as the King's ambitions had grown since his accession in 1611, to carry him now to a battlefield deep inside Germany, increasingly he had to turn to foreign mercenaries to fill his battalions. At Breitenfeld, the proportion of Swedes and Finns in the King's army had shrunk to as little as one-fourth, and many of these were in the cavalry, which was recruited not from conscripts but from volunteers from the most prosperous classes of the population.

Foreign mercenaries, hired out by entrepreneurial captains and colonels in whole companies or even regiments, were the staple of most European armies of the day. Gustavus Adolphus, having hoped for a different kind of army, attempted at least to integrate the mercenaries as well as his native Swedes into his system of increasingly rigorous professional standards of performance by both officers and men—in administration, in tactics, and not least in adherence to a code of the ethical conduct of war. And meanwhile he returned to the recruiting districts of his kingdom to search out from them all the Swedish and Finnish soldiers the economy could spare. He drew these men from provincial regiments that were mainly recruiting pools and that initially had supplied personnel for two or three tactical regiments each; by the time of Breitenfeld, however, the field regiments had become permanent administrative organizations as well as tactical units, and some of the regiments of Gustavus Adolphus's nascent national army survive in the Swedish Army today.

One of the King's means of integrating his mercenaries more fully into his national army was to deal with them as much as possible not as hired units but as individual soldiers. Throughout, individualism was a remarkably prominent ingredient in the Swedish Army, though always of course in counterpoise with the discipline that made this army a reincarnation of the legions. The contrast between Gustavus Adophus's tactical arrangements and his enemies' begins to make this point clear.

The principal rival form of military organization and battlefield alignment to the Swedish, the basis of Tilly's formations that confronted the Swedes at Breitenfeld, was the tercio. During the sixteenth century, the infantry of Spain had become the dominant military force in Europe largely through the cohesive strength of this modern version of the Spartan phalanx or of the late-medieval column of Swiss pikemen. As early as 1505 the Spanish had begun to group several companies together in larger tactical formations under the command of an officer of intermediate rank between the leader of the army and the captains of companies. This officer was the *colonel*, a name derived from *cabo de colunela*, head of a column. The tercio itself probably derived its name from the traditional medieval division of an army into three masses, the van or vavard, the main body, and the rearward. As it matured by about 1534, the tercio combined enough 100- to 250-man companies to create a tactical unit of about 3,000. (The name in fact may have derived from this figure; it may also reflect the tendency for a tercio in its early days to form one-third of a Spanish field army, or the tercio's combination of pikemen, arquebusiers, and musketeers.)

On the battlefield, the tercio comprised a belt of men carrying firearms— the arquebusiers and musketeers—encircling a mass of pikemen and halberdiers, with a rectangular sleeve or shot of musketmen massed at each corner. In addition, a forlorn hope of men with firearms was placed in advance of the main body. In the tactical employment of the tercio, the arquebusiers and musketeers were supposed to soften up an enemy with their firepower before the pikemen charged to achieve a decisive result through shock action. On the defensive, the men armed with guns would fire to weaken the enemy's attack, then—with enough time and skill—retreat within a wall of pikemen.

While the basic tactics were similar to those of Gustavus Adolphus, the tercio was a far more cumbersome apparatus than the Swedish squadron or even the Swedish brigade. It was so cumbersome in fact that it had only limited offensive utility. It afforded almost no opportunities for the exercise of individual soldierly skills, except those of its commander. It confined the greater part of its manpower within its densely packed mass, where most of its soldiers could neither move freely nor even contribute much to the outcome of battle; it was a formation notoriously wasteful of manpower.

Unlike Gustavus Adolphus, who relied for his infantry missile power on the demoralizing effect of three lines firing simultaneously, the Spanish attempted to maintain a continuous musketry fire from the tercio. But the rate of reloading the firearms of the era was so slow that this purpose entailed ranging musketeers at least ten lines deep and training them to fire by successive ranks, each rank countermarching after delivering its fire. Under the pressures of combat this scheme practically never worked; the full ritual of reloading required as many as ninety words of command, which meant that efforts to maintain continuous fire degenerated into chaos. Gustavus Adolphus accepted the inevitability of this degeneration and did not attempt continuous fire.

The tercio standing on the defensive was indeed difficult to break; it was so deep that its front lines had nowhere to go even should they desire to run away. But on the attack the formation not only proved incapable of sustaining the fire that was intended from it; it possessed very little maneuverability. Because it was almost unmaneuverable, the idea of using its pikemen for offensive shock effect gradually declined. The proportion of firearms carriers to pikemen then increased—from one-third arquebusiers and musketeers and two-thirds pikemen, to equality about the end of the sixteenth century, to a two-to-one predominance of firearms men by about 1620. This process placed the offensive reliance of the tercio mainly upon the arquebusiers and musketeers—but seventeenth-century musketry had neither the range nor the accuracy for decisive effect in battle. Tercios would not readily lose battles, but they could not readily win them either, especially in terms of achieving aggressive, positive results. That is why Gustavus Adolphus not only turned to smaller, more flexible and more maneuverable tactical units, but also increased the proportion of pikemen to musketeers—216 pikes to 192 muskets in a squadron—so he could restore shock tactics to the infantry assault.

By the time of the Thirty Years War, the Spanish had improved the tercios by reducing their size to enhance their maneuverability. The Spanish clung so insistently to the tercios as their basic formations that some of them became permanent administrative organizations and the foundations of the regiments of the modern Spanish Army. But as early as 1584 the tercios had been cut to 1,500 men each; by the 1630s the Spanish tercios were smaller still, but the Imperial tercios commanded by Tilly at Breitenfeld remained about 1,500 strong. By this time, furthermore, the tercios were commonly grouped by threes for tactical purposes in a triangle, one tercio in front and two behind, or by fours in a diamond shape with the rearward tercio in reserve. Withal, they continued to be ponderous formations lacking in offensive capacity.

Because the individual soldiers inside the tercios were so severely restricted in their movements simply by the press of their comrades, the armies of Spain and the Holy Roman Empire needed far fewer junior and noncommissioned officers than Gustavus Adolphus used in his numerous small units. This economy was another one purchased, however, at the cost of flexible utility in battle. The Swedes with their numerous small units expected at least some measure of individual initiative from their officers down to the noncommissioned officers. The flexibility of the Swedish Army demanded the application of its members' intelligence, frequently on the part of all officers and sometimes including the rank and file.

Gustavus Adolphus could place the greater confidence in the individual decisions of his officers because they were becoming professionals in the second sense, beyond that of making their careers in the army. The officers of the Swedish Army were among the first since ancient times to be *educated* in the conduct of war. For them, military officership was becoming not simply a matter of learning from experience and from observation of the performance of others, as a craft is learned, but of study, as study based on history and theory is the essence of any modern educated profession.

The return of the legions, the reappearance of armies possessing a discipline and training comparable to the Roman Army, was a product of many factors and especially of the emergence of the nation-state with a sovereign able to pay his soldiers consistently. But it also derived from the renaissance of ancient literature. Gustavus Adolphus, largely self-taught as a soldier, educated himself first by sharing in the European rediscovery of the military writings of ancient and early medieval times. Particularly this rediscovery included the writings of Aëlian, Vegetius, and Leo the Isaurian: the Latin translation by Theodorus Gaza of Thessalonica of the second-century Τακτικῆ Θεωρια, by the Greco-Roman Aëlianus Tacticus, included in the collection *Veteres de re militari scriptores* published in 1487;[4] the *Epitoma rei militaria, sive institutorum rei militaria libri quinque* of the fourth-century Roman writer Flavius Vegetius Renatus;[5] and the treatise on military tactics attributed to the Byzantine Emperor Leo VI (Emperor 886–911) but probably actually written by Leo III the Isaurian (Emperor 717–740).[6]

Vegetius had never been completely forgotten during the Middle Ages; the writings of all three were available readily by the time of Gustavus Adolphus. The ancient writers strongly influenced military critics just before and during the time of the Thirty Years War. Although Aëlian, Vegetius, and Leo had all flourished long after the demise of the citizen-soldiery of the Roman Republic, enough of a conception of the virtues of such a soldiery had persisted in their writings to help inspire in new readers a disdain for mercenaries and a preference for a citizens' militia. Gustavus Adolphus may have drawn from his reading of or other acquaintance with these works part of the inspiration for building his national army founded upon conscription.

The Dutch Republic and the Birth of Military Professionalism

Several European monarchs had anticipated Gustavus Adolphus in attempting to restore the Roman legions to reality. François I and Henri II of France in fact essayed literal recreations of the legion as a tactical formation. In the deeper sense of recapturing the discipline and professionalism of the legions, the United Provinces of the Netherlands preceded the Swedish King and share with him considerable claim to the fashioning of the first modern army.

A scholar in the Netherlands, Justus Lipsius (Joste Lips), from 1579 to 1590 professor of history in the University of Leiden within the Dutch provinces rebelling against Spain, contributed a major landmark to the necessary literary foundation of an educated military profession with *De militia Romana . . . ,*[7] another widely circulated work that almost certainly influenced Gustavus Adolphus. By the time he published the book in 1595, Lipsius had broken with the

4. [With other tracts, separately paginated, in Giovanni Sulpizio (Johannes Sulpitius), ed.,] *Veteres de re militari scriptores* (Roma: Euchatius Silber, January 29–June 7, 1487); *see The Tactics of Ælian, Comprising the Military Sysyem of the Grecians. . . .* With a Preliminary Discourse by Henry Augustus [first] Viscount Dillon . . . (London: Printed by Cox and Baylis, for Kirby, 1814).

5. Also included in Sulpizio, ed., *op. cit.*

6. Leonis Imp[erator]., *Tactica; sive, De re milites: liber. leonnis Meursius græce primus vulgait, & rexus adrieat* (Lvgdvn [Leiden]: Balvorvm apud. I. Baldvinvm, impens L. Elzeuirijn, 1612); see *L'«Extrait tactique» tiré de Léon VI le Sage,* par A[lphonse]. Dain (Paris: Champion, 1942).

7. Justi Lipsi, *De militia Romana libre quinque, commentarius ad Polybivm. E parte primâ historicae facis* (Antverpiae: ex officina Plantaniana, apud Viduam & Ionannem Moritum . . . , M.D.XCVI . . . ; "Liber quintus" has special title page date, 1595). See Polybius, *De Romanorum militia, et castrorum metaticae . . .* Ejudem A. J. Laccaris . . . (Basilum [Basel]: No publisher, 1527). The original is a work of the second century B.C.

Dutch rebellion and its Protestantism and had fled to Antwerp (Antwerpen) and Catholicism. These shifts geographical and spiritual reflected a conservative bent that made his book too thoroughly a paean to the ancient art of war and too little an encouragement to modern innovation to meet most of the practical military requirements of the day. Although Lipsius merits recognition as one of the restorers of military education and tactical discipline, the greater contribution of the Netherlands was in practice rather than theory.

Here the principal credit for military innovation is usually accorded to Maurice of Nassau (Maurits van Nassau), second son of William (Wilhelm or Willem) the Silent and William's heir as Prince of Orange and Count of Nassau. Maurice became the principal Dutch military commander defending independence from Spain during the late years of the sixteenth century and into the seventeenth. William Louis (Wilhelm or Willem Lodowijk) and John (Johan) II, Counts of Nassau and Maurice's cousins, contributed almost equally to tactical reform, however; and notwithstanding political differences, Maurice also worked closely in military administration with the most powerful Dutch civilian leader, John (Johan) van Oldenbarneveldt.

The revolt of the Netherlands against Spain erupted in 1566. Initially it united Roman Catholic aristocrats of the southern Netherlands and Protestants of the north. The purposes of these two groups differed, however, because the aristocrats sought to preserve a traditional local autonomy, while the burghers wanted a new freedom for their cities to conduct commerce as they chose—and for the practice of their religion. More to the point, Spanish military power could operate with greater effectiveness in the southern provinces than in the readily flooded and therefore defensible lowlands of the modern Netherlands. In 1578 the southern provinces, led by the Catholic nobility, came to terms with Spain rather than be drawn into a Protestant-dominated urban society and polity, and rather than go on with a perhaps hopeless rebellion in their less defensible territories. Thereupon the north found itself deprived of the customary nucleus of a European army; throughout the Middle Ages the nobility had been the principal warrior caste.

Such few noblemen as remained in rebellion, conspicuously the princely house of Nassau and Orange, retained military command—mainly having to substitute military for political ambitions, furthermore, because of the political predominance of the burghers. But they had to build a new kind of army. In officers, they had to look to skill and knowledge rather than claims of birth to create a hierarchy of command. Theirs was a predicament with advantages. If without noblemen they had to settle for officers with comparatively little experience, nevertheless they no longer had to put up with status in the nobility as a source of confusion in military rank; in the Dutch Army, higher noblemen were not so likely to contest the commands of men with loftier military rank but lesser aristocratic distinction. The Dutch were able to advance a long way toward establishing a modern military rank structure. In other armies, the technical branches that demanded a mathematical education, that is artillery and engineering, carried disproportionately little weight in command councils because noblemen did not customarily acquire the appropriate education, and consequently the artillery and engineer officers were of inferior social standing. In the Dutch Army, the artillerists and engineers were the social equals of just about everyone else. Not coincidentally, the Dutch developed outstanding gunnery and fortification skills, especially the latter.

To fill the ranks, Maurice of Nassau had to resort to mercenaries, mostly foreign; the urban rebellion had no more military tradition on the enlisted than on the officers' level. Many of the soldiers were English. Volunteers from England began fighting alongside the Dutch in considerable numbers about 1572. Queen Elizabeth I, to keep her Spanish enemies busy and to protect both her own country's and the Protestant cause, sent an expeditionary force under Robert Dudley, fourteenth Earl of Leicester (although the first and last of his family to hold the earldom), to the Netherlands in 1585. In 1594 the United Provinces of the Netherlands absorbed the English companies into the Dutch Army. At the battle of Turnhout on January 14/24, 1596/1597, one-third of the Dutch force was English—fifty companies of foot and sixteen cornets of horse; another eight companies were Scots.

The relative absence of aristocratic pretensions among Dutch officers seems to have had healthy effects throughout the army. Elsewhere career enlisted soldiers had taken on pretensions borrowed from their social betters, on the assumption that all military men were somehow superior to mere laborers. Soldiers consequently considered themselves above stooping to the tasks of laborers; in many armies, mercenaries refused to dig trenches. In the Dutch Army, however, soldiers carried shovels and built the field fortifications that the skillful Dutch engineers designed.

The Dutch also discovered that it was more economical to keep trained soldiers on duty through the winter months when custom and climate called for the suspension of campaigning, rather than to retain the old practice of demobilizing companies and regiments in the autumn and hiring or rehiring in the spring. In this, the Dutch followed the example of the Spanish with many of their most effective tercios. Together, the bitter rivals Spain and the United Provinces set the pattern of the permanent, standing army.

Like everyone of his time who aimed to be an educated soldier, Maurice of Nassau read the Roman textbooks. He created the modern language of drill-ground and command by adapting it from Vegetius. From Maurice, this language passed into the other European armies. Characteristically, Maurice also standardized the caliber of handguns in terms of the number of balls contained in a pound, the source of the "gauge" measurement still used in shotguns. It was a related development that the principal Dutch literary contribution to the founding of modern armies was probably not Lipsius's book but one commissioned in 1596 by John II of Nassau and published in 1607, Jacob de Gheyn's *Wapenhandelinghe*.[8] This is one of the first modern manuals of arms. It includes 116 engravings showing the postures and movements for using the three basic infantry

8. Jacob de Gheyn, *Wapenhandelinghe van Roers, Musquetten ende Spiessen* . . . Figuerlyck vulgebiegt ('s Gravenhage [The Hague]: No publisher, 1607); facsimile edition (New York: McGraw-Hill Book Company, 1971).

weapons—the caliver or arquebus, the musket, and the pike—and a text probably better correlated with the drawings than in any similar work for many years. The appropriate words of command are given for each step in using the weapons. This development of precisely repeatable commands and actions was of course no small ingredient in that rationalization of activity which made the military reforms the heralds of a new social order.

The military system of Maurice of Nassau also led to the founding of the first modern schools for studying the art of war. In particular, John II of Nassau, the sponsor of the *Wapenhandelinghe,* established the Kriegs und Ritterschule at Siegen in 1617.

In 1601, meanwhile, John also accepted a commission from Charles (Karl) IX of Sweden, the father of Gustavus Adolphus, to attempt to transplant the Dutch military reforms. The time was not yet ripe in Sweden—Charles IX had almost none of the military talents of his son—and John returned to the Netherlands after only a year. Nevertheless, in his youth Gustavus Adolphus was introduced to the Dutch military innovations as well as to Roman military literature by his Dutch tutor, Johan Skytte. In 1608 the soon-to-be King received two months' intensive training in Maurice's tactics from a veteran practitioner, Jakob de la Gardie. In 1620 Gustavus Adolphus, King since 1611, met with John II of Nassau at Heidelberg and is supposed to have discussed military issues with the Dutch leader at length. The organizational innovations through which the Dutch sought to give scope to their individual training of officers and soldiers by breaking the bonds of the tercio became the direct foundation of the Swedish organizational reforms.

Maurice of Nassau had substituted for the tercio as the basic tactical unit a battalion of 550 men. He conceived his battalions as a resurrection of the Roman cohorts. He reduced the depth of the pikemen in his array to ten and eventually to five lines. The tercio's girdle of firearms gave way to platoons of musketeers and arquebusiers stationed on the flanks of the pikes. Five deep, the pikes would form a front of fifty men, with three forty-man firearms platoons drawn up on each side of the pike hedge, each platoon deployed in column of fours. Another sixty firearms men were in front as a forlorn hope of skirmishers. Thus the battalion consisted altogether of 250 pikes and 300 firearms. The arquebusiers and musketeers could readily retreat behind the hedge of pikes without throwing the whole formation into disarray. They could also advance, fire rank after rank, and countermarch to reload with much less confusion and much more possibility of actually accomplishing the maneuver than the firearms men of the tercios.

In place of the heavy triangles of three tercios or diamonds of four tercios in which Spain and the Empire wasted much manpower, the Dutch battalions lent themselves to linear battlefield formations in which a much higher proportion of the army's potential strength could be brought to bear. The battalions came to be brigaded in groups of six, to be drawn up usually in three lines of battle. This arrangement also gave the Dutch a much more flexible and economical reserve than the fourth tercio of the diamond formation; units of the Dutch third line could readily be moved to any threatened part of the first line.

In their compact tactical formations and the necessary multiplication of officers and noncommissioned officers that these formations entailed, as well as in their revival of Roman standards of discipline and training and their development of military professionalism in the two senses of the word, Maurice of Nassau and the Dutch took long strides toward creating the first modern army. But Gustavus Adolphus and the Swedes advanced still farther. For the Dutch Army failed to go much beyond its Spanish rivals in achieving offensive power, without which armies must remain only limited instruments of state policy.

This result was inherent, however, in the Dutch situation. Because of the relatively small Dutch population and out of policy considerations, Maurice fought mainly a defensive war against the Spanish opponents of his country's independence. He fought behind field fortifications and with the aid of the numerous watercourses and the marshy ground of the Netherlands. Gunpowder and cannon had rendered obsolete the vertical-walled stone castles of the Middle Ages; the Dutch engineers, led by the especially skillful Simon Stevin, the inventor of the decimal system for expressing fractions, used admirably constructed earthen revetments and, most of all, the country's abundant means of creating wet ditches to take the place of castles in halting the enemy's progress. In military engineering, the Dutch probably progressed farther toward a full-fledged professionalism in the second sense of the word than in any other area. They borrowed once more from the Roman literature, and from the Italian Renaissance theorist Niccolò Tartaglia (or Tartalea).[9] Particularly they adopted and adapted to their own uses from the Italians the basic star fortress that would long dominate fortification design. Their skill in engineering along with the emphasis on drill and tactics in their military literature made the professionalism of the Dutch primarily a technocratic kind of professionalism.

Primarily standing on the defensive, Maurice fought only two pitched battles of any consequence. The first of them, Turnhout (January 14/24, 1596/1597), sprang from an irresistible opportunity to catch a Spanish force in both front and rear as it marched along a low ridge across an inundated countryside. Whatever the limitations of Dutch striking power, in these favorable circumstances Maurice scored a spectacular success, killing some 2,000 of the enemy and capturing 500 prisoners at a cost of about fifty dead in his own force. The second, and bigger, battle of Nieuport (Nieuwpoort) (June 22/July 2, 1600), was significant partly in that the defensive-minded Maurice did not desire it. The States General of the United Provinces pushed him into a more ambitious and aggressive undertaking than he liked, an expedition to capture the ports of Dunkirk (Dunkerque) and Nieuport from which Spanish ships were raiding Dutch commerce. The Spanish responded with a swift concentration of force that reached the sea between Maurice and his base and thus compelled him to fight. But the Spanish threw away much of their advantage by delaying their attack until Mau-

9. Niccolò Tartaglia, *Opere del' famasissimo Niccolò Tartaglia cioè Quesita, Trauagliata inuentione, Noue scientia, Ragionamenti supra Archimede* [Archimedes] . . . (In Venetia [Venice]: Al segno del lione, M.DC.VI); see also *Le Ballistique de Nicolas Tartaglia; ou, Recueil de tout ce que cet auteur a écrit touchant le mouvement des projectiles et les questions qu s'y rattachent* . . . , traduit de l'italien avec quelques annotations par [?] Rieffel (Paris: J. Correard, 1846).

rice had had warning and time enough to deploy for battle. Finally it was a Dutch counterattack that carried the day against enemy formations enmeshed in the confusion that typically followed their aggressive efforts.

Nevertheless, it was the corresponding limitations of the Dutch themselves in offensive war that more than any other factor set the modern Netherlands and modern Belgium upon their separate historical courses. When the fighting between the remaining rebellious provinces and Spain at length subsided in 1609, independence remained confined to the low-lying northern provinces where defensive military engineering had afforded the revolt its greatest advantage. The Dutch and the Belgians became divided from each other not so much by differences of language, culture, or religion; the language of the north still reaches deep into Belgium and divides the country today, while during the rebellion Protestantism was stronger in some of the Belgian provinces than in some of those farther north. Rather, the Netherlands and Belgium were separated by the fortunes of war. Much will be said later in this history about the frequent futility of even the best organized and most tactically effective armies in translating war into a genuinely effective instrument of policy. But the division of the Netherlands is a striking demonstration that the arbitrament of arms sometimes overcomes more fundamental social and cultural forces.

The Weapons of Gustavus Adolphus

On the Dutch foundation of flexible organization and tactics and professional education, Gustavus Adolphus sought to build added offensive power. His tactics at Breitenfeld in 1631 were the product not only of his study of the Romans and the Dutch but of campaigning against Russians and Poles since he was seventeen. For the infantry, his main step toward improved strength in the attack was his substituting of salvos of arquebus and musket fire with three lines shooting simultaneously for the often unattainable goal of continuous volleys. More than that, he enhanced the potential for shock tactics by reversing the trend of the past century with an increased proportion of pikemen to firearms men. He also reduced the weight of the pikes by shortening their length from eighteen to eleven feet (from six to three and two-thirds meters). He trained his infantry in a tactical system whereby the mission of the shot was to soften up the enemy by fire, but the charge and shock of the pikemen would deliver the foot soldiers' main offensive blow.

The Swedish King had recognized more clearly than most the severe constrictions binding seventeenth-century infantry firepower. The short range and the inaccuracy of arquebus and musket assured the indecisiveness of exchanges of infantry fire and condemned Spanish tercios and Dutch battalions alike to a mainly defensive value in most circumstances against any reasonably well-trained and well-armed foe. In range, accuracy, and penetrating power, early hand-carried firearms represented a drastic step backward from the longbow or the crossbow of the Middle Ages. The European continent's most renowned infantry of the late Middle Ages, the Swiss pikemen, had the good fortune never to confront a strong force of English longbowmen in battle. If they had, the

English archers would have mowed them down. But against the first firearms, the Swiss merely dropped to the ground while the bullets passed over their heads, then resumed the advance while the enemy reloaded. The regression in infantry missile-firing was tolerated largely because a man could become acceptably adept in handling an arquebus or musket much more quickly than he could learn to handle a longbow or crossbow properly; skill in archery usually required constant practice from early boyhood, and the decline of the English longbowmen was as much a social as a military phenomenon, involving the decline of England's independent agricultural yeomanry in the face of the first enclosure movement. Nonetheless, the superiority of the crossbow to early firearms has been estimated at forty to one, and because the longbow had a considerably more rapid rate of fire than the crossbow, its superiority would have been greater yet.

Of course, by the time of Maurice of Nassau and Gustavus Adolphus infantry firearms had improved over those against which the Swiss pikemen had simply lain down for a minute or so—but not by much. In its Spanish form the arquebus was usually a ten-pound or five-and-a-half-kilogram, .72-caliber (18.288-mm) weapon shooting a .66-caliber (16.764 mm) ball (to allow for irregularities in the shape of the ball). It had laughable accuracy even within fifty meters or yards and little penetrating power. The musket, weighing about twenty pounds or nine kilograms, was a more formidable weapon, with slightly better range and considerably more penetration; but it was so heavy that it usually had to be aimed from the waist instead of the shoulder to minimize the vicious kick of its recoil, and its muzzle usually had to be supported by a forked rest.

The arquebuses and muskets were still mainly matchlocks; that is, they were fired by lighting a match that dipped into the powder chamber when the trigger was pulled. Pistols were coming to be wheellocks, in which a roughened steel wheel was wound up like a clock with a spanner or key, whereupon the pulling of the trigger released the wheel to rotate against a stone—pyrites or flint—and strike sparks into the powder; but the wheel was so delicate and needed repair so often that it was not particularly practical for a heavy infantry shoulder weapon.

Improved field artillery was another of Gustavus Adolphus's means of trying to infuse greater offensive power into his army, but the cannons like the shoulder arms of his day were so inherently limited that the Swedish artillery has probably received more credit for the King's victorious battles than it merited. Certainly the "leather gun" has captured historical imagination more than its practical value warranted. It was an effort to make field artillery light and maneuverable by binding the barrels with leather and thus cutting down on the otherwise necessary weight of metal; but the experiment was abandoned during the Polish campaigns and before the Swedes invaded Germany. Gustavus Adolphus's more lasting artillery reforms hewed to the same line of thought; he shortened the barrels and lightened the carriages of his field guns to try to make them light enough to be maneuvered in battle, with some small degree of success.

The King also standardized calibers—24-, 12-, and 6-pounder (10.884-,

5.442-, 2.721-kilogram) guns for siege artillery and, in the lighter weights, limited field use, with three-pounders (1.361 kilogram) weighing about 600 pounds or 272 kilograms serving as his famous squadron guns maneuvering on the battle-field. (These guns would have had bore dimensions of about 5.83 inches, 4.63 inches, 3.66 inches, and 2.91 inches, respectively [about 148,082 mm, 117.602 mm, 92.964 mm, and 73.914 mm]). Unlike the mythical fixed cartridges for his infantry shoulder arms, Gustavus Adolphus actually developed fixed ammuni-tion in wooden cases for his artillery, which helped his gunners contrive to fire eight rounds to every six fired by a musketeer.

While the squadron guns assured a modicum of artillery support to the infantry formations, a more fundamental means of enhancing the offensive con-tribution of the guns was to organize the new, lighter and more maneuverable pieces larger than the three-pounders so they could deliver a concentrated fire of maximum intensity at critical points on the battlefield rather than a mere dis-persed cannonade. In the Swedish Army as in other armies, artillery previously had not been formed into permanent tactical units. In 1623, however, Gustavus Adolphus had created a company of artillery, and by 1629 there were six compa-nies that the King combined into a regiment—four companies of gunners, one of fireworks—bombs, grenades, petards, and the like—and one of sappers. Receiv-ing the command of the regiment was Lennart Torstensson, who was to become the greatest cannoneer of the age, through such feats as his massing of seventy-two guns to force the enemy to take cover so that the Swedish Army could cross the River Lech in April 1632, while another eighteen guns commanded the crossing-place itself.

For all that, it was Gustavus Adolphus's cavalry that became the true deci-sive weapon and that most fully bestowed offensive power upon his army. Here his years of experience contributed more than his study of the Romans and the Dutch, and his enemies served as his tutors.

In western European armies until this time, efforts to combine cavalry mo-bility with firearms had not been happy ones. The standard tactical method for employing horsemen carrying guns—almost always light pistols—had come to be the caracole, in which the troopers in successive lines rode to within close enough range to warrant some hope of damaging the enemy, fired, and then quickly turned and rode away to reload. This ritual, however, tended to have even less decision-making potentiality than exchanging infantry volleys. To res-cue the cavalry from tactical futility, the horsemen had to abandon the caracole and return to an emphasis on shock action: the cavalry charge. The Swedish cavalry had adopted the pistol-firing pirouettes of the caracole just as had almost every other cavalry—except the Poles. Acknowledging that cavalry firearms and effective cavalry shock action simply did not mix well together, the Poles still charged with saber and lance. In Gustavus Adolphus's early campaigns in Po-land, the result was that the enemy's horse rode roughshod over the Swedish cavalry. Swedish horsemen who cracked little pistols in their direction could not halt the crunching shock of the Polish mounted onslaught. Therefore Gustavus Adolphus remodeled his cavalry on the Polish design, adding of course his cus-tomary insistence on discipline and intensive training.

NORTH
SEA

KINGDOM OF
DENMARK

BALTIC SEA

BISHOPRIC
OF CAMMIN

HITHER POMERANIA

EASTERN
POMERANIA

Texel

Lübeck ⊚
⊚ Hamburg

Elbe R.

⊛ Bremen

Aller R.

UNITED
PROVINCES
OF THE
NETHERLANDS

ELECTORATE
OF
BRANDENBURG

⊚ Berlin

KINGDOM
OF
POLAND

Spree R.

Weser R.

Magdeburg ⊚

Oder R.

Rhine R.

⊠ Breitenfeld

⊚ Leipzig
Lützen ⊠

⊚ Dresden

DUCHY
OF
SILESIA

⊚ Aachen   ⊚ Köln

C. OF NASSAU

KINGDOM
OF
SAXONY

Koblenz ⊚

SPANISH
NETHERLANDS

⊚ Frankfurt

White Mountain ⊠

⊚ Prague

⊚ Mainz

Main R.

Moselle R.

⊚ Trier

RHEINPFALZ

⊚ Bamberg

KINGDOM
OF
BOHEMIA

⊚ Worms

Rhine R.

Neckar R.

Nürnberg ⊚
Alte Feste ⊠

Moldau R.

DUCHY

OF

LORRAINE

Nördlingen ⊠

Ulm ⊚

Rain
(The
Lech)

Iser R.

ELECTORATE
OF

ARCHDUCHY
OF

Augsburg ⊚

Danube R.

Munich ⊚ ⊚ BAVARIA

AUSTRIA

Lac
Constance

FRANCHE-
COMTÉ

SWISS CONFEDERATION
(Independent of the
Empire 1648)

THE THIRTY YEARS WAR AND GERMANY
AFTER THE PEACE OF WESTPHALIA, 1648

——————— Boundary of the Holy Roman Empire
of the German Nation

—·—·—·— Boundaries between other states

Lac de
Genève

DUCHY OF
SAVOY

DUCHY
OF
MILAN

0   50   100 miles

0   50   100 kilometers

A *Strategy Seeking Battle*

The payoff came in battle. Of all the changes in warfare represented by the military organization and tactics of Gustavus Adolphus, none was more dramatic nor more important in its implications for the future of war than the additional change that the Swedish King brought to the strategic realm, his persistence in seeking and fighting battles.

There are famous battles of the Middle Ages, especially the great battles of the Hundred Years War—Crécy (August 26, 1346), Poitiers (or Poictiers, September 18, 1356), and Agincourt (October 25, 1415). But battles in medieval warfare were nevertheless rarities.

At least until the invention of effective artillery—which is to say, not yet at the time of the first cannon but at some point after 1420—the difficulties of capturing fortified castles meant that castles could generally frustrate the winners of battles and render the outcome of battle almost a strategic irrelevancy. Furthermore, the purposes of war in medieval Europe did not include the decimation of the knightly caste that specialized in the waging of war. All the knighthood of Europe shared an interest in avoiding the killing of knights. It was acceptable enough to slaughter commoners in battle, just as commoners were continually slaughtered, plundered, and ravished during military campaigns whether or not battles occurred; but a battle involving large-scale casualties among the commoners was all too likely to produce the undesirable byproduct of considerable casualties among the mounted knights as well. Therefore battle in general usually appeared undesirable.

On those occasions in war when knights did happen to fight each other, the usual aim of the combat was not to kill or to injure severely but to capture and hold for ransom, thus serving the object of economic gain that was a mainspring of medieval war behind the façade of chivalry. Under the medieval mode of warfare, a supposedly bellicose king such as Henry II of England could go through a lifetime of campaigning without once fighting a battle that amounted to much more than a skirmish. Henry's son King Richard I, Cœur de Lion, presents a yet more warlike image; but in Europe as distinct from the Holy Land—where the Crusades had modes and purposes different from those customary in European war—Richard never fought a battle, with one doubtful exception during his suppression of a rebellion in southern France in May 1176 when he was duc d'Aquitaine.

Among the reasons why medieval warriors did not fight battles there was also a consideration that was to shape the campaigns of no small number of later soldiers. Battles are usually highly uncertain enterprises. All sorts of events beyond a commander's control, all sorts of accidents of weather or mere luck, can undo the best-laid plans and cause a battle to be lost. If the objectives of a campaign can be secured without the always chancy expedient of battle, then the rationally calculating commander will tend to eschew battle.

For Gustavus Adolphus, however, the purposes of his invasion of Germany were not to be secured without battle. The resources of the Holy Roman Empire were too far superior to those of Sweden for the most skillful campaigns of maneuver and of capturing territory to be likely to give the Swedes any lasting claim to hegemony in the Baltic and to that end in northern Germany. For the Swedish King to grasp the hegemony he sought, he needed to inflict upon the Empire a substantial depletion of its power, physically and—for more lasting results—psychologically. And because the Empire's resources could easily outlast his own, he had to do it quickly. These considerations all pointed him to a strategy of seeking battles. Only through battles was he likely to accomplish the rapid destruction of the Imperial armies, which he increasingly seems to have regarded as essential to reaching his hegemonic policy goal.

Moreover, Gustavus Adolphus could contemplate battle with more equanimity than medieval chieftains had done because the professional qualities of his army made battle somewhat less of a gamble than it had formerly been. The professionalism of his army gave him a confidence in it and a control over it that medieval leaders had not possessed. For him, the disciplined tactical proficiency and organizational flexibility of his army meant that even grave mischances might be overcome. This new confidence of military leaders in the reliability and resilience of their instruments of war combined with new strategic purposes to make battle a hallmark of modern war as it had never been of medieval war.

And so we turn to Gustavus Adolphus's first great battle against the Empire.

Breitenfeld

The Swedish King had brought his country into the religious wars of Germany in 1628, at a time when Imperial and Catholic forces had swept across Protestant North Germany to the Baltic Sea and were threatening to extinguish Protestantism at least as a political force in central Europe as well as to foreclose Gustavus Adolphus's ambitions for Swedish preeminence in the Baltic. By the day of Breitenfeld, Gustavus had driven his enemies back across much of North Germany, but the decisive battle he sought had eluded him, and in 1631 under Tilly the Empire had managed to recapture the offensive.

Nevertheless, Tilly's leadership brought consequences promising that Gustavus might now attain his object of battle. For one thing, Tilly had allowed his troops to sack and ravage the city of Magdeburg when after a siege it fell to him on May 10/20, 1631. Fear and horror among German Protestants following the sack of Magdeburg afforded Gustavus Adolphus a new leverage for enlisting allies and thereby enhancing his chances of battlefield success. John George of Saxony came to Gustavus's side when Tilly's army compelled the surrender of the Saxon city of Leipzig by threatening it with the fate of Magdeburg. For another, while Tilly was an experienced veteran soldier and a generally sound commander, he had mismanaged the logistics of his 1631 counteroffensive. Mismanagement of logistics was not difficult, of course, after much of Germany had been the scene of marching and countermarching for many years and had repeatedly been picked bare of subsistence, the Thirty Years War having begun in 1618. By the time Tilly's troops entered Saxony, long neutral and therefore relatively replete with foodstuffs, they were on the edge of starvation. Thus it behooved Tilly to hold his ground around Leipzig, until the unaccustomed plenty of the city and its hinterland could fill his men's stomachs and replenish his stores. Accordingly, the Imperial commander was more willing than usual to fight. When Gustavus Adolphus and John George approached Leipzig from the north, Tilly moved his army to a low ridge some five miles (eight kilometers) north of the city between the villages of Breitenfeld on his left and Stenberg on his right, there to offer the battle that his enemy so heartily desired.

The officers of the Swedish infantry brigades and cavalry regiments moving through the early-morning mists toward Tilly's ridge on September 7/17 had been carefully counseled by Gustavus Adolphus regarding what he expected of them in various contingencies. Yet another reason why battle had so often been avoided was that once the overpowering noise of battle commenced, and with the advent of firearms once the smoke clouds of black powder enveloped the field, no adequate control of events was possible to the high command. Neither couriers nor flag signals nor drum beats nor trumpet calls could be relied on for communication. Only a careful prior understanding between an army commander and his principal subordinates could prevent battle from degenerating into absolute chaos—and a good deal of chaos was inevitable even with the best of preparation. So Gustavus Adolphus took pains to advise his officers of his expectations of them under almost any conceivable developments.

Tilly, accepting battle at Breitenfeld but without his opponent's clarity of strategic purpose, took much less care in preparing his subordinates for whatever he might have wanted them to do.

The combat began as an artillery duel. The Swedes predictably had the better of it, because their guns were not only more numerous but, with Gustavus's fixed ammunition, could get off about three shots to the Imperialists' one.

It should have been equally predictable, had Tilly thought about it, that this galling Swedish gunnery might provoke premature activity from the 5,000 Imperial cavalry deployed on his left wing. Tilly had entrusted this force to his most famous, able, energetic, and also rash subordinate, General Gottfried Heinrich Graf (Count) von Pappenheim, a cavalier in the bold and dashing mold. On an earlier battlefield, that of Wimpffen (or Wimpfen) on April 26/May 6, 1622, Tilly had achieved a dramatic victory by means of a double envelopment, and he may well have had in mind as his principal design for the battle at hand combining a charge by Pappenheim against the Swedish right with a similar thrust under his own direct command on the opposite flank to repeat that result. But the fire of seventy-five massed Swedish guns goaded Pappenheim into attacking before Tilly was ready to make a corresponding move.

The Imperial cavalier imparted about as much vigor as anyone could have to a caracoling attack with pistols. Nevertheless, he made little headway against the Swedish cavalry forming Gustavus's right flank. Assailing Swedish horse meant assailing also the companies of musketeers regularly interspersed among them. When it was the Swedes who were attacking, those musketeers had the troublesome effect of slowing the pace of a Swedish cavalry charge; but for defensive occasions such as this one, their firepower was invaluable. Balked in

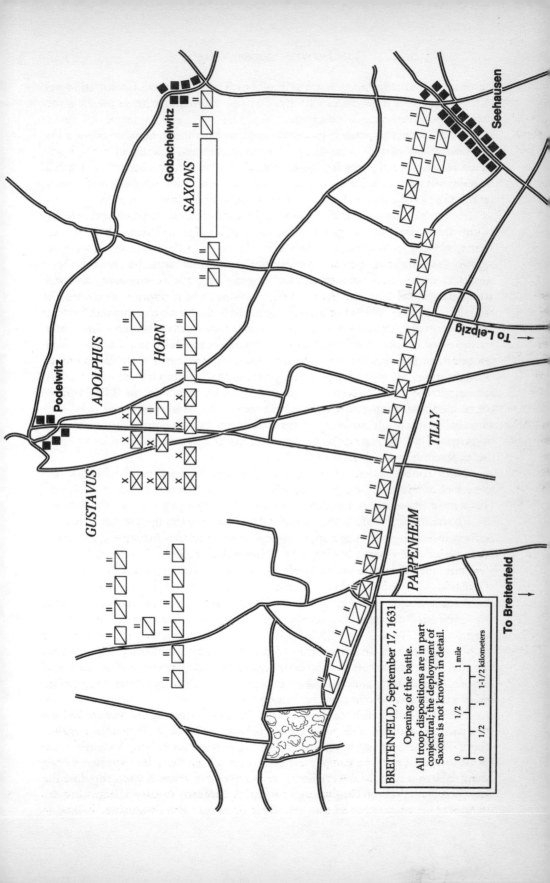

BREITENFELD, September 17, 1631
Opening of the battle.
All troop dispositions are in part
conjectural; the deployment of
Saxons is not known in detail.

Seehausen

To Leipzig →

To Breitenfeld →

Gobachelwitz

SAXONS

Podelwitz

ADOLPHUS

HORN

GUSTAVUS

TILLY

PAPPENHEIM

0   1/2   1   1 mile
0   1/2   1   1-1/2 kilometers

his head-on assaults, Pappenheim skillfully executed repeated extensions of his left to try to curl around the extreme Swedish right, but with equal skill the Swedes countered every such effort.

While Tilly was unable to launch an immediate concerted attack on his other flank, his cavalry detachments there nonetheless took Pappenheim's advance as a signal for them to do likewise. Their assault on Gustavus's left fell most heavily upon his Saxon allies, and indeed soon drove the Saxons from the field. Duke John George had little taste for warfare and seems to have been just as happy to have an excuse for a personal exit. Therefore the premature attacks of the Imperial cavalry seemed about to award Tilly a triumph after all. His veterans began to raise the cry, "Victoria!"

Against any other army of the day but that of Gustavus Adolphus, the cry would almost certainly have found fulfillment. But the Swedes' independently articulated squadrons and their superior training and discipline gave them a capacity unparalleled since the Romans to react promptly to battlefield emergencies, and not simply in a defensive but in an aggressive manner. Fortunately for the Swedes, furthermore, it was Gustavus Adolphus's ablest lieutenant, Gustav Horn, an officer whose skill in the offensive leadership of combined arms rivaled the King's own, who commanded the 4,000 troops forming the Swedish left wing that was exposed by the Saxon retreat. By now Tilly had been able to throw his infantry into the attack behind the cavalry of his right, and Horn saw some 20,000 foot-soldiers and 2,000 horse bearing down on his flank and rear. Forthwith, Horn formed front to his left, a maneuver much easier to execute under Swedish than under Imperial tactics.

Horn also appealed for reinforcements from the reserve and from as far away as the right wing, but until they arrived he would be badly outnumbered. His next response, therefore, was to attack Tilly's onslaught, to hit the advancing Imperial troops before they could thoroughly realign themselves after the confusion inevitably brought on by sweeping through the Saxons. In adversity, Horn played every card that Gustavus Adolphus's professionalization of the army gave him: the alternate musketry volleys and pikemen's charges of the infantry, the shock tactics of the cavalry, the barking of the squadron 3-pounders. With the reinforcements arriving, Horn's troops advanced again, fell back, advanced yet again, fell back again, but slowly began to make their advances exceed their retreats.

Five hours had passed since Pappenheim first attacked the Swedish right. On that flank, Gustavus Adolphus in personal command had prevailed over Pappenheim at last, and the King now perceived that the time was ripe to resolve the battle. The cavalry, his offensive weapon par excellence, would play the critical role. Himself leading four squadrons of horse in the van, Gustavus Adolphus wheeled his right wing inward toward the Imperial cannons stationed where Tilly's center had been before its infantry and cavalry were funneled into his various assaults. Overrunning the guns—mostly 24-pounders so clumsy that each required a team of twenty horses to move it—the King turned these weapons upon Tilly. Their fire was more than the already battered tercios could endure.

Before nightfall ended the pursuit, the Swedes gathered up some 6,000 prisoners. The next day they counted 7,600 enemy dead on the field. Altogether, Imperial casualties may have run as high as 20,000. Tilly himself was among the wounded. Swedish casualties are said to have been only slightly over 2,000 (not including, of course, the 15,000 or so Saxons who decamped).

Nearly two centuries later, Napoleon Bonaparte was to make the battle of annihilation, the thunderbolt of combat so destructive that it shattered whole enemy armies at a single stroke, the hallmark of his own method of war. But Napoleon never achieved a battlefield victory of annihilation more complete than Gustavus Adolphus's at Breitenfeld. And the annihilation of the enemy army that the Swedish King achieved was, as with Napoleon, precisely the goal that the King's strategy intended. The very concept of strategy—in the terms of nineteenth-century warfare, the use of battles to achieve the purpose of war—as yet scarcely existed; the military literature borrowed from the Romans and just beginning to be amplified by contemporary writers was mainly a tactical and engineering literature, a technocratic literature. The very word strategy and its equivalents were not to enter western European languages in common military discourse for about another century and a half. Yet Gustavus Adolphus surely had a conception of how to achieve the purposes for which he had gone to war, and fighting a battle of annihilation fitted conspicuously into his strategy.

THE LIMITS OF
THE NEW LEGIONS:
LÜTZEN AND AFTER

P rotestants all over Europe set their church bells pealing when they heard the news of Breitenfeld. The Swedish King had already gone far toward rescuing the Protestant cause in religiously divided Germany; Breitenfeld seemed to assure the survival of the new faith. In 1629 the Holy Roman Emperor Ferdinand II had promulgated the Edict of Restitution, ordering the restoration to the Church of all ecclesiastical lands secularized since the Peace of Augsburg in 1555; Breitenfeld left the Edict of Restitution a nullity.

Gustavus Adolphus in part shared the popular perception of himself as the Protestant champion. He was a deeply religious Lutheran who tried to fashion his army into not only a professional but a Protestant array, the military embodiment of Protestant ethical and moral convictions. As king, however, he had to concern himself to a greater degree with the more secular concerns of his realm. Even a triumph of the magnitude of Breitenfeld could not altogether ease his worries over those concerns, at a time when his country remained essentially backward and impoverished.

By precipitating the defection of John George of Saxony, Breitenfeld in fact aggravated those worries, because Sweden's campaigns in Germany could not continue without foreign subsidies and without allies. For the present, subsidies from France continued, but the Saxon exodus from the battle reminded Gustavus of the persistent precariousness of his hopes for alliances. He had sought in vain the help of Denmark, but old jealousies separated the Scandinavian kingdoms. He had practically bludgeoned the Elector and Margrave George William (Kurfürst and Markgraf Georg Wilhelm) of Brandenburg into a reluctant partnership—not for the army of Brandenburg, which Gustavus regarded with contempt, but for bases, recruiting rights, and further financial assistance; but Brandenburg was proving a most miserly and distrustful coadjutor. The departure of John George made the cooperation of George William still less certain.

Between Sweden's inherent weaknesses and the paucity and unreliability of allies, Gustavus Adolphus believed he must seek completely decisive results from his German campaign as rapidly as possible. Thus it was a battle nearly of annihilation such as Breitenfeld that he had pursued since his landing in Germany. But the Holy Roman Empire was big enough, rich enough, and resilient enough that destroying the main Imperial army even to the almost literal annihilation of Breitenfeld failed to end the war. To press the Emperor to peace negotiations in circumstances sufficiently favorable to Sweden and to Protestantism apparently demanded also the occupation of Imperial territory, the denial to the Emperor of the resources of much of his domain. It was a matter of no small concern, furthermore, to make as much territory as possible tributary to Swedish logistics.

A march on the Imperial capital at Vienna (Wien) might have seemed the obvious next step after Breitenfeld, to occupy the most critical territorial objective possible. To capture the great city of Vienna, however, might even now demand a prolonged siege, and Gustavus Adolphus doubted that his army could sustain such an effort. Therefore he moved from Breitenfeld not toward Vienna but southwestward toward Franconia and the Rhineland. If he could base himself securely on Protestant areas there, firmly linked in turn with bases in the north on the River Elbe and in Pomerania, he might generate the strength with which to eliminate Bavaria as a bulwark of the Imperial and Catholic cause. Then, reaching next into Württemburg, Baden, and Swabia, he might be able to circle still farther southward to cut off Austria from Spanish and Italian help. With Vienna thus isolated, he might move at last upon the Imperial capital.

His march south and west carried Gustavus Adolphus to a crossing of the Danube (Donau) at Donauwörth and thence to another confrontation with Tilly, who had gathered together remnants of the Imperial forces at the River Lech. On April 6/16, 1632, the Swedes defeated Tilly's army again and this time mortally wounded the enemy commander. He died a fortnight later.

Thereupon the Emperor felt obliged to counter the Swedish strategy of battles of annihilation and territorial occupation by recalling to the command of his armies a general abler than Tilly—and, Breitenfeld notwithstanding, Tilly had been an exceedingly capable general—Albrecht Wenzel Eusebius von Wallenstein (properly Waldstein), Duke of (Herzog von) Friedland, Sagan, and Mecklenburg.

A Strategy of Erosion versus a Strategy of Annihilation

It was Wallenstein's victories that had swept Imperial power northward to the Baltic to precipitate Swedish intervention in the first place. But Wallenstein was too ambitious and mercenary for Ferdinand II ever to trust him, and the two had soon afterward fallen out. For some time before the Emperor decided to return to him, this Bohemian soldier had in fact been negotiating with Gustavus

Adolphus for Wallenstein's possible alliance with the Swedish cause, an association that because of Wallenstein's aptitude for the private recruitment of regiments would have solved almost at one stroke Gustavus's need for more and better partners. In one of his rare errors of judgment, Gustavus Adolphus had allowed the euphoria following Breitenfeld to convince him that he could afford to break off the negotiations. Perhaps nothing could have come of the effort anyway; not only would Gustavus have collided in time with the same qualities in Wallenstein that irritated the Emperor, but in spite of self-centeredness, Wallenstein has sometimes been credited with a Czech patriotism and a vision of a truly unified and progressive Holy Roman Empire that would have stood in the way of any long-term harmony with the Swedes. Nevertheless, even postponing the rapprochement between Wallenstein and the Emperor might have paid incalculable dividends for Gustavus Adolphus.

Reinstated as Imperial military commander on November 25/December 5, 1631, Wallenstein invoked a strategy of erosion and delay against Gustavus Adolphus's strategy of annihilation. After the idea of strategy had become better articulated than it was in the seventeenth century, military critics would see in the opposing methods of Gustavus Adolphus and Wallenstein the classic opposite poles of strategy. For the present, Wallenstein more prosaically perceived in buying time through a strategy of delay the appropriate answer to Gustavus's need for swift results. The Empire would wait out the Swedish King, allow his country's basic weakness gradually to undermine him, and all the while erode his strength with harassing operations.

Predictably, Wallenstein recruited a new Imperial army with impressive dispatch. He then promptly joined forces with the troops of the Catholic League led by Elector and Duke Maximilian of Bavaria. Their combined army totaled about 60,000. With even more impressive dispatch Wallenstein then marched this force northward to interpose it between Gustavus Adolphus's army and the King's allies, such as they were, in Saxony and farther to the north and east.

Whatever their shortcomings, Gustavus had to remain in contact with his allies both to assure against their complete defection and to maintain a line of communications. Already the rigors of long marches distant from his bases had badly eroded his army; he retained with him perhaps only 10,000 infantry and 8,500 cavalry, though he still had seventy guns.

He occupied the fortified city of Nürnberg hoping that Wallenstein might be lured somehow into attacking him there, because with the city's guns added to his own he had about 500 cannons, which would do much to offset his reduced manpower. Wallenstein approached but was much too shrewd to attack, instead taking up a defensive position southwest of Fürth, partly in an old hilltop fortification called the Alte Feste (or Alte Veste).

Through most of the summer of 1632 the rival armies glared at each other from their defenses. Time, however, was not so fully on the Imperial side as Wallenstein hoped; for Gustavus had put in charge of all relief and reinforcement activities a leader with abilities comparable to his own, the great Chancellor Axel Oxenstierna (or Oxenstjerna). By mid-August this prodigy had contrived to funnel enough men to the King that his numbers were not much smaller than Wallenstein's. Gustavus hoped that the reinforcements if nothing else would goad his rival into assaulting the Nürnberg defenses, but the Imperial commander though doubtless surprised and troubled by Oxenstierna's achievement remained faithful to his waiting game. After all, every additional mouth to feed would aggravate Gustavus's difficulties in sustaining his army, especially while it remained immobile.

Logistics and Christian Warfare

The perplexities of provisioning his army had deeply shadowed Gustavus Adolphus's whole campaign long before the patient Wallenstein's return to military command. One of the dimensions of Gustavus's image of himself as the Protestant champion, and indeed of his deep religious convictions, was his intent to march through Germany as the Christian head of a Christian army. Swedish Lutheranism was a faith more activist in its attitudes toward this world than was German Lutheranism. In the spirit of his religion, the King hoped that his Protestant Christian army might become a reforming force beyond the military sphere, helping for example to nurture a new unity among central European Protestants. This hope required, however, the maintenance of a morally admirable army waging campaigns shaped by moral principles. Gustavus must wage war on Christian terms, if such a thing is possible. Yet these lofty aims were forever tending to founder on the grubby realities of logistics.

The discipline of the new Swedish Army—the Articles of War first read to the assembled troops by Oxenstierna as long ago as 1621 and since then read again by every regimental commander to his regiment every month—was not only a military discipline but a moral discipline. It was designed to assure that the Swedes would come to the Baltic countries and to Germany as deliverers and protectors and not as marauders. Swedish soldiers were to behave as moral men among themselves; they were not to swear or blaspheme or fall into drunkenness or consort with loose women. With Gustavus Adolphus's forces, wives went along to the wars, but not, so far as the King could prevent it, the usual rabble of other descriptions of females. Each company as well as each regiment had its chaplain, and there were to be prayers twice daily and a sermon every week. Punishments prescribed for infractions of the code were severe, with the death penalty to be invoked for more than forty offenses. The prayers, sermons, and punishments, moreover, were to assure Christian conduct toward those people among whom the army might march and fight as well as within its camps. "Such as were birds of the Divell's hatching," wrote the King's Scots soldier Robert Monro, "all such were banished from the Army, that was led by Pious and religious *Gustavus* of never dying memory."[1]

Alas for such pious intentions: the Swedes became virtual symbols of the Devil's hatchings deep into Germany as far as Bohemia, where Czech children

---

1. Quoted in Michael Roberts, *Gustavus Adolphus: A History of Sweden* (2 vols., London, New York: Longmans, Green and Co., 1953-1958), II, *1626-1632*, 242, citing Robert Monro, *Monro His Expeditions VVith the VVorthy Scots Regiment* . . . (2 vols., London: Printed by William Jones in Red-Crosse streete, 1637), II, 19.

were warned that Oxenstierna would get them if they were not good. Part of the moral breakdown sprang from the necessity for the Swedes to replenish their losses by recruiting Germans as well as their own countrymen as the campaigns grew prolonged and the battles and marches more costly. Eventually Gustavus and Oxenstierna were contracting for mercenary companies like any other war-lords of the time, and if they wanted to retain the mercenaries, they found themselves unable to impose on them the same discipline as the Swedes; the mercenaries expected their customary perquisites in looting and rapine as well as pay. Yet probably even more important, Gustavus himself had early had to abandon any illusions about how to supply and particularly to feed his troops. The limits of his resources and especially of transport meant that his army must live by plundering the lands through which it campaigned; it was difficult to put any kind of good face on that process.

Some of the logistical achievements of the Swedes were prodigious. By the standards of the time, Sweden developed a respectable metallurgical in-dustry—all the more remarkable in an economy that was in many other re-spects backward—and Gustavus Adolphus's artillery consisted largely of Swedish-made guns. Also, the King created a depot system for storing war materials at strategic points such as Erfurt, Ulm, and Mainz (Mayence), thereby anticipating the logistical methods of a century later. The rise of firearms, furthermore, had added substantially to every army's logistical problems. A victorious army of Roman times had been able to replenish its supply of ammunition by scavenging the battlefield for the spears cast by both friend and foe during the fight; the supply of gunpowder, bullets, and cannon balls in contrast had to be replenished continuously from the rear. Blacksmiths accompanying a Roman army could readily repair damaged weapons in the field; with firearms there could be a certain amount of such improvised repair, but it was much less easy. Also, the weight of the musket, its rest, and powder and balls so much exceeded that of the Roman legionnaire's sword, spear, and shield that the musketeer was able to carry considerably less of the food he ate on his own person than his ancient military predecessor, and so he had to replenish his rations more frequently.

When the soldiers were allowed to roam the countryside to forage for food-stuffs, they became free enough to ravage the people roundabout in other ways as well. The mercenaries seem to have behaved somewhat worse than the Swedes, but that was small consolation for the demise of the King's original idea of a Christian army. The King's religious and moral intentions notwithstanding, any district through which his army marched was soon a wasteland. Nor could the army survive an indefinite period without movement. War as waged by the Protestant Christian champion, like war waged by anybody else in the early seventeenth century, ruined peasants and townsfolk alike as harshly as flood, fire, or plague. And to the discomfiture of Gustavus Adolphus the strategist as well as of Gustavus Adolphus the Christian monarch, logistics forever bent his strategy—which was precisely what Wallenstein had in mind when he took up his strategy of erosion.

Maneuver Leads toward Another Battle

It was another of the Swedish Army's nearly prodigious accomplishments in this logistical wilderness that while the deadlock at Nürnberg dragged on for nearly two months, Gustavus Adolphus's soldiers were still enjoying reasonably adequate nourishment. Salt fell into dangerously short supply, and the horses suffered and sometimes died for lack of fodder, but the Swedes had established an efficient enough depot system and a secure enough line of communications to maintain themselves during several weeks of immobility.

Oxenstierna arrived in person on August 7/17, 1632, with reinforcements to raise the total Swedish force to about 30,000. The King then concluded that there were now too many mouths to feed and that he must move on. Wallenstein's skillful choice of position for the Imperial army dictated in turn that, lest flanks or rear be exposed to the enemy, to move meant to attack.

In the consequent tactical maneuvering for further advantage of position, Wallenstein briefly faltered in a way that gave Gustavus an opportunity to strike when much of the Imperial force was outside fortifications and thus with a fair chance of Swedish success; but the opportunity was missed in large part because Gustavus Adolphus was excessively busy doing almost all of his own reconnaissance. Staff work was a department in which the Swedish Army was not yet modern. The sequel found Gustavus assailing Wallenstein in the Alte Feste after all, when the inadequacies of the Swedish reconnaissance and intelligence systems led the King into the further error of imagining his opponent was retreating from that strong place.

For the Swedes, the battle of the Alte Feste on August 14/24 was a disaster mitigated by little except Gustavus Adolphus's refraining from the commitment of his entire army to what proved to be a series of futile frontal assaults against the hilltop defenses. Swedish casualties totaled some 2,500 against Imperial losses of about 600, and the repulse showed that Gustavus Adolphus was not so invincible as many of his foes had grown to fear.

There was, however, one other mitigating circumstance. Although Wallenstein's army had been throughout the recent operations better situated to supply itself than Gustavus's, Imperial rations were too low and Imperial soldiers too hungry to permit Wallenstein to follow up his victory. Instead, he also was obliged to resume movement looking for territory that had not been marched over so often that it could not longer support armies and their hangers-on. He shifted ground as though to threaten Gustavus's unsteady ally John George of Saxony.

There followed an interval of inconclusive maneuvering before Gustavus decided to return to his strategy of annihiliation by battle. With his rival's strategy as well as his own bending to logistical necessity, Gustavus Adolphus believed in the meantime that he ought to be able to recapture at least a modicum of freedom for strategic maneuver against Vienna before fighting another battle. He proposed to resume his earlier design and to march once more toward the

Danube. He reached Donauwörth for a second time by September 15/25. In that vicinity, however, he discovered that his opportunities for maneuver remained more restricted than he had thought. Word came from Oxenstierna, who had gone northward, that Wallenstein was not only persisting in his march toward Saxony, but with a considerably larger force reassembled than Gustavus had been crediting to him—the intelligence problem yet again. Moreover, another Imperial army of at least respectable strength and led by that dashing adversary Pappenheim, now a *Feldmarschall*, was also converging on Saxony. All along since the fight at the Alte Feste, Gustavus Adolphus and Oxenstierna had been assessing the enemy's gestures in the direction of Saxony as merely diversionary, designed all too obviously to pull Gustavus away from the road to Vienna. But with the Imperial movement proving to include much more numerical strength than had been expected, and with the Alte Feste's blow to Swedish prestige to be considered when weighing the extent of John George's always doubtful loyalty, Gustavus Adolphus decided he must change his mind about trying to maneuver south of Vienna and instead take the bait that Wallenstein was offering him to fight another battle. If only for the sake of the long, thin Swedish line of communications through Germany, Wallenstein had to be faced directly and subdued. And Gustavus's strategy always aimed toward eventual battle in any event.

Yet another factor almost certainly helped precipitate the next major battle, and it was a factor that must be borne constantly in mind by the student of war. To speak of the student of war implies reflection upon war in unwarlike circumstances, in the safety and tranquility of a student's environment. It suggests book-lined walls and soft leather chairs. It suggests also a scholarly temperament in the researcher, writer, and reader of the history of war, the kind of temperament that is always in danger of overemphasizing the importance to a soldier of professional education, professional study, and professional thought.

The student and the scholar are inclined to forget that even in an age when the profession of military officership had become far more fully based upon classroom education and upon intellectualized military doctrine and theory than in the time of Gustavus Adolphus, the hallmark of successful generalship never became studiousness in professional subjects or an intellectual mastery of military thought. The successful military commander has always displayed not only the educational and intellectual attainments appropriate to whatever degree of refinement the profession of officership has reached in his time, but also the temperament of the warrior. He has been a fighting man, with the pugnacious instincts of the fighter.

The profession of military officership, after all, consists of the achievement of professional skills in the conduct of organized violence. Military professionalism is professionalism in directing violence. And the successful practitioner must possess not only mental and educational attainments. He must possess also—indeed, he needs even more—a warlike spirit, the spirit that drives him zestfully into the risks and competitiveness of combat.

Gustavus II Adolphus—nearsighted, stoop-shouldered, and although relatively young inclined toward paunchiness—does not fit easily into stereotyped

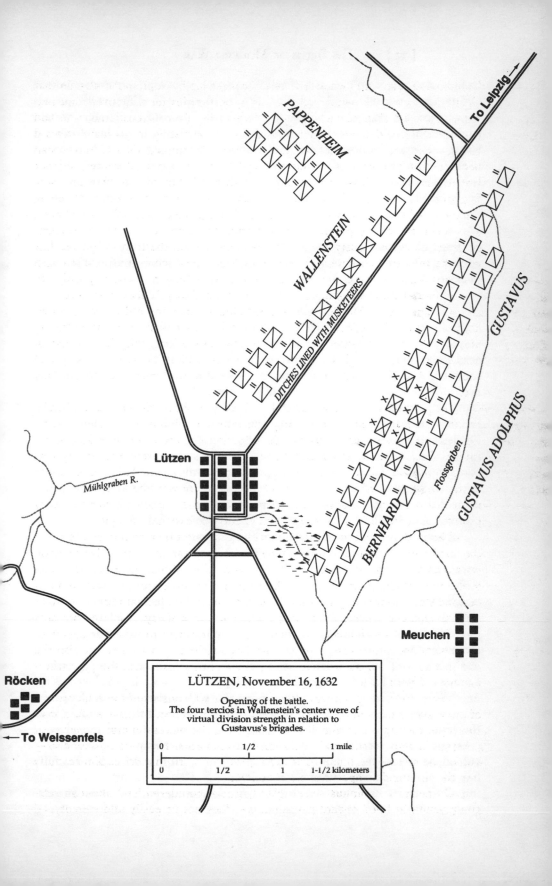

PAPPENHEIM

WALLENSTEIN

DITCHES LINED WITH MUSKETEERS

To Leipzig →

GUSTAVUS

GUSTAVUS ADOLPHUS

Lützen

Mühlgraben R.

Flossgraben

BERNHARD

Meuchen

Röcken

← To Weissenfels

LÜTZEN, November 16, 1632

Opening of the battle.
The four tercios in Wallenstein's center were of
virtual division strength in relation to
Gustavus's brigades.

| 0 | 1/2 | 1 mile |

| 0 | 1/2 | 1 | 1-1/2 kilometers |

images of the fighting man as a physical presence. A casting director would see him rather as the soldier-scholar, if he were to be cast as a soldier at all. But his appearance was deceptive; he was a warrior nevertheless. His strategy sought annihilation of the enemy forces through battle, and in late 1632 his next great battle occurred, because intellect and emotion converged to impel him toward another fight. In the current circumstances, emotion probably outweighed intellect. Gustavus marched his army into another battle less because strategic logic demanded it than because opportunity offered and the warrior spirit demanded that the opportunity be seized.

And opportunity offered not least because Wallenstein, for all his cautious strategic conviction that time was on his side and that delay worked to his advantage, was a warrior too. He also was ready to quench his warrior's thirst for combat.

Lützen

The result was the battle of Lützen, fought amid swirling fog by armies that perforce lunged at each other like blind wrestlers, and with an outcome to match its stygian atmosphere. By November 5/15, 1632, characteristic hard marching had carried Gustavus Adolphus within striking distance of Wallenstein's camp along the high road from Lützen to Leipzig. The King believed that all his recent logistical trials confirmed the necessity for his strategy of annihilation. Provisioning his army in a Germany through which soldiers had ranged to and fro for a decade and a half was growing so difficult, and so badly damaging to his concept of a Christian army, that any prospect of eliminating Wallenstein's force once and for all must be seized eagerly, before the depletion of foodstuffs might compel the Swedish army itself to disperse and to reduce the war to joustings between ever smaller rival detachments. Furthermore, a prompt offensive against Wallenstein might still catch him before Pappenheim joined him.

As the Swedish troops moved out from Naumberg before first light on that day, they collided with a probing force sent out by Wallenstein. This force stubbornly contested the Swedish crossing of a little stream called the Rippach, which consumed several hours and caused Gustavus to postpone his main attack until the next day. The effect was to herald Gustavus's aggressive intentions to Wallenstein and to assure that Pappenheim would be able to join the latter for the battle.

Wallenstein stood in defensive array with his right anchored by a castle at Lützen but with his left hanging in air. To expose a flank in this manner was not uncommon for generals commanding even the scaled-down version of Spanish tercios; Tilly at Breitenfeld, for example, had left his flanks open, because even the latter-day tercios resembled hedgehogs sufficiently to assure considerable inherent flank protection. Nevertheless, the Imperial left was not only the more vulnerable enemy flank, but by turning it Gustavus could rupture Wallenstein's line of communications and of retreat to Leipzig. Therefore, early in the morning of November 6/16 Gustavus led his own right wing, with his main strength concentrated therein, to fall on the Imperial left.

Twice, however, the mists blanketed the prospective battleground so heavily that Gustavus had to interrupt his preparations for the attack. The first time, the court chaplain, Jakob Fabricius, tried to relieve the inevitable heightening of the soldiers' fears by reciting the Protestant prayers that were so closely bound up with the King's vision of what his army ought to be (though by now many of the mercenaries picked up during Gustavus's wanderings were Catholic, if they respected any religion at all). The second delay witnessed only a restless standing to arms. Not until almost eleven o'clock did the sun penetrate the fog enough to permit the battle to begin.

For the Swedes it began well. By noon the Swedish attack had followed its intended progression to the climactic cavalry charge that was Gustavus Adolphus's trump card of aggressive war. Under the swords of the Swedish horse, the Imperial left gave way, and the Swedes rolled up Wallenstein's line toward the infantry in its center. Pappenheim arrived on the field apparently just in time, however, to reverse the tide in the Empire's favor, as though the battle followed a Hollywood script. Believing a well-aimed counterattack would save the Imperial cause, he threw his fresh horsemen into a wide sweep around Gustavus's extreme right toward the Swedish baggage train, to force the Swedes to retreat to their camps.

But battlefield romance was not to prevail on this grim, dark day—for either side. A cannon ball unhorsed Pappenheim before he could drive his assault home. A cart carried him from the field mortally wounded, and the news of his fall in combination with several of the inevitable contretemps of battle was enough to precipitate a panic in his ranks and the disintegration of his attack. At this hour in the early afternoon the fog rolled across the battleground again, so dankly impenetrable that the Swedes could not fully know that Pappenheim's counterstroke had failed and that their own triumph over the Imperial left remained almost as complete as anything they had achieved at Breitenfeld. So the Swedes withheld what could have been a final annihilating blow, and the Imperial army found just enough respite to survive.

Moreover, a secondary Swedish attack against the Imperial right had never gone well. The town of Lützen and its castle obstructed this Swedish advance, the more so because the smoke of burning buildings thickened the fog. Also, Wallenstein had a formidable concentration of artillery in this sector. Gustavus Adolphus evidently learned of the lack of progress around Lützen itself just before Pappenheim's arrival on the field. Because everything to that time seemed to be developing as he wished on his right, the King had hastened with a regiment of cavalry to rekindle the attack on his left.

He rode into a melee around his left center. Almost immediately, a musket ball shattered his left arm. Losing control of his horse, he was carried into the vortex of battle where an enemy horseman fired a pistol shot into his back. Gustvaus fell from his saddle, but with one foot stuck in his stirrup he was dragged across the field. He finally twisted free, but lay exhausted in the mud until someone shot him in the head.

Word of the King's disappearance in the melee nearly provoked a panic among the Swedish cavalry just as Pappenheim's fall about the same time undid his detachment of Imperials. Fittingly, it was chaplain Fabricius who rallied the Swedish left center by religious appeal. Dozens and in time hundreds paused to join Fabricius in prayer, and then the chaplain was able to send most of these men back into the fight. Gustavus's most capable and professional lieutenants were not present: Gustav Horn's abilities had won him a separate, autonomous command along the Rhine (Rhein); Lennart Torstensson had been captured at the Alte Feste. The command devolved on Duke Bernhard of Saxe-Weimar, who had led the left wing in the morning and proven unable to press through Lützen. Bernhard nevertheless rose to the occasion.

Still stalemated on his left and in the center, and informed that Wallenstein had by now contrived to pick up the pieces of the Imperial left for yet another counterattack through the mists where Pappenheim had fallen, Bernhard shook off counsels of retreat and determined on one more lunge into Lützen village and its Imperial artillery. The pastor Fabricius had been attempting to deny the rumor that the King was dead; Bernhard preferred rather to confirm it, and to count on the soldiers' anger for the stimulus that might generate victory where all his earlier efforts had failed.

The Duke judged the Swedish Army well. Late in the afternoon his last thrust, stoutly supported by the battalion guns firing as close up to the enemy as they could be pushed, carried the town and the Imperial battery that guarded it. Local counterattacks here and there along the line continued to threaten Bernhard's victory until well past the November dusk, but Wallenstein believed himself and his army too exhausted to fight on. The Imperial army withdrew. The Swedish army was too shaken by the price of its victory and the loss of its King to pursue. Lützen ended as a Swedish tactical victory but not the strategic triumph of annihiliation that Gustavus Adolphus had wished. The battle's stultification of nearly all power of command and control had dramatized the high risks of choosing battle as the means of pursuing strategic decision.

Swedish casualties amounted to 5,000 or 6,000, about a third of the army. Imperial losses must have been at least as high. When he learned of the death of Gustavus Adolphus, Wallenstein did not attempt to exploit it with a renewal of battle. Instead, battered as both armies were, he believed the occasion called for a redoubled effort to rid Germany of invaders by a surer and far more salutary means than remorseless war: through a reunification of the Germans.

On the Indecisiveness of War

Breaking the alliances of some of the German states with the Swedes and other foreigners and cementing unity around the Emperor demanded, however, in Wallenstein's judgment, conciliatory moves by the Emperor, in particular the withdrawal of the Edict of Restitution. Unhappily for central Europe, concessions did not fit Ferdinand II's notions of what was appropriate when the enemy had been weakened by Gustavus Adolphus's death. Wallenstein's importunities for policy changes had the perverse effect of opening the Emperor's ear to a circle of princes who were actually his enemies, who desired to refuel the Imperial distrust of the general precisely because they thought Wallenstein's policies were likely to strengthen the Emperor's authority. Ferdinand foolishly accepted the blandishments of his secret enemies.

Meanwhile Wallenstein also asserted himself by opposing a suggestion from the Spanish Habsburgs that they aid their Imperial cousins by stationing a Spanish army along the Rhine. The effect of this suggestion would obviously have been to enhance that very foreign presence in Germany which it was one of Wallenstein's highest goals to eliminate. But Wallenstein's position added the Spanish to the ranks of those poisoning Ferdinand's mind against his general. In fairness it must be added that Wallenstein's career had given Ferdinand cause to wonder where the general's solicitude for the Reich left off and his personal ambitions began.

When the passage of an entire year after Lützen and the death of Gustavus Adolphus produced no substantial military gains for the Empire, but only a further blending of Wallenstein's military strategy of erosion with his political efforts to bend events in directions unpalatable to the Emperor, Ferdinand on January 14/24, 1633/1634 signed a secret patent removing Wallenstein from command. On February 8/18 he followed up with a publicly announced patent charging Wallenstein with treason. The Emperor made it no secret, either, that he would not be displeased if someone chose to rid him of Wallenstein once and for all. A week after the issuance of the second patent, an Englishman named Captain Walter Devereux assassinated Wallenstein with a knift thrust.

Meanwhile, without Gustavus Adolphus the inherent limitations of Swedish power were decreeing that this Scandinavian country could no longer hope to act as the arbiter of Germany. Swedish military power began to beat a long, slow retreat from the mainland of central Europe. Even had Gustavus Adolphus survived the battle of Lützen, however, and carried his victory to completion through the annihiliation of Wallenstein's army, the Swedish retreat could at most have been postponed. And no more indeed could have been realistically expected even had Sweden's inherent strength been a good deal greater than it was.

The Habsburg Empire—the hereditary Habsburg domains, partly in and partly out of the Holy Roman Empire of the German Nation—possessed enough reserves of manpower to assure that if Wallenstein had been able to recruit his army of 1632 so readily, other manpower resources still remained to be tapped to raise additional armies should that one fall. It is true that Gustavus Adolphus's strategy of annihilation offered the most promising available means to push aside the Habsburgs and establish a new predominance in central Europe. But the most promising means were not necessarily means that were genuinely likely to achieve their object. Because, as Wallenstein recognized, Gustavus's strategy of annihilation remained susceptible to the tyranny of military logistics over military strategy—albeit less susceptible than a slower-working military strategy—in truth no strategy was likely to permit a foreign army to exert itself in Germany with sufficient strength over a sufficiently prolonged period to overcome the resiliency of the Habsburg Empire.

The case of the permanent separation of the northern from the southern Netherlands because the latter region was more vulnerable than the former to

Spanish military power demonstrates the capacity of armies and war sometimes to override economic, social, and cultural destinies. But the potential of war to effect such an overriding is much smaller than most proponents of the use of war as an instrument of policy have supposed—including as intelligent a proponent as Gustavus II Adolphus of Sweden. This King brought military organization and military tactics alike to about as high a degree of efficiency and effectiveness as was possible in his time. But no conceivable military force of the time, most especially no foreign one, possessed enough efficiency and effectiveness to subdue the political, economic, social, and cultural forces that sustained the Holy Roman Empire. Gustavus Adolphus was the most skillful and foresighted soldier of his day, but he was too much the soldier to recognize that war simply could never suffice as a means of attaining his lofty ambitions. With the history of the first modern armies, the history of war already begins to take shape as a history more often futile than glorious. War almost never achieves the positive goals of policy in pursuit of which ambitious leaders invoke it.

After Lützen, Swedish power went into retreat; but with neither Tilly nor Wallenstein to command his armies, and hindered by his own deficiencies of judgment, the Emperor was crippled as well. The Empire was too strong to be shattered but too unwisely governed to prosper. In these conditions the power best situated to pick up the pieces that neither Sweden nor the Empire could grasp and to emerge with the greatest profit from Germany's chaos was the subsidizer of Gustavus Adolphus, France. Less unlimitedly ambitious at the moment than Gustavus had been for a hegemonic role in central Europe, France might the more readily realize her desire for a more modest degree of preeminence. It reaffirms the lasting importance of the contribution of Gustavus Adolphus to the history of armies and war, however, that to precipitate France's attaining her desires in central Europe was to require a Swedish-style cavalry charge, at the battle of Rocroi.

3 UNDER THE LILY
BANNERS: ROCROI

From the Dutch Republic and Sweden, leadership in the creation of modern armies and the modern military profession and in the waging of a modern fashion of war passed to a state whose population and resources permitted sustaining military preeminence for a much longer time, becoming in many ways the first and certainly the most enduring of the modern great powers.

The French Army as a permanent establishment dates from the latter half of the Hundred Years War of 1337–1453. Its early history was marred, however, by its reversal of a Swedish pattern. Gustavus Adolphus relied on his mobile shock arm, his cavalry, to strike the climactic blow in his battles of annihilation; but the heart of his army's strength always lay in its infantry, the arm that more than any other wore down the enemy for the climactic cavalry charge. The early French Army, in contrast, lacked infantry strength and had to rely disproportionately on cavalry and artillery. The consequent dearth of staying power in battle, of ability to stand up under repeated harsh blows, proved a serious weakness; the most effective armies have been those that combine the enduring and resilient power of infantry with the mobility and shock power of good cavalry. For the foot soldiers necessary to hold the army together in sustained battle, the French relied too heavily on foreigners, and particularly on Swiss pikemen who did not adapt quickly enough to the evolution of firearms tactics that began with the Spanish tercios.

The humiliation of the mounted knighthood of France by the English at Crécy, Poitiers, and Agincourt drove France, before the close of the Hundred Years War, to begin replacing the undisciplined feudal levy with a professional heavy cavalry. Under Charles VII, long-service, paid horsemen called *gen-*

darmes—"men at arms"—were organized into *Compagnies d'Ordonnance du Roi* of 500 men each. The 500 men in turn comprised 100 lances, each lance consisting of a man at arms, a squire, and three mounted archers or two mounted archers and one light cavalryman called a hobilar. Though the men at arms of the *Compagnies d'Ordonnance* were still recruited from the nobility, they became well drilled careerists, and in that sense the *compagnies* became a professional force capable of coordinated maneuvers far beyond the capacities of their predecessor heavy cavalry of the feudal levy.

After the fighting against England ceased, the tendency toward professionalization in France was reinforced by Louis XI's long struggle against Charles the Bold (Charles le Hardi), duc de Bourgogne. Both the French and the Burgundians built their armies around a nucleus of careerist mounted troops, and the progress of each in tactical skill and discipline challenged the other toward still further improvement. The cynical realism of the "spider king," Louis XI, encouraged the process, too, because this monarch entertained no illusions about the values of knightly chivalry.

Nevertheless, and the realism of Louis XI notwithstanding, neither French nor Burgundian society possessed an appropriate tradition of non-noble prowess in arms or an appropriate social class comparable to the English yeomanry to nourish a native professional infantry. Burgundy like France relied largely on foreign mercenaries for its foot-soldiers. It was characteristic of Burgundian attitudes toward infantry soldiers of common birth that at the battle of Montlhéry on July 16, 1465, the Burgundian "main battle" of horse impatiently rode down their own English foot-archers, the more quickly to come to grips with the rival French cavalry. Yet Burgundy was a realm whose financial strength rested ultimately on commoners, the bourgeoisie of the Low Countries and their commerce and industry. With fitting justice the ruthlessness of the Burgundian horsemen opened the way to a French victory, so that at Montlhéry, at least, the cavalry of Charles the Bold suffered the humiliating debacle they deserved.

The French Army and the Creation of Modern Artillery

The technical trade of gunnery had about it, if anything, even less chivalric romance than infantry combat. But necessity can sometimes outweigh even the most stubborn of traditions; and for France to rid itself of the English invaders in the closing phases of the Hundred Years War, necessity decreed the development of an artillery capable of shattering the castle walls behind which the English sheltered themselves in order to maintain strongpoints and bases for marauding expeditions. Therefore, in addition to creating a careerist cavalry, Charles VII also presided over the beginnings of a technically skilled artillery, led by the brothers Maître Jean and Gaspard Bureau. Maître Jean was a lawyer and civil servant of common birth, whose mathematical mind and passion for technology led him to become both master-gunner to the King and his own cannon-founder as well. About 1429 the powder mill was invented, to fashion "corned" grains of gunpowder in which the powder no longer disintegrated, as before, into its components of sulphur, saltpeter, and charcoal. Within ten years of this invention, in 1437, the guns of the Bureau brothers drove the English from their last fortress on the upper Seine, Montereau. Similar artillery triumphs followed at Meaux in 1439, at Saint-Germain-en-Laye in 1440, and at Pontoise in 1441. Surpassing the quality and value of the *Compagnies d'Ordonnance,* the artillery became perhaps even more truly the cornerstone of the modern French Army.

The guns of the brothers Bureau were the predecessors of the equally famous artillery train of Jacques de Grenouilhac, Grand Master of the Ordnance, with which Charles VIII invaded Italy in 1494: 140 bronze 50-pounders (22.222-kilogram) (about 8 inches [20.32 cm] in caliber) and 200 bombards ranging from 2- to 16-pounders (.907 to 7.256-kilogram) (about 4 to 5 inches [10.16 to 12.7 cm]), with 8,000 horses to draw the guns and their supply wagons. For nearly ten years, these guns and their supporting cast of gendarmes and infantry swept all before them.

The Beginnings of Modern French Infantry

In 1503 came a rebuff, however, from the Spanish infantry of *el Gran Capitán,* the Great Captain Gonsalvo de Córdoba (the Italianized name usually given to Gonzalo Fernández de Córdoba). To the extent that toward the end of the Hundred Years War Charles VII had used a native French infantry, which was not very much, he had relied largely on a militia called the *francs-archers.* For the invasion of Italy, Charles VIII was able to draw a small body of professionalized archers from this force, but the prospect of a campaign of long duration and his hope for a high degree of military skill led him to rely still more than his grandfather had on Swiss mercenaries; it was hard to find French infantrymen willing to contemplate a lengthy sojourn beyond the Alps. Charles VIII died in 1498, but his son Louis XII continued the effort to establish a French hegemony in Italy and continued employing the same kind of army, with the artillery as its backbone, career *gendarmes* as its cavalry, and an infantry largely of pikemen from the Alpine cantons.

At Cerignola in Apulia on April 21, 1503 this army confronted a defensive array of the Spanish under Córdoba, positioned behind a ditch topped with wooden stakes. With the confidence born of nine years of almost uninterrupted success the French sent *gendarmes* and pikemen alike attacking recklessly in a simple frontal assault. They piled up in disorder against the ditch. Córdoba's arquebusiers peppered them there, whereupon Córdoba's cavalry followed up in pursuit.

France's Swiss pikemen were destined to score one more major victory, at Novara on June 6, 1513; but the battle of Biscocca on April 27, 1522, was almost a complete repetition of Cerignola, and a convincing enough demonstration of the need for firepower to induce even the Swiss to begin mixing arquebuses among their pikes. Loss of confidence in the Swiss precipitated the experiment of Louis XII's successor, Francis (François) I of France, with a nearly literal recreation—except for weaponry—of the Roman legions. But Francis made the mistake of copying the legions of the Roman Republic, so that what he got was another citizen-soldiers' militia but without the social and economic ingredients that permitted Roman militiamen in the era of the Republic to become a formidable army. Francis recruited from the lower levels of the peasantry rather than being able to draw on independent property-owners as his raw material, and his new legions became distinguished principally for their indiscipline.

The French evidently had to turn to a professional infantry resembling the Spanish model. They proceeded to recruit permanent *bandes*, each drawn from a particular province and numbering from 100 to 2,000 men. By about the opening of the French Wars of Religion in the middle of the sixteenth century, some of the company-size *bandes* were coalescing into permanent regiments, particularly those of Picardie, Champagne, and Le Piémont. These three were formally recognized by 1567. The Huguenots formed the regiment of Navarre, which entered the royal service when Henri de Bourbon, king of Navarre, became Henri IV of France in 1589; it thereupon became the fourth permanent regiment of the French Army.

In tactical quality, however, the French infantry regiments still had to travel a considerable distance to catch up with the Spanish tercios. Although they absorbed some lessons from the Dutch and the Swedes in the early seventeenth century, the French for a time seemed still too far behind even in the second third of the century to exploit fully the potential given them by their national unity, their population, and their resources to emerge as the principal beneficiary of the Thirty Years War.

Rocroi

At the battle of Nördlingen near Ulm on August 25–27/September 5–6, 1634, a combined Spanish-Imperial army under the Cardinal Infante Don Fernando de Austria, brother of King Philip (Felipe) IV of Spain and Portugal, achieved a victory of decisive magnitude over a Swedish army in spite of the combined leadership of Bernhard of Saxe-Weimar and Marshal Gustav Horn. Sweden's foes had modified their tactics in the direction of greater flexibility enough to cope with the Swedes; and with any approximation of parity in tactical quality, the numerical advantage of about 40,000 to 20,000 that the Imperialists possessed at Nördlingen was bound to prevail. It was Nördlingen that practically destroyed the Swedish Army as a model army; thereafter the army retained some distinction in administrative efficiency, but it was no longer preeminently the most professional army in Europe.

From disposing of the Swedes, the Cardinal Infante turned to deal with their bankers, the French. Before 1635 was out, this churchman of uncommon militancy even by the standards of the time had driven from the Netherlands deep into the possessions of the Bourbon Kings and came close to capturing Paris. Had a converging column from Franche-Comté marched with the vigor and resolution of the Cardinal Infante, the French capital might well have fallen. Nevertheless, in the next several years the Spanish reasserted the mastery over the French, and particularly the infantry superiority, that they had developed in the latter phase of the Italian wars. They scored an almost uninterrupted series of battlefield victories in the France-Netherlands border region. The Cardinal Infante died at the siege of Aire in 1641, but while the Spanish had no commander of equal merit with whom to replace him, further victorious battles suggested that it hardly mattered who commanded the *tercios viejos* when it was a matter of outfighting the French.

Still, Spanish logistical problems when making war in northern Europe, along with a continual failure to grasp Gustavus Adolphus's idea of a strategy of annihilation and therefore to exploit battlefield victories to completion, helped assure that the French repeatedly rebounded from defeat. The French and Spanish armies were still jockeying for advantage roughly along France's northeastern frontier when the death of King Louis XIII of France on May 4/14, 1643, inserted a new factor into the political-military equation. The new King, Louis XIV, was not yet five years old. Royal minorities were almost always times of instability and danger, and under the circumstances of repeated French defeats this particular minority might open the door to the overthrow of the recently established Bourbon dynasty, with incalculable consequences for the future of all of Europe.

So at least thought the latest French commander on the northern frontier, who believed it imperative to make the next battle a French victory for a change. This commander was himself a prince of the blood and cousin to the King: the twenty-one-year-old Louis II de Bourbon, duc d'Enghien, son of Henri de Bourbon, prince de Condé, and destined himself to be famous in time as prince de Condé and from 1646 as "the great Condé." His father insisted that Enghien must return to Paris on the old King's death, to help protect the position of the family and the regency of the new King's mother, Anne d'Autriche (Anne of Austria). But Enghien disobeyed his father, because he believed it was not in Paris but against the Spanish armies that the fate of the Bourbon line would be decided.

In May 1643 the Spanish governor of the Low Countries, Don Francisco de Melo, commanding the Spanish Army of Flanders, was laying siege to the fortress of Rocroi, originally called Croix-de-Rau or Rau Croix, some twenty-two miles (thirty-five kilometers) north-northwest of Charleville. At Rocroi a small French garrison guarded one of the numerous strategic hilltops of the Ardennes plateau, that area whose forests and many deeply scored stream bottoms make it less than inviting for travel by armies, but whose location has repeatedly caused it to be a cockpit of war nevertheless. The Rocroi summit commands the area between the Meuse River and the headwaters of the Oise.

Enghien's immediate problem was whether to reach out to the garrison only enough to create an opportunity for successful withdrawal, or whether to seek a battle in the hope of rescuing the place. To approach the Spanish position involved overcoming the obstacles of terrain common to the area. The hilltop, some three and three-quarters miles (six kilometers) wide, was surrounded by woods penetrated only by a narrow marshy ravine. Nevertheless, Enghien decided that the larger context of war and politics called on him to fight.

As evidence that the current enemy commander was less to be feared than the recently deceased Cardinal Infante, the French found the approach route to

Recroi practically unguarded. Whereas the Spanish could have enjoyed the advantage of contesting the French advance through the difficult ravine, they allowed Enghien to gain a position of tactical advantage about equal to their own. To that extent Enghien's boldness in seeking battle won a reward. But there remained the problems of the superior tactical proficiency of the Spanish infantry and of the moral ascendancy that the Spanish had accumulated during their string of victories.

The French had a slight numerical edge, about 23,000 to 20,000. This was not enough to prevent the battle from beginning as if to become yet another Spanish triumph. The aged *maréchal* Francois de l'Hôpital, a veteran soldier who was supposedly present as a mentor to the young Enghien, opened a premature attack on May 7/17 and nearly blundered into a disaster. The day was saved for the French only because Don Francisco failed to reinforce a cavalry counterattack into an all-out exploitation of pursuit.

Spurred by his conviction of the dynasty's need for a victory, Enghien returned to the charge the next day, but again a premature attack crumbled and provoked a cavalry countercharge. Now desperate, Enghien placed himself at the head of his own cavalry and led it in a daring ride around the Spanish left flank and thence behind the rear of the whole enemy line into the strong right flank. This adventure could have been suicidal had the enemy commander simply possessed enough presence of mind to change front to rear and pour fire into the French cavalry's flank, or if a reasonable number of Spanish subordinate commanders had acted on the same principle. But again Don Francisco proved he was not the Cardinal Infante, while the smoke, clamor, and confusion endemic to battle evidently prevented any other Spanish leaders from adequately appreciating what was going on. Consequently Enghien was able to barrel into the Spanish right rear and to rout that enemy flank. He had been lucky, and his luck grew apace; just as the Spanish right wing was on the verge of disintegration, the Spanish artillery began running out of ammunition. The rout thereupon became general. The Bourbon dynasty had attained its perhaps indispensable victory.

Rocroi by no means signaled the end of France's difficulties in finding an adequate infantry, but this triumph of *gendarmes,* good fortune, and superior generalship nevertheless began the process of translating France's potential ability to profit from the Thirty Years War into military actuality. As for the quality of the French Army and particularly of the infantry, Rocroi did not begin a winning streak. Instead, at a second battle of Nördlingen on July 24/ August 3, 1645, Enghien's generalship could achieve nothing better than a costly deadlock against a motley Imperial army, even though the Duke was assisted on this occasion by another rising young star, Henri de la Tour d'Auvergne, vicomte de Turenne, *maréchal de France.* But in spite of that, the leverage given France by national unity and overall resources superior to those of any other single European power, in combination with Rocroi's demonstration of what it might be able to accomplish in war, permitted France to dominate the peace negotiations, which after a generation of struggle had now become imperative.

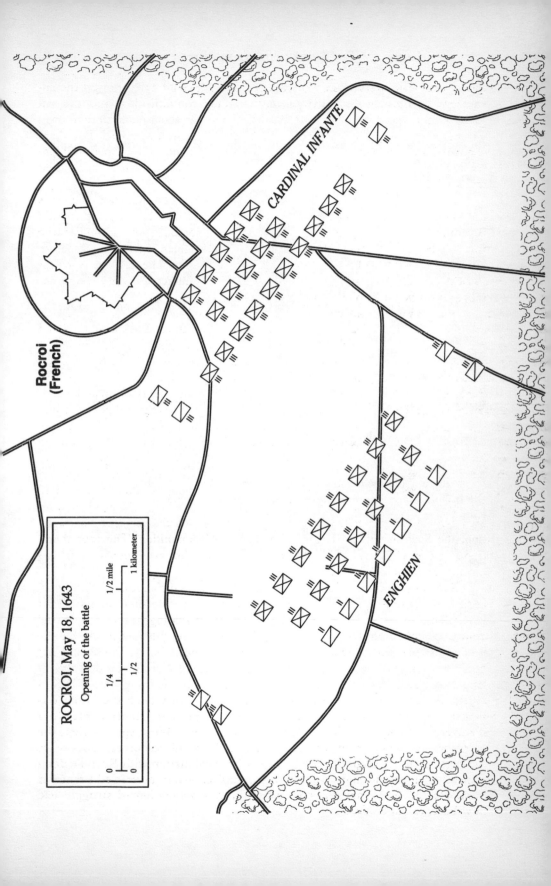

ROCROI, May 18, 1643

Opening of the battle

Rocroi
(French)

CARDINAL INFANTE

ENGHIEN

The Peace of Westphalia

In those negotiations, Sweden did not go altogether unrewarded for the achievements of Gustavus Adolphus, his generals, and the first modern army; the Treaty of Westphalia of 1648 awarded it western Pomerania and other German territory along the Baltic. The Empire paid the severest penalties. The peace arrangements recognized every German prince as a sovereign power, able to make war and peace and to govern his state independently. The Holy Roman Empire of the German Nation became more than ever a shadow, with the practical authority of the Habsburg Emperors restricted to their family domains— though even the mere shadow of the imperial legacy of Rome was to prove of no small consequence in the subsequent transformation of the Habsburg inheritance into one of the great powers of modern Europe.

France, meanwhile, won the Trois-Évêchés of Metz, Toul, and Verdun, the Three Bishoprics that histories habitually describe as strategic because they dominate the relatively short boundary line south of the Low Countries across which France and Germany confront each other directly. France also received the sovereignty of Alsace, except for the free city of Strasbourg (German, Straß-burg or Strassburg). It thus advanced a long stride toward one of the frontiers that its statesmen considered its natural boundaries, the River Rhine. In 1659, moreover, France reached its other "natural" landward frontier, the Pyrenees, when the Peace of the Pyrenees, ending the Franco-Spanish phase of the long war, granted to France the province of Rousillon. France also secured the county of Artois, detached from the Spanish Netherlands. To seal both Franco-Spanish reconciliation and the passing of Spain's former European ascendancy to France, the Infanta Maria Theresa, eldest daughter of Philip (Felipe) IV, was married to King Louis XIV.

Unfortunately for her, the Spanish princess thereupon actually fell in love with her bridegroom, whose own attentions were always to be focused on other ladies and other interests, not only the completion of the march to the natural frontiers but much larger military and diplomatic ambitions than that. In the process, however, Louis took up the work of Maurice of Nassau and Gustavus Adolphus in the fashioning of the modern profession of arms.

4 THE ARMY OF
THE SUN KING

L   ouis XIV began his personal reign at about the time when
         the strong man of the preceding regency, Jules Cardinal
         Mazarin (born Giulio Mazarini), attained through the
         Peace of the Pyrenees the substantial completion of his
own and his great predecessor Armand Jean du Plessis Cardinal de Richelieu's
work of elevating a unified France to European political preeminence. The
King, however, believed himself rightly entitled to hope for much more.
Tradition still strongly linked such preeminence with the Imperial title. France
through her acquisition at the Peace of Westphalia of territories within the
Empire was now invested with the right to vote in the Imperial Diet, and the
proper manipulation of the military power and political influence at her disposal
might bring to Louis election as the next Emperor. Adding to that the marriage
alliance with Spain and the prospect that his heirs might unite the French and
Spanish thrones, Louis could well regard himself as poised to add to the majesty
of France a reestablishment of the grandeur of the Habsburg Charles (Karl,
Carlos) V (Charles I in the Habsburg family territories), who had ruled
simultaneously over the Holy Roman Empire, Spain, and the Spanish empire in
the New World. Truly then Louis XIV would become the Roi soleil, the Sun
King, whose rays would illuminate all Europe.

Louis XIV and European Hegemony

It is a commonplace of histories of war to state that the end of the
Thirty Years War ushered in an era of limited war in Europe. The necessity for the
armies of the Thirty Years War, even for the army that Gustavus Adolphus would

have made the model Christian fighting force, to supply themselves according to the principle that war must be made to feed war left much of Germany a near-desert, ravaged and depopulated. Where towns and farms had been, sometimes only wolves now roamed. The condition of Germany seemed to offer terrifying evidence that the roots of civilization in Europe were still insecure enough, more than a thousand years after the fall of the Roman Empire, that the continent might sink into another long night of barbarism. From this precipice Europe hastily retreated. By an act of will, a prevalent interpretation of the new era of limited war tells us, Europe's statesmen for the next hundred and fifty years limited both the means and the ends of war, to avoid a return to the precipice.

Regarding the means of waging war, it is true that it was in the era following the Thirty Years War that the crucial principle of noncombatant immunity developed as a major feature of the international law of war. But limitations on means are difficult to establish while the ends of war, the objectives, remain barely limited. And the objectives with which Louis XIV commenced his active reign were little less limited than those of Napoleon or Adolf Hitler. To overthrow the Habsburgs and enhance his own candidacy for the Imperial throne, his most Christian Majesty, as Louis's title described him, was not above encouraging the Islamic Ottoman Empire in the assaults that were to carry Turkish power to the walls of Vienna in 1683. If Louis had his way, only he himself would remain in Europe as a military contender against the Turks. All Christian Europe would kneel at his feet.

The Administration of the Army under Louis XIV

Ambitious as he was, however, Louis was not without patience. He had been schooled in that virtue throughout his lengthy wait for the end of the regency and of the power of Cardinal Mazarin, the shriveled old Italian who had doled out a meager personal allowance to the boy King as though the court had been a Victorian orphanage. Louis knew that the foundation of European hegemony must likely be constructed of such prosaic materials as his own considerable capacity for hard work and an administrative apparatus capable of similar hard work; less prosaically, however, he also sought a rationalized efficiency in government scarcely seen before in any era or on any continent. To fulfill his ambitions would require also an improved French Army comparable to the army of Gustavus Adolphus in professional qualities and considerably exceeding it in size. The army itself would require an unprecedentedly rationalized and efficient administrative apparatus. As events turned out, it was to be in military administration more than in conquest that the Sun King made his most lasting mark upon the history of armies and war.

Just as Cardinal Richelieu had accomplished more than any of his predecessors among French statesmen to achieve the unification of the French state, so also Richelieu had established the foundation of centralized French military administration. The Cardinal characteristically relied on middle-class civilian bureaucrats as men who would owe their advancement entirely to himself and the King and whose loyalty would therefore be reasonably well assured. In the military sphere he chose from the ranks of such bureaucrats, and particularly from among the provincial intendants, an *intendant d'armée* as his and the King's representative with each field army. Under the army intendants, *commissaires* of similar background were made responsible for the gathering and storage of equipment and other supplies and for the most important task of seventeenth-century military administration—the basis of the professional as distinguished from the feudal army—paying the troops.

On the other hand, during Richelieu's time the regiments and often the companies remained essentially the private enterprises of their commanding officers. A *colonel général de l'infanterie* and a *colonel général de la cavalerie* proved not so much the effective agents of centralization that Richelieu intended as additional locuses of independent authority. They customarily acquired their offices by purchase, and as the issuers of commissions for their respective branches, they recouped their investments and gained dividends upon them by extracting a brokerage fee on the purchase and sale of commissions. The proof of the incompleteness of Richelieu's centralizing of military authority came when such capable leaders as Condé and, for a briefer time, Turenne joined that last-gasp effort by the nobility of France to regain their former nearly sovereign powers, the Fronde.

The Peace of the Pyrenees extinguished the final remnants of the Fronde because its remaining leaders had allied themselves with Spain. Consequently the stage was set for Louis XIV to build on Richelieu's accomplishments and to further the centralization of the army. Toward this end Cardinal Mazarin had already taken another major step by creating in 1643 the post of Secretary of State for Military Affairs, to which he named the capable intendant of Piedmont, Michel le Tellier. In 1668 the office passed to le Tellier's yet more capable— though also ruthless and unscrupulous—son, Francois Michel le Tellier, marquis de Louvois. Louvois became the primary agent in completing the transformation of the army into an instrument loyal to the King, and the first great civilian war minister in any country.

Louvois found a more than able coadjutor in the principal field commander, Marshal Turenne. Turenne had become preeminent among French generals by the close of the Thirty Years War. While he had joined the Fronde early in its course, he soon returned to the royal allegiance and won the last campaigns of the civil war by overcoming the great Condé. One of Louis XIV's first personal acts on taking the reins of government in 1661 was to appoint Turenne Marshal-General of the Camps and Armies of the King. He offered in fact to revive for Turenne the medieval office of Constable of France, suppressed in 1627, if the Marshal would convert from Protestantism to the King's church; Turenne demurred, although his dismay over the schism in Christendom was to lead him back into the Roman Catholic fold later, in 1668. Turenne might well have been regarded as the foremost battle captain of his era simply because of his victories over Condé, but until his death in battle in 1675 he continually renewed his claim to that eminence. Nevertheless, the military developments behind the front remained still more consequential than Turenne's triumphs along and beyond France's eastern frontiers.

To complete the centralization of military authority required all Louvois's talents as well as his ruthlessness. Autonomous officership could be a profitable business, and its entrepreneurs were scarcely eager to abandon their perquisites. The entrepreneurial captain received from the French state fixed rates of payment for each man in his company, in return for which he undertook to recruit, equip, clothe, and feed his soldiers. The captain's own pay, ranging from about four *louis d'or* per month in the infantry to twelve *louis d'or* a month in the King's Guards (at twenty-four francs to the *louis d'or* the *louis* amounted to perhaps twenty current U.S. dollars), would not in itself afford an adequate return on the purchase price of his commission; it might well fail to meet his expenses. Therefore the captain drove as hard a bargain as he could in the enlistment terms of his recruits, so he could retain as much as possible of the two *louis d'or* that came to him for each infantry recruit or the ten *louis d'or* per cavalry recruit. The surest way to extract a profit from fixed monthly payments per soldier was for the captain to claim more soldiers than he had. If his company muster rolls listed a hundred men but he actually had only sixty or seventy, inspections were usually infrequent enough that he could line up an assemblage of vagabonds and ne'er-do-wells for a small fee on the day when an inspector came visiting. If the inspector happened to be so perceptive or so demanding that mock soldiers would not deceive him, troops could be borrowed for the day from some other captain in return for a similar favor. The imaginary soldiers—the *passe volants*— obviously represented not only a financial abuse but a danger in war, because they gave the War Minister and the King a misleading impression of the strength they could put into the field. (The *passe volants* also make casualty statistics of the era even more misleading than those of other eras; a convenient means for the peculative officer to cover his tracks was to claim periodically that the nonexistent men had been lost in battle.)

The equipment and rations allowances for real soldiers might sometimes be almost as profitable to the captains as those for the *passe volants*. Supplies doled out frugally enough could leave a surplus for resale by the captain. If subsistence for the men and forage for the horses could be lifted from the countryside, the whole of the amount received from the King's magazines might be resold— perhaps back to the King's commissary contractors. At the extreme, captains friendly with each other might not only share each other's soldiers when their companies had to be paraded before inspectors; they might even share each other's company equipment, and thus save considerably on the purchase price.

Orders against these abuses had been issued well before Louis XIV took power; Louvois fought the system with stern punishments as well as orders. In 1663 he decreed that a *passe volant* who was detected would be flogged. Two years later he added branding to flogging. Two years after that he escalated the punishment to execution. According to a modern sense of justice, these punishments seem to strike the wrong victims; but they helped dry up the supply of impersonators, and furthermore Louvois was not content to penalize the latter. He decreed also that any soldier truthfully denouncing his captain for using *passe volants* was to be rewarded with a discharge and a payment of 300 *livres* (there were twenty-four *livres* to the *louis 'd'or*)—the money to be subtracted from the captain's pay. The captain would receive a month's imprisonment. When Louvois learned that a sergeant in the remote garrison town of Belleisle had been imprisoned for reporting his captain's *passe volants,* the War Minister saw to it that the local governor and town major who acquiesced in the arrest suffered stoppages of pay themselves, and that the captain was cashiered. It suggests much about the diligence of Louvois's enforcement measures that his inspector general of infantry was Jean Martinet, *lieutenant colonel,* whose name has become a byword.

Centralizing military administration to curb corruption was only a means to the further end of employing centralized authority to create an efficient army, one trained and disciplined well enough by sufficiently well prepared officers that it might join the Dutch and Swedish forces in meriting the adjective professional. Also significantly, Martinet was a principal director of infantry training.

To maximize the effects of training, Louvois hoped to find recruits of improved aptitude and intelligence. The idea that the rank and file of early modern armies consisted of the dregs of society dragooned into service is another staple of military history, and no doubt many of the soldiers of Louis XIV were the scrapings of jails and gutters, especially when Louis's ambitions spawned wars that chewed up more and more battalions. But reliance on the most shiftless and ignorant members of the population was precisely what Louvois hoped to avoid. He strengthened the supervisory powers of the intendants over recruiting agents and toughened the regulations that guided the agents. Recruits were to be enlisted for four years, a period long enough for adventure and for seeing something of the world, but not a lifetime commitment. The recruits were to be physically fit, bachelors or widowers, and under forty years of age. Louvois's centralization of control and crackdown on officers' peculation had among their other purposes the luring of recruits with the promise of adequate and regular pay. A uniform scale of pay for each arm of the service was established in 1670, and under Louvois's careful direction it was by and large actually enforced. In part for similar motives, the field hospital service was transformed from a scandal into an at least modestly humanitarian operation. In 1674 the *Hôtel des Invalides* was opened to house wounded soldiers, replacing a more haphazard and less appropriate practice of billeting them in monasteries. Moreover, the War Minister hoped to enhance the soldier's status in addition to his physical comfort and well-being; more than a century before the French Revolution, he implicitly anticipated the Revolution's promise that a marshal's baton might some day appear in any soldier's knapsack.

The education of officers was of course yet more important than the training of the men, if only because the latter was finally dependent on the former. Customarily, a youth looking toward an officer's career—almost always in the past a young nobleman—had been attached to a regiment to absorb whatever knowledge he could. Louvois first gave this system a certain regularity by making particular regiments the preferred training corps, especially for staff officers. Such regiments included the companies of the King's household, especially the musketeers, and after 1683 the King's Regiment and beginning the next year the King's bodyguards. Going further, in 1682 Louvois established nine cadet companies in frontier towns, commanded by the local governors and with instructors attached. By 1684 the Cambrai company had graduated some 400 officers, instructed in drill, the manual of arms, fencing, riding, and dancing, but also in geography and the principles of mathematics. Artillery and engineer officers required more advanced instruction; much of this still took place on the job, but after 1679 an artillery school was attached to the Royal Cannoneers.

Cross-currents swirled around the opening of officership to talent rather than merely to noble birth and wealth. Louis XIV preferred increasingly to staff the civilian bureaucracy of France with men of bourgeois origins; they were more amenable to training than the nobility, and more important, if they owed their advancement and their status completely to the King, he in turn could depend on their loyalty. On the other hand, the noblemen had to have something to do to occupy themselves—and to keep them busy enough so they would not try to reassert their independence. In part, the efflorescence of court ceremonies to accompany every daily activity of the King at Versailles was intended to meet this need. But the Fronde had signified the persistence of military ardors and ambitions as well as other kinds of restlessness among the nobility, and both tradition and the weight of actual power still latent in the upper social order left the King and Louvois with no choice but to retain a leading military role for men of noble birth.

Except on a limited scale—in the elite *Gardes du Corps*—Louvois was unable to abolish the purchasing of regiments and companies, a foundation of the near-monopolizing of cavalry and infantry commissions by wealthy members of the nobility. In regard to purchase, Louvois had to content himself largely with attempting to assure that the purchasers were genuinely wealthy men, again to curtail peculation by seeing to it that purchasers would not be obliged to attempt to recoup their investments through corrupt means. Ensigns in the infantry, cornets in the cavalry, and lieutenants, captains, and colonels of the nontechnical arms continued to attain their positions through wealth along with the prestige of birth.

Ingeniously, however, Louvois created another ladder of military promotion in addition to the traditional one, opening this new hierarchy to soldiers of education and merit. He instituted the nonpurchasable appointments—technically, they were not ranks—of major and lieutenant colonel. Only professional ability was to open the way into a major's or a lieutenant colonel's appointment. While the lieutenant colonel was in theory only the deputy to the colonel of a regiment, Louvois saw to it that in practice the lieutenant colonel increasingly administered and commanded the regiment, gradually elbowing the colonel toward a merely honorific status. The major in theory held no command at all; but he was responsible for the administration of the regiment including its discipline and training. In this work he was assisted by one or two subalterns designated *aide-majors*. Furthermore, in 1667 and 1668 Louis and Louvois instituted commissions as brigadiers, inaugurating the equivalent of today's lowest general-officer rank in the United States Army; but brigadiers did not necessarily need to have been colonels, and so promotion to this new position was open to those climbing either ladder, that of education and merit or that of wealth and nobility.

Aided by the new promotion system, Louvois turned his energies also to insisting upon the drilling, exercising, and disciplining of the men. At the outset of the reign, he discovered that many soldiers who went into battle had never fired a musket. Musketry drill for the infantry forthwith became routine. The cavalry, regarded as the decisive arm partly out of realism and partly out of social prestige, had suffered less neglect in training, but with this arm also Louvois insisted upon a stiffened regimen, including camps for the development of new tactics and weapons. One result was the replacement of the sword by the lightly curved saber in 1679.

It further signifies the freedom of Louvois and the King from the old assumption that only the nobility could properly bear arms to find them devoting considerable energy to an effort to create an effective citizens' militia as a reserve for the professional army. Here, too, notwithstanding Louis's conception that the state was identical to himself, lay the germ of the idea of an army that was national—an embodiment of all France—as well as professional. Nevertheless, social cleavages of the *ancien régime,* along with the persisting geographical divisions of the country, defeated the creation of anything but a dubious reserve.

The King's interest in the centralization and professionalization of his army was direct and constant. Louvois was all the more energetic and insistent a reformer because the monarch was always peering over his shoulder. It remained the ambition of the Sun King to grasp the political and military hegemony of Europe. Though fostered by skillful diplomacy and by the economic and fiscal reforms of his head of administration, Jean Baptiste Colbert, the aim would be achieved ultimately by military means. Moreover, as Louis XIV perceived it, he was being propelled to the summit of European power not only by a great army but by one that moreover was commanded by the foremost general of the age: himself.

In truth, Louis was anything but such a general. He was a physically courageous soldier, and his involvement in the military reforms shows that he was a more than competent military administrator. But he was no battlefield tactician in any but the most routine sense, and the limitations of his strategic vision were among the most important of the factors eventually frustrating the achievement of his ambitions. Still, Louis XIV ranks high among the creators of the modern military profession and of modern armies.

On July 15/25, 1661, Louis took upon himself personally the post of Colonel-General of the Infantry. His consequent direct control of what was increasingly the most numerous arm of the service tended to undermine the autonomy of the Colonel-General of the Cavalry and the Grand Master of the Ordnance, a process diligently and craftily furthered by Louvois. The personal contributions of the King to army reform are also supposed to have been as varied as conceiving the beginnings of a retirement system to pension off surplus officers in peacetime—thus creating the roots of a reserve officers' system for mobilization in war—and the introduction of portable bake ovens. It is especially plausible that the bake ovens were Louis's own idea, because they fitted both his fondness for involvement in every detail no matter how petty and his genuine concern for the welfare of his troops.

During one day's halt, the bake ovens could make enough bread for the next six days. They complemented nicely a larger reform of Louvois's, the considerable improvement and regularization of the system of prestocked magazines for supplying armies on the march. Building further upon yet another of the methods of Gustavus Adolphus, the French armies henceforth would base their campaigns on an elaborate, carefully planned system of depots intended to minimize the need to forage from the countryside and to maximize mobility. With provisions for the men and fodder for the horses stored in the fortified magazines, the French could now at least to a limited degree campaign in any month of the year. They did tend habitually to gain a march on their opponents with an early opening of the campaigning season, whereby for example they seized Namur in 1692 before their opponents were ready to repel their initiative.

Of course, the extent to which a well-planned magazine system was a great leap forward ought not to be exaggerated. Horse-drawn wagons still had to haul provisions to the armies from the magazines, and a horse consumed about twenty pounds (about nine kilograms) of fodder a day. The horses therefore ate up much of what they were hauling, and a supply train could usually sustain a field army for only a five days' march, about seventy miles (112.63 kilometers). This estimate assumed reasonably good roads and good weather, neither of which could be relied upon, especially in the mud of late winter. Like almost all the armies that had preceded them and for many years followed them, the troops of the Sun King had no choice but to feed themselves and their animals from requisitions and raids upon the countryside a good deal of the time.

Nevertheless, the magazine system did much to make possible a major increase in the numerical scale of armies during the age of Louis XIV, while the growing selection of officers by tests of education and merit permitted the increase to occur without a simultaneous descent into administrative and disciplinary chaos. Richelieu had expanded the French Army to the largest numbers of any well-organized military force since the reportedly vast military swarms of the ancients; the grim Cardinal bequeathed to his successors a standing force of 100,000 men, about double that which he had inherited. Louis XIV and Louvois, however, not only transformed the army they inherited from Richelieu and Mazarin from what was still largely a congeries of entrepreneurial companies serving under contract into the army of the centralized state, but also raised it to a standing force of some 400,000 by the time of the War of the Spanish Succession at the beginning of the eighteenth century.

Even with their rationalized administration, nevertheless, and remembering that individual field armies still tended to remain under 100,000, the increases in size made armies frustratingly cumbersome to manage. Strategy more than ever became the captive of logistics, particularly of the alternating halts and plodding advances decreed by the magazine system. Moreover, an army of 400,000 was probably too big for the French population of some twenty million to sustain without excessively burdensome strains upon an economy that was just beginning its general rise from subsistence agriculture, and that was trammeled by a nightmare labyrinth of regressive taxes whose only consistent feature was their penalization of enterprise.

The growth of the army occurred disproportionately in its infantry regiments; the proportion of infantry to cavalry in French field armies changed from two to one early in the reign to three to one well before the end of the seventeenth century. This quantitative increase occurred without a commensurate qualitative improvement in the French infantry, which in spite of professionalization continued to prove in combat to be a relatively weak link in the French military system. Moreover, because the mobile arms tend to be the arms of decision in war, a disproportionate growth of the infantry implied a retrogression from the ability of the armies of Gustavus Adolphus to achieve decision in battle.

That retrogression, furthermore, was aggravated by another development of the age of Louis XIV closely linked to the expansion of the infantry and the relative decline of cavalry: the rise of fortress systems and siege warfare.

These developments are closely tied in turn, however, to the name of the most professional of all the increasingly professionalized soldiers of the armies of Louis XIV, that of Sébastien Le Presle, sieur de Vauban.

Vauban

Paradoxically, the two arms of the service already most advanced toward professionalization of officership when Louis XIV commenced his reign, the artillery and the engineers, offered greater impediments than the infantry and cavalry in the extent to which the King and his War Minister could further apply to them their professionalizing reforms. Artillery officership became yet more professional with the development of artillery schools, but until 1672 civilian contractors still hired soldiers to handle the guns, being paid for each gun brought into action, and even later the transporting of the guns to the battlefield was still hired out to contractors.

Nevertheless, the War Minister gradually extended his authority over the artillery at the expense of the Grand Master of the Ordnance. In 1677 Louvois formed the *Fusiliers du Roi*, consisting of six battalions of gunners, escort troops, and appropriate laborers. In 1693 this force was renamed the *Royal-Artillerie*.

Similarly, but with less success, Vauban sought the creation of an engineer corps with its own troops and administration. The branch of the service that was most professional at the top proved for a complex of reasons, rooted in tradition and vested interests, to be yet more resistant than the artillery to removal from entrepreneurial auspices at its working levels.

The sciences of artillery ballistics and the design of fortifications that could withstand artillery projectiles had both been advancing since the time of Simon Stevin. Artillery had long since thrown high-walled medieval castles into the dustbin of military antiquity. Fortress design had become highly standardized. Low-silhouette gun platforms followed a polygonal bastioned trace, adapted of course to the dimensions of the site to be defended and the contours of the terrain. There would be a heavy inner rampart, with a parapet for the mounting of the guns; a broad ditch outside it; and then an outer rampart, the glacis, with an open, gentle slope up which assailants must advance while exposed to the defenders' fire. The key element, however, consisted of the outlying bastions, which were designed to place every potential axis of attack not only under fire but under crossfire, and always to be mutually supporting. The design of the bastions had come to be a matter of applying standard geometric rules, formulated largely by Blaise, comte de Pagan, a mathematical theorist rather than a practicing engineer, and set forth in his *Les fortifications du comte de Pagan.*[1]

The forts designed by Vauban for Louis XIV have come to be divided by historians into three stages of development. Vauban's first system was essentially that of Pagan. The modifications that were to make Vauban the most renowned of military engineers, in his own time and thereafter, came late in his career, after he had already constructed most of his fortresses. Even then, there is debate about the originality of his later designs. But in time the grandiose ambitions of the King came to overshadow the monarch's own considerable professionalism of military judgment, the ambitions through their excesses threatening the French monarchy with ruin, and at that stage it was the geometrically expressed professionalism of Vauban more than any other single military factor that rescued the kingdom and provided an ample foundation for Vauban's renown. Vauban's fortresses saved France from military collapse. Military professionalism does not consistently curb ambition with the moderation of judgment that ought to be nurtured by study; as early as Gustavus Adolphus, the beginnings of professional military education and of a professional outlook had on the contrary encouraged a quest for unlimited victories of annihilation. In Vauban, however, and under the influence surely of the dawning Age of the Enlightenment, professionalism did imply moderation and reason.

Appropriately, Vauban exemplified also the opening of advancement in the French Army to talent and study in place of wealth and birth. At most, the great engineer's family had occupied the lowest rung of noble status. Vauban's bourgeois ancestors had acquired a small fief during the middle of the sixteenth century. Born at Saint-Léger in 1633, Vauban enlisted at the age of seventeen in the rebel forces of Condé during the Fronde. When Condé returned to the King's service, Vauban entered that service as well, in 1653; he was destined to remain in it until a few months before his death in 1707, ceasing his work in the field only when his promotion to the rank of *maréchal de France* on January 4/14, 1702/1703 made him too exalted a personage to engage in the technical work of supervising fortress construction and conducting sieges—although first he carried to a successful conclusion his siege of Alt Breisach.

Between the Peace of the Pyrenees in 1659 and the beginning of Louis XIV's first war of conquest, the War of Devolution, in 1667, Vauban as a young lieutenant and *ingénieur du roi* was busy repairing and improving fortifications. During the War of Devolution, as a lieutenant of the Guard, equivalent to a colonel elsewhere, he displayed a mastery of siegecraft that captured the attention of Louvois. With characteristic decisiveness and dispatch, the War Minister pushed him abruptly upward to be *maréchal de camp,* equivalent to major general, in 1676, and *commissaire-général des fortifications* in 1678. Thenceforth his career alternated between besieging and capturing fortresses during the subse-

1. (Paris: C. Bosogne, 1645).

quent wars of conquest and improving, building, and defending fortresses during periods of peace and military recession.

On the offensive, it was Vauban more than any other practitioner of siegecraft who transformed that endeavor into the formal ritual now synonymous with our conception of the siege in the century preceding the French Revolution. With Vauban, the purpose of formality and ritual was the avoidance of bloodshed. He hoped to make war an extension of policy by means other than the promiscuous destruction of life. Beginning a siege by assembling his men and supplies out of range of enemy gunfire, he proceeded to advance toward the enemy's works by means of elaborate systems of parallel trenches followed by carefully contrived and protected approach trenches followed in turn by additional parallels, all designed to keep the besieging forces under protective cover.

If an assault ultimately became necessary to carry the defender's outer ramparts, the assailants would be shielded as much as possible by painstakingly sited covering fire from behind earthworks; preferably, at this juncture the defender would be driven from the parapet of his outer ramparts by ricochet bombardment. Once in possession of the defender's outer line, the attacker would bring up siege artillery to breach the main defenses. So inexorable was a Vauban-style advancement of approaches from parallel to parallel that, in response to the same methods adopted by his opponents, Louis XIV ruled that a fortress commander might honorably surrender once an initial breach had been made in his citadel and he had repulsed one assault.

Here is an alluring vision of the path that military professionalism might have taken toward the reduction of the violence of war, if professionalism had hewed consistently to Vauban's line of development: ritual substituting for bloodshed as the means of resolving political predicaments that had led to invoking military force. But Vauban's siegecraft did not make sufficient allowance for anger and other passions, including the kind of ambitions that swayed his own military master. In ritualistic siege warfare, the enemy as well as the assailant lived to fight another day; angry and consumingly ambitious warmakers preferred that he should not do so.

Unless the defender could interrupt the siege by bringing a reinforcing army to the scene, the only likely military salvation for the target of a Vauban-style siege lay in the assailant's exhausting his provisions before the accumulated stores within the citadel were similarly exhausted. The introduction of the magazine system into the French Army and its inevitable adoption by other armies notwithstanding, the limitations of wagon transport assured that running out of provisions was always at least a shadow on the horizon. Foraging parties could all too quickly level the resources in the environs of a besieged fortress. Therefore the besieged sought to buy time; to delay the consummation of a siege was at least possibly to prevent that consummation. Vauban's improvements in fortress design consequently had as their essence the beginnings of invoking the principle of a defense in depth.

Before Vauban's second system, the outlying bastions all remained attachments of the main enclosure, the main enceinte. If any of them fell, the citadel itself was immediately threatened. In the second system which began to appear in 1682, Vauban replaced the bastions at the angles of the polygon with small works or towers that were themselves covered by detached bastions. The assailant had to work his way through the latter, and even when he had done so, he did not yet threaten the principal works. Vauban's third system consists in fact of a single fortress, that of Neuf-Brisach in Alsace, reconstructed after 1697, in which almost everything was increased in scale, especially the towers at the angles and the detached bastions.

Vauban had less immediate influence on other fortress designers than his fame might imply. For one thing, the King considered himself master of the art and science of fortification as of other aspects of war—and as usual, with considerable reason in terms of diligent study—but he did not consistently accept Vauban's concepts. In the conduct of war as distinguished from military organization, Louis XIV was surprisingly conservative. For example, in 1687 Vauban proposed what would become the bayonet, a short sword to be mounted on a musket with a socket holding the blade to the side of the barrel so that the musket could be fired; but Louis and Louvois were slow to accept the idea, and one-third of the French infantry remained pikemen until 1703. The King's response to innovative fortress design was similar.

In addition, Vauban's influence was limited by the absence of adequate written or published explications of his principles of fortress design. During his lifetime only two books were published under his name, neither focusing directly on his main legacy. *Directeur général des fortifications*(1685)[2] concerned itself principally with administration. There was also *Projet d'une dixme royale, qui suppriment la taille, les aydes, les douans d'une province à l'autre (1707).*[3] The three treatises that became best known in time were combined and published in a badly edited form only as late as 1737: *Traité de l'attaque et de la défense des places suivi d'un traité des mines.*[4] While the latter work was republished from time to time, publication of editions prepared with suitable care waited until almost the end of the eighteenth century or later: *Traité de l'attaque des places* . . . (1794);[5] *Traité des mines* . . . (1795);[6] *Traité de la défense des places* . . . (1829).[7]

Vauban merits the appellation of professional soldier because he was a strategist as well as a technician. He perceived his fortresses as bases for the offensive as well as anchors for the defense of France. He regularly and copiously advised Louvois on the proper location and interrelationship of strong points for both these purposes, and on the places whose capture should be sought to give France the strongest possible military frontier. During the Dutch War of 1672–1678, for example, for example, his specific suggestions along these

2. (La Haye ['s Gravenhage; The Hague]: Chez Henri van Bulderen, marchand libraire, in de Footen, à L'enseigne de Mezeray, 1685).

3. (Rouen [?]: No publisher, 1707). (See *Projet d'une dixme royale, suivi de deux écrits financiers, par Vauban; publié d'après l'édition original et les manuscrits avec une introduction et des notes*, par Émile Coornaert . . . (Paris: F. Alcan, 1933).

4. (La Haye ['s Gravenhage; The Hague]: P. de Hendt, 1737).

5. (Paris: Magimel, 1794).

6. (nouv. éd., revué, rectifiée, aug. de developpemens considerables . . . par Frédéric P. Foissac, Paris: Magimel, 1795).

7. (Nouvelle édition . . . publiée . . . par M. le Baron de Valazé, Paris: Anselin, 1829).

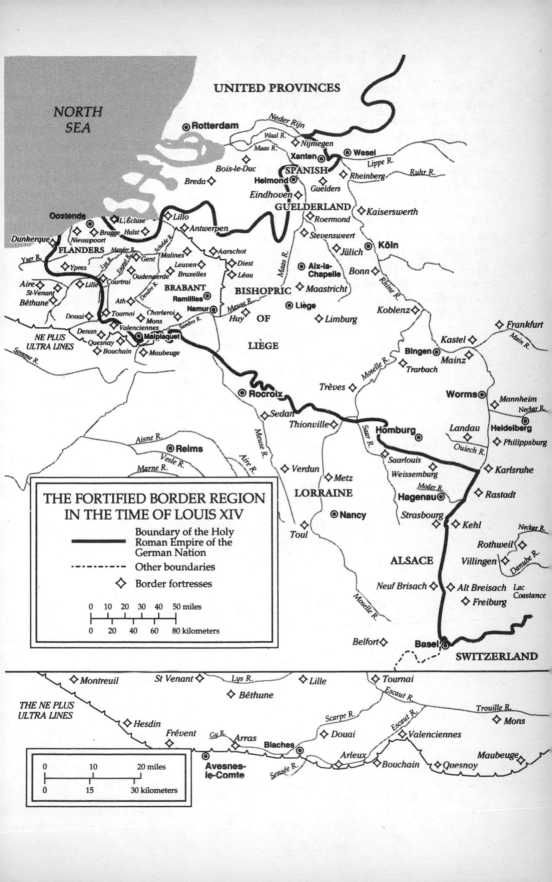

THE FORTIFIED BORDER REGION IN THE TIME OF LOUIS XIV

Boundary of the Holy Roman Empire of the German Nation

- - - Other boundaries

◇ Border fortresses

0   10   20   30   40   50 miles

0   20   40   60   80 kilometers

NORTH SEA

UNITED PROVINCES

Neder Rijn

◉ **Rotterdam**

Waal R.

Maas R. ◉ **Nijmegen**

◉ **Xanten** ◉ **Wesel**

Bois-le-Duc SPANISH *Lippe R.*

Helmond ◇ *Rheinberg* *Ruhr R.*

Breda ◇ Eindhoven ◇ *Guelders*

GUELDERLAND ◇ *Roermond* ◇ **Kaiserswerth**

Oostende L'Écluse ◇ Lillo ◇ *Stevensweert*

◇ Brugge Hulst ◇ Antwerpen ◇ **Jülich** ◉ **Köln**

Dunkerque Nieuwpoort ◇ *Aix-la-* Bonn ◇

FLANDERS Gent Malines ◇ Aarschot Chapelle ◇ *Rhine R.*

Yser R. ◇ Ypres *Lys R.* ◇ Diest ◇ Maastricht ◇ **Koblenz** ◇

Aire Courtrai Oudengerde ◇ Léau BISHOPRIC

St-Venant ◇ Lille ◇ Bruxelles ◇ *Liège* *Frankfurt* ◇

Béthune Ath BRABANT ◇ OF *Limburg* **Bingen** ◉ *Main R.*

Douai ◇ Tournai Ramillies ◇ Huy ◇ **Mainz** ◉

Denain ◇ Mons Namur ◇ LIÈGE *Trarbach* ◇

NE PLUS Valenciennes Sambre R. *Moselle R.* **Worms** ◉ *Mannheim* ◇

ULTRA LINES Quesnay ◇ Malplaquet *Trèves* ◇ **Homburg** ◇ Landau ◇ **Heidelberg** ◉

Bouchain ◇ Maubeuge ◇ ◉ **Rocroix** *Sedan* ◇ *Thionville* ◇ *Saar R.* Saarlouis ◇ *Ouiech R.* *Philippsburg* ◇

Somme R. *Aisne R.* Weissemburg ◇ **Karlsruhe** ◇

◉ **Reims** *Vesle R.* *Verdun* ◇ *Metz* ◇ *Moder R.* Rastadt ◇

Marne R. LORRAINE **Hagenau** ◉

Aire R. *Meuse R.* *Strasbourg* ◇ **Kehl** ◇

◉ **Nancy** *Toul* *Rothweil* ◇ *Neckar R.*

ALSACE Villingen ◇ *Danube R.*

Neuf Brisach ◇ **Alt Breisach** ◇ *Lac Coastance*

Moselle R. **Freiburg** ◇

Belfort ◇ **Basel** ◉ SWITZERLAND

THE NE PLUS ULTRA LINES

◇ **Montreuil** *St Venant* ◇ *Lys R.* ◇ **Lille** ◇ **Tournai**

◇ **Béthune** *Escaut R.*

◇ **Hesdin** *Scarpe R.* ◇ **Douai** *Trouille R.* ◇ **Mons**

Frévent *Gy R.* ◇ **Arras** **Biaches** ◉ *Escaut R.* ◇ **Valenciennes**

◉ **Avesnes-le-Comte** *Sensée R.* **Arleux** ◇ **Bouchain** ◇ **Quesnoy** **Maubeuge** ◇

0   10   20 miles

0   15   30 kilometers

lines led to the sieges of Condé, Bouchain, Valenciennes, and Cambrai, and to the capture of the first two places in 1676 and of the second two the following year. In the Peace of Nijmegen (Nijmwegen) in 1678–1679, France yielded certain Flemish territories to secure additional strategic fortresses, particularly Saint-Omer, Cassel, Aire, and Ypres, while also acquiring Nancy in Lorraine. Because vulnerabilities remained along certain sections of the frontier, Vauban promptly presented an appraisal of the overall defense of the border between the English Channel and the River Meuse. Among the characteristics making a fortress strategically important he emphasized control of the crucial routes into the Kingdom, control of bridgeheads across major rivers, control of internal routes of communication, control of major seaports and good harbors, and control of principal cities capable of contributing to the expense of forts and of helping sustain their own defense as well as otherwise important to the economy of the realm.

Along the northern frontier, Vauban proposed, the roads into France should be guarded by two lines of about thirteen fortresses each, arranged in an approximation of infantry battle order. The first line should be strengthened and linked together by a waterline between the Channel and the Scheldt (Dutch, Schelde; French, Escaut). In general, streams or canals should tie the fortresses together and themselves be protected by outlying defensive works. Relatively small garrisons in such a system of forts would protect the Kingdom from enemy raids. Should an enemy attack with a full army, a French Army would of course be necessary for defense, but the added strength and flexibility imparted to the army by the fortresses might save the Kingdom.

The Early Wars of Louis XIV

Among the enemies cast up by the Sun King's ambitions was a sovereign not unlike himself in administrative and organizing capacities, persistence of purpose, and military knowledge though without exceptional talents in military command. Among Louis's enemies, yet more unfortunately for him, there also emerged two of the most able military commanders in all history. The sovereign was William (Wilhelm, Willem), Prince of Orange, Stadtholder of the Dutch Republic and King of England. The two great commanders were John Churchill, first Duke of Marlborough, and Prince Eugène of Savoy. To thwart rivals of this caliber would require all the enhanced professional capacities of the French Army, and ultimately all the strengths of the Vauban fortress system.

When the Infanta Maria Theresa of Spain became Marie Thérèse, *reine de France,* there came with her to Louis, at least in his own perception, a claim to the Spanish Netherlands upon the death of her father. Marie was a child of Philip IV by his first marriage, to Princess Elisabeth of France, sister of Louis XIII; the heir to the Spanish throne, the future Charles (Carlos) II, was the offspring of a second marriage, to the Archduchess (*Erzherzogin*) Maria of Habsburg, daughter of the Emperor Ferdinand III. In some provinces of the Netherlands the so-called principle of devolution decreed that property descended only to children of a first marriage. Upon that principle Louis asserted that the Spanish Netherlands, so desirable an extension of the French frontiers toward the Rhine, was his wife's and therefore his own share of the legacy of Philip IV.

The Spanish responded that their empire was not a mere landed estate, and they repudiated Louis's claim; but the French monarch thereupon opened the War of Devolution in 1667 by overrunning a number of strategic places in the territory he claimed. For good measure, his army also occupied Franche-Comté in a two-week campaign, demonstrating the improved efficiency of the French forces and ensuring against Spanish reinforcement of the Netherlands by that route. These events naturally alarmed the Dutch, who promptly persuaded England (along with Scotland) and Sweden to join a Triple Alliance against France. With his improvements of the French Army just under way, however, Louis did not yet feel ready for a large-scale war, and in 1668 he agreed to the Treaty of Aix-la-Chapelle, ending this opening round of his military bid for European hegemony. Under the treaty, he disgorged Franche-Comté but retained eleven of the Netherlands towns he had seized, including Lille, Tournai, and Charleroi.

And it was certainly no more than a first round that had ended. Louis took advantage of the financial difficulties that perpetually plagued the small kingdoms of Sweden and England in this era to detach them from the Dutch alliance by means of bribes and subsidies. In June 1672 he abruptly marched forward in the Netherlands once more, striking directly against the Dutch. Taken by surprise, the Dutch had to open the dikes and inundate much of their country to hold back the invader. In desperation, they also rebelled against their current leader, the Grand Pensionary Johan de Witt, and recalled to power the party and house of Orange and Nassau in the person of William, Prince of Orange and Count of Nassau, who was named Stadtholder of the Republic, captain-general, and admiral for life.

When a riotous mob in The Hague ('s-Gravenhage; Den Haag) followed up the coup by murdering Johan de Witt and his brother Cornelius, William rewarded the principal instigators of this outrage. Such coldness and cynicism were to prove typical of the man. Within a small, frail, even consumptive constitution, and behind a baleful, fishlike countenance, William nourished a ruthless determination to preserve the Dutch Republic from the French despot by any means and at any cost.

Other Europeans' fear of France again came to the aid of the Dutch in spite of Louis's financial manipulations. The Habsburg Empire under Leopold I; the Electorate of Brandenburg under yet another ambitious statesman, named Frederick William (Friedrich Wilhelm); Denmark; Spain; and at length even England—notwithstanding French subsidies—aligned themselves with the Dutch. The Dutch War, as this second round is called, witnessed French troops pushing not only into the Netherlands but as far afield as the Rhenish Palatinate. Gradually the forces of the alliance checked their advances, however, and the Dutch War ended with several treaties called collectively the Peace of Nijmegen of 1678–1679. Under its terms the *Grand Monarque* agreed to buy additional time for the further strengthening of his army by settling for the retention this time around of Franche-Comté, while receiving several additional favorable territorial adjustments in the Netherlands. For the present, he gave up the Palatinate.

Reverting to legalistic contrivances similar to his earlier employment of the principle of devolution, Louis next sought to further his territorial ambitions and to secure the strategic sites desired by Vauban through the institution of chambers of reunion, special courts intended to ferret out forgotten titles that he might claim. The Imperial City of Strasbourg, especially recommended by Vauban as a key bridgehead on the Rhine, succumbed to French occupation under this pretext in 1681. Luxembourg fell in 1683, and four years after that, Louis reached again into the Rhenish Palatinate.

Thereby he once more overreached. William of Orange had never rested in his efforts to form new combinations against the French King, and in 1686 his efforts had come to fruition in the League of Augsburg, which united with the Dutch Republic for resistance against France the Holy Roman Empire, Spain, Sweden, and Bavaria. Louis's new advance into the Palantinate precipitated the outbreak in 1689 of the War of the League of Augsburg.

By that time, England and Scotland had rejoined the anti-French coalition, for in 1688 the Glorious Revolution had propelled William of Orange into a share of the English, Scottish, and Irish thrones. As William III he would reign jointly with his Queen, Mary II, the Protestant daughter of the ousted Catholic King James II. For the English Parliament, the purpose was to assure a Protestant succession to the throne. For the Dutch patriot William, the purpose was to unite under his leadership the resources of the British Kingdoms and the Dutch Republic in the battle against the King of France.

The English Army to 1660

The English had been slow to follow the example of continental states in establishing a standing army led by professional officers. The English military tradition combined high regard for officership as a suitable gentlemanly pursuit, a regard inherited from medieval knighthood and passed on in the early modern era to the rural gentry, with an inheritance of a part-time militia soldiery, based on the principle of a universal military obligation owed by able-bodied freemen. This inheritance reached back to the Anglo-Saxon fyrd and to the Assize of Arms of Henry II (1181) and the Statute of Westminster of Edward I (1273). England's island geography nourished the tradition of a part-time soldiery, whether among gentlemen-officers or yeomen militia, by preserving the realm from continuous or near-continuous war. (When the ambitions of England's Kings and ruling families nevertheless generated the near-continuous Hundred Years War against France from 1337 to 1453, there was a temporary divergence toward a professional army.) For the most part, geography permitted Englishmen to believe that war was only an occasional, passing phenomenon and that armies therefore ought to be raised to fit the particular needs of the occasional war and thereafter be disbanded. The early centralization of power in the English monarchy, against which the feudal nobility could not sustain the kinds of challenges that had bedeviled the medieval and early-modern French Kings, similarly encouraged the belief that armies are not permanently required, since the kingdom usually enjoyed relative internal tranquility. The similar absence of continental-style standing armies in Scotland, Wales, and Ireland finally assured the English devotion to militias, not professional soldiers.

During the middle years of the seventeenth century, the military Commonwealth of the Lord Protector Oliver Cromwell appeared from a time to be turning England into a different military direction. The very absence of a standing army had rendered King Charles I vulnerable to the demands of Parliament for a larger weight in the King-in-Parliament combination that governed England. Charles's vulnerability became acute when in 1639 and 1640 his efforts to impose the Church of England upon the Calvinist Scots precipitated war with his northern Kingdom and made him dependent on Parliament for funds and forces to conduct the war. His effort to break loose from that dependence precipitated in turn the English Civil War in 1642, with both the royal and the parliamentary factions employing militia-type armies at the outset. In the course of the war, however, "the army under Sir Thomas Fairfax" on the parliamentary side evolved into the "New Model Army," which merited its description in part because the Puritan religious element in the parliamentary cause gave the army an extraordinary cohesion based upon religious zeal, but also in part because it was a well-trained, well-disciplined, tactically proficient army approximating the new professional standards of the Dutch and the Swedes. These standards were instilled in the army both by leaders who had campaigned on the Continent, such as the Lord General of Scotland, Alexander Leslie, from 1641 first Earl of Leven, who had fought with both the Dutch and Gustavus Adolphus and risen to marshal in the Swedish service, and by diligent self-taught soldiers who learned by emulating those like Leven who had fought in Europe's wars. Oliver Cromwell, by June 10/20, 1645, and through the rest of the Civil War a lieutenant-general, belonged to the latter category.

When the parliamentary forces eventually triumphed in the Civil War in 1649, tensions between the zealous religious independents prominent in the army and the more moderate Presbyterianism that prevailed in Parliament broke into the open. Thereupon the army not only forced the execution of the King but suppressed Parliament as well, establishing a Commonwealth with Cromwell becoming Lord Protector and virtual dictator. To maintain the Commonwealth, the army itself had to be maintained as a standing force, and thus came the new direction of English military history.

In the late 1650s the Commonwealth kept up a standing army of some 40,000 men stationed both at home and abroad. Employing the army not only to ensure domestic order but also as an instrument of foreign policy, and sending some of his best generals to sea to create also a disciplined navy, Cromwell made England a power to be reckoned with in continental affairs to an extent unprecedented since the halcyon days of the Hundred Years War. The expeditionary forces dispatched to the Netherlands by Queen Elizabeth I to help shield England from Spain by keeping the Spanish preoccupied with the Dutch had at best been supported on a shoestring, long before they had to be absorbed into the Dutch Army. Similarly, the various contingents from the British Isles that fought for Gustavus Adolphus and other continental soldiers had been private ventures, not producing any particular political credit for the British Kingdoms. Now, the

First Anglo-Dutch War in 1651–1654 and a similar trade war against Spain in 1655–1658 offered hints of England's imperial glory to come.

The Spanish War brought luster to the newly professionalized English Army; it was fought in alliance with France, and at the battle of the Dunes, fought near Dunkirk on May 24/June 3, 1658, when an Anglo-French force under Marshal Turenne faced the Spanish whose leaders included the Prince of Condé, it was 6,000 red-coated English infantry who bore the brunt of the struggle. This too was a portent of things to come, for the English and British infantry were to prove the backbone of their army in direct contrast to the relative weakness of the French infantry. The immediate effect of the battle of the Dunes was to defeat a Spanish effort to relieve Dunkirk from siege and thus to assure the fall of the town.

Such feats of arms notwithstanding, however, the years of the Commonwealth blighted the prospects for a professional English Army. They associated such an army indelibly with an attack upon the traditions of both Crown and Parliament and with dictatorship. For the long run, the English distaste for standing armies was redoubled; Cromwell's reign became a byword symbolizing the dangers of a standing army forever afterward, wherever the English language and the English political heritage traveled, most notably in the United States of America.

By the time Oliver Cromwell died on September 3/13, 1658, the muskets and sabers of the army could no longer have sustained the Commonwealth without a force of Cromwell's character behind them. After the death of the Lord Protector his elder son and successor, Richard, promptly lost control of affairs, and English politics plunged into turmoil. Efforts of the army to enhance its autonomy helped lead Richard to dissolve the Commonwealth Parliament and to recall the Rump of the Long Parliament that had directed the Revolution against King Charles. When this body proved insufficiently responsive to the army's wishes, Major-General John Lord Lambert on October 12/22, 1659, led still another expulsion of Parliament from its chambers by a body of soldiers.

Thereupon General George Monk (or Monck), commander-in-chief in Scotland, once among the most capable royalist commanders but more recently an able military coadjutor of Oliver Cromwell on both land and sea, led the core of his army of 10,000 men southward to restore order. Monk avoided battle with Lambert until the latter's force began to melt away from lack of political support and thus from lack of pay also. On November 24/December 4 the Republican Council of State named Monk commander-in-chief of the army. Distrusting Monk's still unannounced purposes, other parts of the army along with the navy reaffirmed their loyalty to a parliamentary, nonroyalist regime. When Monk crossed the Scottish border at Coldstream on the Tweed on January 2, 1659/January 12, 1660, however, potential rival detachments of the army either proceeded to disband or prepared to join his forces as he marched toward London. Once in the capital Monk called for a new Parliament, which after dictatorship followed by chaos was virtually certain to have a royalist majority. Monk was already in communication with the exiled Charles II to assure that there would be no untoward action or declaration from that quarter to prevent a restoration of the monarchy. On May 1/10 the new Parliament voted for the return of the Stuart King, and on May 29/June 8 Charles II entered his capital city. The shift in loyalty of one of the best disciplined and most capably led portions of the army had proven all that was necessary to tip the political balance in favor of the King.

General Monk would have preferred to be an apolitical professional soldier, and his intervention in politics had come about only because he perceived no other means to return himself to his role of preference. Nevertheless, the decisive contribution of the army to bringing back the monarchy, just as the army had earlier been decisive in overthrowing it, still further reinforced England's traditional aversion to a standing soldiery and guaranteed that there would be a rapid dissolution of most of the army.

The Beginnings of England's Standing Army, 1660–1688

In spite of the latter circumstances, the modern English Army is often dated from 1661, because the continuous history of the oldest regiments in approximately their present form dates from the Stuart Restoration. On February 14, 1660/February 24, 1661 the Lord General's—that is, Monk's—Regiment of Foot and the Lord General's Regiment of Lifeguards laid down their arms as troops of the Commonwealth army, but they immediately took the arms up again in the royal service, as the Lord General's Regiment of Footguards and the Lord General's Troop of Guards. The former survives as the Coldstream Guards (the Coldstream Regiment of Foot Guards from 1670, the Coldstream Guards from 1817), the latter as part of the Life Guards.

Nevertheless, the remainder of the Commonwealth army was disbanded, with the ready acquiescence of General Monk, the model apolitical soldier. More than that, the Militia Acts of 1661, 1662, and 1663 restored the militia to the role of primary internal police and external defenders of the realm, while a standing army in peacetime came to be regarded as illegal. When Chancellor Edward Hyde, first Viscount Cornbury and first Earl of Clarendon was impeached in 1667, for example, the first charge against him was that he had intended to raise a standing army. In the Declaration of Rights of 1688, Parliament included in its catalogue of the crimes of James II that had led to the Glorious Revolution his keeping a standing army in peacetime without consent of Parliament.

Yet again on the other hand, this trend did not prevent the emergence of several others of the modern British regiments, though hardly of an army in the sense in which the 115 regiments that Louis XIV could deploy in 1688 constituted an army. Before the end of 1661, the regiment of foot guards and the troop of horse guards that had been in Monk's service were supplemented by creating two regiments of foot guards and two troops of horse guards out of the troops that had protected Charles II in exile. In 1665 the latter two regiments of foot guards were amalgamated as the First Foot-guards, which became the Grenadier Guards (the First, or Grenadier Regiment of Foot Guards from 1815), taking precedence over the Coldstream Guards because of its royalist antecedents.

Altogether, English troops in regiments totaled 3,574 men in 1663, with garrisons counting for an additional 4,878. Efforts to raise troops for the Second (1665–1667) and Third (1672–1674) Anglo-Dutch Wars focused on improving the readiness of the militia, without much effect. James II merited the charges against him in the Declaration of Rights about a standing army by enlarging the royal forces to a total of more than 34,000 in his three Kingdoms of England, Scotland, and Ireland. To be sure, he needed to strengthen his forces in 1685, just after the outset of his reign, to suppress the rebellion of Charles II's bastard son, Sir James Scott, first Duke of Monmouth and first Duke of Orkney; but he continued to increase the army, as his critics with probable warrant believed, in order to approximate the status of Louis XIV as an absolute monarch buttressed by military power. The necessary financial resources came from the diversion of funds intended for the militia. The organization and administration of the army were conducted with a skill not unworthy of comparison with that of James's friend the *Grand Monarque*. If Cromwell planted some of the seeds for the eventual—though long-delayed—professionalization of England's army, so did James II.

That King's actions, however, raised anew the specter of military despotism; they also became entangled with England's fears of a restoration of Roman Catholicism. James proceeded unabashedly to catholicize the Army of Ireland; more circumspectly but nevertheless to the perturbation of many, he also commissioned Roman Catholics in the English Army. All these developments of course helped bring about the landing of William of Orange at Torbay on November 5/15, 1688, to consummate the Glorious Revolution. Notwithstanding James's motives for enlarging the army and the alarm he generated thereby, in the showdown he discovered that he could not count on his army to fight for him, and therefore he fled to France.

However much an army of 34,000 preyed upon English hypersensitivity about the dangers of standing armies, James II's military legacy did not afford William III much help at the outset toward his primary purpose, the frustrating of the Sun King. Instead, William had to continue relying mainly on the Dutch and his continental allies for the next several years.

The War of the League of Augsburg

A token English contingent soon went to Flanders, where it proved insufficiently trained for continental war, but the circumstances of William's accession to the British thrones permitted the French to divert the Stadtholder-King himself along with many of his troops to a prolonged campaign in Ireland. The French invested a mere 7,000 of their numerous troops to accompany James II on his return to the British Isles to raise the Irish Catholics against William and Mary. The French soldiers provided a professional nucleus for an Irish army that obliged William to commit some 30,000 English, Dutch, and mercenary troops to Ireland. William eventually won his famous victory at the battle of the Boyne on July 1/11, 1690; but while the outcome at the Boyne caused James to flee to France again, somewhat over yet another year of additional hard fighting followed before the battle of Aughrim on July 12/22, 1691, accomplished the climactic and decisive defeat of the French and Irish.* Even then, Limerick did not fall to William's forces until the following October 3/13. Only after the capture of Limerick, nearly three years after the Glorious Revolution, could William turn his full military attention back to his main purpose.

And at that, his doing so did not prevent the efficiently professional French from advancing with seeming inexorability to the line of the River Meuse in the campaigns of 1691–1693. Freedom from the worst of the Irish distraction did not altogether remedy William's handicap of inferior numbers along the front in the Low Countries; he still had only 17,000 English troops there as late as 1693. Moreover, his generalship was not equal to his determination to thwart the French. After he lost the fortress-city of Namur in 1692 he sought a riposte in an attack against the French at Steenkirk (Steenkerke, Steinkirk, or Estinkerke) in Hainault on July 24/August 3, 1692. He achieved a tactical surprise against François Henri de Montmorency-Bouteville, duc de Luxembourg, *maréchal de France,* successor to Condé and Turenne as the foremost of Louis XIV's commanders. William also achieved a concentration of superior strength on the battlefield, in spite of his overall numerical inferiority. Nevertheless, William and his subordinates mismanaged the attack, while Luxembourg, once alerted, by no means mismanaged the defense. The Allied troops became hopelessly entangled with each other along constricted approach routes, and nothing like the full intended attack force ever got into action. But Luxembourg skillfully hastened reinforcements to the threatened sector of his line. The Allies had to retreat with considerable loss and nothing much to show for it.

The next year William again gave battle to Luxembourg, at Neerwinden on July 18/28. This time neither surprise nor numbers favored the Allies, and the result was predictable. The English monarch counted on marshy ground inhospitable to cavalry to protect his troops from the powerful French mounted arm, but the ground did not hinder the French enough. On this occasion Louis's infantry performed well, and a series of French assaults broke the Allied front. There was not much sophistication about the assaults, and they left Luxembourg's men too exhausted and his units too nearly shattered to pursue, but nevertheless the battle opened the way to the marshal's capture of Charleroi.

For all that, the strain of continual warfare was beginning to tell alike upon France's manpower reserves and its treasury, while the British contribution to the Allied armies gradually swelled as more troops were enlisted—or hauled in by press gangs—and brought up toward continental standards of training. Meanwhile, on May 19/29, 1692, the combined English and Dutch fleets had defeated the French navy off Barfleur or Cap La Hogue (La Hougue) in the Channel, to squelch Louis XIV's dream of supremacy at sea as well as on land, and in the sequel to produce an Allied command of the sea that lasted through the remainder of the war. These circumstances combined to oblige the French to restrict

*The anniversary of the battle of the Boyne is celebrated by Orangemen of Northern Ireland on July 12, even though the New-Style date of the anniversary of the July 1, Old-Style, battle is July 11. The July 12 observance originated as a celebration of both the Boyne and Aughrim.

themselves mainly to the defensive in 1694, Luxembourg nevertheless enlivening the campaign by marching the mass of his cavalry a hundred miles (160 kilometers) in four days to fall on William's flank and cause him to desist from a siege of Dunkirk. But that march proved the last triumph of the last of Louis XIV's great field commanders. Poor health led Luxembourg to give up his command soon afterward, and he died December 25, 1694/January 4, 1695. Louvois having died July 16, 1691, for the present the genius of Vauban was unaccompanied by comparable talent at the head of the War Ministry or of the field armies.

Vauban's principal rival as a military engineer was the Dutch Director-General of Fortified Places, Brigadier Menno, Baron van Coehoorn. At the fall of Namur to the French in 1692, Coehoorn, lying wounded in an outwork called Fort Coehoorn, had to listen to the congratulations of Vauban for designing a fortress that was excellent but not excellent enough. Now, in 1695, Coehoorn enjoyed the satisfaction of supervising a siege that in little more than a month recaptured Namur after Vauban had strengthened it into what many considered the strongest of French fortifications.

Hard pressed to retain his earlier conquests of the war, the *Grand Monarque* was willing to consider the termination of another round of battles and sieges and the opening of another interlude of respite and rebuilding. William III at the same time faced domestic pressure to end the war and postpone his ultimate objective of checkmating the French King. The cold Dutchman was never a popular occupant of the English throne, and the death of his consort from smallpox on December 28, 1694/January 7, 1695, had removed his principal claim to the affections of the people. His circle of Dutch advisers and the spectacle of his Dutch Guards on duty around English castles offended English patriotism; his obvious use of England as a make-weight in his continental strategy was to many Englishmen a much more grievous concern.

It was the Tory party that took up the cry against this strategy, and the Tories shrewdly mixed foreign and domestic issues when they entwined opposition to continental war with opposition to the Bank of England, which was financing the war and simultaneously enriching the urban merchant class; thus the Tories could play on the fears of the country gentry that their ascendancy in English life was slipping away. In 1697 the Tories, led by a master politician in Robert Harley, rode these issues into control of the House of Commons. In 1697 William asked Parliament for an army of 87,440, with the force having risen close enough to that figure that he expected to get it. By two years later, however, the Tories had cut the army to 18,000. For the time being, William had to abandon his wars.

The Treaty of Ryswick of September 10/20, 1697, nevertheless reflected William's resolution and the recent course of the war. Louis XIV had to yield almost all the territories handed to him by the chambers of reunion except Strasbourg, to give up Lorraine and the Palatinate as well, to recognize William of Orange as King of England, and to grant the Dutch a commercial treaty. To seal the outcome, the Dutch were to be allowed to garrison a cordon of fortresses in the Spanish Netherlands, including Ypres and the prize of Namur. Yet William so feared for the future, and the Tories' diminution of the English Army so confirmed his fears—while forcing him to return the Dutch Guard to the Continent so humiliated him—that he considered abdicating the throne and returning to the Netherlands.

Short of that, William at least displayed an unwontedly conciliatory attitude toward Louis XIV when the inflammatory issue of the Spanish succession threatened almost immediately to undo the Peace of Ryswick. With the Tories in power, William doubted that he could lead England to take up arms again; and without England, he believed he dared no longer risk Holland, so much had the center of military gravity in his realms shifted toward the north shore of the Channel during the 1690s.

The Spanish Succession and the Emergence of Marlborough

One principal claimant to the throne of Spain upon the death of the feeble and childless Charles II would of course be the *Grand Monarque's* son Louis, the Grand Dauphin of France, thanks to the marriage of Louis XIV to the Infanta Maria Theresa. In deference to the other European monarchs' concern for the balance of power, King Louis had long recognized that he might have to forgo the potential union of the French and Spanish Crowns by permitting Spain to descend instead to the Grand Dauphin's second son, Philip (Philippe), duc d'Anjou. Through the Habsburg connections, however, the Emperor Leopold also possessed a claim. Both Louis XIV and Leopold I were grandsons of Philip (Felipe) III of Spain, Louis through the latter's first daughter, Anne of Austria, and Leopold through his second daughter, Maria Anna, wife of the Emperor Ferdinand III. Both Louis and Leopold, furthermore, had married their first cousins, the daughters of Philip IV of Spain; Leopold's first wife, dead since 1673, had been the Princess Margareta Theresa. Also in deference to the principle of maintaining the balance of power, however, Leopold was willing to transfer his claim to the Archduke Charles (Erzherzog Karl), his second son by his second wife, Claudia Felicitas, heiress of the Tyrol (dead since 1676; Leopold was unlucky in the health if not the inheritances of his consorts). Nevertheless, with Louis XIV and William III each in a chastened mood after Ryswick, the two of them agreed to the Partition Treaty of 1698, whereby to the anger of the Emperor, Spain was to pass to yet another claimant, the young Josef Ferdinand. In compensation the Archduke Charles was to receive Milan (Milano), and France would acquire Naples (Napoli) and Sicily from among Spain's existing dominions.

Early the next year the Electoral Prince died. The English and French Kings remained in a sufficiently cautious and conciliatory humor, however, that they carved out a second Partition Treaty, making Archduke Charles the principal heir after all, but granting him only Spain, the Spanish Netherlands, and the Spanish Empire overseas, with the condition that those realms should never be reunited with the Holy Roman Empire. Naples and Sicily were now to go to the Grand Dauphin, while Duke Charles of Lorraine was to surrender his province, already from time to time under French control, to France in return for Milan from the Spanish inheritance.

It was Spanish nationalism, however embryonic, that unexpectedly upset this tortuous effort to prolong a peace that neither Louis XIV nor William III felt strong enough as yet to break. Belabored by courtiers intent on avoiding the disruption of the Spanish Empire, Charles II summoned up a last and untypical burst of resolution and energy in his dying days. In October 1700 he named Philip of Anjou the sole heir to his dominions. He added the proviso, moreover, that should Louis XIV not accept this inheritance in Philip's name, it should pass to the Archduke Charles.

On October 22/November 1 Charles II died. For Louis XIV, the proviso added to Charles's testament signified that if he did not accept, France would face Habsburg encirclement all over again—the empire of Charles V virtually reborn—and all his own accomplishments toward French hegemony would become as dust. To decline the inheritance would obviously be intolerable. Even a far less ambitious monarch would almost certainly have done as Louis now chose to do. He repudiated his treaty with William and accepted the legacy of Charles II on behalf of Philip of Anjou.

William still felt too weak to risk war; anyway, even he had to acknowledge that Louis had little choice. William thus joined in recognizing King Philip V of Spain. But Louis, evidently emboldened by his rivals'—and particularly by his one foremost rival's—acquiescence, proceeded to let his old thirst for grandeur draw him too boldly forward. William III was able to present to Parliament documentary evidence of a new French scheme to invade England itself on behalf of the exiled James II. Spain, furthermore, appeared to be offering a French company the Asiento, the sole right to ship black slaves to Spanish America, a commerce in which the English and Dutch had been doing a thriving business under various subterfuges. Joint Franco-Spanish restrictions on English trade in the Mediterranean also seemed to be in the offing. By far the worst, however, beginning in February 1700/1701 Louis used the new relationship between France and Spain as a warrant for marching French troops into the border fortresses of the Spanish Netherlands garrisoned by the Dutch. Ostensibly the purpose was to help protect the possessions of the Spanish Crown. But one by one the Dutch garrisons were overawed by superior force and interned. Namur became French again. All the bastions of Dutch security so patiently and painfully erected by William in the War of the League of Augsburg seemed to be collapsing around him.

William's salvation was the discovery that Louis had gone too far even for the peace-minded Tory leadership of the House of Commons. Enjoined by Parliament to do all that was necessary to preserve the peace of Europe—which under the circumstances meant to prepare to counter Louis by war if necessary—William could begin to restore his forces to readiness for battle and to draw up estimates for military accretions with renewed confidence that Parliament would cooperate. Yet William's never-robust health had so far declined—the recent blows to his defiant spirit also taking their toll—that he knew he would not again become the soldier-King leading his armies personally in the field. For the next round against Louis, a new commander must be found.

The choice was obvious. Political barriers had always prevented personal cordiality and had sustained mutual suspicion between the King and John Churchill, Baron Churchill of Aymouth (or Eyemouth in the Scottish peerage), Baron Churchill of Sandridge in Hertfordshire, since 1689 fourth Earl of Marlborough. As a Tory and a senior officer, already a lieutenant-general, in James II's forces, Churchill had gone over to William's cause only at the last moment, when James refused to heed Churchill's advice to advance against the Dutch forces landing with William and forthrightly to fight them. In the 1690s the general continued overly long in correspondence and other contacts with the exiled Jacobites, for which he was incarcerated in the Tower of London during part of 1692 on suspicion of treason. Nevertheless, there ultimately could be no question in William's mind either of Marlborough's stoutness in the contest against an overweening France, or of his abilities to command in war. Honed in an apprenticeship under Marshal Turenne between 1672 and 1674 when England and France were allies, these abilities had been amply demonstrated from the time when Churchill was the de facto commander of James's forces that quashed the rebellion of the Duke of Monmouth. It was Malborough who broke the last organized resistance against William in southern Ireland. If no equally brilliant continental victories as yet crowned Marlborough's head, William knew at heart that it was because he himself had insisted on direct command of his forces, seconded mainly by Dutch generals. Now, however, William proclaimed Marlborough commander-in-chief of the English forces assembling in the Netherlands and appointed him also Ambassador Extraordinary to the United Provinces, with authority if need be to frame treaties without reference to King or Parliament. Around the activities of William and Marlborough, a new Grand Alliance took shape, successor to the League of Augsburg, for yet another contest against the French drive toward European hegemony.

On Restraining the Violence of War

Through four decades that contest had already raged, with few and brief interruptions. But however much the duel had strained the financial, economic, and military resources of Europe, and especially of France itself, it had created no wasteland of plundered, ravaged territory and massacred populations on anything approaching the scale of the devastation of Germany in the Thirty Years War. However prolonged the wars of Louis XIV, and however destructive of soldiers' lives the occasional battles had been—when William III unsuccessfully fought Luxembourg at the battle of Neerwinden on July 18/28, 1693, the Allies lost 20,000 casualties, the French nearly 10,000—the age of Louis XIV is customarily accounted the beginning of an era of limited war.

There is more than a little reason for this accounting. The mundane matter of inadequate logistical support, perhaps even more than religious hatreds and the brutalization induced by continuous warfare, had transformed the armies of the Thirty Years War into hordes of murdering pillagers—including, as we have seen, the would-be Christian army of the would-be Protestant Christian paladin Gustavus Adolphus. By 1648, the theater of war in central Europe had nearly been reduced to impoverished barbarism. The warning that armed conflict might thus destroy European civilization did not go unheeded. Hugonis Grotius (Huig van Groot in his native Dutch, or Hugue de Groot) codified the historic rules for the limitation and control of war, and particularly for the relative protection of noncombatants, under the threat posed by the Thirty Years War that the alternative to limitation and control was the destruction of civilized life.[8] The counselors who served Louis XIV and his contemporaries as heads of state were aware of Grotius's codification and of the older war conventions that lay behind it, and they appear to have shared the conviction that it would be to the benefit of all concerned to display at least a reasonable adherence to the codified war conventions, and to employ military violence with restraint.

The restraints, it is true, were all too fragile. The notorious *Dragonnades*—Louis XIV's forced conversion of Huguenots by billeting brutal troops among them (the name refers particularly, of course, to dragoons)—indicate that a peculiar ferocity could still poison religious antagonisms, even though the Age of the Reformation and Counter-reformation was gradually giving way to the Age of the Enlightenment. The international law of war did not directly apply to and did not curb Louis's persecution of his own Protestant subjects. Its applicability notwithstanding, international law had little more of a moderating influence on the conduct of his soldiers among the recalcitrant Protestants of the Rhenish Palatinate. That unhappy district, already among the regions scoured by the Thirty Years War, was given over again to semi-authorized plunder, rapine, and murder by the army of Louis XIV through two extended periods: from 1673 to 1679 as part of the Dutch War, and beginning in 1687 as the precipitating cause of and a continuing scar upon the War of the League of Augsburg. During this war, the ancient university city of Heidelberg was twice sacked by French troops running amok.

French atrocities in the Palatinate and on a smaller scale elsewhere provoked cries of outrage all over Europe, to a degree suggesting that Grotius's code and the memories of the Thirty Years War were not without a salutary influence after all; but the rape of the Palatinate also suggests the fragility of the moderating and limiting tendencies in war. It is not peasants or the tradespeople and artisans of Heidelberg who have given us our conception of the age of Louis XIV as the opening phase of an era of limited war. Nevertheless, if the moderating tendencies were fragile, they were also real, if always for reasons of expediency more than of ethical principle. Not only was the fear that unrestrained military violence might threaten civilized life a motive of expediency; it was a more directly expedient concern to Louis XIV and then to the other monarchs whose military systems emulated his that indiscipline would undercut all the professionalizing reforms that were making the new armies increasingly useful tools to serve the ambitions of the state. And to allow soldiers to run riotously out of the control of their sergeants and captains when they sacked a city was to dilute the assurance that their sergeants and captains could control them at other times, especially in the heat of battle.

---

8. Hugonis Grotius, *De iure belli ac pacis liber tres. In quibus ius naturae & gentium: item iuria publici præcipia explicatur* (Parisiis [Paris]: apvd. Nicolavm Bvon [Bion], M.DC.XXV).

It was to assure continuous disciplined control of the troops by their officers as much as out of any other motive that the depot system of supply was improved by Louis XIV and his War Ministry and the improvements were copied elsewhere. While prestocked supply depots enhanced mobility in some seasons, allowing a certain amount of mobility to an army even in winter, they also impeded mobility in good weather, when the army might have traveled more freely and rapidly if it had simply gathered food for the men and forage for the animals from the countryside. But to send soldiers wandering away from the main routes of march was to risk loss of control over them—not only might they desert, but there was the danger of encouraging casual habits of conduct even among those who returned. The retention of the newly established disciplined, centralized, professional control over armies was the most important consideration shaping the increasingly elaborate depot system of supply. It was also the most important motive for minimizing the devastation that soldiers were allowed to inflict upon the territories through which they marched. Just as in the Thirty Years War it was the absence of any other feasible methods of supplying armies that, more even than religious passions, loosed a destructive soldiery upon central Europe, so conversely in the age of Louis XIV it was the rise of more efficient logistical methods that more than any moralistic or legalistic restraints curbed the destructive visitations of war upon Europe's civilians.

Thus, in the age of Louis XIV, the early effects of the emergence of military officership as a profession tended toward limiting the horrors of war. It should be remembered, too, that the spirit of the new professional soldier—the educated soldier who devoted his life to the study and practice of military skills in a manner that increasingly regarded those skills as comprising a science—was exemplified most fully in any one soldier of the era by the great engineer Vauban. And it was of the essence of Vauban's conception of war that the devastation wrought by war should be curbed not only to protect noncombatants but even to protect the lives of soldiers. Vauban's fortresses and siegecraft sought to substitute for the carnage of a battle of Neerwinden a ritualistic resolution of conflict, whereby issues put to the test of arms could be resolved as bloodlessly as possible.

On the whole, it reinforced the tendencies of nascent military professionalism that the two great monarchical rivals of the age of Louis XIV were themselves educated soldiers to a degree that warrants calling them professional officers. While the foundation of a military officer's career was increasingly becoming the refining of talent and intellect by means of education, the education involved was not yet so specialized and so intense that attaining it precluded the King's combining officership and statecraft. Therefore the professional conduct of war was not yet divorced from the policy on behalf of which war was initiated. The soldier-kings Louis XIV and William III shaped war and policy simultaneously. Louis's fury toward various stubborn Protestants notwithstanding, this marriage of war-making and policy by and large encouraged moderation in the methods of employing violence, because stirring up bitterness and hatred in occupied territories could no more encourage the permanent unity with France that was the goal of Louis's occupations than it could enhance military discipline. William III as well sought to use arms in order to solidify lasting alliances. Policy goals and thus the union of statecraft with the conduct of war favored wars of limited destructiveness and violence.

The means by which war was waged in the age of Louis XIV were more limited, however, than the ends, the purposes of waging war. While Louis hoped to conduct war in such a manner as to encourage the building of permanent bonds between France and the territories he occupied, his ambitions were far too large to permit us to speak unequivocally of an era of limited war when we consider the motives behind the wars of the Sun King. Louis's purposes were not the decidedly limited ones of achieving mere territorial adjustments or dynastically advantageous marriages. Although he looked toward the attainment of a frontier along the Rhine as his conception of France's natural eastern border, he was not thinking only of the Rhine frontier either. His goal was nothing less than hegemony in Europe—to become the new Charles V, but on a still grander scale than Charles V had achieved. If he could have had his way, he would have destroyed the independent Netherlands altogether, he would have made the British Kingdoms his satellites through a dynasty dependent on him, and he would have fragmented yet further the Holy Roman Empire—unless he could himself become the Emperor.

But it is unlikely that humankind will ever curb permanently the horrors of war if the curbing depends on doing away with ambitions on the scale of the Sun King's. The serving of ambition and even of grandiose ambition, the persistence of the human effort to attain *la gloire,* will remain central to statecraft until humanity ceases to be humanity as we know it. If we are permanently to curb war, experience affirms that it will be more profitable to focus on means rather than on ends. Wars of ambition will remain with us, but at least we may hope to moderate the destructiveness of their conduct. Toward that object, the nascent professionalization of military officership as it took shape in the army of Louis XIV and other contemporary armies seemed to offer a measure of hopeful promise.

5 MARLBOROUGH'S BATTLES: BLENHEIM, RAMILLIES, OUDENARDE, AND MALPAQUET

There is a strong linkage between curbing the horrors of war and achieving decisiveness in the conduct of war. If warfare degenerates into indecision and deadlock, then the frustration of the rival belligerents may well tempt them to lash out at each other with growing fury and diminishing regard for the principles of the war convention. If war can produce reasonably swift decisions on the battlefield, then the likelihood of the extension of its destructiveness to noncombatants is much less. Gustavus Adolphus initially achieved success in restoring tactical decisiveness to battle. Considerably before his death he must have perceived the unhappy truth, however, that his attainment of tactical decisiveness was unable to win him a comparable strategic decisiveness, that in spite of Breitenfeld he was not on the way to a swift resolution of the issues of the war. But it was after Gustavus's death had eliminated virtually all hope for strategic decisiveness on the part of any of the contestants in the Thirty Years War that the conflict descended finally and completely into the abyss of unrestricted horror.

Dangerously compromising the tendencies of the era of Louis XIV toward the moderation of war under such precepts as those codified by Grotius was the persisting failure of war to attain decisiveness; in fact, not only did strategic decisiveness still elude belligerents as it had done during the Thirty Years War, but battles failed to yield even the tactical decisiveness and therefore the potential and the hope for strategic decision of a Breitenfeld or a Lützen. The indecisiveness of clashes of arms, the failure of any of the major battles of the War of Devolution, the Dutch War, or the War of the League of Augsburg to produce so clear and unquestionable a margin of victory for any of the contending armies as to compel its opponents to make peace, was a principal factor in keeping the long cycle of Louis XIV's wars turning.

Weapons and Tactical Indecision

Reviewing the history of modern war from the perspective of the late twentieth century will return us again and again to the discouraging conclusion that strategic decisiveness in war has been forever elusive. The particular tactical, battlefield indecisiveness of war in the late seventeenth century, however, had a specific cause. It was directly related to the increase of the relative proportions of infantry in the armies of the day. The cavalry, the arm of mobility and shock, without which qualities decisiveness in battle must always be unlikely, had declined again from the level of effectiveness to which Gustavus Adolphus had lifted it. The technology of infantry weapons and the accompanying infantry tactics meanwhile made it even more difficult than in many other eras for infantry to compensate for the limitations of cavalry by applying shock action of its own.

The great Condé and Turenne had employed cavalry less in a manner that exploited its mobility for tactical advantage through exploitation and pursuit than with emphasis on shock, using the momentum of the charge to rupture the enemy's defenses. In England at the same time, Cromwell had made the cavalry the special arm of decision in the New Model Army, and by the same means. The rival Royalist cavalry had employed similar tactics with only slightly less success. But one of the less desirable corollaries of the rise of professional military discipline and control was the fear felt by less than fully confident commanders that they would lose their now much-valued control over their troops, and the headlong cavalry charge is an event peculiarly frightening to the lesser commander who blanches at the prospect that action may attain an uncontrollable momentum of its own. Under commanders of the latter description, the French cavalry reverted to tactics of advancing at a trot to fire pistols or carbines into the enemy's ranks and then to wheel away. At least the full-fledged caracole had been abandoned, and three ranks of horsemen fired at once. But fire from light weapons was scarcely an adequate means of breaking down a reasonably resolute foe, and while the cavalry followed up by drawing swords to seek to engage in a melee, there was no vigorous hurling forward of the weight of a rapidly charging horse arm.

The infantry, it is true, had become more readily maneuverable than they were in Gustavus Adolphus's day, improved weapons technology as well as continuing refinements in tactical training making possible increasing flexibility in battlefield maneuver and with it a growing potential for infantry's own shock action; but the possibilities were still too limited to be recognized and exploited by any officers except those of the highest skills. The changes in infantry developed especially out of enhanced firepower and the decline of the pikemen.

In firepower, there was a gradual replacement of the matchlock musket with various forms of flintlocks. The necessity for the musketeer to fire his weapon by putting a fusecord to the touch-hole to ignite the powder had been a primary impediment to infantry firepower from the beginning. The method was so unreliable that the rate of misfires was about 50 percent. Even the slightest dampness in the weather sent the number of misfires soaring; the effects of wind were similarly disastrous. The musketeer had to burden himself with his stock of cords, or matches, and the match supply of an entire army was so bulky that it constituted a not unimportant logistical problem. Handling a constantly lighted cord—the match—and with it charging a new fuse inside the gun to ignite the powder with each firing was so cumbersome a business that it had always made sustained infantry fire exceedingly difficult; there had to be some five ranks to keep one rank firing while the others prepared to fire, with consequent awkward arrangements for the rank that had just fired to march to the rear while its successor ranks moved forward. Not only because of these marching and countermarching arrangements, but also because the musketeer was holding a lighted match throughout the action, a space of a yard or a meter had to be maintained around each musketeer so that each could use his weapon without interfering with his comrades.

From early in the seventeenth century, armies had attempted to replace the match with some device that would ignite the musket's powder by means of a firing mechanism inside the weapon to strike a spark through friction between rough surfaces. The caracoling cavalry sometimes used wheellock pistols, wherein a mechanism like that of a clockwork toy would turn against a rough surface to ignite the spark. But the wheellock mechanism, notoriously delicate and unreliable, was unsuited to the infantry's heavier weapons. Long before mid-century, several forms of flintlocks had made their appearance. In these simplified versions of the wheellock, pulling the trigger directly struck a piece of flint against a rough steel surface. Difficulties remained. The flint wore down after about ten or twelve firings and had to be replaced. So replacing it had to be easy, but easily seated flints tended to fall out of the weapon during action. If the flint was very short, it could not be counted on to strike a spark; if it was too long, it would break apart.

Nevertheless, these problems were gradually more or less solved, and when they were, the flintlock musket increased infantry firepower over the matchlock geometrically. The number of misfires declined to about one in three, and eventually to about 15 percent. Even the vagaries of the weather, although firing during rainstorms was still usually precluded, were no longer quite so disabling. And the speed of readying the weapon to be refired was cut in half. Furthermore, without a lighted match in every musketeer's hand, the traditional interval of a yard or meter between infantrymen could be closed, and musketmen could stand shoulder to shoulder with a space of as little as twenty-two inches (55.88 cm) allotted to each. Thus the volume of fire in proportion to length of front could also be much increased.

In 1670 the French Army ordered that four men in every infantry company might carry *fusils,* a type of flintlock so called because *fusil* is the French word for the frizzen, the rough steel surface from which the flint struck sparks. The next year the French created *le Régiment des Fusiliers.* The English followed with Our Royal Regiment of Fusiliers (also called Our Ordnance Regiment; from 1689 the

7th Regiment of Foot [Royal Fusiliers]; from 1881 the Royal Fusiliers [City of London Regiment]. Also in 1685, the Scots transformed Colonel [Charles Erskine] the [fifth modern or tenth] Earl of Mar's Regiment of Foot by changing the last word in its name to Fusiliers. Henceforth under various colonels it was——'s Regiment of Fusiliers or, popularly, the Scots Fusiliers Regiment of Foot (from 1707 the Scots Fusiliers Regiment of Foot officially, and from 1881, after numerous intermediate designations the Royal Scots Fusiliers). Other similarly equipped regiments followed in these and other armies. Meanwhile the French increased the number of fusiliers in an ordinary infantry company to eight in 1687 and to twenty-one in 1692. With the latter change, a French infantry company comprised twenty-one musketeers still using matchlocks, twenty-one fusiliers, and ten pikemen. The rise in infantry firepower had brought about the gradual decrease in numbers of the latter, but some pikemen were still thought necessary to repel cavalry attacks.

The introduction of flintlocks and the decrease of both musketeers and pikemen in the French Army might have proceeded more rapidly had not Louis XIV and Louvois displayed a conservatism in regard to weapons at odds with their professionalizing reforms elsewhere. Perhaps as with the cavalry charge, battle and therefore tactical questions posed such severe threats of loss of control over events that caution was again a natural response. The high cost of reequipping the entire infantry with flintlocks was another and more obvious deterrent to change.

The reason for creating separate fusilier regiments was initially to have this special form of infantry escort the artillery. The fusecords used with matchlocks had a nasty way of touching off explosions when they were handled in proximity to the cannoneers' powder supplies. In the French Army, indeed, the fusilier regiments were eventually—in 1720—assimilated into *le Régiment Royale d'Artillerie,* although in the British armies they evolved into ordinary infantry.

Beyond the special needs of the artillery, however, Louis XIV resisted the increase of flintlocks; as late as 1693 he ordered their complete abandonment by the French Army, although he soon cancelled so drastic a retrogression. It was about this same time, moreover, that Louvois was showing at best a lukewarm interest in the efforts of Vauban and others to promote the socket bayonet, which offered to enhance infantry mobility and firepower still further by doing away with the need for pikemen.

The Dutch and English armies showed a greater willingness to shift from matchlocks to flintlocks, but they were impeded, especially the English, by frugal legislatures reluctant to spend much money on the change. In the early 1690s, nevertheless, King William's Musket, a flintlock and a predecessor of the famous Brown Bess or Tower Musket, was standardized in pattern, and the English proceeded with a very gradual rearming of their infantry, a process that dragged on well into the eighteenth century.

Gradually, too, all the European armies accepted the socket bayonet. Plug bayonets had been in use since early in the century. The word bayonet is supposedly derived from *bayonette,* a short dagger made in Bayonne in the fifteenth century. The plug bayonet had to be inserted into the muzzle of the firearm; its disadvantages were manifest. The next experiment, the ring bayonet, attached to the musket barrel by a series of rings, tended to slip back along the barrel or to fall off in combat. With the socket bayonet, a sleeve attached to the bayonet was drawn over the muzzle of the musket or fusil and then given a half turn to be attached firmly by a metal lug affixed near the muzzle.

With the adoption of the socket bayonet, the pikemen virtually disappeared, although officers and noncommissioned officers often carried some kind of bladed weapon—in the English Army, spontoons for officers and halberds for NCOs—as an emblem of rank and to help keep their men's battle alignments straight. The changes in infantry weaponry, giving almost every soldier a firearm of much enhanced reliability and rate of fire, greatly increased the firepower of infantry. Infantry formations also became more maneuverable as the unwieldy pikes disappeared. Soldiers could now march and fight close together, and alignments four or only three ranks deep appeared in place of the old phalanx-like battalions five or six ranks deep.

But most commanders by no means fully exploited the new maneuverability and flexibility. While the British and Dutch led in the adoption of a three-rank formation, other armies retained four or five ranks, sometimes for a considerable period of time. Also, the increased volume of musketry now possible often created an excessive infatuation with firepower alone, and massed infantry firing without much effort toward shock action or maneuver often became the principal reliance for battlefield success. Infantry firepower was of course supplemented by artillery, but the state of the art of gun-founding still left cannon so heavy in relation to the weight of the shot they fired that only small pieces such as 3- and 6-pounders (1.361 and 2.721-kilogram) (2.91 and 3.66 inches, 73.914 and 92.964 mm) could be hauled and manhandled into position effectively in mobile battle. While the resulting hail of fire from muskets and cannon was devastating enough to inflict appalling casualties, at least at close range, it was far from removing the axiomatic need for maneuver in combination with fire to extract decision from battle.

By the closing years of the seventeenth century, battles thus had tended to become primarily exchanges of infantry volleys, supplemented by artillery. The infantry advanced upon the enemy to deliver its fire at close range—the extreme range of its shoulder arms was about 250 to 300 yards (or meters), with reasonable accuracy impossible much beyond fifty yards (or meters). But attacks were only infrequently driven home by means of a bayonet charge and a melee. With the cavalry generally refraining from headlong charges as well, battle degenerated into an indecisive contest of attrition. The battle tactics of the time were not the least of the reasons for the indecisiveness of the War of the League of Augsburg, until both sides succumbed to exhaustion.

Lieutenant-General Lord John Churchill, Earl of Marlborough, resolved to change all that. In military history unlike most other branches of history, the hero in the fullest meaning of the word, the individual who by his own will and accomplishments alters the course of events, still strides across the record of the past. In few areas of human endeavor can one person so shape the course of events that we can assert with conviction that history would have been different without this individual. But the great captain has almost unique opportunities to mold the course of war, and Marlborough so moved the military and thus the political and diplomatic events of his era that he became truly the rare individual without whom the past would be different. But note: he restored tactical decisiveness to the battlefield; he did not achieve strategic decisiveness in war.

Marlborough's accomplishing as much as he did is all the more impressive because he had to use as his principal military instrument the troops of an alliance plagued by all the dissensions endemic to alliance politics. His armies, furthermore, primarily British and Dutch, lacked the professionalism of officership and administration of the rival armies of France.

Like Gustavus Adolphus, Marlborough accomplished his return to tactical decisiveness largely through a reinvigoration of the cavalry and particularly of shock action more than by any other means. Also like Gustavus Adolphus, Marlborough had to cope with daunting logistical problems before he could revitalize tactics; here his achievement surpassed the Swedish King's.

The Outbreak of the War of the Spanish Succession

The renewed war between England and France that had been simmering since Philip of Anjou's ascent to the Spanish throne burst into flames after Louis XIV perpetrated what to English eyes was the ultimate violation of the Peace of Ryswick. He made the death of James II on September 17/28, 1701, the occasion for recognizing James's son James Francis Edward as King of England in place of William III. He followed up by declaring France closed to the importation of British goods; but such decrees could be evaded, and his repudiation of his acceptance of William III was a more hurtful wound.

Almost simultaneously with James's death England, the United Provinces, and the Empire had already completed the formation of a new Grand Alliance. They declared their willingness to accept Philip V as ruler of Spain and the Indies on condition that the crowns of France and Spain should never be united; but they bound themselves to acquire Milan, Naples, Sicily, and the Spanish Netherlands for Austria, and to demand that they should continue to receive the commercial privileges in the Spanish Empire that they had enjoyed under Charles II. On these latter issues, Louis XIV predictably was not forthcoming.

No doubt the changes in the diplomatic and military balance since Ryswick helped inspire the latest expressions of Louis's arrogance. The Spanish succession had shifted the largest empire in the world to his side. As long as he disdained the demands of the new alliance, much of Italy came to him with Spain, and of course so did the Spanish Netherlands. Louis's seizure of the barrier fortresses from their Dutch garrisons had left the United Provinces so exposed that the Dutch had to prepare again for their last defensive recourse— the inundation of their country. Diplomacy supported by Louis's awesome alignment of power had also brought the Archbishopric of Cologne (Köln) and the Electorate of Bavaria into the French camp. Cologne put Louis in a fair way to controlling the lower Rhine and threatened communications between the United Provinces and Austria. Bavaria, although remaining formally neutral at the first onset of war, seemed about to become a French salient thrust deep into the Habsburg domains. Furthermore, Duke Victor Amadeus (Duca Vittorio Amadeo) II of Savoy allowed French troops to occupy the upper valley of the River Po, whence they could join hands with Spanish troops in the Milanese. When to all these circumstances was added the restiveness of the Hungarian subjects of Leopold I, the Empire was sorely threatened from every direction but the north. Even at sea, English and Dutch naval superiority was dangerously undercut by the absence of friendly harbors south of the English Channel; in June 1701 Bourbon diplomacy brought Portugal into alliance with France and Spain.

Nascent English nationalism reacted strongly to these latest French insults and advances in a fashion that was to become typical of the nation and predictable: the English rallied around William III as the symbol of defiance. The Dutch Stadtholder was never so popular in his adopted country as when the war drums beat again in the Low Countries early in 1702. On February 20/March 3, 1701/1702, however, William was thrown from his horse when it stumbled over a mole's diggings at Hampton Court, and on March 8/19 he died of complications stemming from the injuries.

His sister-in-law, the surviving Protestant daughter of James II, became Queen Anne. She immediately appointed Marlborough a Knight of the Garter and declared him captain-general of her armies. Through the Countess of Marlborough, Lady Sarah Jennings Churchill, the Earl's wife and the new Queen's closest confidante, Anne had long felt a friendship for Malborough of which the reclusive and distrustful William would never have been capable. In the Netherlands, there was no direct heir; but the consequent confusion of Dutch politics, while it did not bode well for the future harmony of the Grand Alliance, failed to prevent the United Provinces from appointing Marlborough deputy captain-general of their forces, while the office of Stadtholder and Commander-in-Chief fell in abeyance.

Fighting between Franco-Spanish forces and the Empire had broken out in northern Italy in 1701, but England and France formally went to war only in May 1702. The most skillful members of Louis XIV's new generation of military leaders urged the French King to strike first against the vulnerable Habsburg domains.

The military balance was already barely being maintained in Italy by the ablest of the Emperor Leopold's generals, Prince François Eugène of Savoy. After long service against the Turks, this soldier had remained loyal to the Empire in spite of the new alignment of his native house. Or rather, he had remained hostile to Louis XIV. He had grown up in Louis's court, for his mother, Olympia Mancini, bride of Prince Eugène Maurice of Savoy-Carignano, was a daughter of Cardinal Mazarin's sister Hieronyma Mazarini Mancini; but for some reason Louis had refused him a French commission as a young man, and Eugene forever resented it. His resentment would scarcely be able, however, to save Italy.

Nevertheless, the long struggle against William of Orange had fixed the French King's eyes upon the Netherlands, and Louis preferred to begin by assembling the largest concentration of his forces along the Meuse. To do so, however, was to confer a favor upon Marlborough, who perceived the safeguarding of the United Provinces as his first task, and for whom a campaign in the Low Countries posed far less difficult logistical problems than a march to succor the Emperor.

Logistics and administration promised no small headaches for Marlborough. Not only would he have to deal with both the English and the Dutch governments, and eventually perhaps with other allies as well, but neither of the principal governments he served had brought the supply and maintaining of armies to French levels of efficiency.

English Military Administration

The English government in particular lagged behind. An able bureaucrat named William Blathwayt had since 1683 been developing his office of Secretary of the Forces—military secretary to the King—into a quasi-Cabinet position. By 1702 Blathwayt participated formally in presenting the military estimates to the House of Commons, and in other ways he drew to himself some of the business and prerogatives of a secretary of state. But he was not a Cabinet officer, his prerogatives were undefined,and for questions of policy he served no less than three masters in the Cabinet, the Secretaries of State for the Northern and the Southern Departments in regard to strategy and operations, and the Lord High Treasurer in regard to finance. Because the division of authority between the Secretaries of State for the Northern and the Southern Department was geographical, it was altogether possible for them to give Blathwayt conflicting orders. Meanwhile the Master-General of the Ordnance was the supplier of guns and other war matériel; it at least eased matters that Marlborough was Master-General of the Ordnance as well as captain-general, but there remained the problem that in these capacities he stood at the top of separate ladders of administration. This peculiarly English tangle of overlapping ad hoc arrangements was destined to grow more tangled still before it was remedied more than a century later, but its labyrinths were already obstructive enough.

It did not help that in the English Army each regiment was still virtually the property of its colonel, to a considerably greater extent than Louis and Louvois had allowed to persist in France. The English military system would have to be rescued from its inherent defects by a combination of personal capacities, Blathwayt's talents and Marlborough's ability while overseas to make many of his own logistical arrangements. At the same time, the necessity for Marlborough to take the field overseas rendered his influence over the system, or lack of system, still more tenuous.

Blenheim

It was not beyond the limited capacities of the English military machine, however, to put an army of 12,000 men into the nearby Low Countries, so in June 1702 Marlborough was there to begin his campaign against Louis's con-

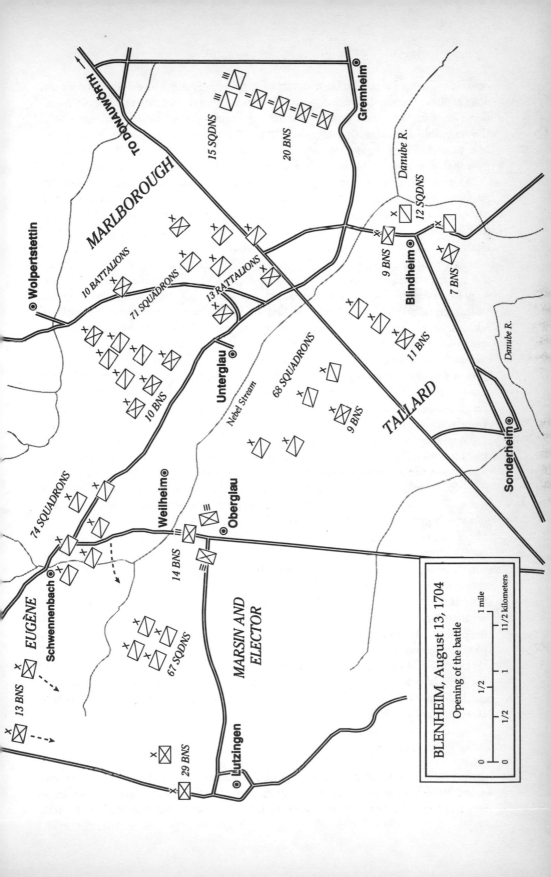

BLENHEIM, August 13, 1704

Opening of the battle

TO DONAUWÖRTH

MARLBOROUGH

Wolpertstettin

15 SQDNS

20 BNS

Gremheim

Danube R.

12 SQDNS

Blindheim

9 BNS

7 BNS

10 BATTALIONS

71 SQUADRONS

13 BATTALIONS

Unterglau

Nebel Stream

68 SQUADRONS

11 BNS

TALLARD

10 BNS

9 BNS

Danube R.

Sonderheim

74 SQUADRONS

Weilheim

Oberglau

14 BNS

EUGÈNE

Schwennenbach

MARSIN AND
ELECTOR

13 BNS

67 SQDNS

Lützingen

29 BNS

0   1/2   1   11/2 kilometers

0   1/2   1 mile

centration in the area. Continental troops, largely Dutch, lifted the Earl's total strength to something over 40,000. His opponent, Louis François, duc de Boufflers, *maréchal de France*, enjoyed the advantage of controlling the fortifications of the so-called Lines of Brabant as well as all the fortresses on the Meuse and Maas below Huy, except for Maastricht (Maestricht), on which to anchor his formidable army of some 90,000.

Upon the mind of a timid general, however, fortresses can exercise a stultifying, confining influence, and Boufflers was no Turenne or Luxembourg. Marlborough neatly maneuvered himself into a position between Bouffler's main mobile force and the Lines of Brabant, which threw the French commander into a panic and gave Marlborough a position whence he might destroy him. Before Marlborough could commence the decisive battle for which he hoped, however, the vagaries of rudderless Dutch politics intervened; the Dutch field deputies, who represented the civil government with the army, forbade risking battle. Within ten days this process repeated itself, Marlborough maneuvering Boufflers into another potential trap, the Dutch government forbidding him to spring it, lest their own casualties prove too high; and much the same frustrating course of events was to occur twice more before the campaign of 1702 ended. Thwarted though he was in his quest for decisive combat, however, Marlborough through maneuver pried Boufflers out of enough of the Low Country fortresses to give the Allies control of the Meuse and the lower Rhine. On December 2/13 Queen Anne rewarded her captain-general by announcing that she would make him Duke of Marlborough.

Honors at home did not assure military success abroad; the campaign of 1703 proved annoyingly similar to that of 1702. Marlborough invaded the Archbishopric of Cologne and carried his conquests up the Rhine as far as Bonn. Returning to the Netherlands, he was on the verge of taking Antwerp when Dutch irresolution again interfered.

The major military events of 1703, however, occurred farther south, and they involved France's capitalizing at last on the vulnerability of the Empire. Notwithstanding Louis XIV's continued focusing of his own major attention elsewhere, and notwithstanding also a series of failures of various French and allied chieftains to cooperate with the designs of the most capable of France's new commanders, Claude Louis Hector, marquis de Villars, *maréchal de France*, by the end of the year Vienna seemed likely to fall into Villars's grasp. This was true, furthermore, in spite of a new reversal of policy by Savoy, this time departing the French camp to join the Grand Alliance.

Villars made use of the Emperor's distraction by rebellious Hungarians and the chronic Turkish danger to the east. Furthermore, the French at last concentrated superior force on the Emperor's western frontier, including the Bavarian Army of the Electoral Prince Maximilian II Emmanuel. Again and again Villars defeated the Imperial armies in the field, and almost certainly it was only the circumstance that the marshal shared with Marlborough the misfortune of irresolute allies and subordinates that saved Vienna from him in 1703. The western shield of Vienna, the fortress-cities of Augsburg, Regensburg (Ratisbon), and Landau, nevertheless fell to the French and Bavarians.

As the campaigning season of 1704 approached, the Emperor appealed to Queen Anne in terms almost of desperation, that unless Marlborough marched to the rescue the Empire might collapse. Marlborough already had been contemplating a shift of his forces southward to campaign on the River Moselle (Mosel). By May 1704 he had resolved that he should heed the appeals of the Emperor and march instead to the Danube. His earlier designs toward the Moselle would offer a convenient cover, for the Dutch were reluctant to see him go even that far south, and his original plan would permit him to make his first southward moves while concealing from the United Provinces—as he was sure he must—his intent to proceed on beyond the Moselle. The possibility of a campaign on the Moselle might also deceive the French about his purposes during the initial stage of the campaign.

His new plans were daring to a degree that was extraordinary in light of the logistical difficulties of the era. He proposed to lead his British troops and those in British pay, about 30,000 men of whom well under half were actually British, on a 250-mile (400-kilometer) march from the Netherlands to the Danube. It would necessarily be a flank march, exposed all the way to a French riposte from the west. The Margrave Louis (Markgraf Ludwig) of Baden, Lieutenant-General (*Generalleutnant*) of the Empire, with his small army would provide a measure of flank protection in the southern part of the journey, but by no means enough for security. The magazine or depot system of logistics with its many halts for resupply tended to limit a campaign of an entire year's campaigning season to a distance of 300 miles (a little less than 500 kilometers); Marlborough could not afford to spend the whole or even the better part of the good weather of 1704 traveling his 250 miles to the Danube, and to escape customary logistical limitations he took his supply arrangements personally in hand. His intent was to march three or four days and then rest for a day, having arranged for the commissaries of friendly states to be waiting with supplies at every resting place. There the soldiers would need only to pitch their tents, draw and cook their rations, and rest, while his wagons were filled for the next leap forward.

Marlborough's march to the Danube proved to be one of the great marches of military history, because both his logistical and his strategic designs were fulfilled almost to perfection. In an army lacking most of the professionalism of the French, Marlborough made up the deficiencies almost single-handed, at least in logistics, and surpassed any logistical achievement of the army of Louis XIV. Or more accurately, he made up the deficiencies with the assistance of one similarly self-created professional among his subordinates, his Quartermaster-General, Colonel William Cadogan. Setting out from Roermond in mid-May, the army reached Koblenz before the end of the month. After pausing there, Marlborough made the turn that astonished friend and foe alike by marching not up the Moselle but over a floating bridge across the Rhine. Through Mainz and Heidelberg, the Duke hastened on, thence across the River Neckar at Ladenburg. By mid-June, Marlborough had completed his march and rendezvoused with both Louis of Baden and the main Imperial Army, to command which in this critical year Prince Eugène had been ordered north from Italy. The Prince was an able and meticulous logistician himself; yet to discover that Marlborough's army had not only accomplished its march but was ready for battle astonished him.

The first fruits of the famous march to the Danube were nevertheless meager. In cold reality Marlborough had effected no more than the concentration of an Allied force that was still inferior in numbers to the opposing French and Bavarians, and with a precarious line of retreat because the French in their chagrin at failing to intercept him were sure to attempt to block the Rhine against Marlborough's return northward. The British general's next move, therefore, was to attempt to capture the fortress of Donauwörth on the Danube—part of its defenses constructed under Gustavus Adolphus—which would give him both a new and more secure line of communications, northward through Nördlingen, and a strategic crossing of the Danube for a further thrust south and east.

Commanded by the fortified heights of the Schellenberg, Donauwörth was a suitable subject for the kind of siege so characteristic of war in the immediately preceding years; but Marlborough lacked the time for that. Instead he assaulted the place, achieving tactical surprise by delivering his main blow on June 21/July 2 against the strongest part of the defenses, the Schellenberg, and carrying this objective swiftly, albeit contributing to the heavy total cost of some 1,400 killed and 3,800 wounded for possession of Donauwörth. The casualties seemed a necessary price, however, for the rapid gaining of reasonably secure lines either for retreat or for moving farther toward Vienna.

Marlborough's principal problem, inferior numbers, nevertheless remained unresolved. To begin to deal with it the Duke embarked on one of the less admirable ventures of his career. He turned his army loose to plunder and devastate Bavaria, with the idea that the cries of his subjects might cause the Elector either to make peace or, at least, to disperse his army for the protection of the countryside. Again we note how much the softening of the horrors of war and particularly of its visitations upon noncombatants since 1648 leaned upon the thin reed of expediency, and how inexact it is to characterize the era following the Peace of Westphalia as a time of limited war. The results of Marlborough's ruthlessness were not what the moralist might like. The Elector nearly came to terms; a separate peace was squelched at the last minute only by the approach of the senior French commander in the area, Camile d'Hostun, duc de Tallard, *maréchal de France*. The more capable Villars had been removed from the scene, partly because of the friction that his very ability and energy generated between him and France's allies. But while Marlborough did not succeed in driving Bavaria out of the war, he did impel Maximilian Emmanuel to disperse most of his army throughout his estates.

Tallard, the Elector, and their principal lieutenants nevertheless believed that they retained sufficient numerical superiority to oblige Marlborough to retreat, leaving Prince Eugène and the Empire in the lurch, they hoped. The precise extent of their numerical advantage is uncertain, but probably it was now less than they imagined; Marlborough consistently enjoyed better intelligence than his adversaries, as usual giving it along with every other matter of importance the close personal attention that he could draw from his amazing stock of energy. (It is worth noting that he was fifty-four years old, about eighteen years older than Gustavus Adolphus had been at the time of his death and eight years older than the Emperor Napoleon at Waterloo.)

The Franco-Bavarians may have had as many as 60,000 men, perhaps only 56,000. The Allies' numbers have been estimated at 52,000 to 56,000. Probably Marlborough's unpleasant Bavarian activities had been instrumental in decreasing the Franco-Bavarian advantage to about 4,000 at most, whatever the totals. Of the Allies' sixty-five battalions of infantry and 160 squadrons of cavalry, only fourteen and nineteen, respectively, were British. In Prince Eugène's contingent, two-thirds of the infantry, probably over 10,000 men, were soldiers of a rising German military power, Brandenburg-Prussia. Their commander, *General-lieutenant* Fürst Leopold I of Anhalt-Dessau, famous in German military history as "the Old Dessauer" (*der Alte Dessauer*), was a skillful soldier noteworthy in particular for having borrowed from the Swedes the recent practice of marching his troops in cadenced step, an example soon to be followed throughout Europe.

Approaching Marlborough and Prince Eugène, Tallard and the Elector pitched camp on a gentle rise of ground behind the Nebel brook, near the villages of Höchstädt and Blindheim and the confluence of the Nebel with the Danube. The site seemed auspicious for the Franco-Bavarians; here, in an action taking its name from Höchstädt, the Elector had defeated an Imperial army some eleven months before, on September 9/20, 1703. The Franco-Bavarian commanders still entertained a delusion of so much numerical superiority that they believed their near approach to the Allies would cause Marlborough to decamp. Notwithstanding this misconception, the village of Blindheim was of course about to give its name to a new battle, anglicized as Blenheim.

The best generals as well as multitudes of their inferiors have tended to fight their battles in stereotyped fashion. They develop a tactical method that suits their character and talents and the weapons technology of their day. It is the ability of the great commanders to play variations on their standard themes so as to differentiate one battle from another and thus keep their opponents off balance that largely accounts for their stature as successful battle captains.

The theme that Marlborough developed at Blenheim and on which he was to play variations through most of his major battles featured the use of repeated strong attacks at places where he did not intend to stage his climactic assault, to draw the enemy's attention away from the eventual focus of decision and to tempt the enemy into weakening the critical sector of his lines. At Blenheim, Marlborough opened the battle on August 2/13, 1704, with a series of assaults against the Franco-Bavarian right and right-center, where the villages of Blindheim on the right and Unterglau (or Unter-Glauheim) about a mile or one and a half kilometers leftward up the Nebel gave the Franco-Bavarians natural rallying points. Here was the strongest part of the enemy line, the Franco-Bavarian guns in the villages being able to sweep the crossings of the marshy Nebel and some open meadows between the stream and their main line of resistance. Thus beginning by hitting the enemy where he was strongest was one of Marlborough's subthemes, a repetition now of the assault on the Schellenberg, and once more it contributed to Marlborough's achieving tactical surprise. Tallard and the

Elector had anticipated neither being attacked nor, in the unlikely event that he should strike them at all, that Marlborough's blow would fall where it did. Therefore the Allied assaults several times came close to penetrating the Franco-Bavarian right, in spite of its intrinsic strength.

Meanwhile, Prince Eugène proceeded to assail the enemy left, to keep the enemy fully occupied also in that sector. From Eugène's far flank to Blindheim was a distance of about two and a half miles or four kilometers, so that the army commander's communications and exercise of control presented severe difficulties, and there was always the danger that an alert and active enemy might turn Marlborough's tactics against him by assailing him in a vulnerable place when his concentrations lay elsewhere. Against these difficulties and dangers, Marlborough kept a staff of couriers close at hand, ready to hasten to any part of the field. This precaution proved its worth when the French not only repulsed an Allied feint around the village of Oberglau on Marlborough's right-center, midway between Unterglau and Eugène's right-flank attack, but drove it back on the Nebel in disarray. Nine triumphant enemy battalions, among them the "Wild Geese," *le Brigade Royal Irlandois,* Irishmen bearing arms for King Louis against the hated English, threatened to rupture Marlborough's line. The Duke rode to the scene himself, and he also dispatched a messenger to Eugène to seek help. Marlborough and Eugène were in fact acting as coordinate commanders; the English general could not give orders to the Imperial general. But Eugène immediately stripped a cavalry brigade from his own attack, and its timely charge repaired the damage.

By mid-afternoon the battle seemed a deadlock. Marlborough's assaults against Blindheim and Unterglau were well contained, while Eugène was making little or no progress on the opposite flank. Furthermore, the French had managed to retain most of their cavalry, their own weapon of mobility and shock and perhaps qualitatively the best troops of their army, in reserve. Nevertheless the battle was going essentially as Marlborough had planned. The enemy infantry was pinned down in defensive struggles. In his center, the Duke had hoarded a grand battery of forty guns, ninety battalions of infantry, and twenty-three squadrons of cavalry. The Franco-Bavarians had retained no comparable strength in this area of the field. When Marlborough learned that Eugène was at length on the verge of curling around the enemy left, he seized upon this opportune moment to launch his climactic stroke.

The forty-gun battery laid down a brief but intense bombardment. The massed infantry of the Allied center followed immediately with an assault. Tallard sufficiently perceived the threat to throw his cavalry reserve into the action. But Marlborough had concentrated overwhelming power on a narrow front. The French cavalry delayed the Allied advance only briefly. Choosing with superb military instinct—the hallmark of the warrior, reaching beyond the intellectual qualities of the educated professional soldier—the moment when the fight was most fluid and ready to be resolved by a fresh effort by either side, Marlborough ordered a general assault and threw in his massed cavalry.

Unlike the French, the Allied horsemen were trained primarily for shock action with the saber; Marlborough restricted his English troopers to three rounds of ammunition, for use when guarding the horses in bivouac. Thus it was with a headlong charge that the Allied cavalry broke the French lines. The enemy army lost its cohesion, Marshal Tallard himself fell into Allied hands, and the shock action of Marlborough's cavalry charge completed at least as decisive a battlefield victory as Gustavus Adolphus had attained at Breitenfeld.

The cost was not low. Marlborough's day-long pounding of the enemy lines to pave the way for the final assault took a heavy toll of his own men as well as the enemy, to say nothing of the losses that had to accompany the frenzy of the climactic blow. Allied casualties were probably about 20 percent of their strength, some 4,500 killed and 7,500 wounded. The Franco-Bavarians, however, probably lost something over 38,000, including 15,000 prisoners. For practical purposes, their army was destroyed. A grateful Empire in April 1706 named Marlborough Prince of Mindelheim of the Holy Roman Empire of the German Nation (after the Treaty of Rastadt [Rastatt] of February 24, 1713/March 7, 1714, he became simply Prince of the Holy Roman Empire of the German Nation).

Marlborough had achieved the supreme consummation sought by a battlefield commander; his next and most perplexing problem, of course, was to translate tactical into strategic decisiveness. From the battlefield of Blenheim he promptly marched west toward the borders of France. He captured Ulm after a brief siege. In the autumn his troops took Landau after a longer siege. Meanwhile Marlborough himself had proceeded to the Moselle, where he also captured Trarbach and Trèves (Trier). There, however, the campaign of 1704 closed down; not even Marlborough could master the logistics of moving a large army in the winter, when the grainfields were bare and the roads often quagmires of mud or sheets of ice. Planning for 1705, however, the Duke studied his maps for a march on Paris.

He did not arrive there. When won against a state possessing the relative strength in population and resources of Louis XIV's France, even the most decisive of battlefield victories proved almost impossible to translate into corresponding strategic decisiveness. In 1705, allies rendered complacent by Blenheim—and the Margrave Louis of Baden rendered embittered by it, because Marlborough, distrustful of his abilities, had denied him a role in the victory—failed to meet promptly their commitments to reinforce Marlborough's army. The Duke decided he must depart the Moselle to relieve Liège from a siege brought on by a French countereffort. Thus the sometimes-glorious Blenheim campaign ingloriously petered out.

English Intervention in Spain

Marlborough's dependence on allies could have been less crippling, and his chances of achieving decisive effects beyond the battlefield greater, if his country had enjoyed less amateurish direction of policy and strategy than it now found everywhere except where the Duke himself held control.

Military professionalism should be the servant rather than the maker of national policy, of course, but the advice of the professionals can serve as an anchor against the drifting of policy into strategic shallows. In England, only the largely self-generated military professionalism of Marlborough offered such an anchor in a sea of military amateurism, and Marlborough alone could not shape all decision-making. It is remarkable that he controlled as much as he did. The absence of professional military advice from any source other than Marlborough made English grand strategy, furthermore, forever susceptible to the changing winds of politics.

The Whigs remained as they had been since they called William and Mary from the Netherlands the party of English commitment to the Continent, to resist the hegemonic ambitions of Louis XIV. The Tories resisted continental commitments. To the extent that the Tories possessed a military policy and strategy, it was to substitute for expensive continental ventures a maritime strategy of employing rising English sea power to erode the periphery of the French empire. By means of a peripheral strategy, the Tories hoped to win strategic advantages at a much cheaper price than Whig continentalism entailed—and with the cost offset or more than offset by deriving commercial contacts and benefits from the excursions of the Royal Navy.

Marlborough himself was for family reasons a Tory, but he and the Lord Treasurer, Sir Sidney Godolphin (from December 1706 first Viscount Rialton and first Earl of Godolphin), were lonely champions of a contentional strategy within their own party. They were increasingly dependent on the Whigs to sustain Marlborough's campaigns on the Continent.

To be sure, the maritime strategy of the Tories, with its use of naval power to attain relatively cheap military advantages while augmenting commercial assets, was to become increasingly a foundation of British world power. It appeared at its profitable best while the Blenheim campaign was in progress in an effort that partially miscarried but yielded serendipitous results.

Through the typical method of backing up business enticement with naval power, England in 1703 had detached Portugal from its French alliance, offering in return an assured market for Portuguese wine—so that henceforth upper-class Englishmen drank port after dinner. With Lisbon (Lisboa) now open to it, the Royal Navy had a base from which to cruise the Mediterranean. In 1704 Rear-Admiral Sir George Rooke therefore was able to lead an Anglo-Dutch fleet past the Pillars of Hercules to operate against the southern coast of France as a diversion in support of Marlborough's Blenheim campaign. Nothing in particular came of that phase of the venture, but Rooke teamed up in July with another squadron under the very able Rear-Admiral of England, Sir Cloudisley (or Cloudsley) Shovel, and together they captured Gibraltar.

The French responded by besieging the place, but "the Rock" held on to become a bulwark of British strategy throughout the era of British world power.

On the other hand, maritime strategy with its prospect of cheap or even money-making victories began early to tempt England into misadventures nourished by the delusion that such a strategy might with patience overcome powerful continental adversaries. This delusion was to plague Great Britain during the whole era of its world power even more than the possession of Gibraltar benefited it.

A case in point developed early, with an intervention in Spain designed to place the Archduke Charles on the throne of that country after all. Early in 1704 an Anglo-Dutch fleet carried to Spain 8,000 British and 4,000 Dutch troops who could well have been used in Marlborough's forthcoming campaign. When in spite of reinforcement by some 30,000 Portuguese soldiers they failed to accomplish much beyond creating a nuisance to annoy Philip V and the French, the Tories refused to admit the limitations of their maritime strategy and instead sent out reinforcements for 1705—once more, troops who might have been employed in the primary areas.

With a total force only slightly larger after attrition than that of the year before, the Allies in Spain won a superficial success by entering Catalonia and taking advantage of the traditional restlessness of that region, a restlessness at present partially directed against Philip V. But the capture of Barcelona on September 28/October 9, 1705, had as its principal effect the provoking of a strong French counteroffensive into Iberia, which revealed the dubiety of the foundations of British intervention. In spite of the Pyreness, it was much easier for the French than the British to maintain an army in Spain, given the conditions of long sea voyages at the time. It was not unusual for more than a third of the passengers on a troopship to perish en route. To make matters worse, in 1706 Louis XIV sent one of his ablest generals to be commander-in-chief in Spain, Sir James Fitzjames, a son of James, ninth Duke of York, fifth Duke of Albany (in the Scottish peerage), first Duke of York and Albany, and twelfth Earl of Ulster—that is, the man who became James II—by Arabella Churchill, sister of Marlborough; in 1687, before the Glorious Revolution, this illegitimate son had been created first Duke of Berwick, first Earl of Teignmouth, and first Baron Bosworth; he was now a *maréchal de France*.

Catalonia, it is true, gave the cause of Archduke Charles substantial support, and there were risings in his behalf elsewhere—but nothing on the scale of the guerrilla insurgency destined to support another British venture into Spain a century later. Instead, the English had grave difficulties in trying to maintain a large field army while also having to scatter troops through much of the country to protect and encourage their friends. By 1708, Parliament had authorized 29,395 men for the Spanish campaign, an astonishing total in light of the numbers given to Marlborough; but only 8,660 British soldiers were concentrated at the battle of Almanza on April 14/25, 1707. There Britain's Portuguese allies took flight, and in the ensuing disaster the remainder of the Allied infantry was almost wiped out. The Tories were not ready to admit failure, and the struggle dragged on; but for practical purposes Almanza ended any possibility that strategic accomplishment might flow from the disproportionately large military investment in Spain.

Ramillies

Having returned to the Low Countries in tacit admission of the strategic indecisiveness of Blenheim, Marlborough opened his campaign of 1705 by employing his standard device of applying pressure in one direction while preparing a climactic effort in another, this time using the device on a grand-tactical or operational scale. His latest opponent, François de Neufville, duc de Villeroi, *maréchal de France*, proved a ready victim of even the simplest of stratagems; he had secured his command mainly through family preferment and possessed nothing of the abilities of a Condé, a Turenne, or a Luxembourg. With Louvois gone and Louis XIV approaching old age, professionalism was becoming badly diluted as a qualification for high command in the French Army.

When Marlborough appeared to be aiming at Namur, Villeroi took the bait and thereby left a path open for the English general to penetrate the Lines of Brabant around Tirlemont. Once inside the belt of French fortresses, Marlborough was able to execute a further advance freely enough to envelop Villeroi's right flank and threaten him from his rear. There Marlborough prepared to give battle on ground that would one day be the battlefield of Waterloo. But yet again the Dutch frustrated him, delaying permission to fight until Marlborough had to withdraw to replenish his supplies.

Nevertheless, Louis XIV found Allied penetration of the Lines of Brabant intolerable, and he pressed Villeroi to begin the next year's campaign by going over to the offensive. That he could contemplate the offensive shows how badly Allied dithering and dispersion of resources in less than two years had squandered the impact of Blenheim. In May 1706 Villeroi with a reequipped French army of about 62,000 crossed the River Dyle to challenge Marlborough where the Allies had penetrated the Lines of Brabant, around Tirlemont.

On May 12/23, 1706 Marlborough with almost equal numbers challenged Villeroi to battle near the village of Ramillies. The French took up an apparently strong defensive position on high ground, with their flanks protected by marshy streams, the River Meshaigne on the south, the French right, and the Little Gheet (Klein Geet) on the north. As at Blenheim, villages scattered along the line gave them defensive bastions. But the villages happened to be too far separated for effective mutual support, and the course of the Little Gheet, running in front of the French left, was such that although it shielded that wing of Villeroi's army, it also tended to deprive Villeroi of the possibility of counterattack in the north.

In spite of the screen provided by the Little Gheet, Marlborough directed his first effort—in fact, the standard feint—in that direction. After thus drawing Villeroi's attention northward, Marlborough struck hard on the opposite flank, the French right, with the bulk of his cavalry. Villeroi was sufficiently perceptive and alert that, the northward feint notwithstanding, he committed most of his own cavalry to the more bitter, southerly action. Here indeed the fighting became so intense that Marlborough himself rode into the midst of it; a not infrequent failing of his was to depart from the role of commander in chief for that of squadron commander, in part because professionalism had not yet altogether eclipsed the attitudes of medieval chivalric warfare.

In the course of this dubious action, Marlborough was unhorsed. Fortunately for his plans, however, he was not too much distracted to order the climactic assault, which was to fall at neither of the two locuses of the battle so far but against the French center around Ramillies, a sector that Marlborough rightly hoped Villeroi would have weakened. For his own part, Marlborough had

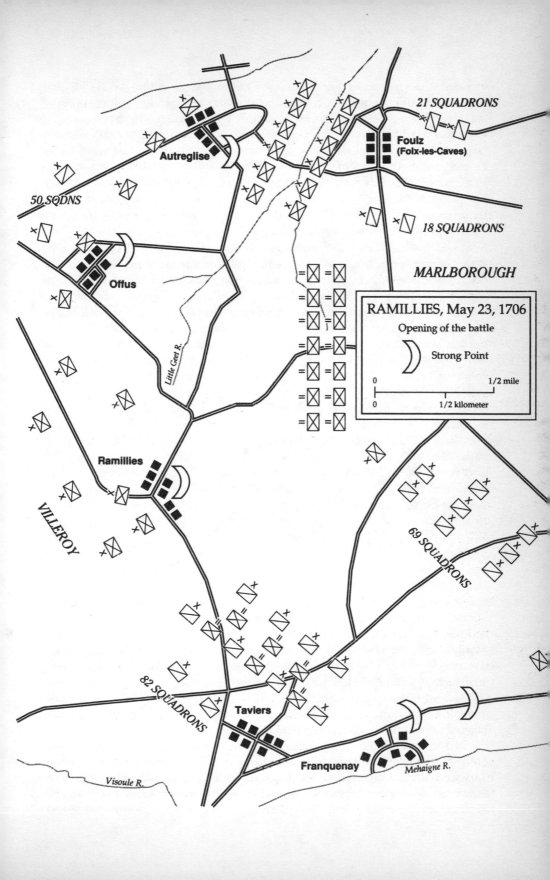

21 SQUADRONS

Foulz
(Folx-les-Caves)

Autreglise

50 SQDNS

18 SQUADRONS

MARLBOROUGH

Offus

RAMILLIES, May 23, 1706

Opening of the battle

Strong Point

0   1/2 mile

0   1/2 kilometer

Ramillies

VILLEROY

69 SQUADRONS

82 SQUADRONS

Taviers

Franquenay

Mehaigne R.

Little Geet R.

Visoule R.

effected what he intended as the decisive concentration in this sector, but characteristically did so only after the battle was under way, stealthily drawing battalions from his right wing. Once unleashed, the resultant overpowering infantry concentration broke the French center. With the French in disarray, Marlborough's cavalry as usual dealt the final blow, rolling up what remained of the French line from south to north. The French fled the field with casualties of some 15,000; they left their cannons behind. The Allied losses were a relatively low 5,000, borne disproportionately by the Dutch, who compensated in part for their hesitancies elsewhere by bearing the brunt of this new struggle to stem the French advance into their homeland.

The battle of Ramillies not only checked that advance but assured the Allied conquest of virtually all of the Spanish Netherlands. Marlborough's troops occupied Antwerp, Brussels (Bruxelles; Brussel), and nearly all the barrier fortresses that Louis XIV had seized on the pretext of aiding their Spanish garrisons. With the United Provinces therefore secure and the *Grand Monarque* humiliated, the Dutch were willing to seek peace. Because of exhaustion, the French were not unresponsive, and the war seemed about to end on terms that left both the balance of power and the Low Countries in about as stable a condition as could be hoped for. But now it was the turbulence of British politics that intervened to prolong the war, however pointlessly. The political leaders hoped to extract from the tactical decision of Ramillies a strategic decisiveness beyond what a realistic appraisal of the military balance would have warranted— a not-uncommon further contributor to the futility of war as an instrument of policy. And while Marlborough would go on commanding in the field, and two of his four great battlefield victories still lay before him, his hold upon British policy-making and strategy had already loosened by the day of Ramillies and was soon almost to fade away.

Oudenarde

We can speak of British rather than English policy-making because among the effects of Ramillies was a patriotic pride throughout Great Britain that encouraged Scottish acceptance of the Act of Union of March 4, 1706/March 15, 1707, to unite the Kingdoms of England and Scotland. But other British political events of 1707 were far less happy. Increasingly the Whigs had demanded that Marlborough and Godolphin acknowledge their dependence on Whig votes in the House of Commons by helping to reorganize the Cabinet around Whig leadership. Queen Anne resisted. The Whigs were, among their other attitudes, the party of relative tolerance for religious dissent, yet the Queen's uneasy sense of assurance that she rather than her half-brother James Francis Edward Stuart, James II's legitimate son, rightly held the throne depended on her unquestioning and intolerant adherence to the Church of England. To the Queen, acceptance of religious dissent implied the possible acceptance of a Roman Catholic dissenter's claim to the throne itself. Thus, while after Ramillies the Queen did acquiesce in a Cabinet reshaped to meet Whig demands, her acquiescence violated her deepest convictions. Psychologically it was a death blow to her already

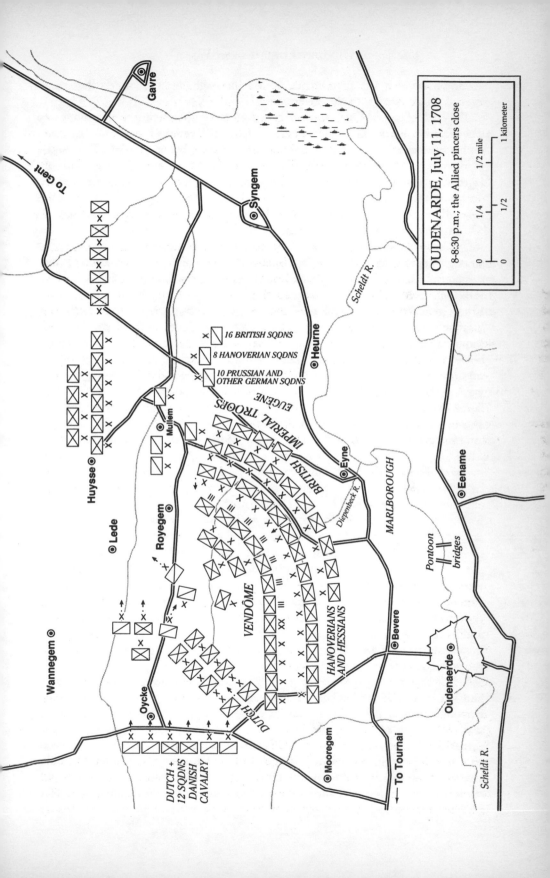

OUDENARDE, July 11, 1708

8–8:30 p.m.; the Allied pincers close

0   1/4   1/2   1/2 mile
0   1/2   1 kilometer

16 BRITISH SQDNS

8 HANOVERIAN SQDNS

10 PRUSSIAN AND OTHER GERMAN SQDNS

Gavre

To Gent

Syngem

Heurne

Scheldt R.

Eyne

Eename

MARLBOROUGH

EUGÈNE

IMPERIAL TROOPS

BRITISH

Diepenbeck R.

Pontoon bridges

Huysse

Mullem

Lede

Royegem

VENDÔME

DUTCH

HANOVERIANS AND HESSIANS

Bevere

Oudenaerde

Scheldt R.

Wannegem

Oycke

Mooregem

To Tournai

DUTCH + 12 SQDNS DANISH CAVALRY

waning friendship with the Duchess of Marlborough, and thus to Marlborough's special relationship with the sovereign.

By 1707 Queen Anne was intriguing with Marlborough's rivals among the Tory leaders, particularly Robert Harley, former Speaker of the House of Commons, against the Duke's leadership. For the time being Marlborough held a place in the Cabinet through threat of resignation of his military command, but at the expense of yet further alienation from the Queen and yet more dependence on the Whigs, a situation that pushed the hitherto more moderate Tories toward the extremists of the anti-Marlborough and anti-continental-war school.

Against this political background, Marlborough the military commander waged only a defensive campaign in the Low Countries in 1707, investing his strategic hopes instead in an expedition by the forces of the Empire, led by Prince Eugène and including the Prussian troops placed at the Empire's disposal, out of Italy and into southern France against Toulon. More frustration followed; the French reinforced Toulon strongly enough that it withstood the combined efforts of Eugène's army and a British fleet. The Dutch meanwhile governed their recently acquired fortress cities in a bungling manner that worsened the estrangement between Catholic and Protestant Netherlanders and helped precipitate *coups d'état* that restored Ghent (Gent; Gand) and Bruges (Brugge) with their strategic waterways to the French. Prince Eugène traveled north to concert his plans with Marlborough's in the spring of 1708, to find the British general close to despair over the entire course of events, political and military.

Eugène supposedly was able to rouse Marlborough both from dismay and from a sickbed. Be that as it may, the two principal Allied commanders together responded to the crisis with a display of unorthodox military boldness that carries considerable claim to representing the apex of their joint efforts in generalship, even when Blenheim is recalled. The current French commanders in the Low Countries, Louis, duc de Bourgogne, grandson of the King, and Louis Joseph, duc de Vendôme, *maréchal de France,* were taking advantage of the auspicious turn of events to march against the fortress of Oudenarde (Oudenaerde) astride the River Scheldt. Aroused again and determined to forestall them, Marlborough along with Eugène hastened their forces across the Scheldt to challenge the French in a meeting engagement with the river in the Allied rear. On two counts—by hastening into battle instead of arranging a set-piece engagement, and by fighting without a secure line of retreat—the Allied generals were violating the precepts of war of their time; on the second count they ran grave risks by the standards of any time.

But they gained the advantage of surprise. The Allies attacked Burgundy and Venôme while the French army was extended in line of march. The French commanders thus also had to feed their troops into combat piecemeal. Nevertheless, the battle of Oudenarde, June 30/July 11, 1708, soon found the French threatening to isolate and destroy the Allied advance guard under William Cadogan, now a major-general. It required skillful and stubborn leadership by Cadogan and an equally stubborn defensive fight by his soldiers—in which the Prussians were once more conspicuous—to preserve the vanguard until the bulk of the Allied forces could deploy to relieve the pressure.

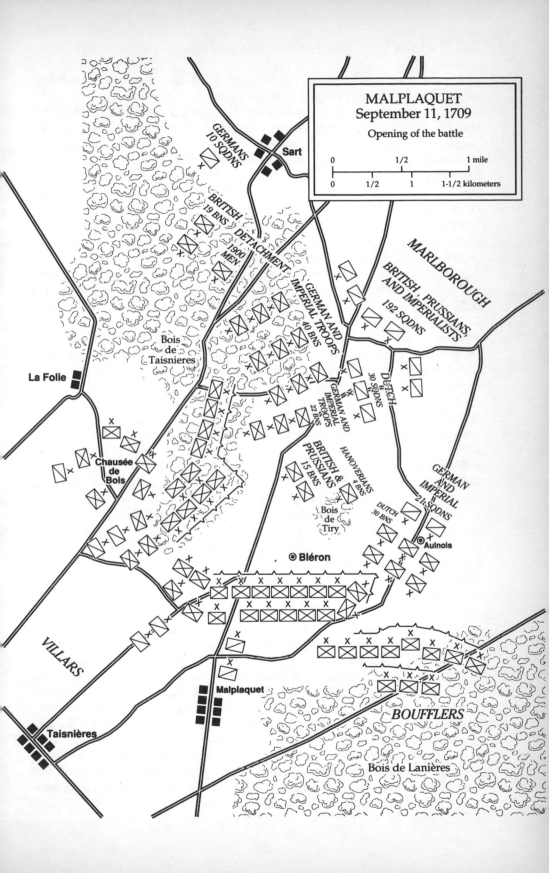

MALPLAQUET
September 11, 1709

Opening of the battle

0   1/2   1 mile

0   1/2   1   1-1/2 kilometers

GERMANS
10 SQDNS

Sart

BRITISH
DETACHMENT
19 BNS
1900
MEN

GERMAN AND
IMPERIAL TROOPS
40 BNS

MARLBOROUGH

BRITISH, PRUSSIANS,
AND IMPERIALISTS
192 SQDNS

Bois
de
Taisnieres

La Folie

GERMAN AND
IMPERIAL
TROOPS
22 BNS

DUTCH
30 SQDNS

Chausée
de
Bois

BRITISH &
PRUSSIANS
15 BNS

HANOVERIANS
4 BNS

GERMAN
AND
IMPERIAL
21 SQDNS

Bois
de
Tiry

DUTCH
30 BNS

Aulnois

⊙ Bléron

VILLARS

Malplaquet

BOUFFLERS

Taisnières

Bois de Lanières

Even in this improvised battle, however, Marlborough was as usual hoarding strength for a climactic blow after the enemy had focused his main strength and his attention elsewhere. After the battle had swirled for several hours around the centers of the deploying armies, Eugène began carrying his and Marlborough's design toward its conclusion with an attack that broke the French left. This, however, was only Marlborough's penultimate stroke. The final blow was an enveloping maneuver, spearheaded by the Duke's cavalry, with Marlborough invoking his favorite assets, mobility and shock, to send his reserve around the enemy's right and into his rear. This maneuver in combination with Eugène's formed nearly a double envelopment, almost enclosing the French army. The rival armies at Oudenarde each mustered about 63,000 men. Marlborough and Eugène extracted from the French casualties of some 6,000 killed and wounded and 9,000 prisoners, in exchange for about 3,000 casualties of their own.

The victory of Oudenarde notwithstanding, Marlborough's political position at home continued to deteriorate. His was a voice for a reasoned middle course in foreign policy when the prevailing views of the rival Whigs and Tories had polarized. It must be conceded, moreover, that perhaps because of weariness the Duke did not bring to bear all of the influence he might yet have mustered in behalf of his professed desire for peace on terms commensurate with the Allies' exertions but not draconian. The Whigs insisted that the war must continue until Spain had been pried away from the Bourbons. The Tories, their peripheral strategy in Spain frustrated, were ready for peace on almost any terms. Louis XIV, older and with yet more cause for weariness than Marlborough, was willing by now to yield Spain to the Habsburgs—that is, to withdraw his troops from the country and leave Philip V to whatever fate might then await him. But Philip had become too closely associated with Spanish nationalism, and therefore the outcome of his abandonment by Louis was too uncertain, for such a recourse to satisfy an Allied policy shaped largely by the English Whigs. The Allies insisted that Louis XIV must force his grandson from the Spanish throne if nothing else would guarantee his departure. They also demanded various French fortresses as hostages to assure the desired outcome in Spain. Thus the Allies overreached themselves; they asked Louis for much too great a sacrifice and humiliation. So the war dragged on.

Malplaquet

The war dragged on, changed now in its basic nature from a struggle to save Europe from French hegemony to an Allied war of conquest against France and Spain. Marlborough, although essentially reduced to the role of field commander, continued to grind away at the lines of barrier fortresses shielding northeast France. After capturing Tournai in 1709, Marlborough and Eugène moved on toward Mons. To the west and south of this fortress-city, the directions from which the Allies approached, a semicircle of wooded and broken ground formed a shield, penetrated by only two passes, that of Jemappes to the west and that of Aulnois to the south. Within the latter pass and in the adjacent woods, around the village of Malplaquet, Marshal Villars stationed his French army to block the Allied advance. The Allies attacked on August 29/September 9. Long practice in military administration permitted each side, war-weariness notwithstanding, to send into the combat an army of 100,000 men, so that Malplaquet was in numbers engaged the greatest battle of European history before the Napoleonic Wars.

It was also the bloodiest. Marlborough employed his customary tactics, but Villars though no Turenne was both reasonably skillful and exceedingly stubborn, the most worthy opponent the French could pit against him. Marlborough opened the battle with an assault against the French left under his own direct supervision, employing the Prussian and Austrian infantry and a British column that he hoped might curl around the enemy flank. But in a desperate combat in the woods, a defense anchored on the ancient Regiments of Picardie and Champagne fought the Allies to a standstill, until on both sides casualties, fatigue, and the woods had broken up the regiments into congeries of detached fragments.

In an effort to crumble the Allied right completely, Villars sent the "Wild Geese," the *Royal Irlandois,* forward in a counterattack. They collided with the British troops who were supposed to have assailed the extreme French flank but were now needed in the holocaust among the trees. The British 18th Regiment of Foot, the Royal Irish, met the *Royal Irlandois.* It was Queen Anne's Irishmen who prevailed.

Before the contest ebbed on this part of the field, Marlborough, Eugène, and Villars all succumbed to the persistent temptation to become battalion commanders again, leading troops personally. Eugène and Villars were both wounded, the French marshal severely, so that after trying for a time to direct the battle from a chair he was carried away unconscious.

By that time the Allies had been assaulting the French right as well, the Dutch forming the core of the effort here. The enemy commander in this sector was Marshal Boufflers, less skillful than Villars but equally brave and stubborn. Again the French repulsed the allies, with casualties so heavy that the Dutch Army was never quite the same again; the vacant ranks could be replenished in time, but the memory of Malplaquet cast a long, dark shadow.

Stereotyped though Marlborough's tactics had become, the French had not been able to avoid weakening their center in the course of warding off his heavy blows against their flanks. In the afternoon, consequently, Marlborough was able to launch Lieutenant-General George Hamilton, fifth (first of the modern line) Earl of Orkney, in the customary climactic assault. Forty guns first bombarded the French center, an Allied infantry attack followed, and the Allied cavalry reserve, 30,000 strong, as usual delivered the ultimate blow with a saber charge. Not as usual, however, Villars and then Boufflers, who succeeded to the command of the whole field, had managed to retain the principal mass of their own cavalry in reserve in anticipation of the Marlboroughean climax.

For a final time, therefore, the outcome of the battle wavered. The French horse seemed for a while to be repelling the Allies. But Boufflers feared that his center had already been too badly weakened to permit him to hold off the enemy indefinitely. Rather than risk a defeat as complete as Blenheim or Oudenarde, he ordered a retreat.

The French withdrew with discipline and cohesion, while the Allies could no longer muster the strength for a driving pursuit. Malplaquet was the fourth—and last—of Marlborough's famous battlefield victories, but it left his army about as sorely staggered as the French. The Allies in fact may well have lost more casualties than the French; the toll probably ran to about 20,000 on each side.

The Ne Plus Ultra Lines

Malplaquet may have been Marlborough's last famous battlefield victory at least in part because after its terrible slaughter, the Duke may have deliberately avoided battle. He and Eugène waged the next year's campaign against Villars as a war of maneuver with only the most half-hearted gestures toward a new confrontation. The United Provinces more than ever wanted to settle for the border security they had already gained before the flower of their army was cut down on the way to Mons. In Great Britain, there was a general election in 1710 that produced a Tory majority in the House of Commons, determined to make peace.

The most auspicious opportunity for peace, however, was the one that had been lost before Malplaquet when Louis would have been willing to meet any of the Allies' terms except the forcing of his grandson from the Spanish throne by his own hands and the surrender of fortresses that were unquestionably French. Now the mood of France and its King had become one of renewed defiance against the possible unnatural humbling of the inherently most powerful state in Europe. Accordingly the new British government found itself obliged to retain Marlborough as its captain-general and to wage another campaign in 1711.

The most tangible embodiment of French defiance consisted of the Ne Plus Ultra Lines, constructed under Villars's direction during the winter of 1710–1711, a system of fortifications, entrenchments, and inundations stretching from the sea along the River Canche, thence to Arras, thence along the River Sensée to Bouchain on the Scheldt, and finally to the River Sambre. Buttressed by the lines, Villars led a larger army than Marlborough's, for the death of the Emperor Joseph (Josef) I, the eldest son of the old Emperor Leopold I and wearer of the Imperial crown since 1705, had brought the Archduke Charles back from Spain to claim the Habsburg dominions, and Prince Eugène thereupon had to shift his army southward to guard against French gestures toward interference with the Imperial election. Marlborough was left with some 90,000 men against Villars's 120,000.

The Duke proposed to rupture the Ne Plus Ultra Lines around Arras and Bouchain by capturing the latter major fortress. To achieve this end while avoiding battle, he once more applied his accustomed stratagems to the grand-tactical or operational level, on perhaps the most ambitious scale of his career. Inundations and swamps in the valley of the Sensée made the approach to Marlborough's targeted sector of the lines especially difficult, but causeways crossed the valley at Arleux and Aubanchoeil-au-Bac. On June 25/July 6, Marlborough achieved the capture of Arleux. He then marched away westward, however, as if to attack next between Arras and the headwaters of the Canche. Villars followed but left a detachment behind to retake Arleux. Receiving a message warning that the garrison there could not hold out, Marlborough sent General Cadogan at the head of a relief column. But Cadogan moved too slowly, and Arleux fell back into the possession of the French. The vulnerability of the place having been demonstrated, however, Villars thereupon destroyed its defenses, so that Marlborough would not be able to use them again.

But the significance of these events was even more obscure than is usual under the fog of war—to everyone except Marlborough. Cadogan was in Marlborough's confidence as was no other Allied leader save perhaps Eugène, and in fact Cadogan had failed purposely, on the Duke's instructions to do so. The object was to deceive Villars about the importance Marlborough attached to the Arleux causeway and Bouchain. In further deceptive maneuvers, Marlborough dispatched part of his army toward Béthune, part toward Douai, and himself continued on the march toward the upper Canche and Arras. There he conspicuously reconnoitered the front in person and with a large retinue, giving instructions for an attack. Villars hurried up artillery from elsewhere along his lines to complete a counterconcentration opposite the Duke.

Thereupon on the night of August 4–5/15–16 Marlborough swiftly and stealthily led his main forces away toward Aubanchoeil-au-Bac. His troops marched across the hills between Vimy Ridge and Arras, so famous or infamous in later British military annals. The column that had shifted toward Béthune rejoined. Cadogan returned to and regained the causeway at Arleux. Marlborough himself led his cavalry spearhead across the other causeway at Arbanchoeil-au-Bac.

The capable Villars alertly marched with similar speed in response, but he arrived in front of Cambrai just too late, and in just too piecemeal a fashion, to undertake an attack that might have driven Marlborough back from his penetration of the Ne Plus Ultra Lines. Villars offered defensive battle, but in his post-Malplaquet frame of mind Marlborough declined the offer. Instead, the Duke maneuvered farther eastward and laid siege to Bouchain. He guarded his rear too strongly for Villars to discover an opening to strike in that direction, and on September 13/24 Bouchain surrendered. Marlborough now commanded an opening through the Ne Plus Ultra Lines wide enough to permit a direct advance against Paris. Less heralded than his spectacular battles, the campaign of 1711 may nevertheless be Marlborough's masterpiece.

His reward was a summons home to face charges of peculation Moreover, the Tory leader Robert Harley, fully supported by the Queen, whose former love for the Duke and Duchess had gradually turned into loathing, engineered Marlborough's dismissal from all his offices. In disgust, Marlborough slipped out of England and back to the Continent, where without power he cooled his heels until the death of Queen Anne in 1714.

The French Resurgence and the Peace of Utrecht

In spite of Marlborough's unhappy fate, and notwithstanding also the Tories' already eager and still growing thirst for peace, it was the Allies who could open the campaign of 1712 with confidence, and the French who were again near despair. Such was the military effect of Marlborough's superb campaign of maneuver into the Ne Plus Ultra Lines. Like the line identified with André Maginot more than two centuries later, the Ne Plus Ultra Lines had been well advertised; their rupture sent waves of demoralization through France. The disaster appeared so great that even the administrative and logistical systems of the army seem to have sunk into lethargy; the troops awaited the campaign of 1712 hungry and in tattered uniforms as well as deprived of much of their defensive shield. Some of the King's ministers urged the removal of the government to a place more distant from the front than Paris and Versailles. As Villars prepared to take up his command in the field, Louis XIV could not help airing an accumulation of both personal and dynastic griefs to the marshal. After thus unburdening himself, the King said: "But enough of this. . . . If disaster overtakes your army, how would you advise me to act personally?"

Taken aback, Villars hesitated. Louis therefore proceeded with his own views: "I know that an army of this size cannot be so cut up that the bulk of it will be unable to fall back on the Somme. . . . What I shall do is to go to Péronne or St. Quentin, scrape up what troops I can, join you, and we will make one last effort, in which we will either die together or save the state."[1]

The Allies, or more accurately the British, saved the *Grand Monarque* from that sacrifice. Prince Eugène traveled to England to try to rally the Tory government for a final campaign but had to depart without assurances, disappointed and dubious about the likely extent of British participation. When Eugène nevertheless laid siege to Landrecies, his doubts were fully realized. Under James Butler, second Duke of Ormonde in the Irish peerage and Marlborough's successor as captain-general, the British contingent of 12,000 on orders from the Cabinet marched away from the Allied camps. Most of those Allied troops who were in British pay refused to follow Ormonde's men, and Eugène still had a force of 100,000. But the Allies were left shocked and off balance, and Villars promptly seized his opportunity.

Eugène protected the rear of the troops besieging Landrecies with the "lines of circumvallation" customary to the siegecraft of the day. By means of espionage, however, Villars learned of a weak spot in those lines north of the Denain crossings of the Scheldt. In a game of deceptive maneuver demonstrating that the French marshal had studied Marlborough's methods well, Villars through skillful feints misled Eugène about his intentions and then marched long and hard to cross the Scheldt and assail Denain. The defenders whom he hit were Dutch, still stricken by Malplaquet and with their morale scarcely improved by the British exodus. Villars routed them, and many drowned when in flight they overloaded and broke down the bridges of Denain. Eugène arrived on the south bank too late to save the day. Villars followed up energetically, break-

---

1. Warren Hamilton Lewis, *The Splendid Century: Life in the France of Louis XIV* (Paperback edition, Garden City, New York: Doubleday Anchor Books, Doubleday & Company, Inc., 1957), p. 35, no citation.

EUROPE IN 1721

Following the Treaty of 1713 and
associated treaties and at the
close of the Great Northern War.

—— Boundary of the Holy
Roman Empire of the
German Nation

- · - Other boundaries

0   100   200   300 miles

0   150   300   450 kilometers

NORWAY   FINLAND

KINGDOM
OF
SWEDEN   RUSSIAN
EMPIRE

SHETLAND ISLANDS

ORKNEY ISLANDS

HEBRIDES   St. Petersburg
                              Bergen ⊙   ⊙ INGRIA
                        ⊙ Christiania   Narva   ⊙ Novgorod
SCOTLAND   Stockholm ⊙   Gulf of Finland
                                              ESTONIA   Moscow ⊙
KINGDOM ⊙ Edinburgh   LIVONIA
Londonderry OF   NORTH   COURLAND Dvina R.
IRELAND Belfast ⊙   SEA   København ⊙ BALTIC   ⊙ Vilna
         Dublin ⊙ GREAT   SEA   Niemen R. LITHUANIA
         Cork ⊙ BRITAIN   PRUSSIA   ⊙ Minsk
Bantry   ENGLAND UNITED   Vistula R. Grodno ⊙ Mogilev
Bay   WALES   PROVINCES BRANDENBURG Warsaw ⊙ Dniester R.
         London ⊙   ⊙ Berlin   POLAND   ⊙ Kiev
Plymouth ⊙   AMSTERDAM ⊙   SAXONY   Kraców ⊙   Vorskla R.
ATLANTIC Dunkerque ⊙ AUSTRIAN   BOHEMIA   Poltava ⊙
OCEAN   St-Malo ⊙   NETHERLANDS ⊙ Prague   Dniester R.   Bug R.
          ⊙ Brest   Seine R. Ulm AUSTRIA
          Orléans ⊙ ⊙ Paris Rhine R. BAVARIA   Prut R.
                     Loire R.   Vienna KINGDOM
          Rochefort ⊙   Buda ⊙ Pest OF
Cape   Lyon ⊙ SWITZERLAND   HUNGARY   BLACK
Finisterre Bordeaux ⊙ FRANCE REPUBLIC   Danube R.   SEA
                            SAVOY OF
          Burgos ⊙ ⊙ Bayonne PIEDMONT VENICE
          Douro R.   Avignon ⊙ ⊙ Genoa ADRIATIC SEA
SPAIN   Rhône R. Toulon ⊙
          ⊙ Madrid   Marseille PAPAL   MONTENEGRO
PORTUGAL Toledo ⊙ Ebro R. CORSICA STATES   OTTOMAN EMPIRE
Lisbon ⊙   Barcelona (TO GENOA) Rome
Cabo   Valencia ⊙ BALEARIC IS.   ÆGEAN
de São   Almanza ⊙   MAJORCA MINORCA SARDINIA   ⊙ Naples   SEA
Vincente Cádiz ⊙ ⊙Sevilla   Port Mahon (TO HABSBURGS 1714,
C. Trafalgar ⊙ Gibraltar Cartagena (TO GREAT TO SAVOY 1720) KINGDOM
          ⊙ Tangier   MEDITERRANEAN SEA BRITAIN, 1713) OF
                                              NAPLES
                                    Morea
MOROCCO   ALGERIA   TUNIS   SICILY   Capo Passero
                              TO HABSBURGS, MALTA   Crete
                              1720-1735

ing into Eugène's supply depots to force the abandonment of the siege of Landrecies.

By this time the British were well on their way toward negotiating a separate peace. The Emperor Charles (Karl) VI (or Charles II within the Habsburg family domains) fought on through all of 1713, but after the French recaptured the fortress of Landau and again threatened Germany he felt obliged to give up the struggle. On February 24, 1713/March 7, 1714 he agreed to the Peace of Rastadt, which is generally regarded as part of the Peace of Utrecht, the name given to the various separate settlements reached by France and its enemies.

In the package, Philip V was allowed to retain the Spanish throne, on condition that it was never to be united with the throne of France. Great Britain was to retain Gibraltar as well as Minorca, which it had captured from Spain; in the New World it received the French colonies of Newfoundland, Acadia, and Hudson's Bay. It also received the Asiento, the slave-trade monopoly with Spanish America, and was privileged to send one additional ship a year for further trade with Spanish America. Austria was compensated for the Bourbon acquisition of the Spanish throne with the Spanish Netherlands—henceforth the Austrian Netherlands—and Milan, Naples, and Sardinia. The Dutch retained the barrier fortresses and received a monopoly of the navigation of the Scheldt.

In an agreement that was to prove of exceptional importance in the future, the Duke of Savoy was rewarded for his shift to the Allied coalition with the title of King and the acquisition of Sicily. (In 1720 he was to trade Sicily for Sardinia, thence styling himself King of Sardinia). Of still greater portent, the Elector of Brandenburg, whose troops had so often contributed conspicuously to the victories of Marlborough and Eugène, was allowed to assume the title King in Prussia, that is, in the part of his domain outside the boundaries of the Empire. Usage, however, would soon glide over into King of Prussia.

Another stipulation will reveal its importance when we turn in detail to naval warfare. The French had infested the Channel with privateers, based especially on Dunkirk. Raiders from that port alone were believed to have taken some 1,600 English and Allied ships. The settlement provided that the forts and harbor of Dunkirk were to be dismantled under English supervision. In consequence, the French not only lost a haven for privateers; more than that, the French Navy was to find itself with no northern port of refuge east of Brest, a circumstance that left the French perennially timorous about challenging the Royal Navy in the Channel, lest they be cut off from safe harbors.

On Decisiveness and Professionalism

When Marlborough first became captain-general, war had descended into protracted indecision, which aggravated its tendencies toward unrestrained violence because indecision bred frustration. Marlborough, ably seconded by Prince Eugène of Savoy, restored decisiveness to the battlefield. At Blenheim and Oudenarde he well-nigh attained the goal that over the centuries has been a will-o'-the-wisp pursued by all resolute commanders, the practical destruction of the enemy army that confronted him on the field. Marlborough even more than

Gustavus Adolphus executed what later military critics and historians would call a strategy of annihilation, particularly one using the instrument of battle to annihilate the opposing army. Nevertheless, a brilliant generalship's restoration of decisiveness to battle proved insufficient to restore decisiveness to war; a strategy of annihilation securing tactical decisiveness in battle failed to prove correspondingly decisive in its strategic impact.

And if Marlborough is truly an example of the earth-shaking hero in history, the rare individual without whose presence the course of events would surely have been much different, there thus remained severe limitations on the extent to which any individual, even one of the greatest of military commanders, could shape the course of history through battle and war. The hegemonic ambitions of France could be broken, and Great Britain could be raised to an eminence among the powers that it could not yet have hoped for without Marlborough. But France as a great power could not be broken.

The France of Louis XIV possessed too large a population, too deep a reservoir of resources, and too much resilience to be undone by a single battle or even a series of four destructive battles, even if battle brought the destruction of one and then another of its field armies. It staggered under its reverses; an economy not yet far advanced beyond subsistence agriculture and a system of taxation worse than archaic made for a resilience considerably less than that of the later great powers of the industrial age. Nevertheless, France's reserves of strength and resolve—and those of the King himself, whose finest hours came in adversity—permitted it to rally from defeat and emerge from the War of the Spanish Succession still the foremost military power in Europe, Blenheim, Oudenarde, and Marlborough's other military victories notwithstanding.

The efficient, centralized, and increasingly professionalized administration and command of the army contributed in no small measure to France's ability to survive its battlefield defeats. New armies could be recruited, trained, and equipped with remarkable dispatch to compensate for losses. The effectiveness and dispatch with which military business was conducted stood in dramatic contrast to most other activities of the French government, such as the counterproductive taxing system or the ritualistic ceremonials that marked almost every aspect of life at court. Only in the military sphere did the French nation-state as yet display the rationalized planning and activity that Europeans and Americans long afterward would flatter themselves was the hallmark of "modern" civilization. The rationalized planning and conduct of military affairs were the essence of those developments that we have described as the professionalization of military command and administration. France could rally from these reverses also because at the time of the Peace of Utrecht no other state had quite caught up with France's rationalization and professionalization of the conduct of war.

However, Great Britain was by no means so far behind as in 1688. The rise of the office of Secretary of the Forces and the activities of Cadogan as Quartermaster-General both signified considerable profiting from the experiences of the French. The gradual evolution in Marlborough's time of a numerical ranking of regiments by seniority, though based in large part at first on the seniority of their colonels, signified a further progression of the army into a coherent body, in contrast to the older system of simply designating regiments by their colonels' names, which reflected the origins of the regiments as entrepreneurial ventures of their commanders.

The fact that by Queen Anne's time red had become the uniform color of the British Army (with a few exceptions) was also not merely of superficial importance, or simply an aid to identification on the battlefield (although it was of immense value in that regard). While regimental commanders were still allowed to choose variations in facings and design, the emergence of the redcoats as the immediately identifiable soldiers of the British line signified further the centralization and rationalization of army administration. "Rationalization" is a particularly appropriate word here; red dyes were cheap, and in an age when the limited range of weapons made camouflage unimportant, red brought highly desirable visibility to help hold the army together amid battlefield confusion at minimal cost.

These generalizations about the British Army apply as well to the other major armies that were trying to catch up with the French. All learned much from the French, and in order to compete with France, all moved toward the French Army's standards. (All moved also to adopt a uniform color at least for their infantry. Considerations of avoiding expensive dyestuffs while fostering high visibility led France with its whitecoats, as well as Austria, the United Provinces, Spain, and Denmark all to adopt various shades of white or gray for their infantry. Sweden and Prussia chose blue, Bavaria sky-blue, and Russia green.)

Of course, it should be emphasized again that it was France's inherent strength and resilience more than its advances in military professionalism that permitted it to withstand the combined assaults of much of the rest of Europe, led by the two ablest generals of the age. If, against a power less inherently strong, battlefield victories approaching Marlborough's in decisiveness could be achieved, then tactical decisiveness might on occasion lead at last into the elusive goal of strategic decisiveness. Such proved to be the fate of a power that even more than Britain in the time of Marlborough had to base its claims to greatness upon the exertions of heroic individuals—Sweden under the Vasa dynasty. But it signifies much for the role of war as an instrument of policy that tactical decisiveness could rise to strategic decisiveness only when a fundamental imbalance of power existed before war began.

6 THE EMERGENCE OF THE GREAT POWERS OF EASTERN EUROPE

Sweden's ascent almost to the summit of European power under Gustavus II Adolphus was a *tour de force,* an achievement of the soldier-King's brilliance in military organization, tactics, and strategy that overcame immense deficiencies in resources. Of course, the Sweden of Gustavus Adolphus had attained, albeit largely thanks to the operations of foreign merchants in her ports, a share of the commercial foundation necessary to sustain large military ambitions. It had become the dominant commercial nation of the Baltic Sea. It also had the advantage of a citizenry generally free from serfdom, which made possible a vigorous military tradition embodied in a cohesive national militia. Thus when Gustavus Adolphus transformed the militia into a recruiting ground for a national standing army, and then applied to that army the new professionalizing training and discipline of the Dutch and the old precepts of the Romans, the King could with relative ease create the first modern national army in Europe. Always, nevertheless, Gustavus Adolphus built his military might on precariously narrow foundations.

Sweden remained basically an impoverished country of bare subsistence-level agriculture. The population was small. The casualties of Gustavus's campaigns promptly began changing the national army into a mercenary multinational army, because the Swedish population could not replenish the losses. The economic base of military power eroded almost as rapidly; Sweden soon became dependent on French subsidies in order to persist in the Thirty Years War.

Nevertheless, Sweden remained the principal power in the Baltic, where all the contending states of the time labored under similar handicaps. It still carried enough weight in European affairs in the closing years of the seventeenth century to be sought after in the alliances that formed and reformed during the wars of Louis XIV. The Swedes rebuilt their nation and in large measure their professional army after the ravages of the Thirty Years War, restoring the army essentially to the cohesion and skill it had possessed when Gustavus Adolphus first led it into Germany. If the Swedish Army was no longer the pioneer of military modernization, it did not lag far behind in the professionalizing developments now led by France.

Charles X Gustavus (Karl X Gustav), the nephew of Gustavus Adolphus (son of the latter's sister Katerina and Johan Kasimir, Pfalzgraf of Zweibrücken), succeeded to the throne in 1654 upon the abdication of the former King's daughter, Queen Christina (Kristina). He was an able soldier; he had learned war under Field Marshal Count Lennart Torstensson. He was a still abler diplomat. It is true that he overreached himself by attempting to conquer Poland. He captured Warsaw (Warszawa) in 1655, but the Poles' successful defense of their national shrine, the fortress-monastery of Czestochowa, in 1655–1656 served to raise up a more powerful wave of Polish nationalism than he could overcome. This setback was largely compensated for, however, by a spectacularly triumphant Swedish campaign against Denmark in 1657/1658, during which the Swedish Army approached Copenhagen (København) by crossing the Baltic on the ice in January/early February, compelling the Danes to cede nearly half their territory for fear that otherwise they would lose their independence entirely; Denmark yielded the three provinces forming Scania (Skåne), the island of Bornholm, and the Norwegian provinces of Baahus and Trondhjem.

But it is not surprising that the legacy of this lesser Swedish soldier-King proved like that of the greater Gustavus Adolphus difficult for so inherently constricted a power to maintain. Charles (Karl) XI succeeded his father at the age of four. The regents proved indolent and prepared him little for either statecraft or war. When he was barely twenty, Denmark went to war against him to regain its lost territories. In spite of a neglected education, however, Charles XI proved to have inherited some of the natural military genius of the Vasa family; at twenty-one, on November 24/December 4, 1676, he thrashed the Danish invaders at the battle of Lund, one of the bloodiest engagements in history, in which over 8,000 men, more than half of those in action, are supposed to have died. On July 5/15, 1678, Charles routed the Danes near Malmö, whereupon Louis XIV as the would-be arbiter of all Europe, seeking to curb the aggrandizement of the Swedes, intervened to save the Danes from a second prospect of complete defeat. The necessity to acquiesce in this intervention notwithstanding, Charles XI had rescued Sweden's stature as one of the major powers, and he had done so by offering a reminder that in war professionalism is not everything, and that the spirit of the warrior counts for much. Furthermore, because when Louis XIV intervened the *Grand Monarque* was still having his way with almost everyone, and because Louis valued Sweden as a military force even while seeking to retain a balance of power in the Baltic, his settlement was generous to the Swedes: Finland, Karelia, Ingria, Estonia, Livonia, western Pomerania, Wismar, Bremen, Verden, and most of the Baltic islands as well as the recent acquisitions from Denmark still flew the Swedish flag, and Sweden controlled the mouths of the Neva, Dvina, Oder, Elbe, and Weser rivers.

Yet once more, however, a royal minority soon seemed to render Sweden still more vulnerable than its inherent limitations already made it. When Charles XI died on March 24, 1696/April 5, 1697, his son, who became Charles (Karl) XII, was two months short of fifteen. Though the new monarch unlike his father had been carefully tutored for kingship—with his father as principal mentor, taking him on many tours of the realm and its industries—the boy was still too young to have found his way into a sure grasp of responsibility. He was known, too, to be headstrong and impetuous; though the Riksdag promptly offered him full sovereignty without a regency, his response was to accept without swearing the customary coronation oath, implying by the omission that he considered himself under no obligation to his subjects.

Those who fretted under Swedish domination of the Baltic readily concluded that this immature youth might well be imposed upon. That category conspicuously included the resentful Danes, but it included also, more ominously, the rising, vast, and mysterious power of Russia to the east.

The Great Northern War

In Russia, since the year of Charles XII's birth, 1682, there had reigned as Tsar one Peter (Pyotr) Alexievich—the Peter who was destined to be called the Great. At the time of the new Swedish King's accession, Peter had just embarked on his Grand Embassy to the West, a tour by Russian dignitaries dispatched abroad to bring back the foundations of western European learning, technology, and particularly military science, the better to transform Russia from a semi-oriental backwater, not so long ago a mere satrapy of the Mongol Empire, into a Western-style great power. The Tsar accompanied the embassy in the guise of a volunteer sailor called Pyotr Mikhailov, so he might see and hear more and particularly learn more about the western art of shipbuilding. His return to his homeland was hastened by news of a revolt of the Streltsy, the palace guard. Eliminating this corps, whose ethos, to the extent that it was military at all rather than political, was too narrowly that of warriors unreceptive to professionalism, would in any event serve as a convenient start toward refashioning the Russian Army on the model of the nascent professionalization of the West. This beginning Peter proceeded to make. But he was not so busy with the killing of the Streltsy that he failed to seize upon the apparent opportunity created by the accession of the young Charles XII of Sweden.

In order to turn westward, Russia needed a port with free access to the Baltic. Peter already envisaged his new capital of St. Petersburg built upon such a port. His vision demanded the expulsion of the Swedes from the mouth of the Neva and from as much as possible of the rest of the eastern Baltic littoral as well.

Next there appeared a carpenter to nail together the Russian and Danish resentments against Sweden for the creation of an alliance. Taking up this chore was a Livonian landowner, Johann Reinhold Patkul, whom the Swedes had deprived of his estates. Patkul was currently serving Frederick Augustus (Friedrich Augustus), Elector of Saxony, who during the eventful year 1697 had been elected King of Poland as Augustus II, and who thus also found his dominions' way to the sea impeded by the ubiquitous Swedes. Patkul was able to make his own master the link between Peter of Russia and Frederick (Fredrik) IV of the Danish royal house of Oldenburg, in an alliance against Sweden whose formation precipitated in 1699 the Great Northern War.

The Allies were repeating the mistake made by the Danes when they had hastily taken on the youthful Charles XI. The mistake was less excusable this time not only because of the memory of Lund and Malmö but because it was generally known that Charles XI had taken pains to prepare his son for kingship. Even a more thoughtful recollection of recent events and of the consistent military abilities of the Vasa dynasty, however, could not have prepared the Allies for the tiger they now took by the tail. Even more than his father, Charles XII embodied the best of the tradition of the warrior, but with the discipline and skills of modern military professionalism readily at hand in his army. For a time this combination was to prove a deadly one.

In warrior fashion, Charles responded to the creation of the hostile coalition by seizing the offensive. He turned first against the nearest and probably the weakest of his enemies, Frederick IV of Denmark. He compelled his protesting naval commanders to attempt the navigation of the supposedly unnavigable eastern end of the Sound between Sweden and Sjælland (Zealand), the Flinterend, and thereby he transported an army to a landing a short distance north of Copenhagen on July 25/August 4, 1700. He might well have completed his father's work and captured the Danish capital had he not been governed, in spite of his warrior impulsiveness, by the difficulties of coping with multiple enemies. Because Frederick was willing to make peace, Charles took the opportunity to extricate himself swiftly from Denmark in order to turn eastward. In the Peace of Travendal on August 8/18, Denmark yielded only limited new concessions to Sweden but promised to engage in no further hostilities against that country.

Charles immediately hastened toward Livonia with an army of 8,000. His intention was to relieve Riga, besieged by the Saxons; but on learning that Narva was more tightly pressed by a Russian siege, under the personal command of the Tsar, he turned thither. His subordinate commanders were appalled when in mid-November he set out along a boggy approach road guarded by three dangerous passes. But he drove his troops through the first two passes without meeting opposition, and at the third, Pyhajoggi, a charge of 400 Swedish horsemen broke perhaps 6,000 Russian cavalry. From the beginning, Charles recognized that decisiveness in battle was to be sought in the arm of mobility and shock.

When Charles thus hastened into Lagena on November 9/19, only nine miles (fourteen and a half kilometers) from Narva, Tsar Peter panicked and fled the scene, leaving his command to subordinates. The next day, the impetuous Swedish King attacked the besieging forces, though he had to advance through a blinding snowstorm and was outnumbered about five to one. Whether it was a matter of fortune's favoring his boldness or of his correctly estimating Peter's progress, or the limitations of it, in modernizing the Russian Army—it was probably a measure of both—Charles was rewarded with a crushing victory, almost a battle of annihilation, in which his climactic cavalry charge turned the Russian survivors into a mass of fugitives.

Charles's hitherto cautious subordinates now counseled him to exploit the Russians' demoralization by pursuing them toward Moscow (Moskva), on the way fanning the discontents raised by Peter's reforms in order to stir up a rebellion that might dethrone the Tsar and push Muscovy back into oriental lethargy. The vision of hindsight creates temptations to endorse such advice, but surely Charles was wise to eschew a plunge deep into Russia while Saxony and Poland were still to be accounted for in his rear. Impulsive though he was, Charles was not merely a berserker—though he would not always remain so wise about the perils of excursions into the East.

His decision to go into winter quarters after Narva and then to turn west against Frederick Augustus may have reflected an overriding desire for vengeance against the principal authors of the hostile coalition. But concern for the security of his communications offered also a sound military motive, and there is no reason to impute the decision to any less rational consideration. In any event, the Narva campaign provided sufficient cause for Charles to believe that his principal opponents to the west constituted a greater military threat than the Russians, however vast Tsar Peter's domains. Such credence as the idea that vengeance was his guiding motive has attained, however, owes much to the conduct of the Swedish King and his armies when they entered Saxony and Poland. After clearing Livonia and occupying the Duchy of Courland to transform it into a Swedish Governor-Generalship in 1701, Charles invaded Poland in 1702. With the combination of audacity and tactical skill now becoming familiar, he readily captured both the capital, Warsaw, and the fortress and coronation city, Krakow. Frederick Augustus thereupon indicated a willingness to accept a conciliatory peace, but the Elector-King had misjudged the youthful Swedish monarch in more ways than one.

Not only was Charles XII proving to be the most formidable Swedish military commander since Gustavus Adolphus; in addition, he nourished grievances and repaid them ruthlessly. He differed from Gustavus Adolphus in sharing none of the latter's aspiration to be the embodiment of Christian kingship at the head of a Christian army. Instead, he set his troops to ravaging the territories of Frederick Augustus with a cruelty and abandon at least the equal of the French atrocities in the Palatinate, in fact presenting a calculated rather than spontaneous repetition of the worst of the outrages of the Thirty Years War. Murder, plunder, and destruction for destruction's own sake became the traveling companions of the new Swedish Army. In eastern Europe, the limitations upon the violence of war grown up since the Peace of Westphalia broke apart even more readily than in the West. Under Charles XII, the organized violence of war was often little different from organized barbarism.

Part of the motive for the policy of calculated horror was Charles's determination to accept nothing less than the removal of Frederick Augustus from the Polish throne. The combination of the threat of continued terror along with Swedish bribes for pliant Polish electors produced the election of Charles's candidate, Stanislaus Leszczynski, to be King of Poland as Stanislaus I on June 21/July 2, 1704. Resistance from the partisans of Augustus II delayed the coronation until September 13/24, 1705, but thereupon the new Polish King entered an alliance with Sweden and promised help against the Tsar.

Meanwhile Charles had essayed another foray into Russia to discourage Peter from mischief. After another fairly easy success he doubled back yet again to invade Saxony in 1706. This venture of course carried him well toward the west. With the War of the Spanish Succession currently in full fury, the Grand Alliance of the opponents of Louis XIV, mindful of the past partnership between Sweden and France, feared in fact that Charles was moving too far west for their safety. The Alliance dispatched no less an emissary than the Duke of Marlborough to sound out Charles on his intentions and to dissuade him from any dangerous designs. A meeting between two of the greatest soldiers of the era consequently occurred at the castle of Altranstädt near Leipzig. Marlborough found Charles preoccupied with his own, eastern affairs and reported accordingly that there was no cause for alarm—although in the sequel, while ensconced in Saxony the Swedish King did take it upon himself to intervene in the affairs of the Empire on behalf of the Protestants of Silesia. Sweden was a guarantor of their rights by treaty, and Charles insisted on Imperial restitution for alleged violations of those rights with so much of his now-customary bellicosity that the western allies of the Empire also felt obliged to become involved, lest the Swedes aid the *Grand Monarque* after all. The immediate outcome was that Charles secured all he demanded for the Silesians.

Meanwhile he also secured the capitulation of Frederick Augustus in the Treaty of Altranstädt of August 31/September 11, 1707, whereby the Elector renounced any anti-Swedish alliance along with his claim to the Polish throne. Charles was now free to move in for the kill at last against his remaining enemy, the Tsar. Thus isolated, Peter was willing to make peace; he sent out conciliatory overtures, but Charles ignored them.

Nevertheless, Peter had employed the time since Narva well. He had continued pushing forward the westernization of his army, and he had also given careful thought to how best to cope with the skillful yet impulsive Charles. The Tsar was about to prove a much wiser adversary than before, and a much more stubborn one, having used the interval also to gain better control over himself. He would not again panic. He would also apply to the war the ruthlessness that he often displayed at home; in preparation for Charles, he sent Tartar and Kalmuk horsemen raiding deep into Poland, ravaging the country and burning farms and villages, to render the Swedes' approach march as difficult as possible—and to illustrate still further how feeble were the limits upon violence in war.

At first, nevertheless, Charles appeared to be on his way to his accustomed triumphs won in accustomed fashion. On New Year's Day of 1708 under the western calendar (December 21, 1707 Old Style) he crossed the River Vistula by literally walking on thin ice. The dangerously fragile surface and Charles's luck both held. His first destination was Lithuania, but instead of taking the customary route through Pultusk he led his army through the Masurian forests and swamps, perhaps to test his luck and determination yet again by going where no army had gone before. Peter advanced to Grodno to prepare defenses there; but hearing of the Tsar's movements, Charles hurried forward with 900 cavalry to try to seize the Grodno bridge over the River Niemen and the Russian fortress there by a *coup de main* before resistance could be well prepared. The Swedes broke through more than twice their number of Russian cavalry and succeeded, entering Grodno just two hours after Peter had hastily departed.

From his own Baltic provinces, Peter removed all the inhabitants whom he suspected of sympathizing with the Swedes, driving old and young, the halt and the lame as well as the able-bodied, from Pskov, Dorpat, and other towns eastward into labor camps. By June, Charles was encamped near Minsk regrouping for what he hoped would be a final drive to Moscow. Moving forward again, he forced a passage of the River Beresina at Borisov at the end of the month, and on June 23/July 4 he split in two a Russian defensive line along the Wabis or Bibitch River near Holowczyn, opening the way to Mogilev on the Dnieper. It was a bad sign, however, that the Russians were obviously fighting with more skill and determination than on Charles's earlier expeditions against them.

Furthermore, there were yet more somber signs. The pause at Minsk notwithstanding, the Swedish Army was beginning to suffer severe supply problems. No modern army had yet solved such problems over distances comparable to those of Russia. Here no depot system could even begin to free an army from the necessity to feed itself from the resources of the countryside; but such resources were sparse at best, and the Tsar's new policy was while retreating to destroy everything that might sustain the invaders. By the time Charles XII reached Mogilev, he was nearing the end of his stores of food and forage, with little in prospect to replenish them.

While Charles pondered his difficulties but utterly refused to contemplate retreat, a tempting path of escape from starvation seemed to appear in the form of overtures from the Hetman (Headman) of the Kazaki, or Cossacks (a term meaning freebooters), Ivan Stepanovich Mazepa- (or Mazeppa-)Koledinsky. Mazepa was an adventurer who had insinuated himself into the close confidence of Tsar Peter. Probably the natural son of a Polish nobleman, he was educated at the court of King John II Casimir (Jan II Kasimierz) and also abroad, but he was banished from service as a page at the Polish court after his alleged seduction of some married lady. A tradition that may well be authentic says that he was tied naked to a horse and dispatched into the steppes. The Cossacks of the Dnieper rescued him, and he soon rose to be one of their leaders. Becoming Hetman, he served Peter in his campaigns that won Azov from the Turks in 1696 and in the early part of the Great Northern War. But as Charles's army rolled into Russia, Mazepa misread the meaning of the Swedes' successes and decided that Peter would lose the war. Mazepa would not have reached his current eminence without one consistency, a regard for his own fortunes at the expense of anyone else's. He was also jealous of rivals for Peter's favor. He would have preferred simply to take the Ukraine out of the war and watch for opportunities from the sidelines. But Peter ordered him to assume an active role in the defense of the

Ukraine, and, pressured also in his secret negotiations with the Swedes, Mazepa felt obliged to agree to welcome Charles's army into the Ukraine and to close off the region to Peter's forces.

Mazepa's reversal of loyalties struck Charles as offering the solution to his logistical crisis. He would postpone his advance on Moscow and march into the Ukraine, to renourish his army on its rich grainstuffs, grasses, and herds. He intended at first to tarry at Mogilev until a reinforcing and resupplying column from Sweden had arrived, but true to his nature, he soon grew impatient and on August 5/16 crossed the Dnieper to foray southward in search of local supplies. He encountered Peter's army at Dobry on August 29/September 9 and again won a battle, but again with much less than the ease of Narva and with only scorched earth awaiting him as he resumed his advance. He was shaken enough to call a council of war, in which he was advised to halt again, await the relief column, and then retreat to winter quarters in Livonia. But his own bolder inclinations were reinforced by an urgent appeal from Mazepa that arrived in the midst of the council: Peter's army had turned its attention to the Cossacks, and Mazepa needed help quickly. The relief column was now only sixty miles (ninety-six kilometers) away, but instead of waiting for it Charles hastened to join Mazepa.

Thereupon Peter turned to intervene between Charles and his reinforcements. The Tsar attacked the relief column of September 28/October 9 at Liesna with a numerical advantage of about four to one. The Swedes were hit so hard that they had to bury their artillery in hopes of preventing the Russians from using it, to burn their ammunition wagons, to mount many of their troops on the wagon horses, and to seek escape by a circuitous route. Of 11,000 reinforcements who had started out, only 6,000 eventually joined Charles, with their resupply sadly depleted. Another Swedish column, marching against St. Petersburg to create a distraction, was repulsed also, with losses of 3,000 men, 6,000 horses, and all its heavy supplies. By this time, many of the Cossacks had forsaken Mazepa and renewed their allegiance to the Tsar, perceiving better than Mazepa which way the wind was blowing. When Mazepa met Charles at Horki on October 28/November 8, only about 1,300 Cossacks remained to the Hetman as the armed force he could contribute to Charles's cause. Meanwhile, the increasingly sophisticated strategist Peter had marched promptly to occupy Mazepa's capital at Baturin before the Hetman could return in company with the Swedes. He occupied the place on November 2/13.

A large magazine of powder and arms had awaited Charles there, and, much more importantly, considerable stores of grain. Thus the rationale for Charles's southward march had collapsed, and his impatience to be on with the march had also deprived him of the help sent from Sweden. Now the Swedish Army might as well have been in the middle of a desert—but an intensely cold desert, for the frosts came early in 1708, and the winter was destined to be perhaps the worst in memory even in frigid Russia. By early November, firewood would not ignite except in sheltered places.

The recent reinforcements, depleted though they were, had raised Charles's numbers to somewhat over 40,000. The indomitable Swedish King would not give up, would not retreat, and resumed the march southward in quest of supplies and a secure base somewhere. By now his warrior spirit may well have hardened into a form of madness, yet somehow he retained a magnetism without which his army would have dissolved. On November 4/15 his troops crossed the River Desna on rafts against Russians in defensive array on the opposite bank, and dispersed the enemy. Thence the Russians cautiously marched parallel to Charles, harrying his flank with Cossack raiders. Nearly starving, the Swedes at last found a store of provisions at the town of Romni on the River Sula, something over a hundred miles (or 160 kilometers) east of Kiev; but now the worst of the winter assailed them, a time so cold that wine froze and saliva congealed as it left the mouth. Yet Charles would not rest. When Peter threatened four battalions of Swedes in a detachment at Gadiatz about fifty miles (eighty kilometers) south of Charles's main body, the Swedish King would not pull in the outpost but instead marched to rescue it with the bulk of his forces. On the march, perhaps 3,000 Swedes froze to death, and many more were disabled by the cold. Moreover, the now-dexterous Peter seized the opportunity to recapture Charles's haven at Romni, and the Russians also struck in force at Gadiatz before Charles could arrive, burning the place to the ground. Once more the Swedes found themselves in a frozen desert.

Somehow about 20,000 of them survived until the winter began to relent at the end of February 1708/1709, though some 2,000 of this number were variously crippled. Charles even contrived to win a few small battles before the spring mud halted almost all movement. Predictably, Charles's generals urged him that when the troops could march again, they should retreat to the friendly territory of King Stanislaus of Poland. Just as predictably, Charles instead sought reinforcements from Stanislaus, and through Mazepa he also won assurances from another band of Cossacks, the Zaporogian Cossacks, that they would harry Peter from the south. He hoped by remaining deep in the Ukraine to bring the Ottoman Turks to his aid as well. At the end of April he moved to invest the fortress town of Poltava, near the crossing of the Kiev-Kharkov Road over the Vorskla River.

The warrior in Charles, driven to at least the fringes of madness, had almost completely eclipsed any measure of military professionalism to which he had once held. His numbers were insufficient to invest Poltava completely. His artillery was reduced to thirty-four guns, and most of his powder had been ruined during the winter. A Russian army of 80,000 was maneuvering in the vicinity even before the siege began.

The Tsar himself was busy putting down the Zaparogian Cossacks, but he reached the neighborhood of Poltava in early June. On June 6/17—by coincidence, Charles's twenty-seventh birthday—Peter staged a feint attack on the besieging force in order to cover movements intended to bring his main army into a better position from which to threaten the Swedes. The feint drew Charles into a personal reconnaissance, during which he was shot in the left foot. The King completed his reconnoitering, but when he returned to his headquarters he discovered that the ball had passed completely through his foot from heel to toes. Surgery was necessary, and after the surgery Charles fell into a coma.

News of his incapacitation reached Peter, whereupon the Tsar decided to invite a showdown battle. He had avoided the general confrontation of his main force against Charles's since the Russian disaster at Narva; now he believed the time had come at least to capitalize on the Swedes' accumulated misfortunes. Some 40,000 of the Russians advanced into a camp that they quickly entrenched just north of Poltava, with the Vorskla River covering them on the east, and woods and rough ground providing protection to the south. Charles meanwhile recovered enough—though he still lay prostrate—to receive word that Stanislaus was too much preoccupied by other Russian forces to leave Poland, and that the Ottoman Turks were keeping their swords sheathed. Consistent in his conduct despite all his adversities, on June 16/27 Charles held a council of war at which he ordered an attack on the Russians' fortified camp for the next day. Detachments to observe the fortress of Poltava, to guard the baggage, and to watch against a flanking counterattack reduced the assault force to only about 12,500, in about equal numbers of infantry and cavalry. The infantry were so short of powder and shot that they would have to rely mainly on the bayonet.

For all that, the consequent battle of Poltava might have become another Swedish victory if Charles had been able to exercise his accustomed personal command. He deputed authority to subordinate commanders but then, in the midst of the battle, rose to try to reassert command himself. Usually he galloped across the battlefield from crisis point to crisis point; now he was confined to a litter and much less mobile than usual. His intervention was a grave mistake, a critical example of his lack of the qualities of the professional soldier. It disrupted all semblance of unity of command, and contradictory orders flowed from Charles and other officers down through the ranks.

The assault struck across relatively open and level ground on the western face of Peter's camp, but the Tsar had strengthened this sector with a series of redoubts that forced the Swedish attack into at least two separate channels. On their left, the still-skillful shock action of the Swedes penetrated the Russian front; apparently Charles was present there. But the right column attempted to carry the redoubts before it by direct assault rather than by sweeping around to their rear; this column not only was halted, but much of it was surrounded. Charles evidently did not understand what had happened on his right; he suspended his successful attack on the left to bring reinforcements to bear on the right—seemingly thinking he was reinforcing success. At about this juncture, another Swedish penetration of the Russian position occurred in the center, but now the confusion in command became complete. Orders from someone halted this latest breakthrough in mid-tide.

By the time Charles was once more reasonably well informed about what was going on and in approximate control, the Russians had restored their lines. Whatever opportunity might have beckoned the Swedes was gone. Charles staged a final frontal assault with infantry in its center and cavalry on the flanks; but by now he could throw fewer than 10,000 troops into the charge, against 40,000 or more Russians supported by about 100 guns. Peter, furthermore, exercised personal command of the defense with conspicuous courage instead of the panic of Narva. Charles's own bravery and skills could not offset the odds against him, though he was so much in the thick of the fighting that twenty-one of his twenty-four bearers and attendants were killed or wounded. His litter was struck by a cannon ball, and he was lifted to a horse to ride from the field in defeat.

At Poltava, it was not only Russian numbers but the increased skill of the Russian Army from Tsar to private soldier that at last overcame Charles XII. The battle heralded the emergence of Russia as a European great power and signaled the end of Sweden's great-power status.

With Charles's magnetism much diminished by his illness, the Swedish retreat from Poltava got out of the officers' control and deteriorated into a virtual rout. Little infantry, in fact, remained to retreat, while most of the survivors, mainly cavalry, surrendered to the Russians on June 19/30. Charles himself, however, along with Mazepa and some 1,000 horsemen managed to flee across the River Dniester into the Ottoman Empire.

The Turks were inveterate enough enemies of the Russians that they welcomed him, and indeed enough remained of the force of his personality that three times between 1710 and 1712 he persuaded the Ottoman government, the Sublime Porte, to declare war against Russia. But Turkish power was in ebb tide, and the Turks lacked the financial resources to conduct a campaign of any length. Therefore such fighting as occurred was altogether inconclusive—Peter was not ready for a major offensive either—and Charles soon began to quarrel with his hosts.

Eventually, on January 21/February 1, 1712/1713, the Turks attacked Charles's camp at Bender on the Dniester and made him a prisoner. After the Russians and Turks made peace in 1714 Charles was allowed to depart, riding across eastern Europe to assume command of the defense of Stralsund, which along with Wismar was by this time one of the only two German possessions remaining to Sweden. Saxony and Denmark were again in the field alongside Russia, and Prussia and Hanover (Hannover)—whose Electoral Prince was also from 1714 King of Great Britain and Ireland—had joined as well in the somewhat jackal-like coalition against the descending Baltic power.

Charles held Stralsund against this coalition through almost all of 1715, abandoning it in late December only when nothing but ruins remained to defend. Returning to Sweden itself for the first time in fourteen years, he rallied a new army with which, to pick up bargaining chips, he attacked the Danish possessions in Norway in both 1717 and 1718. Late in 1718, probably on November 30/December 11, when he had pressed almost to completion the siege of the fortress of Fredriksten, he peered over the parapet of the most advanced trench and was shot in the head. Ulrica Leonora, his sister, was elected to succeed him, but in 1720 she abdicated in favor of her husband, the Prince of Hesse-Darmstadt, who became Frederick (Fredrik) I.

Charles's death made possible the end of the Great Northern War. Sweden concluded peace with Hanover, Prussia, and Denmark in 1719 and 1720, ceding the bishoprics of Bremen and Verden to Hanover and Stettin to Prussia but generally still showing enough sharpness of tooth that the terms were not humiliating. Against the rising eastern power that had won at Poltava, however, the Swedes could not fare so well. By the Peace of Nystad of August 19/30, 1721,

Sweden lost to Russia Ingria, Estonia, Livonia, the Finnish province of Kexholm, and the fortress of Viborg. Even against the Russians, nevertheless, Sweden was still strong enough to insist on the return of Finnish territories west of Viborg and south of Kexholm, as well as an indemnity of two million thalers and a promise of noninterference in its internal affairs.

The twentieth-century British military critic and historian Major-General John F. C. Fuller called Charles XII of Sweden "the most extraordinary soldier in the history of war."[1] As a remarkable embodiment of the warrior spirit combined with just enough professionalism to restrain his berserker tendencies until almost the end of his career, perhaps Charles deserved such an encomium. But the minimal quality of his professionalism meant that he forever flirted with disaster, particularly with logistical disaster; and when the irrational in him became altogether preponderant and he plunged obstinately deeper and deeper into Russia, he brought upon himself and his country one of the most complete defeats in military history. Sweden's stature as a military great power had always rested on a *tour de force* accomplished by a remarkable succession of able monarchs, generals, and statesmen. Limited resources had always made great-power status dubious. After Charles XII, Sweden wisely refrained from aspiring toward military prominence.

Montecuccoli and the Army of the Habsburgs

The intervention of Charles XII in the affairs of the Holy Roman Empire in the midst of the Great Northern War, and the embassy of the Duke of Marlborough to protect the interests of the Empire and its allies, symbolized the vulnerability of another of the powers that like Sweden was at least partly of the East, the Habsburg realm. The geographic position of the Imperial domain was such that through most of the seventeenth and early eighteenth centuries the Habsburgs had to fend off too many enemies at once. Nevertheless, the Empire exhibited a capacity for survival that was already growing proverbial and would in time become more so. In military terms, the army built by Wallenstein and Tilly long outlived the army of Gustavus Adolphus as the military foundation of a great power, notwithstanding the disasters it had suffered at Gustavus's hands, and notwithstanding the excess of burdens that the Habsburg forces perennially bore.

The survivors whom Wallenstein led away from the battlefield of Lützen became the nucleus of an army that was henceforth introduced to the new professionalism primarily by a veteran wounded at both Breitenfeld and Lützen, Raimondo, conte di Montecuccoli (or Montecucculi), from 1657 *Feldmarschall* of the Imperial Army.

Born at the castle of Montecuccolo in Modena and a soldier in the Imperial service from the age of sixteen, Montecuccoli had reached the rank of colonel by

1. John Frederick Charles Fuller, *A Military History of the Western World* (3 vols., New York: Funk & Wagnalls Company, 1953–1957), II, *From the Defeat of the Spanish Armada, 1588 to the Battle of Waterloo, 1815* (1955), 184.

the time he was captured by the Swedes in 1639. Held at Stettin and Weimar for two and a half years, Montecuccoli seized the enforced opportunity to study the rediscovered ancient literature of war and to plan what became his own major work on the art of war, to be based on the ancients and in time on his own accumulating experience. Released, he fought during the waning years of the Thirty Years War in Silesia against the Swedes and in Lombardy against the French, winning promotion to *Feldmarschall Leutnant* and a seat in the Hofkriegsrat, the Imperial Council of War; in Hungary against the rebellious Georg Rákóczy I, prince of Transylvania, who was supported by Sweden and France; on the Danube and the Neckar against the French; and in Silesia again and Bohemia against the Swedes, winning the rank of *General der Cavallerie*.

These travels partially exemplify the breadth and diversity of the military problems besetting the Empire—but only partially. Montecuccoli's next service, which gained him his promotion to *Feldmarschall*, was from 1657 to 1660 against Prince Georg Rákózcy II of Transylvania as well as the Swedes, with the purpose of propping up a Habsburg ally, John II Casimir, as King of Poland. From 1661 to 1664 Montecuccoli fought against the Ottoman Turks, whose crescent was in the ascendant at the time, but whom Montecuccoli defeated in the battle of Saint Gotthard (or Gothard) Abbey on the Raab River in 1663; here his Imperial army was reinforced by French troops, because Louis XIV had not yet settled on his later policy of joining hands even with the infidels if doing so would help humble the Habsburgs.

Montecuccoli's next active command, however, was to be against the army of the *Grand Monarque*. The victory at Saint Gotthard Abbey won him the presidency of the Hofkriegsrat. For nearly ten years thereafter he devoted himself to his military studies and writing and to the professionalization of the Imperial forces along the lines suggested by his studies and experience as well as by the example of the principal rival army. His was a strong voice in favor of a military challenge to the ambitions of Louis XIV, and when war broke out, he became commander of the Imperial troops. In 1673 he outgeneraled Turenne along the Neckar and the Rhine, capturing Bonn and completing a juncture with the forces of William of Orange to present a solid cordon east of the French.

The next year Montecuccoli retired from the army at the age of sixty-five, but successes by Turenne in 1674–1675 ensconcing the French in the Palatinate and Alsace precipitated Montecuccoli's return to command and to the field. In the summer of 1675 he waged a campaign of maneuver against Turenne, a military symphony conducted by two masters; this time the advantage lay with Turenne, but as the opposing armies seemed to be forming up for a climactic battle on Turenne's terms, along the Sassbach (or Sasbach) on July 16/27, one of the first cannon shots of the preliminary skirmishing killed Turenne. The Imperial field marshal was then able to avoid battle and forthwith invaded Alsace instead. Here the great Condé took over what had been Turene's forces, to oppose Montecuccoli in yet another duel between two virtuosos of maneuver warfare. Condé checked the Habsburg commander and thus induced him to cross the Rhine eastward into Germany. There Montecuccoli completed the campaign of 1675 with the siege and capture of Philippsburg in Baden, whereby he returned to German possession a fortress-city that the long-ago Peace of Westphalia had awarded to the French. Philippsburg was to be, however, his last triumph. He and Condé both retired at the end of the year.

Contending on at least equal terms against soldiers of the prowess of Turenne and Condé, Montecuccoli had well earned the titles now bestowed on him of prince and of duca di Melfi, the latter an honor of the Kingdom of Naples whose monarch was the Habsburg Charles II of Spain. He spent the rest of his life further advancing the cause of professionalism within the Imperial army and completing his military writings. He died on October 6/16, 1680, of injuries received in an accident.

In order to qualify for admission to a profession, it is necessary for the candidate to master a body of historical and philosophical knowledge rooted in the liberal arts and then applied specifically to the tasks at hand. After the revival of the ancient military literature that he himself had studied, Montecuccoli's writings form the literary foundation of the military profession in central Europe.[2]

It is a war of maneuver such as he waged skillfully against Turenne and Condé that Montecuccoli urges upon soldiers in these writings. By no means did he believe that decisive objectives can be attained in war without combat,[3] but he believed that skillful maneuver ought to set the stage so that battle can achieve decisiveness. Moreover, Montecuccoli hoped to limit the bloodshed and violence of war in a larger sense than by avoiding unnecessary battle. His forces never perpetrated atrocities in any way comparable to those of the French armies in the Palatinate, and his writings can be interpreted as supporting the proposition that European war after 1648 was at least moving in the direction of curbing violence directed against civilian lives and property. To facilitate the waging of wars of adroit maneuver and limited ferocity, he relied upon an educated, professionalized officer corps and rationalized and thus professionalized military administration and logistics.

Montecuccoli's opportunities for applying his desire for professionalization were more limited in the Empire than were those open to Louis XIV in France. The state that Montecuccoli served was in transition from the medieval Holy Roman Empire to a congeries of dominions held together by the dynastic claims of the Habsburgs. Neither Imperial nor Habsburg sovereignty could draw upon the rudiments of nationalism as could the Bourbon monarchy in France; while nascent nationalism assisted the French steps toward centralized military com-

2. His *L'attione bellica* . . . was published in 1692 (Milano [Milan]: No publisher). The next year it was published in Spanish translation as *Arte universal de la guerra* . . . (Traducido de italiano en español por Don Bartolomé Chafrion . . . , Milano [Milan]: No publisher); this volume was republished (Lisboa [Lisbon]: Impr. de M. Menescal, 1708). It became the first volume of *Memoria della guerra* . . . (3 vols., Venezia [Venice]: No publisher, 1793); see also *Mémoires de Montecuccoli généralissime des troupes de l'empereur; ou Principes de l'art militaire en général; Divisez en trois livres.* (Traduite d'italien en français par * * * [Jacques Adam], Paris: Jean Musie, M.DCCXII.).

3. A disquisition *"Sulle Battaglia"*—"Concerning Battle"—has achieved an excellent modern English translation in Thomas M. Barker, *The Military Intellectual and Battle: Raimondo Montecuccoli and the Thirty Years War* (Albany: State University of New York Press, 1974); Barker's translation "Concerning Battle" is part 3, pp. 187–334. But Montecuccoli nevertheless remained an advocate of setting the stage for decision less by bloodshed than by maneuver.

mand and administration, in the Empire it impeded moves in that direction because in a multinational state it was a divisive force. More than the French, the Habsburg armies had to remain a collection of geographically and ethnically based regiments. The privileges of the various geographic and ethnic divisions of the Empire, furthermore, were in large part the privileges of the nobility of those entities, and they weighed against efforts to establish education and ability as criteria for promotion in the officer corps. Within these limitations, however, Montecuccoli achieved remarkable progress. The troops he led against Turenne and Condé fell little short of the French standards of tactical skill, discipline, efficient administration, and effective logistical support.

To build adequate defenses along the whole of the Empire's vulnerable circumference in central Europe, however, was beyond the ability of Montecuccoli or any other human resources. In fact, Montecuccoli's very successes against the Rákóczy rebellions in Hungary helped precipitate one of the gravest threats to the Empire in its history, developing just after his retirement. The rebellions had sprung from Hungarian nationalism generally and from Hungarian Protestantism more particularly—the Rákóczy princes were Calvinists and their court a haven for east-European Protestants. Despite certain concessions to the Protestants and after 1679 the restoration of the Hungarian constitution of 1656, Habsburg rule was repressive enough that simmering discontent led to a Hungarian invitation to the Turks to intervene in 1683. The Hungarians had for over a hundred years exhibited some degree of preference for the Turks over the Emperors. By 1683, furthermore, Louis XIV had repented of his earlier assistance to the Habsburgs against the Ottomans, and he joined the Hungarians in encouraging a new Turkish march up the Danube. With Hungarian leaders opening the gates of their country, the Turks rolled across the Hungarian plain and by July 1683 were approaching the Habsburg capital of Vienna.

The Habsburg court departed hastily for Passau, leaving the defense of the capital to a force of only about 22,000. Armed forces from throughout the Empire rallied to the defense of the capital more quickly, however, than the conduct of their princes in wars against Christian rivals of the Habsburgs might have suggested they would. West and north of Hungary, the infidel Turk was still a byword signifying terror. Elector Maximilian II Emmanuel of Bavaria led a relieving army, and the reinforced garrison turned back continual attacks persisting through two months. Then by August 28/September 7 King John (Jan) III Sobieski of Poland arrived at the head of additional reinforcements. The Polish monarch had fended off strenuous efforts by the French to draw him into an anti-Habsburg alliance, choosing instead to sign on March 3/13, 1682/1683 a treaty of alliance with Emperor Leopold I against the Turks. This decision may well have been crucial to the fate of Vienna, but, as has so often been true for the Poles, their unhappy country—yet more exposed to external attack than the Empire—gained little directly from it.

On September 2/12, 1683, the Habsburg forces and their allies launched simultaneous assaults from the city and from the nearby heights of the Kahlenberg. The battle became yet another in which the difference between stalemate and tactical decisiveness was a charge by the arm of mobility and shock, in this instance the still-excellent Polish cavalry from whom Gustavus Adolphus had learned mounted tactics, now led by John Sobieski himself. Among those who distinguished themselves in lesser roles during the battle was the young commander of the Kufstein Dragoon Regiment, Prince Eugène of Savoy.

The battle of the Kahlenberg might have been still more decisive had the Christian commanders not proven incapable of preventing many of their troops from taking time to plunder the Turkish camps. As it was, the battle proved a turning point in the relative fortunes of the Habsburgs and the Ottomans. The Turks, failing for internal political and cultural reasons to keep pace with the increasing proficiency of the professionalizing European armies, and soon beleaguered by the rising power of Russia as well as by the Habsburgs, were never again able to mount so formidable a threat along the Danube as in 1683. The Habsburgs, notwithstanding their preoccupations elsewhere in Europe, became able to spare enough strength for a gradual rolling back of the Turkish borders toward the southeast. Budapest fell to the Habsburg forces in 1686. On September 1/11, 1697, Prince Eugène won the battle of Zenta some 133 miles (214 kilometers) southeast of Budapest, a victory complete enough that, in combination with the other troubles of the Turks, it led the Sublime Porte to conclude the Treaty of Karlovici (Karlowitz) of January 16/26, 1698/1699. Thereby all of Hungary except the Banat of Temesvár was ceded to the Habsburgs, along with Transylvania and Slavonia.

John Sobieski, who had contributed so much to this reversal of Habsburg fortunes, met a much less happy fate. He continued with his own campaigns against the Turks in the Ukraine, hoping to extend the borders of Poland as the Habsburgs were extending those of their domains. But he had failed meanwhile in his efforts to overcome Poland's chronic political chaos by substituting an absolute monarchy for the vagaries of government by an unruly nobility, and the failure left his military forces with so little internal support that even the declining Ottoman power sufficed to fend them off. While the leaders of the *Sejn,* the Polish senate, plotted the King's dethronement, and his wife, Marya Kazimiera d'Arquien, wove webs of intrigue that further weakened his position, he sank into disillusionment and the habit of defeat, at home and toward the end in battle as well. He died June 7/17, 1696, to be remembered mainly for one glorious campaign.

Among the means by which the Habsburgs sought to avoid the lamentable fate of Poland, to reduce the vulnerability of their frontiers, and to prevent a repetition of the crisis of 1683 was to maintain and strengthen their military colonies along the Ottoman frontier, and to extend the colonies eventually to cover the entire frontier. The Austrian Military Border—*Militärgrenze* or *Vojna Krajina*—had emerged in the first half of the sixteenth century when various Balkan refugees from Ottoman conquest were taken into Habsburg service as colonists who would perform the dual roles of peasant farmers and part-time soldiers along the Imperial borders, to permit the defense of a frontier where adequate permanent garrisons would otherwise be too expensive to maintain. This method of border defense harkened back to Egyptian, Greco-Roman, and Near Eastern examples in the ancient world; the Romans especially had made much use of armed colonists from the third century A.D. onward.

The Croatian Border—the Krabatische Gränitz, after 1578 often called the Karlstadt or Karlovac Border from what became its main fortress, lay south and west of the Drava Rover and was the oldest part of the Habsburg system of military frontiers. In 1522 the Estates of Inner Austria, fearing Turkish advances, and the Croatian nobility, out of the same fear and unable to pry adequate help from Hungary, petitioned the Archduke Ferdinand I, younger brother of the Emperor Charles V, to defend Croatia. At first sending a mercenary garrison, Ferdinand soon resorted to the less costly expedient of land grants to refugees in return for militia service, and in 1527 he moved to make such a system permanent. By 1550 Croatia and the Inner Austrian duchies were guarded by a line of fortified villages, blockhouses, and watchtowers manned by some 5,000 *Grenzer*. From 1553 a general officer commanded this and the Slavonian Border, the *Windische Gränitz* or *Slovinska Krajina*, later the Warasdin or Varaždin Border for its major town, the latter border lying between the Sava and the Drava. The general officer held both military and civil authority. Eventually there were separate Karlstadt and Warasdin Generalcies and a separate Hofkriegsrat at Graz for the military supervision of the borders.

The separate Hofkriegsrat and chain of command indicate that while their peasant-soldiers were a military asset, the borders through their special military organization and decentralized command also reflected the peculiar military difficulties of the sprawling and heterogeneous Habsburg domains. Some autonomy for the military borders was no doubt a necessity; whether the separation from the principal Habsburg military establishment should have been so complete is dubious. On the credit side, the *Grenzer* remained loyal to their Habsburg overlords during the rebellions in Hungary in the late seventeenth century, and they participated in pushing back the Turks after 1683. On the debit side in addition to the awkward command system, they showed that their fighting qualities were definitely those of a militia rather than a professional force, so that after the Treaty of Karlovici there developed ideas of drastically tightening *Grenzer* discipline. Duke Joseph (Herzog Josef) of Sachsen-Hildburghausen, commissioned in 1735 to investigate the causes of a mutiny in the Warasdin Generalcy, proposed disciplinary reforms sweeping enough to convert the *Grenzer* from a militia to a nation in arms subject to call at any time against any enemy.

In the future, the Habsburg government would push the *Grenzer* in this direction, but there were virtues as well as disadvantage in their not being the complete equivalent of career soldiers. From out of eastern Europe, and particularly from the less than formal tactics of the *Grenzer*, there would move westward in time a refreshing stimulus toward tactical flexibility, to soften the otherwise more and more rigid infantry tactics that the musket and the bayonet proved to impose upon the conduct of battle, and to help to revitalize infantry tactics just when rigidity seemed on the verge of degenerating into outright stultification.

Brandenburg-Prussia under the Great Elector

To be sure, in the military arena rigidity of tactics and discipline, the transformation of thousands of men into an approximation of a well-coordinated machine, can also have its virtues. The values of iron discipline and nearly mechanical battlefield evolutions were about to be dramatized by a new Germanic military power, one that would build upon those values a challenge to the Habsburg Empire for the military leadership of central Europe.

To none of the constituent princes and polities of the Holy Roman Empire had the Thirty Years War brought more humiliation than to the Elector of Brandenburg and his scattered domains. Other parts of Germany may have suffered worse physical devastation—though not much worse, for Brandenburg proper was thoroughly desolated, with many villages reduced to fewer than ten farmers; but few of the middling states of the Empire were so utterly reduced in political status to pawnship to the major powers. In the hope of fending off the perils of war, the Elector George William, who inherited the dominions of the Hohenzollern family in 1619, just after the beginning of the war, attempted first to remain neutral. Under the emotions and pressures of the times, it was an impossible task. Eventually he felt obliged, partly because of his Protestantism and in protest of the Edict of Restitution, much more out of fear of Sweden, to form an alliance with Gustavus Adolphus after the latter crossed the Baltic and landed at Peenemünde to begin his German campaigns in 1629. In fact it was a matter of trying to rescue such dignity as he could in the face of Gustavus's threats that he must at least yield horses, financial aid, and recruiting privileges to Sweden. But the Elector's hesitant and wavering alliance won Brandenburg scant credit, either with the Swedes or with German Protestantism; while the mere fact of the alliance naturally provoked the hostility of the Emperor.

After the death of Gustavus Adolphus and the revocation of the Edict of Restitution, Brandenburg accepted the Peace of Prague (Praha; German, Prag) of 1635, ending its war with the Empire. The terms implied that Brandenburg along with Saxony and other, smaller signatories were now the enemies of the Emperor's enemies. But Brandenburg was no less halfhearted in the new allegiance than in the old, and the Elector had thus earned the contempt of all parties in the war. By 1640 and the death of George William, Brandenburg proper except for Berlin and a few other fortresses was under foreign, mainly Swedish, occupation, and the Elector's other territories were either threatened with similar occupation by nearby forces or in open disaffection against his regime. Hardly a semblance of an army existed to defend the realm, only a few thousand mercenaries who were largely fugitives from more serious armies, unruly *Landsknechte* more dangerous to the people they were supposed to protect than to foes from outside.

The Elector's susceptibility to the threats and pressures of stronger powers may command at least some measure of sympathy when we consider the near-indefensibility of his domains even had he possessed a respectable army, an indefensibility that was extreme even by the precarious standards of central and eastern Europe. The Margraves (Markgrafen) of Brandenburg, Electors of the Holy Roman Empire since the Golden Bull of 1356, or more specifically the Hohenzollern dynasty, Margraves of Brandenburg since 1415, had spliced together a patchwork of scattered territories: Brandenburg itself, in large part a sandy wasteland drained by the Elbe and Oder rivers; the County of Ravensburg near the Weser; the County of Mark; the Duchy of Cleves on the Rhine; and the Duchy of Prussia—all united by no other connection than that of the dynasty. Prussia had passed to the Hohenzollerns as recently as 1618; this duchy was a fiefdom of Poland, lying outside the boundaries of the Holy Roman Empire, a circumstance that was to assume particular significance with the Peace of Rastadt. For the present, Prussia amounted to little but another outlying territory for the Hohenzollern collection, and at that another barren place of sandy soil, limited resources, and a backward agriculture.

There was, however, a Prussian military tradition worth noting. The dukedom had evolved out of the territory of the crusading Order of Teutonic Knights, who had wrested it from heathen Slavs in the thirteenth century and encouraged German peasants, burghers, and nobles to emigrate thither. The defeat of the Teutonic Knights by the Kingdom of Poland-Lithuania in 1410 had ended the heyday of the Knights, and a second defeat led to the Peace of Torun (Thorn) of 1466, whereby the Poles annexed the western part of the Knights' territory and the Grand Master of the Order had to pay homage to the Polish King for the eastern part. The religious motive of the Knights having faded with this absorption by a Christian state, the Grand Master secularized the landholdings of the Order in the sixteenth century. There remained to be passed on to the Hohenzollerns the memories of Teutonic martial prowess in the early days of the Order and the symbols of the Teutonic Knights, a black cross upon a white background and a one-headed black Imperial eagle bestowed upon them by the Holy Roman Emperor Frederick (Fridericus, Friedrich) II.

In 1640 there succeeded to the electoral throne of the tottering Brandenburg domains a twenty-year-old prince determined to revive his polity's tenuous military tradition and by that means to rescue Brandenburg-Prussia from desolation and transform it into a state that the great powers must respect and reason with. Frederick William (Friedrich Wilhelm) was descended through his mother, Elisabeth Charlotte, daughter of Frederick IV, Elector and Count Palatine of the Rhine, from the House of Orange and Nassau. He had spent part of his youth in the United Provinces and acquired an admiration for and knowledge of the professional military system of the Dutch. George William had relied on diplomacy and alliances; Frederick William resolved to rely on arms.

His most immediate problem was to find the means to build adequate armaments. The disasters of the Thirty Years War had almost erased the ability of the Elector to govern within his own realm, particularly to wield any ascendancy over the assemblies of notables, or Estates, in the various parts of the realm. These assemblies controlled taxation and had used that control to extort a host of other privileges from Frederick William's predecessors.

The new Elector began with a gesture that seemed on the face of it to weaken still further his already paltry military force. He purged it of its most mischievous mercenary colonels and undisciplined troops, reducing it to a core of about 2,500 reliable men. The Estates of Brandenburg, mollified at no longer being ravished by their supposed protectors, allowed gradual increases in funding to rebuild the army to 8,000. The existence of a disciplined force of even this modest size largely accounts for the fact that Frederick William was able to secure remarkably generous terms for Brandenburg in the Treaty of Westphalia. In return for surrendering Western Pomerania to Sweden, Brandenburg received the greater part of Eastern Pomerania; and in recognition of its claim on the whole Duchy of Pomerania, it was compensated with the secularized bishoprics of Halberstadt, Münden, and Kammin, along with the reversion to it of the archbishopric of Magdeburg upon the death of its administrator, prince Augustus of Saxony, which occurred in 1680. In addition, the Elector of Brandenburg like the other princes of the Holy Roman Empire received recognition as a sovereign in his own right.

The return of peace rendered the Brandenburg Estates rather less willing to finance the Elector's military programs, and the army was probably reduced to about 5,000; but through the practice of stringent economies, skillful compromise, and evasion of restrictions Frederick William contrived to go on about his military reforming work. Most importantly, in 1653 he entered into a bargain with the Estates that was crucial in establishing a pattern for a polity that might become militarily advanced though it remained otherwise retarded in political, social, and economic modernization. For a grant of 530,000 talers payable over six years, the Elector agreed to the transformation of the estates of the large landholders—the *Junkers*—from fiefs held in return for military and other services into holdings in absolute ownership. Moreover, eliminating certain legal restrictions upon the *Junkers,* the Elector recognized them as the only class permitted to acquire estates, exempting them from the payment of taxes and according them complete control over their peasants. They also received almost complete political authority in local matters.

In 1655, war broke out between Sweden and Poland. Frederick William used the danger of its spreading into Brandenburg to justify accelerated military recruiting throughout his dominions, financed by extraordinary taxes. The Brandenburg Estates did not feel they were in a position to press their objections vigorously. Anyway, there was no general meeting of the Estates after 1653. By September 1655, the Elector had restored the army to 8,000, and by the time the war ended in 1660 he had increased it to 27,000. Thereafter until the next major war involving Brandenburg, Frederick William was able to hold the peacetime force at between 7,000 and 12,000. He began building a reserve by settling discharged soldiers as farmers on his personal holdings.

The Elector had also turned toward wresting approval of his military policies from the other Estates of his realms. He practically compelled acquiescence from the Estates of Cleves, Mark, and East Prussia by threatening military enforcement of his decrees. By the middle of the 1670s, all his domains had been brought into line. By that time, furthermore, he had begun taking an increasingly active role in European politics. He joined the Empire in war against the Turks in 1663. In religious questions he became a champion of Protestant rights within the Empire, meanwhile seeking a reconciliation between Lutherans and Calvinists within his own dominions. At first he held back from joining the resistance to the expansionism of Louis XIV, in fact allying himself with Louis after the close of the War of Devolution in 1667. With the French attack on the United Provinces in 1672, however, he was the first to come to the aid of the

Dutch, although the campaign he conducted the next year on the Rhine brought no instant glory to Brandenburg's arms. It was not yet apparent whether he had achieved any substantial elevation of his state's military power. In 1674, indeed, while Frederick William and his troops were campaigning against the French in Alsace, Louis XIV induced the Swedes to invade Brandenburg itself.

The Elector quickly returned homeward, and on June 18/28, 1675, he won a clear-cut victory over superior numbers of Swedes at the battle of Fehrbellin; Fehrbellin remains well remembered in Germany as the first great day in the modern military history of Brandenburg-Prussia. Frederick William followed up, with Imperial and Danish aid, by driving the Swedes from Pomerania as well as Brandenburg. When the Peace of Nijmegen was followed in June 1679 by the Treaty of St.-Germain-en-Laye between Brandenburg and Sweden, however, the indifference of the Emperor to the Elector's claims on the one hand and the still-considerable power of Louis XIV on the other obliged Brandenburg to restore Western Pomerania to Sweden, in exchange for the payment of 300,000 crowns (75,000 *louis d'or*) by France. The latter subsidy did not draw the Elector out of the coalition of France's enemies. In 1685 Frederick William arranged a new alliance with William of Orange, and in 1686 he allied himself with the Emperor Leopold I, including among his pledges an agreement that in return for a subsidy he would contribute troops against the Turks.

All the while, Frederick William was striving to improve the quality of the army as well as to enlarge it and to assure its financial underpinnings. While sometimes dealing ruthlessly with his Estates for the sake of finance, he also offered them protection from marauding troops, their own as well as foreign soldiers. The army was reminded by its chaplains as well as its commanders that any act of plundering would be punished by the hangman's noose. If any officer attacked a civilian, he would be stripped of his rank for a year and compelled to serve as a private soldier.

At the same time the Elector offered the troops at least a modicum of justice to temper harsh discipline. No court-martial sentence, most certainly no death sentence, could be carried out without confirmation by the Elector himself. Officers and noncommissioned officers were forbidden to beat their soldiers. A traditional punishment of the army, running the gauntlet, was also proscribed.

Predictably, administrative and training reforms followed the pattern developed in Louis XIV's France from the earlier models of Sweden and the Netherlands. Recruiting was centralized in the Elector's hands, rather than remaining with the regiments and their colonels. By this means, Frederick William sought not only to assure himself satisfactory specimens of manhood, but also to leave productive artisans and peasants safely contributing to the economic foundations of his power, foundations that remained all too narrow and therefore needed all the reinforcement they could get. The regiments themselves increasingly became creations of the central government, the Elector striving to avoid specific contracts with individual commanders, the colonels coming to owe their appointments to the Elector. Although the colonels generally continued to appoint the regimental officers, the Elector established his right to veto their choices and ordered that regimental rank be determined by seniority. A *Ritterakademie* was instituted as the basis for a cadet corps and a military educational system, albeit Frederick William was unable to advance it beyond rudimentary beginnings.

The Great Elector still ruled his state and commanded his army in a very personal fashion, but he recognized the need for bureaucratic machinery to govern a larger army, and he created the nucleus of it. Until his time, the troops of the various Hohenzollern provinces had received little coordination. In 1655 the Elector appointed Otto Christoph Freiherr von Sparr to command his troops throughout his domains, in 1658 awarding Sparr the title *Generalfeldmarschall.* Sparr used the *Generalquartiermeister* and his assistants as the nucleus of what would later become the *Generalstab,* the General Staff, to assist in his command functions, particularly with planning studies. (Initially the term *Generalstab* referred simply to all general officers and all administrative personnel not attached to regiments or to the artillery.) Simultaneously the office of *Generalkriegskommissar* took shape in the hands of Claus Ernest von Platen, whom the Elector charged with the assembling, paying, provisioning, and billeting of the army and the management of its stores and magazines. Platen was theoretically responsible to Sparr, but as early as 1657 the latter complained that the General War Commissioner was taking actions without informing him; the uncertainty of the relationship between command and administrative bureaucracies was to remain a troublesome issue into the twentieth century. But Frederick William nevertheless left military command and administration immensely more rationalized than he had found it.

The Great Elector died on April 29/May 9, 1688. He bequeathed to his son an army of about 30,000 men with a reputation for efficiency confirmed by the victory of Fehrbellin and by the unprecedented eagerness with which other powers sought Brandenburg-Prussia's alliance. His immediate accomplishments would have merited in themselves, in the military and diplomatic spheres at least, the appellation "Great." As foundations for subsequent military achievement, his reforms were to prove still more to have earned him that title.

Prussia's Military Tour de Force:
The Approach to Great-Power Status

His successor, the Elector Frederick (Friedrich) III, was great in little besides his ability to spend lavishly on Baroque palaces. But until 1697 an invaluable adviser, Eberhard Donckelmann, helped maintain the Great Elector's reforms until court intrigues brought Donckelmann down. The Elector did see to it, however, that Brandenburg-Prussia remained useful to the anti-French coalition through the troops he contributed under the leadership of Prince Leopold von Anhalt-Dessau. The disciplined Prussian contingent was useful enough, in fact, that it supplied Frederick with the leverage to accomplish a goal that had eluded his father.

In 1692 he raised with the Emperor Leopold the possibility of his receiving the title of King. He renewed the subject in 1698, when the Emperor was beset by the multiple vexations of the issue of the Spanish succession, and this time he got most of what he wanted. The Imperial authorities decided that it was best for the Hohenzollern Kingship to reside beyond the Empire, but on January 7/18, 1700/1701, the Elector was crowned Frederick I, King in Prussia, at the Prussian capital of Königsberg. In return Frederick promised 8,000 troops for the Emperor's assistance. By the time his reign ended with his death on February 14/25, 1712/1713, he had enlarged his army to 40,000 men.

His son, and heir to the new throne, King Frederick William (Friedrich Wilhelm) I, promptly demonstrated that in interests and ambitions he was a throwback to his namesake, the Great Elector—except that many of his contemporaries were to regard his military ambitions as extending to the point of mania. Costly display in architecture and interior decoration ceased abruptly with the beginning of the new reign. One of the King Frederick William's first actions was to order an inventory of valuables in jewels, silver, and rare furniture and the sealing up of these items. Drastic economies were imposed on every kind of court and nonmilitary governmental activity. Civil officeholders who were retained saw their salaries cut by as much as 25 percent; most, however, were either dropped or transferred to the administration of the army.

The Peace of Utrecht of 1713–1715, coming close on the heels of the King's accession, combined with the economies to make possible financing the state without reliance on foreign subsidies. To keep this advantage and yet enlarge the army, Frederick William I continued the process of centralization and rationalization of military as well as civil administration. He carried yet further his grandfather's drive for ascendancy over the provincial Estates, leaving them finally with little to do but to administer the ordinances of the King. He also curbed the influence of local notables over the state bureaucracy. Thus in the political sphere the power of the great landholders, the *Junkers*, was curtailed, though they clung to their economic and social privileges.

He recognized that financial self-sufficiency must rest upon a healthy and expanding economy, and he did all that was within his power to expand that most fragile element of Prussia's strength. The kingdom had benefited from Louis XIV's persecution of the Huguenots by receiving numerous refugees, many of whom had craft and business skills. Frederick William I sought additional stimulation of trades and commerce, especially through royal patronage. He channeled state purchases particularly through the rising Berlin merchants David Splitgerber and Gottfried Adolph Daum, who purchased several arms factories and established new ones. Similarly, a confidant of the King, Johann Andreas Kraut, received royal encouragement to set up a textile factory and warehouse in Berlin to supply uniform cloth for the army.

While expanding the size of the army, the King hoped to minimize the impact of recruiting on economic growth and especially on agriculture. Until Frederick William I promulgated his *Cantonal Règlement* of 1730 and subsequent decrees in 1731–1732, recruiting was a haphazard process, largely a matter of dragooning random unfortunates. The search for recruits extended beyond Brandenburg-Prussia's borders, often into more easterly regions; but within the realm the frequent resort to compulsion also drove citizens to flight into neighboring states. Since the Thirty Years War the Hohenzollern provinces had had a militia system based on a compulsory obligation to defend the state, and the system had received a clear legal foundation in 1701; but the obligation had never been more than erratically enforced and had never created an effective reserve for the regular army, while enrollment in it often afforded a pretext for escaping regular service. In the first year of his reign, Frederick William I abolished this weak program, at the same time announcing that anyone who left the country to escape regular military service would be regarded as a deserter.

This latter decree implied a universal military obligation, a principle that Frederick William sought to make effective in a practical way with his regulations of the early 1730s. Practicality included, however, his concern for the economy as well as for the army. Not surprisingly, the highest ranks of society were exempted, though the landholding *Junkers* were expected to supply the officers. The exemptions reached down to include a goodly proportion of artisans and industrial workers as well as business entrepreneurs.

The canton system divided the realm into recruiting districts with every district associated with a particular regiment. Every young male in the district was entered on the regimental recruiting list. When voluntary enlistments left vacancies in the regiment, it turned to conscription from this list. After basic training, however, the conscript would be subject to only three months' military service per year. Thus the peasants and agricultural laborers on whom the bulk of the compulsory obligation fell would continue to be able to farm through most of the year. Furthermore, behind the mercenary army there grew up a trained reserve, and especially in wartime the Prussian Army could begin to become an approximation of a culturally homogeneous national force.

Even the mercenary troops did not necessarily serve full-time. The officers tended to seek those recruits who were more or less volunteers from the inhabitants of their own landholdings, if only to save money in recruitment. Lest this practice retard agricultural production unduly, the soldiers were allowed to go on leave to return to their farm labors at appropriate seasons. They went without pay from the army, their employers presumably taking up the burden of their support; thereby the army retained funds that could be used to help finance the recruiting system.

The King's solicitude for agriculture helped reconcile the *Junkers* to their loss of political authority. So, in spite of some early friction, did his methods of recruiting officers. At the outset, he declared it illegal for members of the nobility to enter foreign military service. He also gathered lists of all young noblemen between the ages of twelve and eighteen and from the lists personally chose those who were to enter the cadet corps in Berlin; in effect, he was drafting the nobility as well as commoners. But to those who became cadets he offered an education and an assured income in place of the more or less genteel poverty that was all that the barren soil of much of his territory offered to landlords. Within the officer corps, the young gentleman became a member of a band of brothers in which everyone from the King downward wore the same uniform coat, and only generals wore badges of rank—a band of brothers, furthermore, increasingly held in respect by the entire population of the Hohenzollern state and by all Europe as well, and united by bonds of chivalry refurbished from feudal codes of honor. The bargain was not a bad one; some of the more astute among the *Junkers* could foresee that it would carry their class to authority and power throughout Europe.

For the policies of Frederick William I were completing his grandfather's transformation of one of the weakest and least independent of the German states into a great power. By the end of his reign, Prussia was still to rank only thirteenth in population and tenth in territory among the European states; but, its army having grown under Frederick William I from 40,000 to 83,000, it was to be fourth in Europe in numbers of soldiers, and second to none in the efficiency of its army.

The Calvinist Protestantism of his Dutch forebears was strong within Frederick William I. His Calvinism was reinforced by his contacts with the puritanical Pietist movement of Germany in his day, particularly by his association with August Hermann Francke, the Pietist theological leader at the University of Halle. The King's religious convictions made themselves felt in almost everything he did. His thrift and his zeal for economic development were textbook exemplifications of the Protestant ethic at work in the everyday world. His military preparations for the defense of his realm and of its Christian values were consistent with the worship of a stern Old Testament God. If he obviously did not share the pacifist leanings of part of the Pietist movement—pacifism being incompatible with the duties of a ruler of a state—he nevertheless abstained from war through most of his reign, and did so on moral as well as expedient grounds. In unsheathing his sword at last against Charles XII, he could well convince himself that nobler purposes than Prussian territorial aggrandizement alone might be served in ending for good and all the career of that warrior-King gone mad. But to Frederick William I, the sword was not to be unsheathed lightly, and especially not for expediency alone. The memory of the Thirty Years War was too green in Prussia for that; all he knew of that war, and all of his consequent conviction of the necessity to limit war, combined with the King's principles of religious duty in the advice he gave his son and heir: "I beg you not to begin an unjust war, because God his forbidden unjust wars. You must give account for every man killed in an unjust war. Look at history and you will see that nothing good has come from unjust wars. This, my dear successor, demonstrates the hand of God . . . ."[4]

On the Limitations of Early Military Professionalism

Among the great powers of eastern Europe in the first half of the eighteenth century, the decision to wage wars, both just and unjust, still lay firmly with the monarchs. Under a Charles XII, royal power permitted war to be waged beyond the limits of sanity. In part, kings retained their control over the decision for war and the shape of war because their officers' professional expertise was not yet sufficient to discourage monarchs from considering them-

4. Quoted in Hannesjoachim Wolfgang Koch, *The Rise of Modern Warfare, 1618–1815* (A Bison Book, Englewood Cliffs, N.J.: Prentice-Hall, Inc., 1981), p. 132, no citation given.

selves—according to the standards of the era—professional soldiers. The kings' authority could therefore not be challenged on the plea that the officers were privy to a special body of knowledge that the kings did not share.

In part too, the monarch retained this control because the professional expertise of military officers was a tactical, operational, logistical, and administrative expertise but not yet in any noteworthy degree a strategic expertise. The new military literature and schools taught officers how to organize armies with a certain efficiency, how to move them to the battlefield, how to maintain them while leading them in siege or in battle, but not how to devise and apply military strategy, which is the art and science of using battles and campaigns in a systematic, coherent, coordinated way so that the battles and campaigns will attain the objects for which war is waged. The very concept of strategy had scarcely been articulated; the military theory of the day scarcely touched on it.

Thus, except for the battles and campaigns of a Gustavus Adolphus, a Montecuccoli, or a Marlborough, the sequence and circumstances of battle in the wars of the seventeenth and early eighteenth centuries often display little logic or reason; the events of military campaigns often occurred almost randomly. Gustavus Adolphus's campaigns are an exception, because the great Swedish warrior-King seems to have been seeking systematically the strategic purpose of destroying the enemy armies in order to be able to dictate terms ending in Swedish domination of the Baltic and Protestant security throughout Germany. Montecuccoli similarly made systematic planning the foundation of his pursuit of strategic purpose, albeit usually with less ambitious and aggressive aims. Marlborough's Blenheim campaign was designed strategically not only to relieve French pressure against the Empire but to set the stage for a concerted Allied campaign into France itself. But few examples of the era display that much clarity of strategic purpose.

This limitation of the professional expertise of the officer corps to areas more specialized and technical than that of strategy may raise the question whether the professionalization of military officership had yet grown comprehensive enough to be called a profession rather than a trade. Because the expertise of the profession nevertheless encompassed the whole art of war as it was understood at the time, and because despite its limitations it remained an expertise dependent on schooling, the claim that military officership had evolved out of the Dutch Republic and the Sweden of Gustavus Adolphus and especially in the France of Louis XIV into a distinctive modern profession remains justified. We do not deny lawyers the title of professionals if they happen not to reach the level of practicing before the Supreme Court of the United States; so it would seem equally too restrictive a use of the term to deny officership the status of a profession except for those officers who practice strategy. Few officers do so in any era. But questions about the location of the threshold of professional status are especially worth keeping in mind as we turn from the emergence of the profession of miliary officership on land to the rise of the profession of naval officership at sea.

7   THE RISE OF
NAVAL POWER

The development of a profession of officership among navies was a more uncertain process than among armies, and this uncertainty reflected yet other kinds of blurring between the military and the civil in the conduct of war at sea. It was not simply fortuitous that when the international legal code limiting war that grew up after the Thirty Years War was to break down disastrously in the twentieth century, one of the first decisive ruptures occurred in maritime warfare: the violation of the principle of noncombatant immunity during the unrestricted submarine warfare of the World Wars. Submarines came to use methods violating the principle of noncombatant immunity, and in defiance of the war convention civilian lives were taken at sea, in large part because the functions of warships and merchant ships melded too readily together, because merchant ships could make too large a contribution to the waging of war, for submarines to be able to afford fastidious judgments about the difference. In maritime war it had always been thus, that the line between the civil and the military was blurred; in early modern history it was more rather than less so. But the consequences in jeopardizing international restraints upon the depredations of war were to prove to be dire.

As military officership on land had evolved out of the occupation of knighthood—and more than that, out of the social-class status of knights—so military officership at sea arose out of the occupation of merchant sea-captain. The first warships of the early modern era were simply merchant ships with weapons aboard them. The specialized warship required a considerable time to develop out of the armed merchantman, and a profession of naval officership required an even longer time to evolve.

From the beginning of modern military history, war at sea was through the connection with merchant seamanship a more bourgeois endeavor than war on land. Notwithstanding the British Navy's eventual emergence as the principal military foundation of British world power, officership in the army has carried with it more social éclat in Britain than officership in the navy. Army officership descends from feudal knighthood; naval officership descends from merchant seamanship. It is significant that neither England nor any other of the northern European powers began a serious effort to create a navy until the appearance of middle-class merchants began to break the rigidities of the medieval social order. The medieval barons, and with them most of the kings in England and elsewhere in the northern European realms where feudalism held sway, felt no reason to be interested in the sea, except occasionally as they needed to be transported across it to conduct their fighting on land. They were land warriors; they were, above all else, cavalrymen; the sea was too unfriendly to horses for warfare there to be suitably chivalric, in either a literal or a figurative sense. One must speculate, indeed, to what extent the absence of a chivalric tradition in naval war and the origins of war at sea rather in practical-minded middle-class attitudes contributed to the extreme fragility of international restraints upon the conduct of maritime war. The unrestricted submarine campaigns of the World Wars were but the climax of a maritime military history in which navies had long been entangled with piracy, the distinction between them not becoming altogether clear until the renunciation of privateering by the signatories of the Declaration of Paris as late as 1856.

From Medieval to Early Modern Navies

England, destined to reign for several centuries as a sea power without peer, presents the best known case study of the evolution of a navy in concert with the rise of the middle class and the evolution of capitalism, even for the years well before the establishment of English naval preeminence. On the one hand, it is true that the kings of England possessed ships of their own as early as the time of the Plantagenets; the kings demonstrated at least slightly wider views of such broad national considerations as overseas commerce than did the barons. Yet on the other hand English sea power did not genuinely flourish until its destiny became entwined with that of middle-class capitalism.

Under King John (1199–1216), the reluctant signer of Magna Carta and the target of a notoriously and perhaps excessively unfavorable historical press, there was already a Clerk or Keeper of the King's Ships. King John in fact was an exception to the usual pattern of medieval royal indifference to the sea; and if his historical image is ever to be rehabilitated, his claim to be the founder of English naval power would be conspicuous in his list of credits. He called himself Sovereign of the Seas—that is, of the Narrow Seas, the Straits of Dover and the neighboring parts of the North Sea (the German Ocean) and the Channel. But neither John nor his less enthusiastic medieval successors could ever afford enough royal ships to make a fleet.

In naval emergencies the medieval English kings resorted first to the naval contributions of the Cinque Ports—Hastings, Romney, Hythe, Dover, and Sandwich, to which had been added over the years the Ancient Towns of Winchelsea and Rye and in time several other "limbs" or member ports. Secondarily, the kings called on vessels from throughout the realm. Commerce and major maritime war could not be conducted simultaneously, because the same ships were used for both and could not meet both responsibilities at the same time. Nor was King John, let alone any other medieval monarch, free enough from the predispositions of a cavalry soldier to transform naval war into anything beyond a tactical extension of land warfare. The conduct of war at sea remained, as it had been in the ancient world, a matter of bringing rival ships close alongside so that armed men—trained soldiers at best, often seamen with no better than brawling skills—could fight each other from shipboard instead of on land.

It was the Tudor era that brought the first true efflorescence of English mercantile capitalism and the first major reliance of an English royal dynasty on middle-class support. Not coincidentally, the same era also witnessed substantial changes in ship design, naval fighting methods, and naval administration. The administrative changes were instrumental in bringing the building and maintenance of ships more fully into accord with bourgeois business practices. The changes in ship design and fighting methods began to free the navy from landsmen's practices of merely transferring land warriors to the decks of ships. Technological advances in the metallurgy of guns and the design and building of ships were essential to the other changes, but as usual in the history of early modern war the technological innovations of the time were not all that imposing; to a larger extent, ship design and naval tactics altered because the Tudor monarchs depended upon and benefited enough from a rising mercantile capitalism and overseas trade to turn naval warfare increasingly over to genuine seamen whose social and economic origins lay in the middle class.

By the middle of the sixteenth century, improvements in the design and rigging of the sailing ship had cost the various forms of the rowed galley their previous usual predominance in England and elsewhere in northern Europe both as merchant carriers and in naval warfare. In the Mediterranean, oar-driven vessels retained their importance a good deal longer because of their superior maneuverability in narrow seas where the winds were generally light. But in England, Henry VII (1485–1509) added to the royal fleet the *Regent*, the *Sweepstake*, and the *Mary Fortune*, the first of these with four masts and carrying topsails above its courses and a topgallant sail above its main topsail, the *Sweepstake* and the *Mary Fortune* with three lower masts as well as a main topmast although they were relatively small ships.

While the first Tudor monarch's navy remained primarily a fleet of armed transports, designed for "in-fighting"—the traditional boarding tactics derived from land warfare—Henry VIII (1509–1547) introduced naval ordnance of unprecedented power. As early as 1509 the *Mary Rose* and the *Sovereign* were armed, respectively, with five and four brass guns weighing about 3,000 pounds (6,615 kilograms) each. The English followed Italian examples when they mounted the heavy guns low in the waists of the ships and pierced the ships' sides with gunports, thus moving toward creation of the broadside battery. But they used bigger guns than the Italians, and they soon developed the best gun foundries in Europe, which cast cannon especially designed and mounted for use on ships. They also developed the four-wheeled truck carriage for mounting guns on ships' decks. For the first time, warships were intended mainly for "off-fighting" instead of "in-fighting." The navy of Henry VIII had the potential to destroy its enemies from a distance. Henry VIII's largest ship, the *Henri Grâce à Dieu* or *Great Harry,* a four-master of 1,500 tons, was rebuilt in 1540 as a more compact 1,000-ton ship but with a double tier of gunports.

In 1546, Henry VIII established an organization for naval supply that was to evolve into the Navy Board and to be charged with administration of the fleet under the direction of a Lord Admiral. The Clerk of the Ships evolved into the Clerk of the Acts, principally a secretarial position, but the Navy Board gave England the most centralized and effective naval administration anywhere in Europe.

The tactical and strategic implications of these developments emerged only over an extended timespan. In his three French wars, Henry VIII still used his fleet mainly as a means of transport rather than as any sort of independent weapon for controlling the English Channel and the seas more generally. In these same wars, the potential of the broadside guns only barely began to be translated into tactical reality. The warships of the King soon formed an unprecedentedly strong permanent fleet, Henry VIII having added within the first five years of his reign twenty-four royal vessels to the seven he had inherited from his father. Moreover, much larger numbers of merchant ships still reinforced the navy in war. The King's own warships were often hired out to the merchant service in time of peace, especially utilizing their great size and strength for voyages to the distant Levant.

The Levant was one of many areas toward which the first two Tudor monarchs encouraged the development of English trade in English ships. In the background of Tudor naval expansion lay a series of Navigation Acts whose purpose was to restrict imports into the realm to those carried by English, Irish, and Welsh crews, while the Kings also subsidized the building of merchant ships of 100 tons and over. While practical considerations of relations with other maritime powers, in particular the need to propitiate the Hanseatic League for the sake of tranquil commerce with northern Europe, limited realizing the purpose of the Navigation Acts, the early Tudors initiated not only an expansion of maritime commerce but the effort to transfer that commerce from mainly foreign to overwhelmingly English ships. But while the rise of English seaborne commerce was to provide a foundation for eventual English naval supremacy, for the time being it left the navy so closely intertwined with merchant shipping that scarcely the barest beginnings of a military profession could be found at sea. Warships and merchantmen were still interchangeable. So for the most part were their commanding officers and crews. The officers of the King's ships were practitioners of the craft of seamanship; they were not educated in the conduct of war.

As the tactical implications of broadside gunnery began to be realized during the reigns of Henry VIII's successors, the new naval tactics tended if anything to impede further the development of a naval profession. The boarding tactics of "in-fighting" demanded a certain tactical skill on the part of ship captains. So of course did the tactics of "off-fighting," but these latter tactics evolved in such a way that they encouraged an unthinking rigidity detrimental to any professional growth.

The Armada and Broadside Gunnery

Under Queen Elizabeth I (1558–1603), the focus of English naval rivalry shifted from France to the Iberian powers, Spain and Portugal, which were united in 1581 under the kingship of Philip (Felipe) II of Spain (and remained so until December 3/13, 1640, during the reign of Philip IV; these kings were Felipe I and III, respectively, in Portugal). The causes of England's shift lay in the descent of France into internal religious rivalry and confusion, in the separation of the Church of England from Rome, in Philip II's championship of Catholicism against such deviations, and, perhaps most important, in the growing confidence and vitality of the English at sea and their consequent challenge to the Iberian monopoly of commerce with the new worlds just being discovered and explored. Not the English government or the sovereign's navy but privateers first directly challenged Iberian control of transoceanic trade. The privateers, whose profits depended partly on keeping their crews small, also became the first to crystallize the tactical potential of broadside gunnery; so long as enemy ships were outranged and underarmed against English broadsides, gunnery actions would require fewer men for success than efforts to board.

The first naval encounter in which broadside gunnery was decisive may have been the victorious fight of the English privateer *Castle of Comfort* near Terceira in the Azores in 1567. By means of superior gunnery, the English vessel beat off the attacks of seven Portuguese ships in two days.

Superior gunnery could not always prevail against adverse numbers. In the same year John Hawkins (or Hawkyns), a Devonshire captain of characteristically middle-class background, whose father, William Hawkins, had been a notable maritime explorer, began his third slaving voyage to the New World. He led a small squadron that included two of the Queen's warships. After he had sold off his cargo of slaves in the Spanish colonies, bad weather forced him to put in at the port of San Juan de Ulúa in Mexico. There a Spanish treasure fleet that he had allowed to come peacefully into the harbor under an understanding of amicability while both sides sought shelter suddenly embarked against him apparently overwhelming numbers of boarding parties. Hawkins contrived to open something of a gunfire action, in which he sank two Spanish vessels including the flagship. But the enemy's advantage of surprise and Hawkins's inability to maneuver much in the confined waters of the port assured victory for the "infighters"; Hawkins lost his own flagship, and in the end only two English vessels escaped, the royal ship *Minion*, to which Hawkins himself fled just in time, and the fifty-ton bark *Judith*, under a young—probably in his early twenties—Devonshire neighbor and perhaps kinsman of Hawkins, Francis Drake.

The experience seems to have afflicted Drake with a thirst for revenge by means of further exploits against Spanish ships and colonies. In 1577–1580 he carried his raids into the Pacific Ocean and thence completed the first English circumnavigation of the globe. But Hawkins in contrast was evidently so badly shaken that henceforth he little enjoyed the sea. For more than twenty years he mostly stayed ashore. In 1573, however, he succeeded Benjamin Gonson, father of Katharine Gonson whom Hawkins had married, as Treasurer of the Navy, and soon afterward he became Controller as well. As such, he was the principal administrator and ultimately the principal shaper of Queen Elizabeth's fleet.

The Spanish learned to respect and then to emulate English broadside gunnery aimed low at an enemy's hulls. When the English added assistance to the Dutch rebellion to their other offenses against Spain, and relations between the two countries thereby degenerated into open war, Philip II included in the maturing of his plans to squelch both England and Protestantism the building of an Armada featuring heavily gunned ships on the English model. As much as possible, Philip fitted these ships with the superior cannon cast in England's own foundries. The Spanish did not, however, adopt the four-wheeled truck carriage, employing instead a cumbersome single-axled carriage that made it much more difficult to haul a gun inboard for reloading. (The method of allowing the gun's recoil to carry it inboard, restrained by a breeching rope, was not developed until the next century.) Furthermore, the Spanish preferred long guns for which their decks did not provide adequate space for inboard reloading. Possibly they reloaded outboard, that is, with the reloader precariously straddling the barrel outside the gunport. Evidently they could not reload efficiently and quickly, and their guns could get off few shots in a broadside gunnery action.

Nevertheless, Philip II hoped his ships could wrest from England the naval control of the Channel and then escort transports to invade Elizabeth's realm with much of the Spanish army from the Netherlands. Once the Spanish were ashore in England, the English would find themselves with scant military force to resist the tercios.

While the Spanish Armada neared completion, England's preparations to defend the Narrow Seas and prevent invasion were threatened by a controversy over the best way to design ships to take advantage of the new gunnery. The first Tudor warships had been "high-charged" vessels, with lofty forecastles and poops, their towering decks designed to facilitate the old boarding tactics. The development of broadside gunnery had encouraged a shift toward vessels with lower decks, especially without towering works fore and aft, and longer in proportion to their beam, altogether more seaworthy as well as better suited to gunnery tactics. These tendencies had partially conditioned the rebuilding of the *Great Harry*. Nevertheless, Sir William Winter, who as Master of the Ordnance and Surveyor of the Ships occupied two of the five seats on Elizabeth's Navy Board, and his brother George, who occupied a third seat, still held out for high-charged ships through the 1570s and into the 1580s. William Borough, appointed Clerk of the Ships, took the same line. John Hawkins was the champion of ships designed for long-range broadside gunnery. He met resistance at every turn, but gradually he succeeded in inaugurating a new era in shipbuilding design (and at the same time in lower costs).

The *Felicssima Armada* began to set sail out of Lisbon on April 29/May 9, 1588, commanded by *Capitán-General del Océano Mar* Don Alonzo Pérez de Guzmán el Bueno, seventh Duque de Medina Sidonia. The core of the Armada consisted of some forty heavily gunned sailing warships. The English had about the same number, with comparable design characteristics except for the superior maneuverability and reloading capacities of the English guns, and also larger numbers of guns. They were commanded by the Lord High Admiral, Charles, second Baron Howard of Effingham, with Vice-Admiral Sir Francis Drake and Rear-Admiral John Hawkins, who was to be knighted in the course of the coming battles, among his subordinates.

The largest English galleons, the *Triumph* and the *White Bear,* mounted forty to forty-five guns. The remaining major warships carried from twenty to thirty-four guns. Overall the English had about a two-to-one superiority in numbers of long-range guns. During the battles in the English Channel, however, as Queen Elizabeth's fleet harried the Armada on its way to the Netherlands, the English vessels somewhat surprisingly scored no marked advantage in the gunnery duels, because they approached the awesome Armada cautiously and fired at excessively long range.

Neither side had an adequate system of signals; thus neither side had an adequate system for the exercise of the senior officers' command at sea. The English suffered especially on this account because they were the aggressors and in greater need of tactical coordination. The difficulties here displayed in the first major battles of ships relying on broadside gunnery were to plague naval warfare until the coming of radio in the twentieth century and to exert a baneful influence on naval officer professionalism. For the present, battles tended to deteriorate into uncontrollable melees.

The Armada lost only three vessels during the fighting up the Channel. The decisive turn of events came only after the Spanish anchored off Calais for their junction with the army. Then, on the night of July 28/August 7, the English launched eight large fireships to be borne by wind, floodtide, and current into the midst of the Armada. The bigger Spanish ships drew too much water, over twenty feet (over six meters), to have entered any of the shallow ports that are the only harbors in the narrowest waters of the Channel. The only suitable port nearby, Flushing (Vlissingen), was in Dutch hands. The Armada therefore could not anchor in sheltered waters where it might have been relatively safe from the fireships. The latter vessels in fact sank nothing anyway, but their appearance caused the Spanish to panic. Having dropped double anchors, many of the Spanish crews now cut or slipped their cables in their confusion and haste to escape. One of their great ships, the *San Lorenzo,* had its rudder broken in a collision with another ship and ran aground. By morning the Armada was scattered up a long stretch of coast.

Meanwhile there was no sign of the flotilla of flat-bottomed transports that was to bring out the army. These ungainly craft in fact embarked the troops during July 29–30/August 8–9 but could not come out because they needed the best of weather to be seaworthy, yet the wind was freshening and the skies darkening.

The Spanish fought skillfully to reconcentrate their warships. They riddled the English *Revenge* of thirty-four guns with forty shot, for example, obliging it to retire from the action. But their Flemish pilots assured the Spanish commanders that the quickening winds meant they must leave their position along a lee shore, or all their vessels would go aground. With the wind from the northwest, the Spanish could not, however, follow this advice. Then on September 30/ October 10 a shift to the southwest precipitated a decision to try to save at least part of the Armada by sailing in the apparently wrong direction: northward, to return home by the long and perilous voyage around Scotland and Ireland.

It was then that gales and heavy seas completed the crippling of the once-mighty Armada, so that Protestant England could believe that Catholic Spain was undone by the hand of God Himself. Fewer than half the ships of the Armada, and about a third of the crewmen, returned to Spain.

Despite the manner of the undoing of the Spanish fleet, by fireships, wind, and tide more than by English guns; despite the indecisiveness of the gunnery duels in the Channel; despite the indecisiveness, also, of the remainder of the Anglo-Spanish War, with England unable to capitalize on the defeat of the Armada in any notable further triumph at sea save a raid on Cádiz in 1596—for all that, the campaign of the Armada assured the supremacy in naval war of the sailing ship armed primarily with broadsides of long-range guns. No other kind of fleet could have saved England by driving the Armada onto the lee shore where its impotence could be sealed; any other kind of fleet could have been victimized by Spanish in-fighting tactics.

The Anglo-Dutch Naval Rivalry: The Early Phase

After the Spanish War at last ended in 1604, England not surprisingly sought respite from its prolonged strains, and the navy sank into a decline. At least nominally, the English government also prohibited privateering, so that private entrepreneurs as well as royal warships no longer posed the obstacles to hostile depredations on English shipping, territorial waters, and even ports that they had in Elizabeth's day. Mariners' complaints about piracy in home waters became chronic; many of the ships that prompted the complaints now ranged northward from the Barbary ports of North Africa, a Moorish pirate ship being captured in the Thames itself in 1617.

Signs of an English naval revival appeared in 1620, when James I (James VI of Scotland) sent a squadron into the Mediterranean: a historic turning point, for it was the first English naval expedition into that sea. The Barbary pirates provided the ostensible objective of the squadron, but in fact renewed troubles with Spain represented a deeper motive. As events turned out, the squadron retired with no particular accomplishment.

From his accession on March 27/April 6, 1625, Charles I attempted the further renewal of the fleet. Unhappily, the effort helped precipitate his break with Parliament, because when the House of Commons refused to vote the necessary funds, the King claimed ancient privileges to levy a "ship-money" tax on the seaport towns in 1634. The seaports had traditionally been expected to contribute to maintaining the fleet, but now, instead of contributing vessels, they were to pay for new ships. In 1635, furthermore, the King extended the tax to the inland counties. The returns were by no means proportionate to the resistance and resentment that Charles aroused, and his naval projects remained hampered by lack of funds throughout his troubled reign.

The ship-money squadrons were noteworthy in that they consisted entirely of warships built for the purpose, without accompanying armed merchantmen. Unfortunately, however, a comparatively small number of large warships could not keep the seas around the British Isles free from pirates, nor did the improvements in the navy prove sufficient to cope with a rising maritime threat from a former ally: the United Provinces of the Netherlands.

The defeat of the Spanish Armada had opened the waters surrounding Europe and the wide Atlantic as much to Dutch as to English ships. The Dutch were sure to press this opportunity, because fisheries and maritime commerce were the necessary foundation of the economy of those provinces of the Low Countries that had made good their claim to independence. By the time James I ascended the English throne as of March 24/April 3, 1602/1603, numerous Dutch vessels were already fishing the east shore of England and Scotland as well as swarming over the Dogger Bank and, in search of whales, voyaging far into the Arctic Ocean. In the carrying trade, the Dutch not only supplanted the Hanseatic League in northern European but went far toward taking the place of Venice (Venezia) and Genoa (Genova) in the Mediterranean. Already erecting their own Oriental empire upon the ruins of Portugal's, the Dutch established their East India Company in the year of James I's accession to the English Crown. To develop Holland's eastern ventures, the company was capitalized at the equivalent of about half a million pounds sterling, whereas the English East India Company had been chartered on December 22, 1600/January 1, 1601, with a capital of only £72,000.

The Dutch drove the English from the Indonesian archipelago except for a small post at Banten on the island of Java, planted trading posts on the shores of Africa and Brazil, and founded a Nieuw Amsterdam at the mouth of the Hudson River in North America. The Dutch takeover of the East Indies was a process further embittered for the English by the "Amboyna massacre" of 1623, in which the Dutch made captives of ten Englishmen they found on the island of Ambon (Amboina, Amboyna) in the Moluccas, tortured them to extract confessions of various almost certainly nonexistent misdeeds, and at length executed them. The Dutch government apologized, but in England Amboyna became a watchword signifying resentment of the Dutch for decades.

On the model of England, meanwhile, the Dutch founded upon their seaborne mercantile expansion a navy, drawing officers and ships at first from the merchant marine, then gradually increasing their numbers of naval careerists and warships. Of course, it was a navy of broadside gunnery vessels, and of exceedingly well-designed ships at that.

In 1635 the United Provinces entered into an alliance with France that merged the old but still-smoldering Dutch-Spanish conflict into the Thirty Years War. This development helped lead in turn to the greatest series of naval battles since the defeat of the Spanish Armada, occurring, however, in circumstances that humiliatingly underlined the decline of English sea power since 1588. In February 1638/1639 Lieutenant-Admiral Martin Harpertzoon Tromp of the United Provinces surprised a Spanish fleet off Gravelines and destroyed it. Later in the year, a Spanish-Portuguese fleet numbering some seventy sail and carrying a large reinforcement of soldiers for the Netherlands ventured up the English Channel. Tromp attacked again, off Beachy Head on September 6/16, and during the next two days, despite an apparently overwhelming Spanish advantage in numbers of ships, drove the Spanish into the Downs—that is, into English territorial waters.

The English fleet arrived to watch but did nothing more to assert the sovereignty of Charles I, while for more than a month the Spanish and Portuguese remained in place and the Dutch hovered nearby. Thus the international law bearing on neutrality was demonstrated to be yet another among those limitations upon war that seemed to enjoy little respect when running contrary to a military force's exigencies of survival. At length, early on October 11/21, Tromp sailed in among the Iberian vessels and shattered yet another enemy fleet. Only about a dozen of the Spanish and Portuguese ships escaped sinking or capture. The battle of the Downs was even more decisive than the battle of the Armada in at least a strictly military sense, because it terminated for good Spain's ranking as a principal sea power.

Already thus so sorely reduced that other navies could ignore it with impunity, the English fleet soon split in two. In 1648, as the Parliamentary party sought to assert control over the navy, a number of vessels under Royalist captains fled to Holland. The next year they formed a squadron under the command of a leader already proven in land battles as the paladin of the Royalist cavalry, James I's grandson Prince Rupert (Ruprecht) of the Rhine, in England first Duke of Cumberland, claimant to be Count Palatine of the Rhine (Pfalzgraf von der Rhein) and Duke of Bavaria (Herzog von Bayern) as the son of Count Frederick (Friedrich) of the Palatinate and his wife, Princess Elizabeth, daughter of James I.

Rupert led the Parliamentary vessels on a merry chase from Kinsale to Lisbon to Toulon to the West Indies, displaying sterling qualities of seamanship and boldness, but accomplishing nothing in particular save to embarrass the Parliamentary fleet and to get in some raiding against the rival party's West Indian commerce. To stop such indignities, but also with an eye to the permanent reestablishment of English maritime power, Parliament took firm control of those parts of the fleet that were accessible to it and used them as a foundation for rebuilding. Navy Commissioners presided over by Sir Henry Vane insisted on efficient and economical building and rebuilding of ships and vigorous, dedicated leadership. They even contrived to inject a modicum of honesty into the buying and selling of ships and stores, a surprising achievement in a business that was notorious for graft, overpricing, inferior workmanship and materials, and every other conceivable kind of fraud—notorious even in an era of questionable ethics throughout the burgeoning capitalist system.

Just as the Royalists found a naval commander among their land-force lead-

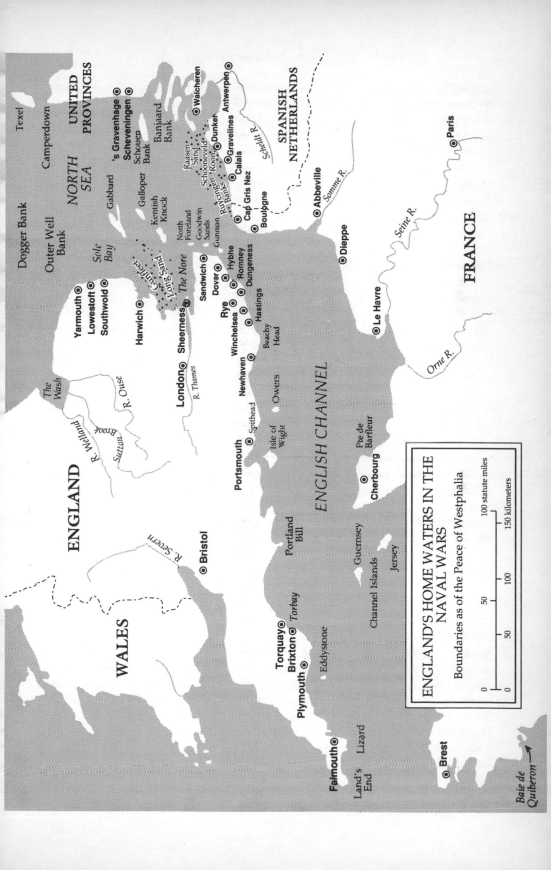

ENGLAND'S HOME WATERS IN THE NAVAL WARS

Boundaries as of the Peace of Westphalia

ENGLAND

WALES

FRANCE

SPANISH NETHERLANDS

UNITED PROVINCES

NORTH SEA

ENGLISH CHANNEL

Texel
Camperdown
Dogger Bank
Outer Well Bank
's Gravenhage
Scheveningen
Waicheren
Antwerpen
Banjaard Bank
Schouen Bank
Gabbard
Galloper
Raasen Sand
Schooneveld
Roon
Dunkerken
Gravelines
Calais
Cap Gris Nez
Boulogne
Ruytingen Banks
Kentish Knock
Goodwin Sands
Gunfleet
North Foreland
Sole Bay
Gunfleet Sand
Long Sand
The Nore
Yarmouth
Lowestoft
Southwold
Harwich
Sandwich
Dover
Hythe
Romney
Dungeness
Rye
Winchelsea
Hastings
Newhaven
Beachy Head
London
Sheerness
R. Thames
The Wash
R. Ouse
R. Welland
Sutton Brook
Bristol
R. Severn
Portsmouth
Spithead
Isle of Wight
Owers
Pte de Barfleur
Cherbourg
Portland Bill
Torquay
Brixton
Torbay
Plymouth
Eddystone
Falmouth
Lizard
Land's End
Channel Islands
Guernsey
Jersey
Abbeville
Somme R.
Scheldt R.
Dieppe
Seine R.
Le Havre
Orne R.
Paris
Brest
Baie de Quiberon

100 statute miles
150 kilometers
50
100
50
0
0

ers, so Parliament appointed Edward Popham, Robert Blake, and Richard Deane as generals-at-sea. In the transition, Rupert proved a more clever and wily naval chieftain than his opponents, but they gradually wore down his strength until in 1653 he returned from the West Indies with only a single warship left to him, with which he took asylum in France.

Sober patience rather than cleverness was both an appropriate hallmark of Puritan naval leadership and a stronger asset than cleverness for the long run. Between 1649 and 1651 the Parliamentary government practically doubled the strength of the navy, adding forty-one new vessels. Throughout the period of Parliamentary and Cromwellian power, more than 200 new vessels joined the fleet. The Commonwealth created far and away the largest peacetime navy that England had ever possessed; it was significant of the roots of maritime power that this stride forward was the work of a middle-class government. Following up the earlier English naval penetration of the Mediterranean, the Commonwealth also established a more or less regular escort service for vessels in that sea—a measure intended to stifle the North African pirates but not so incidentally aimed at challenging incipient French naval power in the Mediterranean as well. A Convoy Act of 1650 looked toward similar protection of other sea routes. Perhaps of most importance, the famous Navigation Act of 1651 limited seaborne commerce between England and its growing overseas empire to English and colonial ships. The purpose obviously was to stimulate still further the growth of the English and colonial merchant marine for the benefit of the whole empire, and just as obviously to encourage the further growth of the navy.

All these developments worsened relations with the Dutch. If a rising capitalist economy in England increasingly took strength from maritime trade, still more did the very existence of the Dutch depend on such trade, because agriculture could feed only a minority of the Dutch people. Furthermore, the Dutch and the English competed in the same trading routes and markets. Both shipped out wool and textiles and the harvests of the same fishing grounds for the wines of southern Europe, the silks and spices of the Orient and the Mediterranean, and the timber, naval stores, and furs of the Baltic. Much of Holland's invaluable carrying trade was in fact with the English colonies in America. The Navigation Act therefore struck directly at Dutch well-being. It was an almost certain prelude to Anglo-Dutch war.

The war was precipitated, as great wars often are, by an otherwise trivial incident. A tradition reaching back to King John's thirteenth-century claim to be Sovereign of the Seas had English warships insisting that in the Narrow Seas—the Straits of Dover and adjacent parts of the North Sea and the Channel—all foreign ships must on encounter strike their flags and lower their topsails in salute. On May 2/12, 1652, a Captain Young, an English naval officer, stopped a Dutch convoy and demanded the salute. He was refused. Promptly the Dutch government prepared to assure Dutch freedom of navigation in the Straits of Dover by sending thither forty sail under Admiral Tromp. Eight English ships from Dover and fifteen others under Robert Blake from near Rye did battle with Tromp on May 9/19, each side afterward accusing the other of commencing the action. The fighting was indecisive, but war had begun.

The Dutch had a more desperate need to win the war, but they also faced grave handicaps. All their trade except that of the Baltic and northeastern Europe had to pass close to English shores. Now and over the coming centuries, the strategic geography of England was destined to enhance English sea power in more ways than by the simple advantage of insularity. Because of that geography, the Dutch always felt pressure to dissipate their naval strength in convoy duty rather than concentrating it to meet the English fleet. Moreover, strategy and policy decisions of this kind were especially difficult for the Dutch to reach and adhere to because their government was much less united and coherent than the English Commonwealth. Also, the Dutch Navy still relied on a higher proportion of armed merchantmen than the English; partly for that reason, the Dutch were armed with considerably fewer long-range guns. The English, indeed, had among their ships the *Royal Sovereign,* launched in 1637 as the *Sovereign of the Seas,* and renamed after a rebuilding in 1660, the principal embodiment of a belated effort by Charles I toward further naval renewal; rated at 1,637 tons, it was the first full three-decker, the first warship to mount three complete decks of guns, at least a hundred of them. Outgunned, the Dutch were also likely to be outmaneuvered; the shallow waters of the Netherlands coast decreed that their ships must be relatively flat-bottomed, and therefore English vessels sailed faster on a wind and could tack and veer more handily. The Navy Commissioners had also brought the crews of English ships to an apparently higher level of training and discipline than the Dutch.

The Dutch also suffered from bad luck, the ultimate curse of the military man. In the summer of 1652 Blake sailed to raid the enemy's Baltic commerce and his fishing fleet off the north of Scotland. Tromp with some hundred vessels prepared to follow him and bring him to battle, but contrary winds frustrated the Dutch admiral. Tromp thereupon turned instead to deal with a small English force guarding the Thames estuary and commanded by Admiral of the Irish Seas Sir George Ayscue; but an abrupt change in the wind saved Ayscue from probable disaster. A surely exasperated Tromp then looked toward Blake again and sailed northward. On July 15/25 he caught sight of Blake's fleet off the Shetland Islands, only to have another contrary wind intervene. A heavy northwest gale scattered the Dutch fleet, while Blake rode out the storm sheltered under the lee of the Shetlands.

Tromp had to return to port to refit, and the Dutch government made the mistake of replacing him with Rear-Admiral Cornelius de Witt, Governor or *Ruwaard* of Putten and Bailiff of Beierland and a weighty political figure as an ally of his yet more influential brother Johan de Witt, who within a year—July 13/23, 1653—was to become Grand Pensionary of Holland. A further series of indecisive engagements followed. Rear-Admiral Michiel Adriaanzoon de Ruyter beat off a superior force under Ayscue to protect an outbound convoy on August 6/16 and then contrived to outmaneuver the English, offsetting inferior ships with superior leadership, while protecting an inbound convoy a few days later. Blake defeated de Witt on September 18/28 at the Kentish Knock at the mouth of the Thames but by no worthwhile margin.

The latter battle was significant nevertheless because of the manner in which it was fought and the importance of that manner for the future of naval warfare. To try to extract the maximum power from their broadsides and yet to deal with the issues of command and control in a way that would avoid the disorderly melees of the Channel battles against the Armada—signals had not yet been improved much, and in a fight it was difficult to see them anyway—the rival fleets sailed in line ahead while hammering at each other. That is, they cruised past each other in parallel lines in slow, stately procession. They did relatively little damage to each other despite their weight of gunnery, the English especially suffering little, but the line-ahead formation by maintaining order minimized risks and therefore appealed to naval commanders charged with the responsibility for costly ships.

The Dutch meanwhile had tried to compensate for their own misfortunes and English successes in the North Sea by dispatching to the Mediterranean a stronger fleet than the English had there. The English Mediterranean squadron felt obliged to take refuge in the neutral port of Leghorn (Livorno), and without its protection English commerce in the Mediterranean nearly halted. Therefore, after the battle of the Kentish Knock, the English ordered Blake to detach twenty warships southward. The Dutch seized this opportunity with a vengeance, however, meaning that they showed the good sense to restore Admiral Tromp to command of the eighty-five vessels they could now oppose to Blake's remaining forty-two or so.

Blake's numbers were so small partly because the English government, with less reason than the Dutch, had chosen for the time being to focus on protecting convoys instead of concentrating for command of the contested seas. Blake had had to make a further detachment of ships to guard North Sea commerce, sending to command this force Vice-Admiral William Penn, an exception among the Commonwealth's senior naval officers in that he was not a former soldier but a sailor of Bristol merchant and seafaring stock.

Blake was still further handicapped because the Council of State had ordered him to draw away from the Dutch coast. Consequently, when Tromp emerged with his fleet and some hundreds of merchantmen in convoy down the Channel, Blake had no chance of bottling him up before he could get his superior numbers into relatively open waters. Those numbers commanded by an admiral of Tromp's skill went far to assure Dutch success when the fleets engaged off Dungeness on November 20/30; the English lost two ships and might have lost more except for the lefthanded good fortune of timidity on the part of several captains. The English defeat was severe enough that the Dutch were now able to persuade Denmark to close the Sound against the English, which threatened to cut off Baltic timber and other naval stores.

Such were the penalties of an almost complete absence of coherent English strategy, a reflection in turn of the absence of almost any degree of military professionalism in naval affairs above the level of gunnery; if the rulers of England's navy possessed a measure of professionalism at all, it was only in seamanship, not in the military employment of ships.

The Commonwealth could not solve such problems overnight, but it could and did display vigor in its areas of competence to attempt to remedy setbacks that should not have been suffered. Sir Henry Vane and the other Navy Commissioners redoubled their efforts toward efficient and honest administration. They introduced new reforms involving more generous pay and prize money and better food supplies and medical care. In December 1652 the government promulgated the first Articles of War for the English fleet, not only laying the foundation for all subsequent legal oversight of the navy but announcing that henceforth merchant captains would not be allowed to command their ships in action; all fighting vessels would go to war under naval officers—an important step toward professionalism, even if the naval officers themselves lacked much in that regard.

More immediately, the Council of State determined to intercept Tromp when he convoyed a homebound merchant fleet. Penn returned from the north, George Monk joined the cadre of "admirals and generals at sea," and some eighty sail under Blake's command awaited Tromp by the middle of February 1652/1653.

It was when he returned up the Channel with about eighty fighting ships of his own convoying some 150 merchantmen that according to legend Tromp hoisted a broom at the top of his mainmast to proclaim his intention to sweep the English from the sea. Nothing more than legend sustains the story, and in fact the Dutch admiral must have known that shepherding his convoy would be perilous. A running fight known as the Three Days' Battle began off Portland Bill on February 8/18. The Dutch merchantmen sailed between the French coast and Tromp's fighting ships, which were aligned in a protective obtuse angle. The first two days were indecisive. Tromp fought with his usual tactical skill, but he was to complain of the undisciplined conduct of several of his captains. Partly because of such indiscipline, the English managed to break his line off Cap Gris Nez on February 10/20 and to capture about sixty merchant vessels. Tromp then took the risk of sailing close in near the French coast—a lee shore with the wind at northwest—while the English, with the rigging of many of their ships badly damaged in the fighting, decided they ought not to accept the similar risk of following closely. They deemed the Dutch situation desperate anyway; Blake's pilots assured him that the Dutch would not be able to weather the shore.

With darkness, the wind quickened. But Tromp was so skillful a seaman that he accomplished the apparently impossible, using the turn of the tide to slip his fleet around Cap Gris Nez so that by morning most of his ships were anchored safely inside the Polders off Gravelines. Evidently still more strenuous efforts by the leaders and administrators would be necessary if the Dutch were to be crushed, in spite of the English advantages in geography and ship design.

The Tactics of the Line Ahead

The better to address the difficult issues of command and control in naval battle, to avoid disruptive melees and to whatever extent possible to avoid the unsettling effects of meeting the unexpected, on the heels of the Three Days' Battle the English Navy issued its first Fighting Instructions. The Fighting Instructions of early 1653, destined for many subsequent editions and variations but embodying a basic principle that was to endure for over a century, comprised a guide to battle tactics whose fundamental injunction was to make the line ahead obligatory.

All modern armed forces have recognized that major advantages are to be found in prescribing standard accepted tactical and operational methods—what the twentieth century was to call doctrine. The Fighting Instructions commendably reflected this truth. Less fortunately, however, the Fighting Instructions regarded the difficulties of command and control in naval battle as so formidable that their proposed remedy limited officers' initiative so rigidly as to impose a nearly insurmountable obstacle to the development of a profession of naval officership—or for that matter, to decisiveness in battle and naval war. In fleet actions, there simply was to be no deviation from the line ahead. Thereby the fleet commander could always know where his ships were and what they were doing, no matter how primitive the signals available or how dense the smoke of battle. But thereby, also, almost no tactical initiative remained to any officers except the fleet commander. With ship captains obliged to sail slowly and close-hauled in line ahead during fleet actions, the English Navy and then its competitors and copiers allowed so little room for officers to develop naval fighting skills that they had little choice but to remain merely seamen, rather than to become military professionals at sea.

Throughout the rise of military professionalism, tactical expertise has tended to emerge first, with larger operational and strategic expertise built upon it. Because the Fighting Instructions stultified the growth of naval tactical skills as distinguished from seamanship, they also stultified professional growth in the higher levels founded upon tactics, in operations and strategy.

Other navies, furthermore, did tend to follow the English example. The dead hand of the Fighting Instructions was perhaps the single most critical direct influence causing the evolution of naval officership as a profession to lag behind the evolution of military officership on land. Of course, the nature of the Fighting Instructions was a symptom as well as a cause of the limitations hedging the naval officer's world view. The leadership of the middle class in creating the new modern navy naturally brought with it characteristic deficiencies as well as advantages. In land warfare, the legacy of medieval officership, with its origins in the knightly practices, the jousting, and the castles of the nobility, included a romanticism that was not merely impractical. Rather, romanticism could encourage a breadth of imagination and thus even of strategic outlook—the breadth, for example, that had conceived the campaigns of the Crusades—conducive to an escape from rigid, stereotyped military ideas. Modern naval warfare, in contrast, may have had its roots so firmly planted in the mercantile world of account books and ledgers that its attitudes were practical and hardheaded to excess. The leaders of the navy desired the minimization of risks and the maximization of businesslike efficiency and control. They valued imagination less than they valued predictability. Thus they issued the Fighting Instructions.

But risks and unpredictability lie close to the essence of warfare. To attempt to avoid the unsettling effects of the unexpected, the best method is to avoid war itself. If war is to be chosen as an instrument of policy—a dubious choice anyway except in extraordinary circumstances—then at least it should be recognized that the unexpected is part of the bargain, that the unexpected must be somehow prepared for by encouraging imagination and flexibility in command. To invoke rigid systems as a means of countering the unpredictability that is at the heart of war is in fact to make the unpredictable yet more dangerous; only flexibility can hope to cope with the unexpected.

England was saved from the worst evils implicit in insistence on the rigid line ahead by the rival navies' mistake of copying the system. When once there arrived naval commanders bold enough to break the rigidities and capable enough to find other ways of maintaining command and control, then for the opponents of such officers clinging to the line ahead was a prescription for disaster. For the present, however, the line ahead prevailed, and the stultification of naval professionalism was an important outcome. Nor could naval battles offer even so much hope of decisive effects as battles by land—but that, too, could help rescue England from the defects of its tactical system, because it retained its inherent naval advantages.

The Anglo-Dutch Rivalry: The Middle Phase

For the present, furthermore, the tactics of the line ahead served the English just well enough to escape hard questioning and to encourage emulation. Notwithstanding Tromp's brilliant engineering of the escape of his fleet and most of his convoy, the Three Days' Battle persuaded the Dutch that the Channel had become a deathtrap for them and that accordingly they must accept the severe—but, they thought, the lesser—hazards of sending their convoys around the north of the British Isles. Tromp carried two large convoys through this circuit successfully, but the dangers helped turn the States-General of the United Provinces to a new conviction that their fleet must apply its first priority not to convoy duty but to an effort to gain control of the sea. Therefore Tromp appeared with about a hundred sail around the mouth of the Thames before the end of 1653 in open challenge of the English.

Part of the English fleet was still inside the river refitting, while its commander, Blake, was still recovering from a severe wound suffered in the Three Days' Battle. But Monk and Deane sailed out to meet Tromp with a fleet about equal to his own in numbers and still superior in gun power, though the Dutch by now were hastening to remedy their deficiencies in weight and range of metal. Battle broke out off the Gabbard on May 23/June 2, 1654. The tactics of the line ahead made it more important than ever that a fleet going into action should try to seize the weather gauge, that is, to sail with the wind blowing it toward the enemy, the better to be able to control the opening, the pace, and the closing of the action. The English commenced the battle of the Gabbard in possession of the weather gauge, and Rear-Admiral John Lawson led their van in bearing down on the Dutch.

Tromp, conscious of his handicaps in gun power and wind, drew away while ordering his gunners to aim at the English rigging to try to cripple their ships. When the wind abruptly shifted, however, Tromp turned to counterattack, not imprisoning himself in the concept of the line ahead but endeavoring to concentrate the bulk of his strength upon Lawson's vanguard. Then the wind shifted yet again, and Monk and Deane seized the return of the weather gauge and the opportunity that Tromp's close approach had given them to open a general action all along the length of their line-ahead formation. Their superior firepower gave them the better of it, though Deane was killed—Monk, at his side, throwing a blanket over his mangled body—and Tromp had to retreat toward the shelter of his own coast.

Meanwhile Blake had hastened to participate in the action with as many additional ships as he could find ready, and on May 24/June 3 he reinforced the pursuit of Tromp with thirteen sail. Blake's arrival sealed English preponderance, and in all Tromp lost some twenty vessels before he reached the refuge of his harbors. He reaffirmed to the States-General that they must build heavier and better-gunned ships.

Instead, the Dutch sought peace. But they found themselves not yet ready to acquiesce in all of Cromwell's demands, which amounted to acceptance of English maritime preeminence. The English demands rested, however, on a virtual close blockade of the Dutch ports, where forests of immobile masts bespoke a near-paralysis of Dutch commerce and the threat of complete economic collapse, if not starvation. Having to choose between surrender and one more naval effort, the Dutch refitted and as best they could reinforced their fleet, and they sent Tromp out to fight again.

The Dutch had refitted in two squadrons, one of eighty-five ships under Tromp himself in the Maas River, another of thirty-nine ships under de Witt in the Texel. Blake's wound had compelled him to go ashore again, so it was Monk who cruised off the Dutch coast to prevent a junction between the squadrons. By now it was predictable, however, that the superb seamanship and tactical skill of the great Dutch admiral would unite his squadrons anyway. On July 16/26 Tromp sailed out from the Maas and contrived to draw Monk southward in pursuit. De Witt thereupon emerged from the Texel, prompting Tromp to reverse course under cover of night to join de Witt on July 30/August 9. The Dutch, with the weather gauge, then stood out to sea to challenge Monk, and the rival fleets battled off Scheveningen on July 21/31.

Monk tried to take away the weather gauge, while Tromp maneuvered to retain it. When the fleets passed each other on opposite tacks, the Dutch dispatched fireships into the English line, but without success. At length, the superior sailing qualities of the English ships permitted Monk to score despite his adversaries' skills. The English broke the Dutch line. Part of the Dutch fleet, thus cut off, returned to the Maas. Tromp felt obliged to withdraw into the Texel. The gunnery exchanges had been heavy, and no less than six of Monk's captains were killed. Now Tromp was slain by a musket shot during his retreat.

It was Tromp's abilities that had permitted the Dutch to compensate for their less weatherly ships, their lighter gunnery, and all their other handicaps to the remarkable extent that they did—those abilities, of course, set off also against the dearth of English strategic sense. Without Tromp, the Dutch acquiesced in the conclusion that they must make peace even at the cost of humiliation. The war ended with the Treaty of Westminster of March 26/April 5, 1654, whereby the Dutch promised compensation for the Amboyna Massacre, acceptance of the Navigation Act, and recognition of England's right to be saluted in the Narrow Seas.

The Anglo-Dutch Rivalry: The Final Phase

In matters naval, the later Stuart Kings were almost everything that the early Stuarts had not been. Upon the foundations laid by the Commonwealth, Charles II raised the English Navy to heights from which its coming dominance over all others could be glimpsed not far ahead. His brother, James, Duke of York—the future James II—contributed substantially to this development as Lord High Admiral. About 1670, significantly, the English fleet began to be called the Royal Navy. But in the end, political questions largely extraneous to the navy sorely compromised all the naval progress of the Restoration.

Almost as important as the royal brothers in the effects to improve the Stuart navy was the Clerk of the Acts of the King's Ships. The holder of this awkward title was primarily responsible for building the ships, supervising the dockyards, and feeding and clothing the crews. Upon the Restoration, patronage awarded the position to a young cousin of Edward Montagu (or Mountagu), from July 1660 first Earl of Sandwich, a general-at-sea who early in 1660 had carried the fleet over to the side of the King. The cousin was Samuel Pepys, who knew nothing about ships but needed the money that went with the appointment. Pepys was very different, however, from the run-of-the-mill spawn of patronage. He set out with the intention of transporting himself from near-penury to riches, as was customary in a patronage post, and he gladly accepted payoffs in return for jobs dispensed or other favors done; but he also lavished upon his office a prodigious capacity to learn and to work. Often he rose at four in the morning to study and worked halfway through the night (though not always, for he possessed additionally a similar amplitude of ability to enjoy himself). He could not root out the corruption that was endemic in contracting for King's ships—not only was he part of the system himself, but he scarcely could have transformed the whole climate of the age—but he set out to have good ships built in spite of profiteering, and to a considerable extent he succeeded (although English vessels remained superior to Dutch mainly because of the geographic constraints under which the Dutch labored, and when the rivalry shifted to France, French ships were to prove consistently better).

Neither could Pepys transform the officers of the navy into military professionals, even had the idea occurred to him (and from the Dutch and French examples in land warfare it might have); but he could at least become the scourge of the lazy and the incompetent. This task became more difficult because the Restoration developed a tendency to replace the middle-class ships' commanders who had created the modern navy with "gentlemen captains" awarded the privilege of striding a quarterdeck through influence at court. The influx was sufficient, and sufficiently discouraging to the old seamen-captains, that in the Second Dutch War of 1665–1667 the Duke of York and other leaders who were determined upon improving the navy had to struggle to prevent it from declining again instead through want of enough captains able to handle their ships properly. Already, however, the Duke of York had taken a step toward a long-term solution. When a young man named Thomas Darcy entered the navy under royal patronage on April 27/May 7, 1661, he was awarded the title and pay of a midshipman. This title had hitherto applied to a noncommissioned officer serving under a boatswain, but henceforth it came to designate a young gentleman learning the trade—as it still was, rather than the profession—of naval officership through service at sea, at first as a "Volunteer," later as a "King's Letter Boy." Capitalizing upon this useful innovation, Pepys in time was able partially to combat the problem of gentlemen captains by instituting an examination for promotion from midshipman to lieutenant.

A small but significant detail of Pepys's administration involved cartography. When war with the Dutch resumed, the English were still using, as they had done in the previous war, their enemy's charts even for England's own coasts. Pepys appointed Captain Grenville Collins to survey the coasts and harbors of England, and out of Collins's labors there came in time charts better than the Dutch possessed, beginning a process whereby in the nineteenth century the British Admiralty produced the charts relied upon by navigators all over the world.

But war with the Dutch did resume. The Restoration Parliament reaffirmed and strengthened the navigation laws of the Commonwealth with its own Navigation Acts of 1660, 1661, and 1663. In 1664 an English expedition seized the Dutch town of Nieuw Amsterdam and the surrounding colony of Nieuw Nederland on behalf of the Duke of York, who became proprietor of the new city and colony of New York. There had already been renewed English raids on Dutch trading stations in West Africa, and now the Dutch retaliated with counter-raids. On February 22, 1664/March 4, 1665 England declared war on the United Provinces.

The Grand Pensionary Johan de Witt had achieved a rebirth of the Dutch fleet not unlike the accomplishments of the Stuarts in England, and Dutch commerce had revived enough to help put the Dutch government in considerably better financial condition than the Stuarts'. Dutch ships were now much more uniform in design and considerably better gunned than they had been in the preceding war. In 1665, the English fleet was able to win a battle off Lowestoft on June 3/13 but not to exploit the victory for any decisive strategic advantage. In January 1665/1666 the ambitions of Louis XIV drew France into the war on the side of the Dutch, a curious permutation of the main course of the politics of the era, but one heralding England's next principal rivalry at sea. The French intervention prompted the English into the mistake of detaching twenty sail under Prince Rupert into the Channel and away from the main fleet, which confronted the Dutch from the mouth of the Thames. Commanding the main English fleet was Monk, now Baron Monk, first Earl of Torrington and third Duke of Albemarle, who sallied forth with his remaining fifty-seven sail to challenge the Dutch under Admiral de Ruyter off the coast of Flanders. He thus precipitated the Four Days' Battle of June 1–4/11–14, 1666.

Albemarle sought to substitute boldness for numerical strength. On June 1/ 11 he struck the enemy's van with the bulk of his own force; but he failed to inflict as much damage as he hoped, and during the next two days the rival fleets engaged in formal line-ahead fashion, with the Dutch extracting the advantage implicit in their numbers. The English lost the *Prince* of 100 guns, run aground as Albemarle attempted to withdraw late on the 3rd/13th; they might have lost much more had not Rupert rejoined that evening. The English casualties by the time they were able to get away to the shelter of the Thames included twenty ships and 6,000 men. De Ruyter now blockaded the Thames, and England feared a French invasion.

Essaying a riposte, Albemarle and Rupert together were able with good luck and good seamanship to work the whole fleet out into open water on a single tide and to give battle off the North Foreland on July 15/25. The English scored enough of a victory to break the Dutch blockade for the time being, but the enemy's ships cruised off English ports again, albeit in smaller numbers, after the great fire of London virtually paralyzed the English war effort in September.

Altogether, the Second Dutch War was a less than auspicious baptism of fire for the Restoration navy, the efforts of the King, York, and Pepys notwithstanding. By December 1666, Pepys was rejoicing inordinately over the arrival of a mere four ships carrying masts from New England, the Dutch having cut off the Baltic trade in naval stores. While a convoy slipped through from the Baltic soon afterward, arriving on December 19/29, these latter events hardly sufficed to reverse the course of the war. The following June de Ruyter was able to taunt the English by sailing down the length of the British coast from the Firth of Forth to the mouth of the Thames. On June 10/20 he sent a landing party ashore at Sheerness and plundered the magazines and storehouses. Entering the Thames, on the 11th/21st he sent out another detachment that forced the entrance of the Medway and burned the dockyard at Chatham and six large ships while capturing a flagship, the *Royal Charles,* 100 (the number of the ship's guns according to the standard rating system that had now come into use). Thereafter de Ruyter continued to patrol off the mouth of the Thames, and again English shipping was threatened with paralysis.

It was the Dutch distrust of their ally, Louis XIV, rather than the English Navy that saved England at this juncture. Lest his embrace grow too close, the Dutch proposed a compromise peace to which the English under the strategic circumstances had to prove agreeable. For the present the French decided to agree also. In the resulting Treaty of Breda of July 11/21, 1667, the English finally windrew from the Spice Islands—mainly Indonesia—and undertook to limit their Oriental trade to India, while also yielding Surinam on the coast of South America to the Dutch and Acadia in North America to the French. England, however, retained New York and some Dutch slave-trading stations that it had captured on the coast of Africa. More important, England also retained the Navigation Acts.

Before England took its place at Holland's side against the danger that had engendered the Treaty of Breda, as England's nascent policy of opposition to any potentially hegemonic contintenal power decreed, there was to be yet a Third Dutch War, in 1672–1674. In this final conflict of the series, the curious alliance of the Second Dutch War underwent an almost equally curious reversal, and it was England that fought in partnership with the potentially hegemonic France of Louis XIV. Because of this anomaly, however, England fought without the broad middle-class support that commercial rivalry with the Dutch had generated for the earlier two Dutch wars.

Specifically, the Third Dutch War grew out of the secret Treaty of Dover arranged by Charles II and Louis XIV on May 12/22, 1670. The avowed object in fighting the Dutch yet again was to resolve the commercial rivalry once and for all in England's favor. The real purpose, however, was to ease Charles's difficulties in squeezing funds out of Parliament; under the secret treaty, Louis was to grant Charles an annual subsidy during the war and also to lend long-run support toward a monarchical despotism in England on the French model, complete with the reestablishment of Roman Catholicism. A supplementary religious compact indeed assured Charles an additional £150,000 for announcing his conversion to the ancient faith.

The renewed friction between the Stuart monarchy and Parliament that motivated the Treaty of Dover and the Third Dutch War had reached the point, in fact, where the rebuilding of the English Navy foundered for lack of funds in spite of French subsidies. Even by dint of defrauding creditors, Charles could not scrape together enough money to put more than a relatively small fleet to sea. On May 18/28, 1672, de Ruyter attacked the Duke of York, commanding the principal English fleet of only about sixty sail, in Sole Bay. A French fleet of about forty vessels was close at hand; but, seeking to deal with his two enemies separately, de Ruyter managed to concentrate the bulk of his force against one of the two English divisions. On this occasion Dutch fireships were effective, and the *Royal James,* 100 guns, flagship of Pepys's patron the Earl of Sandwich, was among the vessels burned; the Earl was killed and his disfigured body recovered three days later, identified only by a scar on his face. The Duke of York himself had to shift his flag from the *Prince,* 100 guns, to the less badly battered *St. Michael,* 90. When the English forward division tacked to come to the support of the embattled second division, de Ruyter circumspectly retired, but the Anglo-French fleet had to enter port to refit. The English grumbled about the French, sometimes alleging that they had deliberately withheld their support; French naval inexperience was a more likely explanation for their ineffectuality. Once again, nevertheless, the English themselves had come out second-best against the sturdy Hollanders.

Once again, also, the Anglo-Dutch War was resolved by considerations external to it. In 1673 Prince Rupert took over direct command of the English fleet from the Duke of York but, though again combining with the French, failed to bring de Ruyter to decisive action. By now the Dutch fleet was only half manned, because sailors had to be drawn off to help garrison the Republic's land defenses against the French. Yet de Ruyter won the better of it in the principal maritime clash of the year, on August 1/11 off the Texel. Meanwhile, however, the terms and purposes of the Treaty of Dover were threatening to leak out;

Parliament passed the Test Act of 1673 to quash the prospect of a Catholic restoration (thus obliging the Duke of York to relinquish his command, because unlike his brother he was an avowed Catholic); and the wily Charles decided he must abandon both the French alliance and the war before they pushed him down the disastrous path that his father, Charles I, had trod. The Treaty of Westminster of February 1673/1674 restored the *status quo ante bellum,* except that the hard-pressed Dutch agreed to pay England a modest indemnity.

The divergence between the Stuarts' dynastic interests and the interests of the governing classes of the English nation did not, however, cease with the ending of the Third Dutch War. This divergence in turn prevented the efforts of the King and his brother to enhance the skills and power of the navy from having the fullest possible effects.

It is true that the neutrality of England after 1674 while war between the French and the Dutch resumed and persisted gave a new impetus to English maritime commerce at the expense of the United Provinces. Also, the stimulation of commerce eased the financial difficulties of the monarch, as customs revenues flowed into his coffers. Largely thanks to these developments, Pepys was able in 1677 to lead the way in persuading Parliament to adopt a naval expansion program that would add thirty ships of the line, as the two- and three-decker warships capable of standing in the line of battle came to be termed. But all these gains produced less naval power than they should have after the suspicions nourished by the Stuarts' indulgent policies toward the French and the Roman church erupted in the "Popish Plot" frenzy of 1678. After Titus Oates claimed that he knew of a Jesuit plot to kill the King, presumably because Charles would not follow his brother into an avowal of Catholicism, and also to burn London, invade England with French and Irish troops, and massacre all Protestants who refused to turn Catholic, the monarchy and its naval forces both tottered.

The Whig caucus that engineered the tale of the plot saw to the exile of the Duke of York and Pepys's removal from office and imprisonment in the Tower of London. A commission of seven men mostly ignorant of maritime matters took over the administration of the navy, and there set in a deterioration staggering in its rapidity and completeness. The ships of the line were allowed to rest—and rot—at their moorings, the thirty new ones if anything more neglected than the old. The fleet in being became nothing more than some twenty frigates—cruisers for commerce-raiding—and some fireships. The officer corps split into partisan factions of the friends and enemies of the Stuarts.

The navy of the Restoration was vulnerable to such decay because it was too narrowly the product of the royal family's enthusiasms, particularly those of York and Prince Rupert, and of the work of their favored protégés. It signified how much the higest ranks of English society had changed their attitudes since the Middle Ages and now recognized the potential contributions of the sea to the country's greatness that the Restoration monarchy cared as much as it did about the navy, where previous sovereigns except for the Tudors had generally cared little. Nevertheless, the solid foundations of the modern navy lay with the middle class, and any prospects for a stable rate of growth depended upon the support of the middle class. Too close an identification with the Stuarts, the use of the navy in the Third Dutch War to serve purposes more French than English, and the less than glorious showing of the navy in both the Second and Third Dutch Wars in spite of the Stuarts' patronage all served to erect a barrier between the fleet and the English middle class. The permanent prosperity of the Royal Navy had to await a return of harmony between the regime and the merchant capitalists.

Charles II weathered the storm over the Popish Plot with the help of new subsidies from Louis XIV and the eventual discrediting of the Whig leaders by their own prevarications. But the permanent revival of the navy could not yet be at hand so long as it was attached to so precarious a dynasty. With all due credit to Samuel Pepys, this remained true despite his return to his former duties in the spring of 1684 under the new and more grandoise title of Secretary for the Affairs of the Admiralty of England. It was true also despite the return of the Duke of York essentially to his former duties notwithstanding his inability, because of the Test Act, to retrieve the title of Lord High Admiral. When York became King James II in 1685, Pepys proposed a Special Commission to oversee the revitalization of the navy. With Pepys himself doing most of the work of the commission, the ships were repaired, the greater part of the navy's debt was paid off, and a new beginning was achieved upon which the next monarchs could build, with the indispensable added assurance that the regime would come to be in harmony with the interests of the middle class and of the English nation at large.

Colbert and the Rise of the French Navy: The Battle of Beachy Head

On October 1/11, 1688, King James II ordered his fleet to rendezous at the Buoy of the Nore to ready itself to resist the apparent intention of William of Orange to cross the Channel with a Dutch fleet and to assert his and his wife's claims to the English and Scottish thrones. In command for James was Admiral of the Fleet George Legge, first Baron Dartmouth; he was a Protestant, one of the many religious concessions James had made to the tide of indignation and suspicion about his possible design to reestablish Catholicism. Dartmouth chose to anchor his ships off the Gunfleet within the Thames estuary, not a particularly opportune place from which to intercept the Dutch. In spite of the efforts of Pepys, a victualling crisis occurred before October was out; and the supply of guns and ammunition, the responsibility of the Master-General of the Ordnance rather than being within Pepys's grasp, also fell considerably short of adequacy.

After a long and trying wait for a fair wind, William sailed on the evening tide on November 1/11. An English naval officer, Vice-Admiral Arthur Herbert, commanded his fleet. Anticipating this event, Dartmouth had tried two days earlier to clear the Galloper and enter the open sea to intercept, but he had failed. The wind then turned strongly east, leaving Dartmouth's ships windbound. The "Protestant wind" carried William and his fleet to a landing at Torbay on November 5/15 unopposed. Protestant though the wind might have been, Dartmouth for whatever reason had taken little precaution against such a contingency, and his efforts to bring on a confrontation with William's fleet seem to have been halfhearted throughout. Given the conditions on which the navy's ultimate prosperity depended, it is scarcely surprising that the attitude of the fleet and its officers toward protecting James II was decidedly ambivalent.

The coming of William and Mary meant both a more stable foundation for English naval growth and a firm focusing upon France as the primary naval enemy. The Anglo-French rivalry was destined to remain the axis around which world naval history revolved for the next 200 years.

By 1688, Louis XIV had built an impressive navy from a beginning of virtually nothing. Characteristically, he had also advanced the military professionalism of his naval officers beyond anything attained in the English Navy. It must be remembered, however, that in the handling of a fleet of warships, military professionalism is far from being everything. Even though the stultification of English naval tactical doctrine withered in turn the growth of naval strategy and the whole emergence of a profession of naval officership, naval tactics and strategy could scarcely go far without seamanship. The Anglo-French naval rivalry was long to remain one in which the English were stronger in seamanship while the French were stronger in military professionalism, in the officers' study and knowledge of the art of war.

The French were also to be stronger in the quality of their naval architecture and shipbuilding and in centralized naval administration, the latter representing the fountainhead from which other French naval assets flowed. In 1669 the naval ambitions of the *Grand Monarque* led him to appoint as Minister of Marine an already proven administrator, Jean-Baptiste Colbert. Thoroughly loyal to the King (although from about 1677 their personal relations became strained) and sharing Louis's ambitions for France, Colbert was soon to be the King's deputy in practically every branch of national administration except that of the army. In particular, he became Minister of Commerce and of the Colonies as well as naval minister, and he thoroughly understood the interdependence of his responsibilities. Colbert proposed to make France a colonial as well as a continental power, its empire bound together by maritime commerce whose development would both foster and be protected by a powerful navy. For these purposes, France could of course draw on the resources of a homeland much richer and more populous than England, including a wealth of forests for shipbuilding.

Colbert established naval colleges at Saint-Malo, Toulon, Rochefort, and Brest for the education of naval officers along lines parallel to the growing professional education of French army officers. Naval as well as army officers studied, in fact, at the artillery school founded at Metz in 1668. Vauban designed fortifications to protect major Atlantic and Mediterranean naval bases at Brest and Toulon.

In addition to these principal base sites, Colbert also improved many of the other harbors of France to accommodate naval squadrons. He died August 27/September 6, 1683, but he had set French naval progress on so sure a course that his passing caused little immediate loss of momentum. In 1688, France had the best warships, the best navy yards, the best naval tacticians, the most professional naval officers, and even the best maps and charts in Europe.

In that year Louis XIV proclaimed that his officers should demand a salute to the French flag from all ships except English. English vessels might not long be exempt. On March 2/12, 1688/1689, a French squadron landed James II with an army of 5,000 at Kinsale in Ireland, to begin a campaign for James's reconquest of England, Scotland, and Ireland. When Admiral Herbert challenged the escorting French squadron of twenty-four ships of the line with twenty-two of the line in Bantry Bay on May 10/20, the outcome was less than decisive, but the French had the better of it. Their landing of troops and suppliers had escaped interference.

On July 13/23, 1689, Anne-Hilarion de Cotentin, comte de Tourville, *vice-amiral du Levant* and *lieutenant général des armeés navales,* one of the rare senior French naval officers who was a true seaman, dealt Herbert (since May the first Earl of Torrington) another blow by evading his larger force to lead twenty sail of the Toulon fleet into Brest, to reinforce the principal French fleet. Early the next year a French expedition got out of Brest before the English were at sea and deposited another 7,000 troops in Ireland. By the summer of 1690, Tourville was able to lead some seventy-five sail into the Channel against no more than fifty-six sail in a combined English-Dutch fleet under Torrington.

Torrington believed he should avoid action unless circumstances brought him some exceptional means of overcoming the numerical disparity. The English government, however, shaken by setbacks not only at sea but in Ireland—the battle of the Boyne had yet to be fought—feared that the fate of the new monarchy might depend on prompt positive accomplishment. Furthermore, a small squadron from the Mediterranean, another from Ireland, and a valuable merchant convoy were approaching the English Channel, any or all of which would be easy pickings for Tourville's big fleet. Torrington therefore received orders to engage the enemy under any favorable wind. On June 30/July 10, consequently, off Beachy Head, Torrington ran down on the French. The Dutch in the Allied van charged with so much spirit, while Torrington for a complex of reasons was so slow in bringing his center and rear into action, that Tourville was able to break through the Allied line and encircle the Dutch. He battered them hard. The Dutch felt new cause for bitterness toward the English, and the French could rejoice at the battle of Bévéziers, as they called it (their version of the name Pevensey), as a signal victory that might herald many more.

Many Allied vessels were roughly handled in the battle, but it was in the pursuit, after the cautious Torrington acceded to his distaste for the entire enterprise by breaking off the fight, that Tourville scored most heavily. As many as fifteen Allied ships, by the French count, and up to eight, by the English count, had been too badly battered to be able to keep pace even with a withdrawal that was timed so it could float on a favorable turn of the tide, and ran aground to be burned.

The news of the battle of Beachy Head touched off a panic in England. Government and public alike saw it as the harbinger of a French invasion. The militia were called to active duty for home defense, and the Earl of Marlborough deployed for the same purpose such regular troops as remained at home.

In fact there was no danger of invasion. The French had no troops available for an enterprise of England. News of a French victory at Fleurus in Flanders on the day after the naval battle intensified the panic in England but showed why no invasion was in the offing. The French Army was otherwise employed. Not only that, but French strategy and policy were also otherwise engaged. At this level lay the crippling imperfection in the remarkable naval advances that Louis XIV and Colbert had achieved; at this level, the French Navy's potential for success was to be yet more fatally undermined when the operational, tactical, and technical strengths of that navy might be less assiduously maintained.

In England, the maritime crisis of 1690 probably helped stimulate additional efforts toward administrative improvement of the Royal Navy. The Admiralty Act of 1690 laid the foundation of the modern Board of Admiralty. The statute vested in the members of an Admiralty commission all the prerogatives that without it would have belonged to the Lord High Admiral of England. Except for the brief periods 1701–1709 and 1827–1828, the commission, evolving into the Board of Admiralty, thereafter governed the Royal Navy. Some administrative functions remained with the old Navy Board until it was amalgamated with the Board of Admiralty in 1832, but the operational responsibilities gravitated to the new board. Within it the office of First Lord of the Admiralty developed as the center of the board's responsibilities; the First Lord was a Cabinet member responsible to Crown and Parliament for all naval matters. There also developed First and Second Naval Lords, an Additional Naval Lord and Controller, and a Junior Naval and Civil Lord; these latter four directed the machinery of administration, while in time the Admiralty Board evolved into a bureaucracy with differentiated staff functions.

The comparable French administrative machinery was more effectively rationalized at an earlier date, but all the naval efforts of Louis XIV nevertheless were undercut by an additional disability at least as crippling as flaws in seamanship, one that largely emptied of significance even such a victory as Bévéziers. Ultimately, the French Navy lacked a strategic purpose. Louis XIV created and supported it to enhance his grandeur, but to no more tangible end. If the critical object of his strategy and policy was to bring down England—and now that William of Orange had made England the linchpin of all combinations against Louis, such a focusing of French purposes would have fitted well the political and military realities—then the French Army and Navy alike should have been harnessed first to the task of knocking out England. The navy should have been given the strategic mission of controlling the Narrow Seas; a substantial portion of the army should have been readied to invade England once such control was assured. It is understandable that as a continental power France was distracted from such certainty of purpose by the requirements of her landward frontiers. Yet Louis XIV and Louvois had so completey elevated the French Army to European preeminence, and Vauban's fortifications so amply seconded the army's regiments in protecting the eastern borders, that Louis could well have spared the military resources for an invasion of England while going over to the defensive on the Continent. Once he had driven England from the lists, then the possibilities of further continental advances would have widened beyond foretelling. But Louis was too continental a statesman and soldier to perceive the opportunity for decisive strategic action that his navy thus afforded him.

To be sure, if the France of Louis XIV thus failed to integrate its military and its naval power into a comprehensive strategic design, it was by no means alone in this failure. Neither the United Provinces nor England had yet achieved such an integration of the land and maritime elements of their power, and in all modern military history few nations have done so. Even in the more recent history of Great Britain, during which the Royal Navy was the principal military support of British world power, misunderstandings and misperceptions have been more common in army-navy relations than trust and cooperation. Nevertheless, the lack of coherent naval strategy and of purposeful integration of land and naval power in the France of Louis XIV is exceptionally noteworthy because it contributed to the loss of exceptionally large opportunities.

The reasons for a persistent lack of integrated purpose for both land and naval power, in Louis XIV's France and elsewhere, have gone beyond the obvious divisive factor, which is the competition between army and navy for limited national resources. They have lain in part in those prejudices of ground soldiers regarding naval war that reach back to the time when most knights cared little about war at sea because it had nothing to do with horses. These prejudices include those derived from the origins of military officership on land among the nobility and the aristocracy, while naval officership has been largely bourgeois. More profoundly, the difficulties of army-navy cooperation also have had to do with the stunted development of the profession of military officership at sea. Even in France, where progress toward an educated profession of naval officership was most conspicuous by the late seventeenth century, the technical difficulties of sailing a ship got in the way of military professionalism.

In France as well as in England and the Netherlands, moreover, naval tactics got stuck on routinized and inhibiting adherence to the line ahead. With tactics inflexible and uninnovative, the operational and strategic thought that among ground officers has historically been built upon tactical thought failed to flourish. Even in France, consequently, the evolution of naval professionalism fell short of a flowering of a coherent body of thought about the use of ships in the art of war—of tactical and operational thinking, let alone of naval strategic thought. Strategic thought was the least developed aspect of professional military thought on land as well, but there was more of it among the commanders of armies than among admirals. As long as strategic thought remained almost nonexistent among naval officers as well as limited among army officers, any dialogue between the two kinds of military officers also had to remain sorely limited—because it is in the strategic realm that the purposes of armies and navies most closely converge. Army-navy cooperation has to be less a matter of tactics than of operations and strategy, and regarding these areas army and navy officers were slow to speak the same language.

The stultifying effects of tactical adherence to the line ahead continued to involve specific and immediate as well as long-run consequences. Tourville's pursuit of the Allied fleet after Beachy Head might have been a good deal more ruinous still to the English and Dutch if he had not insisted on his ships' holding their places in line during the chase. When in addition Tourville contemplated the fact that completing his victory would necessitate following the English into the Thames estuary, with some of his own ships already damaged and no base for him nearer than Brest, he broke off the action. Some urged him to attack Plymouth and thereby possibly cut off the English ships expected from the Mediterranean and the approaching convoy; but the English had begun fortifying Plymouth—because their rivalry with the French had shifted their attentions westward they were about to construct a major base on the Hamoaze there—and Tourville decided he had best go home to Brest. Beachy Head won the French Navy prestige but not much more.

The Confirmation of English Naval Ascendancy: The Battle of Barfleur

The real danger to the English after Beachy Head was not invasion but French attacks against English convoys, especially those shuttling between England and Ireland. In fact, however, French naval strategy did not extend even to a systematic commerce-raiding scheme. The next year the English themselves thought to interrupt France's traffic with Ireland in turn. But Tourville not only exploited France's superior dockyards and logistical support to put to sea earlier than the English in the spring of 1691; he also maneuvered more adeptly, so that with a fleet now inferior in numbers to the Allies he kept his adversaries so far out to the west, and so consistently held the weather gauge, that they failed of their aim. More importantly, however, by the end of 1691 the land fighting in Ireland had completed the crushing of any hope that with French support James II might return to London by way of Dublin.

This disappointment for the French and the Jacobites led the next year to a belated attempt to extract some strategic capital from the victory of Bévéziers by mounting a direct cross-Channel invasion. James II was to participate.

The project produced for France, however, a humiliating public display of the inability of French naval professionalism, admirable as it was in various technical and tactical respects, to attain an intellectual dimension worthy of being called strategic thought.

Louis XIV and his ministers ordered Tourville to escort a fleet of transports across the Channel to Torbay without first defeating the English and Dutch fleets, and then to keep cross-Channel communications open. The French counted on their technical capacities not only to repeat the achievement of putting to sea ahead of the Allies but also to permit them to unite their Brest, Toulon, and Rochefort squadrons before their enemies were ready for them. This landsmen's plan failed to take into account the vagaries of wind and weather as they might affect the converging of the squadrons, and it also overlooked the perils of exposing troops and transports to a fleet that had enjoyed time to recover from Bévéziers and would have to be beaten anew for the design to succeed. Nevertheless, Tourville's orders gave him little discretion, indicating that he must sail promptly whether ready and reinforced or not, and that if he met he enemy he must fight no matter what the numerical odds. Tourville, though he was the officer responsible for implementing the plan, was never consulted in its making.

The nemesis lurking in such procedures made its predictable appearance. Contrary winds kept the Toulon squadron from rendezvousing with Tourville before the campaign had already been resolved. Although French preparations were supposed to be secret, word of them reached the enemy—another virtual inevitability in so large an enterprise—and the English and Dutch responded by going to sea earlier than the French had counted on. Tourville meanwhile had to sail from Brest to Le Havre (Havre de Grâce) where he was to meet the transports, with twenty ships left behind because 2,000 additional men were still needed to complete their crews. Then he found that he must delay for more than a month at Le Havre because the transports were not ready to sail. When he finally put to sea on May 2/12, he commanded only forty-four warships and, some observers thought, did not command his own temper, because his government had accorded him so little of the respect that his previous accomplishments merited.

Off Barfleur he sighted the Allies, ninety-eight warships under the command of Admiral of the Fleet Edward Russell (later, from 1697, first Earl of Orford). Impelled alike by his orders and probably by his exasperated and even reckless state of mind, Tourville attacked. There is a story that a council of war advised him to retreat but he drove forward anyway; he seems not to have bothered with the formality of consulting such a council. But if his mood was bad, his tactics and leadership were much better, albeit hardly flawless. He had the weather gauge, and he evidently expected that with superior design and gunnery his ships could deal harder blows than they took, following which, having carried out the letter of his orders, he could use his possession of the wind to break off the action.

Up to a point Tourville succeeded in this scheme, and magnificently so. The battle of Barfleur or La Hogue (or La Hougue) rumbled on for some twelve hours on May 19/29, during which the outnumbered French did not lose a ship. The chief flaw in Tourville's conduct, however, and one that may have been partially induced by his smoldering over his treatment at the hands of the French higher command, was that, like the landsmen in their strategic plans, he had not given sufficient allowance in his tactical plan to the vagaries of the wind. When at midnight he sought to withdraw, Tourville had lost the weather gauge: there was pratically no wind at all. A dreamlike, slow-motion French retreat and Allied pursuit thereupon commenced.

With each flood tide the ships had to anchor to avoid losing whatever gains they had made in the ebb tide. Throughout the day following the battle, Tourville once more probably set too much store on keeping his fleet well closed up, this time in part because he wanted to protect his flagship, the *Soleil Royal* of 104 guns, which had absorbed heavy pounding. In the evening he at length shifted his flag to the *Ambitieux*, 96, and thereupon gave the signal for what amounted to a general flight. He had been trying to make for the race between Alderney and the French coast into Saint-Malo, the Raz Blanchard, a dangerous channel for sailing ships because of strong crosscurrents; twenty-two of his ships succeeded in getting into the race and navigating through it to safety. Several more reached Brest. But others, borne along by the flood tide against which they had difficulty anchoring, went into the open bays of La Hogue and Cherbourg, where the enemy followed them and during the next few days cut out and destroyed fifteen warships, including the *Soleil Royal,* and the French transports.

Barfleur proved more decisive than Beachy Head in large part because the French unlike the English did not really try to retrieve their psychological loss. They built new ships, but they did not return to the enterprise of challenging English supremacy. Their failure to do so was another symptom of the shallowness of their naval endeavor. Perhaps if Colbert had remained alive, the sequel would have been different; but Louis XIV was easily distracted from the sea by discouragement, and because France lacked the vital maritime interests of England or the Netherlands, there was no strong underlying corrective to his distraction.

Tourville took seventy sail out to sea in 1693, but this time he had no unequivocal orders to do anything in particular with the ships, nor did he in fact do much except lead a naval procession. The French fell back on a commerce-raiding war, led most notably by the redoubtable Jean Bart, a Dunkirk fisherman's son with a fisherman's language and manners who had served with the Dutch and now became the greatest of French privateers. When in later centuries there developed at length a systematic body of naval strategic thought, the kind of *guerre de course* to which the French now resorted was to be widely despised among the strategists—except, appropriately, among most of those who were French—because commerce-raiding could allegedly never achieve decisive strategic effects. Actually, there have been occasions on which commerce-raiding contributed no small part toward twisting a belligerent's arm to end a war, especially if the war was not profitable in other ways either; American disruption of British shipping during the War of 1812 offers a case in point. For the present, it was true enough that the French *guerre de course* in the last years of the seventeenth and the first years of the eighteenth century did not deter King William III and Queen Anne from their policy of resisting the hegemonic ambitions of Louis XIV. But Jean Bart and his coadjutors were a serious threat rather than a mere nuisance to the commerce on which England's economy increasingly depended. Once more, if the French had been willing to commit somewhat larger resources to the war at sea, albeit now to a different form of maritime war rather than the quest for command of the sea, they might have attained disproportionately greater results.

The Triumph of the Royal Navy

French naval weakness and inertia helped motivate the English during the War of the Spanish Succession to press their naval advantage far beyond the coasts of their home island. In 1710 they mounted a combined naval and military expedition against Port Royal, the capital of French Acadia in North America, and on September 14/25 they captured the place. The next year they went so far as to mount a similar expedition against the principal French citadel in North America, Québec, but this effort was mismanaged and failed. More importantly, the English carried the struggle against Louis XIV into the Mediterranean, with the expeditions whose main features we have already described. With their Mediterranean ventures, the English helped lay the foundation of what was to become a strategic tradition of dubious merit: the belief that a major continental adversary can be dealt with primarily by means of naval and amphibious operations against his shipping and his maritime periphery, at less cost in money and lives than would be required by confronting him with an army on the Continent. For the most part, the British resources applied to the Mediterranean, especially those poured into Spain, would have contributed much more efficaciously to the defeat of Louis XIV if they had instead gone directly into Marlborough's campaigns. Nevertheless, the War of the Spanish Succession was a turning point in the rise of British naval power toward eventual mastery of all the seas around the globe. The capture of Gibralter on July 24/August 4, 1704, and its subsequent successful defense symbolized and sealed the arrival of England as an enduring Mediterranean power. And reaching out to the Mediterranean proved the first step in reaching around the world.

For while sea power tempted the English—and after 1707, the British—to neglect sometimes the strategic importance of continental land power, still it was sea power combined with maritime commerce generating it and protected by it that more than any other factor transformed the island kingdom from a minor state on the periphery of European affairs into a major European and then global economic, political, and military force. Maritime commerce protected by naval force gave Great Britain access to the resources and the financial means to challenge and soon to excel France as the most powerful of all the nation-states.

It is one of the most impressive achievements of history that the British erected so much wealth and power on a foundation of no more than a collecction of wooden, square-rigged sailing ships, at their biggest about 200 feet or seventy meters in length, their maximum speed running before the wind no more than about seven knots, their smoothbore guns possessing a maximum range of only about 2,500 yards (or meters), each ship so clumsy an instrument of war that its guns could be aimed effectively only by turning the whole ship to bring its broadside to bear upon an enemy, the possibilities for such maneuver being drastically limited by the fact that a square-rigged vessel could head no closer to the wind than fifty degrees.

The sheer difficulty of sailing a seventeenth- or eighteenty-century ship of the line and handling it in battle goes far to explain the fascination that tales of naval warfare in the age of fighting sail have always held even for the reader who is nothing of a sailor. The magnitude of the edifice that Great Britain built upon its wooden ships also explains much of the fascination. For all that, the edifice of British Empire might have been built more expeditiously on its naval foundation if only naval war had acquired greater strategic direction in place of improvization, which means if only naval officership had earlier become more of a military profession and less a matter of seamanship alone. A more vigorous growth of a naval profession and of naval strategic thought might not only have helped Great Britain use its naval power more efficiently and effectively; it might also have guarded against the delusion of expecting too much from naval power, that delusion which tempted Britain to neglect land armies as an essential element of military power.

Part Two

THE EIGHTEENTH CENTURY: THE CLASSICAL EPOCH OF MODERN WAR

THE BATTLES OF FREDERICK THE GREAT

Historians of warfare have often presented the period from about the third to the ninth decades of the eighteenth century as an era of limited war, limited in aims and means alike and gentlemanly in conduct. It is true that after the wars of religion ended, Europe was able to draw back from the precipice at the bottom of which lay barbarism. The warring states for the most part offered renewed obeisance to the historical limitations of the international war convention upon the violence of war, particularly the principle of noncombatant immunity. Similarly, the subsiding of Louis XIV's and Charles XII's grandiose ambitions early in the eighteenth century permitted a yet further withdrawal from unrestrained violence, symbolized by the less permissive nature of Emerich de Vattel's 1758 codification of the war convention as compared with Grotius's of 1625.[1]

But the histories of the eighteenth century's limited wars were not written by the peasants who dwelt along the paths of marauding armies; if they had been, the prevalent impression about the extent of noncombatant immunity in the mid-eighteenth century might be less complacent. Nor was war much limited in frequency; the European states and particularly the great powers remained about as frequently at war as when the state system had been agitated by the designs of the French and Swedish monarchs. Perhaps most important, the checking of certain French and Swedish ambitions did not herald a universal reining-in of the aims of war—and the limitations of aims is almost certainly the

---

1. Emerich (sometimes Emer, Emeric, or Émeric) de Vattel, *Principes de la loi naturelle, appliqués à la conduite & aux affaires des nations & des souverains* (À Leide [Leiden]: Aux depens de la Compagnie, 1758). For Grotius, see Chapter Four, note 8, above.

critical element in making possible the limitation of means. Instead, the continuing rise of Prussia to military and diplomatic power disproportionate to its population and resources provoked an effort by the rival states of France, Austria, and Russia to eliminate it from the ranks of the great powers—no very limited aim. The most important war of the mid-century, the Seven Years War aimed at the humbling of Prussia, was therefore by no means a paradigm of limited conflict.

For all that, the eighteenth century from the Peace of Utrecht to the outbreak of the wars of the French Revolution nevertheless constituted an era of limited war by comparison with almost any other era. Apart from dealing with upstart Prussia, the objectives for which the European states waged war were severely confined to limited territorial acquisitions. As European empires expanded overseas, the territories contested were often vastly larger than in Europe, but on the fringes of the European world such stakes did not seem inordinately high. Usually waging war for limited objectives—albeit with the Seven Years War representing a major exception—the European states could more readily settle for limited means. More even than in the late seventeenth century, the means were primarily careerist soldiers led by professional officers and conducting their campaigns in such a way that injury and disturbance to noncombatants were minimal. The period was marred by virtually no departures within Europe—and apart from civil war—from the principle of noncombatant immunity that could approach the notoriousness of the ravages of Louis XIV in the Rhenish Palatinate.

But even limited war must remain war in quest of decision, and in the era of relatively limited war the most promising instrument of decision continued to appear to be the battle. As usual, the promise was rarely fulfilled, but the eighteenth-century age of limited war was decidedly a phase of the age of battles.

Frederick the Great
and the Shape of Eighteenth-Century Battle

The impression is vivid among us that eighteenth-century war resembled a prolonged parade. This impression is not the least of the reasons why we readily grow nostalgic when we contrast the comparatively civilized warfare of the eighteenth century with the barbarities of our own time. Battles were tournaments between serried ranks of colorfully uniformed toy soldiers come to life, advancing toward each other to the beating of the drums. Once the opposing armies began firing, their casualties indeed became severe, because they fired against close-ordered lines at short range. But while we must compel ourselves to remember that the battlefield was a more dangerous place then than now (short of tactical nuclear war), the notion of battlefields as paradegrounds is not altogether deceptive. That international quarrels were resolved in such arenas confirms as well as symbolizes the considerable degree of truthfulness in conventional descriptions of an age of limited war.

The same sort of confirmation and symbolism are implicit in the fact that it was Frederick (Friedrich) the Great of Prussia who became the foremost soldier

KINGDOM
OF
DENMARK

BALTIC SEA

WEST
PRUSSIA
(1772)

Königsberg

EAST
PRUSSIA
(1618)

Lübeck

Hamburg

Elbe R.

AST
EESLAND

Aller R.

Bremen

BRANDENBURG

Oder R.

Vistula R.

MINDEN
(1643)

Minden

LINGEN
(1702)

RAVENSBURG
(1614)

Braunschweig

Wolfenbüttel

Magdeburg

Berlin

Spree R.

Frankfurt

Zorndorf

Kunersdorf

Posen

Warsaw

Weser R.

SEE INSET

MARK
(1614)

MANSFELD
(1780)

Halle

Torgau

KINGDOM
OF
SAXONY

KOTTBUS

Kanth

Liegnitz

Leuthen

Glogau

Breslau

KINGDOM
OF
POLAND

Leipzig

Rossbach

Hochkirch

Hohenfriedberg

Mollwitz

Oder R.

Koblenz

Frankfurt

Dresden

Lobositz

Mainz

Rhine R.

Main R.

Prague

Kolin

Chotusitz

BOHEMIA

MORAVIA

KINGDOM
OF
HUNGARY

Moselle R.

Regensburg

Danube R.

Moldau R.

AUSTRIA

Ulm

München

KINGDOM
OF
BAVARIA

Wien

Danube R.

Buda

Pest

UNITED
PROVINCES

LINGEN
(1702)

KLEVE
(1614)

MARK
(1614)

GELDERS
(1713)

Köln

Rhine R.

REPUBLIC
OF
VENICE

Koblenz

ADRIATIC
SEA

THE WARS OF FREDERICK THE GREAT

—————— Boundary of the Holy
Roman Empire of the
German Nation

– · – · – · – Other boundaries

/////// Brandenburg-Prussia

0   20   100   200 miles

0   50   150   300 kilometers

of the age. This was largely on the strength of the superior training of his army, which enabled it to execute the linear battle tactics of the day with machinelike precision, and also because of a relatively slight modification Frederick introduced into paradeground-style battle tactics, the oblique order of battle, which took form gradually and continued to evolve during his reign.

To an even greater extent the various facets of Prussian military excellence inherited by Frederick appear at first glance to have been simply matters of detail, but they were critical matters nevertheless at a time when no European army possessed a superior weapons system over its enemies. The Prussian Army unlike most European armies before 1740 had a system of drill that was uniform throughout the army. This system, continually practiced, devoted much attention to marching in step even under combat conditions, to retain a coherent line while advancing against the enemy. In most armies, the theory of marching in well-dressed lines during the attack broke down in practice; it would sometimes do so in Frederick's army also, but to a considerably lesser extent.

The Prussians intensively rehearsed loading and firing until a Prussian infantry battalion could get off five rounds per minute, which in most other armies was an achievement only of elite units or of occasional individual soldiers. Under battle procedures, firing in unified volleys—each Prussian battalion had eight platoons each of which was a firing unit—also tended to break down in practice, but again practice diverged from theory a good deal less in the Prussian Army than elsewhere. To maintain a high rate of fire, the Prussians adopted an iron ramrod; the traditional wooden ones frequently broke during reloading.

The Prussians had also modified their march formations so that the files forming columns of march could more readily transform themselves into lines of battle, thus hastening the cumbersome task of deployment on which the outcome of a battle might well depend.

Frederick in Silesia: The Battle of Mollwitz

Frederick William I bequeathed to his son Frederick II in 1740 an army that he had increased from 40,000 to 83,000 men, the fourth largest in Europe. The old King had distrusted his heir as too Frenchified, even effete, in manners and habits, and young Frederick in fact had sought in 1730, when he was eighteen, to run away from his austerely military father and to look for refuge at the English court; foiled, he had been imprisoned for his pains. By the late 1730s the Prince began to show a measure of soldierly interests and promise, but his friends remained too intellectual and otherwise too diverse for his father ever to feel comfortable about his prospects. Yet he was to prove in significant ways more tough-minded than Frederick William I. The father was almost sentimentally loyal to the Empire, so that he sent a contingent of troops to fight in the Rhineland for the Empire against France in 1734 although he would risk his precious army in active campaigning almost nowhere else; the son was dedicated to no loyalties except to his own royal house and his Prussian state. The father preferred to use the army as a makeweight in diplomacy; the son believed that for the army to be worth its cost, it must fight.

On becoming King, the son promptly eliminated the one ornamental extravagance that his frugal father had permitted himself; he did away with Frederick William's Guard of Giants, a corps of some 3,000 extraordinarily tall men. Almost as promptly, the son also displayed the most important difference between his and his father's conceptions of statecraft.

Prussia was still a collection of scattered, disparate territories exceedingly difficult to defend. If the kingdom could not be consolidated geographically, Frederick II believed, then its diligently cultivated new weight in the international scales could hardly be expected to endure. And an opportunity to begin the geographic consolidation of Prussia presented itself at the very time when Frederick became King.

The Habsburg Emperor Charles (Karl) VI had labored for a number of years to avert the prospect of a War of the Austrian Succession on the model of the War of the Spanish Succession. The danger arose because he had no direct male heir. He cajoled and bribed the monarchs of Europe, including Frederick William I of Prussia, to accept a Pragmatic Sanction guaranteeing the inheritance of the Habsburg lands intact by his daughter Maria Theresa as Archduchess (Erzherzogin) of Austria and Queen (Königin) of Hungary and Bohemia, with her husband, Francis of Lorraine, Grand Duke of Tuscany, to become Emperor. Maria Theresa would then be Empress (Kaiserin) in terms of practical power. Frederick II of Prussia, however, cast covetous eyes toward the rich Austrian province of Silesia, whose prosperity probably exceeded that of any single part of his domains and whose acquisition would help round out his kingdom into a more defensible entity. The Elector Joachim II of Brandenburg had arranged a treaty in 1537 whereby three Silesian duchies—Liegnitz, Brieg, and Wohland—were to be united with Brandenburg upon the death of the last of the then-current dynasty in the duchies, the Piasts. This line had actually died out in 1675, but the Habsburgs had then taken possession of the duchies. Frederick discerned in these circumstances a sufficient pretext to grasp all of Silesia.

Frederick negotiated with both France and Great Britain, seeking the support of either by offering Prussian military aid at a time when the War of Jenkins's Ear between Great Britain and Spain, which had broken out in 1739, was threatening to expand into a British conflict with both of the Bourbon powers. Charles VI died on October 9/20, 1740, while the negotiations were still in process, and Frederick decided he could not wait for them to be concluded. The Russian Tsarina Anna had also just died, so Russia would be unlikely to intervene in any action he might take. Two days after the Emperor's death, Frederick informed his principal military commanders of his determination to invade Silesia. He hastened preparations in secret, but the justification he was ready to offer once his armies struck was that the Pragmatic Sanction could apply only to lands rightfully belonging to the house of Habsburg, and that in any event the Habsburgs had failed to carry out various undertakings to his father that had accompanied Prussia's accession to the Pragmatic Sanction. Frederick was also willing to profess a concern for the liberties of the Silesians, on the ground that the Austrians were not strong enough to protect them—as indeed they were not.

Without a declaration of war, Frederick sent his army across the Silesian frontier on December 5/16, 1740. The Prussian standing army was virtually at war strength; the Austrians, in contrast, had to call up reserves. Consequently the Austrian commanders believed they could do no more in Silesia than hold garrisons in a few fortresses, while the bulk of their troops fell back to the Sudeten Mountains along the borders of Bohemia. The retreat of the Silesian forces was ably conducted, however, by *Feldmarschall Leutnant* Maximilian Ulysses Reichsgraf (Imperial Count) von Browne, the scion of a transplanted Irish family that had fled the Protestant ascendancy. Browne's resourcefulness provided time for the Austrians to mobilize their armies promptly enough to limit their losses to what Frederick's audacity had made inevitable. Under the circumstances, nothing could have prevented the Prussians from soon going into winter quarters with the fortresses of Glogau, Brieg, and Neisse invested, and Silesia otherwise overrun. Glogau fell on February 28/March 11. Only by that time did the Austrians have an army in the field sufficient to challenge Frederick.

Displaying like Browne no little operational skill, the principal Austrian commander, *Feldmarschall* Adam Albert Reichsgraf Neipperg, contrived to overcome snow-covered ground as well as the larger adversities engendered by tardy preparation to relieve Neisse and in the course of his subsequent march upon Brieg to put his troops astride the Prussians' line of communications. This maneuvering compelled Frederick to give battle to Neipperg at Mollwitz on March 30/April 10. While Frederick had eschewed his father's custom of using his army mainly as a showpiece, he differed from most commanders of this age of battles in professing to regard a battle as a desperate resort, claiming to believe the jeopardy into which combat losses were bound to throw the fragile Prussian edifice of army and state to be only rarely tolerable. So by' forcing battle upon him, the Austrians under Browne and Neipperg had achieved a considerable recovery.

In its beginning, furthermore, Frederick's first battle seemed about to confirm the opinion of those who still held the Prussian Army in low esteem because it had garnered so little combat experience during the past generation. Frederick and his father were both essentially infantry commanders. Neither had bestowed on the cavalry anything approaching the tactical thought and training they gave the infantry, yet it proved to be the cavalry on the Prussian right that had to bear the first major shock of action, because against it the Austrians struck first. They routed it, and *Feldmarschall* Karl Graf von Schwerin persuaded the King that he must flee the scene.

Schwerin, left in command with the Prussian infantry apparently about to break next, responded by grasping the colors of the First Battalion of the *Garde* and under that standard rallying the foot-soldiers and leading them in a counterattack. So thoroughly had they been drilled that they indeed advanced almost as if on parade. Prussian discipline prevailed. Infantry volleys mowed down the repeated efforts of the Austrian horse to duplicate their initial triumph, and eventually the Austrian army gave way as well. Neipperg withdrew to Neisse, leaving Schwerin in possession of the field and with Prussian communications restored. Mollwitz was the first demonstration of what the Prussian Army could achieve through a simple superiority in the conditioning of its troops in cohesion and in precise maneuver.

The Prussian victory revitalized Frederick's efforts to find an ally. King Louis XV of France sent Charles Louis Auguste Fouquet, comte de Belle-Isle, *maréchal de France,* to negotiate with Frederick as part of a French scheme to win the election of the Elector Charles Albert (Karl Albert) of Bavaria as Holy Roman Emperor and further to reorganize the Empire in ways beneficial to France. The Prussian King and Belle-Isle came to terms, whereupon the Silesian War was transformed into the more general War of the Austrian Succession. The French, however, refrained from open belligerency except by joining in Spain's colonial war against Great Britain. On the Continent, the French fought through proxies, with French officers wearing Bavarian cockades.

Although Mollwitz thus led to a French alliance, it had also freed Frederick from any urgent need for allies. He cared for nothing but Prussia's security, and for the present he desired only to assure his hold upon Silesia. Therefore he was willing to conclude with Neipperg on September 28/October 9, 1741, the agreement of Klein Schnellendorf, whereby Neisse surrendered after the performance of the rituals but without the substance of a further siege at that place, and the Austrians agreed to leave Frederick unmolested in return for his freeing Neipperg's army to face the Empire's other opponents, mainly the Bavarians, the Spanish, and the Neapolitans.

Unfortunately for Frederick, the Austrians succeeded so well against these foes that Maria Theresa decided to divulge the terms of Klein Schnellendorf in order to drive a wedge between her other enemies and Prussia. The war thereupon resumed in full vigor. But Frederick had put the interval to good military use by reorganizing and strengthening his cavalry. His heavy cavalry, the cuirassiers, had been retrained to use lighter horses so that their tactics could become swifter and more flexible; while the light cavalry, hussars with sabers and dragoons trained to fight with either blade or firearms, were expanded in numbers.

Against the musketry and bayonets of well-drilled eighteenth-century infantry, cavalry lacked the power it had displayed in Gustavus Adolphus's day. But for the cavalry flank guards to be so vulnerable to attacking infantry as Frederick's had proven at Mollwitz was of course a recipe for disaster, and on the attack the mobility and the shock effect of cavalry might still be put to good effect under appropriate circumstances. Frederick may have been slow to recognize the necessity to combine a strong mobile arm with his excellent infantry to secure decisive tactical results (though by emphasizing hard marching, he showed from the outset an appreciation of the value of mobility in the infantry). Driven by Mollwitz to acknowledge the need for a strong mounted arm if only for flank defense, he would soon display a growing perception of the offensive values of mobility and shock.

At the battle of Chotusitz or Czaslau on May 6/17, 1742, Frederick's mounted troops contributed as impressively as the infantry to a Prussian victory. They achieved a feat much praised in military textbooks but rare in fact, a vigorous pursuit. Partly for that reason, the success was decisive enough that on May 31/June 11 Austria and Prussia concluded the separate Peace of Breslau, Maria Theresa ceding Silesia to Frederick.

Hohenfriedberg and the Oblique Order of Battle

The Empress of course did not do so gladly, and Frederick soon had ample information suggesting she intended to try to regain the province at the first opportunity. Frederick responded characteristically by arranging a preemptive strike. He secretly concluded a new alliance with Louis XV, intended to bring France into open war against Austria. The French took the field for this purpose in 1744—motivated by a return at least in part to the hegemonic ambitions of Louis XIV—and with the Empire therefore occupied, Frederick broke the Peace of Breslau and invaded Austria again in August, thus opening a Second Silesian War.

Three Prussian columns marched into Austria almost unopposed, one through Saxony, one through Lusatia, and the third from Silesia. The bulk of the Prussian forces converged on Prague on August 20/September 2 and compelled the surrender of the Bohemian capital six days later. But this latest exercise in Frederick's cynical *Realpolitik* nevertheless failed to work as smoothly as its predecessor. Louis XV, personally commanding the French armies, took sick, and French activity practically ceased. The Austrians became able to concentrate their principal forces against Prussia after all. Frederick gave up Prague and was hard put to lead his troops safely back into Silesia in the face of capable maneuvering by Austrian armies under Prince Charles of Lorraine and *Feldmarschall* Otto Ferdinand Reichsgraf von Abensperg und Traun. It was disheartening too that, encouraged by British subsidies, Saxony shifted from a Prussian alliance to the side of the Habsburgs. It was yet more disheartening that some 17,000 men deserted from the Prussian Army—many were other kings' subjects and felt no loyalty to Frederick—as the campaign began to fall apart.

In none of his campaigns so far had Frederick distinguished himself in maneuver; continuing this pattern, he was now compelled once again to resort to the dangerous expedient of battle with its risk of calamitous casualties. It should never be forgotten in this regard that he worked from a far more fragile foundation of resources than any other great captain of the age of battles except Gustavus Adolphus. Nevertheless, in battle, at last, he could count on the sturdy discipline of his army as a possible touchstone of escape from the difficulties besetting him. In the middle of March 1745 he personally took direct charge of the intensified training of his army for the battle he had decided he must invite.

Frederick's diplomatic isolation had worsened. On January 9/20, 1744/1745, the Elector Charles Albert of Bavaria died; since 1742 he had been recognized by the enemies of Maria Theresa as the Emperor Charles VII. Simultaneously, the Austrians inflicted a series of defeats on the Bavarians, so that the new Elector, Maximilian III Joseph (Maximilian III Josef), felt constrained to agree to the Peace of Füssen, April 11/22, 1745, whereby the Austrians recognized his title to the Bavarian dominions in return for his acknowledgment of the Pragmatic Sanction. Louis XV of France had returned to the field but was concentrating on Flanders. Austria remained free enough to concentrate against Frederick that

Prince Charles of Lorraine could lead a combined Austro-Saxon force of 85,000 against Frederick's 65,000.

Prince Charles crossed the Sudeten passes into Silesia between Hohenfriedberg and Pilgramshain, confident of victory. But battle was Frederick's last trump card and, altogether contrary to Austrian expectations, the Prussians attacked, initiating the battle of Hohenfriedberg (Hohenfriedeberg or Striegen), May 24/June 4, 1745. Once more the Prussian cavalry proved how well Frederick had spent his time in improving it. Forty-five Prussian squadrons defeated sixty enemy squadrons poised to meet them, thus clearing the way for the Prussian infantry to do its work. In the infantry battle, Frederick's object was to roll up the enemy right flank, for which purpose he built up a strong concentration on his left, one of the first demonstrations of his principal tactical innovation, the oblique order of battle. He was of course by no means the first general in history to weight one flank more heavily than the other and to deploy *en echelon* with this weighted flank advanced, in order to roll up the enemy. Marlborough had employed weighted flanks habitually. But deliberate training in an oblique deployment to attack with a weighted flank echeloned forward was new to the linear, paradeground tactics of Frederick's era.

This "oblique order of battle" was to be Frederick's major contribution to tactics and a principal source of his reputation for generalship, but it worked to considerably less than perfection at Hohenfriedberg. The Prussian left advanced with unwonted irregularity. A gap opened between the left and the center, where fortunately ten squadrons of Dragoon Regiment No. 5, the Bayreuth Dragoons, were in the vicinity to close up the line. Frederick's infantry assault wavered under eight close-range volleys from a determined Austrian defense. At length, nevertheless, superior Prussian discipline under fire again made itself felt, and the Austrian defense became uncertain. Sensing the critical moment, the leaders of the Bayreuth Dragoons charged upon enemy regiments already fearful of being overborne and isolated. The ten Bayreuth cavalry squadrons, some 1,500 sabers, shattered six infantry regiments and captured 2,500 prisoners; their own casualties were ninety-four.

Their right wing broken, the Austrians fled the field. The Bayreuth Dragoons had displayed again the decisive tactical effect that cavalry shock action and mobility could still add to infantry warfare. Against unwavering infantry, their charge might have been suicidal; but against foot soldiers already wavering, the swift and awesome onset of horse could turn fright into panic.

Hohenfriedberg was Frederick's most impressive and certainly most personal battlefield victory so far. In spite of his own professed distrust of the wager of battle, he had left subtlety in maneuver and even the strategic initiative to his rivals, to stake everything on superior discipline and tactics. The flaws in implementing his oblique order of battle notwithstanding, the added strength on his left may well have been indispensable to his prevailing. Frederick would devote much of his forthcoming exercises to honing these tactics.

For the present he pursued Prince Charles cautiously, because his infantry regiments in the crucial assaults had by no means been so fortunate as the Bayreuth cavalry in the numbers and proportions of their casualties, and he could not be sure about the extent of discouragement in the Austrian Army. The Austrians were able to recover enough to revert to a campaign of maneuver, which they dragged out through most of the rest of the year. Thereby they impressed the Imperial Electors sufficiently to cause the election of Maria Theresa's consort, as Emperor Francis (Franz) I on September 2/13. The Elector of Brandenburg—Frederick—dissented, but he was nevertheless willing to accept the result in return for his continuing real interest, recognition of his title to Silesia, and on the heels of the election the Austrians and Prussians negotiated a new treaty to that effect. Still, Maria Theresa remained unwilling to bid Silesia good-bye without at least one more effort, and a succession of battles additionally testing Prussian tactics proved necessary to convince her. None of these engagements was a victory on the scale of Hohenfriedberg, but none was a Prussian defeat either. On Christmas Day (December 14 Old Style), Austria at last acquiesced, and the exchange of Prussian recognition of Francis in return for Silesia was formalized by the Treaty of Dresden. Frederick returned eagerly to the drillfield.

Military Preparations and Diplomatic Revolution

For the next decade, Frederick organized his maneuvers largely around the purpose of improving the oblique order of battle. His conquest and retention of Silesia at the expense of the apparently superior power of the Empire had begun to attach the sobriquet "der Grosse"—"the Great"—to his name; but he had to realize how precarious his and his kingdom's condition remained. In spite of the addition of Silesia, Prussia was still the least of the great powers in population and resources. Maria Theresa and her court would surely grasp any opportunity to regain Silesia and to punish Prussia effrontery. Russia was emerging from a bout of dynastic distraction and at best had to be counted as an unpredictable giant too close to Prussia for comfort; in 1746 Russia arranged a defensive alliance with Austria.

Even in the most narrowly military perspective, Frederick's triumphs constituted a *tour de force* of exceptional training and discipline and, toward the end of the Silesian Wars, of a superior system of tactical deployment; but these military strengths had rarely if at all been undergirded by comparable excellence in operational and strategic direction, and mere disciplinary precision combined with a simple tactical innovation could all too readily be duplicated by Prussia's rivals. Fragility marred the entire Prussian edifice. Prussia's very status as a great power was as precarious as Frederick's victories. And meanwhile the Austrian enemy had been diligent in digesting the experiences of its Prussian wars, introducing and rehearsing a uniform drill throughout the army, engaging in maneuvers of large formations, and altogether coming to approximate its adversary in precision and discipline.

Frederick's dependence on battle to compensate for other weaknesses rendered his situation all the more tenuous, furthermore, in that his battlefield triumphs had not been and he could not aspire for them to be victories of annihilation such as even Gustavus Adolphus had been able to aim for and at

Breitenfeld had nearly achieved. With numerical inferiority the likely lot of Frederick's army on any battlefield, superior discipline and training along with the oblique order of battle could not offer compensating advantages sufficient to make for more than a narrow margin of victory. Thus Hohenfriedberg, though Frederick's greatest tactical triumph so far, had to be followed by an exceedingly cautious pursuit and an exhausting campaign of maneuver and further battle. Perhaps Frederick was enough a product of his age that a predisposition toward moderating the ferocity of war would have restrained him from waging battles of annihilation even if his resources had permitted them. The cool cynicism with which he grasped Silesia makes one doubt, however, how much he would have restrained himself voluntarily. If he had been strong enough to annihilate Prince Charles's army at Hohenfriedberg or in the pursuit, Frederick would have done so. But fragility remained inherent in his system and status.

Thus he might well labor to carry his training system still further toward machinelike perfection, and at the same time to build still further improvements into the military administration and logistics his father had bequeathed him. He turned the civilian administration of the Prussian state still more fully to military purposes. He made the civilian *Landräte* largely responsible for billeting troops and establishing and maintaining supply depots throughout the kingdom. He cut in half the time required for logistical mobilization for war, so that only six rather than twelve days' notice would be required to make a regiment fully ready for campaigning.

There may have been a brief moment after the Treaty of Dresden when Frederick hoped that he would not need to go to war again and that, while maintaining military preparedness, he could turn much of his attention to the literary and philosophic studies that he loved. His hopes cannot have lasted long. The Austrians were too industrious in their diplomatic activities against him. The Austro-Russian alliance of 1746 was too ominous a cloud on the horizon.

That alliance went far, too, toward rescuing the Austrians from their French and Italian adversaries. The War of the Austrian Succession, though Frederick had ignited it, had acquired an intensity of its own that kept it aflame to the west and south after the Treaty of Dresden. The French in fact enjoyed the maturing talents of a military commander fully worthy of comparison with Frederick himself, Arminius [Hermann]-Maurice, comte de Saxe, *maréchal de France*, for whom in 1747 Louis XV revived Turenne's old title of Marshal-General of the Camps and Armies of the King. On April 30/May 11, 1745, Saxe defeated a British-Hanoverian-Dutch army at the battle of Fontenoy, and for three years thereafter the French won an almost unbroken series of victories against the Austrians as well as their other opponents, the more readily because after Fontenoy the Scottish rebellion of 1745 compelled the British to withdraw almost all their troops from the Continent. In 1748, however, the Habsburgs' new alliance brought a large Russian army westward to the River Meuse—a remarkable foreshadowing of the eventual power of the rising Muscovite empire. Thereafter the French and their opponents alike were willing enough for a respite, and a general peace was sealed by the Treaty of Aix-la-Chapelle (Aachen) of October 7/18, 1748.

The general peace encompassed the colonial rivalry of Great Britain against

France and Spain, with a return to the *status quo ante bellum*; but statesmen sensed that this long-standing rivalry was approaching a showdown. To free their hand to deal better with the French overseas, the British in 1755 concluded a treaty with Russia whereby the Russians committed themselves to defend the Electorate of Hanover, the continental seat of the new dynasty that had ascended the British throne in 1714 in the person of George I. The new Anglo-Russian bond threatened Frederick of Prussia with encirclement, and he responded by negotiating his own understanding with George II of Great Britain and Ireland, the Convention of Westminster signed by Frederick on January 15, 1756, stipulating the neutrality of Prussia in a renewed Anglo-French conflict. Frederick hoped that the effect would be to neutralize also Hanover's guarantor, Russia; he did not realize that the Tsarina Elizabeth (Elisabeta) Petrovna, who had received the Russian crown in 1751, and her councilors feared the rising new power to their west at least as much as the Austrians feared the threat to their north, and were at least as determined to expunge it. Nor did he foresee the immediate backfire effect of the convention, which, leaving Austria unsure of British support, greatly encouraged the project of Maria Theresa's Chancellor, Wenzel Anton Reichsgraf von Kaunitz-Rietburg, to achieve a diplomatic revolution: an alliance of the Bourbons and the Habsburgs.

Kaunitz had been fostering this project since 1749, as Ambassador to France from 1750 to 1752 and since then as House, Court and State Chancellor. He had persuaded Maria Theresa—the contrary advice of Emperor Francis I notwithstanding—that an alliance with the premier continental power rather than with British sea power offered the most expeditious means of resolving Austria's most pressing political problem, the chastisement and humbling of Prussia. The Franco-Prussian alliance expired in April 1756. Spurred on by the Convention of Westminster, Austria the next month replaced that alliance with a new one with its old antagonist, France.

But Kaunitz and Westminster were not the only spurs to Vienna's reversal of alliances. Elizabeth of Russia was also pressing Maria Theresa, and the Tsarina's assurance that Russia was ready to march against the upstart Frederick no matter what Austria might do, while offering Austria 80,000 men should a partnership be formed, presented an opportunity not to be missed. By 1756, Russian military preparations were so obvious that Muscovy's British partners expressed concern, to be told that the preparations aimed only at fulfilling Russia's commitment to London. In fact, Russia sought nothing less than the elimination of Prussia as a major power. The next war would not fit a pattern of limited means employed for limited objectives. The Seven Years War, as it came to be called, took shape as a war hardly less aimed at the complete humbling of Prussia than World War II came to be aimed toward the complete humbling of Prussia's successor-state, Germany.

It scarcely requires comment that, in both instances, it was the fears aroused by the focusing of almost all the energies and resources of one country on the attainment of military superiority that largely animated a policy of eliminating that country's power. Thus did worship of military power recoil upon the worshippers.

Lobositz

Disappointed in the failures of Great Britain to restrain Russia, and shaken still more by the loss of his most potent partner, France, to the embrace of Maria Theresa—standing indeed alone against all the principal continental powers, with Sweden and Saxony also thrown into the balance against him—Frederick once more decided he must seize the military initiative. He mobilized an army of 150,000 men, a strength achieved in large part by a greatly increased recruitment of foreign soldiers, not only Germans from beyond the borders of Frederick's kingdom but many French, Italians, and Swiss. As Prussia's diplomatic troubles mounted, every regiment had sent officers and NCOs ranging abroad to gull and inveigle the displaced, the needy, and the credulous into wearing Prussia's blue coat. Infantry Regiment No. 45, denominated the Dossow Regiment in 1743 and the Hesse-Cassel Regiment in 1757, became a notorious depository of criminals scraped from the latter principality's jails.

Frederick deployed 11,000 troops in Pomerania to guard against Sweden, 37,000 in Silesia under Field Marshal Schwerin, 26,000 in the east to check the menacing Russians (a boldly economical force), and 70,000 under his immediate command in three columns ready to march into Saxony. On August 29, 1756, he marched.

Even after their previous experience with him, Frederick's opponents had not expected so daring an initiative. The Austrian Army was scattered and unable to advance promptly to the Saxons' relief. The Prussians entered the Saxon capital of Dresden on September 10, while the Saxon Army fell back on entrenched positions parallel to the Elbe River at Pirna on a high, almost inaccessible plateau near the border with Bohemia. Frederick left detachments to cover Pirna while he led his main body farther up the Elbe to deal with any Austrian relief column that might appear. When word arrived that such a column was under way under Reichsgraf von Browne, now a *Feldmarschall*, Frederick pressed forward his advance to meet it.

The resulting battle of Lobositz on October 1 might well have confirmed the Prussian King in his old professions of reluctance to give battle, from which on this occasion he had departed in spite of the lack of a crisis comparable to those that had precipitated Mollwitz and Hohenfriedberg. The armies collided in a heavy fog, which reduced the affair to a confused melange of localized encounters. Prussian discipline again prevailed to the extent that the Prussians held the field while the Austrians retreated; but losses were about even, some 3,000 on each side, and Frederick was unable to conduct a pursuit that might have won any commensurate strategic gains. The Austrians had not yet concentrated sufficient strength to have relieved Pirna in any event.

With no such relief in sight, the Saxons surrendered on October 14. Frederick appropriated their army into his own service while transferring the civil government of Saxony to Prussian administrators. The dubious battle of Lobositz notwithstanding, Frederick had opened his new war against the fearsome French-Austrian-Russian coalition with a success comparable to his Silesian Blitzkrieg of 1740.

Prague and Kolin

Unfortunately for Frederick, against his combination of adversaries he had already reached the limits of what his bold initiative could gain. The principal strength of the opposing coalition was obviously intact, and the winter of 1756–1757 afforded leisure for its mobilization. He would soon again be in the position of having no alternative to the expedient of battle, with all its implicit dangers for a kingdom that still depended on the fragile *tour de force* of maintaining an army disproportionate to its resources, and therefore one ill able to afford heavy losses. Frederick's Saxon initiative of 1756 proved a remarkable achievement but was not enough to save Prussia from mortal danger.

As usual, Frederick's response to adversity was to retain the initiative. The next result of this response was to be a bloodier battle, probably, in its proportions of casualties to strength engaged than any other hitherto fought in modern military history—the battle of Prague of May 6, 1757. On April 18 Frederick sent a field force of about 116,000 deployed in four columns upon an invasion of Bohemia aimed at its capital, Prague. Two of the columns were to converge in the rear of Prague, while the other two would come under Frederick's immediate command for a direct assault on the capital. The Austrians responded, however, by concentrating their own forces upon Prague, and Frederick's latest initiative was promptly oppressed by a surfeit of difficulties. The King had hoped he might successfully lay siege to Prague as he had to Pirna, by beguiling the Austrians into disposing of their forces elsewhere. Instead, one of the Austrian columns moving toward Prague, under *Feldmarschall* Leopold Josef Reichsgraf von Daun (or Dhaun), spoiled the game by placing itself astride Frederick's line of communications, so that he became the one who would have to go elsewhere. Daun's maneuver in itself would have precluded a siege, but in addition Frederick received reports indicating he must hasten to make new deployments against the French, the Russians, and the Swedes. Meanwhile the Austrian main body under Prince Charles of Lorraine stood on high ground between Frederick and Prague, almost certainly too firmly positioned for direct assault. Field Marshal Daun, only some twenty miles (thirty-two kilometers) away, threatened the Prussian rear. Prussian resupply was highly uncertain. Frederick had to risk battle.

He left a secondary force to screen Charles while during the night of May 5–6 he marched to deploy a force of some 64,000 at a right angle to the right flank of Charles's 66,000. In the morning, Frederick attacked, hoping to roll up the Austrian right. But he had no time for proper reconnoitering, and although the fog of Lobositz did not reappear, there was a mist heavy enough to throw the advance into confusion. And the ground in front proved to be a morass in which the Prussians bogged down while the Austrians, alertly realigning, used the open marsh as a glacis across which their artillery fire withered their assailants. With Frederick's attack disintegrating, Field Marshal Schwerin once more as at

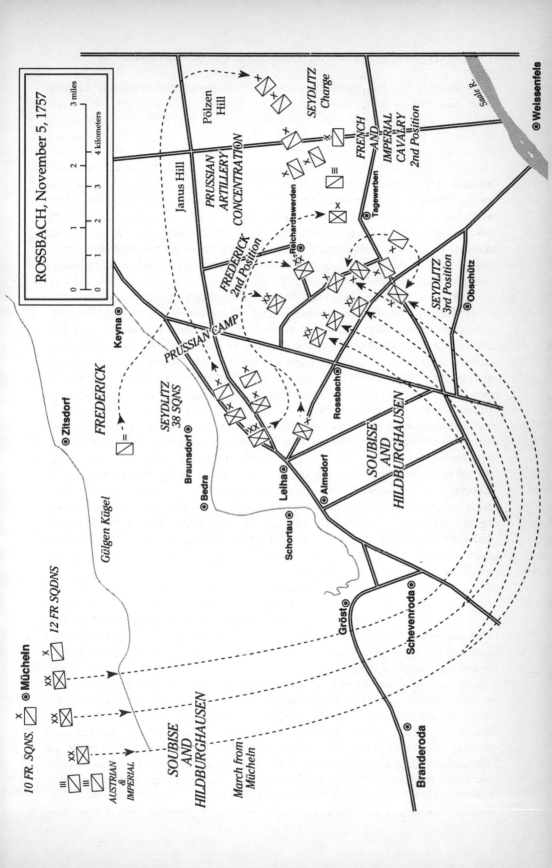

ROSSBACH, November 5, 1757

Mollwitz grasped a regimental standard and took on a battalion officer's task of personally rallying troops and leading a renewed charge. This time Schwerin died in the attempt. But Frederick, steadily improving as a battlefield tactician, was less dependent on Schwerin's heroics than at Mollwitz. The King had taken the precaution of sending his main cavalry force on a wide sweep beyond his left. The horsemen assailed the Austrians' new right flank just as a second wave of Prussian infantry was coming abreast of the faltering first wave. Under this double blow it was again Austrian discipline and coherence that proved inferior to Prussian. The Austrians retreated into Prague. They lost about 10,000 killed and wounded and 4,275 prisoners, a casualty rate of some 21.6 percent. The battle of Prague cost Frederick 11,740 killed and wounded and 1,560 prisoners, 20.8 percent of his force. These proportions at least equal and may well have exceeded even those of Malplaquet.

For Prussia, such a rate of losses implied a victory more costly than it was worth. This verdict was assured when Frederick turned to deal with Daun in order that he might free his line of communications and perhaps return to the idea of besieging Prague. He attacked Daun at Kolin on June 18. Daun was a strongly entrenched, so Frederick attempted to march past him and assault his right on the model of the battle just ended. This time, however, subordinates opened the Prussian attack so prematurely that it became a frontal assault, and in these favorable circumstances the Austrians turned the Prussians back. Frederick lost another 6,710 killed and wounded and 5,380 prisoners out of 33,000, while Daun's losses were some 6,500 killed and wounded and 1,500 prisoners out of 53,500.

Daun's name was to become a byword for caution in generalship, and Kolin offers a major reason why. Pursuits are notoriously easier for military critics to suggest than for armies to execute just as they emerge from the debilitating mental and physical strains of battle, but if there was ever a combination of circumstances auspicious for pursuit, Daun enjoyed it after Kolin. Nevertheless, he chose not to follow up.

Rossbach

Daun knew enough, though not all, about the stormclouds ever more threateningly shadowing Frederick that he might partially be excused for thinking that the *coup de grâce* was about to fall without him. Frederick would surely have to abandon his efforts to take Prague. It was almost as certain, and it happened in fact, that the Prussians would yield up all of Bohemia; Frederick fell back on Bautzen. The preparations of the Russians, which had done so much to precipitate the war, at length had ponderously sent forward an army of 100,000 into East Prussia, where 30,000 Prussians were conducting delaying actions against them. Sixteen thousand Swedes had invaded Pomerania. A French force of 24,000 was advancing through Franconia to unite with a heterogeneous Army of the Holy Roman Empire of some 60,000 troops largely of the lesser German states. The main French army, another 100,000, was marching against Hanover, where the captain-general of Great Britain's land forces at home and in the field, William Augustus, third Duke of Cumberland (also first Marquis of Berkhamsted, first Earl of Kennington, first Viscount Trematon, first Baron of Alderney), third son of King George II, commanded 54,000 defenders. One month and eight days after Frederick's defeat at Kolin, the French defeated Cumberland at Hastenbeck.

Frederick judged this latter setback to his only major ally—and only major source of financial aid—to be the problem most in need of prompt rectification, so he left another screening force—this one only 13,000 men—in Silesia while he began marching across Germany to assist Cumberland. At Leipzig on September 1, however, he heard that his East Prussian force had been beaten at Gross-Jägerndorf on August 30, which new calamity was followed almost immediately by word that at Klosterzeven on August 8 Cumberland accepted a convention stipulating the complete evacuation of Hanover and the disbanding of his army. Frederick was left almost completely alone.

Toward which of the besetting ring of evils should he turn next? Where might he be most likely to accomplish anything? Perhaps rapid action might prevent a full juncture between the French, possibly including now the troops no longer needed in Hanover, and the Army of the Holy Roman Empire. At least Frederick might crush the latter army before the French could aid it. Animated by this design, Frederick turned southward again even before Cumberland's capitulation was final. From September 1 to 13 the King drove his troops 170 miles (274 kilometers). The forced march achieved only partial success. Rather than offer the Prussians the chance to smite it, the Army of the Holy Roman Empire withdrew into the forests of Thuringia and Franconia. Disappointed in not accomplishing more, Frederick had to swallow yet another bitter pill in the form of news that Silesia was badly threatened. Hastening there, he was greeted by the yet worse news that a force of Austrian raiders had actually entered and plundered his capital of Berlin.

A Prussian cavalry expedition quickly dispersed the raiders, but in the meantime the Army of the Empire with at least limited French reinforcement was on the move again, advancing toward the Saale River and threatening Frederick's hold on Saxony. The attrition of marches and countermarches had reduced this enemy concentration to 50,000, but Frederick believed he could spare only 20,000 to lead against it.

More than ever, obviously, Frederick had to count on the consistent trump cards left to him, the quality of his troops and of his own generalship. As for the latter, he could find a certain consolation in recognition that his immediate opponents were leaders of decidedly mediocre qualifications. At the head of the Army of the Holy Roman Empire was a resoundingly titled nonentity, Joseph Frederick William (Josef Friedrich Wilhelm), Herzog von Saxe-Hildburghausen, *Generalfeldzeugmeister* of the Empire. His French coadjutor was Charles de Rohan, prince de Soubise, *maréchal de France,* who owed his position to the favor of Jeanne Antoinette Poisson le Normant d'Étoiles, marquise de Pompadour, the King's most persuasive mistress.

Nevertheless, Frederick's opponents maneuvered with fair skill as the rival armies converged, preventing the Prussians from securing any advantages of position. On the morning of November 5, in fact, the opposing forces lay en-camped in Saxony some eight miles (thirteen kilometers) southwest of Merse-burg, with the Allies able from their advanced posts to look from high ground down on the entire Prussian force. The latter faced west between the villages of Bedra on the north and Rossbach (or Rosbach) on the south. Rossbach was about to give its name to one of Frederick's most masterfully fought battles.

In view of their advantages of position and numbers, Hildburghausen and Soubise decided to attack. They disagreed, however, about the scope of the effort, Hildburghausen wanting an all-out engagement, Soubise apparently fear-ing Frederick enough to hope for a cautious, tentative action that might be broken off if matters went awry. The French commander's misgivings seem to account for the Allies' hesitating through much of the morning before commenc-ing their movements, and then their forces proved to be so unwieldy that break-ing camp consumed about three hours. After 11:00 A.M., however, they were finally on the march to attempt to play against Frederick the very game that he had employed at Prague, by marching across his front to form a new line perpen-dicular to his flank—albeit his left rather than his right—and then to roll up his line.

Frederick for some time deceived himself about the enemy's intentions, assuming that the Allies were retreating southward. The Allied van was nearly abreast of his left before he discerned the truth, but then he resolved immedi-ately to attack. Prussian discipline and training permitted his army to break camp and be on the move in half an hour, one-sixth the time the Allies had required. His opponents' complacent disregard of the differences in the qualities of the armies helped keep them unconcerned about the imminence of Freder-ick's riposte even when they learned that the Prussians were bestirring them-selves. The Allies plodded onward in column of march, two main columns, the first line of infantry on the left (nearest the Prussians), the second line of infan-try on the right, the reserve artillery between them, the reserve infantry farther to the right, the right-wing cavalry at the head of the columns, the left-wing cavalry patrolling the rear.

Frederick planned to march south and then west, either himself repeating his Prague maneuver by rolling up the enemy right if the Allies had deployed facing northward by the time he struck, or smashing the van of the enemy column if the Allies were still moving eastward. He actually hit them as they were beginning their turn to deploy northward, an awkward moment for them; and the Prussians were aided also by the fact that in the course of the Allies' earlier wheeling movement to bring themselves astride his original flank, their columns had fallen into confusion, getting too close together and even intermin-gled, and with some of the reserve infantry blundering into the path of the reserve artillery.

The Prussians advanced in their now-standard oblique order of battle, weighted toward the left, the better to roll up the enemy. On the extreme left came the Prussian cavalry under *Generalmajor* Friedrich Wilhelm Freiherr von Seydlitz, who had just crowned an already impressive combat record by helping lead the relief of Berlin, and to whom Frederick had entrusted overall command of the horse only that morning. Seydlitz was an inspirational battle captain; under his leadership thirty-eight squadrons of Prussian cavalry caught the van of the Allied army, mostly its own cavalry, in front and by the right flank. Achieving tactical surprise, Seydlitz's troopers enjoyed exactly the right circumstances for the exploitation of the mounted arm. Only a few enemy cavalry squadrons found time to deploy to meet them, and they swept the Allied vanguard into chaos.

By the time the first melee had ended and Seydlitz was rallying and reforming the horsemen, the Prussian infantry, weighted to complete the ruination of the Allied right, were descending upon enemy infantry already at least halfway demoralized by the spectacle of the rout of their cavalry. Again, a few Allied regiments managed to deploy, and several French infantry battalions displayed a tactic with which the French were experimenting, going into battle in column instead of in line, so that a heavy weight of troops from the rear could help sustain the momentum of the spearhead (although the column was likely still to retain more breadth than depth, a battalion column often forming up twelve deep with at least four times as many files as ranks of depth). The confusion into which the Allies had fallen when their march columns converged and became partially entangled with each other was too severe, however, to permit the deployment of an ordered defense, especially under the impact of fear. The Prussian infantry broke the countercharges of the French columns, and then Prussian musketry and artillery fire poured into the dense and already disordered enemy main body.

The Allies broke, and Seydlitz's cavalry returned to the charge at just the right moment to turn flight into another rout—yet one more display of the value of the refurbished Prussian mounted arm in a manner that extracted the highest possible advantages from a weapon whose utility was limited but could be decisive when its shock power and mobility were properly employed.

Except for the cavalry, little of the Prussian army was engaged at close quarters for any prolonged period in the battle of Rossbach. Frederick's losses were only about 550 against Allied casualties of some 7,700. Here at last was a Prussian battlefield victory of which it could be said that Frederick had contrived to impose the penalties of the expedient of battle mainly upon the enemy, while he himself scarcely suffered those penalties at all. Such an achievement alone would go far to raise Frederick the Great into the highest ranks of generalship.

The achievement was no ephemeral one, either. For once a decisive tactical triumph yielded comparable strategic advantage. Rossbach was at least as much an Imperial as a French defeat, but the lost battle proved to abate considerably such enthusiasm as the French had been able to generate for their unaccustomed alliance with the Habsburgs. Frederick had by no means swum out from his sea of troubles, but he could comfort himself that the shore might be in sight. France became a decidedly less active menace to him hereafter.

Rossbach developed an even longer-range significance in future years, when it came to be regarded as the first major victory of German arms over French, and as such it served as a foundationstone of German nationalism during the nineteenth century. This view of the battle obviously involved further disregard of the reality that Rossbach was at least as much a victory of Germans over

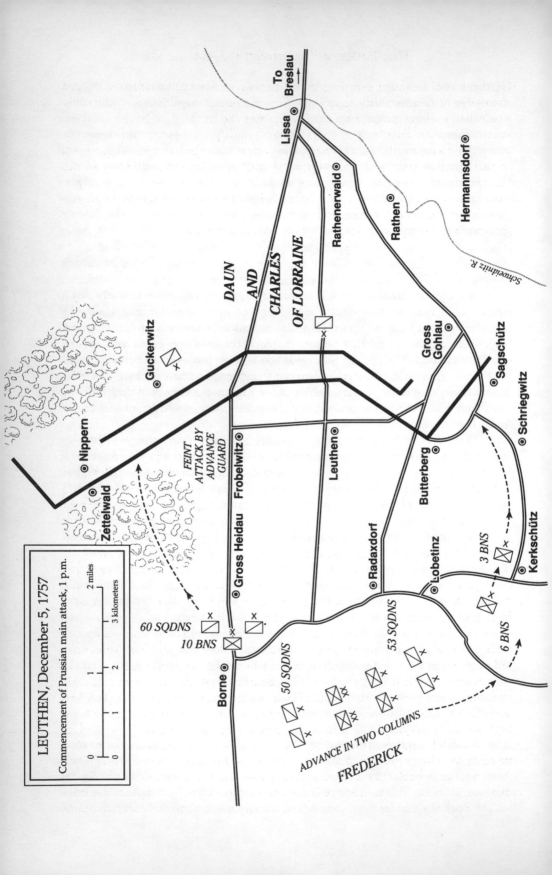

LEUTHEN, December 5, 1757

Commencement of Prussian main attack, 1 p.m.

2 miles

3 kilometers

2

1

1

2

0

0

To Breslau

Lissa ⊚

Rathenerwald ⊚

Rathen ⊚

Hermannsdorf ⊚

Schweidnitz R.

DAUN *AND* *CHARLES* *OF LORRAINE*

Gross Gohlau ⊚

Sagschütz ⊚

Schriegwitz ⊚

Guckerwitz ⊚

Nippern ⊚

Zettelwald ⊚

Leuthen ⊚

Frobelwitz ⊚

Butterberg ⊚

FEINT ATTACK BY ADVANCE GUARD

3 BNS

Kerkschütz ⊚

Gross Heidau ⊚

Radaxdorf ⊚

Lobetinz ⊚

6 BNS

60 SQDNS

10 BNS

50 SQDNS

53 SQDNS

Borne ⊚

ADVANCE IN TWO COLUMNS

FREDERICK

Germans as of Germans over French. To cast Frederick the Great in the role of champion of German nationalism was ironic, furthermore, because culturally Frederick strained to be French; French was his favored language, and he looked down his long nose at the German language as boorish. Yet Rossbach proved by no means the only occasion on which the advancement of the interests of the Prussian state was to be confused with advancing the interests of the German nation; far greater muddlings of those two interests were eventually to shape the movement toward a German nation-state, and the failure to distinguish what was good for Prussia from what was good for Germany was to have incalculable consequences for the history of war and peace.

Leuthen

Without the victory of Rossbach, Prussia's problems might have proven fatal. Even with Rossbach, Frederick had to press yet another march of 170 miles (274 kilometers) in twelve days to attempt to rescue Silesia. Prince Charles of Lorraine had led the Austrian Army to a series of small victories over the Prussian defenders of the Silesian duchies, pushing them across the Oder. Even while Frederick marched he learned that Breslau, encircled by the Austrians, had fallen to them. Urgency left the King no recourse to any semblance of supplying his marching columns from depots; the army candidly foraged off the land. The necessities of retaining a defense in the west allowed Frederick to bring fewer than 20,000 men, and when this force linked up with the Silesian army his total strength was only about 43,000, against some 72,000 Austrians. Nevertheless, the King decided he must attack. Because the circumstances were so bleak, he assembled his generals to explain to them this resolve while offering the opportunity to resign to any who thought his decision too much a surrender to desperation.

The small, stoop-shouldered, bulbous-eyed King in his habitually snuff-stained bluc uniform was not an imposing figure; but his defiance of adversity had lent him a magnetism well beyond the aura of kingship itself, and naturally no general resigned. Thus on December 5, 1757, Frederick led his army into the battle of Leuthen, named for a village in the center of the strongly entrenched high ground along which Charles's army lay, astride the road leading from the Prussian camps back to Breslau. Shielded from direct enemy observation by rolling hills, Frederick moved his forces to deploy in the customary oblique order of battle, weighted this time against the enemy's left, or south, flank.

A feint attack toward the Austrian center caused the enemy to focus his attention there. When the Prussian main attack came forward in echeloned battalions against Charles's left, consequently, the assailant again had the advantage of tactical surprise. The infantry combat nevertheless became heavy and its issue doubtful, until Austrian cavalry from Charles's right attempted to exploit mobility by riding around into the right rear of the Prussian infantry assault. The Austrian horse neglected adequate reconnaissance and instead of striking an exposed Prussian flank, found themselves ridden down by the hitherto concealed Prussian cavalry rear guard. The cavalry clash sent the Austrian horse retreating into their own infantry, which served to break the infantry's resistance and to award Frederick another triumph. Austrian casualties numbered about 25,000, including 20,000 prisoners taken by the Prussians along with 116 guns and 51 colors when the Austrian withdrawal collapsed into disorder. But Leuthen was not Rossbach; the Prussians themselves lost 6,200, which brought their total casualties in the battles and skirmishes of 1757 well over 50,000.

Still, Leuthen became another famous victory. Rossbach had already touched off a wave of admiration for Frederick in Great Britain, the islanders characteristically cheering for the underdog in a wave of enthusiasm that did not subside until in far-off Pennsylvania it planted a tavern whose identifying sign accounts for the curiously named Philadelphia suburb of King of Prussia. With Leuthen following close upon Rossbach, the British government in turn was encouraged enough to reach an agreement with Prussia in April 1758, promising Frederick an annual subsidy of £670,000 and pledging both powers not to conclude a separate peace.

Zorndorf and Hochkirch

The harsh casualty toll of 1757 meant that Frederick's position was nevertheless scarcely less precarious than ever. The Russians, however ponderously, had overrun much of East Prussia and were busy replacing any civil officials who failed to swear fealty to the Tsarina. Because first winter and then the mud accompanying the spring thaws would largely immobilize the Russians and also the Swedes for some months to come, Frederick chose to follow up Leuthen by continuing to campaign against the Austrians, beginning with the substantial reconquest of Silesia and pressing on into Moravia. But there the Prussian advance got stuck in front of the fortress city of Olmütz, which gave the Austrians the chance to use their irregulars from the Balkans—Croats, Pandours, and such, of whom they had hitherto not availed themselves in this war as they might have—to harry the Prussian line of communications. The result was that Frederick had to turn back against the Russians after all, lest they erupt from East Prussia and unite their forces with the Austrians.

A plundering Russian march that showed little regard for the notions of noncombatant immunity or of mitigating the horrors of war had advanced to Posen and into Neumark and had brought Küstrin under siege. The approach of Frederick's army prompted the Russians, about 42,000 strong, to lift the siege and take position on high ground behind the Mutzel River, facing north, about five miles (eight kilometers) northeast of Küstrin. There on August 14/25, 1758, Frederick challenged them, in the battle of Zorndorf, named for a village initially behind the Russian lines that eventually became a focus of the battle.

It became such because Frederick, as usual finding the enemy's prepared positions too formidable to assault directly, in equally customary fashion sought to march his 36,000 troops around their flank. On this occasion he reached the enemy rear, so that the Russians had to reverse the direction of their front. When Frederick struck them, they were deployed in three irregular squares, each on high ground but separated by marshy defiles.

Far from becoming another Rossbach, Zorndorf proved a yet more costly hecatomb than Leuthen. The Russians demonstrated themselves to be a more stubborn, indomitable soldiery than any Frederick's armies had yet faced— qualities destined to impress themselves on the Germans whenever they had the misfortune to contend against the armies of Muscovy no matter what the nature of the current Russian regime, however incompetent or brutal.

Frederick first attacked the westernmost square, but after prolonged fighting it was the Prussian and not the Russian infantry who were wavering—until Seydlitz, having worked his way with great difficulty across the Zaberngrund, a marsh shielding the Russians, managed to drive home a charge. Once more Prussia's premier horse-soldier intervened at the psychologically crucial moment, and the Russian square broke into retreat.

A similar conflict was already raging around what had been the Russians' central square, into which Frederick now threw much of the infantry from his left. Again it was the Prussians who first wavered, some of their units shattered and fleeing, and again it was Seydlitz's cavalry whose timely intervention reversed the momentum of the battle. While the Prussians then pushed forward energetically enough to rupture the square as a formation, however, they did not this time break the tenacity of the defenders. It was nightfall that halted the combat, not victory for either side.

The Prussians had lost 12,500 killed and wounded and about 1,000 missing, a casualty rate of 37.5 percent. The Russians lost a staggering 50 percent, 21,000 casualties. So Zorndorf was even worse than Prague in proportions of casualties and approached Malplaquet in absolute numbers of losses. Yet on the morning after, the Russians were standing again in defensive array a few miles north of the Zorndorf battlefield, while Frederick believed his army was too battered and weary to resume the attack.

After Zorndorf had dramatized again how desperate an expedient indeed the choice of battle as the means of seeking decision could be, the war again transposed itself into a series of maneuvers. Frederick fell back on relying on his position in the center of his adversaries—in the military lexicon as it was developing at officers' schools, his possession of the interior lines—to fend off enemy thrusts one by one (as the lexicon would have it, to deal with his enemies in detail). With Prussia's limited manpower resources already badly depleted, and with marching, fighting, and countermarching imposing a continual attrition, the plight of the Prussian kingdom became steadily more grave. Casualties had to be replaced by soldiers not yet trained to the usual Prussian standards. The loss of thirty-five general officers killed since 1756 put a greater burden than ever on the King himself, though in fact he had always tried to keep a tight personal hold on the reins of command and never relied much on the professional qualities of his subordinates. Frederick's sterling and maturing military abilities—drained, however, by a severely worsening case of gout, as well as by accumulating discouragement—could accomplish no more than to improvise one short-term remedy after another to prop open closing jaws that seemed more and more likely to clamp shut upon Prussia no matter what he might do.

From Zorndorf the King turned to face the Austrians and Daun. After a series of maneuvers during which that Austrian commander showed evasive skill but seemed to confirm his reputation for extreme caution, Frederick and some 37,000 Prussians were encamped on October 13, 1758, at Hochkirch in defense of Dresden. Daun lay in front of them with about 90,000 whom Frederick planned to assault in spite of the disparity in numbers. The Prussian camp was unforti-fied because of Daun's reputation; only a part of the cavalry even kept their horses saddled. Reassuringly, the Austrian watchfires remained burning through the night. But about five in the morning of October 14 Daun's troops came bursting in upon Frederick's camps from almost every direction.

As usual, Prussian discipline saved Frederick's army, not from defeat this time but at least from irremediable disaster. Such cavalry units as were reason-ably ready to fight were able to hold open an escape route, and through this avenue most of the army eventually contrived to withdraw, leaving behind 101 guns and losing 9,450 mean dead, wounded, or captured. Prussian discipline cost Daun 7,500 men in turn, but Austria could far better afford the loss.

Kunersdorf, Minden, Torgau

During the winter of 1758–1759 Frederick managed to hang on to Dresden in the face of Daun's siege; but when good campaigning weather re-turned in the spring the Austrians and Russians both planned to unite substan-tial portions of their forces and actually accomplished this purpose, notwithstanding Frederick's best preventive efforts. The juncture seemed to leave Frederick no alternative but to risk another battle; and so, as the enemy approached Frankfurt-an-der-Oder, Frederick marched to attack them.

He could muster only some 53,000 troops against an Austro-Russian force of 70,000. He found the Allies entrenched on sandhills above Kunersdorf, where he struck them on August 1/12, 1759. He delivered his main blow against the Rus-sians, who were especially well positioned and with their artillery on command-ing ground. Moreover, the Russians had devised an effective response to the oblique order of battle, which Frederick weighted against both their flanks in an effort to accomplish a double envelopment. The Russians had heavily weighted their center, making it an almost impregnable bastion, and one from which they could dispatch reinforcements as needed to either flank. Their design worked all the better because Frederick's attacking forces on both flanks lost their way in woods along the approach routes, so that the Prussian assaults were not deliv-ered simultaneously.

Frederick's first attacks failed, as did a series of subsequent blows, each delivered in a mood of growing dismay. The Prussian cavalry intervened but found the enemy insufficiently weakened to be moved, and any possible magic the horsemen might have woven departed when Seydlitz fell wounded. Instead, it was the Austrian cavalry that charged at the critical moment when the Prus-sians were despairing. The Prussian front broke. Frederick himself, who already had had two horses killed under him, clutched a regimental standard to help rally the troops; but he failed. The Prussian Army fled westward toward the

Oder. It had suffered 20,720 casualties and left behind 278 guns and 28 colors. Allied losses were about 15,700.

Prussian discipline, diluted though it now was, reasserted itself to permit the rallying of the army. Frederick nevertheless despaired of his cause. He informed Dresden, still under Austrian pressure, that it could expect no help; on September 12 the capital of Saxony capitulated. Yet Frederick's own rallied army proved strong enough for the time being to avert further calamity, with the aid of divergent Russian and Austrian war aims. The Russians would have liked to march to Berlin; the Austrians preferred to reconquer Silesia; the victorious partners of Kunersdorf went their separate ways.

A measure of relief came also from the west, where the French in 1759 had at last bestirred themselves to resume serious campaigning after their reverse at Rossbach, but where the British had also renewed their efforts on the strength of the impetus that William Pitt as Principal Secretary of State and virtual head of the government, the King's First Minister, was giving to the war against the French around the world. The victories that Pitt's energy had conjured up in North America helped encourage the British Cabinet to believe it could spare military resources for the Continent as well. On August 1, 1759, consequently, a combined Anglo-Hanoverian-Prussian army gave battle to the French at Minden (Münden) near the River Weser. The Prussians again faltered, but a brigade of British infantry drove home successfully an attack that they delivered at all only because of confusion in orders, and the Anglo-Prussian alliance won the day. Largely on the strength of this partial atonement for Kunersdorf, the Prussian and British governments initiated peace overtures in November.

The Austrians, for whom 1759 was a year of expanding hopes nourished at relatively low costs, led the way in rejecting a settlement, so that Frederick had to resume his weary dashes across the interior lines in 1760. His maneuvers were sufficiently adroit to permit him to avoid any costly battles through most of the year. But while he was fending off his enemies' major armies, Berlin fell again, to a mixed force of Cossacks, Austrians, and Imperial troops on October 9. Frederick's rapid march to its relief precipitated an Austrian concentration against him under Daun, whom Frederick chose to attack at Torgau on the east bank of the River Elbe on November 3.

Of all Frederick's full-scale battles, Torgau is the most difficult to explain in terms of the balance of the risks of battle to Prussia's fragile great-power status against any available advantages. As usual Frederick was outnumbered— 44,000 Prussians to 65,000 Austrians—and it is hard to imagine what he thought he might accomplish against the defensive capacities of Daun in, as usual, a well-entrenched position. To make matters worse, without Seydlitz the Prussian cavalry, scheduled to create a diversion to assist the main infantry attack, was itself diverted into a combat with the enemy's light troops. Predictably, the Prussian infantry assaults deteriorated into successive waves of slaughter. Late in the day the Austrians were driven back into the fortress of Torgau, whence they crossed to the west shore of the river, but Frederick achieved no gain in any way proportionate to his loss of 13,120 casualties (in exchange for 11,261 Austrian casualties).

The British, whose contingent of 20,000 helped again to hold off the French in 1760, had by now attained most of their overseas objectives against France and were growing understandably discouraged over the prospects of their continental ally. In 1761 they reduced their European troop contingent and threatened to discontinue their financial subsidies. With the Anglo-Prussian alliance thus tottering, the French overran Braunschweig (Brunswick) and Wolfenbüttel. In the east, Frederick's maneuvering could not ward off another juncture of the Austrians and the Russians, who for a time cut the communications between Frederick's main army in Silesia and Prussia itself. When William Pitt resigned as virtual head of the British Cabinet on October 5, Prussia's abandonment became practically complete. By this time the drain on Frederick's manpower had reduced the proportion of his own subjects in his army to about one-third of the total, and despite strenuous efforts in foreign recruitment the King would face 1761 with only some 60,000 soldiers.

The Miracle of the House of Brandenburg

As the embattled German Führer, Adolf Hitler, was often to recall in the early months of 1945, Prussia nevertheless escaped the disaster that even Frederick had come to believe inevitable. The miracle of the House of Brandenburg was precipitated by the death of the Tsarina Elizabeth on December 29, 1761/January 9, 1762. Her nephew and adopted son, the new Tsar Peter III (Pyotr Carlovich), happened to be a good-natured weakling who hero-worshipped the Prussian King because of Frederick's possession of qualities opposite to his own. Almost immediately Peter offered peace, and on March 5/16 Prussia and Russia agreed to an armistice. The subsequent agreement formalizing the peace was followed on June 8/19 by an offensive-defensive alliance, whereby the Tsar returned to Frederick all the territories that Russia had conquered and agreed to defend Frederick against all his enemies. Forthwith a contingent of 18,000 Russians was placed at the Prussian King's disposal.

Russia's defection from the anti-Prussian alliance also pulled Sweden out of the war, because that kingdom could not risk a new contest against Russia. Neither of Frederick's remaining enemies, Austria and France, was now much more eager for battle than the Prussians. French finances had been drained by a losing colonial struggle against Great Britain; and if Austria was far from being so sorely strained as Prussia, neither its military manpower nor its treasury could be described as robustly healthy. With Seydlitz again in the saddle and playing a conspicuous part, the Prussians won the relatively small-scale battle of Freiberg over the Army of the Holy Roman Empire on October 29.

Before that event, however, a fresh spasm of danger had shaken Prussia with another eccentric turn of events in Russia. Despotisms are unreliable partners; their policies can be overturned too quickly by overturning the despot. On June 28/July 9 Tsar Peter's wife, née Princess Sophia Augusta Frederica (Fürstin Sophie Auguste Friederike) of Anhalt-Zerbst, now called Catherine (Yekaterina) Aleksyevna, and her friends staged a coup d'état that compelled the feeble Tsar to abdicate. Nevertheless, the Tsarina Catherine II had no more desire to renew the spending of Russian resources for what she perceived as Austrian interests than to spend them for Prussian interests; for the present, Russia simply withdrew into isolation. The spasms of renewed peril subsided.

No one else still considered the game of destroying Prussia to be worth the candle, either. Had they been empowered to foresee the future, the leaders of Prussia's rivals might have thought otherwise. As it was, the conclusion of a separate peace between Great Britain and France at Fontainebleau on November 3, 1762, opened the way to both the Treaty of Paris of February 10, 1763, establishing a general peace with France, and to the Austro-Imperial-Prussian Treaty of Hubertusburg of February 15, 1763. For Prussia, the settlement essentially restored the *status quo ante bellum,* including retention of Silesia and acceptance as one of the great powers.

This acceptance did not of course change the fragility of Prussia's great-power status. Even with the extraordinary abilities and exertions of Frederick the Great, Prussia at the beginning of 1762 would probably have been doomed to inconsequence had the Tsarina Elizabeth lived. Within another half century Prussia was to be virtually swept from the European chessboard. But by that time the memory of Frederick the Great had brought a new dimension to Prussia's role in Germany. The aura created by Frederick had grown to shield physical brittleness with a moral strength and resilience such that the elimination of Prussia as a major power could no longer be permanent. Inspired by the image of Frederick as the great German soldier and by the military-political *tour de force* that his predecessors from the Great Elector onward had begun and that he had brought to so imposing a fruition, yet bolder and more imaginative military reformers were to raise the Prussian Army from the ashes of near-extinction and thereby to raise the Prussian state itself—its fate still inseparable from its army—to a new vitality.

But the vitality was to remain distinctly military in almost all its sources of energy, and the fact was to be of fateful importance to the entire world. Under Frederick, Prussia, living by the sword, had nearly perished by the sword. The brush with disaster did not, however, impel this modern Sparta to change its ways. Its claim to greatness continued to be principally one of greatness in war. And on that foundation, inspired also by the memory of Frederick the Great and by the legend that he had won the first modern German military triumphs over the French, was to be built in time a unified German state. This state would command far greater population and resources than Frederick's Prussia; but like Prussia, it was to live and die by the sword. In the process, the Prussian-German state was also to refine the standards of the profession of officership to an unprecedented degree, and that development in turn was to influence greatly the coming shape of war and particularly the effort to limit the violence of war.

Armies and Warfare in the Time of Frederick the Great

Frederick contributed little directly to the development of the profession of officership. He did seek to instruct his officers through written codification of his military precepts as well as through personal instruction of his senior commanders and by maintaining Prussia's military schools. In time his military writings came to be much studied among professional officers.[2] As a military commander, however, Frederick kept so close a control over almost every detail of his army and its campaigns—superintending as carefully as distance permitted even those armies that were fending off whichever enemies he was not himself confronting at any given moment—that the professional and intellectual development of his officers was decidedly restricted.

Of course, the professional attainments of his officers were honed by experience and by reflections on the experience. But otherwise, the development of officership as a profession was remarkably stagnant in the Prussia of Frederick the Great. In addition to preferring his own detailed control of both operations and administration over the development of responsibility and discretionary authority among his subordinates, Frederick favored aristocratic lineage over education as a criterion for entry and advancement in his officer corps. The essential simplicity of his military methods, the precise and resilient discipline of his soldiery and the tactic of the oblique order of battle, permitted this relative neglect of intellect and study. So did the strategic reality that through most of his campaigns Frederick was improvising under pressure, devising short-run solutions to immediate emergencies, rather than applying coherent long-range designs. It is significant that Frederick's most famous subordinate was the cavalry commander Seydlitz, a bold battle captain outstanding for the instinctive timing of his attacks and for gallant inspirational leadership rather than for acuteness or depth of intellect.

For the further development of the profession of officership, we must turn to armed forces less spectacular in their eighteenth-century feats of valor than the Prussian Army, and probably a degree less meticulous in the preciseness of their training and battlefield evolutions, but for various reasons more generous in their encouragement of the thoughtful officer.

Although the wars of Frederick the Great had grown for a time grandiose rather than limited in aim, with the intent of at least some of Frederick's enemies to destroy Prussia as a great power, the means of waging war had remained more restrained and more in harmony with the conception of the just war than they had been through much of the era of Louis XIV. The contest between Frederick and those who sought the downfall of Prussia remained a contest whose principal means consisted of careerist armies, with little resort to other instruments and little violation of the critical limiting principle of noncombatant immunity by the contending armies.

That culture of the French Age of the Enlightenment which spanned the military rivalries between Versailles and Potsdam saw the universe as a structure

---

2. See in particular Friedrich II, *Œuvres de Frédéric II, roi de Prusse. Publiées du vivant de l'auteur* . . . (4 vols., Berlin: Voss et fils . . . , 1787); *Instruction militaire du roi de Prusse pour ses generaux.* (Traduit de l'allemand par M. [Georg Rudolph] Faesch, lieut. col. des troupes saxones . . . , Frankfurt [an der Oder] & Leipsic: No publisher, 1761), a translation of *Die Instrukcion Friedrichs des Grossen für seine Generale von 1747* (Berlin: No publisher); *Military Instructions from the Late King of Prussia to His Generals. To Which is Added, (By the Same Author) Particular Instructions to the Officers of His Army, and Especially Those of the Cavalry.* (Translated from the French, by Lieut. [Thomas] Foster, Sherborne: W. Cruttwell, [1797]).

of balance and harmony, wherein rational humankind ought to bring its institutions into consistency with the rational functionings of a world governed by natural law. The possibly irrational desire of Vienna to lay low the upstart in Berlin notwithstanding, the armies of the middle eighteenth century and their method of warfare attained a remarkable congruence with the other institutions and values of an age trying to guide itself by the light of reason. If disputes between states became sufficiently intractable that they had to be submitted to the arbitrament of war, still the arbitration did not entail any all-consuming destructiveness; it was conducted rather by men who had more or less volunteered (less rather than more among the rank-and-file soldiers) to take upon themselves the risks of arbitration by violence. And these risk-takers confined their violent attentions mainly to each other. In the Age of Reason, the irrationalities of war were at least strenuously and strictly confined.

More specifically, this Age of Reason saw little resort to economic warfare, to blockades and restraint of trade. European business went on remarkably little affected by the military rivalries. Restraint of cultural interchange was even more minimal; Frederick's court remained a center of admiration for and patronage of French Enlightenment thought throughout, with French continuing as the language of the court. The opposing armies maintained rules against unnecessary endangerment of noncombatant lives and property, especially against plundering civilians, and they sought with fair success to enforce the rules. The limitations of supply using wagons over primitive roads from depots laboriously constructed in the rear necessitated frequent subsisting of armies from the foodstuffs of the territories through which they campaigned, or at least supplementing depot supply in that manner, but vigorous efforts were made to feed men and animals through orderly purchases and not by plunder. When in 1757 Louis François Armand du Plessis, duc de Richelieu, *maréchal de France,* allowed his Army of the Lower Rhine to become marauders through the countryside from which the formation took its name, such conduct was enough out of the ordinary that Richelieu came to be known disparagingly as *Père la maraude.*[3] (It made no difference that the logistical system supporting him had broken down largely through no fault of his, and that his army was destitute.) Europeans of the eighteenth century were expected to wage war with moderation and within civilized limits.

3. Lee Kennett, *The French Armies in the Seven Years' War: A study in military organization and administration* (Durham, N.C.: Duke University Press, 1969), p. 84, citing Charles Duclos, *Mémoires secrets sur le régne de Louis XIV, la régence et le régne de Louis XV* (Nouvelle Édition, Augmentée . . . , 2 vols., Paris: J. Gay, 1864), II, 287.

THE FRENCH AND BRITISH ARMED FORCES FROM THE RHINE TO THE ST. LAWRENCE

The Spanish, seeking under the aggressive political leadership of Giulio Cardinal Alberoni to recapture their former preeminence in the Mediterranean, poured troops into Sicily early in 1717 in violation of the peace terms of Utrecht. Their purpose was to reconquer from Savoy this island that had in the past been a sparkling jewel in their crown. Their venture precipitated a rare moment of cooperation among all three of the greatest powers, France, Austria, and Great Britain, to prevent so early a rupture of the recently reestablished equilibrium of European power.

On July 19/30 a British fleet under Vice-Admiral Sir George Byng sighted a Spanish squadron in the Straits of Messina. The Spaniards fled, and Byng ordered a general chase. The pursuit continued through the night, and the next morning the leading British ships at last began to overtake the sternmost Spanish off Cape Passero. A running battle ensued, in which the circumstances precluded fighting in line-ahead formation. Instead, the chase resolved itself into multiple small duels, in which the British gradually overwhelmed their opponents by weight of numbers. The battle of Cape Passero was probably the first in modern naval history in which the chase was the principal tactic employed. Unfortunately for the possibilities of stimulating naval professional growth, the shape of the combat was so much dictated by circumstance that this battle brought no loosening of the tyranny of the line ahead.

But if naval professional development remained as stagnant as the professional growth of the officer corps of Frederick the Great, events at sea nevertheless colored almost everything else that occurred militarily in the two westernmost European powers during the eighteenth century. France in this century shifted its main ambitions from the continental designs of Louis XIV to its imperial rivalry with Britain overseas; witness the halfheartedness of the French contribution to the struggle against Frederician Prussia. Yet in the imperial contest, the French Army's continued impressive professional development upon the foundation laid by the Roi soleil could avail little without naval success. And at sea, the eighteenth century witnessed Great Britain's sealing of the naval verdict of the War of the Spanish Succession by establishing an enduring naval preponderance. The Royal Navy's increasingly assured mastery of the seas frustrated the efforts of the French Army to assert its professional leadership in the wars for overseas empire. Behind the shield of British naval power, furthermore, the British Army proceeded to develop its own contribution to the rise of the British Empire, a contribution substantial in spite of the small scale of the army. Indeed, in quality there was more to the British Army than the bumbling amateurism that is all that some historians have perceived in it.

The Royal Navy in the Early Eighteenth Century

The grasp of British sea power encompassed more and more of the globe. In the Mediterranean, the sequel to Byng's victory at Cape Passero was the same admiral's convoying an Austrian army to Sicily to chase the Spanish home. Almost simultaneously, the Royal Navy intervened in the Great Northern War, somewhat paradoxically on the side of Cardinal Alberoni's principal ally, Sweden. The governing consideration in the north, however, was assuring Britain's supply of Baltic timber, spars, hemp, and tar, essential to the Royal Navy notwithstanding considerable success in developing alternative, North American sources. By 1716 the Great Northern War had already created a shortage of naval stores, by curtailing shipments from both Sweden and Russia. It was vital for Britain to maintain Swedish sources; it was highly desirable to prevent any one power from dominating the Baltic and thus potentially monopolizing the supply. Therefore in 1716 Britain concluded a mutual assistance treaty with Sweden, and an Anglo-Dutch squadron sailed into the Baltic to help protect Sweden in the naval phase of its war, which meant especially against the Danish fleet. British intervention contributed to Sweden's surviving the backlash stirred up by the ambitions of Charles XII. From the Great Northern War onward it became the settled policy of the British government to assert a naval presence in the Baltic whenever the balance of power there might be threatened.

The substitute North American sources meanwhile were being developed under the stimulus of an act of Parliament of 1705 for the encouragement of the naval stores industry in the Northern colonies. This measure provided bounties for the colonial production and shipment to England of pitch, resin, tar, turpentine, ship timber, masts, and hemp. It placed these products on the list of enumerated articles, which were permitted to be exported only to England and its possessions and colonies (after the Act of Union of 1707, Scotland came to be included). It also provided that pine trees in the forests of New England, New Jersey, and New York should be reserved for naval stores; agents under the energetic John Bridger were soon axing the symbol of the King's arrow into selected specimens of such trees, and increasingly—despite the unpopularity of this restriction among colonial entrepreneurs—it was North American pine trees that towered up as the masts of the Royal Navy.

The outward reach of British naval power was by no means shaped by consistent strategic conceptions. Strategic thought remained stunted—certainly in part because of the dearth of tactical thought on which to build—and too often the uses to which sea power was put were eccentric and unproductive. In the imperial war that broke out against Spain in 1739—the War of Jenkins's Ear—in 1744 merged into the War of Austrian Succession, the most conspicuous British naval effort was decidedly ill conceived. It was the Cartagena expedition of 1741. Vice-Admiral Edward Vernon was dispatched to assail the largest and richest city in Spanish America, Cartagena (or Carthagena) in the Viceroyalty of New Granada (Nueva Granada). Vernon arrived on February 26, 1740/March 8, 1741, just in time for the fever season. He landed over 8,000 troops in marshes near the city, 3,600 of them newly recruited and scarcely disciplined Americans. The principal outcome was to sicken and kill the soldiers with tropical fevers and occasional futile assaults, until the expedition withdrew—but not before the commanders forced the sick and the sickening to languish for days in hot and overcrowded ships lingering at anchor in Cartagena harbor, thus aggravating the death toll. Of the Americans, no more that 600 survived, and the mortality rate among the British soldiers was little less severe. Followup attacks on Santiago de Cuba and Panamá became only slightly less tragic fiascos. (Admiral Vernon himself nevertheless impressed sufficiently one of the American officers at Cartagena, Captain Lawrence Washington, that Washington named his Virginia plantation Mount Vernon).

With strategy thus given over to enterprises of doubtful long-range value even had they succeeded, tactical thought under the dead hand of the line-ahead principle proved hardly more efficacious. In this respect matters went from bad to worse in the aftermath of Admiral Thomas Mathews's battle of January 31, 1743/February 11, 1744, against the French Toulon fleet along with a Spanish squadron of twelve of the line.

Mathews was both naval commander in the Mediterranean and plenipotentiary to the King of Sardinia and the other courts of Italy, with no discernible qualification for either position save social influence. He was of so furious a temper that the Italians call him *Il Furibondo*, and he was not on good terms with several of his immediate subordinates, most notably the second in command, Vice-Admiral Richard Lestock.

Great Britain and France were not yet officially at war; but when the Spanish squadron, transporting troops to Genoa, was forced by the British into Toulon, Louis XV ordered the Toulon fleet of sixteen of the line to escort them the rest of the way—but without fighting the British. With the latter proviso in mind the French wanted to scatter the Spanish ships among their own. The Spanish, however, refused, and the vessels of the Bourbon allies sailed forth in three divisions, French ships in the van, more French ships in the center but with two Spaniards bringing up their rear, and Spanish ships alone forming the third division. Admiral Mathews with thirty sail of the line came up with this aggregation at daybreak off Hyères. He went into action at 1:30 in the afternoon, when his leading ship was abreast of the center ship of the enemy. Accounts differ regarding the signal or signals Mathews hoisted. With his own, central division of the British fleet, in any event, he broke the sacred line ahead and closed upon the Spanish. He may have been concerned that the French ships, fresh from the yards and with clean bottoms, might outsail any effort to continue his pursuit until he caught up with them; he might have wanted to fight only the Spanish because his country and France were not formally at war. Whatever his signals and intentions, he created confusion in much of his fleet. Admiral Lestock lagged behind with the British rear division and remained merely an onlooker.

Mathews nevertheless gave the Spanish ships a heavy pounding, and one of them, the *Poder*, 60, was captured (but then recaptured and finally sunk by the British). The French van meanwhile engaged the leading English division in spite of the absence of formal war and of the King's instructions, but at medium to long range and relatively harmlessly. When the French attempted to come about to catch the British between two fires, Mathews ordered his ships to turn as well and thus broke off the battle; by now his flagship, *Namur*, 90, was badly damaged.

It is an understatement, and an indication of the self-satisfaction with which Great Britain by now expected nothing less than undiluted triumph in every naval battle, to say that Parliament and Court were displeased by the tininess of the dividends from this action and particularly by the contributory indecision and disarray of the British fleet. No less than twenty courts-martial and a parliamentary inquiry issued from the event. One of the trials was that of Admiral Lestock, who was acquitted on the ground that he had obeyed Mathew's orders, which was probably the literal truth. Then Mathews himself was brought to trial, convicted of numerous breaches of duty, and cashiered. The long-term result, however, was the deleterious one of strengthening the grip of the line ahead, for the basic verdict against Mathews was that he should not have engaged until his van ship was abreast of the leading ship of the enemy. That is, the court assumed that clinging to line-ahead tactics would have avoided the confusion, and thereby the court warned all subsequent naval commanders that they departed from the line ahead only at grave legal risk.

Altogether, the naval battle of Toulon implies that the Royal Navy's eighteenth-century supremacy rested, beyond mere numbers of vessels, less on the qualitative attainments of the British fleet than on the generally worse ineptitude of the enemy. Granting that at Toulon the French were also constrained and confused by the ambiguous diplomatic situation, the French fleet did not garland itself with tactical laurels either; the British easily evaded its maneuver when it attempted to double up on them.

The Rising of "the Forty-Five"

To be sure, not every British naval leader was out of the same mold as the indecisive Mathews. In command of the Channel Fleet was Admiral Sir John Norris. Norris saw to the alert observation of France's Brest fleet, which was under the command of Jacques Aymar, comte de Roquefeuil, *chef d'escadre* (roughly the equivalent of a British rear-admiral). The Channel Fleet was ready to respond promptly to any French movement when in February 1743/1744 Roquefeuil emerged with twenty sail, intending to rendezvous at Dunkirk with an army under the formidable Marshal Saxe, to embark that army for a Channel crossing and the invasion of England in anticipation of a declaration of Anglo-French war. The "Young Pretender," Prince Charles Edward Stuart, grandson of James II, had come to Gravelines from Italy to join in the expedition and assert his claim to the British throne.

In spite of Norris's vigilance and readiness, Roquefeuil succeeded in making his rendezvous and embarking most of Saxe's army, accomplishing the latter part of his task in spite also of the difficulty of doing so across the open Dunkirk beaches (a difficulty imposed, it will be remembered, by the Peace of Utrecht). But on February 25/March 7 Norris arrived off Dunkirk with twenty-five sail of the line. His intent was to hit the troopships first.

Unfortunately for the British, the turn of the tide in the afternoon obliged Norris to anchor before he could attack. Roquefeuil, however, had been nervous from the beginning about challenging the British in the Channel (in part another legacy of the Peace of Utrecht, which left the French Navy with no haven in these waters nearer than Brest). Immediately upon Norris's arrival, Roquefeuil had already decided to take flight; the deficiencies of the enemy again came to the assistance of the British. In late evening the French fleet weighed anchor or cut its cables and without lights began to drift silently down the Channel on the ebb tide. In the process, the troopships were abandoned. About midnight a strong wind blew up, quickly freshening to gale force and continuing through the next day. The gale scattered both of the rival fleets and wrecked and grounded a number of the French transports. Roquefeuil's ships gradually straggled into Brest, but Norris's vigilance, abetted by the kind of weather to be expected in the Channel in winter, had squelched France's design for invasion.

The Young Pretender, "Bonnie Prince Charlie," was not, however, squelched. In the autumn of 1715 his father, "the Old Pretender," Prince James Francis Edward, had landed in northern Scotland, his standard as James VIII of Scotland having already been raised by John Erskine, sixth or eleventh Earl of Mar. The Stuart line after all had been first a Scottish dynasty; the Scots were restive under the Hanoverian succession of 1714, and many of them considered James their King over the water. Mar's bungling leadership had begun to turn this rising of "the Fifteen" into a fiasco even before James arrived, and the Old Pretender had soon fled; but Charles thought he could manage better. Undeterred by the unwillingness of the French to try again after the Dunkirk episode, the Prince sailed from France in the summer of 1745 in the privateer *Du Teillay*, escorted by the French warship *Elizabeth*, 60, with nine companions and some weapons and money. On July 12/23 he landed on the Scottish island of Eriskey.

The way was supposed to have been prepared for him by a Jacobite association, but in fact this group had accomplished little in Scotland and almost nothing in England. Rather, they had grown thoroughly discouraged about their

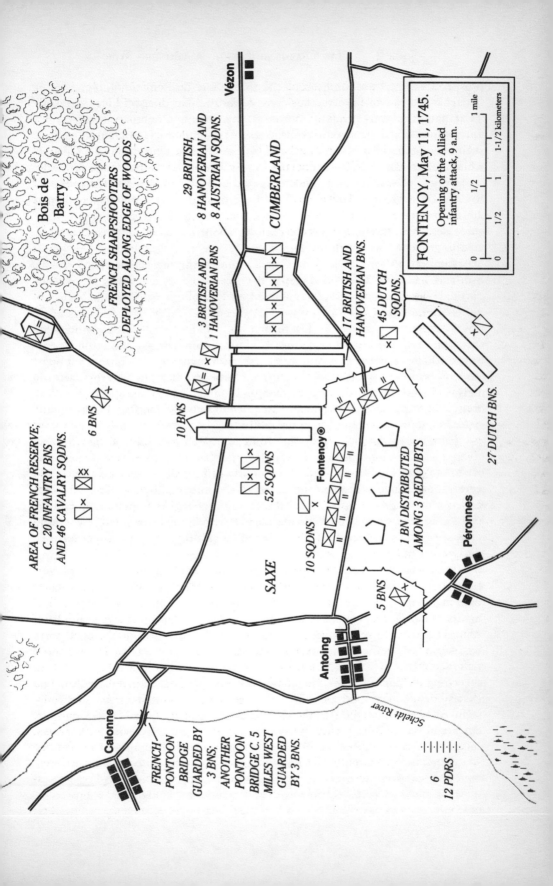

Bois de Barry

FRENCH SHARPSHOOTERS DEPLOYED ALONG EDGE OF WOODS

Vézon

29 BRITISH, 8 HANOVERIAN AND 8 AUSTRIAN SQDNS.

3 BRITISH AND 1 HANOVERIAN BNS

CUMBERLAND

17 BRITISH AND HANOVERIAN BNS.

45 DUTCH SQDNS.

27 DUTCH BNS.

FONTENOY, May 11, 1745.

Opening of the Allied infantry attack, 9 a.m.

| 0 | 1/2 | 1 | 1-1/2 kilometers |
| 0 | 1/2 | 1 mile | |

AREA OF FRENCH RESERVE; C. 20 INFANTRY BNS AND 46 CAVALRY SQDNS.

6 BNS

10 BNS

52 SQDNS

Fontenoy⊙

1 BN DISTRIBUTED AMONG 3 REDOUBTS

10 SQDNS

SAXE

5 BNS

Péronnes

Antoing

Calonne

FRENCH PONTOON BRIDGE GUARDED BY 3 BNS; ANOTHER PONTOON BRIDGE C. 5 MILES WEST GUARDED BY 3 BNS.

Scheldt River

6 12 PDRS

prospects and had tried to head off the Prince's arrival with a lugubrious letter that chanced not to have reached him. Nevertheless, the appealing, debonair spirit and handsome, athletic person of the Bonnie Prince—not yet turned twenty-five—soon attracted recruits. Some Highland chiefs brought in parts of their clans, especially MacDonalds and Camerons; and after raising his red-and-white silk standard at Glenfannon, the Prince was presently marching south with some 1,300 men, albeit mostly little trained and ill armed. At Perth a veteran soldier, Lord George Murray, joined the rising; the Prince appointed him a lieutenant-general, and he was to prove the architect of the rising's military successes, even though he was too realistic about the ultimate prospects to be able to get along well with the Prince.

Lieutenant-General Sir John Cope, commanding the Hanoverian forces in Scotland, had fewer than 4,000 men in the entire country, excluding garrisons of "invalids," veterans more or less disabled, at Edinburgh, Stirling, and Dumbarton Castles. All of Cope's troops were of uncertain quality, and there was not a Royal Artilleryman in the lot. Distrusting his strength—the civil authorities ordered him into the Highlands against his better judgment—Cope responded to Prince Charles's advance by retiring quickly into Inverness. His retreat left open the road between Charles and Edinburgh. On September 5/16 the rebels accordingly occupied the Scottish capital unopposed, and Charles was able to establish himself in the Palace of Holyroodhouse. (The Grand Union flag, however, still looked down on Edinburgh from the castle.)

Cope meanwhile had taken ship from Aberdeen to Leith and then formed his troops at Prestonpans to resist Charles's further advance. There on September 10/21 Cope's judgement about the quality of his troops was confirmed; they were routed. Cope probable contributed to the outcome by overestimating the Prince's force of some 2,500, about the same number that Cope himself had on hand, as at least 5,000 strong; this idea and their general's redoubled discouragement seem to have seeped down to many of Cope's men. But the main source of Hanoverian military weakness in Scotland and the real foundation for the rising of "the Forty-Five"—as distinguished from the feeble efforts of the Jacobite association—were to be found elsewhere. Most of the British Army's best troops were in Flanders. General Cope promptly became a figure of ridicule, but the quality of his soldiers and his lack of guns and gunners meant that it would have required a commander of exceptional ability to halt the Jacobites' initial progress. Cope was certainly not such a general, but neither was he a dunce or a coward.

Great Britain's further military problem was that Marshal Saxe had not lapsed into idleness after Dunkirk but instead had mounted an overland campaign eastward, into the Austrian Netherlands, which Louis XV proposed to annex and which therefore had become the point of friction assuring the extension of the War of the Austrian Succession into an Anglo-French conflict. On the Continent, the backdrop to the Forty-Five was the fiercely contested battle of Fontenoy, of April 30/May 11, 1745, a classic among battles in its case-study demonstrations of certain problems of command, and in the high drama of its incidents.

Fontenoy

Saxe had begun by laying siege to the fortress city of Tournai. To the relief of Tournai marched an Allied army, English, Scottish, Hanoverian, Austrian, and Dutch, under the command of George II's captain-general and second son, the Duke of Cumberland. Cumberland had been raised to become Lord High Admiral and had sailed in 1740 under Sir John Norris; but he had not found the sea to his liking, and in 1742 shifted to the army. Commissioned a major-general in December, he fought in company with his father at Dettingen, where on June 16/27, 1743, George II defeated the French in the last major battle in which a British monarch personally took part (in fact an almost pathetic incident; the King was a small, dull, unimpressive personage who waved his sword about to no particular purpose). Cumberland was wounded at Dettingen, but not before displaying bravery and tactical capacities that made his prompt promotion to lieutenant-general, and then to captain-general for 1745, not simply the fruits of nepotism. Now at twenty-four the Duke marched against Saxe with the English portion of his army, at least, bonded by its leader's combination of discipline stern enough to rival the Prussians' together with inspirational energy and command presence. Cumberland had studied and prepared for war from boyhood, and he possessed remarkable qualities of resolution and decisiveness for one so young, along with an acute eye for tactical advantage.

When word of Cumberland's approach toward Tournai reached Versailles, King Louis XV and the Dauphin Louis hastened to join Saxe in confronting him. Saxe, a bastard son of King Augustus II of Saxion, had been present at Malplaquet with the army of Prince Eugène. He was fifty-one and prematurely aged by hard campaigning and hard living as well as by dropsy; but while he could no longer mount a horse he could still dominate a campaign. A student of the art of war, he represented the best of the professional attainments that Louis XIV had nourished in the French officer corps. With exemplary speed he responded to Cumberland's advance by selecting and strongly fortifying a position on a high plateau along the right bank of the River Scheldt.

Here his line formed a rectangle, one side of it stretching two and a quarter miles (three and a half kilometers) northeast to southwest between the villages of Ramecroix and Antoing. Thence the line ran east somewhat over a mile (about one and three-quarters kilometers) to the village of Fontenoy, thence almost due north to the Wood of Barry, and thence less than a mile (a bit more that a kilometer) back to Ramecroix. Antoing and Fontenoy were especially heavily fortified; three redoubts were established between these two villages. Two redoubts protected the Bois de Barry where it formed a tip pointing toward Fontenoy. But Saxe deliberately refrained from fortifying the half mile (.8 kilometer) between Fontenoy and the wood, because he did not want to waste resources, and he believed that the marshy ravine that ran through this sector was for practical purposes impassable. He did, however, deploy the brigade-strength *Gardes Françaises* in front of the ravine as insurance.

Louis XV arrived to endorse Marshal Saxe's dispositions, to visit his troops, and to spend the night of April 29–30/May 10–11 in spirited conversation with their chieftains. The King was only thirty-five, the Dauphin fifteen, and they recalled that not since the battle of Poitiers on September 18, 1356, had a French King and his son fought side by side. The omen was not a cheerful one, because Poitiers had been a humiliating French defeat during which the English had captured King John (Jean) II (while King John's son and comrade the Dauphin Charles had not lived long enough to ascend the throne). But the French were optimistic that under Saxe's leadership they could hardly fail to win the battle they anticipated for the next day. In spite of the memory of Marlborough and of the recent defeat at Dettingen, they did not recognize that the probably superior qualifications of Saxe over Cumberland might not compensate for the persisting superiority of the British infantry over the French in discipline and tactical proficiency.

The Allies had about 46,000 men on the field, the French about 50,000. Preliminary skirmishing had revealed to Cumberland the gap in the French fortifications between Fontenoy and the Bois de Barry. The plan on which he and his commanders determined called for the Dutch to attack between Antoing and Fontenoy, while Cumberland with his British troops attacked Fontenoy and the opening between that village and the wood. Initially, there was also to be a cavalry attack swinging around to the north of the wood, but this element was abandoned when on the evening of the 29th/10th the Allied light cavalry drew fire from the southern edge of the wood. Cumberland then ordered the cavalry to form a screen for the infantry in front of Fontenoy. The disposition of the shock arm with its potential for decisiveness was to prove critical in the events that followed.

Only the next morning did the Allies discover that there was a redoubt at the top of the Bois de Barry. Opening a series of attacks about 5:30 A.M., Cumberland ordered Brigadier James Ingoldsby's Highland brigade to assail this strongpoint; but French troops concealed in the wood and covering the redoubt were not discovered until they poured a devastating fire into the Highlanders, and this development along with less than energetic leadership by Ingoldsby caused the attack to fail. Similarly, the Dutch failed to push home their attack against Antoing. British and Dutch troops together, while pressing farther forward more resolutely than the other Allied forces, failed to make any real headway against Fontenoy. Briefly, success seemed about to reward the charge of a battalion newly recruited in the Scottish Highlands in the hope of diverting the clans' thirst and talent for war into Hanoverian service—the Black Watch, at the time the 43rd Regiment of Foot; but there was not enough support.

These setbacks reinforced Cumberland's resolve to stage his main attack along the ravine that Saxe thought practically impassable—a resolve that was about to produce one of the most dramatic episodes of British military history. The Duke formed some 15,000 English, Scottish, and Hanoverian infantry into a compact mass probably of some 500 yards (or meters) by 600 yards (or meters). The English infantry initially deployed into two lines, with the Hanoverians on their left. But the narrowness of the defile through which the attack must pass caused the latter to form a third line behind the English, while the Scottish battalions of Ingoldsby's brigade—Ingoldsby himself was out of action, wounded—formed on their flanks. Closing on their center, the Allied infantry next compressed their formation further still so that three ranks became six. A few guns were to accompany them, and cavalry was to follow. The Duke of Cumberland, a believer in personal leadership, already paunchy of girth and unhealthily florid of countenance but physically vigorous for all that, put himself at the head of this compact column of assault; such a procedure, however inspirational, would no longer have been recommended by the more astute professional officers, for reasons that will become apparent.

The purpose, of course, was to strike the French line with so irresistibly compact a formation that the line would break. The fate of this kind of infantry attack, like Frederick the Great's infantry assaults, was now as it had been since the invention of the bayonet likely to be determined by firepower and discipline. The enemy infantry would all be armed with muskets, except for NCO's and officers who still carried edged weapons as emblems of rank; there were no longer pikemen to dilute the defender's ability to lay down volleys of fire, and the question was whether the discipline and training of the attacking infantry would prove sufficient to sustain their cohesion so that they could rupture the defender's line. Artillery would play a part, but guns mobile enough to be transported to and maneuver on the battlefield—largely three-pounders (1.361 kilograms) (2.91 inches or 73.914 mm) or six-pounders (2.721 kilograms) (3.66 inches or 92.914 mm)—were still small enough and limited enough in their range that the artillery role was rarely decisive (though at Prestonpans the soldiers of George II might not have broken if they had enjoyed any semblance of adequate artillery support; there the artillery role had perhaps been decisive in a negative sense).

To enhance the prospects of breaking the defenders' line, the attacking infantry still came forward marching as if on parade, the better to foster cohesion, and with drums beating and colors flying—and among Scottish troops with pipes skirling—the better to overawe the defenders. Because the accurate range of muskets and artillery remained minimal, there was no question of concealment, and uniforms remained brightly colored and much ornamented not only to ease identification of friends or foes but also to assist in creating an imposing spectacle that might demoralize the defenders.

The configuration of the ravine leading to the French line was such that Cumberland's majestically advancing column was subjected to flanking fire from the beginning and soon fully enfiladed by French guns laying down a converging fire. The effect was to drive the attacking infantry, discipline notwithstanding, to form still more tightly on its center, its column growing yet more compact.

At Fontenoy, this pattern of battle as spectacular theater reached an apogee as Cumberland's advance paused on reaching a low crest. At this point the French commanders decided that their fire had done enough damage to Cumberland's numbers and morale that the time was ripe for the *Gardes Françaises* to rise up and advance to meet the attack, adding the shock effect of their own charge to the havoc already wrought by defensive firepower. As the French came forward, Captain Lord Charles Hay of the First (Grenadier) Guards is supposed to have run out in front of his troops, doffed his hat to the enemy, and pulled out a pocket flask to toast them, saying, "We hope you will stand till we come up to you, and not swim the river as you did at Dettingen."[1] He then led his men in three cheers. The French knew not what to do except to shout a counter-cheer. Tradition has it that Captain Lord Hay next invited the French to fire first, an invitation that was declined.

If the legend is true, the invitation need not have been merely a quixotic gesture, for if the French fired first the Allies would have tried to drive home their charge while the French were still engaged in the time-consuming process of reloading. For this reason, in fact, the *Gardes Françaises* had long been under orders not to fire first. In this particular instance, however, withholding fire was not necessarily a wise tactic, because the French, having advanced from their defenses to meet the British, were as exposed as the British. The British forthwith fired a series of volleys by companies, a curtain of fire that is supposed to have struck fifty officers and 760 men of three leading French regiments. The French survivors fell back.

The Allied column now pressed on, firing disciplined volleys into the French second line, 300 paces behind the position where the first line had opened the struggle. The advancing Allies were now far enough forward that the French guns no longer enfiladed them, and victory seemed about to crown their banners. French conterattacks were unavailing. The *Régiment du Roi* broke itself against a battalion of the Second (Coldstream) Guards; the British Guards had bested the *Gardes Françaises*.

Some of Louis XV's advisers urged him to flee, but the King and the Dauphin were determined instead to rally their army. It was to be the one great hour of the King's reign. Meanwhile Saxe rode off in his wicker chariot to gather the cavalry.

Now the fatal flaw of Cumberland's personal leadership exposed itself. Firepower and discipline decided most eighteenth-century infantry actions, and the Allies had shown that at least on this day British firepower and discipline remained superior to French. Decisive triumph in the battle as a whole nevertheless still depended as it had in Gustavus Adolphus's day on the shock action of the mobile arm, the cavalry, to follow up infantry success and to prevent the enemy infantry from regrouping. Fire and movement in combination remained the inseparable keys to tactical decisiveness. But the Allied cavalry, now a mile in the rear, could not make its way through the ravine and the heavy infantry column to the front where it might have begun an exploitation before Louis and Saxe could mount a counterstroke. With Cumberland in the front of the infantry, furthermore, the Allied commander was in no position to capitalize on his attack between Fontenoy and the wood through efforts elsewhere.

Cumberland's infantry column thus had to spend the early afternoon beating back the assaults of the French cavalry, some thirty-eight squadrons. Aided by the piecemeal nature of these assaults—for which Saxe deserves some cen-

1. Quoted, without further citation, in Jacques Boudet, "Fontenoy, 1745," in Cyril Falls, ed., *Great Military Battles* (New York: The Macmillan Company, 1964), p. 52.

sure—the tough British and Hanoverian infantry succeeded in this task; as usual, steady infantry were proof against cavalry charges, and therefore for the French unlike the Allies the time was not ripe for the shock action of the mounted arm.

But eventually the time was no longer ripe for the Allies either. The French infantry, free from serious pressure anywhere else along their perimeter, could rally and redeploy to assail both flanks of Cumberland's hedgehog column. They formed up especially heavily on its right, the Irish Brigade conspicuous among them. In front of the British column there formed the French King's personal artillery units and the infantry protecting them, the *Maison du Roi* and the *Gendarmerie*. About two in the afternoon Saxe ordered a general attack by all these forces. The British and Hanoverian hedgehog, weary and much depleted in numbers, at length gave way and retreated, Cumberland predictably fighting with the rear guard.

The British have liked to think that if the Allies had properly supported Cumberland's column, Fontenoy would have been a famous British victory. Certainly Cumberland's attack demonstrated that not even the Prussians could much excel, if they excelled at all, the battlefield proficiency of the British battalions. The Dutch contingent, on the other hand, lost only 7 percent casualties; they did not fight hard. But it remains true also that Cumberland might have prevented the French from concentrating against his column if he had adhered to the role of captain-general instead of behaving like a battalion commander.

Both sides suffered heavily, but as the Dutch casualty rate suggests, disproportionately among those troops engaged in mounting or repelling Cumberland's assault and much less elsewhere. Allied casualties have been estimated between 7,000 and 10,000, French between 5,000 and 7,000. The three British battalions of Foot Guards that fought as the Guards Brigade—including the Third Regiment of Foot Guards, the Scots Guards—take pride that while their casualties were otherwise heavy, they had none missing.

Saxe's personal guard of Saxon Uhlans helped the sick marshal climb upon his horse to meet the King and be embraced by him in reward for the victory. Louis XV also reportedly took time to show the Dauphin the field littered with the dead and the suffering, to urge him to remember this reality of battle and not to play lightly with his subjects' lives. As it turned out, this Dauphin also was not destined to live to rule France, so we do not know how well the salutary lesson was learned.

Culloden

Attractive a figure as he was, Bonnie Prince Charlie might be accused of such play with his adherents' lives in the cause of his father, the still-living Old Pretender, because Jacobite hopes were delusions of considerable transparency. Fontenoy meant that the Prince had chosen his hour as well as was possible, and the capture of Edinburgh and the battle of Prestonpans were heartening events to be followed for a time by a still more spectacular Stuart progress into England; but George II could bring home much of the sturdy army of Fontenoy despite the costs to his European alliances, and he did so.

After Prestonpans, the Jacobite army plunged into England. All Scotland now lay in the control of Prince Charles Edward, except for the castles of Edinburgh, Stirling, and Dumbarton and a collection of forts and barracks on Loch Lomond and in the Highlands. For a time the Prince could persuade himself that England might return to the old allegiance as well; rising in numbers to some 5,000 foot and 500 horse, the Jacobite army swept through Carlisle while the royalist army, deceived by a feinting maneuver, remained idle around Newcastle-upon-Tyne. On November 18/29 the Jacobites captured Manchester. Meanwhile in October four French ships had landed at Montrose and Stonehaven to debark arms and equipment, including six Swedish field guns and French gunners to man them.

But no truly substantial French aid was forthcoming, nor was there anything approaching a large-scale rising of the English in the Stuarts' behalf. By the time the Prince's army entered Manchester, a tough-minded officer like Lord George Murray, and to some degree even the Prince himself, recognized that the Scots had accomplished about as much as they could in the Jacobite cause. They had won Scotland and carried the rebellion into England; now either a French army or an English rising must help them. Instead of either of these indispensable new developments, however, the Jacobite army faced the Duke of Cumberland with an army rapidly growing as the three battalions of Foot Guards, eighteen line regiments, nine squadrons of cavalry, and four artillery companies returned from Flanders. On the far side of the Pennines, moreover, Field-Marshal George Wade maneuvered the army that had been beaten at Prestonpans, transformed however by numerous reinforcements including 6,000 Dutch troops.

The Jacobite army executed one more deft maneuver of its own, inducing Cumberland to open the road to further penetration of England, to Derby. Here Prince Charles Edward and his advisers assembled on November 24/December 5. At a council of war the next day, however, the Prince acquiesced, with dismay—in fact, with an ungrateful and ungraceful display of pique—in the advice that his army should retreat. Such was the advice of Murray and of all other voices of common sense; the Prince's ingratitude to sturdy friends aside, there is much to be said for the proposition that common sense never had anything to do with this rising anyway, and that if there existed any chance of success, it lay in the rash but conceivably winnable gamble of a desperate march on London, which just might have induced a panic flight away from the not overly beloved new German dynasty.

Though the Jacobites' mood thus grew bleak, the sober Lord George Murray conducted the retreat with the skill to be predicted of this orthodox soldier. At Clifton on December 1–2/12–13 he actually fought a successful rear-guard combat, contrary to the Prince's orders, to permit continuing the retreat through the night down a narrow lane and a road enclosed between high walls. By now defying the Prince's orders was also almost predictable; Charles Edward and his military commander were barely on speaking terms, the Prince sensing that however well qualified Murray might be in a professional way, his advice had probable deprived the rising of its only hope of ultimate victory.

The small rebel victory of Clifton meanwhile spawned an insidious rumor, that the Jacobites were following a policy of giving no quarter and murdering the King's wounded soldiers. Cumberland may have believed it; he was to retaliate as if he did.

Once back in Scotland, the Jacobites again overcame their drooping morale to win a more substantial success than Clifton, at Falkirk between Glasgow and Edinburgh on January 6/17. They embarrassed Cumberland's advanced force of some 8,500 men under Lieutenant-General Henry Hawley, a ruthless killer of rebels real or suspected who deserved embarrassment. Murray astutely chose tactics, position, and timing: an abrupt charge, when Hawley expected the out-numbered rebels to await his initiative; a surge to grasp high ground, Falkirk Hill, before the enemy could ensconce himself there, Lord George knowing that his Highland troops put a premium on holding the hilltops and felt much more secure if they could possess them; the attack opening just as a storm was sweep-ing across the field from the Jacobite rear and obscuring the redcoats' vision. But while Murray's generalship thus gained yet one more round, because of his earlier insistence on retreat the success had to be accomplished in spite of deteriorating discipline among the Jacobites' clan regiments that assured there could be no pursuit—the storm probably would have prevented it anyway—and that augured ill for the approaching showdown with Cumberland's main body.

That showdown occurred when the Prince's army, after retreating on across Scotland and deep into the Highlands, chose to stand on Drummossie Muir (or Moor) near a modest mansion called Culloden House, in order to defend the Highland capital of Inverness. On April 4/15, 1746, Cumberland approached the moor with his King's Army in Scotland, as the Hanoverian force was now styled, almost 9,000 strong with eighteen guns. Prince Charles Edward's army had now about 5,400 men, had abandoned most of its artillery during the long retreat, and had seen its never well-organized logistics collapse almost completely; its troops were near starvation, and bone-weary besides.

Cumberland had prepared for the climactic battle by training his troops in a tactical innovation much simpler even than Frederick's oblique order of battle but in the context just as effective and important. The tactical reliance of the Highlanders, consistently and most recently at Falkirk, was upon a wild, head-long charge. The charge was little disciplined even when their morale was at its best, and underarmed because the clansmen wielded mostly swords, axes, and pikes with few firearms—yet hard to resist because of the ferocity of the oncom-ing, yelling Highland warriors, and more importantly because the redcoats' bayo-nets had typically gotten caught up on the attackers' protective shields. Cumberland consequently trained his men each to aim his bayonet not at his immediate attacker but at the unprotected right arm and shoulder, the sword-carrying arm, of the clansman just to his right, counting on his comrade to dispose of the man directly charging him by doing the same. It was an excellent tactical scheme.

Lord George Murray, emboldened again by the desperation of a last-ditch defense of the Highlands, wanted to lead off not only with another charge of the clans but with a night attack the better to use shouts and bagpipes and a fierce reputation to recapture psychological ascendancy. But by now it was the Prince and most of the other leaders who were too discouraged to attempt anything bold, and indeed almost all cooperation among the Highland chieftains had ceased. Murray got a night march under way, but when he was ready to command the charge, he found he had no spearhead strong enough to make the effort worthwhile. Thus all that came of his design was the still further wearying of some of the clansmen in a stumbling march and a dreary countermarch.

Back to the moor Lord George's column straggled, to a field of battle badly chosen by the Prince and whichever of his lieutenants had joined him in the choosing. The dimensions of the open moor were such that the larger King's Army in Scotland might readily stretch beyond the Highlanders' flanks, and there was a stone wall along the Jacobite right from which the Hanoverians might then lay down an enfilading fire.

Nevertheless, as the King's Army advanced on April 5/16, the Highlanders responded by launching yet one more charge, most strongly on their right where Murray directly commanded the men of Atholl, the Stuarts of Appin, the Camerons, and the Frasers. In spite of Cumberland's tactical innovation, Murray's charge broke the Hanoverian first line, pressed against the second line, and finally retired in good order with bagpipes skirling. But Cumberland's tactics helped weaken Murray's charge enough to deprive it of decisive momentum, and the same tactics did much to ensure that no Highland penetration occurred anywhere else. Cumberland's army was too strong and the Duke's tactical training and leadership too sound to be denied—while the Hanoverians' artillery alone came close to pounding the Jacobites into submission. As the Hanoverians went over to the attack all along the front, the Duke himself once more displayed his personal bravery in urging troops forward, and his infantry for the most part displayed again the same kind of resolute discipline that had nearly defeated a more formidable opponent at Fontenoy. The government troops in Scotland had been close to demoralization when Cumberland first arrived from Flanders, and even the Flanders veterans were shaken when Falkirk followed on the earlier Jacobite successes; but Cumberland's hearty leadership had restored their spitits, and his training had restored their effectiveness.

Along with Cumberland's leadership, however, it was his artillery and the deterioration of the Highland army that were the keys to the outcome at Culloden. In the course of the battle, only the action of the Jacobite right wing produced much close-quarter fighting. Most of the troops on both sides were never closely engaged. Cumberland's army lost only fifty killed, 259 wounded, and one missing; the Jacobite casualties have been estimated at a thousand killed and wounded and 558 captured. Many of the Jacobite dead must have fallen not during the battle but during the flight afterward. The principal damage was done by Cumberland's artillery and by the disintegration of Jacobite cohesion *before* the battle.

Culloden was destined to be the Duke of Cumberland's only victory. He turned twenty-five the day before the battle, but his early corpulence presaged health problems, and by his early forties he was to be afflicted by failing eyesight, asthma, and a stroke. He died October 11, 1765, at the age of forty-four. Even among the government's friends his reputation was blackened, furthermore, by the events that immediately followed Culloden, which gave him the sinister sobriquet of "The Butcher." He had restored his army's morale, but the troops were nevertheless bitter about having to wage a winter campaign in the Highlands with much hard marching and galling weather against opponents they regarded as traitors. There was also the canard, circulated by the Duke himself, that the rebels gave no quarter, Cumberland did nothing to discourage his troops' venting their bitterness in wanton killing of the Jacobite fugitives. Noncombatants were not spared if they chanced to fall into the path of Cumberland's pursuit. A man and his little son were murdered when government cavalry came upon them in a plowed field; two old weavers were similarly slain. Total numbers are predictably uncertain. Many Jacobite leaders who escaped the random killings soon felt the hangman's noose instead. Prince Charles Edward and Lord George Murray never saw each other again after the day of Culloden, but after going their separate ways in hiding in Scotland, both eventually escaped to live out their years in exile on the Continent.

Cumberland and his friends could palliate their ruthlessness by pointing to Jacobite threats of a turn to irregular war—what would now be called a guerrilla campaign—but in fact the Forty-Five collapsed altogether with the defeat of Culloden. The violence of the retribution owed much to the particular circumstances of civil war. Traitors were not afforded the protection owed under the international war code to soldiers and subjects of recognized governments. But the aftermath of Culloden is yet another indication of the fragility of the limits upon warlike violence that had grown up since the Thirty Years War, just as along with the less than limited arms of Prussia's enemies in the Seven Years War the dénouement of the Forty-Five blurs the conception of the eighteenth century as an age of limited war. And the eighteenth-century limitations upon the conduct of war were in decidedly less than full vigor outside Europe.

The British Soldier from Minden to Québec

The Duke of Cumberland did not return to command in Flanders until 1747, when he faced Marshal Saxe again and lost to him again, at the battle of Lauffeld or Val on June 21/July 2. This time the shortcomings of Cumberland's battalion-commander style of generalship showed up still more plainly than at Fontenoy, and his adherents could not claim he would have won if only his allies had supported him properly.

After the Peace of Aix-la-Chapelle, Cumberland spent his energies as captain-general on efforts to bring up the whole British Army to the standards of battlefield discipline that had nearly carried him to victory at Fontenoy. While his declining health was transforming his bluff heartiness into harshness, nevertheless the supervision of training and drill brought out his best military talents, and he did much to solidify the British Army's stature as second only to the

Prussian in skill and dependability in battle. The conduct of the army in the Seven Years War was to furnish yet more evidence that, for all Cumberland's faults, the British could have found a far worse senior commander than he.

When the combined Anglo-Prussian army fought the French at Minden on August 1, 1759, it was the Prussian infantry that was faltering in close-quarter action, when a charge by the British Brigade—the 12th, 20th, 23rd, 25th, 37th, and 51st Regiments of Foot—turned the course of battle. The impress of Cumberland's training decided the outcome of Minden, and the Duke could feel that much satisfaction even though he lost his own final battle, Hastenbeck on July 26, 1757, to a superior French army.

The virtues of the Duke of Cumberland's training and drill as they permeated the British Army displayed themselves conspicuously also in the campaigns of the Seven Years War overseas, which ended by confirming the global ascendancy of the British Empire over the French. Major-General Edward Braddock's battle of the Monongahela on July 9, 1755 has become notorious as a symbol of British ineptitude in American wilderness warfare, but to a large degree undeservedly so.

The two regular regiments that marched with Braddock toward Fort Duquesne at the Forks of the Ohio River were the 44th and 48th of Foot. The facts of the expedition are that these troops pressed steadily through the forests of the Appalachians from Wills Creek, Maryland (or Will's Creek, the present accepted spelling), on the upper Potomac River. They carved out a road as they went and maintained such firm discipline and such excellent march security that the French at the fort came to regard them as an almost inexorable tide, while Colonel George Washington of the Virginia Militia, accompanying the expedition as an aide-de-camp to Braddock, marveled at the ease with which these regulars overcame the obstacles of geography in contrast to provincial troops he had commanded on much the same journey the year before. The French and their Indian allies—numbering only some 750 and 650, respectively—ventured forth to meet Braddock's 1,400 British regulars and their 1,100 Virginia and Maryland auxiliaries at the crossing of the Monongahela River, with the French disheartened by the British performance so far and anticipating only a face-saving gesture before they lost Fort Duquesne.

The battle that followed was less the ambush that was often depicted than a meeting engagement as the British vanguard emerged from the river crossing. If at the first encounter officers leading the British van had pushed ahead to grasp either a clearing not far distant or a rise of ground to the right, the redcoats probably would have had the opportunity to form line of battle and would almost certainly have administered to the French the beating they anticipated.

It was a failure of officers to seize the favorable ground that betrayed the British troops, forcing them to bunch up in an increasingly unwieldy mass devastatingly vulnerable to the enemy's fire from behind cover. General Braddock reached the head of his column and the scene of the action too late to retrieve a proper deployment. He fell mortally wounded while trying to rally his men, and the expedition retreated. But Colonel Washington emerged from the defeat with a lasting admiration for the discipline of British regulars. Ever after, he sought to

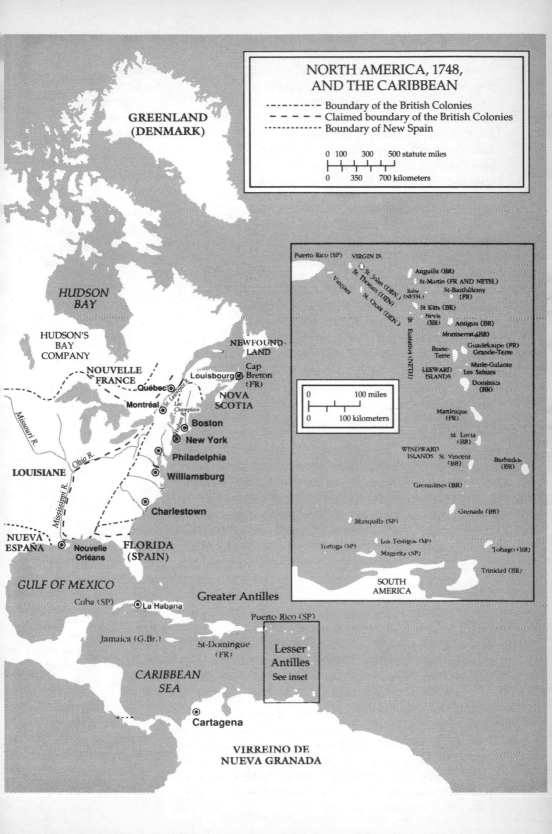

NORTH AMERICA, 1748,
AND THE CARIBBEAN

········· Boundary of the British Colonies
- - - - - Claimed boundary of the British Colonies
·········· Boundary of New Spain

0   100   300   500 statute miles

0   350   700 kilometers

GREENLAND
(DENMARK)

HUDSON
BAY

HUDSON'S
BAY
COMPANY

NOUVELLE
FRANCE

Québec

Montréal

St. Lawrence R.

Lac
Champlain

Hudson

Missouri R.

Ohio R.

Mississippi R.

LOUISIANE

NUEVA
ESPAÑA

Nouvelle
Orléans

NEWFOUND-
LAND

Cap
Breton
(FR)

Louisbourg

NOVA
SCOTIA

Boston

New York

Philadelphia

Williamsburg

Charlestown

FLORIDA
(SPAIN)

GULF OF MEXICO

Cuba (SP)

La Habana

Greater Antilles

Jamaica (G.Br.)

St-Domingue
(FR)

Puerto Rico (SP)

Lesser
Antilles
See inset

CARIBBEAN
SEA

Cartagena

VIRREINO DE
NUEVA GRANADA

Puerto Rico (SP)   VIRGIN IS.

St. John (DEN.)   Anguilla (BR)

Vieques   St-Martin (FR AND NETH.)

St. Thomas (DEN.)   Saba   St-Barthélemy
                    (NETH.)   (FR)

St. Croix (DEN.)   St Kitts (BR)

                    Nevis   Antigua (BR)
                    (BR)
St. Eustatius (NETH.)   Montserrat (BR)

                    Basse-   Guadeloupe (FR)
                    Terre   Grande-Terre

LEEWARD   Marie-Galante
ISLANDS   Les Saintes

                    Dominica
                    (BR)

                    Martinique
                    (FR)

                    St Lucia
                    (BR)

WINDWARD
ISLANDS   St. Vincent   Barbados
          (BR)   (BR)

Grenadines (BR)

                    Grenada (BR)

Blanquilla (SP)

Tortuga (SP)   Los Testigos (SP)

            Margarita (SP)   Tobago (BR)

                    Trinidad (BR)

SOUTH
AMERICA

0   100 miles

0   100 kilometers

instill in any troops he commanded as close an approximation as possible to the training and discipline of the first regular soldiers with whom he served.

A similarly disciplined British advance against Fort Duquesne in 1758 succeeded where Braddock had failed. This time the British reduced their vulnerability as they approached the fort by establishing depots along the way, reducing their logistical strain and creating refuges to which they might retreat without abandoning the whole expedition. This time their march appeared so inexorable that the French evacuated the fort without a fight.

In the colonial contest as at Fontenoy, the training and discipline of the British Army's rank and file tended to surpass the professional capacity of the officers; the troops showed a tactical proficiency not equaled by most of their senior officers' professional attainments in command. The British had yet to install any system of schooling for infantry and cavalry officers comparable to the French; many officers were sufficiently dedicated to their careers to be respectably self-schooled, but too many after purchasing commissions advanced through further expenditures of their wealth and on the strength of their social standing.

A costly instance of misuse of capable soldiers by incapable officers was Major-General James Abercromby's wasting of a 15,000-man expedition against the French Fort Carillon at Ticonderoga on Lake Champlain on July 8, 1758. There were only 3,500 defenders and various possible approaches to the fort. Abercromby had artillery with him and might have placed guns on an eminence commanding the fort from the south, the means that the more capably commanded British expedition of Major-General John Burgoyne in 1777 was to employ against American-held Fort Ticonderoga. Instead, Abercromby chose to hurl his infantry forward in frontal attacks against the enemy's outer defense.

These defenses featured a wall of logs along a ridge running the entire width of the narrow peninsula on which the fort stands, the logs piled horizontally two and three deep with loopholes for muskets. Since some of the logs were three feet (about one meter) or more in diameter, and the wall was crowned with sandbags, the works were six to seven feet (two meters or more) high. A glacis—a sloping defensive field of fire—had been formed by clearing the ground across a hundred yards (or meters) in front of the wall; and an abatis—a defensive obstacle—created by piling up a hedge of tree tops and branches, sharpened ends toward the attackers, loomed up across part of the glacis. Manned by seven battalions of French regulars as well as auxiliary troops, this wall left the attackers with nothing like the fighting chance they had had at Fontenoy. In utterly futile charges, Abercromby lost 464 killed, 1,117 wounded, and 29 missing. The Black Watch alone, redesignated since the Peace of Aix-la-Chapelle as the 42nd of Foot, the numeral under which it would win its greatest fame, lost 203 killed and almost 600 wounded, more than half its strength.

But there was a growing number of British officers in whom such sturdy fortitude among the troops helped inspire a sufficient willingness to reflect upon experience and a sufficient study of the art of war that they might offer the soldiers the quality of leadership they deserved. One such was Brigadier-General James Wolfe, who with the local rank of major-general was given in 1759 the command of the troops of an amphibious expedition to sail up the St. Lawrence (Saint-Laurent) against the citadel of New France, the fortress-city of Québec.

Thirty-two years old and a veteran of Dettingen, Falkirk, and Culloden, as well as of a successful expedition against Louisbourg on Cape Breton Island in 1748, Wolfe had seen enough of the run-of-the-mill leadership of the British Army to be contemptuous of many, indeed most, of his fellow officers. A scholarly, sensitive man, he did not have much use for the hard-bitten scrapings of country lanes, jails, and gin mills who filled the enlisted ranks either; but he was determined that his expedition would not become another waste of their bravery. To that end he made no secret of his distrust of the capacities of his subordinates, including his three brigadier-generals all of whom were older than himself. Wolfe was so earnest that he was less than fair; these three men, Robert Monckton, George Townshend, and James Murray, were well above average in quality and themselves good examples of the rising breed of more professional British officers. But because of his sense of superiority, Wolfe took little counsel with anybody, and few officers were so widely disliked throughout the army. Nor did it help his popularity that in no way did he look like a soldier; tall, painfully thin, and ungainly, he stared at the world through pale blue eyes bulging from a pallid face otherwise marked by an arrowlike nose and a startlingly recessive chin. Still, the new First Lord of the Treasury, William Pitt, had personally chosen Wolfe as the man to take Québec.

British sea power carried Wolfe and his small army of 900 regulars and 400 Rangers—the latter were largely woodsmen recruited in North America—to anchor on the south side of the Île d'Orléans, within sight of Québec, on June 26, 1759. But now Wolfe had to find a way to enter the city, and more than two subsequent months of futility set his subordinates to even more grumbling about his aloofness and conceit and seem for a time to have left Wolfe himself confused and for once self-doubting.

The city of Québec frowns down upon the St. Lawrence River from V-shaped bluffs, 200 feet (about sixty meters) above the water, framed between the confluence of the St. Lawrence and a tributary, the St. Charles. On the St. Lawrence side the bluffs are almost sheerly perpendicular. A wall guarded the city from the westward reach of the lofty plateau on which it sits. From the beginning Wolfe believed that the way to approach Québec was across this plateau from the west, the wall notwithstanding; but reaching the relatively level area just outside the city wall, called the Plains of Abraham (Plaines d'Abraham), appeared to be an insoluble problem.

On June 30, Monckton landed troops on the south shore of the St. Lawrence at Point Lévis and began planting cannon there to bombard the city across the half mile (.8 kilometer) of the river, but this effort was unlikely to force a surrender. Wolfe considered landing on the north shore of the St. Lawrence below the mouth of the St. Charles and trying to circle above the city, but gestures in that direction proved to be fiascos. He landed most of his army below the Montmorenci River, another tributary of the St. Lawrence east of the St. Charles, but a reconnaissance up the Montmorenci produced forty-five British killed and wounded in return for evidence of rough and dubious terrain. On July

31 Wolfe mounted an assault on the easternmost French redoubt, near the Montmorenci; but although the redoubt fell, the troops capturing it immediately came under intolerable fire from a bluff above; and a frontal assault against that position became a miniature Fort Carillon disaster, with 210 killed and 230 wounded for no gain.

About the only hopeful development of Wolfe's first weeks in front of Québec was that beginning on the night of July 18, British ships had found that they could sail up the river past the city in spite of the best efforts of the defending guns. Nor were French fire ships or floating batteries able to do much damage to the British fleet.

The French commander, Louis Joseph, marquis de Montcalm de Saint-Véran, *lieutenant général,* shared Wolfe's perception that Québec's western wall was the weak point of the city, but he had not believed that British ships could make their way up the river past his batteries. He had therefore concentrated on using his garrison, somewhat larger than Wolfe's army but including many irregulars, to defend the St. Charles–Montmorenci area east of town. Now Montcalm had to worry a bit more about his western defenses, and also about his line of communications to Montréal. Nevertheless, he was still confident that Wolfe could find no way to ascend the cliffs from the St. Lawrence to the Plains of Abraham.

With Townshend circulating malicious cartoons of Wolfe to the other officers' sardonic delight, the commanding general condescended to hold a council of war with the brigadiers on August 29. They argued that getting atop the cliffs somewhere west of Québec offered the only hope. Wolfe acquiesced, though he shared no further planning with his subordinates. On September 7 he sailed upstream with an assault force. He spent the day scanning the cliffs with his telescope in search of a place to land. By evening he had found one, apparently with the aid of an intelligence officer who told him about a cave a mile and a half (two and a half kilometers) or so above the city—the place now called Wolfe's Cove—whence a path led through a cleft, the Anse de Foulon, up the face of the cliff from the river. Reportedly, the path was guarded by only a small redoubt at the top garrisoned by a weak detachment of Canadian troops. The way was barricaded at several places by felled trees and was steep and slippery; artillery most certainly could not negotiate it, and it would demand a long and exhausting climb for infantry. But by now Wolfe saw no alternative. There was urgency, furthermore; not only would winter soon close in, but Wolfe thought he had reason to fear that if he did not press Montcalm harder, the Frenchman might actually send reinforcements to Montréal, now threatened by another British force under the commander-in-chief in North America, Major-General Jeffrey Amherst. Wolfe had carried his aloofness to the extreme of sharing little information with Amherst and keeping himself as remote as possible from Amherst's direction. But with his own confidence shaken by a summer of frustration, he nevertheless remained determined to cast any feasible throw of the dice and not to fail to capture Québec.

Montcalm dispatched a detachment to watch the movements of the British ships carrying Wolfe's troops, but the British sailed well upstream from the cove to draw away suspicion. About one in the morning of September 13 Wolfe's force began to drop downstream on the ebb tide in the naval squadron's boats. Four times their movements attracted challenges from sentries in shore, but responses in French gave the impression that the boats were merely carrying provisions to the city, and no shots were fired; a provision convoy had been scheduled for that night but cancelled, yet word of the cancellation had not been passed on to the city. The ebb tide proved so strong that it carried the landing force past Wolfe's Cove, whereupon rather than waste time trying to return, the vanguard leapt from the boats and straggled ashore wherever they could. Rather than search for the path, they also began clambering up the cliff wherever it offered any semblance of a foothold. The garrison of the redoubt at the top resisted but was easily overcome, though its commander, *Capitaine* Louis de Vergon, was able to send a message into Québec. The sound of musketry also carried into the city. Through misinformation and possibly through treachery, however, the civil authorities in Québec delayed informing Montcalm. By dawn Wolfe had completed the assembly of some 4,400 British troops, all regulars, on the plateau west of the city.

Ill-served in terms of information, Montcalm had also been distracted during the night by a cannonade from much of the British fleet and a feint by about a thousand British soldiers against his positions to the east. At daylight, nevertheless, Montcalm rode into Québec from the east—and in dismay saw a long double line of British troops deployed on the Plains of Abraham. The French commander had plenty of men, almost 14,000; but only about 2,500 of them were regulars, and about 3,000 had gone upstream to meet the threat posed when the British ships moved in that direction. While this westerly French force might conceivably have attacked Wolfe from the rear, Montcalm was sufficiently shaken by Wolfe's coup in reaching the approaches to the weak city wall that he decided he must counterattack at once. Immediately he sent militia to harry the British lines. By about ten he had assembled some 4,500 additional troops, only half regulars, whom he ordered forward in three main formations, on a front about a half mile (.8 kilometer) wide and in most places six men deep, with greater depth in the center. French artillery opened fire in support.

The French advance, however, did not achieve much of an approximation of Prussian-style regularity and discipline. Montcalm's infantry opened fire when the distance to the British line had narrowed to 150 yards (or meters), but this was still too long a range for accuracy. Some British soldiers fell, and the French shouted in triumph and quickened their pace. They continued firing, and more of the redcoats fell; but Wolfe set an example of steadiness for his men, and gaps in the British ranks closed up quickly. Wolfe had ordered that there be no firing until the French came within sixty yards, and his lines remained silent.

The French advance, now more than a little ragged, was in fact within fifty yards when Wolfe himself, bleeding from wounds in the wrist and stomach, gave the order to open fire. Six British regiments blazed forth with volleys so well controlled that they might have been the firing of six cannon. The French wavered. The British fired another series of almost perfectly controlled volleys. Reloading, they then advanced twenty paces and fired again. After several minutes more the redcoats slackened their fire to allow the smoke to clear. When it did, they confronted only a desolation of silent or groaning bodies and a few scattered pockets of French fighting men. Most of the enemy were in flight.

Montcalm was mortally wounded in the chest during the retreat and died the next morning. Wolfe also suffered a chest wound, and this, his third wound of the day, ended his life within a few minutes. The French force from the west appeared shortly, but Townshend ordered the British to change front and thus frightened it away. The change of front permitted Montcalm's survivors to escape across the St. Charles, whence they circled westward to join their comrades who had arrived from that direction. The battle on the Plains of Abraham had cost the French at least 644 casualties, perhaps many more. The British lost fifty-eight killed and about 600 wounded.

A garrison remained in the city, against which the British opened a formal siege. But Québec was already short of provisions, and the garrison surrendered on September 17. Then it became the turn of a British garrison to run short of provisions during the winter, after the British fleet sailed away. A corollary of the relative scarcity of British officers, army or navy, who studied their profession as earnestly as Wolfe was a severe weakness in logistical and administrative planning, which now almost took away Wolfe's triumph. On April 28, 1760, François Gaston, chevalier de Lévis, *général de brigade,* led a French and Canadian force of 11,000 against the city. Brigadier-General Murray counterattacked on the Plains of Abraham with fewer than 3,900 troops, and French flank attacks this time caused the redcoats to break. This event, usually called the battle of Sainte-Foy, was bloodier than the more famous engagement that had preceded it; the British lost 259 killed and 893 wounded, the French 193 killed and 640 wounded. It was now Lévis and the French who besieged Murray and the British in Québec. But on May 15 a British naval squadron arrived, and Lévis had to give up. Amherst sent an additional two regiments to Québec from Louisbourg, while he himself prepared to resume his efforts against Montréal via the Lake Champlain route from New York.

On July 15, Murray with 2,200 men opened his own campaign on the St. Lawrence toward Montréal. While his hope of capturing that remaining French stronghold unaided was excessively ambitious, he happened to arrive at Varenne, just below Montréal, on August 31, exactly a week before Amherst landed on the western end of the island occupied by the city. On September 8, Montréal and its garrison surrendered.

The critical victory at Québec in September 1759 had been a triumph of Wolfe's flexibility and boldness over his own failings in leadership as well as over the formidable geography of Québec. Once Wolfe had deployed his troops where they could strike effectively at the city, the battle of the Plains of Abraham became in addition a further triumph of the discipline and training of the British infantry. Notwithstanding the battle of Sainte-Foy, where superior numbers permitted the French to pressure the British flanks, the North American campaigns of the Seven Years War—the French and Indian War, as the British colonists in America called it—confirmed the battlefield superiority of eighteenth-century British infantry over French, and in fact the stature of the redcoat lines as second only to the Prussians in combat prowess—if indeed they were not practically the equals of the troops of Frederick the Great.

With the British as with the Prussians, a superbly trained rank and file proved able to win battles and wars in spite of the limitations of their army's officer professionalism. Marlborough had first fashioned the British tradition of tactical excellence, and if the Duke of Cumberland had won only a single victory in battle he nevertheless strengthened the tradition. But excellence in drill and training was more directly the work of junior officers and especially of noncommissioned officers than of the higher ranks, and in both the British and Prussian armies it was in no small degree a substitute for officer professionalism rather than an expression of it. Both armies were destined in the long run to display the limitations of tactical proficiency in combat unaccompanied by a thoroughgoing professionalization of the officer corps in administration, logistics, operations, and strategy.

The British Sailor from Minorca to Cartagena

The Royal Navy's command of the sea was of course the most fundamental assurance of the triumphs of Wolfe and Amherst in North America. As the narrative of the trials of Frederick the Great has suggested, the French came to regard the Seven Years War more as an imperial struggle against the British than as a contest for continental power. With the attention of the court of Versailles focused less on the Rhine than overseas, France might have dispatched to America enough regulars to overcome with quantity the qualitative edge of the British infantry. But while France was able to carry 3,000 regulars across the Atlantic immediately after learning of General Braddock's expedition thither, the British at once responded with a blockade in European waters and patrols in American waters that precluded any further major reinforcement for the rest of the war. However badly the imperial contest began for Britain on land, with Braddock's defeat and Abercromby's fiasco at Fort Carillon by no means the whole of a tale of early disasters, sea power left the ultimate result never in doubt—provided only that Great Britain retained the will to persist in the war.

The Royal Navy continued to resemble the British Army in that the capacities of the men in the lower ranks—in the navy, their excellent seamanship—were expected to compensate for the limited military professionalism and therefore the limited administrative, logistical, operational, and strategic skills of the officers. Naval professionalism indeed continued to lag considerably behind that of such army officers as Wolfe and his brigadier-generals. The Royal Navy's command of the sea was too completely assured by numerical superiority in addition to seamanship for the French ever to pose a serious threat during the Seven Years War. Nevertheless, the shortcomings of officer professionalism produced a maritime equivalent of the Monongahela or Ticonderoga, in the unhappy affair of Rear-Admiral John Byng, fourth son of Sir George Byng of the Cape Passero battle, who had died on January 17, 1732/January 28, 1733, having become Rear-Admiral of Great Britain, First Lord of the Admiralty, first Baron

Byng of Southall in the County of Bedford, and first Viscount Torrington in Devonshire.

Maintaining command of the seas stretched the Royal Navy thin. At the beginning of the Seven Years War, the British had about a hundred ships of the line ready to put to sea, the French forty-five, not all of them fit for action. Accordingly the war never witnessed a genuine threat of French invasion of the British home islands—though the French assembled an army for that purpose early in the war—because there was never a question of British control of the Channel. In general, North American waters were also securely British. The West and East Indies posed no naval challenges more severe than those of protecting commerce. But with British maritime responsibilities so widespread, in the early part of the war the Royal Navy lacked sufficient plenitude of power to make the Mediterranean altogether secure. Early in 1758, therefore, the French used a show of activity in the Channel to distract the British while twelve ships of the line ventured from Toulon to convoy a fleet of transports bearing 15,000 troops to Minorca, where the British had maintained a Mediterranean base since 1708. Commanding the French squadron was Roland-Michel, Marquis de La Galissonière, *lieutenant général,* scion of a seafaring family and himself a forty-six-year veteran of naval service whose uncertain health did not seriously compromise a capacity in seamanship rare among French officers and worthy of challenging the British. La Galissonière landed the troops on the western end of Minorca, and his ships took up a blockade of Port Mahon across the island.

Minorca's garrison had been allowed to dwindle, and the island would not be able to hold out long without assistance; but in spite of the strategic importance of the place for British power in the Mediterranean, the government allowed itself to be hoodwinked by French sleight of hand in the Channel sufficiently that intelligence of La Galissonière's move in the Mediterranean when it was impending prompted only the dispatch of ten ships of the line from England on April 5, Admiral John Byng commanding.

Picking up such reinforcements as he could in the Mediterranean, Byng still could assemble only thirteen of the line. He arrived off Minorca on May 19, and the French stood out to meet him. La Galissonière actually had a slight advantage in number of guns, especially since the *Deptford,* 50, did not join in the action until almost the end of the battle that ensued. This fight occurred on the 21st, when Byng attacked in spite of his lack of superior weight.

There was some confused, indecisive sparring, the indecisiveness caused by the display of a considerable amount of tactical and seamanlike skill on both sides, with offsetting effects. In the early afternoon a shift in the wind gave Byng the weather gauge, and he came down on the French in a "lasking" maneuver, that is, in line ahead but on a diagonal so that his ships would receive minimal exposure to French fire as they approached. La Galissonière responded with characteristic adroitness by swiftly adjusting the direction of his own line to regain a course parallel to the British. At this juncture of a nice balance in skill as well as in weight between the rival fleets, British tactical control proved to unravel first.

The proximate cause was that perennial plague, the inadequacy of the available means of communicating from ship to ship while in action, particularly of the available signals. Nevertheless, caution on Byng's part and the memory of Mathews's battle off Toulon in 1714 also had baleful effects. Byng was determined to attack with his entire squadron in hand and in line ahead or not at all. Fearing loss of control, he held back when the French responded effectively to his lasking maneuver. But misunderstanding his intentions, the British van did not slacken its speed correspondingly, instead continuing to bear down on the French line. The leading British ships still had somewhat the better of a duel with their counterparts until French gunnery brought down the foretopmast of the *Intrepid*, 64, sixth ship in the British line. The *Intrepid* became unmanageable, and the gap between the British van and the rest of Byng's line widened. The British concentrated three other ships to cover their cripple, thus discouraging further French efforts against her, and the action broke off.

Byng had scarcely covered himself with glory, and he may have missed an opportunity to gain a clear victory by failing to follow up the advantage that his van was gaining despite the troubles of the *Intrepid*. But there was no sufficient cause for his battle to turn into a British disaster—except that Byng's onset of caution in the midst of the fight swelled up into a panicky decision to retreat to Gibraltar. This withdrawal left the French in control of the approaches to Minorca, and on June 28 the isolated garrison of Fort Mahon surrendered. The British had lost one of the principal fruits of the War of the Spanish Succession; Minorca would no longer assist their maritime strategy in the Mediterranean.

On the heels of Braddock's defeat and other setbacks in America, the loss of Minorca provoked an outcry by press and public—particularly by powerful merchants with interests in the Mediterranean—that demanded a scapegoat. Although the Cabinet of Sir Thomas Pelham Holles, fifth (modern, or fifteenth) Earl of Clare and fourth Duke of Newcastle-upon-Tyne, might have blamed itself for allowing French feints to mislead it into sending so small a force to the relief of Port Mahon, doing so would even less have fitted the style of Newcastle than of most politicians. He would gladly throw anyone to the lions to save himself. Admiral Sir Edward Hawke sailed forthwith to replace Byng, and the latter came home in close arrest. A mob nearly succeeded in seizing him at Portsmouth, and effigies of him were hanged across the land—all with the encouragement of the merchants. Byng was brought to trial by court-martial for neglect of duty. The court acquitted him of charges of personal cowardice or disaffection, but it convicted him for having failed to do his utmost. The sentence carried the death penalty, and while the court recommended clemency and Newcastle's Cabinet left office, no one saw fit to risk a new outburst of public and mercantile wrath. On March 14, 1757, in Portsmouth harbor, Byng was shot on the quarterdeck of the flagship *Monarque*, 74. The stultifying sanctity of the line ahead had this time helped create not only another naval failure but a martyr.

By the time of Byng's execution, Admiral Hawke was already back in England from the Mediterranean. There with an energy and boldness far superior to Byng's he had assured the safety of Gibraltar and done much to restore British commerce, descending heavily on French privateers and overawing superior numbers of French warships so that they stayed at Toulon. He was not given the resources to recapture Minorca, but the prospect that the consequences of its loss would not after all be overwhelming was demonstrated not only by his success but also by the fate of the architects of its capture. The expedition to take Minorca had been mounted by the joint efforts of Marc-Pierre de Voyer, comte d'Argenson, Minister of War, and Jean-Baptiste Michault d'Arnouville, Minister of Marine. Their reward for organizing the most successful French amphibious expedition in a century was almost immediate dismissal, because meanwhile they had failed to display the expected deference to Madame de Pompadour. So much for any chance of consistent French success against the often ill-managed but in quantity and seamanlike skills inexorable maritime power of Great Britain.

About the same time, moreover, the British Cabinet underwent a change whose implications were diametrically opposite those of the French Cabinet shakeup. Newcastle gave way on November 10, 1756, to a ministry nominally under William Cavendish, fourth Duke of Devonshire, but actually dominated by William Pitt as Principal Secretary of State and leader of the House of Commons. Pitt began coordinating British military and naval operations worldwide into a coherent strategy designed both to assure continued control of the seas and the grasping of the colonial fruits thereof and to sustain Britain's continental ally, Frederick the Great. The ministerial arrangement was prompted by Pitt's unwillingness to serve under the petty politician Newcastle; but without Newcastle's nevertheless considerable skills in managing Parliament, the Cabinet fell as early as April 6, 1757. Pitt soon thereafter conceded, however, the necessity to combine his talents with Newcastle's, and on the following June 27 the two joined forces with Newcastle as First Lord of the Treasury and thus titular head of the government, while Pitt as Principal Secretary of State took practical control of army, navy, and foreign affairs.

In the Newcastle-Pitt Ministry, Admiral George Anson, first Baron Anson of Soberton, returned as First Lord of the Admiralty, having deserted that post briefly in the political and naval turmoil of late 1756 and early 1757 after holding it since 1751. Anson must share the blame for the faulty deployments that weakened the Mediterranean and led to the loss of Minorca—it was conspicuously for him along with Newcastle that Byng had been a scapegoat—but in spite of that lapse he was among the most able naval administrators of British history, and an invaluable second to Pitt. His reforms, now resumed, included yet another effort to regulate the dockyards better to enhance the quality of the ships and reduce corruption, an effort that as was customary under earnest reformers produced at least a short-term and modest improvement. Part of the reason lay in the inauguration of dockyard inspections. A much-needed system of financial accounting was also instituted, affecting particularly the Navy Board. Promotions to flag rank were rendered less capricious. In 1755, Lord Anson fathered the Corps of Marines, to give the navy a properly trained landing and infantry force as well as shipboard police.

Through 1757 the navy was not quite dominant enough to maintain a rigid blockade of the French coast, and occasional enemy convoys escaped with reinforcements to prolong the war in North America, though never in major strength. Pitt's first move to tighten the blockade became an embarrassing failure, moreover, when a combined army-navy expedition against the port of Rochefort on the Bay of Biscay in September 1757 collapsed despite weak defenses and ideal weather conditions, because a council of war even more irresolute than such bodies proverbially tend to be could not make up its mind to order a landing. From 1758 onward, however, the blockade became almost impenetrable; a few driblets got out of Brest in 1758, but nothing of any consequence.

In March of that year Admiral Hawke, now commanding the Channel Fleet, entered the Bay of Biscay. He was responding to intelligence advice that the French would dispatch therefrom a convoy to Louisbourg. Hawke intercepted the Rochefort squadron and vessels that it was escorting and drove them onto mud flats.

Anson himself, announcing that his principle was to guard North America by maintaining a fleet to the west of any French concentration around Brest, personally commanded the ships off Ushant through the summer months of 1758.

In the Mediterranean, the British had frustrated an attempt to reinforce from Toulon a French squadron sheltering in the neutral Spanish port of Cartagena. On February 28, 1758, Rear-Admiral Sir Henry Osborne's squadron fell in with the French Toulon squadron, drove ashore a sixty-four-gun ship (*Orphée*), captured a fifty-gun ship (*Oriflamme*), and in a running fight beginning at dusk won a measure of revenge for Port Mahon: Captain Arthur Gardiner, Byng's flag-captain in the 1756 battle, led *Monmouth*, 64, against *Foudroyant*, 80, the French flagship in Byng's battle; Gardiner was killed, and both sides were badly mauled, but the *Monmouth* so nearly crippled its superior adversary—his mizzenmast was down, his decks in chaos, and his guns nearly silenced—that when other British ships came up, the French mainmast was quickly toppled and the *Foudroyant* struck the colors. Thereafter the French withdrew from Cartagena.

The Battle of Quiberon Bay

As Pitt and Anson were well aware, so complete a British mastery of the seas assured eventual triumph at Québec and Montréal. The French of course were equally aware, and the customarily lethargic court of Louis XV bestirred itself in 1758 to seek a French equivalent to Pitt, nearly finding one in an army officer, Étienne François, duc de Choiseul, *lieutenant général*. (To be sure, it was critical to Choiseul's selection as Minister for Foreign Affairs and in effect director of the war effort—from January 1761 he was formally War Minister as well—that he was smiled upon by Madame de Pompadour.) Choiseul responded to the need for a dramatic reversal of the balance at sea by resurrecting the notion of a thrust into the very heart of British power: an invasion of England.

Moreover, Choiseul offered an ingenious plan. After considering and rejecting a proposal simply to ferry 50,000 troops across the Channel in barges from the Boulogne-Ambleteuse sector of the coast, he turned to a scheme featuring elaborate diversions and a principal landing directed to a vulnerable part of the English coast in close proximity to London. The first diversion was to involve the combined Brest and Toulon squadrons' convoying 20,000 troops from Brittany to a landing in the Firth of Clyde. Reversing the track of the Spanish Armada, the fleet was then to sail around the north of Scotland and down the British east coast. Meanwhile a squadron of light ships would raid Ireland—the second diversion—as the main fleet rendezvoused with transports carrying 20,000 men from Ostend (Oostende). Those would descend upon the coast of Essex at the mouth of the Blackwater River for a rapid march on London.

British intelligence, an object of Pitt's and Anson's zeal for improvement, got wind of the plan and also of Choiseul's hope to enlist the Dutch, Swedes, and Russians—neutral in the Anglo-French war—in it. British diplomacy, reinforced by such threats as the sovereign of the seas could readily utter, obviated the danger from the neutral powers; the Royal Navy looked to nip the invasion project itself in the bud. Edward Boscawen, Admiral of the Blue, sailed south in April 1759 to reinforce and take command of the Mediterranean squadron in order to cancel out the Toulon squadron's part in the project. Unable to lure the French out from Toulon, however, with three ships damaged by shore batteries during one of the attempts to do so, Boscawen sailed to Giblraltar to refit and replenish his stores, arriving on August 3. The French forthwith slipped out of Toulon and passed through the Strait of Gilbraltar on the night of August 17–18 for their juncture with the Brest squadron—predictably, however, under prompt British observation. With commendable dispatch Boscawen's ships got under way in spite of being in various stages of repair; the squadron commander was at sea by ten o'clock on the night of the 17th.

On this occasion it was the French signaling system whose limitations led to disaster. Part of their fleet put in at Cádiz. Their main body was in the Baia de Lagos off the coast of Portugal when, seeing several sail approaching, they assumed it was the Cádiz detachment, which had been signaled to resume the voyage north. The approaching vessels were actually the British. A running fight developed, in which Boscawen captured three French ships of the line and—ignoring Portuguese neutrality—burned two that went aground, the flagship L'Océan, 80, and Redoubtable, 74. The remaining French took refuge in Cádiz. The battle of Lagos Bay wrecked the Toulon part of Choiseul's plan.

British fears stirred by word of French invasion preparations nevertheless ran high. Accounts of forced-pace building of invasion barges all along the enemy coast from Havre de Grâce (Le Havre) to Brest agitated the press. If the French should come, Britain had little with which to stop them except the fleet. There were no formidable fortifications on the English coast. The army, however reliable, was small and already for the most part occupied elsewhere—27,000 troops in America, 10,000 in Germany, 5,000 at Gilbraltar. Especially alarmed was Newcastle, whose earlier timidity over France's mere gestures toward invasion had helped set up the Minorca debacle. In the circumstances, Admiral Hawke, commanding the Channel Fleet, had decided on a close blockade of Brest rather that the customary cruising to the north and west. Given the hazards of the islands and reefs studding the approaches to Brest and the frequent strong

ENGLISH CHANNEL
(La Manche)

◉ Morlaix

Ushant

Passage du Four

Pte de St-Mathieu

◉ Brest

Île Molene

Black
Rocks

Goulet

Rade
de
Brest

Pte de Toulinquet
La Parquette

Baie de
Douarnenes

Chausée
de Sein
(The Saints)

Passage du Raz

Bec du Raz

Baie de Audierne

Pte de Penmarch

BRETAGNE

Bay of Biscay
(Golfe de Gascogne)

Île de Croix

L'Orient
◉

◉ Port Louis

Auray ◉

◉ Vannes

Morbihan

Vilaine R.

Ì de
Conguel

Pte de Quiberon

Passage de Teignouze

Ì Dumet

Ì Houat

Baie de Quiberon

Belle-Isle

Ì Haedic

Loire R.

LES
CARDINAUX

HAWKE CONFLANS

LE FOUR

QUIBERON BAY, November 20, 1759,
about 2:30 p.m., and
the APPROACHES TO BREST.

0   10   20   30   40 statute miles

0   10   20   30   40 kilometers

winds in the area, this decision was feasible only because of Hawke's well-founded confidence in the seamanship of his captains and sailors—that trump card of the Royal Navy akin to the reliable discipline of British soldiers.

Hawke arrived off Brest on May 24 and found eleven enemy sail out of the harbor and in the roads. By June 4 there were seventeen sail in the roads. The next day a heavy gale blew up, forcing Hawke to retire toward Torbay on the 6th. He returned as soon as he dared, on the 11th, in winds still so strong that three of his ships suffered badly damaged rigging. The prompt return established his pattern; although his orders had called on him to employ more traditional methods, Anson so fully supported Hawke's course that the First Lord spared no effort to assure the provisioning and cyclical refitting of the ships on close station and the health of their crews.

In early July Rear-Admiral George Brydges Rodney, just invested with flag rank on May 19 and a man to watch, bombarded Havre de Grâce and destroyed many of the invasion barges and much other invasion matériel gathered there. The French responded by stepping up their activity at the Brittany ports other than Brest, to which Hawke responded in turn by extending his blockade to those ports. In September, the invasion transports at Nantes contrived to slip out of the Loire escorted by three frigates, but a British squadron of four fifty-gun ships and four frigates under Commodore Robert Duff pursued them into Quiberon Bay on the south coast of Brittany and compelled them to take refuge in the narrow channels leading to Auray. There, nevertheless, the transports at least had the advantage of proximity to the potential army of invasion, now assembled at Vennes in southern Brittany, whence by the waters of the Morbihan they might be carried into Quiberon Bay and on to the open sea.

Hawke warned the Admiralty of the obvious: that when the gales of late autumn and winter arrived, he might not be able to maintain station. Meanwhile intelligence warned of French preparations to take advantage of those coming conditions.

On November 7 a westerly gale forced Hawke, as he had feared, to abandon his station off Brest and, after trying vainly to regain his place, to make for Torbay on the 9th, leaving several frigates to watch the French. On the 7th, meanwhile, the same westerly gale brought a French squadron returning from the West Indies into the waters off Brest. Finding the main British fleet gone, this squadron put into harbor and reported Hawke's absence to the commander there, Herbert de Brienne, comte de Conflans, *vice-amiral du Levant* and *maréchal de France*. Acting under orders governing his conduct should the British blockading force draw away, Conflans put to sea, sailing for the Morbihan and a junction with the army of invasion and its transports. Conflans had shown himself an able enough captain during the War of the Austrian Succession, but unlike that other veteran French seaman La Galissonière, he had drawn from an exceedingly long naval career—fifty-three years—less of skill than of weariness and short temper.

Hawke put out from Torbay on November 12, but a renewed gale drove him back again on the 13th. Not until the 14th was he able to stand down the Channel toward Ushant; but the same wind that carried him also carried the French warships toward their rendezvous with the transports in the Morbihan. On the 16th, Hawke met a British victualling vessel, the *Love and Unity*, whose captain reported that the day before he had seen eighteen French ships of the line and two frigates some seventy miles (about 110 kilometers) west of Belle-Isle, the island guarding the entrance to Quiberon Bay. The ships were making for the bay. This information confirmed other reports that Hawke had already received from British intelligence. Hawke immediately took up the pursuit, and on November 18 and 19 he caught winds favoring his own course southeastward toward Belle-Isle.

The next morning Commodore Duff, watching the French transports, received warning that France's Brest fleet was nearing the south point of Belle-Isle. Duff had little choice but to attempt to escape from Quiberon Bay as the enemy entered it, which would not be easy. One of his ships made its way around the north shore of Belle-Isle, but that course was so dangerous with shoal waters that the rest chanced passing close to the jaws of the French south of the island. Their seamanship saved them from an effort to cut them off, but the French were pursuing them when at half past eight the frigate *Maidstone*, 28, in advance of Hawke's fleet signaled that the French fleet lay ahead. The French in turn soon spotted Hawke's van and gave up the pursuit of Duff.

The French actually had twenty-one ships of the line, the British twenty-seven once Duff's four smallish ones—his fifties—joined Hawke. Fearing the combination of superior British numbers with British seamanship, and wearily lacking confidence in the invasion enterprise, Conflans stood about to regain the sheltered waters of Quiberon Bay. He thought that by forming line of battle there he might have a better chance of surviving than at sea. Hawke promptly hoisted the signal for a general chase, and by the middle of a day of blustery, continually changing winds his ships were rounding the south point of Belle-Isle, where fearsome swells were breaking against the cliffs, while similar geysers of spray leapt from a myriad of rocks and small islands ahead. The French had local pilots to guide them through these perils as the wind blew increasingly hard from the west-northwest and frequent rain showers and squalls obscured every lookout's vision; Conflans believed—or he hoped—that without pilots a British pursuit past the rocks called the Grand Cardinals to the left and the Four Shoal (Le Four) to the right would be suicidal. In Hawke's place, he himself would certainly never have pursued in such waters when the wind was now blowing a gale. But Hawke maintained the chase. Where French seamen could lead, he felt confident, English seamen could surely follow. He had watched his ships and men through all the vicissitudes of his close blockade; he knew that they could accomplish near-miracles. He had also taken accurate measure of the quality of his adversary.

And Hawke was more than a skilled seaman. He was a strategist, in that his object as he conceived it was to achieve not merely the frustration of the current invasion attempts but Great Britain's victory in the war. To that end, he proposed to destroy the French fleet in battle, leaving it never again a factor in this war.

For the second time in his career, Hawke was aided by the circumstance that in a chase the rigid tactics of the line ahead were not required to be applied. He was free to hurry his ships into Quiberon Bay and to let them find their targets of opportunity. His strategic goal and his freedom from the line ahead had to be pursued at the cost of fighting under unprecedented conditions for a major naval battle—in gathering darkness, among rocks, under gale-force winds, and against a lee shore. Never in history was an admiral bolder; never was the quality of British seamanship more harshly tested.

Entering the bay, three of the leading British ships collided with each other, wrecking their jib-booms and spritsail yards and briefly delaying the pursuit. The French *Thésée*, a new vessel of eighty guns, was engaged by Captain Augustus Keppel's *Torbay*, 80; a small squall laid the *Thésée* on its beam ends with its gunports open for firing, and it immediately filled and sank, taking down some 600 men. Hawke's flagship, *Royal George*, 100, made as directly as possible for the French flagship, *Soleil Royal*, 80. The two flagships exchanged broadsides, and several other French vessels joined in engaging the *Royal George*—whose size, like that of the *Soleil Royal*, made it one of the few ships distinctive enough to be identifiable. One of the French challengers, the *Superbe*, 70, foundered under two broadsides from Hawke's ship.

Hawke's initiating a general melee had rendered impossible Conflans's hope to form line of battle in the bay. Impatience and indecision were corollaries of the French admiral's fatigue and absence of confidence, so he now put the *Soleil Royal* about to try to lead as many of its consorts as could see and follow it back out of the bay and in flight to open waters. The flagship collided, however, with two other French vessels and was thus thrown off course by the time it was five o'clock and almost completely dark. Seven other French ships meanwhile sought escape in the opposite direction, by sailing up into the shallow estuary of the little River Vilaine.

No one could have known the full state of affairs when the fitful visibility of late afternoon faded altogether, but in fact two French ships were sunk, *Thésée* and *Superbe*; another, *Formidable*, 80, was a wreck in British hands; and a fourth, *Juste*, 70, had made for the sea after suffering heavy damage and soon wrecked itself near the mouth of the River Loire; another, *Héros*, 74, had run aground and would be at the enemy's mercy at daybreak. In the darkness Conflans in the *Soleil Royal* anchored amidst the British, then tried to slip away and ran aground also. During the fighting Hawke's bold gamble against wind, rocks, and the enemy had cost his fleet no major loss: as certain a vindication as there could be of the qualities of the Royal Navy in which he had put his trust. But about ten o'clock at night the *Resolution*, 74, scraped onto the Four Shoal, and when morning came and the *Essex*, 64, tried to join in completing the enemy's destruction, it too grounded itself on the same obstacle.

The persistent gale blew so hard on November 20, in fact, that Hawke had to abandon further pursuit and strike topgallant masts, spending the day using boats to rescue as many seamen of both nationalities as could be found. The *Resolution* and the *Essex* proved hopelessly breached, but most of their crews were gotten off. The next day's weather was little different, but five of the French ships that had made for the mouth of the Vilaine managed, by tossing guns overboard and with the aid of the high tide and the volume of water blown into the bay by the gale, to bump across the bar into the safety of the Vilaine. No ships of their size had ever entered this stream before—albeit the *Inflexible*, 64, broke its back in the process.

The next day the weather moderated, and Hawke dispatched three of Duff's vessels to burn the *Soleil Royal* and the *Héros*. The few crewmen still aboard the French flagship—Conflans had long since debarked—set fire to it before the British arrived, so the British settled for burning the *Héros*. Hawke then turned toward the Morbihan, and the two French vessels remaining near the mouth of the Vilaine contrived to cross the bar into that river. Hawke spent several days trying to devise means to get at them—preferably using fireboats—but eventually gave up. He then returned to England.

His failure to penetrate the Vilaine did not much matter; the French ships in it remained immobilized for most of a year, and another three of them broke their backs in the mud. Altogether, the battle of Quiberon bay (or Les Cardinaux, as the French call it from the one of the perilous rock outcroppings near the entrance) had cost the Royal Navy the two ships stranded on the Four Shoal and some 300 to 400 men; the French directly lost seven ships, plus the three eventually ruined in the Vilaine, and some 2,500 men. The French had also lost all chance of invading Britain or reversing the naval balance of the war. In quick succession, Québec and Quiberon Bay had climaxed a year of British victories that also included Minden and the capture at last of Ticonderoga as well as Fort Niagara in North America. In the West Indies, the British had captured the island of Guadelupe. In India, French naval leadership in the unenterprising mold of Conflans failed to exploit superior numbers; instead, the East India Company's Governor of Bengal, Sir Robert Clive, was allowed to assure British predominance in the subcontinent. The Year of Victories had sealed the transformation of England from a second-rank power on the periphery of Europe to the greatest of the world's maritime and imperial powers.

And the most important of the year's victories was Admiral Hawke's at Quiberon Bay. In the following century, when naval officership would at length become a profession comparable to army officership, the foundation would be the study of strategy, and professional critics would come to focus on the dictum that the primary object of a navy in war ought to be the destruction of the enemy fleet. That destruction would assure the command of the seas, whereupon naval power could yield all manner of additional benefits—the ability to constrict the enemy's economy by blockade, the ability at the same time to draw upon the resources of the entire world for oneself. Without the destruction of the enemy fleet, however, even an inferior navy in the enemy's hands can embarrass and hinder the strategy of a superior sea power, as the French Navy in the Seven Years War plagued the British by capturing Minorca and by continually diverting attention from imperial goals with the threat of an invasion of the British home islands—until Quiberon Bay. In one stroke, Hawke eliminated all capacity of the French to threaten Britain itself or to obstruct its ventures overseas. Sir Edward Hawke was therefore to be a hero to the nineteenth-century critics of naval strategy, and Quiberon Bay a model of the proper use of naval power in war.

Colonial Wars and European Wars

The immense gains that the British Empire wrested from the Seven Years War might seem to give the lie to the argument that war almost never offers dividends proportionate to its costs. But the gains were possible not in the ordinary course of war but because of exceptional circumstances not to be found anywhere in the world today, and not to be found in the cockpit of European war in the eighteenth century but only outside Europe.

The expansion of the British Empire in the mid-eighteenth century was less a matter of expansion through success in conflict than of moving into vacuums. The areas in which Great Britain planted its new empire offered a vacuum in terms of military power; the native populations of North America, of the sugar islands of the Caribbean, and of India did not yet possess the social cohesion or the sense of nationhood, apart from their relative backwardness in military technology, that would have enabled them to halt European aggression. In spite of occasional instances of dramatic resistance by the North American Indians to the European invasion of their homeland, the Native Americans in general were so weak militarily that the British colonies expanded at their expense less by means of military force than through the appropriation of land by means of planting towns and farms. Native resistance was weak enough that the British imperial frontier in North America was less a soldier's than a settler's frontier.

The prime military weapon of weaker peoples against the military great powers in our own time, guerrilla warfare, was scarcely available to the eighteenth-century victims of British overseas expansion, because while guerrilla resistance does not require military and technological capacities equal to the invader's, it does demand social cohesion and an ability of leaders to articulate and of the people to understand shared purposes that can be realized only by expelling the invaders. It is significant that the first major guerrilla resistance to the British Empire came not from any of the indigenous inhabitants of the colonies but was to develop after the close of the Seven Years War, in the War of the American Revolution, among the European inhabitants of British North America. Europeans transplanted to America possessed the social, cultural, and political requisites to mount a guerrilla uprising; the North American aborigines did not.

The British Empire was able to expand into the military vacuum of the non-European world, moreover, thanks to another vacuum or at least near-vacuum; not even in Europe was there a rival power able to challenge more than sporadically that mastery of the oceans which permitted the British to travel freely to and from their new imperial domains. France was too much bound up in European politics, diplomacy, and war to generate a consistent opposition to British supremacy at sea, and therefore France lacked the access to overseas territories that might have allowed it a more than occasionally effective resistance to British supremacy in America and Asia as well. The Netherlands and Spain no longer commanded the economic and financial resources to compete seriously with Great Britain for naval mastery. No other European state even attempted to become a competing naval power. Thus for most of the middle eighteenth century Britain operated without major military hindrance in conquering its empire overseas, because its navy occupied what was otherwise a naval vacuum and thereby shielded the building of the empire from European interference.

Among the European great powers, competing with approximate parity of strength in war on land, wars of armies as instruments of state policy persisted in their incapacity to produce gains proportionate to their costs. Their dominant characteristic continued to be their indecisiveness. War had never rewarded Guistavus Adolphus or Louis XIV to anything like the extent they desired, their considerable professional improvement of their armies notwithstanding; war did not richly reward any eighteenth-century European land power either. (Frederick the Great was the one possible exception, but the strains of the Seven Years War went far to undermine the advantages his army had seized at the beginning of the War of the Austrian Succession.)

It was not sea power as an instrument of war that built the British Empire, however glorious was Hawke's victory at Quiberon Bay, so much as sea power as a means of moving into power vacuums.

10   TOWARD WARS OF NATIONS: THE WAR OF AMERICAN INDEPENDENCE

T he British victories of 1759 led to the Treaty of Paris, signed February 10, 1763, whereby France formally acquiesced in British imperial ascendancy. Guadeloupe was returned to France to sweeten the pill of surrendering Louis XV's vast North American empire, but otherwise the treaty was a ratification of Great Britain's military triumphs by land and by sea. Even Minorca reverted to British sovereignty; having learned, however, that Gibraltar could offer adequate basing in the western Mediterranean, the British never again invested much in the recovered island, and Spain was to take possession of it during the next war.

In another Treaty of Paris signed little more than twenty years later, September 3, 1783, Great Britain lost much of its North American prize along with its traditional North American colonies, and France gained a measure of revenge, in the War of the American Revolution that resulted in the independence of the Unites States of America. This reversal of fortune was not the product of any major reversal in the Anglo-French balance of military power or of any significant diminution of the British military virtues that had won the victories of 1759 and the treaty of 1763. It is true that the British allowed their navy to deteriorate sadly in numbers and quality of ships between the Seven Years War and the War of American Independence, overconfidently letting too many vessels molder in drydocks, and neglecting the maintenance even of those that continued in active service. It is true also that the French Navy in the interval, spurred by the humiliations of Quiberon Bay and similar disasters, underwent another of its periodic spasms of reform and rejuvenation; but the French may already have had superior quality in ships in 1759, the sources of British naval supremacy lying elsewhere.

It is true, too, that Britain's waging of the war of 1775–1783—first, against the rebellious colonies; from June 17, 1778, against France as well; from June 21, 1779, against Spain; from December 20, 1780, against the United Netherlands— was wracked by administrative inefficiency and an absence of coherent strategic direction. A crazy quilt of agencies, evolving over decades, by now divided the administration of both the army and the Royal Navy; and in the absence of William Pitt—since August 1766 the first Earl of Chatham and first Viscount Pitt; but in shattered health and on May 11, 1778, dying—the crazy quilt wrecked any hope of strategic coherence. Yet this machinery of government had been scarcely better during the Seven Years War, except for Pitt's personal influence and perhaps Anson's at the Admiralty, and the gears had often clattered and clanked in that war as well. Moreover, administrative inefficiency was not crippling enough to prevent extraordinary achievements during the new war in the logistical support over trans-Atlantic distances of armies bigger than those deployed by Pitt. Because the countryside of the rebellious American colonies turned so hostile that foraging for provisions there became an uncertain enterprise, even foodstuffs for the army in America were in large part shipped across some 3,000 miles of ocean. The British war machine of the late eighteenth century functioned more effectively in fact that any diagram of its structure on paper would have suggested was possible.

The Conduct of the War of American Independence

In any event, it was neither strategic incoherence nor administrative inefficiency that lost the war; almost certainly no strategy and no excellence in military administration could have prevailed against the American rebellion. Nor was the war lost by a lack of professional qualities in the officer corps of the British Army and Navy. Indeed, the higher British Army commanders in the War of American Independence could boast of impressive self-education in writings on strategy and military history. This was especially true of General (his local rank; his permanent rank was major-general) Sir William Howe, commander-in-chief in the rebellious colonies from April 1776 to May 1778. According to his own expressions of his purpose, Howe shared the strategic insight that had served Admiral Hawke so well, a focus on the destruction of the enemy force in battle as the direct path to victory. If he did not so consistently apply this clarity of vision in his actions, it was at least in part because of the inherently ambiguous nature of his role in America; he and his elder brother, Vice-Admiral Richard Howe, first Viscount Howe (an Irish title; in 1782 he received the United Kingdom title of First Viscount Howe of Langar), were peace commissioners to the rebels at the same time that they were also, respectively, the army and navy commanders against the rebellion. To press battlefield victories too hard always appeared in General Howe's mind to risk undercutting his hopes for conciliation.

And especially during General Howe's tenure in command, British battlefield victories were numerous. It was no loss of the disciplined tactical proficiency of the British soldier that cost Britain the War of American Independence either, nor in the Royal Navy any loss of the superiority in seamanship that so long had been the key element in curbing the French. In the battles on land, the British Army could throughout the war feel confident that in any action pitting approximately equal numbers of their own troops—or even moderately inferior numbers—against the rebels in conditions of approximately equal tactical advantage in terrain and position, British discipline and tactical skill would produce a British victory.

It reflects creditably on the American rebels, in fact, that by the later years of the war they made deep inroads into this British tactical superiority, and that toward the end the British margin had become an exceedingly narrow one. A few units of the rebels' Continental Army, notably the Maryland and Delaware Lines—as the various state contributions to the army were styled—cut the margin altogether and attained parity with the British in soldierly skills. The ability of the Continentals to progress so far toward equaling an infantry that only the Prussians may have surpassed, and to do so in a few short years after beginning with a few commissioned officers and proportionately far fewer sergeants experienced in European drill and discipline to train the troops, was a tribute especially to the tenacity with which the Commander-in-Chief of the Continental Army, General George Washington, pursued the goal of creating a new army on the British model. From his service with Braddock in 1755 onward, Washington regarded British regulars as the embodiment of an almost ideal military discipline. As military commander of the American rebellion, he believed that the dignity of the American cause, the pursuit of liberty, demanded nothing less than an army of a skill worthy of the cause. With the aid from 1778 onward of a drillmaster who possessed first-hand experience of the Prussian system, Major-General Friedrich Wilhelm Augustus Baron (Freiherr) von Steuben (he frequently came to style himself de Steuben), and against the limitation of time and of the ability of any two individuals to manufacture an entire army, Washington nearly succeeded in raising the Continental Army to the qualitative level of the enemy. He bequeathed to the American Army a legacy of tactical excellence from its beginning.

Washington and Steuben nearly succeeded—but not quite. The British margin became narrow, and against elite American units nonexistent, but for the rival armies as a whole the margin remained to the end of the war. The source of British defeat did not lie in tactical lapses.

In part, the sources lay rather in a new kind of war, for which European military skills of the eighteenth century did not prepare the British Army. This was unconventional, partisan war, the kind of war that later would be commonly termed guerrilla warfare. Major-General John Burgoyne's British invasion of New York State by coming southward along the St. Lawrence River–Richelieu River–Lake Champlain–Hudson River route in 1777 ended with Burgoyne's surrender of his army at Saratoga on October 17 largely because of the operations of semi-irregular militia against his line of communications. Between the headwaters of Lake Champlain and the Hudson there was wooded and marshy country that greatly aided such operations. The raiders were part-time soldiers, essentially civilians, and thus although they often wore some sort of uniform, they met one of the criteria of what constitutes a guerrilla, the blurring or erasure of the line between combatant and noncombatant so that the warrior can disappear at his convenience into the surrounding society at large. It was the ruination of Burgoyne's logistics by the combination of irregular raiders and inhospitable terrain more than battlefield defeats—though toward the end he suffered those, too—that destroyed his expedition.

In the South, in the Carolinas and Georgia, the British were undone by a still closer approximation of modern guerrilla warfare. There the British contrived almost to reconquer three of the rebellious provinces in the course of 1779–1781, but their reconquest turned sour when the harsh treatment of former rebels and suspected rebels—a lamentable strategic error—provoked an expanding series of guerrilla uprisings to harry lines of communications and isolated garrisons. Spearheading the uprisings were the South Carolina Brigadier-Generals Francis Marion, "the Swamp Fox," who operated mainly in the low country near the coast, and Thomas Sumter, "the Gamecock," who operated mainly in higher country farther inland. British tactical skills being what they were, if the British could run the guerrillas down they could usually beat them in fight. For that reason the uprisings might in time have been suppressed had not the American cause been favored from October 14, 1780, by the presence of Major-General Nathanael Greene in command of the Southern Department.

Greene proved to possess an intuitive strategic grasp akin to Admiral Hawke's, but a more subtle one. He readily perceived effective means of blending together the operations of the partisans with those of his small force of Continentals and militia. Particularly, he impaled the British upon a classic dilemma of any army seeking to repress a guerrilla insurgency that is assisted by regular forces. If the occupying army concentrates itself to deal with the opposing regulars, then it leaves the countryside and its small garrisons vulnerable to the guerrillas. If on the other hand the occupying army scatters to deal with the guerrillas, then it exposes its dispersed detachments to destruction by the guerrillas' regular allies.

Furthermore, Greene was not too proud to adopt even for his Continentals an essential tactic of the guerrilla; to run away rather than risk destruction, and if possible to use running as a weapon. In the Race to the Dan from early January to February 14, 1781—the flight of Greene's army to relative security north of the Dan River in southern Virginia—Greene seduced the main British army in the South into exhausting marches with most of its baggage left behind, while Greene could find fresh provisions and other supplies awaiting him in Virginia. The chase so weakened the British that promptly afterward Greene felt free to countermarch into North Carolina and to meet their tired troops in battle, at Guilford Courthouse on March 15. The British won the battle, but barely, and their battlefield casualties combined with their fatigue and shortage of supplies drove them to retreat to the coast.

In the Race to the Dan, Greene capitalized on the rival commander's possession of what is usually a military virtue; the very aggressiveness of Lieutenant-General Charles, second Earl Cornwallis, an able soldier sufficiently self-educated and sufficiently committed to his army career to approximate professionalism, carried Cornwallis toward his downfall against Greene by impelling him to pursue the rebels to the Dan. And through their resort to unconventional warfare first against Cornwallis and then against subsequent British commanders, Greene and the partisan bands stripped the enemy of what had seemed his most promising achievement of the war, his reconquest of three of the rebellious provinces, Georgia and the Carolinas.

Even the difficulties of the British Army in confronting its first major test in guerrilla war were not, however, the principal sources of defeat in the War of American Independence. Of thirteen provinces in rebellion, only three were reconquered by the British even briefly, and in two of those—Georgia and South Carolina—there had always been an exceptionally strong Loyalist element as a potential aid to reconquest. In the remaining ten rebellious provinces, the British never came close to suppressing the Revolution. Their failure to do so in the bulk of the disputed colonies points toward the crux of their problem in the American Rebellion, which the tactical and disciplinary virtues of their battalions could not overcome. The British were probably fighting an inherently unwinnable war.

Because the Continental Army never quite matched the British in tactical proficiency, General Washington lost most of the battles that he fought. By late 1776 he had grown sufficiently aware that such was his fate that thenceforth he usually declined battle against the main British forces rather than go on losing. By declining battle, he kept the Continental Army alive and thus believed he could keep the Revolutionary cause alive. To try to sustain Revolutionary morale while eroding British morale, Washington substituted for full-scale battles between the rival armies a vigilance for opportunities to strike hit-and-run blows against relatively weak enemy detachments, tactics akin to those of guerrilla war but employed not by irregulars who faded into the citizenry but by his regular soldiers. His strikes against Trenton on December 26, 1776, and Princeton on January 3, 1777, were his principal triumphs of the type; the actions at Stony Point, New York, on July 16, 1779, and Paulus Hook, New Jersey, on August 19 of the same year are further examples of the method. But Washington's strategy for keeping the Revolution alive by avoiding large battles while occasionally stimulating Revolutionary moral and chipping away at British morale and resolve was simply his skillful way of exploiting the more fundamental American advantages and British disadvantages inherent in the nature of the struggle.

From the outbreak of the war at Lexington and Concord on April 19, 1775, the rebels controlled almost every acre of the thirteen rebellious colonies except those few where the British Army was present. The rebels continued thus to control almost every acre of the country throughout the war, except in Georgia and the Carolinas for a time before the successes of Nathanael Greene and the partisan warriors. From the beginning of fighting, Revolutionary sentiment was so preponderant that the British could reassert control of a district only by occupying it with their troops. But the American rebels were in their own country, while the British Army was not. The British had nothing remotely approaching the number of soldiers needed to occupy indefinitely all of the infant United

States. Sooner or later their troops had to evacuate a district and immediately thereafter the rebels came back into control. Sooner or later the British Army had to go home, and then the rebels would control their own country. Here was the problem that no amount of British tactical or strategic skill could overcome. The essence of the American challenge for the British Army, like the heart of many subsequent contests of counterrevolutionary war, was that the fundamental issues were not military but political.

To say all that is not, however, to say that a firm majority of the people in the rebellious colonies consistently supported the Revolution. A firm majority of that kind rarely existed in any part of America, and certainly not throughout the new United States. Loyalty to the Crown was distinctly a minority position in all but a few areas, but genuinely zealous support of the Revolution was almost always also the attitude of a minority, and perhaps not much bigger a minority than the Loyalists. There is good reason to suspect that at least half the population desired mainly to be allowed to go about their daily business, unmolested by either side. But a desire to be free to carry out one's own trade and live one's own life made for at least an inclination toward American independence rather than a restoration of British authority, and that inclination was enough to permit the zealous Revolutionaries to dominate the scene almost everywhere and almost all the time. Particularly it was often true that by applying a modicum of organizing skill, the Revolutionaries were able almost everywhere throughout the war to control the part-time military organizations of citizen-soldiers, the militia, and the slightly more professional volunteer armies that had been established earlier for defense against the Indians, the French, and the Spanish.

This assertion of control over the provincial military forces gave the Revolutionaries a monopoly of organized armed force almost everywhere that the enemy army was not physically present. It meant that from the beginning of the war the Revolutionaries were in control of almost all of the original United States, and that from the beginning the British were not engaged in retaining what they already possessed but in the more difficult task of reconquest. Under these circumstances, for Great Britain to win the War of American Independence was almost impossible.

Almost—but not quite. The likelihood that the largest single bloc of the American population was relatively indifferent to the outcome meant that the Revolution was always fragile. At the outset, simply wanting to go about one's own business meant a slight leaning toward the Revolutionary cause, which promised all Americans freedom to control their own affairs. Once the war became prolonged, however, and brought with it troublesome economic dislocation, then the indifferent might turn toward favoring the British cause, in that they might well blame the Revolutionaries for their discomforts, while a restoration of British authority might come to seem the shortest route toward a return to stability. By the summer of 1781 the war that had begun in April 1775 had grown prolonged indeed, and severe economic dislocations had developed, especially runaway currency inflation as well as disturbance by marching and sometimes marauding armies. By that time both British and American leaders, particularly Washington himself, were coming to believe that the Revolution had lost its momentum, that it was approaching death through inertia. If by the seventh year of the war some dramatic new development did not infuse a generous accession of new hope and energy into the American cause, the cause seemed about to wither away. The British might yet win the war, if the Americans became so indifferent to their liberty that they would resubmit to British authority and continue to do so after the bulk of the British Army went home.

Fortunately for the Revolution, the dramatic event that might have been necessary to resuscitate the American cause took place in the autumn of 1781. It proceeded from a most unlikely source—a French naval victory in American waters.

The Capes of the Chesapeake and Yorktown

From the outset of the French alliance, Washington hoped that a French fleet in North American waters might sufficiently embarrass Great Britain's already strained lines of communications to provide the occasion for some sort of Franco-American military triumph that might reverse the Revolution's faltering momentum and bring a favorable end to the war. The French early complied with his hopes to the extent of dispatching various naval contingents, but until 1781 French naval intervention proved as ineffectual as the entire recent history of the Anglo-French rivalry at sea might have suggested it would be. In any event the French were more interested in using their navy to defend and perhaps enlarge their West Indian possessions than to do anything directly for the American rebels.

In August 1778 Admiral Lord Howe had followed his brother, the general, homeward to defend their conduct of their American commands to critics in Parliament. The choice of Admiral Howe's successors suggested a certain naval complacency in Great Britain; none was especially distinguished, certainly not Rear-Admiral Thomas Graves, who took over the American fleet on July 4, 1781. While Graves maintained the tradition of skillful seamanship, he was in all other respects a lackluster commander, especially in terms of energy and resolution.

The French, in contrast, sent out in 1781 François Joseph Paul, comte de Grasse du Bar, *lieutenant général*, an imposing figure over six feet tall whose sense of purpose was as impressive as his presence. De Grasse reached Martinique on April 28. While he was obliged to remain primarily concerned with the West Indies, he early indicated to Washington through the French Army commander in North America, Jean Baptiste Donatien de Vimeur, vicomte de Rochambeau, *lieutenant général*, that he would be eager to cooperate with the land forces along the North American coast, especially in the late summer and early fall when the hurricane season struck the West Indies.

The main British troop concentration against the American rebellion was now in New York City, under the immediate command of General Howe's successor, General Sir Henry Clinton. General Lord Cornwallis had decided after Guilford Courthouse to operate in Virginia rather than the Carolinas; he could readily persuade himself that Virginia was one of the primary centers of the rebellion, but there is also the suspicion that he no longer wished to tangle with Nathanael Greene and the Carolina partisans. Combined military-naval operations against Clinton in New York or Cornwallis in Virginia might be possible for the French and Americans. Washington favored an effort against the main target, New York. De Grasse preferred the lesser risks of striking against Cornwallis in Virginia.

As early as May 3 Sir George Brydges Rodney, first Baronet Rodney, Admiral of the White and commanding the British West Indies fleet, warned the North American fleet that de Grasse might sail north. Rodney himself was preoccupied, however, with the division of the rich spoils of the Dutch island of St. Eustatius, which had been the major transshipment point for European goods bound for the American rebels until, on learning of the Netherlands' entry into the war, Rodney had captured it on February 3. To say that Rodney was preoccupied is in fact an understatement; usually an admiral of high competence, he had grown obsessed with enriching himself by garnering the largest possible share of the spoils. His health as well as his mind became for the time being unhinged, and on August 1 he returned home to England to convalesce.

His fixation on St. Eustatius had already aided the enemy immeasurably. De Grasse had arrived in the West Indies with his ships of the line encumbered by a large convoy of merchantmen, and Rodney might well have intercepted him to windward of Martinique and brought him to battle under conditions exceedingly favorable to the British. Failing that, with twenty-nine of the line Rodney might still have tried to force an action with de Grasse in the spring or early summer. Now, before departing for home Rodney dispatched Rear-Admiral Sir Samuel Hood with fourteen of the line to join forces with Graves, whom he advised to unite with Hood along the Virginia coast. But he himself did not consider the issues critical enough to delay his trip to England. Thus the mediocre Graves would be the senior officer and commander of Hood's force and his own five servicable ships of the line.

Hood, sailing for Chesapeake Bay by a direct route while de Grasse followed a circuitous one through the Bahama Channel to elude observation, arrived off Virginia before the French. He looked into the Chesapeake and, finding it empty, proceeded to New York. There he met Graves, and their combined fleet returned forthwith to the Chesapeake, where General Lord Cornwallis had plunged himself into a predicament upon which the Americans and the French must not be allowed to capitalize. On August 22 the Earl had moved his force of at least 9,750 men into defensive positions at Yorktown, on the south shore of the York River on the Virginia Peninsula between the York and the James, with a small part of the force in a supporting position at Gloucester across the York. Cornwallis felt confident that his project to reconquer Virginia was important enough that Clinton would have to send him reinforcements. But Clinton and he had been quarrelling about the matter, and there was now a good chance that overwhelming enemy forces would arrive before any succor from New York.

A rebel force of something over 3,500 already had Cornwallis under close observation and could restrict his movements. Much more than that, Washington had already resolved to march to Yorktown with 2,500 of his own troops and

Rochambeau's entire force of 4,000, having concerted plans with de Grasse to rendezvous in the Chesapeake. The Franco-American march from the Hudson began on August 19, carefully screened from British intelligence. The British did know, however, that a powerful French fleet was headed for the Chesapeake. Furthermore, a French squadron based on Newport, Rhode Island, had sailed with eight ships of the line—along with Rochambeau's siege train—to join forces with de Grasse and his twenty-four of the line. Unless Graves and Hood could shoo de Grasse away, Cornwallis was about to discover that he had entered a trap.

Graves and Hood arrived off Cape Henry at the entrance to the Chesapeake on September 5. De Grasse had been engaged in landing troops since September 2; he had brought 3,000 from Saint-Domingue to help ensure closing the trap and had landing forces totaling 800 available from his own fleet. As soon as the approaching British were spotted, de Grasse naturally suspended his landing operations and prepared to put to sea, hoping to round Cape Henry and reach open water before the British fleet could begin to engage; he was no Conflans, timidly depending on sheltered waters to assist him. His boldness might have proven excessive, however, for the British had a following wind, and Graves came within range when only the leading French ships had rounded the cape, while most of de Grasse's fleet was still far astern in the bay. Graves had the opportunity to crush the French van with superior weight of numbers and metal.

Yet he did not do so. The dead hand of the line ahead gripped a British fleet once more—along with Graves's timid concentration of his attention not on his opportunity but on the superior total numbers of the French. Close action began between the leading ships of the rival fleets, but Graves did not press hard to exploit his initial advantage, and the French immediately tried to veer away. Graves might have emulated Hawke and ordered a general chase after the vulnerable French vanguard. Instead, he hoisted a confusing succession of signal flags, flying alternately the command to close upon the enemy and the command to keep the line ahead. Not knowing what was expected of them, all the more because most of them had just joined Graves and were unfamiliar with his methods, the British captains failed to bring the French to decisive action. Hood, with the rear division, never engaged at all, which brought about prolonged recriminations between him and Graves.

The battle of the Capes of the Chesapeake was a tactical victory for the French by no clearcut margin, but it was a strategic victory for the French and Americans that sealed the principal outcome of the war. In exchanges of gunfire lasting about two and a half hours and ending at darkness, only the eight leading British ships and the first fifteen French ships to emerge from the Chesapeake were significantly engaged—although the French thus achieved numerical superiority despite Graves's opening advantage. The British ship *Terrible*, 64, was so badly battered that it had to be scuttled on the night of September 9–10. De Grasse's flagship, *Ville de Paris*, 100, so punished its counterpart, the *London*, 98, that all its masts had to be replaced. The French lost 220 killed and wounded, the British 90 killed and 246 wounded.

The rival fleets remained in contact for the next two days without renewing the battle. In the process they drifted southward to the Cape Hatteras area. Concerned about assuring that the Newport squadron with its siege artillery should arrive safely inside the Chesapeake, de Grasse turned north on September 8, maneuvering also for the weather gauge. The next morning Graves's ships were no longer in sight, but during part of the day de Grasse's ships followed a squadron whose identity they could not discern. They eventually lost sight of these ships also; but on reentering the Chesapeake on September 11, de Grasse discovered that the Newport squadron had entered on the 10th; it was this squadron he had seen on September 9. Graves, also returning northward, dallied off the Virginia coast for several days. But with de Grasse reinforced, there was little chance of Graves's fighting him to good advantage. On the 14th the British made sail for New York. The battle of the Chesapeak Capes had decided Cornwallis's fate.

Washington and Rochambeau, riding ahead of their forces, reached the Peninsula on the same day that Graves departed. The advance of their armies approached within a mile of Cornwallis's defensive works by nightfall two weeks later. A formal siege commenced. Guided by foreign officers, the Americans by now had their own competent service of military engineers to work with the French. On the evening of October 14, simultaneous French and American attacks captured two key British works, Redoubts Number 9 and 10, respectively. Two nights later Cornwallis attempted to ferry his main force across the York River to Gloucester to try to escape, but a shortage of boats and a severe storm frustrated him. Meanwhile General Clinton had resolved to mount a relief expedition; but by the time the damage done to Graves's ships had been repaired (while a new naval commander-in-chief, Rear-Admiral Robert Digby, replaced Graves), it was October 27 before Clinton arrived off the Virginia Capes with the fleet and 7,000 troops.

Cornwallis, despairing after his inability to flee to Gloucester, had already surrendered his army, on October 20. There was nothing left for Clinton and Digby to save. Even if the rescue effort had come earlier, it probably could not have broken de Grasse's defensive line of ships protecting the siege operations.

The French Navy had given the American Revolutionary cause the additional moral impetus that was almost certainly indispensable, while in Britain Cornwallis's surrender proved to shift the parliamentary balance to factions favoring peace. Almost all concerned in those factions still resisted American independence. When peace, however, proved procurable only along with recognition of the independence of the United States, the thirst for peace eventually prevailed in spite of the bitterness of the draft that had to be drunk.

Eventually, but not quite yet; the War of American Independence did not end with the surrender at Yorktown in October 1781. Before the freedom of America was recognized, moreover, Admiral Rodney shook off his illnesses both physical and mental to strike a mighty blow for a different kind of freedom, that of the Royal Navy from the paralyzing dictum of the line ahead.

The Battle of Ushant

The effort to escape that paralysis, following up Hawke's triumphant liberation from it at Quiberon Bay, had persisted sporadically from the outbreak of the new war but with disappointing results. The French began this latest round of the maritime struggle in 1778 with the strategic idea that had increasingly fascinated them during the last war, until Hawke squelched the idea. They proposed the most direct strategy, an invasion of England.

They hoped that Great Britain's preoccupation with subduing the American Revolution would prove a far more effective diversion than French Mediterranean operations had ever been, and it was for this diversionary purpose rather than with the notion that for France the western hemisphere could represent the main arena that the French dispatched fleets and armies to the New World. Therefore almost as soon as hostilities commenced the French put to sea a fleet of thirty-two ships of the line to challenge the British Channel Fleet. The French commander, as was becoming habitual, was a veteran to a perhaps excessive degree, Louis Guillouet, comte d'Orvilliers, *lieutenant général*, sixty-eight years old with fifty years' experience at sea. As with Conflans, the hope was that experienced seamanship would compensate for any infirmities of age. The British Channel Fleet, under Augustus Henry Keppel of Quiberon Bay fame, flying the flag of a vice-admiral, was quickly reinforced from twenty-one to thirty ships to counter the French. The years since Quiberon Bay had been a time of almost frenzied efforts toward improvements in the French Navy and of complacent neglect in the British, yet the balance of force was remarkably little affected.

After the rival fleets first sighted each other they were swallowed up by fog for several days, and two of the French ships became separated and returned to Brest. D'Orvilliers had thus lost his numerical superiority by the time he went into action on July 27.

The fleets had found each other again about seventy nautical miles (about 130 kilometers) west of Ushant. The wind was southwesterly, and the French had the weather gauge. Keppel ordered his ships to beat against the wind in a general chase to bring the French to battle. Cautiously, however, the British formed the conventional line ahead as they came into action. D'Orvilliers concluded from Keppel's initial direction that he was trying to concentrate against the rearward French ships, so the French commander ordered his ships to wear in succession in a way that brought the two fleets into action in parallel lines. D'Orvilliers's seamanship was vindicating his selection to command, for now the gunnery of the French, honed in the course of the reform efforts, proved superior. The *Ville de Paris* under Luc Urbain de Boüexic, comte de Guichen, *chef d'escadre*, foreshadowed its role off the Chesapeake Capes by doing especially heavy execution. Finding his better-maintained ships pulling ahead of the British, d'Orvilliers wore his ships again so that the hostile lines passed each other on opposite tacks, still cannonading.

At this juncture both commanders lost control of the action—which meant again that the uncertainty of flag signals and of almost every other aspect of naval combat nullified the very purpose for which the stultifying line ahead was allowed to prevail, the purpose of assuring the commanding officer's control. D'Orvilliers signaled one of his divisions to wear yet again, in order that this division should come to leeward of the British and bring them under a crossfire. But the line ahead was as sacred in the French Navy as in the British—a sense of

inferiority may bind one to mimickry of one's assumed superiors—and consequently the division commander receiving the order refused to believe it (even
though he sent a boat to confirm it) and did not obey. This headstrong conduct
probably owed something to the fact that the commander in question was a
Bourbon of the Orléans branch, namely Louis Philippe Joseph, duc de Chartres,
lieutenant général, the future (from November 18, 1785) duc d'Orléans who during
the French Revolution was to become known as Philippe Egalité.

On the British side, Keppel also tried to bring his ships about, in an effort to
concentrate against the French rear after all. But French gunnery this day continued to be excellent. It had aimed, according to what was now French custom,
at the enemy's rigging (the British tended to aim at the hulls), and some of the
British ships proved so badly damaged that they could not tack. This disability
apparently afflicted in special measure the *Formidable*, 100, flagship of Rear-
Admiral Sir Hugh Palliser, commanding Keppel's rear division. Keppel waited
for Palliser, and by the time he had reformed his line, daylight was fading and
the action broke off.

The aftermath of this indecisive battle of Ushant was more spectacular than
the battle. The British public and press, nervous over the latest invasion scare
and sufficiently spoiled by Quiberon Bay as to be satisfied with nothing less than
a repeat performance—the same sort of mood that punished Admiral Mathews
for the battle of Hyères—raised an outcry against the navy in general and who-
ever might be blamed for the indecisive outcome more particularly. This latter
blame threatened to settle upon Palliser. To Keppel's misfortune, however, Palliser—with whom his relations were already strained—happened to be a member of the Board of Admiralty. Therefore Sir Hugh was able to exert enough
influence to divert the attack upon himself into a court-martial of Keppel. There
followed, in the last days of 1778 and until February 11, 1779, a much-publicized
five weeks' trial (of an officer who, incidentally, had been a member of the court
that convicted John Byng, following which he had campaigned conspicuously for
clemency for Byng). Keppel was acquitted and his conduct at Ushant com-
mended; whereupon part of the still-nervous public, angry that favoritism in
government had nearly turned an old hero into a scapegoat, rioted through the
London streets, tearing the Admiralty gate off its hinges and sacking Palliser's
house in Pall Mall while burning his effigy on Tower Hill.

The government had little choice but to court-martial Palliser next. When
he also was acquitted, both he and Keppel resigned their commissions. A number of flag officers, including Admiral Lord Howe, expressed their disgust over
the whole affair and the deficiencies of naval administration that it symbolized
by announcing that they would refuse to accept commands until the Admiralty
was reformed from the top. Through most of the rest of the war the Channel
Fleet fell to the command of admirals about as elderly as their recent French
counterparts. The combination of the infirmities of age with the cautionary message of the courts-martial deterred these commanders from any vigorous action.
Hawke's system of close blockade of the French ports fell into discard, and
during the winter the principal British ships took shelter in their harbors. Periodic invasion alarms continued to agitate England. Nevertheless, the sheer

weight of numbers of the Channel Fleet remained sufficient to prevent any of d'Orvilliers's occasional spasms of aggressiveness from presenting a genuine danger of invasion.

The prevailing unhappy combination of British naval complacency and diffidence also permitted the Spanish with French naval support to threaten British control of Gibralter by grasping the Rock in a siege that lasted from July 1779, the first month after Spain entered the war, all the way to January 1783. By the final weeks of 1779 the garrison was not far from starvation; but in this crisis Admiral Rodney spearheaded a relief effort, and by winning a moonlit battle off Cape St. Vincent on January 16–17, 1780, opened a path for victualling ships into the Gut of Gibraltar. The victory was a product of Rodney's seamanship assisted by an innovation that suggested the beginnings of the desired Admiralty awakening, the coppering of ships' bottoms to enhance their speed. In spite of such glimmerings of change, Gibraltar had to undergo several further brushes with starvation and disaster before Lord Howe of Langar was persuaded to return to active service and to take its relief in hand late in 1782. Howe insisted on receiving enough ships and support to establish a continuous naval presence off Gibraltar, thereby vindicating at last the stubborn and skillful defense conducted by the army and persuading the Spanish to abandon the siege.

D'Estaing and Byron in the West Indies

The preceding long period of neglect had permitted a strong French squadron under Charles Hector Théodat, comte d'Estaing, *vice-amiral*, to sail past Gibraltar unmolested in the late spring of 1778 on its way from Toulon to the western hemisphere. While its outward voyage was a further blot upon the British naval record in the War of American Independence, the squadron did little further to cause cheering in Paris or in the rebellious American colonies. D'Estaing disappointed George Washington by intervening only halfheartedly and ineffectually in North America, and although such conduct was understandable in light of France's greater interest in operations in the West Indies— source of some 30 percent of French imports and the destination of about 35 percent of French exports—the squadron earned more criticism than plaudits there as well. D'Estaing allowed the British to capture the island of St Lucia (Ste Lucie) late in 1778 though it was only thirty nautical miles (about fifty-six kilometers) from his main Caribbean base at Fort Royal on Martinique. When he tried to win a retaliatory triumph the following summer, he scored an initial success but ultimately accomplished little but to pile up more troubles.

His riposte was aimed at the island of Grenada, where on July 2, 1779, he landed an invading force whose transports were escorted by thirty-five ships of the line. Two days later the local British garrison surrendered to him. But counterretaliation was swift in arriving.

The best of Admiral Howe's generally undistinguished successors in Britain's American naval command was Vice-Admiral the Honourable John Byron, who had recently taken charge of the combined western Atlantic and West Indian fleets. Byron promptly led twenty-one of the line escorting troop transports of his own to recapture Grenada. He sighted d'Estaing's fleet off St George's, the capital of the island, soon after dawn as early as July 6. D'Estaing had heard of Byron's approach and had engaged in the dangerous maneuver of threading his way out of the narrow harbor in the darkness of night, one of his ships, the *Dauphin-Royal*, 70, running aground in the process. Byron perceived that the rearward French vessels had not yet emerged fully enough from the harbor to have formed line, so he signaled for a general chase to run them down while they were still in disarray. The chase would carry him into St George's Bay, the wider but nevertheless somewhat constricted opening of the harbor, but he thought that any disadvantages in entering relatively narrow waters would be offset by the encouragement his appearance would give to the garrison, of whose surrender he was not aware.

"Foul-Weather Jack" Byron shared the family penchant for impetuosity that was to shape the career of his grandson the poet, George Gordon Byron, sixth Baron Byron. His impetuosity had helped make the relief effort so prompt, but it was about to serve him less well. His general chase led to his three foremost ships' sailing so far ahead of their consorts that they had to do battle with eight of d'Estaing's vessels, and French gunnery splintered their rigging badly. Another three fast British vessels were carried to leeward against the French van, which was well formed in line; passing this French formation on the opposite tack, the three British ships were also thoroughly shot up. Moreover, when the chase carried into St George's Bay, the fleur-de-lis banners flying from the fortifications revealed the unpleasant circumstance that the garrison had already surrendered. Byron had led his fleet into a potential trap, between the enemy ships and a hostile shore.

He naturally signaled to go about, and he also called to his aid three ships that he had left to guard the convoy. D'Estaing should now have been able to go in for the kill. But the doctrine of the line ahead once more undid the French as it had so often frustrated the British, and its ill effects were now abetted by the psychological ascendancy that nearly a century of British naval supremacy had established to palsy almost every French commander. To reestablish an orderly line, d'Estaing formed it on his most leeward ship, which had the effect of taking the hostile lines nearly out of range for a brief but critical interval. Then d'Estaing religiously maintained the line rather than concentrate against the several nearly dismasted British ships that lagged increasingly behind. Given Byron's nature, going for these ships would likely have brought the British admiral around to attempt a rescue whatever the perils, playing still further into d'Estaing's hands. Instead, d'Estaing's view of the British cripples allowed him to persuade himself he had done enough for one day, and he returned to St George's Bay while Byron escaped.

For France, such acquiescence in indecision when genuine victory should have been close at hand was not good enough. France needed positive achievements to undermine British naval supremacy in the West Indies, but the battle of St George's Bay left the naval balance of power essentially unchanged and therefore much favoring the British—all the more because the earlier British capture of St Lucia left the Royal Navy staring down the throat of the French base at Martinique. True, France retained Grenada until the peace treaty, but losing it then was foreordained under the circumstances. D'Estaing had fallen short of hopes and possibilities once again. The long Franco-British naval rivalry offers the best of confirmations of a standing principle of military history: By its accumulated moral force a tradition of victory breeds more victories, while a tradition of defeat so surely breeds further defeats that even in the most auspicious conditions the cycle is almost impossible to interrupt.

Rodney in the West Indies: The Dominica Channel and The Saints

And to make matters worse for the French, the kind of inspired leadership that sometimes accomplishes the nearly impossible was about to appear not on their side but among the British. When he was being bad, Admiral Rodney could be very bad indeed; but when he was good, when his mind was not clouded by the kind of mania brought upon it by the wealth of St. Eustatius, he could also be an exceedingly admirable naval commander—perhaps the best tactician in British naval history before Nelson.

Appointed to the West Indies command in October 1779, Rodney hoisted his flag there the following spring. With twenty-one of the line, he promptly brought the rival French fleet to battle on April 17, not quite thirty nautical miles (fifty-six kilometers) west of the Dominica Channel which runs between Dominica and Martinique. The French were escorting a convoy to Saint-Domingue; their commander now was the comte de Guichen, probably as close a challenger to Rodney in tactical skill as their navy produced.

Rodney maneuvered successfully for the weather gauge, no doubt achieving it in part because de Guichen was willing to let him have it. Aiming as they did for the enemy's rigging, the French found it convenient to have the assistance of the wind in their faces as they aimed high; de Guichen in particular was a defensive tactician who seems to have preferred the lee position. The fleets sailed northward in line ahead, the wind as usual from the east. As the French began to outdistance the British, Rodney signaled his captains to alter course eight points to port and engage. His evident intent was to remain within the letter of the line-ahead doctrine yet to concentrate against the enemy's rear in order to break free from the pattern of indecision. De Guichen perceived the intent, however, and ordered his own ships to wear together so that once the British were in range the two lines would again be broadside to broadside in the classic pattern.

Rodney thereupon ordered a further eight-points-to-port alteration in course, and after de Guichen responded the rival fleets presently were sailing southward, again both in line-ahead formation. The French, however, not only tended once more to draw away from the British, but relatively large intervals opened between some of the French ships. Rodney thought that by keeping his own line well closed up he could take advantage of these circumstances for another effort to concentrate toward the enemy's rear. Still staying within the letter of tactical doctrine, he ordered his ships to bear down, each steering for its

opposite in the enemy's line—an order that while observing the line-ahead doctrine would tend under the immediate circumstances of a closed-up British line
and a looser French line to effect the desired concentration. Unfortunately,
however, Rodney had devoted less thought to the persistent problems of communicating at sea than to tactics. He had not given his captains beforehand
enough indication of this intention to break free from the stereotyped line to
permit them to understand his purposes readily, and in the midst of action the
signal flags were as usual inadequate for conveying any message at all subtle.

In response to Rodney's order but laboring still under the fetish of the line
ahead, his captains stretched their own formation to keep up with the French
van and engage ship to ship. Rodney tried to persist in his purpose, and in his
flagship, the *Sandwich*, 90, he actually sailed through the French line. But he did
so virtually unsupported. The *Sandwich* was pounded so hard that he had to shift
his flag, and the battle broke off in indecision and British confusion.

The British had borne the worst of the damage, but de Guichen, more
perceptive than the British captains, chivalrously informed Rodney that he was
aware that the British plan would have brought him to disaster if only it had been
executed properly. De Guichen also resolved that Rodney was too dangerous to
allow him to have the weather gauge again.

The next French misfortune was that de Guichen no longer commanded
and thus could neither exercise his resolve nor repeat his excellent tactical performance when the time came to fight Rodney again. Rodney exercised his fleet
in his tactics in a fury after the battle of the Dominica Channel, but his extraordinary lapse into inaction and incompetence during 1781 postponed that time
until the spring of 1782, when Rodney returned to the West Indies from his
recuperative sojourn in England. The French commander now was de Grasse,
admirable in resolution and strategic grasp and perhaps the savior of the independence of the United States, but considerably less able as a tactician, as he
proceeded to demonstrate on two occasions in quick succession even before
there could be a showdown with Rodney.

On January 11, while Rodney was still on his way westward across the Atlantic (having departed Plymouth the preceding day), the French invaded the British island of St Christopher, or St Kitts. Rear-Admiral Sir Samuel Hood
embarked such troops as he could find—a small number—from Barbados and
Antigua and sailed to relieve St Kitts. With twenty-two ships of the line he found
de Grasse with twenty-six in control of the island's harbor, but with deft tactics
the British maneuvered their way past de Grasse and into the harbor; the French
commander had contrived through excessively complicated signaling to confuse
his captains enough that some of them never got into action to resist Hood's
incursion. Hood promptly discovered, however, that he had neatly replicated
Byron's predicament at Grenada, putting his own neck into a noose. The St Kitts
garrison was too small and his reinforcement too weak to permit the island to
resist the French invaders much longer. Hood took astute advantage of the
configuration of the harbor to deploy his fleet in a defensive line that de Grasse
feared was too strong to attack, but the British ships would soon be trapped
between a hostile fleet and a hostile shore.

Hood managed to escape, however, by resorting to one of the simplest of ruses. He had riding lights strung on buoys in such a way that they appeared to be on his ships. Then, while those lights remained bobbing in place, he led his unlighted ships, their cables cut, gliding out to sea by night.

After Rodney arrived, he stationed his ships at St Lucia to intercept de Grasse when he set out, as intelligence correctly predicted he would, to join the Spanish West Indian fleet for a combined expedition against Jamaica. De Grasse sailed from Martinique on April 8 with thirty-three ships of the line convoying transports, store ships, and merchantmen. Rodney, fully prepared, sailed at once in pursuit. The next morning, however, the French fleet and its convoy were north of Dominica and propelled by the winds blowing through the Dominica Channel, while most of the British found themselves becalmed under the lee of Dominica. Hood, leading Rodney's van with nine ships of the line, one-fifth of the British force, was far enough ahead to catch the winds, and he bore down on two French ships, the *Ardent*, 64, and the *Zélé*, 74, that had been carried to leeward. De Grasse responded by detaching fifteen of the line to deal with Hood, while he ordered his convoy into Basse-Terre roadstead off Guadeloupe to free his warships for battle. De Grasse did not, however, exploit Hood's exposed position to strike for the kill. Hood hove to, but for about four hours the French had him at their mercy while Rodney remained becalmed; yet the fifteen-ship squadron assigned to deal with Hood contented itself with cautiously bombarding him from a distance in a stately series of parades past him. By the time Rodney arrived to rescue him, Hood had suffered considerable damage, but not too much to repair it at sea; while a French sixty-four, *Caton*, considered itself too badly hurt to sail on and without permission resorted to Guadeloupe.

In a subsequent court-martial, de Grasse's failure to destroy Hood was exonerated, chiefly on the ground that it fitted what had become a French strategic predisposition as fixed as the tactical predisposition to fire at the enemy's rigging. Consistent naval failure had led the French to regard their fleet as an adjunct to land power. Far from sharing Admiral Hawke's guiding vision that the first strategic object of a navy ought to be the destruction of the enemy navy, whereupon all the benefits of command of the sea would follow automatically, the French believed that the first duty of the navy was to support whatever land forces it was assigned to assist. So de Grasse's court-martial affirmed, accepting that he was faithful to his duty in persisting with most of his ships toward his junction with the Spanish and the invasion of Jamaica. This strategic conception notwithstanding, de Grasse was about to pay dearly for his successive failures to destroy major portions of the enemy fleet. His debt came due in the battle of The Saints on April 12.

De Grasse now continued beating westward through the Dominica Channel, twenty-three nautical miles (forty-three kilometers) wide between the tips of Guadeloupe and Dominica, but as a practical matter narrowing to about thirteen miles (twenty-four kilometers) between Dominica and a group of small islands called The Saints (Les Saintes). On the night of April 10 the *Zélé* collided with the *Jason*, 64, and the latter had to join the *Caton* at Guadeloupe. The next night the *Zélé* had another collision, this time with de Grasse's flagship, the *Ville de Paris*. The *Zélé* was so badly damaged that de Grasse had to have the frigate *Astrée*, 36, tow it to Guadeloupe.

His encumbering convoy notwithstanding, de Grasse until now had maintained a reasonably comfortable distance between himself and Rodney's pursuit. It took a good deal of time to get the *Zélé* under tow, however, and at daybreak of April 12 it and its companion were within sight of both fleets. Rodney signaled to Hood to detach several fast ships to run it down. Seeing this pursuit, de Grasse came about to the rescue, ordering his ships to form line of battle. This boldness, however, was misplaced, embodying no strategic principle whatever, because it forsook the mission of persisting toward the rendezvous with the Spanish and the invasion of Jamaica while offering no good prospect of a decisive French victory, with de Grasse now reduced to thirty ships of the line against Rodney's thirty-six.

Rodney recalled the ships pursuing the *Zélé* and formed his own line. But he had already given ample indication that he would not bind himself to the stultification of the line ahead, and his captains now were better aware of his intentions than they had been in his earlier battle nearby.

The events of the preceding night had thrown de Grasse's fleet into a measure of disorder before the commander signaled to form line. Under the circumstances the French line was again a straggling one, with wide intervals between many of the ships. The wind was easterly, and de Grasse sailed as if to cross the head of the British line and win the weather gauge, apparently having absorbed some of de Guichen's reflections on how to deal with Rodney. At first matters went well for the French, de Grasse winning his way across the British van by a near margin and gaining the weather gauge. Rodney nevertheless signaled for close action, and firing began about 7:45 A.M. when the ninth French ship in line, *Brave*, 74, came alongside the leading British ship, *Marlborough*, 74, and opened fire. Initially the rival lines passed each other in customary fashion on opposite tacks, firing as they went. The British had somewhat the better of the first exchanges, largely because they had received new gun-locks that permitted more rapid fire and new carriages that widened the arc of fire—like copper-bottomed ships, signs of recovered vigor in British naval administration.

Nevertheless, events seemed to be moving toward the customary indecision until there was a sudden shift toward a southerly wind about 9:15. The shift turned the bows of the French ships somewhat to starboard and thereby enlarged the gaps in their line. Rodney promptly grasped the opportunity to break the customary pattern. His flagship, the 100-gun *Formidable*, sailed straight through the French line between the *Glorieux*, 74, and the *Diadème*, 74, blasting both with its broadsides. The *Diadème* lost way and obstructed the ships following it. The five British ships next astern of Rodney followed the *Formidable* through the enemy line, while the *Duke*, 90, next ahead of Rodney, broke through farther forward, and the *Bedford*, 74, sixth astern of the *Formidable*, did the same farther back.

Thus broken in three places, the French line fell into confusion. Rodney continued along its weather side. Along with the *Duke* and the *Namur*, 90, the *Formidable* poured a series of broadsides into a group of ships stranded behind the *Diadème*. De Grasse signaled to his ships to close on him and form line, but most could not or did not do it. The British continued to develop superior concentrations against small groups of French ships, and among the victims was the *Ville de Paris*. De Grasse himself—one of only three men left unwounded on the upper deck—surrendered with his ship, one of six captured by the British as, disabled, they fell astern of their fleet.

By breaking his own line and thereby the enemy's as well, Rodney had won the sort of decisive triumph that had eluded the Royal Navy all through the current war, and since Hawke had gained such a victory by departing from the line ahead in 1759. In his strategic grasp Rodney was not quite a Hawke, however, and he did not follow through as he might have done by raising Hawke's signal of Quiberon Bay, general chase.

He has been much criticized for this lack of pursuit, the critics including Admiral Hood, who expressed his disappointment candidly and directly to Rodney the following morning on board the *Formidable*. Surely the French were ripe for more losses; another four of their ships of the line had been badly damaged by British firepower, and three other injured by collisions. Rodney was sixty-four years old and had not fully recovered his health, while during the pursuit of de Grasse he had gone four nights without sleep before the battle. On the other hand, pursuit after a victory in battle tends to pose one of the most vexing problems of warfare, whether by land or by sea. Victorious commanders again and again have suffered the tarnishing of their laurels by accusations that they should have pursued more vigorously. But while critics who call for pursuit without being burdened by direct responsibility are legion, examples of successful pursuit, and particularly of pursuits that transform victories into triumphs yet more grand, are decidedly rare.

Even the most capable military commanders more often than not have failed to pursue with the zeal that might seem commendable after reflection at leisure. A primary reason lies in the fatigue, horror, and demoralization that attend the aftermath of all battles, including the most successful. Decks awash in blood and resounding with screams and groans, rigging so tattered that ships can only with great difficulty be steered, pumps straining below decks to keep apace of the flooding from shot-holes, all these accompaniments of battle have usually discouraged younger and healthier admirals than Rodney.

As it was, Rodney learned after putting in at Port Royal, Jamaica, that nine of his ships of the line would have to go home for repairs, because there was a local shortage of masts. They included the captured *Ville de Paris*. He sent them along with some frigates, escorting a large convoy on their way, all under the command of Admiral Graves. Off the Grand Banks the convoy met a storm that sank four 74s—*Ramillies*, *Centaur*, and the captured *Hector* and *Glorieux*, while the great *Ville de Paris* had to be abandoned and was blown up.

Hood meanwhile blockaded the French ships that had fled to Guadeloupe. The *Canton* and the *Jason* slipped out of Basse-Terre one dark night—the *Zélé* was too damaged to be moved—but Hood caught them and sank them.

From his captivity in England, de Grasse began to deliver public recriminations against his captains. A series of courts-martial followed his return to

France, with a few convictions but more acquittals. De Grasse's effort to transfer blame for the defeat failed. He retired to his estates under explicit warnings of royal disfavor, and he died January 14, 1788, never appropriately rewarded for his victory off the Capes of the Chesapeake. Rodney, in contrast, was rescued by the battle of The Saints. The memory of his conduct the previous year had caused the Admiralty second thoughts about sending him back to the West Indies for 1782, and it had been decided to replace him before news of the victory arrived. Now he became a hero and by patent of June 19, 1782, first Baron Rodney of Rodney Stoke in the County of Somerset. The rewards were deserved; pursuing or not, he had won the most decisive victory since Quiberon Bay, assured British naval supremacy in American waters at least for the remainder of the war, and helped open the way for the future professional growth of the navy by confirming that the key to decision in naval war lay in breaking the tactical straight-jacket of the line ahead.

Suffren

De Grasse's recriminations against his captains were not so ill founded as the acquittals suggest, particularly in the matter of their general failure to comply with his order to close on the flagship after the British had broken his line. His disgrace seems especially unjust in the light of a historical perspective indicating that only one French naval commander of his century has been ranked by naval critics and historians as assuredly his superior. And even this single claim to superiority may be unwarranted, as we are about to see. Unfortunately for the French, moreover, de Grasse's one possible superior in ability among their naval leaders of the day led a squadron only in a peripheral theater, and never with sufficient resources to afford his talents their full possible scope.

Pierre-André de Suffren de Saint-Tropez, *capitaine* as well as *chevalier-commandeur* of the Sovereign Order of the Knights of Malta (the Knights of the Order of the Hospital of St. John of Jerusalem), had served with much credit under d'Estaing against Byron. He was outspokenly critical of d'Estaing's less than resolute conduct of his western hemisphere campaigns, not hiding his sentiments in his communications to the admiral himself; but with uncommon largeness of spirit d'Estaing responded by suggesting Suffren for command of a squadron of five ships of the line to serve in the Indian Ocean. Suffren was fifty-two years old, young by contemporary standards for senior French naval commanders. But he had a wealth of experience in naval warfare reaching back to the action off Toulon in 1744 as a cadet, and including the battle against Admiral John Byng off Minorca as a lieutenant, as well as d'Estaing's battles. He had also endured two interludes as a British prisoner of war.

More to the point as far as the evolution of naval officership is concerned, Suffren was not only experienced but reflective upon his experience. He was also a student of naval history and strategy, who took as his special model the Dutch Admiral de Ruyter. When other naval officers were at best seamen rather than military professionals, Suffren was self-educated to professional skills in strategy, operations, and logistics.

His studies were especially important in leading him to challenge the doctrinal corollaries of France's accumulated sense of naval inferiority, particularly the tendency to acquiesce consistently in a defensive strategy or at least defensive operations and tactics, and the tendency to subordinate naval activities to the interests of the land service, as de Grasse had done when he sacrificed his opportunity to destroy Hood's squadron in favor of persisting toward the invasion of Jamaica. Suffren reached, or confirmed, through study the conclusion at which Admiral Hawke had arrived more intuitively: that the strategic goal of naval operations ought to be first the destruction of the enemy fleet; and that further objects, such as the conduct of amphibious operations of blockades, can be accomplished with assurance once the undisputed command of the sea is attained, but if the latter object is postponed for the sake of ulterior purposes, then those purposes will also be jeopardized. To destroy the enemy's fleet, furthermore, offensive battle is essential.

When de Grasse sailed for the West Indies from Brest in 1781, Suffren's squadron parted company with the main fleet. Of Suffren's five of the line, two 74s and three 64s, four were copper-bottomed; that is, they benefited from the new technique, in which the French characteristically had anticipated the British but then had not consistently kept pace with the British, for preventing the accumulation of barnacles to foul the bottom of the ship, and thus for maintaining the ship's speed and maneuverability. As the coppering implied, Suffren commanded sound, well-fitted, and well-kept ships. They would need these advantages, for they would have few others, and especially they would lack an adequate base.

Because the United Provinces had entered the war, Suffren's first mission was to aid the Dutch colony at the Cape of Good Hope against a British expedition intended to seize it and thereby to go far toward blocking French passage around Africa to India. Suffren accomplished this mission by defeating Commodore (usually called Governor) George Johnstone's weaker squadron at Porto Praya in the Cape Verde Islands on April 16, 1781. The French commander then proceeded to the Cape, and his anchoring in its harbor and landing a detachment of troops caused Johnstone to abandon his plans against it altogether. The attack at Proto Praya had violated the neutrality of Portugal, which was sovereign in the Cape Verdes, but the outcome was so successful and so important to communications with the Far East that when the news reached France, Suffren was promoted to *chef d'escadre*. The Knights of Malta advanced him to the high rank of *bailli* in their order, and it is as le bailli de Suffren that he is customarily known.

He next proceeded to Mauritius, or the Île de France, in the Indian Ocean, where he arrived October 25. He soon succeeded to France's overall naval command in Indian waters. Thereby commanding a total of twelve ships of the line, he arrived off Madras on February 15, 1782, to challenge the British for control of the Indian Ocean, the Bay of Bengal, and by implication India itself.

The British, the predominant European power in India at least since the Seven Years War, had opened the new war by attacking successfully the French settlements at Chandernagore, Pondicherry, and Mahé, with the fall of which

France had been removed from the subcontinent. At the beginning of 1782, the British had also captured Negapatam near the southern tip of the mainland and the valuable port of Trincomali (Trincomalee) in Ceylon from the Dutch. These energetic offensives had borne partially counterproductive results, however, by helping to arouse powerful resistance from Hyder Ali (Haider 'Ali Khan Bahadur, born Haider Naik), a soldier who had seized control of Mysore, and from the Mahratta Confederation, to which name it is customary and accurate to prefix the adjective warlike.

Confronting Suffren in February 1782 was a British squadron of nine ships of the line under Rear-Admiral Sir Edward Hughes. Two days after Suffren's arrival off Madras, he attacked Hughes in what proved to be the first of a series of battles: February 17, 1782, south of Madras; April 12, near Trincomali; July 6, off Cuddalore; September 3, also near Cuddalore; and June 20, 1783, off the east coast of the Deccan. While Suffren's squadron was stronger, his lack of a base for refitting did much to offset this advantage (although following the battle of July 6, 1782, he established himself in the anchorage of Trincomali, compelling the garrison of the place to surrender on August 31). As a tactician, furthermore, Suffren was capable but fell short of his strategic reach. He displayed a bold tactical aggressiveness unparalleled among the senior French naval commanders of his era, but his boldness often overstepped the boundary of rashness. Also, he relied on intricate tactical combinations frequently beyond the abilities of his somewhat mediocre captains to execute. And finally, execution depended on at least equaling the customary first-class seamanship of the British. In all the battles except that of July 6, it was Suffren who was the attacker; but in all of them Hughes held his own, and he did not lose a single ship.

By the battle of September 3, Hughes had been reinforced to twelve ships of the line with which to oppose Suffren's line now grown to fifteen, including a newly arrived large (forty-gun) frigate that he had inserted into the line, the *Consolante*. In that action, however, the French line lost its cohesion, and Hughes was able to isolate and to concentrate upon Suffren's center. The British dismasted Suffren's flagship, the *Héros*, 74, except for the foremast and inflicted the same damage on the *Illustre*, also 74. Suffren had to return to Trincomali with some of his ships under tow. There another 74, the *Orient*, was wrecked by poor seamanship on entering the harbor, and a 64, *Bizarre*, was soon afterward similarly wrecked off Cuddalore.

It is one of the major items to Suffren's credit that he could fight his last battle, that of June 20, 1783, at all. By that time his squadron featured a patchwork of improvised repairs; but in the battle it held its line under severe cannonading, and the outcome was a draw. Hughes presently sent a flag of truce with a message that word had reached him overland of the signing of preliminary articles of peace between Great Britain and her French and Spanish rivals in January. In August Suffren received confirmation from France; the preliminary articles of peace had in fact been signed on January 20, and on February 4 the British government had declared a cessation of hostilities. Suffren also received orders to take all but five ships and two frigates home, along with the consolation prize of his promotion to *lieutenant général*. A greater consolation prize was to be his elevation in history to a pinnacle among French admirals; but in fact he had accomplished nothing substantial to delay the rise of British power in India. Astute as was his strategic vision and remarkable as were his logistical accomplishments, they had been undone by his own tactical shortcomings—and of course by the greatest constant of the modern age of naval power under sail, the skilled ship-handling of British captains and seamen.

The Peace Settlement

The war would probably have ended earlier—the outcome in North America having been substantially decided at Yorktown in 1781—had it not been for Spain's persisting in the hope of capturing Gibraltar. Not until late 1782 did Admiral Lord Howe's relief expedition open the way to peace by eliminating that hope.

The Treaty of Paris of September 3, 1783, between Great Britain and the United States of America, along with related treaties ending Great Britain's wars with France and Spain signed at Versailles the same day and preliminaries with the United Provinces signed at Paris the preceding day, left to the British a much truncated North American empire but otherwise changed remarkably little the verdict of the earlier Treaty of Paris of twenty years before. Great Britain's imperial supremacy remained unquestioned.

The French had hoped that by supporting American independence they might take advantage of Britain's distraction not only to taste the emotional satisfaction of revenge against the island kingdom but also to win more tangible assets, perhaps new possessions in the West Indies or trading stations in India, and at the least a permanent anti-British makeweight in international politics in the form of Britain's lost American colonies, nominally independent but it might be hoped actually clients of France. Except for the transitory satisfaction of revenge, these French aspirations foundered in every respect. Notwithstanding the possibly indispensable assistance of France, the United States proved by no means merely nominally independent. Instead, exceptionally able American leadership combined with the remoteness from Europe and the sheer size and potential wealth of the new republic to permit it to follow immediately a foreign policy of shrewdly calculated self-interest. Moreover, the ties of history, language, and culture began drawing the United States and Great Britain together again as soon as peace was concluded; in fact, through generosity in ceding to the United States the expansive territory between the Appalachian Mountains and the Mississippi River to which the Americans could make only the most tenuous of military claims, the British perspicaciously encouraged renewed harmony within the Treaty of Paris itself.

Much friction had yet to be eased in relations between Britain and America, and in 1812 another war would erupt between them. But restored maritime commerce promptly began to reinforce other links to bind the English-speaking nations together again, and as early as the renewal of warfare between Britain and France in the 1790s, the French were to discover to their dismay a tilt of United States policy in favor of the British.

The imperial contest between Great Britain and France had remained fundamentally a naval contest, and in spite of often superior naval administration and of ships often technically superior and better maintained, the French Navy had again in the war of 1778–1783 consistently succumbed to the superiority of the British in seamanship, in the handling and maneuvering of ships—with consistent defeat then adding to the handicaps of the French a reinforced crippling sense of naval inferiority and a consistent crippling subordination of naval strategy and operations to ulterior military and political objects. But the decline of France from the glorious pinnacle attained under the Sun King had not been a naval imperial decline alone. Even the French Army by the middle of the eighteenth century was consistently failing to match the tactical proficiency not only of the Prussians but of the British as well. By the time of the War of the American Revolution, some Frenchmen were giving careful thought to the discovery of the sources at least of the military decline, and often of the political decline as well. Their reforming efforts would soon contribute to a dramatic rebirth of French military greatness, and then also of French political preeminence in Europe. And along with France's military reforms would come a new stimulus to the professionalization of military officership all through the European world, together with consequent major changes in methods of waging war. Particularly, however, and to the world's immeasurable misfortune, the advances achieved since Louis XIV's ravaging of the Palatinate toward curbing the violence of war would once again prove imperiled.

W hy had the armies of France deteriorated so precipitously since the era of Louis XIV? During at least the first half of the reign of the Grand Monarch they had led all the armed forces of Europe in fighting quality and logistical and administrative efficiency, and their quality had been built upon the most advanced professional standards of any army in Europe. They had borrowed the foundations of officer professionalism laid first by the Dutch and then by the Swedes and had expanded those foundations diligently through the encouragement of military study among their officers and through a growing tendency to relate promotion and the awarding of responsible commands to merit. No other army, in fact, had yet matched the professional standards achieved by the French Army in the late seventeenth century. The military prowess of Prussia sprang less from professionalism among the officers than from the discipline of the rank and file and the tactical genius of Frederick the Great; the remarkable accomplishments of the small British Army similarly sprang first from the still larger genius of Marlborough—who surpassed Frederick the Great in the strategic scope he united with superb tactical skill— and from the disciplined proficiency of the rank and file. Yet the French Army of the mid-eighteenth century could not match the skills of the Prussians or the British, and probably fell short of the battlefield toughness and resilience of the Russians and Austrians as well. What had gone wrong?

The Military Decline of France

In spite of the encouragement of professional development among the officers, the army of Louis XIV had been an excessively centralized institution. The King's energies drove everything. Essentially what went wrong was that Louis XIV's capacities declined with age, and Louis XV never possessed similar capacities. Louis XIV never prepared the army to function with any mainspring but himself, abetted to be sure by Louvois. When the original mainspring was gone and an inferior substitute took its place, the mechanism functioned erratically.

Louis XV was not without personal bravery, as he showed when he took the field for the campaign of Fontenoy. But he possessed only a fraction either of the intelligence or the energy or the driving ambition of his great-grandfather and immediate predecessor on the throne. He was indolent, bored, probably timid, fond only of luxury, the hunt, and his mistresses. His indifference to matters of state grew worse in the eighteen years of the reign of Madame de Pompadour as his principal favorite, from 1746 to 1764. Pompadour herself tried to supply a measure of the forcefulness and energy the King lacked. In particular, she sought to invigorate the conduct of the Seven Years War. But she possessed neither the knowledge of politics and war nor the ability to appraise politicians and soldiers that might have made her intervention effective.

No Cardinal Richelieu, no Cardinal Mazarin, no Louvois rose up to grasp the leadership that the King had abdicated. The nearest approximation to such a leader was Choiseul, but he came to the forefront only after the Seven Years War was practically lost, and his political and strategic vision was less consistent than that of any of the three statesmen just mentioned.

The leadership vacuum allowed the holders of the purse strings—specifically, the court bankers—to assume a disproportionate role in the conduct of the Seven Years War. Preeminent were two brothers who embodied at least the virtue of representing the possibilities of upward social and economic mobility in spite of the constraints of the *ancien régime*, products of the Dauphiné small-business class who had first grown wealthy on bread contracts for the army during the War of the Spanish Succession. One of them, Jean Paris de Montmartel, supplied the financial direction without which the ramshackle Bourbon taxation system could not have supported war at all. The other, Joseph Paris Duverney, conducted both the provisioning of the army and, as much as anyone, the supervision of the whole war effort by the time of the Seven Years War. Paris Duverney was close to Pompadour, and with her assistance he came to dominate not only all logistical activities but much of the direction of the campaigns.

During the War of the Austrian Succession and into the earliest part of the Seven Years War, the War Minister was capable enough to retain a share of the authority that was properly his and thus to maintain a semblance of appropriately constituted as well as coherent administration of the war effort. This minister was Marc-Pierre de Voyer, comte d'Argenson. Unfortunately, after holding his office since 1743, he was dismissed in February 1757. His first successor was his nephew, Marc-René, marquis de Paulmy, a young man who had some experience of the workings of the ministry but not enough force of personality or prestige to resist the encroachments of Paris Duverney. In March 1758 Paulmy gave way to Marshal Belle-Isle, duc de Belle-Isle since the end of the War of the

Austrian Succession in 1748, who notwithstanding his rank was similarly lacking in forcefulness, obviously not because of youth, but for the opposite reason.

Generals in the field could expect directions, sometimes contradictory, from a variety of sources. Paris Duverney or the Minister of War, especially if it was Marshal Belle-Isle, or in spasms of energy the King himself, might all send orders, or sometimes orders in the guise of suggestions. In theory, field commanders were accorded the generous degree of discretionary authority that the professionalism of the best of them and their on-the-spot knowledge merited; in practice discretion was sorely limited, especially when Versailles felt nervous. The uneasier the mood at court the more likely it was that the proper chain of command would be intruded upon and confusion be compounded through direct orders from one of the highest officials to subordinate commanders in the field, bypassing the senior field commanders.

With Paris Duverney exercising disproportionate influence over operations, the command system was further disjointed by the consequent increase in the autonomy and authority of the intendants. The intendant assigned to each field army was charged with much of the administrative direction of the army in order to leave the operational commanding officer freer to deal with combat considerations from tactics to strategy. Known as the *service*, the intendant's domain included supply, transport, finance, hospitals, and military police. The intendant initially organized a field army, its commander arriving only after it had been brought into existence. Nominally the intendant was subordinate to the army commander, but he carried a royal commission and had the right of direct appeal to the King. Obviously, the conduct of a campaign depended upon cooperation between intendant and commander. Under this system it was natural that the commanders had always looked with suspicion on the intendants, who were civil functionaries, recruited from the *noblesse de robe*. By the time of the Seven Years War the intendants were in fact all beholden to Paris Duverney, and therefore their subordination to army commanders had become yet more uncertain than before. Dual or multiple control from Versailles found its counterpart in dual command of the armies in the field.

The field commanders themselves, and the entire corps of officers, were more vulnerable to inroads upon their authority because their professionalism had declined since the heyday of Louis XIV. Louis XV and his favorites honored social distinctions still more and ability in those of bourgeois or more humble birth a good deal less than had the Sun King. The highest nobility of France, the *noblesse de cour*, had fended off any forays by those of non-noble birth toward the general officers' ranks. Of 181 general officers on duty in Germany in 1758, every one bore a name containing the noble particle. Among them were three Princes of the Blood Royal, five other princes, eleven dukes, forty-four counts, thirty-eight marquis, fourteen chevaliers, and six barons. The lesser *noblesse d'épée* were practically unable to break into the inner circle of officership, but they probably crowded out non-noble talents from the lesser commissioned grades to a much greater degree than in the middle years of the reign of Louis XIV. Nevertheless, the grades of major, lieutenant colonel, and brigadier still offered an upward ladder bypassing the captaincies and colonelcies that were the preserve of titled gentlemen, and perhaps one-third to one-half of the officers during the Seven Years War were non-noble. But the decline in quality of the French Army had been almost certainly in large part the result of a decline in the abilities of the officers conjoined to a resurgence of noble privilege. And protégés of the powerful—of Paris Duverney in particular—could get away with misconduct and ineptitude to the point of criminality without losing rank or privilege.

Financial abuses that had plagued even the armies of Louis XIV at their best had also not been remedied and if anything had grown worse. Captains continued to receive too little pay to permit them to meet those expenses of their companies that continued to fall directly upon their own pocketbooks, so they still maintained understrength companies with fictitious soldiers on the rolls—borrowing men from other companies when inspections necessitated it— in order to economize. An infantry captain was allotted 125 livres to cover the costs of enrolling a recruit, but the sum was insufficient. The regulation enlistment bounty of thirty livres was only one-half to one-third of the going rate. Thus many captains could no more afford to recruit their companies up to regulation strength than they could maintain them at such strength, and all but the exceptionally wealthy were doubly driven to pad their rolls. For what it was worth, the demands upon the officer's purse at least helped open the way to some well-to-do bourgeois officers in place of impecunious nobles. But wealth was usually no better an index of talent than birth.

It followed, of course, from inflation of the company rolls that French commanders and staffs were utterly incapable of reaching correct estimates of the numerical strength of their own forces. The tactical consequences were not propitious.

Notwithstanding the enlistment bounty, the military pay scale was so low that only the most impoverished subjects of the King could have found it tempting. The daily wage of the common soldier on campaign was five sous, eight deniers; it was somewhat less in garrison. But there were various deductions before the soldier saw any money, for bread, for clothing, for necessary expenses such as polish and hair powder. These deductions left about two sous a day actually given to the soldier, about thirty livres a year, enough to buy one good suit of clothes.

The French Army, unlike its Prussian adversary, depended for the most part on such voluntary enlistments as its decidedly modest pay scale and the companies' and regiments' recruiting efforts could scrape up. The recruiting regulations applying to most of the line regiments provided for enlistment of men between the ages of sixteen and forty, at least five feet one inch in height, for a period of six years. One of the deterrents to recruits was the army's failure to observe the six-year limit consistently. Army recruiters also had to compete with the militia, for which about 100,000 men were raised in total in the levies of 1756, 1757, and 1758. To reduce the army's manpower problems, militia levies were suspended after 1758. Nevertheless, dependence on ill-paid volunteers meant that the French Army of the Seven Years War was modest in size in proportion to the national population and compared with the armies of rivals with smaller populations. The deterioration of officer professionalism and administrative efficiency since the time of Louis XIV was probably among the factors affecting numerical strength, because the forces were smaller than they had been in the past, though the population had grown. Under Louis XIV France had achieved a maximum strength of about 450,000 men in the land forces out of a population of some 19,000,000. France's maximum land-force strength during the Seven Years War was just under 330,000 in line units and about 80,000 in the militia, out of a population of some 22,000,000. Great Britain, similarly dependent on voluntary recruitment, fielded an army and marines totaling about 180,000 from a population of about 8,000,000. During the War of the Spanish Succession France had sought some 50,000 additional recruits annually; during the War of the Austrian Succession it sought about 49,000 annually; by the Seven Years War it lowered its sights to about 38,000 annually, and not because casualties were so much lighter.

The French envied Frederick the Great his ability to squeeze recruits even from among conquered peoples, and in 1759 they tried to do likewise in an occupied Prussian dependency, the County (Graftum) of Hanau. When they essayed a forced levy of militiamen, however, the potential draftees fled the scene, either hiding or escaping into other parts of Germany. When the French attempted to recruit 1,000 Hanau volunteers, they failed again.

Nevertheless, about one-fifth of the French Army consisted of foreign regiments, mostly infantry: fourteen German regiments, thirteen Swiss, five Irish, five Hungarian—Hussars—and one Scots. The Swiss regiments in particular were conspicuous for remaining up to strength, unlike the French; they did their own recruiting. Elsewhere, local authorities obstructed French recruiting efforts, even in the Empire when Vienna gave permission to recruit for France's German regiments. (And Maria Theresa herself refused further enlistment of Hungarian hussars.)

In combination, these circumstances brought on a manpower crisis during the closing phases of the Seven Years War. The most populous state in western Europe and the richest and most fertile was hard put to keep an army in the field. The 1760 recruits not only arrived late and in inadequate numbers, but many soon deserted—many having by now made desertion and subsequent collection of new enlistment bounties a career.

Besides officership and enlistment, another area in which the relative decline of the French Army was conspicuous involved the provisioning system. The French continued to rely on private contractors, whose profits could be maximized by supplying the least satisfactory foodstuffs at the highest prices the army would pay, and who acted accordingly. The favoritism that permeated almost every aspect of military administration permitted the *munitionnaires*—the bread suppliers—and the other provisions contractors to work the system to their own advantage without much interference. Among the other major military powers, only Russia continued into the later eighteenth century to rely largely on private contractors, and even the Tsars had a mixed system of government and private supply, directed by a General War Commissariat and a Provisionmaster, that seems to have established tighter regulation than the French methods. With Prussia leading the way, the other powers moved to rationalize and unify all logistical functions under competent governmental authorities. Austria created government boards to control military provisioning and supply during the 1750s, so that its reformed system was in place by the Seven Years War. Great Britain reorganized its provisioning system on the Prussian model in 1760.

One of the worst corollaries of the French persistence in provisioning by contract was the absence of incentives to modernize methods. In Louis XIV's day, France had pioneered a workable system of bake ovens that followed the armies, offering fresh bread. Brick ovens were customarily built about three days' march from a grain supply and two days' march behind an army. Convoys delivered the bread to the army. To supply 100,000 men some forty ovens were required, and building them used up so many bricks that bricks fell into short supply. For that and other reasons, French operations even at the height of French military power had tended to fall hostage to the pace at which ovens could be built, and projected advances stumbled while waiting for the ovens. By the middle of the eighteenth century, the Austrian and Prussian armies developed portable iron field ovens, but the French failed to follow their example. Consequently, French tactical maneuvers remained restricted to within five days' march of an army's grain supply, while the rival Prussian armies extended their radius of operations sometimes as far as ten days' march from their source of grain.

The Prussians had superior logistics in part because their officers did not regard paying attention to administration and supply as beneath their dignity. Most French officers did. An inflated sense of self-importance indeed marked almost every aspect of the lives of Louis XV's officers, further to the detriment of an effective army. The officers insisted on approximating the luxuries of Versailles in the field. During the War of American Independence, the Revolutionaries were astounded—and also amused and contemptuous—at the lavish style in which certain British generals fed and comforted themselves and their retinues on campaign; but in such matters if not in tactical proficiency the French far excelled the British. A British lietuenant-general was allotted thirty men's rations, a French officer of equivalent rank eighty men's rations. The generals' pay scales were commensurately inflated; in 1758 the 182 French general officers assigned to Germany received more than 500,000 livres for six months' campaign service, enough to pay 20,000 soldiers.

And to make matters worse, the favoritism imbuing the relations of the French Army with the court spawned an excess of generals and of officers of all ranks. As early as 1740, the French Army had one officer for every eleven soldiers, while the Prussian ratio was one to twenty-nine. The inflation of the officer corps and of its cost to the taxpayer proceeded concurrently with a worsening debility of French finances. The French Army was disproportionately expensive to maintain, and the already creaky French taxation system approached the breaking point under the strain of the Seven Years War. The War of American Independence completed the journey to the breaking point, requiring eventually the convening of the Estates General (États-Généraux) to seek remedies, and thereby precipitating the French Revolution.

While the decline of the French Army was thus in large part a reflection of the decline of the French state under the *ancien régime*, that was not the whole story. The same financial abuses within the army had already been prevalent in the late seventeenth century but had inflicted less insidious wounds upon the army; the same was true for the rickety French financial system. While military forces must necessarily be to a considerable degree the mirrors of the governments and societies that they serve, there have been many armies that have organized and operated far more effectively than the political and social apparatus of their civilian states might suggest they would—the army of Louis XIV having already offered a prime example of this phenomenon.

No doubt the French Army of the War of the Austrian Succession and the Seven Years War suffered many of its ills simply because neither the government nor the articulate and influential portions of the nation at large had their hearts in these wars. European hegemony for France and its King no longer constituted the primary issue; it scarcely seemed attainable. Instead, only relatively peripheral issues were at stake for France in Europe. French victory in the War of the Austrian Succession would profit Prussia more than it profited France. To an even greater extent, in the Seven Years War France had been maneuvered into fighting more for the sake of Austria's desire to humble Prussia than for any interests of its own. It was the elusiveness of the possible gains in the continental warfare of the mid-eighteenth century that prompted the French to shift their main interests to the conflict against the British on and across the oceans. Yet the fumbling government of Louis XV lacked the capacity to improve the French Navy sufficiently for success in this conflict also.

It tends to remain a mistake nevertheless to look too deeply into a nation's political and social system to find the causes of military failure. Armies can generate a considerable vitality of their own, and conversely the beginnings of French military decline were already apparent by the final half of the reign of Louis XIV, when in nonmilitary matters France remained far and away the preeminent state in Europe. In no small measure, the decline of French military fortunes can be traced to a relatively simple and apparently superficial problem that had always plagued the French armies, even during Louis XIV's greatest years.

The French infantry had always been the weak link in the French Army. The tactical strength of the army had resided in its artillery—with a tradition reaching back to the brothers Bureau; in its engineering—the most imposing figure of Louis XIV's army remains Vauban; in the professionalism of Louis XIV's officers—and especially in the generalship of the Great Condé and Turenne; and to a lesser degree in the cavalry. The French infantry had never attained the ascendancy over rival infantries once held by the Spanish and then by the Swedes. At best, the French Army had triumphed in spite of the marginal quality of its infantry. From the tardiness of France in adopting the flintlock to replace the matchlock musket at the end of the seventeenth century there dated an increasingly severe decline in the ability of the French infantry to stand up to rival infantries. First the British and in some degree almost all the Allied infantry under Marlborough attained superiority over the French, largely through Marlborough's recognition and exploitation of the improvements in infantry combat power implicit in the flintlock and the bayonet. Then Prussian tactical discipline and training gave the infantry of Frederick the Great a still wider margin of superiority over the French.

A strong infantry alone, as we have seen demonstrated repeatedly, can rarely achieve decisive results in battle. Such results require that a powerful mobile arm be added to the infantry to exploit the damage wrought by infantry firepower and the shock of the infantry assault with the enhanced shock effect conveyed by mobility, and with the capacity of a mobile arm to shatter an already wavering resistance. Nonetheless, if an effective mobile arm is a prerequisite for waging decisive battle, infantry steadiness and combat power is also essential for battlefield victory. The French infantry had never been quite good enough to assure a sustained succession of battlefield triumphs. Louis XIV had been fortunate in his early years that war had become so much a matter of sieges and thus of engineering skills. When in Marlborough and Eugène he encountered opponents who insisted upon battle, the weakness of his infantry proved fatal to the fulfillment of his ambitions.

Because French military difficulties sprang so much therefore from tactical shortcomings, the other flaws in the military system notwithstanding, French military reformers who emerged following the disappointments of the Seven Years War tended to emphasize the remedying of tactical deficiencies. In part the reformers hoped to overcome the historic weaknesses of the infantry; in part they hoped to enhance existing strengths, as in the artillery. Their efforts proved to lay one of the foundations for a renewed bid for French military hegemony in Europe, the old goal of Louis XIV that had seemed out of the question in the reign of Louis XV but was soon to be attained far more fully than even the Grand Monarch had grasped it. This achievement was to be that of a new, revolutionary France, driven forward by energies beyond those that the *ancien régime* could have hoped to tap. But the achievement was to be made possible also by fundamental tactical reforms that might well have generated a revival of French military glory, albeit on a more modest scale than that of 1792–1815, even without the added impetus of the French Revolution.

Toward a Renewed French Army: Broglie and Guibert

Probably the most capable of the *maréchaux de France* during the Seven Years War was Victor-François, duc de Broglie. It was characteristic of the management of military affairs under Louis XV, however, that Broglie never enjoyed an opportunity to display how far his talents might have reached. He commanded the Army of the Lower Rhine in the campaigns of 1760 and 1761, but that was after France had ceased to play an energetic role in the anti-Prussian coalition. While his family was influential, and his uncle the Abbé Charles de Broglie in particular was close to the King, his connections did not save him from being sniped at continually by lesser soldiers, notably Belle-Isle and Soubise. When in 1761 a failure of cooperation by Soubise provoked Broglie to present a memorial to the King justifying himself and attacking Soubise, he fell sufficiently afoul of the latter's champion, Madame de Pompadour, to precipitate his dismissal from the army command.

Nevertheless, Broglie's fortunes revived enough thereafter that he was able late in the 1760s, with the support now of Choiseul, to become the principal supporter of one of the most critical of all modern innovations in military organization and tactics. Marshal de Saxe had advocated the creation of divisions within armies, but beginning with the establishment of the prototype of this form of organization in 1759, Broglie became the father of the modern division.

Hitherto field armies had tended to fight battles as single mass formations. At best, they were divided only temporarily into wings or what might be called divisions; but because these formations had no ongoing identity they could develop little inner cohesion and only a most limited capacity for independent maneuver. Broglie's innovation was to organize divisions as permanent formations within the army. The implications were far disproportionate to the simplicity of the idea.

By marching in divisions, an army could increase the number of roads it used and the breadth of the front it presented to the enemy, accelerating its pace of advance yet reducing its logistical difficulties. At the same time, because the division was a lasting, cohesive entity—at its best a miniature army, including all the combat arms in appropriate proportions—a single division meeting the enemy had the ability to give battle for a reasonably sustained period until it was reinforced by other divisions. One or a few divisions might hold an enemy army in place while others maneuvered against its flanks, rear, or line of communications. Subordinate general officers leading divisions could relieve some of the burden of command and control resting on the commander in chief.

While the division was still only a matter of experiment in practice, its potentialities began to be explored in theory by Jacques Antoine Hippolyte, comte de Guibert, *colonel*, in his *Essai général de tactique* . . . (1772).[1] Guibert was only twenty-one when this book appeared, but he had served with Marshal de Broglie's staff during the Seven Years War and earned his colonelcy on an expedition to Corsica in 1767. Troubled by the return to indecisiveness in recent continental wars as well as by the military decline of France, Guibert sought remedies through a return to an emphasis on mobility in warfare. Apparently recognizing the limitations of the traditional arm of greatest mobility—the cavalry—against infantry firepower, however, he hoped to make the infantry more mobile in a strategic sense: Strategic mobility in the infantry was to be the key to a renewal of decisiveness. His book's title, in fact, was by no means intended to confine his scope to tactics. In his day, the term grand tactics usually encompassed what we call strategy, a word barely beginning to enter the military lexicon; and to Guibert himself, the tactics of his title encompassed the whole art of war, including the organization and recruitment of armies and their relation to society and the state.

While Guibert failed to distinguish clearly between the new permanent divisions and the temporary tactical formations of the past, he recognized especially the possibilities that the division opened for highly mobile strategic ma-

1. Jacques Antoine Hippolyte comte de Guibert, *Essai général de tactique* . . . (2 vols., Londres [London]: Chez les librairies associés, 1772).

neuver. Until now armies had marched to battle with the order of march determined by the place that the various units would occupy in the line of battle. Guibert urged freeing marches and maneuver from this dependency. Rather, each division should march as a separate column. Not only could an army marching in columns move more rapidly than a unitary army and widen its front, but it would enjoy infinite possibilities for distracting and confusing the enemy. The divisions could then concentrate on a chosen battlefield. On this field, the articulation of the army into divisions would permit the commander increased flexibility to adjust to and exploit variations in terrain as well as to maneuver for decisive effect.

Guibert found warfare still under the spell of Vauban, and he believed that the effects generally were not desirable. The engineering skills of Vauban had caused fortifications to be excessively valued. Appropriate maneuver by the kind of mobile army Guibert advocated could bypass fortifications and nullify their value by cutting their lines of communications. Such bypassing would be possible because an army organized into divisions could itself break free from dependence on a single depot of supply. Therefore the value of fortifications would doubly diminish, for to defend great supply depots had been one of the principal reasons for creating fortresses. Without a need for elaborate fortifications, warfare would become less costly—no small consideration for the nearly bankrupt French government—but more important, a war of mobility would become a war of decisive results. Not again would France need to waste its resources in prolonged campaigns leading nowhere, like those of the continental war just ended.

Further to assure decisiveness, Guibert also developed a larger theme. The Age of Enlightenment and Reason had already brought forward the idea that all institutions of government ought to be in harmony with the spirit and desires of the people. From this idea, Guibert drew the concept of a citizens' army. If the armies of France could embody the vigor of the French nation at large, then indeed France could resume its former glorious place in the European military constellation. Thus both the constitution and the army of France ought to be reformed to enlist the participation and pride of the citizenry.

It was reform, however, that Guibert hoped for; he neither advocated nor envisaged a French Revolution. He neither advocated nor foresaw the rising of the nation in arms that was to accompany the Revolution. He believed that modern, civilized European peoples had grown too soft, too fond of luxury, for any such strenuous upheaval to be possible. But he hoped that political and military reform might enlist in the service of the French King enough of the energies and abilities of the French people that the French Army could fight again with a verve and élan it had lost.

Far from encouraging either revolution or a true *levée en masse,* Guibert retreated from the mere suggestion of such phenomena. The citizens' army suggested Sparta, and so thoroughly militarized a state repelled him. The citizens' army also suggested releasing the unreason of crowds of ordinary men into the waging of war, a thought that neither fitted Guibert's underlying accord with the Age of Reason nor truly promised much for the use of war for the betterment of France. Rather, even the hint of a war of mass armies conjured up in Guibert's reflections the loss of those limitations that confined the destructiveness of eighteenth-century war mainly to the career soldiers who waged it. The war of mass armies was likely to become a war of mass destruction of the resources, property, and people among which and whom it blazed forth.

Nourishing these misgivings during the 1770s while he grew older and, having become a celebrity through his *Essai*, was taken up by the French establishment and court, Guibert grew comfortable and satisfied, not to say satiated. In 1773 he traveled to Prussia and met Frederick the Great, discussing the art of war with the Prussian King, observing Prussian military exercises, and developing a new respect for the Prussian military system based on a relatively small, careerist army. From 1773 until her death in 1776 he was the object of the intense amorous passions of one of the darlings of the fashionable salons, Mlle. Jeanne Julie Eléonore de Lespinasse. He read with interest about the American Revolution, and it speaks well for his acuteness but also for the influence of his Prussian travels that he discerned the weaknesses of the American rebels' approximation of a citizens' army and readily acknowledged the superiority of the British regulars over the American citizen-soldiery in battle. He attributed British defeats not to the quality of the British Army but to weaknesses elsewhere in the British system of politics and command.

All these growing reservations about the citizens' army he set forth in a second book, published in 1779, *Défense du système de guerre moderne; ou, Réfutation complete de la système de M. . . . D . . .* [François Jean de Grainloge d'Orgeville, baron de Mesnil-Durand], *par l'auteur de l'essai général de tactique.*[2] Herein Guibert defended the prevailing European system of war on every level from the tactical—asserting the efficacy of the traditional linear tactics against a growing belief among military reformers that columns of attack might shatter the line—through the organizational—emphasizing his new conviction of the battlefield superiority of long-term soldiers over an armed citizenry—to the philosophical. War as conducted by kings and hired mercenaries, he perceived, might be irrational in its ritualistic formalities, but war as expanded by the unleashing of nationalistic emotions would grow far more irrational; it would race toward unlimited destruction of resources and lives alike. Even the slow-moving warfare of fortifications and siegecraft had its redeeming features. If such warfare was indecisive, this very quality tended to restrain the ambitions of would-be conquerors. If military aggression was far more likely to yield stalemate than victories, then the temptation to initiate aggression ought to be small. By implication, the failure of the ambitious goal of destroying Prussia as a military power in the Seven Years War would discourage the pursuit of similarly inordinate goals in the future. Everything in the existing system of war tended to keep war limited in both means and ends, and the advantages of limitation and restraint in war were infinitely preferable to any advantages that might be gained through a quest for military decisiveness.

2. (Neufchâtel: Privately printed, 1779). The work was a response specifically to Mesnil-Durand's *Fragments de tactique; ou, Six mémoires* (Paris: Chez C.-A. Jombert, 1774).

From 1775 to 1777 Guibert was enlisted by a reforming Minister of War, Claude Louis, comte de Saint-Germain, *lieutenant général* (former field marshal in the Danish service), to assist in the improvement of the French Army through the introduction of the Prussian standards of training and discipline. The reforms of Saint-Germain included, however, a return to certain of the professionalizing tendencies of Louis XIV, including a reduction in the number of officers and their privileges, which soon precipitated rumblings of discontent and the resignation of the minister in September 1777. Saint-Germain's downfall was Guibert's as well. He was promoted to *maréchal-de-camp*, the equivalent of a major general, but shunted off to a provincial staff assignment. His *Défense du système de guerre moderne* was among other purposes part of his continuing defense of the work of Saint-Germain. As the Revolution approached he was recalled to the Ministry of War to help palliate discontent through renewed reform, but by that time his reformism was too tepid for the purpose. In 1789 his failure to secure a seat in the Estates-General effectively removed him from any further role in the onrush of events. He died on May 6, 1790, in a mood of frustration, disappointment, and perhaps fear over the changes that his early advocacy of the citizen army seemed about to help produce.

The Problem of Indecisiveness in Battle: Infantry and Cavalry

Guibert's changing assessments of the merits of Frederician infantry tactics reflected in fact not weak inconsistency but the acuteness of his mind— an intelligent critic's appreciation of the existence of a quandary. Assuming that French infantry could be brought up to the tactical standards of the Prussians and the British, the effect was likely to be no more than to confirm a battlefield deadlock marked by heavy casualties, such as had already tended to appear in those battles of the Seven Years War that had pitted against each other infantry forces of approximate parity in skill, and such as had always characterized infantry warfare in conditions in which the mobile arm was unable to intervene decisively.

Frederick the Great's infantry had become preponderant in the battles of the War of the Austrian Succession because of its superior training and discipline, particularly its superior rate of fire and its excelling in cohesive maneuver and in ability to retain cohesion under pressure. To these ingredients, Frederick had added the oblique order of battle as a device for exploiting the assets of his troops. By the time of the Seven Years War, however, the Austrian infantry had come close enough to matching the strengths of the Prussians that Prussian preponderance nearly disappeared. Even the Russians, though lacking the finely honed skills of the Prussians and Austrians, displayed so much sheer tenacity and capacity to bear up under casualties that the Prussians could establish no appreciable tactical ascendancy against them either. In short, the infantry training and tactics of Frederick the Great did not alter the fundamentals of infantry warfare in his time. They achieved only a temporary advantage for his army, which was lost once rival armies approximated his methods of drill.

Meanwhile, however, the firepower of infantry equipped with the bayonet-carrying musket—the bayonet permitting every infantry private to carry a fire-arm—proved to be of sufficiently devastating volume that cavalry could not shatter an infantry formation unless the infantry had already suffered physical and moral attrition almost to the breaking point. It was still essential for armies to maintain effective mounted arms, and the cavalry could on occasion transform a deadlock into a decisive encounter if it charged at precisely the right moment, as Frederick and his great horseman Seydlitz had several times demonstrated. But it was only against already beaten or wavering infantry that the cavalry charge was likely to prove effective. Properly employed, furthermore, the cavalry of a faltering army could shield its infantry comrades against the rival infantry. Thus the overriding tendency of battle pointed toward stalemate.

Gradually there had developed among tactical reformers a hope that the tendency might be altered and stalemate averted through a change in infantry tactics more basic than any of Frederick's. Such reformers looked to the infantry's own capacity for shock action in the shape of the bayonet charge. In place of the customary fighting in linear formation employed by the infantry of all the major powers, the reformers advocated that attacking infantry charge in a deep column, *l'ordre profond*. The depth of the column and the momentum generated by the pressure of its rear ranks upon its van, they contended, could create a shock effect sufficient to rupture the enemy's line.

Firepower, however, remained the watchword of the opposing faction, the persisting advocates of the line, *l'ordre mince*. A line of three ranks firing volleys in rapid succession could spew forth such a hail of bullets as to halt any column, whose firepower would in contrast be diminished by the narrowness of its front. Already in his *Essai Général*, Guibert essentially accepted the force of this conservative view; he was never so radical a reformer as an overly hasty reading of his *Essai* might suggest. Against the two debating tactical schools he offered *l'order mixte*, but this plan leaned toward the arguments of the linear school. Thus, Guibert would have used the column for maneuver and for the approach to the enemy, but he adhered to the line for fighting. By the time of the Revolution, Guibert's cautious compromise formula was accepted French tactical doctrine. Fundamentally conservative as it was, however, it accepted the column sufficiently to bear the seeds of further change.

The tactical reformers seeking an escape from deadlock could also conjure with the possibilities raised by light infantry and skirmishing tactics. The best advertised source of those possibilities among historians in Great Britain and the United States has been forest warfare against the North American Indians. The red Indians did not fight in European-style lines but instead used the concealment offered by the vast forest covering most of eastern North America to shoot from cover against their opponents—increasingly using European firearms. Employing fluid, flexible maneuver, they often simply wore down their adversaries with successive hit-and-run actions. In response, the citizen-soldier militias of the British and French colonies and to some extent the British and French regulars in North America also developed tactics of fighting not in lines but in scattered concealment, taking aim when firing, and advancing against the enemy by making their way as skirmishers from cover to cover.

Yet there has been a tendency to exaggerate the tactical changes imposed by American experience upon European armies fighting in America. The British Army developed several regiments trained as light infantry, that is, with emphasis on skirmishing tactics, notably the 60th of Foot, the Royal American Regiment. Throughout the British Army, not only in America, it became customary to include one company of light infantry alongside the line companies of ordinary infantry in a British battalion. (There was also customarily a company of grenadiers; the light infantry company comprised agile men readily adaptable to skirmishing and irregular tactics, the grenadier company tall, strong men with a talent for throwing hand grenades, the original specialty of the company.) In some infantry regiments, there was a new emphasis on training all the companies for independent maneuver, thus enhancing the tactical flexibility of battalions that had hitherto maneuvered mainly as entire battalions. For all that, nevertheless, the disciplined cohesion of British regulars was almost as indispensable in fighting Indians as against European adversaries; the climactic battle of the Franco-British contest for North America, at Québec in 1759, was as we have seen fought in the European manner and its outcome determined largely by the superior European-style skills of the British infantry. And General George Washington fought the War of American Independence mainly with as close as possible an approximation of the rival British Army as he could make of his Continental Army.

Nevertheless, much of the impetus toward employing light infantry in skirmishing tactics rolled across Europe not eastward form North America but westward from the Ottoman Empire. The Turks like the North American Indians made much use of unconventional tactics, skirmishing, concealment, and ambuscades, but with rather more forethought, discipline, and tactical control than the Indians usually managed. In response, their European adversaries adopted similar irregular tactics. The Croation, Serbian, Vlach, Hungarian, Romanian, and sometimes German *Grenzer* of the Habsburg Empire's Turkish borderlands led the way. Perceiving the utility at the very least of inconspicuous reconnaissance troops and patrols in the van and on the flanks of an army, as well as of occasional ambushes and of skirmisher swarms to harry an enemy, other European armies took up the pattern. Other German armies, conspicuously including the Prussian, established *Jäger*—literally, hunter—regiments. Farther west, the *Jäger* tended to become *chasseurs*. In eastern and central Europe, furthermore, the rise of light troops extended to cavalry, an arm that played little part in the eighteenth-century American wars. Frederick the Great's hussars wore eastern-style uniforms in addition to bearing an eastern European name; as many of them as possible were recruited from Hungary, Poland, and Saxony; their roles on campaign were mainly in reconnaissance and raiding—but while they were irregular troops, they were nevertheless developed into an elite. Similar units appeared in most armies. But in this extension of unconventional infantry and cavalry tactics from east to west, the British shared relatively little; North American experience notwithstanding, the British Army often lagged behind in the development of more flexible tactics.

The development of light infantry and the new forms of light cavalry could measureably improve reconnaissance and flank security for the army on the offensive, while also increasing opportunities for the defender to harass both the enemy's main body and his lines of communications. Light infantry advancing as skirmishers in front of the main infantry assault might conceivably lay down a volume of fire sufficient to soften up the defenses in useful measure before the main assault struck. Nonetheless, light troops remained of secondary importance. They did not offer a solution to the principal tactical problem posed by the continental battles of the Seven Years War, how to break the stalemate into which land battle had once more deteriorated.

The Problem of Indecisiveness in Battle: Artillery

Larger possibilities for enhancing the decisiveness of battle lay in artillery improvements. The impact of artillery in battle had continued to be limited by the fact that guns larger than 6–pounders (2.721 kilograms) (3.66-inch [92.964-mm.] in British service) tended to be too cumbersome for effective tactical maneuver. Siege guns could do effective work once they were hauled laboriously into position; the greater difficulties lay in finding satisfactory mobile field guns. Lack of standardization in calibers and other aspects of design had also impeded the artillery's usefulness by making maintenance and especially the storage of ammunition supplies excessively complicated. If standardized 12-pounders (5.442 kilograms) (4.63-inch [117.602-mm] in British service) could be made light, durable, and maneuverable enough to be employed flexibly in battle alongside the infantry, then the guns might be able to blast away infantry resistance enough to produce a quantum leap forward in the prospects of rupturing field defenses.

The foundations for a more effective field artillery had begun to be laid well before the Seven Years War; the reformers of the 1760s, particularly in France, found the elements of impressive improvements already at hand. We speak here of the two principal types of guns into which field artillery had evolved: cannon, which were long-barreled and intended to fire a solid round shot along a relatively flat trajectory; and howitzers, short-barreled and designed to throw an explosive shell along a relatively curved trajectory.

In the first half of the century, an English mathematician and engineer of Quaker parentage, Benjamin Robins, had established what may well be considered the beginnings of the modern science of ballistics. He did so by combining mathematical theory and calculation with experimentation. He developed the ballistic pendulum, with which the velocity of a projectile can be measured by hurling it against a pendulum of considerable weight, having determined the velocity required to displace the pendulum from its position of rest. He studied the resistance of air to the motion of projectiles and the force of gunpowder, computing the velocities imparted by gunpowder to projectiles under various circumstances. From his theories and experiments he devised practical rules regarding the range and impact of artillery fire. More than ever before, gunnery began to realize its two-centuries-old aspiration to attain the precision of a science rather than to remain a mystery and an art.

While Robins was at work, Dutch founders developed new methods of casting gun barrels. Hitherto, guns were cast hollow around a core. The core, however, tended to move during the process of molding, which caused irregularities in the alignment and circumference of the barrel. By 1747, the Dutch had learned how to drill a barrel that had been cast solid, thus producing a better aligned bore with closer tolerances for receiving shot inserted into it. When to this improvement there was added more precisely cast round shot, the windage of artillery pieces—the difference between the diameters of bore and shot—could be much reduced. Thereby less of the gas pressure generated by the explosion of gunpowder would escape, so that smaller charges could propel shot with greater accuracy over a given distance at a given velocity. Reduced charges in turn opened the way to lighter and shorter barrels, a prerequisite for the more maneuverable field guns that were desired. As is customary in such matters of advancing military technology, the Dutch tried to keep their inventions secret but failed to do so; the European gun-founding industry as a whole was soon ready to apply the new processes.

The Austrians responded to their setbacks at Prussian hands during the War of the Austrian Succession not only by improving their infantry drill but also by seeking to use superior artillery to trump Frederick the Great's infantry. In 1744 *Feldmarschall* Wenzel, Fürst Lichtenstein became Director General of Artillery; at his new artillery school at Budweis he developed both theoretical and practical experiments akin to Robins's, out of which came designs for standardized light, maneuverable 3-pounder (2.91-inch, 73.914-mm.), 6-pounder (3.66-inch, 92.964-mm.), and 12-pounder (4.63-inch, 117.602-mm.) cannon and also some excellent howitzers. (It will be recalled that these guns fired balls of 1.361, 2.721, and 5.422 kilograms, respectively.) In service by the beginning of the Seven Years War, these guns helped regain battlefield parity for Austria against Prussia. The Prussians in fact adopted the Austrian 12-pounder, and the French were to copy the Austrian light howitzer as late as 1803.

Frederick the Great responded to the Austrian advances and to the declining effectiveness of his infantry by devising his own artillery improvements. By the close of the Seven Years War, he was employing almost six field pieces for every thousand men in his army, an unprecedentedly high ratio and one that exceeded even the high reliance that Napoleon would soon place on artillery. He saw to the development of a Prussian 12-pounder even while also adopting the Austrian gun of that size. Already during the War of the Austrian Succession Frederick had sometimes brought heavy siege guns to the battlefield to enhance his battering power, and he persisted in doing so whenever circumstances allowed it. Conversely, he fielded in 1759 a mounted artillery force—horse artillery—that could ride into battle with his cavalry. While others had equipped such an arm with very light "galloper" guns, the Prussian horse artillery employed 6-pounders. The other powers naturally began to follow the Prussian example.

In 1757 Jean-Baptiste Vaquette de Gribeauval, *lieutenant colonel* in the French Army and an artillery specialist, was lent to the now-allied Austrian Army. He rose to the rank of *Feldmarschall Leutnant* (major general) in that service and after returning to his own country received the equivalent rank there, *maréchal-de-camp*. In 1764 he became Inspector of Artillery and in 1765 a *lieutenant général*. Building upon what he had seen in Austria, he sought to restore the artillery of France to the predominance it had enjoyed from the time of the brothers Bureau and for many generations thereafter. Encountering a strong conservative opposition— scarcely surprising in the privilege-laden French Army—he nevertheless rose to the still higher post of First Inspector of Artillery in 1776 and thereafter was able to realize most of his purposes. He created the artillery arm that was again and again to prove the mainstay of another artillery specialist, Napoleon.

Gribeauval's artillery consisted of standardized weapons for field, siege, garrison, and coastal service, complete with standardized carriages, limbers, ammunition chests, and tools. The field guns were 4-pounders, 1.814-kilograms (3.21-inch, 81.534-mm. bore), 8-pounders, 3.628 kilograms (4-inch, 101.6-mm.), and 12-pounders, 5.422 kilograms (4.4-inch, 117.602-mm.), accompanied by howitzers of 6-inch (152.4-mm.) and 8-inch (203.2-mm.) bore. Gribeauval's gun carriages had iron axles for durability, but his weapons and equipment also took advantage of the improvements in gun founding and in metallurgy more generally to reduce weight to about half that of older French artillery pieces of equivalent power. With a thinner and shorter barrel than its predecessor, the new 12-pounder weighed 1,600 English pounds (1,455 *livres*, 1 *livre* equaling 1.1 English pounds; 725.62 kilograms). Such a gun was reasonably maneuverable in the field.

Gribeauval installed calibrated rear sights and graduated tangent sights at the breech that could be set to compensate for the dropping trajectory of the projectile. To ease the task of aiming and thus the use of these sights, he also installed an elevating screw mechanism, a solid screw placed under the breech permitting gunners to raise and lower the muzzle readily.

Other improvements widespread in the European armies of the 1760s further enhanced the effectiveness of Gribeauval's artillery. After 1765 a new quick-match vent tube fashioned from either tin or a reed or a quill, filled with an explosive mixture and inserted into the vent of a gun, provided a much stronger ignition flash than the slow match previously inserted into the tube. Prepacked charges containing the appropriate weight of powder per projectile came into widespread use at the same time. In 1783 the French government offered a prize for the industrial production of saltpeter or potassium nitrate, the critical and hitherto relatively scarce ingredient in gunpowder; this stimulus made itself felt early in the next round of warfare, when Nicolas Leblanc operated a saltpeter factory at Saint-Denis near Paris between 1781 and 1794.

The technological advances in artillery helped assure that, unlike the infantrymen of Frederick the Great, gunners could not be conditioned to become automatons. They needed mechanical skill and also a measure of problem-solving intelligence and initiative. In Austria and France, enlisted soldiers of the artillery as well as officers attended schools, sometimes sitting with officers in the same classrooms. The officers also continued to be selected less for their social credentials and more for their talent and intelligence than in any other service except the closely related engineers. The Austrian and French reforms strengthened the status of the artillery as a special stronghold of professionalism within armies and officer corps. Because the artillery reforms also opened the way for a more pivotal artillery role in battle, they implied also possible further major advances in the professionalization of the whole conduct of war.

The French Army and the Outbreak of Revolution

To the *noblesse de cour*, improving the efficiency of the French Army could scarcely seem so important as maintaining the privileges of the *ancien régime*. The intrinsic strength of France in population and wealth assured that however severe was the decline in the relative prowess of the French Army from 1660 to 1760, the independence of France to follow its own course in domestic and foreign affairs could not be seriously challenged—and an independent course of upholding traditional aristocratic rights and perquisites within France took high priority for the court nobility over any ambitions beyond their country's borders. Therefore the power of the nobility sharply circumscribed the capacity of the reformers to go on advancing professionalism and thus improving the army.

The death of Louis XV on May 10, 1774, ended a reign devoted to its own pleasures above all else. The old King's grandson, now Louis XVI, felt a conscientious dedication to the welfare of his subjects. At first this dedication expressed itself in modest support for reformers both military and otherwise, exemplified by the financial reforms of Anne Robert Jacques Turgot, baron de Laune as Comptroller-General from August 24, 1774, and of Jacques Necker as Director of the Treasury from October 1776, a title he changed in 1777 to Director-General of the Finances. But the forcing of Turgot's resignation as early as May 12, 1776—in a complicated intrigue that unhappily enlisted Necker against Turgot—and then Necker's own dismissal on May 19, 1781, signaled the shallowness of any royal commitment to change. Queen Marie Antoinette, bearer to France of the most rigid political orthodoxies of the Habsburg court, helped bring down Turgot, while the fall of Necker inaugurated a period of her ascendancy over court politics. In the military, this restoration of conservatism produced in the same year, 1781, a royal edict requiring that henceforth officer candidates had to prove their possession of at least four generations of noble ancestors. Professionalization of officership had apparently been thrown back to the days before Louis XIV.

But the expenses of the War of American Independence, piled high upon those of the Seven Years War, had created a financial crisis rendered insoluble by the termination of Necker's efforts to rationalize taxation. The crisis required the assembling of France's provincial *parlements* by 1787 to receive the King's appeals for financial assistance. When the *parlements* balked at subsidizing the reversion toward the Middle Ages, they proved to command popular support so deep that even the nobility's control of the army could not overcome it. On June 7, 1788, troops attempted to enforce a royal edict dissolving the *parlement* of

Grenoble, capital of Dauphiné. The populace of the town and the peasants of the neighboring countryside, the latter summoned by ringing the tocsin, thereupon seized control of Grenoble, overcoming the garrison with a hail of roof tiles, the soldiers displaying no eagerness to resist the populace anyway.

The *Journée des Tuiles*—the Day of Tiles—precipitated a resolution by the less conservative of the Dauphiné nobility along with the clergy and the commoners of the Third Estate to reassemble the old Estates General of the province, suspended since 1628, on July 21. Because the Third Estate had won the victory on the Day of Tiles, it received representation in the new Estates equal to that of the other two orders combined, with agreement also that voting should be by individuals and not by classes. These organizational developments proved to offer exceedingly important precedents. Meeting at Virille when the government contrived to prevent assembly at Grenoble, the Dauphiné Estates General joined in August in a growing demand for the summoning of the Estates General of France. The province of Dauphiné had moved toward initiating a revolution and was practically under the control of revolutionaries.

Louis XVI had already decided that he must agree to a session of the Estates General of the nation, and his call went out on August 8. On the 25th of that month, furthermore, the King restored Necker to office, this time as Secretary of State and member of the Royal Council. Necker persuaded Louis to announce on December 27 that the coming Estates General should follow the model of Dauphiné with the members of the Third Estate equaling in numbers those of the other two orders.

The reaction against the return toward feudalism had already renewed the impulse toward army reform; the officership edict of 1781 must surely prove impermanent. In 1787–1788 a War Council sat with Guibert as its secretary to codify and extend the reforms begun in the 1760s. The Council completed the reorganization into divisions by demarcating France into twenty-one divisional districts to correspond with the same number of permanent divisions. It similarly equalized regimental establishments. It took aim at one of the most egregious evils of the old military system by reducing drastically the number of commissioned officers, from some 36,000, of whom at most 13,000 were on duty, to 9,578 with the regiments and 2,500 on detached service or retired.

The War Council reviewed and helped put in the final form what became the *Règlement concernant L'exercise et les manœuvres de L'infanterie du premier août 1791*. This drill regulation adopted the essentials of Guibert's tactical suggestions to which he had adhered since his *Essai générale*. Mobility remained the principal desideratum for improving infantry effectiveness. Therefore the *Règlement* stressed not an effort to resolve the controversy over *l'ordre mince* versus *l'ordre profond* but an ability to employ rapidly whichever formation was suited to a given tactical situation. It emphasized rapidity of deployment from column into line and from line into column.

The *Règlement* approved, however, the tactical use of the battalion column of divisions (the latter word in this context needing to be differentiated from "division" meaning the new tactical and administrative organization). The battalion column of divisions drew up the companies of an infantry battalion one behind the other with divisions in the sense of short intervals between them. The battalion columns could not only advance rapidly toward the enemy and then deploy rapidly into line (the first company standing fast and the others deploying to right and left), but they could also close with the bayonet without necessarily shifting into line. Thus the column as a battlefield, tactical formation, hitherto employed for the most part only spontaneously, was to become a favorite device of the French for adding momentum and staying power to bayonet attacks.

To complete the combination of flexibility with speed, the infantry were now to march at a Quick Step of 100 to 120 paces per minute. The latter is standard modern marching cadence, but previously the cadence had usually been restricted to seventy-five paces per minute in order to help preserve tactical cohesion and alignment. To the French reformers, rapidity of movement seemed more important, the most likely means of breaking the deadlock between cohesive but slow and inflexible infantry forces.

The French Army in 1791 seemed poised to recapture its former preeminence in quality among the armies of Europe, perhaps even to grasp an infantry preeminence that had traditionally eluded it. But whom the army would serve, and for what purposes, became increasingly doubtful after the Day of Tiles. Reform was accelerating into revolution.

Part Three

THUNDERSTROKES OF BATTLE: THE FRENCH REVOLUTIONARY AND NAPOLEONIC WARS

12 THE FRENCH REVOLUTION: TRANSFORMATION AND CONTINUITY IN WAR

When the Austrian and Prussian monarchies went to war in 1792 to turn back the Revolution in France (albeit the French initiated hostilities against Austria), they themselves unwittingly contributed to an additional dimension of revolution. They did so by taking a portentous step toward enlarging the objects of warmaking.

By threatening the liberty of the French people to choose their government for themselves, the monarchies gave them a popular, deeply emotional cause such as the territorial and dynastic wars could never have generated. With the old French Army of the Bourbon monarchy disintegrating, and French finances even more chaotically in peril than they had ever been under the *ancien régime*, the Revolution nevertheless proved able to defend itself against such ambitious aims. It could do so by calling upon the people whose grievances and aspirations it embodied. It could enlist the might of the nation in arms. Thereby it could, and did, immensely increase the usual size of armies. It thus increased also the difficulties of supply and made restraints upon wholesale destruction by marching armies more difficult to enforce. By enlisting mass emotions it also made the embattled nation-state more resilient and war much more difficult to end, while doubling the tendency to rupture restraints upon the violence of war by stoking the fires of hatred among peoples.

The French Revolution also brought new complexities to civil-military relations. The officer corps of the old monarchies, to whatever degree they had become professionalized, and to whatever degree they permitted the advancement of talent without advantages of birth, had consisted of men tied by self-interest to the regimes they served. Those of bourgeois or very occasionally lower origins owed their rise to the favor of the kings to whom their loyalty was pledged. They had little reason to expect greater favor from political changes that until 1789 had in any event been barely conceivable. With the Revolution, however, any change became conceivable, not only in France but also by implication anywhere else in Europe. With politics suddenly fluid as never before, military men could entertain political ambitious of their own as never before, either individually, or as a corporate professional body that might become a state within the state. To guard against the political aspirations of soldiers, the revolutionary government of France introduced in turn a new kind of political penetration into the army from outside, dispatching to military posts and commands so-called Deputies on Mission to supervise the politics of the soldiers, and often to intervene in tactical and operational decisions.

The consequent revolution in war, however, was not so revolutionary as it has sometimes seemed to have been. The history of armies and warfare displays greater continuity from before and through the French Revolution than the high drama of the revolutionary era, playing upon our own emotions, has often led us to imagine. Most importantly, in spite of the efforts of the pre-revolutionary military reformers and the considerable application of their ideas during the Wars of the French Revolution, warfare retained its intractable and disastrous propensity to lead to deadlocks rather than decisions. The battle remained the favored means of seeking an escape from deadlock.

Revolution Generates War

Heated emotions generating skewed perceptions had a great deal to do, also, with causing the first eruption of European war as a sequel to the acceleration of reform into revolution in France at the beginning of the 1790s.

With the French monarchy nearly bankrupt in prestige as well as in the literal financial sense, and its army not a reliable instrument for domestic police purposes, the convening of the Estates General of France by Louis XVI in the *Salle des Menus Plaisirs* at Versailles on May 5, 1789, proved to set in motion an apparently unstoppable engine rushing more and more swiftly toward change—change of everything connected with the *ancien régime*, sometimes seemingly change for change's sake.

On June 15 the Third Estate and a few members of the Second Estate—the clergy—transformed the Estates General into a National Assembly that hastened toward constitutional government, drastically curbing the powers of the King in the name of the sovereignty of the people. This National Assembly behaved indiscreetly, to say the least, in its management of foreign affairs. While it proclaimed admirably that it desired only peace with foreign nations, it also declared null and void all treaties not sanctified by the national consent. Thus it threw into question every treaty entered into by the French monarchy; no other power could feel confident of the status of its relations with France. Abolishing feudal tenure in France, for example, the National Assembly trod harshly upon the rights of various German princes in Alsace that were guaranteed by the Treaty of Westphalia. The Assembly offered financial compensation, but when the princes declined this recompense it paid no further heed to their grievances. Similarly, when a large part of the population of the papal territory of Avignon sought union with France, the Assembly eventually—in this instance there were cautious second thoughts for a time—declared Avignon annexed to France.

Nevertheless, even after Louis XVI attempted to flee on June 20, 1791, and then became practically a prisoner of the Assembly, the governments of his fellow monarchs showed no haste to intervene on his behalf. War did not at first seem a necessary concomitant of revolution; the sort of people's war that revolution might logically generate merely hovered in the wings, for if no war came there could be no people's war.

On August 25, 1791, it is true, the Emperor Leopold II and King Frederick William (Friedrich Wilhelm) II of Prussia met at Pillnitz, near Dresden, and declared their readiness to intervene in France should the other powers call for their assistance. But they knew that neither Great Britain nor Russia would do so. Leopold II, son of Maria Theresa and Francis I, and only since early 1790 successor to his brother Joseph (Josef) II, particularly desired no war. He entered into the Pillnitz Declaration with great reluctance, yielding to it only because it seemed unavoidable that he offer at least a gesture in favor of the German princes who had been aggrieved by the French. Meanwhile Leopold tried to dampen the appeals both of those princes and of aristocratic émigrés from France, in October 1791 ordering the dispersal of armed émigrés who had assembled in the Austrian Netherlands. When on September 14, 1791, Louis XVI had sworn to the new Constitution voted by the National Assembly eleven days earlier and reducing him to a constitutional monarch, Leopold professed to believe that the revolutionary turmoils had been settled, and he virtually withdrew the Declaration of Pillnitz. A reforming Grand Duke of Tuscany before he ascended the Imperial throne, he might have proven a great Emperor, preserving peace and extending his Tuscan work throughout the Habsburg dominions. But on March 1, 1792, Leopold suddenly died.

Restraining presence though he was and might have continued to be, furthermore, with the Declaration of Pillnitz he had committed a mistake. The declaration gave the new French government a pretext for feeling itself wronged, and there were many men of influence among its leaders who were desirous of such a pretext and even of war. Some moderate conservatives hoped that international conflict would rally the French people patriotically to the Crown and thus limit the Revolution. Many leftists hoped for the opposite effect from war against foreign kings: the discrediting of monarchy and therefore the opportunity to abolish it in France. Leaders further to the left hoped not only for that consequence but also for the export of republicanism eastward. The King, though vacillating, on the whole hoped for a war that would lead to the defeat of the revolutionaries and his rescue by his fellow monarchs; he had already so informed his brother-in-law, Leopold II, in private communication.

Still, there were strong forces in France opposing war. Much of the extreme left feared the very result for which the right hoped, the restoration of patriotic loyalty to the King. Moreover, the recent reforms of the army appeared to be flowing away on a tide of military disintegration. The army's rank and file, hopeful that the liberalization of the regime meant better food, pay, and disciplinary conditions for them, grew restless when such benefits did not promptly appear. The noncommissioned officers hoped that liberalization meant opportunities for promotion into the commissioned ranks, and they also became restless when such benefits came more slowly than they had hoped. Commissioned officers, largely noblemen obviously distrustful of the turn of events, thought their fears were being realized even if the immediate hopes of their subordinates were not when the soldiers were encouraged to join political clubs and to form regimental committees to safeguard their interests. Some of the committees jailed their officers. Many other officers naturally joined the exodus of émigrés from France, some preparing to return in arms to suppress the Revolution. By early 1792, the officer corps was depleted by about half. Throughout the army, discipline was eroded and desertions multiplied.

Nevertheless, the prowar factions persuaded the Diplomatic Committee of the new Legislative Assembly to report on January 14, 1792, that the Emperor ought to be required to give satisfactory assurances of his attitude and conduct toward France by February 10. The Assembly postponed the deadline to March 1. On February 7, however, the Emperor entered into a defensive alliance with Frederick William of Prussia, a measure to which Leopold felt obliged to resort despite his continuing determination to resist war and despite the fact that both his and the Prussian government were at least as much interested in their current rivalry over the fate of a dying Poland that had already been largely partitioned among them and Russia; Austria preferred to preserve what remained of a now innocuous neighbor, while ambitious Prussia desired to complete the division of the spoils. The March 1 deadline came and went without further action from the French Assembly, but it was also the day of the Emperor's unexpected death, an event that removed a possibly indispensable agent of restraint.

There was no immediate successor to the Imperial throne. The hereditary Habsburg dominions passed to Leopold's son, later the Emperor Francis (Franz) II; but this young man of twenty-four possessed only limited abilities, and for the present the Empire was adrift. The elderly Count Kaunitz tried to manage policy, but the most conservative and anti-French circles of the court felt restraint removed, and their maneuvers in turn gave fuel to the ascendant war factions in France.

There the indecisive King was at the moment attempting to restrain the movement toward war, but the principal effect of his intervention in policy-making was a ministerial crisis that on March 15 elevated to the head of the Ministry of Foreign Affairs a soldier, Charles François Dumouriez, *lieutenant général*. Dumouriez had demonstrated considerable military talent while earning a captaincy in the Seven Years War, and he already possessed diplomatic experience of a sort—he had been a member of the *Secret du Roi*, the secret service, of Louis XV. Dumouriez was of the persuasion that war would reunite the nation around the King (while incidentally advancing the Minister's own power). Thus his elevation had the contrary effect from the one that the King himself had intended by reentering the political arena to secure. Pressured by Dumouriez and the rest of the new ministry, Louis XVI changed course again and on April

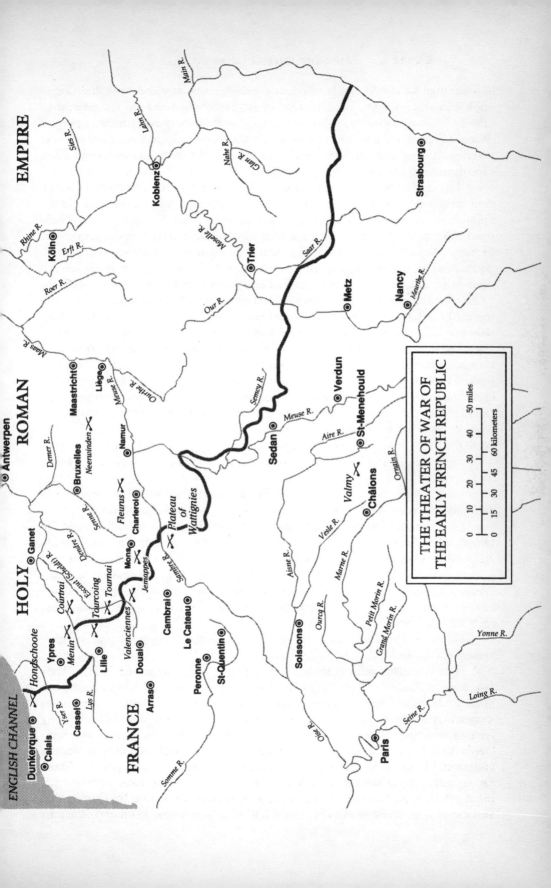

THE THEATER OF WAR OF
THE EARLY FRENCH REPUBLIC

50 miles

60 kilometers

20 went before the Assembly to propose a declaration of war against the King of Bohemia and Hungary—that is, against the Habsburg monarch but not against the Holy Roman Empire, in hopes of splitting other German princes away from Vienna. The declaration carried by acclamation. But as for the hopes of dividing Germany, Frederick William of Prussia agreed forthwith to join the Austrians in an invasion of France.

In the French Army, meanwhile, the emerging Revolution had generated not simply disruption but also some additional genuine reforms, particularly the diminution of the colonels' and captains' proprietary rights over their regiments and companies and the further nationalization of the army. To emphasize a new national homogeneity, regional regimental designations were changed to numbers running serially through the army. The *Maison du Roi* was abolished. To compensate for desertions, conscription had begun to be suggested as early as 1789, but the revolutionaries insisted initially that a free people must have a freely enlisted army—an army of volunteers. On the coming of war, the Assembly called for 100,000 volunteers from the National Guard, the bourgeois militia that had been playing a prominent part in political events, to join the army for a single campaign, electing their officers and receiving higher pay than the regulars. The response to this call was less than satisfactory, but Dumouriez believed that the army retained enough of the strength of the old army, had benefited enough from the recent reforms, and had taken on enough new élan from the Revolution, that he dared launch an aggressive campaign.

Valmy

Dumouriez proposed to begin with an invasion of the Austrian Netherlands, where along with national objectives he seems to have hoped to carve out a domain for himself. But his methods initially backfired as badly as had the King's in seeking to prevent war. Opening on April 28, 1792, the invasion accomplished nothing but to reveal that the disintegration of the French Army was far worse than the leaders of the nation had imaged. Three columns of invasion entered Belgium, the columns grandly denominated the Army of the North, the Army of the Center, and the Army of the Rhine and totaling some 130,000 men. Yet all three armies returned with their tails dragging—the first having fled on sight of the enemy, the second being routed, and the third thereupon choosing judicious retreat.

The Austrians consequently entered France and laid siege to Lille. They were not sufficiently strong, however, to mount a full-scale invasion; from 1788 to 1791 the Habsburg Empire had been engaged in yet another round of debilitating warfare against the Ottoman Empire, and troops had to be retained both along the eastern borders and in Hungary to guard against renewed troubles there. To strengthen itself in the west, Austria called upon Prussia to join it under the terms of the recent alliance. Prussia acceded, but before the Hohenzollern monarchy was ready to participate in a westward campaign it insisted on a resolution of the Austrian-Prussian disagreements over Poland. After much discussion, the Austrians acquiesced in Prussia's initiating another partition, in which in 1793 the

Prussians and Russians shared without the Habsburgs, who were to seek compensation in the west. So the distractions afflicting the monarchies saved France from the possible consequences of its own worse distractions; these included a mounting republican campaign to destroy the authority of the King altogether and remove him from his throne.

By midsummer of 1792, there nevertheless had assembled on the Rhine an Allied army of about 130,000 intended for a major invasion of France,. Its troops were about half Prussian, one-third Austrian, and the rest Hessians and French *émigrés*. The commander was Karl Wilhelm Ferdinand, Duke of Brunswick (Herzog von Braunschweig), *Feldmarschall* in the Prussian Army as well as ruler of his own dukedom. Small auxiliary armies formed on both of Brunswick's flanks, the whole under the command of the King of Prussia, Frederick William II. The French resolved themselves from three into two principal armies, that of the North under Dumouriez himself, that of the Center under François Christophe de Kellermann, *lieutenant général*.

Basing himself on Koblenz (Coblenz), Brunswick entered France on August 19 to commence a leisurely but for a time apparently inexorable invasion. The ill-maintained fortresses of Longwy and Verdun fell to him readily. But on July 25, against Brunswick's wishes, the Allies had prefaced their invasion with a proclamation asserting the inviolability of the French monarchy and thus denying the rights of the French people to control their own destiny. The announcement was couched in such bald and offensive terms that Brunswick was certain it could only put iron into the French resistance; if Leopold II had been alive it almost certainly would not have been issued. An enlightened sovereign in his own domain, Brunswick had little heart for his current enterprise anyway, and now he felt yet more discouraged. As he moved forward ponderously, the weather turned bad, raining almost incessantly; the sicknesses of damp weather soon scourged his ranks. King Frederick William, accompanying the army, proceeded to quarrel with the leaders of the Austrian contingent. And the French began to display the resentment and consequent renewal of resolution that the German field marshal had feared.

Dumouriez had been toughening his troops in a series of small forays around Valenciennes. He now accomplished a rapid flank march through the defiles of la Forêt de Argonne, practically under the eyes of the Prussians of Brunswick's vanguard, to attempt to interpose between the Allies and Paris. He also summoned Kellermann to his aid. Before the two French armies could converge, however, Brunswick demonstrated something of the skill with which during the Seven Years War he had earned his high Prussian rank, forcing and turning Dumouriez's northern flank. Dumouriez then had to change front to face north, along a line stretching from the Argonne in the east through Châlons. The road to Paris was thus opened, but fearing the French presence on his left, Brunswick moved to cut Dumouriez off from Châlons.

Kellermann, having linked up with Dumouriez's force and in temporary command of both French armies in Dumouriez's absence, countered by taking up a strong defensive position between Saint-Menehould and Valmy on the wooded heights of the Argonne. Here Brunswick halfheartedly attacked on September 20. The action is famous as the Cannonade of Valmy, and it proved to be little more than a cannonade. Brunswick's infantry advanced toward the French hoping to overawe their inexperienced troops, but the French did not falter, and Brunswick was unwilling to press his assault to a conclusion. He allowed everything to hinge on an artillery duel, but in this the improved French gunnery arm had the better of it, all the more readily because in the traditionally bourgeois artillery there had been relatively few officer defections.

With his logistics in disarray along the rain-sodden roads behind him, Brunswick was prepared to abandon his last vestiges of confidence should the French show any appreciable stiffness in front of him. They had certainly done so, and ten days after the cannonade the Allied army began to retreat. Dumouriez was content to remove them from the country less with a vigorous pursuit than with subtle and obscure negotiations that presently displaced all their troops from the soil of France. In the meantime Sardinia had invaded southern France in support of the alliance, but there matters went even better for the French, who counter-invaded and conquered Savoy and Nice.

On the day of the cannonade, furthermore, a newly elected National Convention assembled in Paris. Responding in part at least to the Allies' ill-advised proclamation of July 25, the Convention next day proclaimed France a Republic. Thus a series of hesitant, reluctant, and misguided Allied efforts in the diplomatic and military spheres had helped precipitate a seismic shift in France's internal history.

But there was no immediate change in the pace of events beyond France's borders. In the new Republic, the subsiding of the foreign danger brought a subsiding also of military preparations. Louis XVI was gone from his throne and soon to be tried for plotting against the new Constitution and beheaded, but corresponding upheavals in warfare still hung in uneasy restraint.

Even as the French mobilization effort relaxed, however, France's leadership displayed symptoms of a euphoria over the victory of Valmy well beyond anything that the limited nature of the triumph and the still uncertain effectiveness of the troubled French Army would have warranted. To the south of Brunswick's line of retreat, Adam Philippe Custine, *lieutenant général*, with a new Army of the Vosges—in fact too small a force to deserve this designation—went over to the offensive in September, crossed the Rhine from Alsace, captured Mainz, and went on to take Frankfurt am Main as well. Dumouriez meanwhile abandoned the tentativeness of his immediate post-Valmy conduct and resumed the invasion of the Austrian Netherlands. The Austrians had gone into winter quarters, in which the French general surprised 14,000 of them at Jemappes near Mons on November 6 with an attack by 40,000 troops. Much of the neighboring Belgian population now hailed the French as liberators, and Dumouiez entered Brussels (Bruxelles) without meeting further resistance. Custine was encountering similar popular welcomes in Germany. Its euphoria consequently inflated, the National Convention voted on November 19 to extend the aid of France to all peoples seeking liberty—in effect, to export republicanism and revolution. On December 15 the Convention hardened this policy by declaring that all people freed by its assistance should carry out a revolution on the French model or be treated as enemies.

Carnot and the Nation in Arms

Yet even now, such declarations notwithstanding, no one showed real eagerness to translate revolution in France into a firestorm of war across Europe. Consistent not with its latest resolutions but nevertheless with the principal direction of French foreign relations sine 1789, the Convention now allowed its army to subside into winter quarters, and many of the emergency volunteers, claiming leaves of absence, to go home. It also neglected to supply its armies of occupation adequately, which reinforced the homeward movement and also precipitated a wave of plundering that quickly discouraged the recent Belgian, German, and Savoyard welcomers of occupation. And the neglect of supply struck hardest against the old regiments of white-coated regulars, the backbone of the army; the quartermasters and commissaries favored such new revolutionary units as remained on hand. The motive behind the aggressive proclamations had been less zealous than it seemed; the Convention was less interested in the export of ideology than in the more mundane purpose of seeking allies.

On January 21, 1793, however, with its recent conquests from Antwerp to Savoy now garrisoned mainly by the remnants of the old regulars, the French Republic guillotined Louis XVI. In combination with the announced, albeit somewhat unreal, threat to export the Revolution, this horrifying event abruptly crystallized the international resistance to France that had hitherto remained amorphous and halfhearted. Henceforth, the exporting of French republicanism seemed equivalent to the exporting of murder—the murder of kings and, as the Reign of Terror began to take shape, the murder of all members of the traditional ruling classes and of all dissenters as well. In opposition to this specter there rose up the First Coalition against France. The oddly muted tones of the overture had but barely suggested the fury of the drama now to come.

In Great Britain, William Pitt the Younger as King George III's First Lord of the Treasury had exerted restraint against hasty action as judiciously as Leopold II. But in the folly of their euphoria the French went out of their way to make Pitt's labors of restraint as difficult as possible. Dumouriez, it will be remembered, had entertained notions of extracting from the occupation of Belgium an independent domain for himself; when opposition from both the Belgians and the French government predictably frustrated this scheme, France concluded that the best way to resolve the perplexities of occupation of neighboring territories—and to restrain ambitious occupation commanders like Dumouriez—was to annex the territories. Province by province, Belgium was incorporated into France. A similar policy was instituted for the Rhineland. France declared that the Rhine and the Alps as well as the Pyrenees constituted its natural frontiers. Its government's purposes were the enhancement of security and the assurance of civil control over the military, but the policy was nonetheless reckless in its apparent challenge to monarchy in general and to historic British sensitivities about the Low Countries in particular.

As if to aggravate the threat to those sensitivities, the French turned to the question of the River Scheldt. The navigation of the Scheldt had been closed by the Treaty of Westphalia and various other international agreements in order to divert commerce for the benefit of the Dutch. Great Britain had joined in the guarantee of its closure. On November 16, 1792, France unilaterally declared the Scheldt open to navigation.

Soon afterward the French annexed Savoy, a traditional makeweight of English policy against France in the Mediterranean. From Paris there also flowed glosses upon the Convention's resolutions of November 19 and December 15, specifically threatening to attack Great Britain in aid of English republicans. When the execution of Louis XVI followed close behind these assorted provocations, the British government felt obliged to order the departure of the French diplomatic mission from London. Concluding that the annexation of Belgium made war with Britain inevitable, but regarding the abandonment of Belgium without a contest as worse than a British war, France on February 1, 1793, declared war on Great Britain—and for good measure, on the United Provinces also.

The execution of the French King meanwhile had driven Charles (Carlos) IV of Spain away from yet another of the international efforts to conciliate the French revolutionaries—in this instance an effort motivated by hope of French support for a revival of Spanish colonial power. The Spanish King naturally had to denounce the killing of his fellow Bourbon monarch. Consequently, on March 7 France also declared war against the kingdom across the Pyrenees, again assuming that a conflict was inevitable anyway. Presently the Papal States, Naples (the Kingdom of the Two Sicilies), Tuscany, Parma, Modena, Sardinia, and Portugal joined the anti-French grouping. The Imperial Diet declared war in April. (But in January 1793, it must be noted, Prussia and Russia had invaded the remaining rump of Poland, a diversion that limited any Prussian contribution to the coalition armies, caused the Austrians also to hold back forces to keep an eye on the Prussians, and detained Russia from joining the coalition.)

Against this league, the French had left themselves with little means of resistance save their emotional fervor. Mismanagement had sunk Dumouriez's army in Belgium close to disintegration. When Dumouriez nevertheless invaded Holland, he merely left Belgium open for rapid reconquest by an Austrian army of some 42,000 commanded by Prince Josias of Saxe-Coburg as *Feldmarschall*. With the Austrians driving in the detachments that covered his right flank and rear, Dumouriez had to retreat toward the Meuse. He gave battle at Neerwinden on March 18. The French still contrived to muster a slight numerical superiority, but they had nothing like the Austrians' old-order discipline and coherence. They were routed.

Thereupon Dumouriez turned his coat, declaring himself opposed to the Republic and trying to persuade the remnants of his army to defect with him. His persuasion failed, and on April 5 he fled into the Austrian lines; but his former army was now retreating in almost complete disarray. Unable to reform in sufficient strength to hold the old border fortresses of the age of Louis XIV, it streamed back to Valenciennes and still farther, to form clusters around Bouchain, Lille, Dunkirk, and Cassel.

France was now in far worse military condition than it had been when the Duke of Brunswick advanced. A strong push by Coburg could almost certainly have carried quickly into Paris. But as various Allied contingents joined the Austrians, Coburg began to feel distracted and impeded by the customary conflicting counsels of a diverse partnership. More than that, as a commander of a Habsburg army he had to fear also that too aggressive an advance would precipitate the execution of Louis XVI's Habsburg Queen, Maria Theresa's daughter Marie Antoinette. Like Brunswick before him, furthermore, Coburg felt a considerable measure of sympathy for the early Revolution; he admired the Constitution of 1791 and had no wish to become the agent of complete reaction. He was willing to settle for, and seemed most likely to keep all the partners in harness if he restricted himself to, the capture of some major fortresses such as Valenciennes and Lille. The logistical support particularly of his Austrian forces was so difficult—the distance from Vienna so great—that acquiring a fortress to serve as a major depot seemed imperative whatever the larger strategy. Beyond moving toward such a base, initially by laying siege to Condé as a preliminary objective, Coburg negotiated.

Thus the coalition powers were behaving at least as haltingly as before—but the French were not. Knowing far better than the Allies how thin and brittle their defenses had become, the revolutionaries at last began to inject into the war some of the fervor that at home had carried them to the extreme of killing the King. The cry of "*La Patrie en danger*," taken up the year before but then acted on as if it had been less than the literal truth, now sounded forth again and in earnest. During the winter the National Convention had voted a levy of 300,000 men, but many exemptions were granted, and allowing the sending of substitutes threw the military burden as usual upon the lowest orders of society; of 100,000 sought for the regular army and 200,000 for the supposed volunteers, only 180,000 were raised. The effort to apply large-scale conscription, moreover, had provoked a large-scale uprising in La Vendée, the area along the west coast south of the Loire, as well as counterrevolutionary insurrections in many other parts of France. The French Revolutionary Wars became a civil as well as an international struggle; especially in La Vendée, officers and soldiers of the old army organized the counterrevolution into a full-fledged military force that required a corresponding full-scale field army merely to contain it and only slowly to repress it during 1793 and on into 1794.

Nevertheless, invasion and defenselessness now touched off a dramatic rally by the Revolution. The radical Jacobins were now displacing the moderate Girondists from the direction of affairs. In January 1793 committees from the various departments of state formed a united Committee of National Defense to take in hand the war effort; in April this group was transformed into the smaller and more efficient and energetic Committee of Public Safety—the mainspring of the gathering Reign of Terror, but also of the salvation of France.

Lazare Nicolas Marguerite Carnot was a former captain of engineers in the royal army who had entered into the military reform movement of the 1780s but carried his reformism too far by criticizing the fortification designs of the sacrosanct Vauban. This indiscretion actually put him into prison for a time, ostensibly on the charge of fighting a duel. When the Revolution broke out, Carnot expanded his quest for improvement into politics. In 1792 and early 1793 he served repeatedly as a commissioner from the revolutionary government to the armies, and he was instrumental in reestablishing some semblance of organized defense after Neerwinden. He now became the member of the Committee of Public Safety concerned primarily with military matters. In that capacity he continued to travel tirelessly between Paris and the battlefronts. In August, the ponderous invasion of the coalition partners having come to a temporary focus on an Anglo-Hanoverian attack on Dunkirk, Carnot took personal charge of the defense and ordered the opening of the sluices to flood much of the ground around the port, splitting in two the army attempting to invest it. Before the month was out, Carnot had so inspirited the French and discouraged the Allies that the defenders of Dunkirk began to go over to counterattacks.

But Carnot found the military commanders still without much confidence in the maneuvering or the offensive abilities of their forces, and no doubt rightly so. Thus in the meantime Carnot also drove through the National Convention one of the most portentous legislative measures in all military history, the *Réquisition* Law of August 23, 1793. In place of the compromised gestures toward a national levy thus far adopted by the Revolution, this law declared a true *levée en masse* of all unmarried and widower citizens between the ages of eighteen and twenty-five. More than that:

> ARTICLE I. From this moment until that in which our enemies shall have been driven from the territory of the Republic, all Frenchmen are permanently requisitioned for service in the armies.
>
> Young men will go forth to battle; married men will forge weapons and transport munitions; women will make tents and clothing, and serve in hospitals; children will make lint from old linen; and old men will be brought to the public squares to arouse the courage of the soldiers, while preaching the unity of the Republic and hatred against kings.[1]

Here was the first forging of the thunderbolt of a new kind of war—the total war of nations pitting against each other all their resources and passion. The French even now did not apply the *levée en masse* altogether literally; but from the *Réquisition* Law of August 1793 the French Republic was able to raise field armies of half a million men by the end of the year, made possible by the French people's conviction of their united national stake in the survival of the Revolution. Though often thrown into battle hastily trained, the French Revolu-

1. Quoted in Chapter 4, Crane Brinton, Gordon A. Craig, and Felix Gilbert, "Jomini," Edward Mead Earle, ed., *Makers of Modern Strategy: Military Thought from* [Niccolò] *Machiavelli to Hitler* (Princeton, New Jersey: Princeton University Press, 1943), p. 72, citing *Réimpression de l'ancien Moniteur depuis le Réunion des États-Généraux jusqu'au Consulat (mai 1789–novembre 1789)* avec des notes explicatives par M. Léonard Gallois (32 vols., Paris: Bureau central, 1840–1847), 25 août 1793, XVII, *Convention nationale* (1840) 478.

tionary armies henceforth overpowered the precisely drilled and disciplined armies of the monarchies with sheer numbers and zeal—and increasingly, as time went on, with the advantage gained by opening officership to talent virtually without reservation, wiping away almost all vestiges of the noble and aristocratic preference that had diluted professional officership from its Dutch, Swedish, and French beginnings.

At the outset, the new armies were probably more advantageous politically than militarily, an unprecedentedly powerful means of stimulating nationalist fervor. The French were to regain the military initiative through sound generalship using what remained of the old army plus relatively modest accretions before the conscripts had been even partially trained, in the autumn of 1793. But the new armies assured the safety of Revolutionary France, and then, to eliminate the monarchical menace altogether and with missionary fervor to carry the blessings of the Revolution to all of Europe, the new armies afforded France ample strength to advance once more into the Low Countries, into Italy, to the Rhine and beyond into the Germanies, in time even into Russia. In 1796 the Revolution propelled Napoléon Bonaparte (until that year, Napoleone Buonaparte), still *général de brigade,* to the head of the Revolution's Army of Italy. Thenceforth, the thunderbolt forged by the Revolution and by its great War Minister, Lazare Carnot, "the Organizer of Victory," was to be the weapon of Bonaparte.

Hondschoote and Wattignies: The Emergence of Jourdan

Throughout the country in order to supervise enforcement of the *Réquisition,* and to all the armies to assure an appropriately ardent use of the new forces, the National Convention and the Committee of Public Safety dispatched Deputies on Mission; these men must infuse the whole army with the full, passionate zeal of the Revolution. Here was an idea with immense implications for the future evolution of the profession of military officership, particularly for the limiting of professional autonomy. For the present, however, relatively little French military professionalism had survived to undergo limitation by the Deputies.

On September 6–8, Jean Nicolas Houchard, *général de division,* carried the Army of the North to a sufficient approximation of a victory at Hondschoote to cause the Allies to raise their loose siege of Verdun; but the success had required political intervention to order an assault when Houchard was unwilling to do so. On September 15, moreover, one of Houchard's detachments suffered a defeat near Courtrai and was then driven in rout from Menin. The Deputies on Mission thereupon accused Houchard of treason, and he was carried to Paris under arrest. He was a veteran cavalry trooper who bore scars received at the battle of Minden; his rise to command an army represented the danger that the Revolution might fly to the opposite, equally antiprofessional extreme when it broke the grip of the nobility upon the army: that it would advance tough old soldiers who offered the credentials of humble birth but not of military education. Poor

Houchard was out of his depth at the head of 45,000 men and more. Brought to trial, he proudly displayed his scars when one of the accusations proved to be cowardice; but then he lapsed into uncomprehending lethargy, was convicted, and on November 16 executed. Before the year was over, sixteen other generals paid the same penalty. They had failed to give the Revolution victories, and an insatiable appetite for victories was the corollary of the very zeal that in the *Réquisition* Act had transformed the language of law into eloquence.

Jean-Baptiste Jourdan reluctantly took over Houchard's command—reluctantly not least because it was he who had led the assault ordained by the politicians at Hondschoote, and also because he had a sober sense of sharing Houchard's lack of professional credentials. He had been a soldier during the War of American Independence, was invalided out of service in 1784, and then after volunteering for the armed forces of the Revolution rose from subaltern at the beginning of the 1792 campaigns to *général de division*. Jourdan's modesty, however, was in part also an expression of an intelligence that was to prove more than capable of compensating for deficiencies in experience and formal education.

His first battle, nevertheless, demanded little more than revolutionary zeal. With a two-to-one numerical advantage—44,000 to 22,000, a beginning of the dividends of the *Réquisition* Law—and with Carnot again on the scene, Jourdan's army attacked the Allies on October 15 and 16 in a series of head-on assaults whose sheer unremitting energy at length broke the enemy's left flank on the plateau of Wattignies, the landmark that gave the battle its name. Carnot, Jourdan, and the Deputies led charges in person. The battle persuaded Coburg to lift another of the Allied sieges, that of Maubeuge, a key fortress on the way from the Low Countries to Paris. Jourdan followed up cautiously, but Carnot felt emboldened for yet another round of revolutionary planning to carry the promises of liberty into the Low Countries, to the Rhine, and beyond. This time the plans were not to go awry.

The Revolutionary Armies on the Offensive: Tourcoing, Tournai, and Fleurus; Souham, Pichegru, and Jourdan

Carnot could envisage the offensive because the Allies had squandered their opportunities of 1793 as prodigally elsewhere as in the Low Countries and northwest France. On the Rhine, a Prussian-Hessian army of some 63,000 had driven Custine from the River Main back into the valleys of the Saar (Sarre) and the Lauter, and an Austrian force under *General der Cavallerie* (Lieutenant General) Dagobert Sigismund Wurmser (or Würmser) also invaded Alsace. But here the Allies' incorrigible frittering away of time and opportunity allowed a nemesis to arise in the energetic if as usual professionally unschooled personage of Lazare Hoche. Corporal of the *Gardes françaises* when that royalist elite was broken up in 1789, Hoche by 1793 was a *général de division*. Apparently inspired to a new zeal rather than daunted by his recent arrest on suspicion of complicity in the treason of Dumouriez, Hoche at the head of the Army of the Moselle persisted in counterattacking despite several defeats at the skilled if somewhat palsied hands of the Duke of Brunswick. Not his tactical shortcomings but his vigor most impressed the accompanying Deputies on Mission. His storming of the lines of Fröschweiler on December 22 (2 Nivôse An II in the new revolutionary calendar inaugurated the preceding September 22 [1 Vendémiaire An II]) led to the addition of the Army of the Rhine to his command. Thereupon on December 26 (6 Nivôse) he drove Wurmser from the lines of Weissenburg and thence advanced into the Palatinate. His successes opened the way also for French recapture of Mainz.

The Sardinians in the Alps and the Spanish in the Pyrenees did even less than their confederates in the north to take advantage of the French distractions of 1793. On December 19 (30 Frimaire), after a siege of several months, the French recaptured Toulon from a royalist uprising much strengthened by a British fleet and British, Spanish, Sardinian, and Neapolitan troops; the young Corsican-born revolutionary artillerist Napoleone Buonaparte so distinguished himself in the struggle for Toulon that he won rapid promotion from captain to major to lieutenant colonel and, as a reward for victory, to *général de brigade*.

It was the manpower hastened into the armies by the *levée en masse* that permitted Hoche to mount his assaults against entrenched positions and push them until they prevailed, and the *levée* that permitted Carnot to plan a resumption of the offensive all along France's eastern frontiers for 1794. To conduct the new campaigns, Carnot organized no fewer than eleven field armies, in addition to an Army of the Interior. The three largest armies, of the North, the Moselle, and the Rhine, carried on their muster rolls 245,822, 102,323, and 98,930 troops, respectively. The remaining armies varied from 22,000 to 60,000 men. In January the Republic also saw to the completion of the *amalgame* first ordered February 22, 1793: all the troops, conscript and volunteer units as well as the remaining old regulars, were now amalgamated into a unified army clad in the blue uniforms formerly distinguishing the bourgeois National Guard; the Bourbon whitecoats were no more. This unified army was reorganized into new regiments called demi-brigades, one regular and two new battalions to each, with the demi-brigades in turn formed into divisions.

The coalition partners planned to anticipate the French offensives of 1794 with new invasions of their own, particularly on France's northwestern and west-central frontiers. Coburg's chief of staff, Colonel Karl Mack von Leiberich, was a Bavarian of middle-class Protestant background who had risen from the enlisted ranks and amidst the past year's Allied lethargy sufficiently sensed the crescendo of French fury—aided perhaps in his perceptions by not being a nobleman— that he had been conspicuously urging prompt action to annihilate the revolutionary armies as the only appropriate way to deal with them. Without such a departure from the usual customs of eighteenth-century warfare, Mack believed, there would be no containing the revolutionary inferno. The Allied command actually professed to accept this reasoning; the British commander, Major-General Frederick Augustus, twelfth Duke of York and eighth Duke of Albany (third Duke of York and Albany) and fifteenth Earl of Ulster, second son of George III, in particular joined in favoring a vigorous campaign. (But his government never provided him with sufficient troops to permit a proper contribution to such a campaign; his maximum British strength was not much over 15,000.) In spite of earnest professions, however, the actual Allied advance into Belgium displayed much of the ponderosity of the preceding two years; the Allies may have been less uncertain of purpose this time around, but their very determination to strike an overpowering blow committed them to unwieldy columns too dependent on their depots to advance with any of the energy likely to be necessary to accomplish annihilation.

For a time they appeared to be marching toward a considerable success anyway. Joseph Souham, *général de division,* who had enlisted in the French Army as a private in 1792, was in temporary command of the Army of the North. Twice when threatened with entrapment between separate Allied columns, first near Rousselaey and then around Tourcoing, Souham essayed the astute scheme of falling on one of the enemy pincers with a major portion of his own troops while endeavoring to amuse the other enemy threat with a light screening force. This kind of employment of the interior lines, the shorter chord inside a longer arc formed by the enemy, to accomplish the defeat of the enemy in detail, was soon to be a principal stock in trade of the Toulon hero, General Buonaparte, as he emerged as one of the greatest military commanders of this or any age. But Souham failed to carry through his sound conception because he lacked Napoleon's finesse in keeping occupied the enemy force that he was attempting to hold off with smaller numbers. All the Allies continued pushing remorselessly forward. By May 18 (29 Floréal An II) the Austrians were crossing the River Lys near Menin.

That day, however, Souham with 60,000 men counterattacked a similarly sized Anglo-Austrian force under York and Coburg at Tourcoing. The counterattack represented Souham's reversion to Hoche's straightforward reliance on aggressiveness and élan. Thanks largely to the idleness of about two-thirds of the Austrians—their generals apparently inhibited by rumors of a peace settlement—the French won enough of a victory to cause the Allied invasion to falter yet again. The Allies lost about 4,000 killed and wounded and 1,500 prisoners along with sixty guns; French losses were probably heavier, but the effects of the *Réquisition* Law were now coming into full force.

Four days later, on May 22 (3 Prairial), the French counterattacked another time, under the leadership of Charles Pichegru, former lieutenant colonel of artillery in the old army, now *général de division.* Pichegru had originally been assigned the Army of the North for the year's campaign but only now assumed command. Assaulting the fortress and city of Tournai into which Coburg's main force has retired, the new general was repulsed with some 6,500 casualties to the enemy's 4,000. Nevertheless, the battle of Tournai confirmed that the French had grasped the initiative. Pichegru was undaunted and simply looked for a new focus of attack, which he found by investing Ypres on June 1 (13 Prairial). His efforts meanwhile had caused Coburg to draw on reinforcements from farther south. In that sector Carnot launched a new offensive against the weakened Allied forces, hurling forward across the River Sambre toward Charleroi on June 12 (24 Prairial) the right wing of the Army of the North along with the Army of the Ardennes and the Army of the Moselle, all under Jourdan—and all about to become the famous Army of the Sambre and Meuse.

By investing Charleroi, Jourdan brought Coburg racing southward to bring relief. Thus already the French had thrown the Allies off balance. Coburg arrived too late to save the city and fortress, which fell to the French on June 25 (7 Messidor). The next day Coburg attacked Jourdan in an effort to recapture Charleroi—or rather to relieve it, because Coburg was not yet aware that it had surrendered. The resulting battle of Fleurus was the greatest of the war thus far.

Jourdan commanded about 73,000 men, Coburg 70,000, larger forces than had fought on most battlefields since Marlborough's time. On neither side, however, had the generals yet learned how to exercise effective command and control over such numbers. The French formed up in a semicircle shielding Charleroi. Coburg sent forward five separate assaults against this circumference, and the action mainly resolved itself into five separate battles. A better coordinated method might have won victory for the Austrians, for as it was they broke the French center until the republican artillery saved the day by checking the Austrian advance until fresh infantry and cavalry could mount a counterattack that proved successful. Similarly, the Austrians also ruptured the French right, and only Jourdan's ability to send reinforcements because the enemy's lack of coordination afforded him breathing space saved the French there—that, and the growing tactical efficiency that the French were by now adding to their revolutionary zeal. In the end, Jourdan held his ground while extracting about 10,000 casualties from the enemy, losing about 7,000 himself. The successful tactical defense awarded the French strategically offensive results; Coburg felt his army shattered by its casualties, and the Allies virtually abandoned Belgium. On July 9 (21 Messidor), Jourdan's and Pichegru's armies converged to capture Brussels.

Well might Pichegru have pressed forward in spite of his setback at Tournai, for the guillotine's toll upon insufficiently vigorous generals was to total sixty-seven in 1794. But indeed it was more than numbers, zeal, and the terror that drove French advances in mid–1794, the final months of the revolutionary year II. The French had grown more and more adept in exploiting the rapid redeployments from column to line and back again made possible by training under the Regulations of 1791. In the first battles fought by the new and incompletely trained armies, French commanders made much use of the battalion assault column in shock action, relying on the impetus of the troops toward the rear to push forward the vanguard despite losses and the trauma of collision with the enemy. In such actions, however, the losses were almost always severe, and well-drilled old-style infantry lines learned to contain the French assault columns, especially when enemy leaders backed up their infantry with strong cavalry forces ready to counterattack against any penetration.

The French thereupon turned increasingly to the possibilities inherent in the prewar reformers' interest in light infantry, to send clouds of skirmishers roving forward in advance of their main assault to build up a screen of fire that could severely weaken the enemy before the attack drove home. Whole battalions often deployed as skirmishers. Then the flexibility of the 1791 regulations permitted the main force following up the light infantry either to deploy as skirmishers themselves or to charge in assault columns.

Supporting improved tactical skills, furthermore, was an increasing abundance of equipment of good quality. Early in the Revolution, the logistics of the French Army had fallen nearly into collapse along with everything else, but the spirit of the *Réquisition* Law had been seized by the Committee of Public Safety to mobilize the making and delivery of military supplies. By 1794 government workshops were producing 750 muskets a day, almost as many as all the rest of Europe. The Convention voted large sums both to subsidize the creation of new arms manufactories and to enlarge and purchase from old ones. Much of the French economy became tied to the direction of the republican government and to the support of the war. The twentieth-century reader must remember that the economic demands of war remained decidedly limited when compared with those of a contest between rival gross national products in the manner of World War II; the wants even of large armies remained relatively simple, and the principal problem in supplying armies continued to be simply that of feeding men and horses. Nevertheless, by 1794 the French Revolutionary armies were beginning to outweigh their opponents in quantity and sometimes in quality of weapons and ammunition as well as in numbers and fervor.

Thus sustained and equipped, the armies of the Republic were able to swim forward with the military tide in spite of renewed political turmoil behind them. On July 27, Pichegru's troops entered Antwerp and Jourdan's captured Liège. Under the new calendar, this date was the 9th Thermidor—the day of the coup that removed Maximilien François Marie Isidore de Robespierre from power as the dominating figure of the Committee of Public Safety, ended the Reign of Terror, and opened the way to the Thermidorean Reaction, the establishment of a relatively conservative, consolidating government under the Constitution of the Year III and headed by a five-man Directory. Fortunately for the war effort, Carnot continued as the organizer of the armies, for a time exerting his influence indirectly, then as one of the original members of the Directory.

Successes farther south, along the Rhine, followed quickly in train after Fleurus. Earlier in 1794 the French had decided they could afford a relatively passive defense here, because Prussia had again fallen out with Austria over eastern questions, particularly and predictably over Poland, concerning which Vienna had entered into a new partnership with Moscow to minimize Berlin's share of the spoils. Prussia's newest eastern troubles had culminated in the late summer and early autumn of 1793 when Russian troops forestalled the effort of 50,000 Prussians to capture Warsaw. Austria and Russia then moved toward a final partition of Poland—eventually completed on January 3, 1795/December 23, 1794—-in which Prussia received only such crumbs as the two larger powers chose to allow it. The French Revolutionary government thus required no special astuteness to discern that by the beginning of 1794, Prussia was not only strained by the necessity to keep up large troop concentrations in the east but also disinclined to do anything on the Rhine that would help maintain Austrian sovereignty over Belgium. As the French expected, the Allies attempted nothing on the Rhine early in 1794 beyond advancing minor probes. But after Fleurus assured French success to the north, the Republic reinforced its Rhine and Moselle armies to a total near 90,000.

In mid-July (Messidor-Thermidor) these forces began pushing the unenthusiastic Prussians back toward the Rhine, whereupon Austrian forces had to join in the retreat lest their flanks be uncovered. A brief Austro-Prussian counterattack in mid-September (Fructidor An II–Vendémiaire An III) quickly gave way to an October (Vendémiaire-Brumaire) campaign in which the Army of the Moselle under a recently minted soldier, Jean Victor Marie Moreau, a student leader at the University of Rennes early in the Revolution and now *général de division,* cleared the enemy from the left bank of the Rhine. Yet farther south, the Armies of Italy and the Alps had held Sardinia in check and begun to penetrate the Alpine passes. Along the Pyrenees, French troops repelled a Spanish invasion and began to advance into Catalonia.

Pichegru's finest hour may have been his leadership of the march beyond Belgium into the United Provinces. The disheartened enemy, including the Duke of York's British force, mounted nothing more than a fighting retreat; but when winter came, and the country became bare of subsistence, while the many water obstacles crisscrossing it impeded both resupply from the rear and continued advance across icy or flooded streams and canals, Pichegru nevertheless pressed resolutely onward. Inexorably he captured the famous Dutch fortresses that had resisted Louis XIV. On January 20, 1795 (1 Pluviôse An III), Pichegru's forces entered Amsterdam and proclaimed a Batavian Republic. A French cavalry detachment found the Dutch fleet icebound in the Texel and galloped across the frozen Zuyder Zee to capture it; thus when on the following May 16 (27 Floréal) the Batavian Republic declared war against Great Britain, fifteen ships of the line and thirty smaller vessels of a navy that for more than a century had been firmly allied to Britain joined the Royal Navy's enemies.

The British expeditionary force retreated across northeastern Holland into Germany. Although it sacrificed German allied forces to try to assure its own safety, its cohesion had almost disappeared by the time the Royal Navy embarked its remnants from Bremen and Kuxhaven in April. The Hanoverian subjects of the British King did not take a charitable view of this desertion.

The French Republic's military triumphs of 1794 were not only powered by far stronger forces than those that had won the ephemeral triumphs of 1792 and 1793—the French nation in arms was beginning to strike terror through all Europe—but this time the victories were to prove of long-lasting consequence. The Habsburgs had ruled Belgium since the marriage of the Archduke Maximilian of Austria, the subsequent Emperor Maximilian I, to the Duchess Mary of Burgundy (*la duchesse* Marie) in 1477; but the Habsburg whitecoats would never mount permanent garrison there again. Stadtholder William (Willem) V fled to England, and it would be two decades before a member of the House of Orange reigned again in the Dutch Netherlands; for this the Stadtholder had himself partly to blame, because in England he authorized the British to occupy all Dutch colonies and passed word to Dutch political liberals that he would offer no constitutional concessions in return for efforts to restore him to power, thus undermining his own people's incentives to resist the French. For practical purposes, France had won the Rhine frontier that had eluded Louis XIV, and decades would elapse before it yielded it—or the mastery of northern Italy that its troops in the Alps stood poised to assert.

General Bonaparte on the Horizon

These consequences proved enduring in spite of that relaxation on the morrow of great victories that we have so often observed; the reader may especially recall the alternating cycle of victories and relaxation in Marlborough's wars. In 1794–1795, although the overthrow of Robespierre had not immediately diluted the zeal of the French armies, the Thermidorean Reaction could scarcely have avoided lending a measure of encouragement to the almost inevitable waning of military momentum after triumphs as great as Fleurus and its immediate successors. During 1795 the Revolutionary forces fit for action dwindled from 700,000 to 450,000.

Nevertheless, these forces remained formidable enough to support an aggressive French diplomacy that went far toward dissolving the First Coalition. From November 24, 1794 (4 Frimaire An III), the French were in secret negotiation at Basel with representatives of Frederick William II of Prussia. The combined spectacles of France's military prowess and Austro-Russian cooperation to exclude Prussia from major gains in the Third Partition of Poland, and perhaps to injure Prussian interests elsewhere in the east, persuaded the Prussian King that he had better husband on the opposite border from France the limited military resources on which Prussia's great-power status rested; he was more likely to accomplish something substantial against adversaries whose military organization was at least as traditional as his own than against the fury of the French. On April 5, 1795 (16 Germinal An III), French and Prussian emissaries signed the Treaty of Basel. France received control of the entire west bank of the Rhine except for Mainz, which the Austrians happened to be holding again. In return for this Prussian recognition of the long-coveted Rhine frontier, France agreed to abandon its conquests east of the Rhine. A secret article provided that if France's possession of the west bank proved permanent when the Republic made peace with the rest of the Holy Roman Empire, then Prussia and other states losing territory on the left bank should be allowed compensation on the right. A further, supplementary agreement of May 17 (27 Floréal) called for the neutralization of German territory north of the Main River, with Prussia to be the guarantor of neutrality.

Soon thereafter Tuscany left the war, and Spain felt obliged to follow Prussia's example. The Spanish had hoped to exploit France's troubles to obtain a buffer north of the Pyrenees; at the beginning of negotiations at Basel, they sought a Bourbon kingdom south of the River Loire. But the French response was to press the invasion of Spain, carrying the new republican tricolor banners to the Ebro. Moreover, the Spanish had begun the talks largely out of concern that by renewing British sea power the war had accelerated British encroachments upon Spain's colonial preserves. A fresh Royalist outbreak in Brittany and La Vendée caused the French to relax their own demands enough that on July 22 (4 Thermidor) another Treaty of Basel eliminated another member from the coalition. (The Spanish may have come to terms just in time; the day before, General Hoche had destroyed the mainspring of the largest Royalist uprising, an émigré force that had landed at Quiberon Bay.) France agreed to evacuate mainland Spain but retained the Spanish half of the island of Saint-Domingue (Santo Domingo).

France's military relaxation showed up more clearly in the late summer and early autumn campaigning against Austria in the Rhineland. The Austrians repulsed offensives by both the Army of the Sambre and Meuse under Jourdan and the new Army of the Rhine and Moselle under Pichegru. The loosening of the generals' moorings of loyalty in the face of the Revolution's turmoil may again have been part of France's problem, as it had been with Dumouriez. Evidence was to emerge later that Pichegru had accepted money from a British agent and negotiated for the restoration of the Bourbons.

For a time it appeared as if the Austrians and Sardinians were about to contain the French in Italy as well. There in June (Prairial-Messidor) the Allies repulsed and drove back a French penetration that had crossed the Appenines. But as they had already done so often, the Allies failed to follow up with a knockout punch when they had the French staggering. Instead, they made early preparations to go into winter quarters. The French Army of Italy under Barthélemy Louis Joseph Schérer, *général de division,* thereupon struck back with a surprise offensive and a victory at Loano on November 24 (3 Frimaire An IV). Schérer was less than competent in spite of having emerged from the excellent prewar artillery service; the Army of Italy was gradually disintegrating logistically and in morale under his stewardship, as it had seemed about to collapse on the battlefield. The real architect of Loano was General Buonaparte, who had planned the countermoves in Italy while serving in the Topographical Bureau of the Committee of Public Safety during late September and early October (Brumaire). Also instrumental in winning the victory, and present at the scene, was André (or Andrea) Masséna, *général de division,* who knew the area and led a flanking march through a mountain pass. In any event, Loano assured the French the control of the passes of the Ligurian Alps and left them still poised for further conquests in Italy.

This proved to be the stage setting for one of the most spectacular campaigns in all military history. On March 26, 1796 (6 Germinal An IV), Buonaparte took over the Army of Italy from Schérer and began an energetic rehabilitation of its administration and morale. He was about to display other, more impressive talents.

The Campaign of Germany in 1796: Jourdan and Moreau versus the Archduke Charles

Lazare Carnot was again in direct charge of the war effort (which in 1793 and 1794 he had conducted, functioning as a modern chief of staff as well as War Minister, while still technically a captain; in 1795 he was promoted to *commandant*—major—in the engineers). He was the primary designer of France's strategy for 1796. To eliminate the principal remaining continental member of the coalition, he planned that the centerpiece of the year's military activities should be another effort on the Rhine. Indeed, his plan was essentially a repetition of that of the failed Rhineland campaign of 1795, which he had also largely devised. He had formed a penchant for attacks against both of the enemy's flanks; even though the problems of cooperation and especially of timing between the two attacking forces in such a scheme, and of conceding the enemy the advantage of interior lines, had contributed as much as the dubieties of Pichegru's generalship to the setbacks of 1795, Carnot proposed that in 1796 the Army of the Sambre and Meuse should invade Germany from the Rhine while the Army of the Rhine and Moselle attacked down the Danube, the two armies supposedly driving back both of the Austrian flanks and converging upon Vienna. Because Pichegru had resigned his command early in the new year—suspicions were gathering about him, though he was welcomed on his return to Paris—Moreau would lead the latter army.

Carnot intended the new campaign along the Rhine to be the decisive campaign of the Revolution, destroying Austria's military power and thus breaking the remains of the coalition irretrievably while guaranteeing French retention of the Rhine frontier. The design was to founder on several obstacles, not least of them the fact that Jourdan and Moreau were to demonstrate that, without sinking into the treason of Dumouriez (or Pichegru), the new generals could still lose the fine edge of revolutionary zeal. While Carnot's own operational concepts had acquired a somewhat mechanical repetitiveness (not necessarily a fatal flaw, as Marlborough's career had indicated), Carnot himself retained all the fervor of the early Revolution. He was by no means blind to the danger implicit in granting the enemy the interior lines, and in fact he warned his commanders to be cautious on that account; but he intended that this danger should be obviated by the speed and flexibility of movement of which the French armies were still almost uniquely capable, as well as by his generals' seizing upon their numerical superiority to press events beyond simply rapid and flexible maneuver into decisive battle. It was by translating French revolutionary fury and the numbers of the nation in arms into the weapons for remorseless battle that Carnot intended to make the new campaign on the Rhine the climax of the war and the assurance of France's European hegemony.

Unfortunately for this design, the numerically inferior Austrian armies opposing Jourdan and Moreau were commanded by a young man of twenty-five who was destined to prove the most capable commander of the Habsburg troops since Prince Eugène. The Archduke Charles (Carl Ludwig, sometimes Karl Ludwig), Erzherzog von Österreich, Herzog von Teschen, third son of the Emperor Leopold II, had inherited a wisdom and breadth of vision at least the equal of his admirable father's. As a general, he was to become an opponent not unworthy of Napoleon; as a military thinker and writer, he was to rank with *Generalmajor* Carl von Clausewitz and General Antoine-Henri, baron de Jomini, as one of the chief of the galaxy of commentators on Revolutionary and Napoleonic wars who created the modern conceptualization of military strategy and in doing so achieved a quantum leap forward in the depth of the professional literature on the study of which the profession of officership was founded. Already a *Feldzeugmeister,* in effect a lieutenant general, on the basis of accomplishment as well as hereditary privilege, Charles entered the campaign of 1796 with the exalted rank of *Reichsgeneralfeldmarschall* conferred on him in February. He was explicitly conscious of the opportunities that possession of the interior lines might offer him and determined to exploit them to offset his numerical disadvantage; he began the campaign with only about 56,000 men, against 72,000 under Jourdan and 78,000 under Moreau.

All this is not to say that the Archduke Charles was altogether the equivalent of the coming Napoleon in strategic insight. Like Souham's, Charles's perception of the uses of interior lines did not yet reach to recognizing the possibilities of containing one of the enemy forces with a segment of his own while striking at the others; in part, this limitation reflected the fact that the articulation of the Austrian Army into self-contained divisions had not yet proceeded as far as the French had gone. It was to prove enough, however, that Charles's scheme of campaign was that he should retreat before both superior enemy armies, allowing their very advance and the stretching of their lines of communications to weaken them while his falling back into his bases strengthened him, and awaiting the best opportunity to unite his forces against one of the enemy armies, hoping with good fortune to muster superior or at least equal Austrian strength by the time and at the point of the collision. In the sequel, moreover, events were to modify the Archduke's design to include a Napoleonic containing force after all.

At first, falling back was the only reasonable option open to the Austrians, although they accepted occasional clashes of arms. The French advanced so easily that they appear to have grown increasingly careless of Carnot's warning about the enemy's interior lines. Moreau was of such a temperament that carelessness attended him all too readily, but by August (Thermidor) it was Jourdan's army moving from Forchheim through Nürnberg that presented Charles with the kind of opportunity he had been awaiting. Jourdan was intent on turning the inner, southern flank of the Austrian force around Amberg, commanded by *Feldzeugmeister* Wilhelm Graf von Wartensleben. The Austrians had been reinforced to about 68,000; the friction of campaigning had shrunk Jourdan's army to about 45,000 and Moreau's to about 50,000. Exceptionally alert Austrian cavalry reconnaissance on August 13–14 (25–26 Thermidor An IV) apprised Archduke Charles that Jourdan's flanking movement was being executed in such a way that it exposed his army to a descent upon its rear. Charles with admirable intuition had already issued orders anticipating this development; he was ready to use his main force to envelop the Army of the Sambre and Meuse.

At the critical moment, however, Moreau in turn pressed Charles so closely that he decided he had no choice but to leave some 30,000 troops under *Felzeugmeister Leutnant* (Major General) Maximilian Graf Baillet de Latour to entertain the Army of the Rhine and Moselle while he himself struck Jourdan. So circumstance led Charles to modify the customary eighteenth-century fashion of exploiting interior lines and to anticipate Napoleon's favored refinement of the method by dividing his own force in the face of the enemy, thus depriving himself of the possibility of striking one of his foes with all his force, but the better assuring that the enemy could not exploit his willingness to give battle by concentrating against him in turn.

These maneuvers produced the battle of Amberg of August 24 (7 Fructidor An IV). Wartensleben had been a somewhat refractory subordinate, resentful of his only recent subjection to Charles's command, but he fought stoutly enough with about 34,000 men in Jourdan's front while Charles with about 27,000 assailed the French in right and rear. In spite of Charles's display of strategic skill, however, the battle was no better managed on either side than Fleurus had been, and it was an Austrian victory more because of Charles's preparations for it than because of anything that happened on the field. While Charles imperiled Jourdan's communications, moreover, he did not rupture them as he intended, Jourdan contriving to elude the full force of the maneuver against his rear.

Thereupon Charles began a second turning movement to attempt again to get astride Jourdan's lines of support. This maneuver resulted in another collision in battle, at Würzburg on September 3 (17 Fructidor). Würzburg replicated Amberg; the battle was an Austrian victory, but the French were able to escape any disastrous consequences, retreating to the Lahn River and then to the Rhine. Moreau meanwhile had continued to advance against Latour, but when he heard the news of Jourdan's misfortunes he also retreated, eventually all the way to Strasbourg.

Thus, notwithstanding the Archduke's superior strategic and operational generalship, the Austrian margin of tactical victory at Amberg and Würzburg was narrow enough that it might have been reduced to nonexistence if the French armies had fought with anything like the original revolutionary fervor that Carnot personally still felt and that he expected would bring them triumphs of annihilation leading to a decisively successful climax of the war. Transformed from defenders of their country and its people's government into invaders, however, and led by generals similarly drained of revolutionary zeal, the French armies in Gemany in 1796 allowed themselves virtually to be defeated by mere maneuver, with battlefield combat becoming almost irrelevant at a time when hard fighting might still have produced the decision to which Carnot aspired. Or perhaps the onus of such irresolution ought to be shifted primarily to the French generals; Moreau in particular allowed himself to be defeated psychologically when his troops had won almost all the fighting in which they engaged, and when determined leadership of the Army of the Rhine and Moselle might yet have reversed the verdict of Amberg and Würzburg.

While the French thus did much to defeat themselves, due credit should also be accorded to the Archduke Charles both for his strategic and operational perceptions and execution and also for the stout fighting qualities that he had helped instill in the Austrian troops under his command. In the English-speaking world, we tend to remember mainly the prolonged British resistance to Revolutionary and Napoleonic France as the obstacle against which the renewed French drive for hegemony finally crumbled. The French Empire, however, was a continental empire, and however important the contributions of British sea power to eroding its strength, its military defeat had to be accomplished primarily on land. There, the contributions of the British were too often either nonexis-

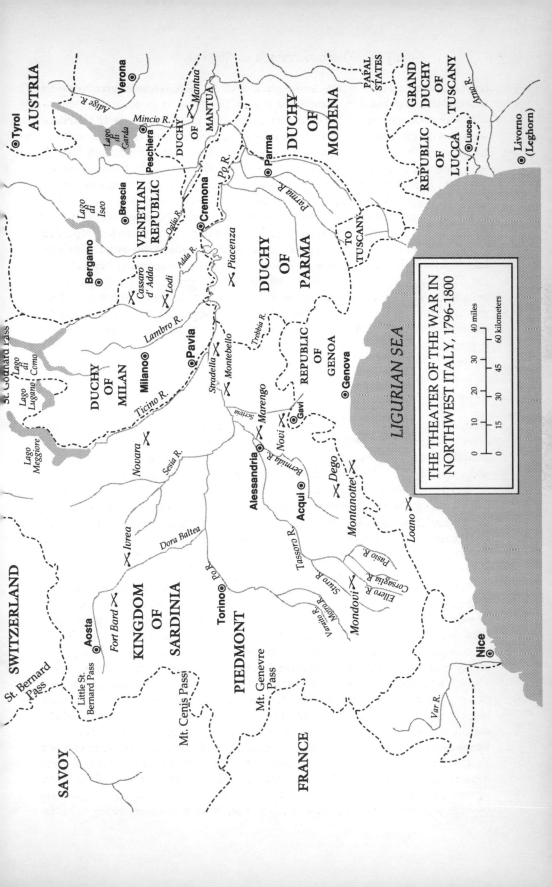

THE THEATER OF THE WAR IN
NORTHWEST ITALY, 1796–1800

tent or as feeble as those that the Duke of York had led. While ultimately Great Britain would send into the lists land armies approximating those that its population and resources would have implied as its due, it was the Austrians who on land most steadfastly and with the most consistent courage and skill kept the resistance to French hegemony alive. On land, the Austrians were to be Napoleon's most resolute, most resilient, and in generalship most skillful opponents. The 1796 campaign of the Archduke Charles was a harbinger of these things to come.

But in 1796, the Archduke Charles did not confront Napoleon directly; and against the ability of that solitary figure to reawaken the fervor that Moreau's and Jourdan's armies had lost, and to harness it to a generalship unparalleled at least since Marlborough, the Austrians like all the other opposing nations were frequently to falter. They faltered badly in Italy in 1796, where General Napoleon Bonaparte, as in this year he came to style himself, transformed what Carnot had intended as the secondary theater into the primary one. Frustrated in the main arena, Revolutionary France found the back door to Austria opened to it by General Bonaparte.

Bonaparte in Italy, 1796: The Bridge at Lodi

At the outset, the new commander of the Army of Italy discovered all around him the evidences that Paris considered his a secondary theater. His army had barely been sustained even on a scale deserving to be called secondary. In spite of the battle of Loano, his forces were in a delicate strategic situation and a worse logistical plight. While Loano had opened the passes of the Ligurian Alps, superior numbers of Austrian and Sardinian troops still lay just beyond the passes, restricting the French army's practical logistical and operational area to the Riviera coast. The Army of Italy had little space from which to gather provisions, and such space and lines of communications from either Genoa or France as it possessed were almost entirely within cannon range of the Mediterranean, should the Royal Navy choose to bestir itself in adjacent waters. The French army's horses had been receiving only half rations for a year. The troops had not fared much better, and many companies had sunk to the condition of little more than autonomous plundering bands, roaming in search of something to eat. For once in military history, even the generals were not well fed.

Bonaparte immediately set out to feed and clothe his troops, driving away corrupt contractors and borrowing funds from Genoa. But he perceived that he could work little logistical improvement until he could tap richer resources more directly, escaping his currently constricted supply lines, and therefore he concluded that logistics must await the verdict of strategy—the reverse of the usual relationship. His soldiers must go into action still hungry, many of them still barefoot, many of them without shoulder arms. The weaponless must capture weapons in the course of the campaign. The army must restore its logistics by conquest. To sustain it in the meantime, it now had Bonaparte's own magnetic presence, continually roving among the troops, a presence so forceful, as the general soon demonstrated, that it could inspire shoeless men to go right on marching past a wagonload of new boots. Their reward, he promised, awaited them in the fertile valleys and rich cities of Italy.

This charismatic, magnetic, inspirational quality even more than any strategic, operational, or tactical grasp was the taproot of Napoleon's greatness as a military commander. It was the quality that more than any other set him above even a Gustavus Adolphus or a Marlborough. Successful as those commanders had been in winning the loyalty and inspiring the self-sacrifice of their soldiers, they could not match Bonaparte in this. Napoleon found the revolutionary fervor of the French nation flickering, and he breathed it back into full flame. But its new flame was a different flame. It was not alone to preserve and extend the people's own government, the people's own revolution, that the soldiers henceforth fought. It was to share in the glory that radiated from Napoleon Bonaparte. Indeed in time this motive would animate men of many nations besides the French; under Napoleon's leadership, the nation harnessed in arms would no longer be the French alone.

To be sure, Bonaparte also confronted his enemies with an unsurpassed strategic and tactical mastery. From the outset of his campaign in Italy in 1796, he exploited the advantages of interior lines with a fullness of understanding of that advantage far exceeding Souham's and excelling even that of the Archduke Charles. He applied also with a skill not seen since Marlborough the great English general's favorite principle of husbanding his troops in order to bring to bear superior forces at decisive points, an axiom applicable in strategy, operations, and tactics alike.

Bonaparte applied the exploitation of interior lines particularly in order to discomfit his two major initial adversaries, the Austrians and Sardinians, by dividing them from each other and isolating the Sardinians to expel them from the war. Raising his field force to about 40,000 by adding men from coastal defense fortifications, and being sure to include two divisions of cavalry despite having to mount them on half-starved horses—he recognized the value of mobility in tactics as well as in strategy and operations—he set out first to deliver a blow against the Austrians heavy enough to reduce them to relative passivity while he eliminated the Sardinians. His two enemies had bestowed on him the favor of so positioning themselves that he enjoyed an interior position between them. He intended to use the interior lines to assure himself the desired superiority at decisive points. Unlike Souham, who had led about 90,000 troops to his enemies' 70,000, Bonaparte was facing total enemy forces larger than his own, about 50,000 Austrians and Sardinians. But he proposed to maneuver along his interior lines in such a way that he would always have the greater numbers when he fought a battle, and in the outcome he succeeded in this purpose.

In fact, he found the Austrians sufficiently scattered that he was able to employ the principle of interior lines on a subsidiary scale against them alone. A detachment of his army amused the Austrian main force while he fell on a secondary force first at Montenotte on April 11–12 (22–23 Germinal An IV) and then at Dego on April 14 (25 Germinal). The latter fortified place proved to be crowded with Austrian supplies, and even Bonaparte could not prevent his victorious troops from plundering and gorging themselves instead of pursuing the beaten army, so that a counterattack drove them out of the town, and Bonaparte had to spend the next day rallying them and capturing Dego a second time. Once these actions were over, however, the Austrian detachment under direct attack had been virtually annihilated, and events were to prove that Bonaparte had gained his initial object of rendering the Austrians temporarily harmless. Moreover, he had greatly enhanced the morale of his still badly supplied Army of Italy. The troops were not altogether aware that they had crushed only a portion of the Austrians; they thought they had thrashed the enemy's main body, and they also thought a good deal more highly of themselves than when they had been starving and idle.

Thus Bonaparte could turn his principal attentions toward the Sardinians. Because the Austrian counterattack at Dego had left him uncertain about just how badly frightened the Austrians were, Bonaparte was slower than he would have liked to be in concentrating against the Sardinians. This delay increased the danger that the Austrians might recover, and it was fortunate for Bonaparte that as he gained in experience during the months to come, his intuitions in such matters grew surer. Nevertheless, the perceptions of the still young (he was not yet twenty-seven) and relatively inexperienced general proved acute enough. By April 22 (2 Floréal) he had built up a concentration of two to one against the Sardinians at Mondovi and by skillful maneuver was threatening their rear; the *manœuvre sur les derrières* was to become another standard Napoleonic weapon, of tremendous psychological advantage beyond its threat to deliver physical ruin. The battle of Mondovi turned into a rout, and on April 27 (7 Floréal) the Sardinians agreed to the Armistice of Cherasco whereby they practically withdrew from the coalition and the war.

The defeat of Sardinia left Bonaparte with a numerical superiority of about two to one over his remaining enemy; he would no longer have to maneuver for simply relative superiority. Logistics were still troublesome, however, so he intended to maneuver nevertheless, for access to territory and resources as well as to complete the downfall of the Austrian army opposed to him. His immediate geographic objectives were the mastery of the rich river valley of the Po, the most fertile in Italy, and the capture of the city of Milan. To these ends, he insisted that the Sardinians grant him the right to cross the Po at Valenza. Naturally, the Austrians learned of the insistence, and accordingly they concentrated to resist a crossing around Valenza. Bonaparte then moved rapidly to cross elsewhere, at Piacenza, and did so successfully.

The Austrians retreated to the Adda River, intending to build up a new defense along that obstacle. Following with his now predictable rapidity, Bonaparte with his van on May 10 (21 Floréal) reached the town of Lodi on the Adda, opposite which they saw an Austrian force whose guns commanded the town's bridge. The enemy evidently intended to prevent the French from using the bridge as long as possible, in order to shield the process of concentration beyond the river.

Bonaparte's troops overran the town, but 200 meters of open ground then remained between them and the bridge, which was another 250 meters long. A few hundred meters still farther on stood some 4,000 Austrian infantry with fourteen guns. Bonaparte apparently thought this force was considerably stronger than in fact it was, believing it was a major part of the enemy army. Nevertheless, acting on an inspiration that he was to consider a turning point of his life, he decided to risk an assault upon the bridge. He hastened forward all his available guns to lay down a barrage that would prevent the Austrians from destroying the structure. He sent cavalry to turn the enemy's right flank by crossing a ford upstream. He then waited two hours for the horsemen's movement to evolve, but he might as well have attacked immediately for all that the cavalry contributed. At length, impatient, he sent 4,000 grenadiers charging forward in column to assail the bridge. The width of the bridge limited the front to no more than about thirty men. The assailants charged successfully across the open ground between Lodi and the river, but half way over the bridge they faltered under continuous blasts of artillery fire. Bonaparte himself and the sturdy division chieftain Masséna—hero of Loano—pushed to the forefront to urge the attack onward again. Some men leapt into the river to wade through it on both sides of the bridge. Drawn once more by Bonaparte's magnetism, others resumed the head-on charge. They carried the bridge, broke through the enemy's artillery, and scattered the Austrian infantry.

The significance of the bridge at Lodi, the reason Napoleon thought the event a turning point, lay in its stimulation of his already considerable confidence in his battlefield impulses and instincts. Without a plan to do so, he had intuitively decided he must assault the bridge, though for all he knew—in fact as he supposed—it was much more strongly defended than it proved to be. Henceforth his confidence in his inspiration would give shape and timing to the climactic assaults on more than a score of battlefields. Notwithstanding his misconception of the enemy's strength at Lodi, Napoleon's intuition surely involved more than imagination and guesswork; he was a genius in waging war, and his genius no doubt encompassed an instantaneous grasp of tactical circumstances surpassing even his own rational understanding. Through many battles, his intuition served him and France well. But the overweening confidence in less than rational perceptions spawned at Lodi would in the end play no small part in destroying him, when age and physical ailments assailed him prematurely and his intuitive perceptions began to fail, but he stubbornly refused to recognize their failure.

As all of the preceding implies, Napoleon Bonaparte was scarcely the model type of the professional soldier. He had studied at a cadet school at Brienne and had been commissioned in one of the two most professional arms of the French Army, the artillery. He was by no means without knowledge of the professional military literature of his time, and especially he had read widely enough beyond his formal schooling to possess a respectable knowledge of tactical and operational history. Nevertheless, his place in the intellectual evolution of military officership is not that of an outstanding professional but that of a genius, whose mental and intuitive powers reached far beyond any understanding that schooling alone might have supplied. His place in the intellectual evolution of military officership is also that of the general whose accomplishments of genius became the stimulus to the next major advances in professional study, as critical studies of his strategy, operations, and tactics assumed a central place in the curricula of all European and American military schools for a century and more to come. While this book has contended that the modern profession of military officership began with the Dutch and the Swedes around the beginning of the seventeenth century, it can be argued with much persuasiveness that it was the articulation of the elements comprising Napoleon's genius by military critics who followed him, that first created an adequate educational basis for the military profession.

Yet Napoleon himself remained a general both of strategic, operational, and tactical axioms and of intuition. On the one hand, his campaigns exemplified such principles as the value of concentrating strength at decisive points and of exploiting the interior lines with such crystal clarity that they readily became the stuff of scholarship. On the other hand, at the core of his triumphs—and in time of his failures—there were always his intuitive reliance on momentary inspiration and the charismatic magnetism he exerted upon the men who followed him.

Bonaparte in Italy, 1796–1797: Arcola and Rivoli

Lodi assured that the Austrians would again retreat, fast and far enough for Bonaparte to occupy the area Parma-Pavia-Milan (except for a time the citadel of Milan), whence at last he could feed, clothe, and complete the arming of his troops. He grasped supplies, money, and even art treasures—commencing by obliging the Duchy of Parma to disgorge twenty paintings that became a nucleus of the collections of the Louvre—so ruthlessly, however, that he soon had to cope with a rash of rebellions throughout the occupied territory. His ruthless confiscations did not impress the Italians as the sort of liberty that Revolutionary France had seemed to promise the peoples of Europe. Bonaparte quelled the uprisings with equal ruthlessness; he executed the principal leaders, dispatched lesser figures to France as hostages, and allowed his troops further license to plunder and loot.

Simultaneously he faced other political troubles, because the Directory, having for ample reason grown wary of headstrong generals, sought to remove him from the command of northern Italy and to divert him to a campaign in the south of the peninsula distant from the main Austrian enemy. In the ensuing clash of wills, Napoleon threatened to resign yet also refused to obey the order to yield his command. It was his will that prevailed over the Directory's.

He had to deal also with a strengthened enemy, an Austrian army reinforced to some 55,000 in the field in addition to garrisons, and given a strong overall commander in General Wurmser, despite his seventy-two years and his earlier cautious performance in the north a skillful military practitioner of the earlier eighteenth-century type. The renewed campaign came to focus upon the fortress of Mantua (Mantova), an indispensable point if Bonaparte was to march on to Verona, into Friuli and Carniola, and eventually into Austria itself. The Austrian garrison of Mantua gave so much indication of stout resistance that Bonaparte resorted to an approximation of a traditional siege, although he could not fulfill the customary plan of husbanding sufficient supplies in his encircling lines to outlast the garrison, or of enclosing himself with outward-facing lines of

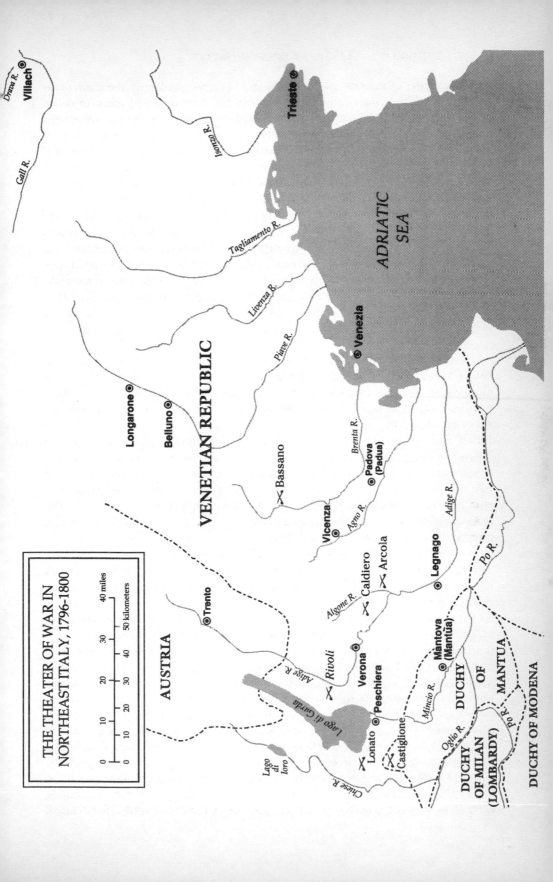

THE THEATER OF WAR IN
NORTHEAST ITALY, 1796–1800

0 10 20 30 40 miles

0 10 20 30 40 50 kilometers

ADRIATIC
SEA

VENETIAN REPUBLIC

AUSTRIA

DUCHY
OF MILAN
(LOMBARDY)

DUCHY
OF
MANTUA

DUCHY OF MODENA

Drava R.
Villach
Gall R.
Isonzo R.
Trieste
Tagliamento R.
Livenza R.
Piave R.
Venezia
Longarone
Belluno
Bassano
Brenta R.
Padova
(Padua)
Vicenza
Agno R.
Caldiero
Arcola
Legnago
Adige R.
Algone R.
Po R.
Trento
Rivoli
Verona
Mantova
(Mantua)
Adige R.
Peschiera
Mincio R.
Lago di Garda
Lonato
Castiglione
Oglio R.
Po R.
Chiese R.
Lago
di
Ioro

circumvallation against a relief expedition, because continued restlessness in occupied Italy left his supply-gathering and his lines of communications too precarious to expend resources in such ways. In consequence, Wurmser was able to mount the kind of campaign at which he was best, a series of maneuvers threatening to isolate the various detachments with which Bonaparte was endeavoring to shield the siege. Wurmser's numerical strength was such that a direct march on Mantua and the forcing of a battle might have served him better still, but at least since Lodi the reputation of Bonaparte and the French in battle was too intimidating for that. Nevertheless, Wurmser's maneuvers played so dexterously upon Bonaparte's fears of the effect upon his soldiers should they have to return to reduced rations that the French general not only abandoned the siege but did so hastily enough that he had to spike 140 valuable siege guns.

For Bonaparte, however, giving up the siege proved a blessing in disguise. Freed of the necessity to guard a fixed point, he could revert to his own skill in maneuver and particularly to the exploitation of interior lines, since Wurmser's maneuvers had produced the additional effect of scattering the Austrian army over a wide front. In these circumstances, the consistently dependable Masséna practically annihilated one of Wurmser's columns around Lonato on August 4 (17 Thermidor An IV), which paved the way for Bonaparte's bringing superior numbers to bear to whip the enemy main body at Castiglione the next day. Wurmser retreated into the Tyrol, and Bonaparte resumed the siege of Mantua (without siege guns).

It was not the Austrians but the Directory who next interrupted any single-minded prosecution of the siege. The government ordered a march into the Tyrol to try to establish cooperation with Moreau to the north. Little came of this effort except to accord the Austrians a breathing space in which to dispatch a new army of reinforcement to Italy under *Feldzeugmeister* Josef Graf Alvintzi; the abilities of the Habsburg empire to mobilize army after army have been much less heralded than the French mobilization of the nation in arms, but the resiliency of this bastion of Europe's *ancien régime* was nonetheless remarkable (and increasingly facilitated, not of course by appeals to the defense of liberty such as the Revolution could raise, but by a growing fear of the apparently limitless expansionism of the French).

The other principal result of Bonaparte's venturing toward the Tyrol was to spread his divisions in a manner that renewed the vulnerability to defeat in detail that had plagued them during their earlier effort to provide a screen for the siege of Mantua. For Bonaparte, a retreat along converging routes was the obvious method of regaining relative safety, but he feared the effects of retreat upon the recently renewed revolutionary zeal of his troops and upon his own mystique as well; the Army of Italy remained something less than a veteran army of the old professional type, and Bonaparte was almost certainly correct in thinking that a withdrawal that the old French Army might have accepted stoically would stir up mischief in one of the new armies.

Thus with his largest single body of troops, under his own command, he chose to stand up to 28,000 Austrians under Alvintzi at Arcola, where a bridge offered a strategic crossing of the Alpone River. Not only were Bonaparte's numbers slightly inferior to those of Alvintzi, but his left was in danger of being turned if another French force of 10,000 should retreat too rapidly before an Austrian force of 18,000 that was pressing it. Moreover, Wurmser was in Bonaparte's rear with the Mantua garrison of 23,000. Because the threat to his left made time critical, however, Bonaparte's idea of how to make a stand against superior numbers at Arcola was to attack.

The battle of Arcola saw him attacking for three successive days, November 15–17 (25–27 Brumaire An V). Like Lodi, Arcola was less an expression of Napoleon's intellectual mastery of the art of war than of his intuition and his personal magnetism. His conviction that with the kind of army he led it was better to fight than to retreat was confirmed—along with, once more, the extraordinary inspirational effect of his mere presence—when his troops rushed more heartily to the assault on the second and third days than on the first. Nevertheless, although the Austrians yielded the bridge under the third day's attacks, the battle had remained not much better than a deadlock until Bonaparte invoked one of the simplest of ruses. By that third day, he had no strength remaining for *la manœuvre sur les derrières* save a few trumpeters, but he decided to make do with them. He sent them to blow calls in the enemy's rear, implying the presence there of a heavy French force. With enemy generals and soldiers alike tottering under the fatigue of three days' intense exertion and strain—the French of course were in no better condition, but they had Napoleon—this stratagem did its work. The Austrians broke in panic, and Arcola was won. It was won just in time, because the enemy on Bonaparte's left was now poised to pounce upon both the Verona and the Mantua roads and thus block a French retreat. Bonaparte turned to deal with this newly arrived enemy force on the 19th, but with his troops' self-confidence again inflated, he won another victory, generally considered part of the battle of Arcola, to insure his communications.

Alvintzi made one more attempt to relieve Mantua in the first month of 1797, but Bonaparte won yet another victory at Rivoli on January 14 (25 Nivôse An V) in a classic tactical application of the principle of interior lines. The Austrian commander thought he was coming in contact with only a single French division and spread his 26,000 men in a wide net to envelop both French flanks. Bonaparte resisted the flanking pincers with minimal force, only enough to delay them sufficiently so that his 10,000 troops could be reinforced by two approaching divisions, one of which was Masséna's. With most of his available strength well in hand, he then attacked Alvintzi's center with superior numbers at the scene of the collision. The numbers along with French confidence and élan decided this part of the battle. Then Masséna's artillery helped part of the French center dispose of the Austrian left pincer, while the two French reinforcing divisions ended the battle by completely crushing the right pincer between them. In these two latter phases of the battle, the speed in marching and deploying that reformers since Guibert had been instilling in the French Army represented another critical factor; the two reinforcing divisions had reached the scene earlier than the Austrians thought likely or even possible.

Wurmser surrendered Mantua and his part of the Austrian Army on February 2 (14 Fluviôse An V). He had conducted the defense with a stubbornness and skill that went far to compensate for his initial failures in the north and vindicated Vienna's decision to send him to Italy in spite of his age. But Austrian resourcefulness in mobilizing new armies had reached at least a temporary limit, so that after Wurmser's surrender not even the dispatching of the Archduke Charles to Italy could halt Bonaparte's advances. The *Reichsgeneralfeldmarschall* could do no more than fight cunning rear-guard actions and go through the motions of mounting against Bonaparte's rear threats that the latter instantly recognized as mere bugaboos. On April 18 (29 Germinal An V) the Austrians and Bonaparte ended the fighting by concluding the Armistice of Leoben, a general armistice for all fronts of the war negotiated by the commander of France's Army of Italy on his own initiative, to the chagrin of the Directory and of General Hoche, who had taken over the Army of the Sambre and Meuse and in a renewed offensive from the Rhine was in the process of ruining the Austrian forces in his front.

Nevertheless, the Directory was willing enough to complete the disruption of the First Coalition by agreeing to the Treaty of Campo Formio of October 17, 1797 (26 Vendémiaire An VI). Thereby Austria ceded the Austrian Netherlands to France, abandoned Lombardy to French disposal, accepted the existence of the Ligurian and Cisalpine Republics as French satellites in northern Italy, accepted also French possession of Corfu (Corcyra) and the Ionian Isles, and in a secret clause agreed to French occupation of the left bank of the Rhine. In partial compensation, Austria received Dalmatia, the Frioul, and Venetian territory east of the River Adige.

Now it remained only for France to deal with Great Britain. Already, the acquisition of distant Corfu and the Ionian Isles reflected a deterioration of British naval predominance in the Mediterranean as a byproduct of Bonaparte's victories. They also might form part of a scheme germinating in Bonaparte's brain to dispose of the remaining enemy, the great naval power, not by frontal assault but by a grand strategic *manœuvre sur les derrières*: to exploit British naval deterioration by moving through Egypt to a now-indispensable pillar of British wealth and power, India.

To Bonaparte, India of course was more than the back door to England. It called forth visions of conquest not only European but worldwide, and of victorious generalship crowned by Oriental wealth and splendor. The loosening of the moorings with which the hereditary French monarchy had restrained military tendencies toward independent policy-making had already given the French Republic hints of how difficult it might become to keep headstrong generals in harness with the Republic's policies when the legitimacy of all except forceful authority had become questionable. But no Dumouriez could have prepared the Republic for the grandeur of the ambitions of Bonaparte. The same reliance on charisma, intuition, and his own sense of destiny that shaped Bonaparte's generalship more than did rational principles of war was to shape also the boundless political adventurism on which he was now ready to embark. With the Treaty of Campo Formio and the destruction of the First Coalition, no active external enemies remained in the path of such ambition except Britain, no active major military force save the Royal Navy.

G reat Britain alone of the First Coalition remained in active opposition to France after October 1797, but Britain's part in the war against the French Republic thus far had been considerably less than distinguished, except for a few brief moments. As was becoming habitual, Britain had relied primarily upon its navy to accomplish against a continental adversary military purposes only dubiously within the grasp of sea power. And as was also habitual, the accomplishments of the Royal Navy had themselves been flawed by the prevalent failure of its officers to combine with skillful seamanship the operational and strategic conceptions of the true military professional.

As First Lord of the Treasury and King George III's chief minister, William Pitt the Younger had displayed admirable restraint when he was still seeking to fend off war with Revolutionary France. His restraint had stemmed in large part, however, from his failure to perceive the measure of fury that underlay the Revolution and thus its threat to British stability. Once he and his country were drawn into the war, he remained slow to perceive the dimensions of that fury, and thus to prosecute the war in earnest, which was less admirable a policy than his previous effort to keep peace. His failure to take the Revolution and the war as seriously as they deserved reinforced his typically British hope of avoiding the expenses and casualties of a large army and a large-scale continental military involvement, thus helping to render futile the participation of the Duke of York and his British army in the early campaigns in the Low Countries. But Pitt also managed the early phases of the naval war with similar offhandedness, and allowed the Royal Navy itself to do the same.

The Glorious First of June

It was not that Pitt neglected the material strength of the navy. On the contrary, during most of the decade before the war he had enforced a policy of economy of the navy (as well as on the rest of government) that enhanced rather than detracted from its effectiveness, in ship for ship strength and in its traditional virtue of seamanship. In such matters Pitt had strongly supported the Comptroller of the Navy, Admiral of the Blue Sir Charles Middleton (from April 1805 first Baron Barham), since 1778 a beacon of efficiency in a naval administration otherwise not noted for honesty and industriousness. Twenty-five ships of the line, fifty frigates, and thirty lesser vessels were in commission when war was declared, and more than twice that number were being prepared for sea and could be ready quickly because Middleton had seen to the allocation of ample reserves of naval stores for that purpose. To find crews for the ships was as usual more difficult; the press gangs set to work in seaport towns with unprecedented vigor, aided by Orders in Council of February and March 1793 that prohibited unarmed ocean-going vessels from sailing until the current naval preparations were complete, and thus keeping vessels in port to be boarded and combed out.

The French Navy, furthermore, was in sorry condition. By the beginning of the war with Great Britain, about three-quarters of its officers had been lost to exile or the guillotine. Ships and stores were neglected, sanitary precautions ignored, many seamen sick, indiscipline everywhere. Shiphandling skills would be less easy to improvise anew than the ability of soldiers in column to charge forward with élan. Somewhat less than thirty out of eighty ships of the line were in commission, with all in doubtful readiness.

Nevertheless, the stimulus of war against the ancient maritime rival in combination with the fervor of the Revolution soon permitted the French to display energy if not first-rate efficiency in getting frigates to sea to prey on British commerce, and even in assembling a squadron of ten or more of the line off the south Brittany coast to prevent foreign aid from reaching the rebels in La Vendée and adjacent areas. The command of the British Channel Squadron, furthermore, went to Admiral Richard, sixth Viscount Howe (in the Irish peerage), first Viscount Howe of Langar, and since 1788 first Baron and Earl Howe, an officer immensely popular in the fleet but sixty-seven years old and never a believer in the close-blockade system of Sir Edward Hawke. To conserve the seaworthiness of his ships, Howe preferred to lie at anchor in the harbor of Torbay rather than see his vessels buffeted off the enemy coast. He put his squadron, fifteen of the line plus auxiliaries, to sea by mid-July 1793 and kept it there as long as the weather was good, but storms sent him back to his sheltered anchorage. Several times in 1793 his lookouts sighted parts of the French fleet on the horizon, but his ships were never able to overhaul them. In mid-December Howe returned to port for the winter, leaving only frigates off Brest. His open blockade denied his captains and crews the honing of their seamanship and discipline that Hawke's methods would have offered, denied them also the accumulation of an intimate knowledge of the French coast, and posed always the danger that the French would go to sea while the Channel Squadron was too far in the rear to intercept them.

Late in 1793 two French ships of the line and three frigates sailed from Brest to escort both a large grain convoy from America and another convoy from the West Indies homeward in the coming spring. These ships left Hampton Roads on their eastward journey on April 11, 1794 (22 Germinal An II). On the same day another squadron of five of the line left Brest for a station some 300 nautical miles or 555 kilometers west of Belle-Isle to meet the ships from America. Presently this squadron encountered the British Newfoundland convoy and captured many of its ships.

On May 16 (26 Floréal) Louis Thomas Villaret de Joyeuse, one of the relatively few senior officers of the old French Navy still in service, a veteran of Suffren's campaign in Indian waters (as a lieutenant commanding the corvette *Naiade*, 20) and newly commissioned *contre-amiral*, put out from Brest with twenty-five of the line to rendezvous with the Belle-Isle squadron and ensure the safe arrival of the grain convoy. Admiral Howe had departed his winter haven on May 2 with thirty-two of the line. Off the Lizard he had detached eight of these ships to escort merchantmen as far as Cape Finisterre. Then he had looked into Brest, found the French fleet still there, and sailed westward to try to intercept the grain convoy. Not finding it, Howe visited Brest again on May 19 and discovered that Villaret had also eluded him.

Howe proceeded to quarter the likely approach routes in search. On May 28 (9 Prairial) his frigates at last signaled a fleet to the southwest. Through that day the British beat to windward to intercept the French. The next morning the French were sighted again, about six nautical miles (eleven kilometers) distant but on the weather bow. During the next two days, Howe pursued and contrived to capture the weather gauge, an accomplishment as usual of British skill in seamanship. Through the next night, however, rain and fog settled in. The British fleet hung close to its prey, another accomplishment of British seamanship, but it was not until midday of May 31 (12 Prarial) that the fog lifted. Then "Black Dick" Howe with exemplary patience decided to postpone battle to the next morning so he might have a full day of combat to complete his work.

Remarkably, the three ships of the line of the Belle-Isle squadron had joined Villaret in the fog, along with another ship arrived from France. Villaret then had twenty-six of the line to the same number retained by Howe after his various detachments. With these forces the rival fleets did battle when June 1 (13 Prairial) proved to dawn a clear day with a moderate southerly wind and a smooth sea: Sunday, the Glorious First of June as it was to be remembered in British naval annals.

Conservative though he was in strategic judgments, in tactics Howe had abandoned the old line ahead. His plan was to overhaul the enemy line and then to have each of his vessels cut through that line under the stern of an enemy ship and engage it from leeward. Thereby each of his ships would be able to throw a raking fire into its opponent's hull as it passed through the French line, and French retreat would be cut off because a disabled sailing ship could retire only to leeward.

The trouble with this otherwise excellent design was that it overtaxed even British seamanship. Indeed, it was partially impossible, because some of the French ships sailed too close together for anything to penetrate between them. Only seven British ships actually pierced Villaret's line. But this was enough to touch off a melee from which the French could not readily flee. Those of Howe's ships that did not cut through the line engaged their French opposites from varying distances. Such cutting of the line as did take place divided the French fleet into scattered and uncoordinated groupings. French gunnery proved no longer a match for British.

At about half past ten in the morning the smoke of battle briefly cleared enough that Villaret could gain some notion of the condition of his fleet, and it was not good. He signaled to close on his flagship, *Montagne,* 120, with the intention of terminating the battle. When his signal was not altogether obeyed, he felt obliged to close on those ships that were surrounded by the enemy in the hope of somehow helping them to get clear. At length, Villaret managed to break off the action with five of his badly damaged ships in tow. Howe captured six of Villaret's ships and sank a seventh.

He could certainly have captured more if he had pursued vigorously; two of his ships were about to capture two dismasted Frenchmen when his orders recalled them. But old as he was, Howe was worn down from the strain of the search for the French and the grueling four days' chase that had preceded the battle. When Villaret displayed no small skill in disengaging in such a way as to shield his injured vessels to maximum effect, Howe had not the heart to press the issue further.

Two British ships had been dismasted, and Howe's flagship, the *Queen Charlotte,* 100, which was among the seven that broke the enemy line, had lost its topmasts. Other British vessels had suffered much damage to their rigging. Altogether, while the fight of the Glorious First of June was certainly a British tactical victory, and while the balance of casualties greatly favored the British at some 1,148 to 5,000, the affair was not all that glorious; strategically it was least glorious, because Villaret's mission had been to bring home the grain convoy, and in that he succeeded.

In spite of the priority of the convoy in French eyes, however, it would seem unfair to criticize Howe for not seeking out the convoy instead of the fleet; certainly the French fleet was more important in the long run than any grain convoy. But the escape of the convoy was symptomatic of the larger laxity of the Royal Navy's strategic grasp at this stage of the war and in the persisting absence of a true military professionalism at its head. At the least, the grain convoy was important enough to France that the British should have tried to cut it off at the start, in or outside Chesapeake Bay. Short of that, Howe had hoped that when on May 28 he sent home the *Audacious,* 74, partially disabled in an exchange of gunfire on the first day of contact with Villaret, its report would bring out ships from Plymouth to deal with the convoy. The ships in fact sailed, under Rear-Admiral George Montagu; but instead of sending his frigates to look for the convoy, Montagu also focused on Villaret, yet nevertheless retired before him when he approached Brest. Montagu had only nine sail of the line and was thus overmatched by Villaret by about two to one despite the latter's condition. Still, if Montagu had stood to fight in front of Brest and Howe meanwhile had pursued with reasonable vigor, the French fleet might have been gored to destruction by the two horns. Instead, Montagu accomplished neither of the achievements possibly open to him.

The weary Howe resumed his strategy of open blockade. This questionable strategy did the British no further harm even though a refurbished French fleet of more than thirty of the line took advantage of his winter retirement to Torbay by putting to sea at Christmas time (early Nivôse An III); the weather proved so bad that the French in their foray injured only themselves, losing no less than five of the line and suffering heavy damages in many other vessels.

The Irish Expedition of 1796

Early in 1795 Howe relinquished practical command of the Channel Squadron to a slightly—but only slightly—less elderly officer, Vice-Admiral of the White Sir Alexander Hood, recently made first Baron Bridport of Cricket St Thomas in Somerset in the Irish peerage as a reward for his role as Howe's second in command on the Glorious First of June. Admiral Lord Bridport made no improvements in Howe's strategy of open blockade. Instead, he allowed the blockade to degenerate into still worse laxity, and by 1796–1797 he was mostly directing his ships from London. In consequence there occurred a series of embarrassing French forays from Brest, culminating in the winter of 1796–1797 with something more serious than embarrassment, a French expedition to Ireland that distracted Britain from the main war and in whose eventual fate the lackluster Royal Navy had little part.

The French Revolution had awakened the inevitable sympathetic echoes in Ireland, where the nationalist leader Theobald Wolfe Tone responded by founding the Society of United Irishmen in 1791. With the British garrison reduced by drafts for the Continent and home defense, the Irish nationalists could commence an almost public program of arming themselves. In France, the idea of strongly reinforcing the Irish armament sprang from the lively mind of General Hoche when in 1796 he was fresh from the suppression at last of the revolt in La Vendée. On December 16, 1796 (26 Frimaire An V) 20,000 troops under Hoche's command sailed from Brest in a naval expedition exceptionally well prepared and fitted out by the standards of Revolutionary France, including seventeen ships of the line, thirteen frigates, several smaller vessels of war, and twenty transports, all under Justin Bonaventure Morard de Galles, *vice-amiral* and a veteran of service under Suffren as a lieutenant. The transports carried the horses and military equipment and stores; the troops mostly sailed on the warships. Wolfe Tone was also aboard.

Exceptional preparation did not prevent confusion bordering on chaos when a sudden shift of wind led to a change of orders while the ships were about to negotiate the difficult exits from Brest under gathering darkness. In a rare stroke of British naval energy, Captain Sir Edward Pellew in the frigate *Indefatigable*, 44, risked entering the Brest waterways and there stirred up additional confusion. Pellew had also dispatched word of the French activity to the fleet, but as usual under the current strategy the weight of the Royal Navy was too far east to do much good.

The French had become separated into two main groups, which managed to find each other on December 18 (28 Frimaire). Unfortunately for them, the frigate *Fraternité*, 38, remained lost, with both Hoche and Morard on board. Early the next morning, nevertheless, most of the French fleet arrived off the entrance to Bantry Bay, inside which they were to make their Irish landing. Here additional misfortune greeted them, because a strong easterly wind, helpful in speeding their progress until now, was a head wind in the bay, and it soon blew more furiously than before, driving snow and sleet. Trying to approach their landing sites—far up the bay, because its waters were exceptionally deep for its width—the French vessels had to tack and tack again, over and over, barely making way. British seamanship would have been hard-pressed, and the navy of the French Republic had by no means attained that standard yet.

For days on end—through Christmas Eve (4 Nivôse)—the French remained locked in this predicament, sails and clothes ripping and men nearly freezing all the while. The *Fraternité* turned up but was blown out to sea again—a final disaster, because on December 24 the winds moderated just enough that a landing should have been possible for the troops farthest up the bay, and if Hoche had been at hand he almost certainly would have ordered it. That was the end. By Christmas Day it was blowing a full gale again, with no relenting on the 26th, and by now ships, crews, and troops were in such bad condition, seasickness everywhere, that the alternatives seemed to be return to Brest or complete catastrophe. The French struggled back to Brest.

Predictably, they returned with little interference from the British—except for one ship that encountered Pellew. The *Droits de l'Homme*, a 74-gun battleship, was blown away from its consorts and met the *Indefatigable* and another frigate, the *Amazon*, 38, about 150 nautical miles (284 kilometers) southwest of Ushant. The frigates were inshore and made sail to head off the Frenchman. A heavy wind was still blowing, though now westerly, and a squall carried away the French ship's fore and main topmasts. This damage caused the *Droits de l'Homme* to roll so heavily that its main battery could not fire, so Pellew and his companion closed on it and continually raked it until all three were blown into Audierne Bay. There the battleship and the *Amazon* both grounded and were battered apart, but Pellew with good seamanship and the dash of luck usually essential to military success, in the form of a shifting wind, got the *Indefatigable* out to sea with a ruined battleship to his credit.

Thus the British had a small moral victory to accompany their greater moral victory of the Glorious First of June. If British naval strategy at the outset of the Wars of the French Revolution had left the avoidance of disaster in the Atlantic and the Channel largely at the mercy of the weather and the vagaries of French seamanship, however, events in other theaters were demonstrating that strategic ineptitude could also reap its more just reward of military and political defeat. In the West Indies, that ineptitude practically annihilated one of Britain's own armies. In the Mediterranean, it made possible Bonaparte's resuscitation of the

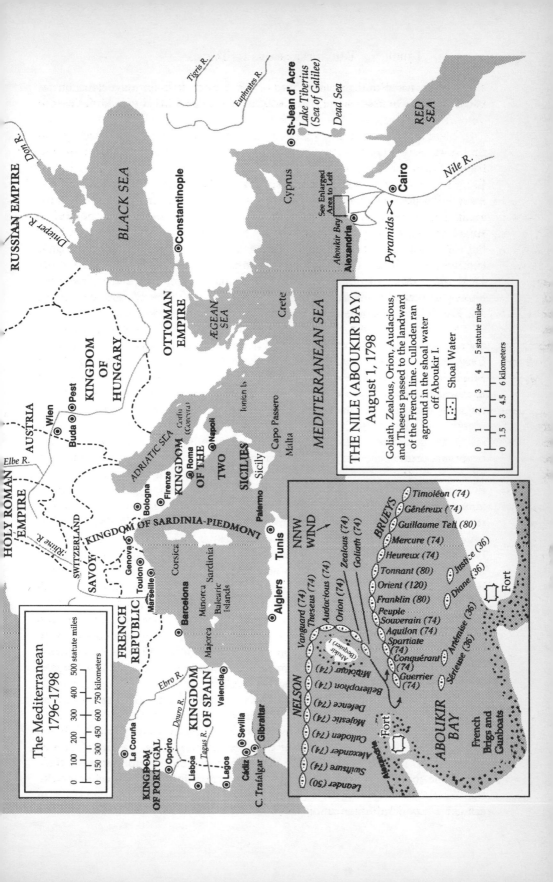

Army of Italy and thus the launching of a career that would plague Britain for two decades. The cost of the absence of naval professionalism could be high.

Land Power over Sea Power: The Mediterranean, 1796–1797

One of the manifestations of Pitt's failure to take the war against the French Republic as seriously as France's expansionist energies merited was his focus on the West Indies. He saw the war largely as a continuation of the old Anglo-French commercial rivalry. When the French drive toward European hegemony warranted sending to the Low Countries a British military contingent comparable to those led by Marlborough at his peak of strength, Pitt starved the Duke of York's expeditionary force but found enough troops for attacks on Saint-Domingue (Haiti, Hayti, or Haïti), Martinique, Sainte-Lucie (St Lucia), and Guadeloupe. Between 1793 and 1796 40,000 British soldiers died of disease in the Caribbean and an equal number were disabled by the same tropical maladies. In return, the expedition to Haiti was a flat failure, Guadeloupe was soon retaken by the French, and a tenuous hold on the two sugar islands of Martinique and St Lucia was all that Pitt had to show for the near-ruination of the British Army—because not only were the immediate casualties more than the army could afford, but fear of being sent to the West Indies almost paralyzed recruitment.

Pitt's colonialist and commercial perception of strategy might at least have been expected to encourage British control of the Mediterranean, but offhandedness generated failure there as well. The war began badly with the unsuccessful effort to hold Toulon in company with French Royalists, a fiasco that we have already noted as contributing much to the rise of Bounaparte. Beyond the protection of British and Allied Mediterranean shipping, the Royal Navy's strategic priority after Toulon should have been attacking France's precarious line of communications with its troops in Italy, a line that because it clung to the narrow Riviera coast was exceedingly vulnerable to rupture by naval gunfire and naval landings.

In the autumn of 1795 a small British squadron was assigned to cooperate with the Austrian Army in this area. This squadron received an exceptionally energetic commander in the person of Commodore Horatio Nelson, thirty-seven years old. Nelson had distinguished himself in his first battle, the action of Cape Poli on March 13–14, 1794 (23–24 Ventôse An II), when as captain of the *Agamemnon*, 64, he had poured a double-shotted broadside into a French laggard, the 84-gun *Ça Ira*, and thus played the principal part in bringing about the capture on the second day of both *Ça Ira* and another enemy ship of the line, the *Censeur*, 74, which had taken its injured consort in tow. But the British Commander-in-Chief at Cape Poli, Vice-Admiral of the Red (and soon full Admiral) William Hotham, had refused to press either this or subsequent opportunities for a decisive battle that might have ruined the French Navy in the Mediterranean. Nor upon Nelson's receiving his squadron did Hotham offer it enough ships or enough support to capitalize on its commander's energy. Nelson later thought that if he had been properly seconded in attacking the French Army's Riviera communications, Bonaparte's Italian triumphs could never have occurred. He was probably right.

Because Bonaparte's triumphs were not aborted but did occur, the Royal Navy's white ensign nearly disappeared from the Mediterranean for lack of basing facilities. This outcome could no longer be prevented even by a far abler Commander-in-Chief than Hotham, Admiral Sir John Jervis, the later first Earl of St Vincent, who raised his flag on December 3, 1795. Jervis vigorously elevated standards of discipline and seamanship that had been sadly lagging in his fleet, and he took up his own station with the bulk of his ships to blockade Toulon, while Nelson worked in the Gulf of Genoa. But the French had accumulated enough, albeit minimal, supplies to launch Bonaparte's campaign of 1796, and that general soon broke free from his perilous logistical dependence on the Riviera coast. Thus it was too late for Jervis or Nelson to halt by naval means the descent of the Army of Italy upon the seaports of the Italian northwest coast, most importantly Leghorn (Livorno), a major naval base as well as a commercial port. The British promptly blockaded Leghorn, but their consequent limiting of French use of its facilities did little to offset their own loss of them.

Worse, Bonaparte's continuing march of conquest, now unimpeded from the sea, did much to cause Spain to waver in its adherence to the First Coalition and then on August 19, 1796 (2 Fructidor An IV) to sign a treaty of alliance with France, soon afterward completing its reversal of allegiances by declaring war against Great Britain. A British squadron that had been operating around Cádiz therefore found itself threatened by the Spanish fleet and, contrary to Jervis's instructions to join him should that situation develop, fled to England. Thus stripped of one-third of his force, Jervis was unable to prevent the Spanish from uniting with the French fleet in Toulon. Thereupon the continuance of the British blockades of Toulon and Leghorn became almost impossible. Pitt's Cabinet ordered the evacuation of the Mediterranean.

British naval traditions have long imbued the English-speaking world with almost awestruck respect for the ability of ships never seen by armies to strangle those armies' logistics and thus in time to bring them to their doom. This attitude is one of the foundations of the British habit of thinking that large armies are unnecessary and that continental powers can be undone relatively inexpensively through the employment of ships, money, and allies, the experience of the wars against Louis XIV to the contrary notwithstanding. The United States has shared much of this attitude. In 1796, however, it was Bonaparte's land power that by depriving the Royal Navy of its bases and allies undermined the workings of sea power. After Jervis withdrew to Gibraltar, throughout 1797 not a British ship of the line and very few British frigates ventured into the Mediterranean.

Bonaparte was free to contemplate a further triumph of Behemoth over Leviathan, by capitalizing on French control of the Mediterranean for a march into Egypt and thence to India, hoping to bring down the British Empire by hammering against its back door.

Cape St. Vincent: Jervis and Nelson

Jervis established his main base at Lisbon, suffering losses from uncommonly severe storms on the way and from the problems of the difficult passage in and out of the Tagus River after he had arrived, aggravated by inadequate repair facilities at his new base. By the beginning of February 1797 he was reduced to ten ships of the line; fortunately the Admiralty responded promptly to the easing of the threat to Ireland at the turning of the year—though turmoil inside the island was still growing—to dispatch another five of the line that joined Jervis on February 6.

The reinforcement was all the more fortunate because Britain's emboldened enemies were reaching out from their new-found control of the Mediterranean for yet another, and much more formidable, Irish foray, this one built upon the combined French and Spanish fleets to be assembled in Brest. Already France's Toulon fleet had safely exited through the Strait of Gibraltar while Jervis was preoccupied with the storm that battered his passage to Lisbon. At the time he received the reinforcement, Jervis was cruising off Cape St. Vincent to intercept the Spanish Cartagena fleet under Teniente-General Don José de Córdoba y Ramos as it sailed to join the rendezvous at Brest.

Nelson in the frigate *La Minerve*, 38, rejoined Jervis on February 13. He was returning from the mission of evacuating a British garrison and naval stores from Elba, and he had just threaded his way through Spain's Cartagena ships in order to find Jervis. With Nelson's fresh information, the admiral prepared to give battle the next day, and he persisted in his determination even when, as a morning fog lifted, his lookouts reported that the enemy fleet included no less than twenty-seven sail of the line. He believed that faulty strategic direction from London had brought the fleet to a juncture where a victory in battle was indispensable if only for a recapture of prestige and moral ascendancy. And he relied on the abysmal deterioration of Spanish seamanship since the days of the Armada.

Jervis flew his flag in the *Victory*, rated 100 guns, actually 110, laid down in the glorious year of victories 1759. On rejoining, Nelson had shifted his commodore's broad pendant to the *Captain*, 74. A clear day with a light breeze west to south followed the disappearance of the fog, and the British saw the Spanish sailing northward in two somewhat disorderly lines. Jervis formed line ahead southward into the gap between the two Spanish lines, intending the ships of his van to tack westward in succession at the appropriate time to assail the windward Spanish line, while his rear ships kept the other Spanish line occupied until half the enemy fleet had been disposed of.

In anticipation of a method of command that we shall meet again with Nelson, Jervis thought he had imbued his captains with his own ideas and spirit enough that almost any of them could lead the way into this design. The choice fell to one of the most promising of them, Captain Thomas Troubridge in the *Culloden*, 74, who demonstrated his insight into the admiral's intentions and spirit by anticipating Jervis's signal to tack. Troubridge had the appropriate flags already run up ready to be unfurled instantly at the moment when he received the signal from Jervis. One by one the British ships went into action raking the Spanish windward division.

The enemy's lee division failed in an effort to break through Jervis's line to join their consorts, suffering some heavy damage in the attempt. As the British ships sailed on southward and eastward, however, the Spanish windward division saw an opportunity to tack to the east and pass astern of the British to reunite their fleet. When they began this maneuver, Jervis was far to the south and enveloped in the smoke of the cannonade. Nelson in the *Captain,* however, was third from the rear of the British line, and he quickly perceived what was happening and put about to try to block the Spanish maneuver.

He laid his ship in the path of three enemy three-deckers, the *Santissimia Trinidad* of 130 guns and the *Salvador del Mundo* and *San Josef* of 112 guns each, which were soon joined by the *San Nicolas,* 84, and the *San Isidro,* 74. The *Captain* lost its foretopmast and wheel, but with remarkable alertness Troubridge led the *Culloden* to its aid, and together the two British 74s held off the heart of the Spanish fleet long enough to be joined by a substantial number of their consorts and thus to bring on a general melee. In this action yet another of Jervis's captains, James Saumarez of the island of Guernsey, joined the quest for laurels. In *Orion,* 74, he compelled the huge *Salvador del Mundo* to strike its colors. Nelson, his sails and rigging torn apart, nevertheless laid the *Captain* alongside the *San Nicolas,* which was entangled with the *San Josef,* and with boarding parties captured both ships. Saumarez had worked the *Orion* abreast of the *Santissima Trinidad* and had forced it to surrender also when Jervis signaled to break off the action, whereupon the largest ship in the world made its escape after all.

But Jervis had his triumph to restore moral ascendancy, with not a British ship lost and four Spaniards as prizes, the *San Isidro* having struck to Captain Cuthbert Collingwood in the *Excellent,* 74. The Commander-in-Chief received a pension of £3,000 a year and his peerage as the Earl of St Vincent. Nelson had already been gazetted to rear-admiral of the blue and become a Knight of the Bath. Ireland was reasonably safe from external interference, with the French now incapable of supplying more than token assistance to the uprising of 1798 in which the current spasm of restlessness erupted, but which the redcoats readily and ruthlessly suppressed.

But the French still dominated the Mediterranean. The battle of Cape St. Vincent, like every other victory of the Royal Navy thus far in the French Revolutionary Wars, was too much a triumph merely of superior naval tactics and seamanship, and not enough a triumph infused with strategic purpose, because the naval war effort still lacked strategic coherence.

Camperdown

Nor was the battle of Cape St. Vincent even a sufficient stimulus to morale to prevent a series of mutinies, breaking out first in the Channel Fleet on the April 16 following the victorious St. Valentine's Day, but erupting almost simultaneously in St Vincent's own force off Cádiz as well, and spreading through the navy. The sources of the mutinies lay in the harsh conditions of the life below decks into which thousands of the seaman had been pressed, and in the lack of any compensating rewards, with pay low and prize money for the occasional victories maddeningly slow to disgorge from the Treasury. The government chose to respond to the mutinies not with any substantial alleviation of hard labor, repulsive rations, and filthy and overcrowded living conditions all under the shadow of the cat o' nine tails, but with still further applications of stern discipline—although a Seaman's Bill hurriedly moved through Parliament to offer at least minimal concessions, and "Black Dick" Howe heroically put aside the infirmities of age to visit the ships and stake his considerable personal credit on assurances that the slim promises of the Seaman's Bill would be kept and that the most unpopular officers would be removed from sea duty. Nevertheless, seamen's defiance of orders continued to break out intermittently half way through 1798.

The French meanwhile had assembled an army of fearsome numbers adjacent to the Texel with the apparent intent of using the Dutch fleet to ferry it across the Channel for an invasion. All through the warm months of 1797, the Admiralty had to keep one eye on the mutinies and the other on nautical and martial activities in the Netherlands, and somehow throughout the mutinies a semblance of a blockade had to be maintained off the Texel. When there were not enough ships with crews reliable enough to keep the blockade real, signal flags rose and descended energetically on the halyards of the vessels just offshore to suggest the presence of numerous others below the horizon. But through most of the early summer there was a British wind, one blowing persistently westerly and thus into the face of French hopes; and while there was a brief interval of easterly breezes in July (Messidor-Thermidor), during which French troops actually began to board transports, the threat from the Texel was in fact at least as illusionary as the blockade against it. From August (Thermidor-Fructidor) onward, the French had explicitly abandoned an Irish invasion, and their true intent against England involved no more than a raid.

The sixteen Dutch ships of the line available to them were less powerful than equivalent British ships, and when they chose to avail themselves of an easterly wind shift to test the outcome of venturing to sea on October 6 (16 Vendémiaire An VI), the sequel was the battle of Camperdown (Kampereiland) on the 11th. Camperdown was yet another tactical triumph of British seamanship, in which the British North Sea Fleet under Admiral of the Blue Adam Duncan equal in numbers to the Dutch but sailing in two columns broke the Dutch line into three segments and with their heavier armament obliged nine of the Dutch to surrender.

This battle destroyed for the present any semblance of a threat of French invasion of England, but in fact the ships and seamanship of the Royal Navy in the Channel had continuously assured the chimerical nature of such a threat in spite of all British strategic failures, mutinies, French troop deployments, and nervous London newspapers. The absence of coherent British naval strategy continued to have its major consequences not in the Channel but in the Mediterranean.

Bonaparte versus Nelson:
The Egyptian Expedition and the Battle of the Nile

In the spring following Camperdown, the Cabinet and the Admiralty became apprised of another set of ominous French troop concentrations, these along the coast of Provence and down the Italian coast as far as Civitavecchia, accompanied by the assembling of transport vessels in the same ports. There was also a scurrying to gather anew a French Mediterranean fleet at Toulon. The British had few clues regarding the French intent. In fact, General Bonaparte had too keen an eye to have discerned any practicability in the recent plans for a cross-Channel foray—especially in that he himself was absent from that scene—but had matured his alternative idea of striking at Britain's warmaking capability by completing its exclusion from the Mediterranean with a conquest of Egypt and the Levant, proceeding thence to strike at India and thus to chop off the large and very lucrative Oriental limb of British commerce and finance. Without India and the trade with the East Indies and China that was dependent upon India, there was some reason to believe that Britain would not be able to afford to persist in the war. Besides, the image of himself transformed into an Oriental potentate was much to Bonaparte's taste.

The French preparations at Toulon and elsewhere along the coast of the Mediterranean persuaded the Admiralty that it must take the risk of reinserting British naval power into that sea, notwithstanding that the earlier shortcomings of British strategy had deprived the navy of adequate bases for the purpose. On May 2, 1798, consequently, orders were sent to St Vincent to dispatch a squadron eastward past the Pillars of Hercules, preferably with Nelson in command. Eight vessels freed from watching the Irish coasts were to be sent to the Cádiz blockade to facilitate the detachment. Lately so indifferent to the implications of failing to use the navy against Bonaparte's communications, the Admiralty now warned St Vincent that the fate of Europe might depend on his ability to overcome the risks of the new deployment.

St Vincent was far too astute to need such a warning. In fact, on the very day when the Admiralty was writing to him, he acted on his own initiative to send Nelson back into the Mediterranean with three 74s and three frigates. The mission was to observe the Toulon fleet and if possible to discover its purpose.

Unfortunately for the British, on May 20 Nelson's expedition encountered gale-force winds that dismasted the flagship, the *Vanguard,* and separated the frigates from the rest of the vessels. The *Orion* and the *Alexander* escorted the *Vanguard* to the anchorage of San Pietro, on the south coast of Sardinia, where it was jury-rigged in four days, a remarkable Nelsonian exertion. Nevertheless, it was too late to gather much information at Toulon; the enemy fleet assembled there, and its convoy of troop transports from around the northwestern Mediterranean, had already departed Toulon the day before the storm, May 19 (29 Floréal An VI).

St Vincent had prepared ten ships of the line under Captain Troubridge to reinforce Nelson. Along with the 50-gun *Leander*, they joined him in the Gulf of

Lyon, the established rendezvous, on June 7, giving him fourteen of the line including *Leander*. The French meanwhile had continued to keep their destination a remarkably well-guarded secret, and Nelson had little notion of where they had gone. Not until June 14 did he receive a report that they had been seen ten days before off the southwest coast of Sicily and bearing eastward. With this news, however, Nelson immediately divined that they might well be bound for Alexandria and thence for an expedition into Egypt; his imagination could leap as far as Bonaparte's. Pressing on sail, Nelson hastened to Naples, where he was told that the French had landed on Malta and seized possession of it from the Knights of Malta. This latest word was reaffirmed when Nelson was off the coast of Sicily on June 21—but with the misleading addition that the French had departed Malta on the 16th (28 Prairial An VII), when in fact they had left only on the 19th (1 Messidor). Nelson now felt virtually certain that Bonaparte must be bound for Egypt. Driving his squadron with almost frantic nervous energy, he reached Alexandria on June 28—too early. The French were not there.

Bonaparte commanded the entire French expedition, ships as well as troops, but the warships were more directly under the control of François Paul Brueys d'Aigalliers, *vice-amiral*. They included thirteen sail of the line, three of them three-deckers, and six frigates. In spite of the busy preparations that had attracted the attention of the British, they were undermanned and under-supplied, and such crews as had been assembled were in large part hastily trained and poorly disciplined. Three of the 74s, *Guerrier, Peuple Souverain,* and *Conquérant*, were so old and ill-conditioned that they probably should not have gone to sea, and the last had received a complement of lighter than usual guns so that firing them would not cause it to disintegrate. The warships themselves were packed with troops, and they escorted enough transport vessels so that together they carried an army of almost 36,000 soldiers, with 160 guns and 1,200 horses. The combination of dubious naval power with heavy responsibility for Bonaparte's formidable land armament made Brueys as nervous as Nelson but for different reasons.

For a time, nevertheless, the French admiral was lucky. While the winds had injured and hampered Nelson, the French encountered favorable breezes for an eastward voyage. While Nelson's energy combined with British seamanship nevertheless soon closed the distance between the rival squadrons—on the night of June 22–23 (4–5 Messidor An VI) their paths actually crossed and the French could hear the firing of British signal guns—Nelson did not discover Brueys, and the French voyage proceeded uninterrupted. When Brueys entered the harbor of Alexandria on July 1 (13 Messidor), the British had just departed.

Against Nelson's energy and British seamanship, however, French luck could not persist. Bonaparte had overstretched the strategic possibilities opened to the French by earlier British ineptitude in the Mediterranean. Without the frigates that should have been scouring the sea on his behalf, Nelson spent the better part of another month in futile voyaging after his departure from Alexandria—while the French Army overran Egypt. Thinking he might have misjudged the direction of the French effort, Nelson beat his way back to Sicily against unfavorable winds, arriving only on July 18. Learning nothing there, he turned east again to the coast of Greece, where at last on July 28 Troubridge of the *Culloden* and Captain Alexander Ball of the *Alexander* separately intercepted two vessels that reported that the French fleet had been seen sailing southeastward from Crete four weeks before. Immediately Nelson sailed again for Alexandria, where in midafternoon of August 1 (14 Thermidor An VI) the topmasts of the French were sighted in one of the sheltered reaches of the delta of the Nile, a bay some fifteen miles (twenty-four kilometers) east of Alexandria called Al-Bakir or Aboukir.

Thus far Nelson had attained his prominence mainly through exceptional boldness and diligence, not through any demonstration of professional military qualifications that would have distinguished him from the run of British naval officers who were good and sometimes excellent seamen but did not possess the strategic, operational, or even tactical learning and insights that would have made them professional officers by the standards of land warfare. The discovery of Brueys's fleet, however, gave Nelson the opportunity to display for the first time the unwonted skills in the most distinctively military aspects of naval command, beyond seamanship alone, that entitle him to undisputed first rank among the naval officers of his era. These skills he derived, of course, from his own insight and experience, not from any formal professional education, which was still almost altogether lacking in the Royal Navy. His professional skills revealed themselves particularly in his solution to those problems of commanding and controlling squadrons and fleets while in action that had spawned the rigid tactics of the line ahead because those tactics had seemed the only alternative to chaos.

Other British naval commanders had begun to escape the rigidity of the line ahead, but they had not yet found an acceptable safeguard against chaos, and the danger of the descent into chaos was one of the main reasons why even an aggressive admiral such as Jervis at Cape St. Vincent cut off the action short of complete victory—to make sure that at the close he would still have his fleet in hand. Nelson's solution was, like many solutions in the conduct of war, exceedingly simple in concept but hitherto largely untried, because the simple concept was not so simple to put into practice.

During the weeks of apparently futile chasing and searching after the French fleet, Nelson had not only drilled and exercised his crews continually in preparation for battle, as would any highly competent commander; he also assembled his captains as frequently as possible on the quarterdeck of his flagship, there to rehearse with them his proposed tactics for every conceivable contingency in which the enemy fleet might be encountered. Through discussions and questioning, Nelson made sure that his captains had assimilated his ideas as their own, to act and cooperate as he would have them do under every possible circumstance. The limitations of the language of signal flags would not hamper his coming battle. He and his captains shared what a later age would call a common tactical doctrine, which remains in war the touchstone for making possible both flexibility in tactics and coordination of neighboring ships, companies, or battalions.

Once Bonaparte had captured Cairo, he ordered Brueys to sail to the island of Corfu in the Ionian Sea. The general felt logistically secure for the time being, and at Corfu his supporting fleet would be less subject to entrapment by the British than on the Egyptian coast. But the courier carrying the orders was killed by Arabs on the way to Brueys, and while the vice-admiral was aware of the Corfu possibility and even of Bonaparte's leaning toward it, he remained at Aboukir Bay because he feared his food supplies would not last the voyage—or more accurately, because he was simply timid and adopted the timid commander's customary solution, that when in doubt one should do nothing.

To protect himself where he was, Brueys counted mainly on the shallowness of Aboukir Bay. A sandbank reaches eastward from the northern point of land forming the bay, and on an island—Aboukir Island—at the eastern tip of this sandbank Brueys erected a protective battery. He then drew up his thirteen battleships in line ahead, the foremost of them just offshore from and somewhat shielded by the battery, all anchored in nearly shoal-water along the northward and westward sides of the bay; four frigates that were with him (the rest being at Alexandria) anchored inland from this line. He relied on the island battery and the shoals to prevent the British from passing to the landward side of his line. Therefore he counted on concentrating the efforts of his guns and manpower to blast any assailant as the assailant passed along his bayward flank. This ability to concentrate artillery fire against an enemy to starboard while riding at anchor should enhance the French asset of gunnery skill, in which the French Navy had traditionally shone and had not entirely lost its edge since the Revolution, while minimizing French deficiencies in seamanship. So sure was Brueys of his advantage of position that he did not even clear his ships for action on the landward side, allowing the batteries there to be cluttered with stores. Brueys evidently expected Nelson to sail back and forth in futile procession past his bayward guns, the French artillery battering the British until they had to withdraw.

It was late in the day—past 6:30 in the afternoon—before Nelson could close enough that his leading ship, the 74-gun *Goliath* under Captain Thomas Foley, came under fire from the first two ships in the French line. To expedite action at this late hour, however, Nelson's understandings with his captains were so complete that the only signals he had to raise in the course of the battle were to clear for action and, at the end, to anchor by the stern. Troubridge's *Culloden* grounded on the sandbank near Aboukir Island, and three other ships fell well behind, but the other ten British ships bore down undaunted. Nelson had emphasized that where there was enough depth of water for a ship to swing to moorings there was depth also for another ship to squeeze past, so Foley sailed across the bow of the leading French ship, *Guerrier*, raking it with his broadside as he passed, and then proceeded along the French line *inshore* of it. The next four British 74s, the *Zelaous, Orion, Audacious,* and *Theseus*, followed forthwith, and Brueys was thus assailed where he was utterly unprepared. Nelson in the *Vanguard* led the other five ships to assault the enemy's opposite side simultaneously.

The British slowed to concentrate their fire first on a few ships of the enemy's van, and their overwhelming barrage dismasted the *Guerrier* in under twelve minutes and similarly disabled two other 74s, *Conquérant* and *Spartiate*, in another ten minutes. Brueys's only conceivable chance of righting the situation would have been a prompt signal to his rearward vessels, generally his stronger ships, to weigh anchor and close on his van to rescue it; but his ships were sufficiently immobilized and encumbered that by the time the action took shape it was probably too late for any remedy, including this one.

The French center and rear nevertheless put up a sterner fight than the van, and when the British 74 *Bellerophon* came abreast of Brueys's flagship, the 120-gun *Orient*, the latter's broadside soon dismasted it and sent it drifting from the fight, its decks cluttered with the dead or mangled bodies of about a third of the crew. Nevertheless, the unspoken coordination of Nelson's captains quickly produced a superior concentration against the French center, the *Leander* distinguishing itself by moving into a gap opened when the *Peuple Sourverain* went adrift, so that the 50-gunner could enfilade both the *Orient* and the 74-gun *Franklin*. Moreover, even in the quality on which Brueys had counted heavily—skill in gunnery—Nelson's carefully drilled crews were proving superior to the French. Brueys was killed when he was shot for the third time. The *Orient* caught fire; to avoid the blaze, the next French ship astern, the *Tonnant*, 80, cut its anchor and drifted to leeward. The next two ships, the 74s *Heureux* and *Mercure*, followed this example, and no semblance of a French line remained.

It was now too dark, and most of the British crews were too tired, for much further action. At sunrise the three French ships that had lain behind the *Mercure*, the *Guillaume Tell* of 80 guns under Pierre Charles Jean Baptiste Silverstre Villeneuve, *contre-amiral*, and the 74s *Généreux* and *Timoléon*, got under way to escape. The last of them ran ashore, where her crew set it on fire before abandoning it. The *Zealous*, 74, tried to prevent the escape of the other two, but there was no other British vessel in good condition close enough to provide support, and the flight succeeded; Villeneuve would be heard from again. (He has been criticized for not having led the three serviceable ships of the French rear forward into the action the night before, to inflict whatever redeeming damage he could; but it is doubtful that he could have accomplished more than to add his ships and crews to the casualties.)

The escape of two ships was small consolation to the French. Nelson's exceptional method of command and control had earned its proper reward in one of the most decisive naval battles of all time, for the French fleet was practically destroyed. Except for Villeneuve's ship and its consort (and the frigates, which also got away), every other French vessel was a wreck or a prize.

The battle of the Nile, as the British called it, or of Aboukir, as the French called it, therefore left Bonaparte's Army of the Orient out on a limb severed from the trunk of French power. Nelson's operational and tactical skills had reversed the consequences of faulty British naval strategy. On October 6, Nelson became Baron Nelson of the Nile and Burnham Thorpe in the County of Norfolk.

Mediterranean Anticlimax

Without hope of reinforcement or substantial resupply, Bonaparte nevertheless had to protect himself and his destiny from the possibility of the destruction of his army. When the forces of the Ottoman Empire, the suzerain of Egypt, marched down the eastern Mediterranean coast to suppress him, therefore, the Corsican characteristically seized the initiative, hastening northward into Syria to meet them. He captured El Arish and Jaffa, ordering the execution of the prisoners taken at the latter place because he could not feed or guard them, and on March 17, 1799 (27 Ventôse An VII), he commenced a siege of the historic fortress city of Acre.

But on the preceding day the naval squadron that had still been giving Bonaparte a modicum of support, the surviving French frigates, had been defeated offshore by a British flotilla under Captain William Sidney Smith. The latter naval officer thereupon took charge of the defense of Acre and, animating the Turks, he held Bonaparte at bay until on May 20 (1 Prairial An VII) the French general abandoned the already futile siege. Retreating to Egypt, Bonaparte won a consolation prize in a land battle adjacent to Aboukir Bay, defeating 18,000 Turks with a mere 6,000 French troops on July 25 (7 Thermidor An VII). Under the illusory glory that this victory afforded him, Bonaparte with a tiny naval squadron sailed for France. There, however, the illusion proved so amazingly compelling that in the guise of an Eastern conqueror he was able to propel himself to the position of First Consul and prospective dictator of the French Republic in the coup d'état of the 18 ème Brumaire An VIII (November 9, 1799).

The French Navy of course was too painfully conscious of the outcome of the naval battle of Aboukir to be dazzled in the fashion of the public and of opportunistic politicians. Instead, it strained itself in the months after Brueys's defeat to assemble a fleet that might rescue the Army of Egypt. Nelson had so completely as well as abruptly shifted the Mediterranean naval balance, however, that only small blockade-running vessels could carry supplies to Egypt (or take Bonaparte out). In late April 1799 (Floréal An VII) the French Navy arranged for the British to capture a false dispatch and thereby deceived Admiral Bridport into relaxing the blockade of Brest to chase northward after an imaginary new attack against Ireland. Thereupon, on the 25th of the month (6 Floréal), Eustace Bruix, *vice-amiral*, led twenty-five ships of the line, six frigates, and a few smaller vessels, perhaps the best-outfitted French fleet of the war, out to sea from Brest.

Most of this fleet actually managed to pass Gibraltar and reach Toulon. It helped the enterprise that Admiral St Vincent had gone to Gibraltar for reasons of ill health, leaving the Cádiz blockading squadron in lesser hands, and still more that Nelson, after providing for a blockade of Alexandria, had himself sailed for Naples. In the capital of the Kingdom of the Two Sicilies, moreover, the victor of the Nile met and promptly fell into his notorious infatuation with Emma Lyon, Lady Hamilton, wife of Sir William Hamilton, the British Ambassador to the kingdom. The infatuation was sufficient to cause Nelson to be otherwise occupied when Bruix's squadron found its way to Toulon. It had also helped bring about his involvement in an ill-conceived Neapolitan effort against the French in Rome, which had ended disastrously with the Neapolitan court and the British Ambassador fleeing from the mainland to Palermo in Sicily, where Nelson thought he should remain to protect what was left, not so inciden-

tally continuing in the company of Lady Hamilton. As evidence of his friends'—
or friend's—continued influence at the Sicilian court, however, on August 13,
1799, Nelson became Duke of Brontë in Sicily.

For all that, the Toulon venture became yet another in the long succession
of French naval fizzles. All that Bruix accomplished was to carry reinforcements
and supplies to French troops on the Ligurian coast and to effect a junction at
Cartagena with the Spanish fleet usually based on Cádiz, which had entered the
Mediterranean after Bruix distracted the blockaders. The Spanish, however,
refused to join in an expedition to strengthen the French hold on Egypt. Consequently, there seemed nothing for Bruix to do but to sail back to Brest. Persuading the Spanish to accompany them thither, the French did at least possess
thereafter some insurance against the otherwise strong possibility of Spain's
growing weary of the war; the bulk of the Spanish fleet would lie henceforth
under the guns of French warships and French harbor fortresses.

Ebb and Flow in the Channel

On the day when Bruix reentered Brest, August 13, 1799 (26 Thermidor An VII), the British North Sea Squadron sailed from the Downs escorting a
transport fleet carrying British troops along with soldiers of a recently acquired
ally, Russia. Their purpose was to drive the French from the Netherlands. The
troops began disembarking south of the Helder at dawn on August 27 (10 Fructidor An VII) and initially pushed back the French and Dutch. Thereupon the
naval squadron penetrated the channel between the Helder and Texel Island
and on August 30 received the surrender of the entire remaining Dutch fleet as it
lay at anchor, seven of the line and thirteen smaller vessels; the Dutch sailors
had refused to fight for the Batavian Republic. This elimination of the most
seamanlike of the enemy naval forces went a long way toward compensating for
the embarrassments of the Bruix episode.

Unfortunately for the British, the naval success failed, as had become usual
in continental waters, to find a counterpart on land. Although 40,000 soldiers
were eventually landed in the Netherlands, three-quarters of them British, and
although the Duke of York came over to command them, a march on Amsterdam
was repulsed, and in November the army was evacuated.

Nonetheless, the success of the North Sea Squadron put to shame the
recent ineptitude of the Western Squadron, the main Channel fleet, unable
either to keep Bruix in Brest or to prevent his returning. The obvious solution to
such troubles was to bring to the command of the Royal Navy's most important
fleet its most successful senior admiral. His health at least nominally restored
after a recuperative interval in England, Lord St Vincent consequently hoisted
his flag over the Western Squadron in the spring of 1800. He was apprised that
his arrival had been preceded by seamen's grumblings about the likelihood that
he might restore stern discipline where it had been lacking since the mutinies,
because rigorous discipline had again become a hallmark of his command in the
Mediterranean. Accordingly he reiterated every disciplinary order that had applied in his previous command; he meant to put the mutinies behind indeed, and

to do everything possible to reestablish efficiency. But he also bestirred himself conspicuously to improve the diet and medical care of the fleet, among other things insisting on a regular issue of lemon juice that almost eliminated scurvy. He was to regard his improvement of the health of his sailors as his most important accomplishment.

The reliable transshipment of better rations to the blockading vessels was essential to St Vincent's goal of maintaining his ships at sea and off the enemy's ports more continuously than had any Channel commander since Hawke. In spite of his physician's misgivings, like Hawke he himself stayed at sea with the fleet, restoring Hawke's strategy of the close blackade. Almost at the beginning of his tenure, commencing on the night of May 16–17 (26–27 Floréal An VIII) and lasting through the next day, gale-force winds lashed St Vincent's fleet, partially dismasting several of his capital ships and to some degree injuring all. He established a rendezvous where henceforth the fleet was consistently to seek safe anchorage—at Torbay, a spacious sheltered harbor with an entrance almost four miles (six and a half kilometers) wide, about a hundred miles (160 kilometers) west of Portsmouth and therefore better suited to a quick return to Brest, but easier to reach under the prevailing winds than the yet more westerly port of Falmouth. From Torbay, St Vincent had his fleet patrolling off Ushant again in a matter of days.

When winter came, St Vincent at length felt obliged to heed his doctor's advice and go ashore. Here he turned much of his attention to the dockyards, to make certain that they did their part to keep his ships at sea as continuously as possible, hastening necessary refitting but also attempting to assure that a vessel once refitted ought not to have to return to port soon again.

In February 1801 St Vincent became First Lord of the Admiralty. On the 9th of that month (21 Pluviôse An IX) the Second Coalition against the French fell apart when Austria, which had returned to the fray in spite of the Treaty of Campo Formio only to be defeated badly in Italy again by the returned Bonaparte—now Napoléon, *Empereur* of the French—acceded to the Treaty of Lunéville. But after the naval as well as diplomatic vicissitudes of the past nine years, the presence of St Vincent at the Admiralty meant a new stability at least at sea: he was to establish the most complete British naval supremacy since the Seven Years War, if not to surpass that measure of preeminence. Impressive as were St Vincent's accomplishments in the Mediterranean, his command in the Channel in 1800–1801, albeit without spectacular victories in battle, had proven at least as devastating to the French. The Channel was the pivot on which all European naval power turned.

The Armed Neutrals and the Battle of Copenhagen

St Vincent's reassertion of unrelenting British mastery in the Channel redeemed practically all naval deficiencies elsewhere, except for the problem of the carrying trade of the neutral states, including the Baltic countries and the United States of America. This carrying trade, to the extent that in spite of the Royal Navy it could reach into and replenish Napoleon's dominions, was not sufficient to threaten the balance of the war, but for Britain's commercial prosperity it was important to control as completely as possible such trade with the Continent as London might choose to permit, and to divert as much as possible of the profit of continental trade into British pocketbooks. Such profits in turn helped finance the Royal Navy, the country's allies, and the war in general.

The principles of international law applying to neutral shipping in wartime were highly controversial. The neutrals on the whole endorsed the principle of free ships, free goods so well known in the early diplomatic annals of the United States—that goods carried by neutral ships are neutral goods and not subject to seizure by a belligerent naval power, unless they constitute contraband of war, that is, materials directly useful in waging war. The British sought to undermine the principle of free ships, free goods by asserting the rival legal principle that neutral ships are not entitled to pursue in war avenues of commerce denied to them in peace, for example, the part of the French coastal trade that France ordinarily restricted to its own vessels. Similarly, the neutrals took a restricted view of the sort of goods to be considered contraband of war, the European neutrals in 1800–1801 seeking to exclude naval stores. The British preferred instead to extend the list of contraband goods.

The issues of international law at sea were not unrelated to those involving efforts through international law to curb the violence of war on land. The legal principles championed by the neutrals would have restricted severely the ability of warriors to injure noncombatants, in this instance not only noncombatant individuals but the ships and fleets of noncombatant states. For example, they would have freed neutral vessels under convoy of a neutral warship even from a belligerent's right of search, let alone any right to seize cargo.

Since the late seventeenth century, the steady rise of British sea power had brought an equally steady practical erosion of neutral maritime rights, under the demands of the Royal Navy that it be permitted to restrict maritime traffic that might aid Britain's enemies. To justify their policies the British asserted their own interpretations of international law as well as the claim that their version of belligerent rights was necessary to support a naval ascendancy that was in turn essential to their survival. The neutrals could perceive, however, that another, less elevated form of British self-interest was also involved, as is customary in efforts to erode legal protection for noncombatants. This other form of self-interest was the exploitation of claims of wartime necessity not so much to eliminate all commerce with the enemy as to regulate the commerce in a manner that would turn its profits primarily into the coffers of British merchants.

Late in the War of American Independence, in 1780, Russia, Denmark, and Sweden had formed a League of Armed Neutrality to resist the erosion of neutral maritime rights in the face of British sea power, particularly to insist that neutral ships by definition carried neutral goods and that they might trade in naval stores with Britain's enemies. All the European neutrals of any commercial consequence joined in the effort, and already hard-pressed in the American War, Great Britain yielded concessions to the armed neutrals. Early in the wars of the French Revolution the occasional presence of Russia among the belligerents hampered a repetition of the campaign of armed neutrality; instead, Russia initially acquiesced in British interpretations of maritime law that it had challenged in 1780. When larger setbacks for Russian forces in central Europe along with the souring of the British alliance amidst the sands of Holland produced Russia's defection from the crumbling Second Coalition, however, the government of Tsar Paul (Pavel Petrovich) I was ready to execute a 180-degree turn.

In December 1800 Russia joined with Prussia, Denmark, and Sweden to revive the League of Armed Neutrality. Bonaparte, whose coup d'état of the 18th Brumaire had made him First Consul, was instrumental in inspiring the creation of the new league by playing upon the admiration felt for him by the young Tsar, an admiration that had undermined Russia's place in any anti-French coalition beginning with Paul's accession to the Imperial throne in 1796. On paper, the armed neutrals presented a daunting challenge to the British naval preponderance that was being so stoutly reinforced by Lord St Vincent. While Prussia had no fleet, the Russian Navy counted the extraordinary total of eighty-three ships of the line. The Danes had another twenty-three of the line, the Swedes eighteen.

Fortunately for the British, they could count on more than their usual advantages in seamanship to help offset these numbers. The focus of the contention with the armed neutrals was the Baltic, but the Russian ships were partly at Archangel and partly in the Mediterranean, while twelve of those in the Baltic and fit for service were at the moment immobilized in the ice at Reval. The main Russian strength was at Kronstadt, some thirty-six of the line—the number actually fit for service was not clear—and also for the time being ice-bound. The Swedes had only eleven of their ships of the line actually ready for sea, the Danes seven or eight. The obvious British strategy was a rapid move to strike the neutrals' fleets while they remained divided and incomplete.

The Admiralty therefore hastened into the Baltic a squadron of fifty-three ships, including eighteen of the line. The command went to Vice-Admiral of the Red Sir Hyde Parker, who became a knight bachelor in 1779 as a captain in the American War, particularly by breaking the defenses of the Hudson River in 1776. Parker had shown little enterprise since then, however, displaying indeed a distinct aversion to sea duty and rising in rank largely through the combination of longevity and the demand for senior officers created by the French War. Parker was in every way an odd choice to lead an expedition in which boldness would be at more than its usual military premium. The oddity was compounded by assigning as his second in command the altogether bold hero of the Nile, since January 1, 1801 vice-admiral of the white, Lord Nelson.

Sir Hyde Parker seems to have desired to avoid even so much as a penetration of the Kattegat. According to legend, Nelson won him over to at least that measure of venturesomeness with the gift of an excellent turbot caught while the fleet was passing over the Dogger Bank. That story is probably apocryphal, but the two vice-admirals somehow got along well enough that Nelson helped prod Parker northward through the Kattegat to approach on March 22, 1801, the entrance to the Sound, the narrow, three-mile-wide (five-kilometer) channel between Kronborg Castle, guarding the approach to Copenhagen (Köbenhavn) on the Danish shore, and the city of Helsingborg on the Swedish shore. Reaching this place required in fact no small amount of seamanship as well as resolution, because the time was the worst of the year for approaching the Baltic, and the squadron had had to beat its way against northeasterly winds through fog and snow, its spars and rigging coated with ice.

The British anchored to allow Parker to carry out his orders to serve upon the Danish government an ultimatum to depart the coalition of neutrals within twenty-four hours. Denmark's refusal arrived on the afternoon of March 23. The refusal was accompanied by a disturbing report of vigorous Danish preparations to make Copenhagen impregnable with a combination of ships, forts, and complex coastal geography. Though brushing aside the notion of impregnability, Nelson urged a council of war to bypass Copenhagen and sail directly through the Baltic to meet the Russians, the main enemy. When Parker rejected this proposal on the not inconsequential ground that the Danes and Swedes should not be left to threaten the British rear, and the council broke up in indecision, Nelson composed a forceful written appeal for the next boldest option, an assault on Copenhagen directly through the Sound and past the eastern shore of the island of Zealand (Sjœlland), on which the city stands. This approach would send the British through a narrow passage between Zealand and shoal water and bring them head-on against the principal fortification of Copenhagen, the Trekroner (Three Crown) Battery, as well as against the Danes' strongest ships, stationed at the northern end of the Copenhagen waterfront.

Perhaps Nelson's purpose in suggesting a plan so evidently calculated to alarm a timid superior was to prod Parker at least into some sort of activity, any action being preferable to a continuation of the council of war's indecision. If so, the ploy succeeded, for Parker now agreed to yet another of Nelson's suggestions, that part of the squadron bypass Copenhagen through a relatively wide passage east of the shoal, not to go on to Russia but to turn back against Copenhagen, approaching it from the south where the waterfront was covered by armed hulks and relatively small gun- and bomb-vessels. Nelson said he could subdue the Danes and command the waterfront of their capital if Parker gave him ten of the line for the trip south and thence northward again. The rest of the fleet should support him with a diversionary effort through the Sound. Parker not only agreed but gave Nelson twelve of the line.

Nelson sailed southward on April 1, having transferred his flag from the *St George*, 98, to the *Elephant*, 74, because the operation would carry into waters too shallow for a three-decker. With a favoring southeast wind he went into action against the southern defenses of the city the next morning. The Danes responded with a heavy fire, but the channel is shallow for a considerable distance off the coast of Zealand, and consequently Nelson's ships in large part could not help but stand outside the range of the shore guns. Gradually Nelson prevailed over the hulks and the gun- and bomb-vessels. The leading British ship, the *Defiance*, 74, approached nearly to the Trekroner.

But the same southeasterly wind that favored Nelson prevented Parker from making his diversionary approach from the north. Characteristically fearful that Nelson might therefore be annihilated, Parker dispatched his flag captain, Robert Walter Ottway, to him in a rowboat, with authorization to withdraw if he saw fit. Generously intentioned if hardly resolute, Parker next decided it would be fairer to Nelson if Parker himself took the responsibility of hoisting the signal to discontinue action. The senior admiral did so. Nelson responded by placing his telescope to his blind eye, and of course failed to see the signal. Having thus amused himself and a few officers near him, Nelson in fact acknowledged but otherwise ignored Parker's order. The wind direction also meant, after all, that Nelson's only avenue of retreat would have been to parade his ships straight under the guns of the Trekroner.

For those of Nelson's subordinates who could discern Parker's signal there was nevertheless an awkward dilemma. The young and capable Captain Edward Riou, commanding the frigates, had advanced to the north of the *Defiance;* his vessels were being hard hit, he himself was wounded, and there was no question but that he could see Parker's signal. Reluctantly, he ordered the frigates to obey the senior admiral; as his own frigate, the *Amazon,* 36, turned to proceed toward Parker's squadron, its own guns no longer firing and the vessel no longer shrouded in gunsmoke, the Danes raked it and one of their shots cut Riou in two. But Nelson's battleship captains risked the opposite resolution of the dilemma and remained in action.

Nelson soon judged the time right to try to end the fighting, however, and he addressed to the Danes a message seeking a truce, but threatening to burn the hulks he had taken—without being able to save their crews—if the Danes did not comply. The Danes acquiesced and were referred to Admiral Parker. Nelson took the opportunity of the cease-fire to attempt to withdraw past the Trekroner. The process showed how disastrous this effort would have been under fire; the *Defiance* and Nelson's *Elephant* went aground on shoals (three others of the line had already run aground while going into action). Fortunately, there was no more firing. The armistice stretched into a peace.

The Danish government had been not so much enthusiastic about armed neutrality as pressed by the Russians, and the Danes soon learned that on March 12/24 Tsar Paul I had been assassinated; the new Tsar Alexander (Aleksandr Pavlovich) I was virtually certain to reverse his father's pro-French policy. The motives of the Swedes had been similar to those of the Danes, and they had not and did not send their warships to sea. Nelson and the British squadron set sail for Russia on May 6, but there they were met with a cold civility rather than with further war.

It was Nelson who led the squadron into the Baltic—the three-deckers lightened so they could pass the shoal waters between Zealand and Sweden— because when the British government learned the details of the battle of Copenhagen, it promptly recalled Sir Hyde Parker. (The news of the recall reached the squadron on the afternoon of May 5; it is not surprising that with Nelson in command the ships weighed anchor at next daylight.)

Thanks to Nelson's leadership. Copenhagen is remembered as a sterling exploit of British sea power, but as so often was the case with the achievements of a Hawke, a St Vincent, or Nelson himself, leadership of an exceptionally high order on the part of at least one individual was indispensable if the professional deficiencies of the Royal Navy at large were to be overcome. In the American

War, that kind of exceptional leadership had been lacking until Rodney supplied it at The Saints, too late, and the war had been lost. The war against the second League of Armed Neutrality had been in a fair way to being lost as well, Nelson's skills producing the victory of Copenhagen by an uncomfortably narrow margin. The vacillation and indecision that so much characterized the British Navy's activities around Copenhagen until March 31–April 1, in a situation so obviously demanding swift action before the Russian fleet could escape the ice and the Baltic navies could unite, could have occurred only in a command system where the professional study of military strategy was almost nonexistent. For Parker's council of war to have broken up with no decision whatever at a time when rapid decision was imperative—when almost any action was preferable to no action—is a crushing indictment of the absence of professional military attainments in the Royal Navy's officer corps. Military men schooled in strategy also make mistakes; the chronicles of modern war are filled with them. But it would be hard to find an instance of genuinely professional officers' blundering in so mindlessly egregious a fashion as Sir Hyde Parker's council of war until Nelson asserted himself.

The End of France's Egyptian Adventure

In the Mediterranean, after the departure of St Vincent and during Nelson's distractions, the Royal Navy had to make do without quite possessing one of its most essential remedies for professional deficiencies, that is, individual genius; but by 1801 Rear-Admiral of the Blue Sir James Saumarez, first Baronet Saumarez, afforded a reasonable facsimile.

Meanwhile it did not much matter, because St Vincent and the pre-Naples Nelson had left the French close to maritime bankruptcy in the inland sea. The British clamped Malta under the blockade that could not be impeded by Napoleon's arranging to have Paul I of Russia elected Grand Master of the Knights of Malta, one of the sources of the League of Armed Neutrality. French relief efforts failed to break through the blockade, and on September 5, 1800 (18 Fructidor An VIII), a starving French garrison surrendered Malta to the British.

More ambitious French efforts to relieve the Army of Egypt met no better success, while in 1801 the British sent 18,000 troops to Egypt and arranged to cooperate with the Turks. Bonaparte launched a last attempt to retrieve his Oriental adventure on June 13, 1801 (24 Prairial An IX), when three French sail of the line ventured from Toulon to join a Spanish squadron at Cádiz for a joint relief expedition to Egypt. Learning that Saumarez was cruising off Cádiz with a superior British squadron, the French put into the Bay of Gibraltar and anchored off Algeçiras. Contrary winds cost Saumarez an initial repulse and a partially damaged squadron when he entered the bay on July 6 (17 Messidor); but after the Spanish Cádiz squadron took advantage of the injuries to his ships to join the French and then sail back in their company toward Cádiz, Saumarez attacked again on the night of July 12–13 (23–24 Messidor), notwithstanding uncompleted repairs and odds of four British ships of the line against four French (the *Saint-Antoine*, 74, having come with the Spanish) and four Spanish. In the ensuing battle, two of the Spanish battleships caught fire and blew up, partly because they had been shooting at each other, and the *Saint-Antoine* surrendered. Saumarez's victory assured the gradual surrender of the French troops in Egypt, a process completed by October 1801 (Vendémiaire An X).

Nelson and the Preliminaries to Trafalgar

Nelson returned from the Baltic to land at Yarmouth on July 1, 1801. In England he displayed an admirable consideration for the feelings of Sir Hyde Parker, going out of his way to avoid public airings of the Copenhagen events that might embarrass his former chief, as well as conciliating him personally; but Parker got no reward for Copenhagen, while Nelson learned that on May 22 he had been elevated to a viscountcy. The new viscount also returned, however, to another less than glorious interval, a renewal of the infatuation with Lady Hamilton and a frustratingly dull command, a squadron of thirty vessels, frigates and gunboats, charged with watching the coast from Beachy Head to Orfordness against a threat of French invasion. Beginning March 3 (12 Ventôse An IX), Bonaparte had been busily assembling flat-bottomed boats at Boulogne, apparently to convey a *Grande Armée* across the Channel against his last remaining active enemy.

Nelson was thoroughly bored, and to break the tedium and in part perhaps out of jealousy of the latest hero, Saumarez, with whom his relations had not been notably cordial, he led some of his vessels over to Boulogne on August 1 (13 Thermidor)—the anniversary of the Nile—to have a look at the French preparations and to destroy some flatboats if possible. He expended a few lives and a good deal of mortar ammunition in learning that Boulogne was well defended, which makes it exceedingly difficult to understand why he ventured a similar but more ambitious crossing on the night of August 15–16 (27–28 Thermidor). He led a reinforced flotilla of seventy boats in four divisions, of which one division never arrived and the other three were repulsed without any gain, at a cost of forty-four dead and 128 wounded.

This lapse into futility is all the more puzzling because it had long been apparent to the British—and certainly should have been to Nelson after August 1—that Bonaparte was merely trying to apply diplomatic pressure, while entertaining no serious thoughts of invasion. With the Second Coalition dead, even Great Britain was ready to try the experiment of peaceful coexistence with a Napoleonic Europe. An armistice was signed in London on October 1 (9 Vendémiaire An IX), preparing the way for the Peace of Amiens of March 27, 1802 (6 Germinal An X). British sea power and French land power had reached a kind of stand-off—albeit one reflecting the limitations of sea power employed against an adversary who commands continental resources, for Napoleon dominated most of Europe.

On reflection and with accumulating experience of the implications, Great Britain found this result to be not one with which it was prepared to coexist indefinitely. Although British purposes were vague, because London was nevertheless unprepared to compensate for the limitations of sea power in the only effective military fashion, by mobilizing a formidable army, the British drifted toward renewed war against France. The struggle officially resumed on May 16, 1803 (26 Floréal An IX).

Thereupon Bonaparte resumed his boat-collecting endeavors at Boulogne in much greater earnest. Previously some 240 invasion craft had been assembled. The Emperor—for as such Napoleon was crowned on December 2, 1804 (11 Frimaire An XII under the republican calendar that the new regime soon disposed of, on 10 Nivôse An XIV—January 1, 1806)—in slightly more than two years after the resumption of hostilities collected some ten times that number of boats. They continued to be flat-bottomed craft capable of being rowed to the English coast, though many were ship- or brig-rigged. Yet-stronger batteries than those that Nelson had met in 1801 covered the transit of the vessels to Boulogne and their assembly there, where the harbor was too shallow to permit British battleships or even frigates to enter and assail them. By the summer of 1805, Napoleon's Grand Army mustered some 130,000 troops encamped around Boulogne and ready for the invasion.

It would require two tides for the transport flotilla to emerge into the Channel. Because no interval of calm was likely to last that long to immobilize the British fleet, the French Navy would have to be concentrated to escort the Channel crossings. Such concentration would require bringing together at least most of the warships scattered from Brest through L'Orient, Rochefort, El Ferrol, and Cádiz to Toulon. From late 1804 Napoleon would also include the Spanish fleet in his reckonings; after the resumption of war, Spain had made monthly payments to the Emperor for the privilege of remaining neutral, but the British had retaliated for those payments by seizing Spanish treasure ships from the New World, whereupon Spain declared war against Great Britain on December 12, 1804.

Napoleon's ingenuity when applied to the problem of concentrating his warships produced a series of schemes each more complex than the last. Here was a sure sign that in confronting a maritime venture the Emperor felt himself at sea in more ways than one, because a usual hallmark of his military genius on land was an essential simplicity, which merely appeared complex in the eyes of befuddled opponents. The subsequent French naval operations were conducted throughout with an amateurish ineptitude that Napoleon would never have tolerated on land, and that amply redeemed the British Navy's own shortcomings in professionalism of command.

The Napoleonic scheme that was actually set in motion began with Vice-Admiral Villeneuve sailing from Toulon on March 30, 1805 (9 Germinal An XIII). Villeneuve commanded eleven ships of the line, with which he was to proceed to Cádiz, there to pick up the *Aigle*, 74, which the vicissitudes of war had carried to the Spanish port, along with any Spanish ships fit for sea and campaign. Thence he was to hasten to, of all places, Martinique in the West Indies; strategic complexity was about to run riot.

As he had done earlier in the year, Villeneuve succeeded readily enough in getting out of Toulon; the British blockade there was now commanded by Nelson, whose policy it was to allow the French to emerge so that they might be brought to battle and eliminated. Villenueve made first for Cartagena, hoping to pick up a Spanish squadron there; but the Spaniards refused to join him. The winds favored the French, however, even if some Spanish did not, and from Cartagena Villeneuve found smooth sailing to Cádiz. There he did acquire the reinforcement of six Spanish battleships as well as the *Aigle*. The British block-aders of Cádiz had to move aside because they were only four of the line; Nelson had heard rumors of another French attempt upon Egypt, and procrastinating while he investigated this news—he seems to have been almost as awestruck as Napoleon by the visions conjured up by the Orient—he did not learn until April 18 that Villeneuve had passed through the Strait of Gibraltar. By that time the French admiral had already sailed from Cádiz for Martinique, departing on April 11 (21 Germinal).

Five French ships of the line were already in the West Indies, as a result of one of Napoleon's earlier naval schemes. The French hoped that Villeneuve might pick them up at Martinique, and there he was to wait for forty days for Honoré Gantéaume, *vice-amiral*, with the Brest fleet of some twenty of the line. Thus most of the French Navy along with some Spanish warships would be brought together, albeit suffering the wear and tear of a trans-Atlantic voyage, upon which event Gantéaume was to command another trans-Atlantic voyage, eastbound to the Channel and the invasion of England.

One difficulty in the way of this design was that Gantéaume was expected to get away from Brest for the West Indies without fighting. Yet off Brest the British again maintained a close blockade in the manner of Hawke and St Vincent, so that a French escape depended on an easterly wind strong enough to blow the British away. No such wind developed within the requisite time period. Nevertheless, the French missed an opportunity. On March 24 (3 Germinal) Gantéaume informed Napoleon that the blockading squadron off Brest had fallen to fifteen of the line, so that he could come out with superior numbers and a fighting chance; but the Emperor forbade it.

Villeneuve's progress to the West Indies was slow, because his Spanish vessels proved to be poor sailors, four of them dropping out of sight and rejoining him only at his destination, while many of his French ships and crews, too long ashore, were not much better. The problem of his fleet in bearing up through the ocean crossing underlined the dubiety of Napoleon's latest concentration plan. In the process, Villeneuve expressed many complaints about the unreadiness of his ships and men for serious work, but he effected little improvement.

Arriving at Fort de France on Martinique on May 14 (24 Floréal An XIII), Villeneuve did not find the five of the line that had preceded him to the West Indies. Those ships had in fact sailed for France after a profitable round of commerce-raiding (an activity that Villeneuve neglected despite arousing much fear about his intentions among the British). The five returning ships put in to Rochefort six days after Villeneuve's entry into Fort de France; French coordination was breaking down everywhere. On June 1 (12 Prairial), however, Villeneuve did encounter two battleships recently departed from Rochefort. They brought him fresh orders to wait thirty days for Gantéaume—more time wasted when the good weather for an invasion of England was fast slipping away. If the Brest fleet did not arrive after thirty days Villeneuve was to sail for Ferrol, join with a batch of French and Spanish vessels still lingering there, and then himself proceed to Brest to drive off the blockaders so Gantéaume could come out. From auxiliary to the Brest fleet, Villeneuve's ships were now turned into the main force.

Three more days—to June 4—and Nelson was also in the West Indies, at Barbados. On learning of Villeneuve's passage through Gibraltar and that he was bound for the West Indies, the commander of the British Mediterranean Squadron had decided without orders to take ten ships of the line in pursuit of the French to the New World. Nelson's motives probably included consideration of the economic importance that the sugar islands retained from the eighteenth century and fear that Villeneuve might plunder those flying the British flag, along with—more importantly—the belief that sound anti-invasion strategy called for bringing Villeneuve's fleet to battle, and that he himself was the best man to lead in the battle. Unfortunately, Nelson's unauthorized departure from the Mediterranean threw the British Admiralty into almost as much disarray as the French. For a while no one knew where Nelson had gone. In its ignorance the Admiralty dispatched Vice-Admiral of the Blue Cuthbert Collingwood with twelve of the line to follow Villeneuve to the West Indies, and it was only through a chance encounter with other British warships that Collingwood learned where Nelson had gone and decided himself to take station off Cádiz. Here he covered the entrance of the Mediterranean and ensured that the enemy's Cartagena squadron would remain separate from the rest.

Making Nelson's unauthorized trans-Atlantic voyage a still more questionable venture was the fact that, as he himself lamented, his vessels had been at sea for an average of two years and badly needed refitting, which meant that with Villeneuve's head start the chances of Nelson's forcing the battle he wished were not brilliant. Nevertheless, British seamanship permitted Nelson to make the ocean crossing in twenty-four days while Villeneuve's main body had consumed thirty-four. Thus although Villeneuve's most recent orders also enjoined him to attack British islands, as Nelson feared he might, the French admiral never had a chance to put this belated part of his instructions into effect. Instead, Villeneuve upon capturing a British convoy heard of Nelson's presence at Barbados as early as June 8 (19 Prairial) and decided to make for Ferrol forthwith. He had fought at Aboukir and therefore knew Nelson too well; dissatisfied with his own ships and men, he had no desire to loiter in accordance with his orders and to end up once more fighting the victor of the Nile.

Nelson probably could have forced a battle anyway had not faulty intelligence passed on by the army sent him chasing toward Tobago and Trinidad, which Villeneuve was supposed to have attacked. The island garrisons thereupon mistook Nelson's fleet for the expected French assailants, so that a battle between friends was narrowly averted. In a mood of surpassing disgust at bungling colleagues as well as bitter disappointment, Nelson decided that Villeneuve must have departed for France, so the British turned eastward from Antigua for Gibraltar on June 13. Nelson assumed that Villeneuve was probably bound for Toulon, but the vessel that he sent toward England with his dispatches for the Admiralty, the sloop-brig, *Curieux*, 18, sighted Villeneuve on June

19 making for the Bay of Biscay. This news, hastened to the recently appointed First Lord of the Admiralty, Admiral Lord Barham, in itself went far toward elevating Nelson's somewhat frenzied round trip into something more than a wild goose chase.

Barham at the Admiralty: A New Direction for Naval Strategy

Lord St Vincent had made the mistake of carrying his zeal for rigorous performance of duty into the business of timber contracts for the Admiralty, whereby he had trespassed upon an ancient domain of privileged corruption and obliged the King's First Minister, William Pitt, to remove him as First Lord of the Admiralty. The removal had been easier because in fact St Vincent's passion for reform had overridden his preparation of the navy for the resumption of war and delayed the latter. Unluckily, Pitt chose as St Vincent's successor Henry Dundas Melville, first Viscount Melville and first Baron Dunira. Melville seemed at an initial glance an excellent choice, because he had been elevated to the peerage in 1802 after service as Treasurer of the Navy from 1782 to 1800, a post that he had surely held long enough to learn almost everything there was to know about the inside of naval administration. But a cloud that had already begun to form over Melville's head with the formation of a Committee of Naval Enquiry burst forth presently in revelations of his mishandling of funds while he was Treasurer. To patch up the mess, Pitt had Sir Charles Middleton enobled and brought in as what many considered a mere stopgap First Lord, since Barham was nearly eighty years old and furthermore a Methodist without most of the customary family and social connections.

Instead of a stopgap, Barham proved one of the great Admiralty Lords of British history. Like Melville, he possessed a vast experience of naval affairs. He had been a captain when Nelson was an infant. He had become Comptroller of the Navy in 1778 (succeeding Captain Sir Maurice Suckling, whose one distinguished service had been to bring into the navy his nephew Horatio Nelson). As Comptroller, Middleton had done more than any other individual to rescue the navy from the doldrums into which it had fallen by the early years of the War of American Independence. He was a businessman as well as a sailor, and in fact he was already connected with the Dundas family of Scots shipbuilding contractors from which Lord Melville and his scandals had sprung. But while grasping—if not necessarily for great personal wealth at least for security, influence, and power—Middleton was also decidedly efficient.

An indefatigable worker, he reformed naval administration through centralization, even overcentralization, in the Comptroller's office. The Navy Board, which had hitherto arrogated to itself increasingly centralized power—especially over the dockyard contracts and their profits—was pushed and goaded by Middleton to act swiftly and thereby as much as possible to do his will rather than its own, not simply because of the board's own corruption but because Middleton deplored its lack of professionalism. He wanted the Admiralty and particularly the First Lord to ride herd on the Navy Board and overrule the autonomy of its decision-making powers in order to create a cohesive administration with something approaching professional standards in everything from ship architecture to formulating strategy for war. He was, in the words of Piers Mackesy, distinguished historian of military administration and strategy during the War of American Independence, "a forerunner of the administrators who were soon to turn the archaic racket called government into the efficient instrument which transformed Victorian England."[1] Whatever his age upon becoming First Lord, such a man could hardly confine himself to minimalist expectations for his tenure.

Becoming First Lord, however, Barham chose to subordinate his earlier principal emphasis upon administrative efficiency, even his earlier advocacy of the First Lord's inserting his fingers into every pie, to free himself from day-to-day detail so that he might concentrate on strategy. How to reconcile the conflicting demands of administration and strategy is a perennial dilemma of the wartime military administrator. Barham's choice ran counter to most of the earlier direction of his career, but it was the obvious right choice for the time of crisis of the invasion threat and the naval war.

Barham had learned on April 25 that Villeneuve was west of Gibraltar and that the blockade of Cádiz had been raised. Promptly he sent out prescient orders for the reinforcement of the blockading squadron off Ferrol but also for a host of possible contingencies, strengthening the Western Squadron and providing if necessary for the withdrawal of the Ferrol and Cádiz squadrons to reinforce the Channel. On July 9 Barham learned of the midocean sighting of Villeneuve's fleet eastward-bound for the Bay of Biscay. With Villeneuve's slow ships still surely at sea, Barham ordered the Ferrol squadron to station itself so as to intercept. He had not thought himself able to reinforce that squadron above fifteen of the line, however, and with its various accretions Villeneue's Combined Fleet now had twenty of the line. In a confused action off Cape Finisterre fought in a fog on July 22 (3 Thermidor An XIII), Villeneuve lost two of his Spanish battleships, but the next day he was able to break free, to put into Vigo Bay on July 28. Barham's careful planning and direction had temporarily misfired, but the old sailor remained indefatigable still.

Nelson reached Gibraltar on the day of the battle off Finisterre but of course could do nothing about it. Villeneuve was nevertheless utterly discouraged. He reported to Paris that he had at least 800 sick and that everything capable of going wrong was doing so. He retained enough enterprise that on July 29 (10 Thermidor) he made his way to Ferrol, leaving behind two of the slow Spanish ships and the *Atlas,* 74, which had been badly damaged, but by uniting at last with the Ferrol ships concentrating eighteen French and eleven Spanish sail of the line. Still, Villeneuve's dispatches dripped so many tears and complaints that Napoleon should have removed him rather than place any further reliance on him in behalf of the great invasion.

Instead, the Emperor had sent him further orders, which reached him off

1. Piers MacKesy, *The War for America, 1775–1783* (Cambridge, Mass.: Harvard University Press, 1965), p. 164.

Ferrol, not to enter that port because it was difficult of egress but to call out the warships in it and then to make for Rochefort. There he was to effect his long-delayed junction with the five of the line that had preceded him to and from the West Indies, and thence he was to set sail for the Channel to frighten the British into maneuvers that would spring free the Brest squadron. If there should occur some unforeseeable misfortune, Villeneuve was authorized to fall back on Cádiz, to join with the Spanish ships still there. But the Emperor anticipated nothing of the sort; instead he exhorted Villeneuve to hasten boldly to the Channel and win control of it for three days or even one, so the Grand Army could proceed finally to the invasion on which all the history of Europe would turn.

Villeneuve, however, was not the man to be inspired by such exhortations coming from so formidable a source. Rather, they frightened him and deepened his mood of depression. To carry the fate of Europe on his shoulders appalled him. Nevertheless, he put in to Corunna (La Coruña), across the Rio de Betanzos from El Ferrol, and displayed apparent energy and resolution in ready-ing his ships for sea. He put out on August 15 (27 Thermidor An XIII). On August 22 (3 Fructidor An XIII) Napoleon received the news that Villeneuve had sailed for the Channel. The Emperor immediately ordered Gantéaume in Brest to be ready to depart to join Villeneuve without losing a day, and he exhorted Villeneuve again to plunge swiftly and boldly into the Channel with the united squadrons.

Napoleon all the more enjoined swiftness and boldness because new factors caused time to press increasingly hard upon him. Pitt had been busy attempting to build a Third Coalition with too much success for the Emperor's comfort. Napoleon had developed a hobby of busily rearranging the map of Italy, espe-cially for the benefit of his relatives, and thereby stirred anew the distrust that both Austria and Russia felt for upstart revolutionaries. Tsar Alexander I was especially troubled by Napoleon's high-handed arrest of Louis Antoine Henri de Bourbon-Condé, duc d'Enghien, in neutral Baden on March 15, 1804 (25 Ventôse An XII), and by the Duke's subsequent trial for treason, without benefit of defense counsel, and his execution. Both the Habsburg Emperor and the Tsar were mobilizing their forces. If Napoleon could invade England now, there ought still to be time to dispose of the island kingdom's little army quickly enough to negate fears of what the Eastern princes might do in the meantime. But the hours were growing precious, as Napoleon stood on the high ground above Boulogne with his eyes fixed on the horizon of the western Channel, watching for French mastheads.

And Villeneuve did not appear. Oppressed both by his responsibilities and his distrust of the quality of his French ships—to say nothing of the torpid Spanish—Villeneuve seized upon the discretionary orders with which Napoleon should never have favored him. When Villeneuve set sail on August 15, his actual destination proved to be not the Channel but Cádiz.

When he learned the truth about Villeneuve at the end of August, Napo-leon indulged himself in a momentary outburst of fury, then immediately or-dered the disbanding of the invasion flotilla at Boulogne and a march of the Grand Army toward Austria. The uncharacteristic hesitancies and overcomplexity of his strategic judgment when he faced toward the sea had combined with the deficiencies of his navy and its commanders and the solidity of the Royal Navy to save England.

But the naval war was not over. The Brest fleet began to receive orders to break up into divisions that would harry British colonies and trade. Villeneuve was to lead the Combined Fleet into the Mediterranean to cooperate there with the overland attacks against Austria. And Lord Barham, at the center of an unaccustomed coherence in British naval strategy, still hoped to maneuver his own squadrons in a manner that would eliminate Napoleon's maritime strength for good and all.

Trafalgar

The news that Villeneuve's Combined Fleet had put into Cádiz reached England on September 1. Barham immediately resolved to concentrate all available force there to make possible an annihilating blow, and to put in command the hero of the hour, who had returned on August 18 to be feted as though he had just won another great victory: Nelson. Whatever the real merits of that admiral's trans-Atlantic chases that lay behind this applause—and Nelson had surely helped generate Villeneuve's fatal mood of despondence—the victor of the Nile and Copenhagen was undoubtedly the most likely architect of the kind of destructive battle for which Barham hoped.

Admiral Collingwood with three ships of the line was watching Cádiz when Villeneuve's Combined Fleet arrived there on August 20 (2 Fructidor). Collingwood stood away in the face of Villeneuve's superior force, but he was determined not to be drawn into the Mediterranean unless he drew the Allies in with him, and at this moment they were unwilling to pursue so far. Villeneuve was now 2,000 men short—1,700 sick, 300 deserters—and he still found much to complain about in the condition of his ships. He took his whole fleet into Cádiz, and Collingwood promptly resumed his station offshore. Barham had arranged for his swift reinforcement, and by August 30 he had twenty-seven ships of the line. Those already in Cádiz added to the existing Combined Fleet gave Villeneuve thirty-three that were serviceable. Nelson arrived on September 28 (6 Vendémiaire An XIV) with three more of the line, headed by his flagship *Victory*. The next day happened to be Nelson's forty-seventh birthday.

It was on September 17 (27 Fructidor An XIII) that Napoleon had dispatched his latest orders for Villeneuve, to enter the Mediterranean in support of the forthcoming continental campaign. The admiral received the orders on the day of Nelson's arrival—which latter was an event unknown to him, because Nelson had carefully sent word ahead that there should be no salutes fired or other advertisements of his coming. Even without awareness of the presence of his old nemesis of Aboukir Bay and the trans-Atlantic crossings, Villeneuve sought to procrastinate over putting to sea. But Napoleon's orders were categorical, and a Franco-Spanish council of war convened by Villeneuve on October 5 (13 Vendémiaire) concluded unhappily that there was nothing to do but essay a sortie. Unfavorable winds dictated further delay until October 14, and even then

Villeneuve continued to mark time until the 18th, when he received word that the Emperor had at last decided to relieve him from command. The mortification proved enough to propel him into action before a successor could arrive. A light land breeze helped the Combined Fleet to make its way out of the harbor on October 19 (27 Venémiaire).

Between various reinforcements and detachments, Nelson's fleet now numbered thirty-two of the line, but four of them that had been maintaining a close-in blockade of Cádiz until October 7 had had to sail to Gibraltar to renew provisions and water and had not yet returned when Villeneuve sailed, while the *Prince of Wales*, 74, had gone off to a court-martial. Thus Nelson had twenty-seven ships of the line, while Villeneuve brought out his thirty-three.

With his inshore squadron gone except for two frigates, Nelson was some thirty miles or fifty-six kilometers west of Cádiz harbor and could not close upon the enemy immediately. By October 20 the Allied ships were all clear of the harbor and proceeding southward toward Gibraltar in five squadrons, three nearer the land than the other two, Villeneuve in direct command of the center landward squadron. Teniente-General Don Federico Gravina, the senior Spanish officer present and decidedly several cuts above the usual run of Spanish sailors (rumored to be an illegitimate son of the late King Carlos III), led the forward westerly division from the flag cabin of the largest ship in the world, the so-called four-decker *Santissima Trinidad* of 130 guns. The winds, now westerly, grew very light and continued so into the night of October 20–21; when the British fleet approached and as the rival forces began jockeying for position, some of the slower Allied vessels began to straggle. By the morning of October 21 the breeze was so light that only the most expert crews could maneuver effectively, a decided bonus for the British. At dawn, the Combined Fleet was about twelve miles (twenty-two kilometers) off Cape Trafalgar, the British some ten to twelve miles—nineteen to twenty-two kilometers—farther west.

Nelson had set forth his plans in a memorandum of October 5. He had assumed that Villeneuve would come out on a strong easterly wind, giving the Combined Fleet the weather gauge, and that the rival fleets might have been greatly reinforced, to some fifty French and Spanish and forty British. Nevertheless, the principal features of the memorandum remained applicable; Nelson planned for the unpredictable. The line ahead was of course in the discard. The British fleet was to form up in the order in which its ships lay when the enemy was sighted, losing no time in closing and in particular not delaying to form a precise line. The fleet was to attack in two divisions, Nelson's second in command, Collingwood in *Royal Sovereign*, 100, assailing the Allied rear while Nelson hit the center and van and assured that no help reached rearward enemy ships that were cut off. With the Combined Fleet broken into at least two parts, the British would seek to concentrate superior force against inferior enemy divisions. But Nelson noted that chance would do much to shape the outcome, and he urged his captains above all to place their ships alongside the enemy's and then to fight.

The British were confidently ready to do that very thing. They were impatient over their recent inability to bring the enemy to decisive battle, and from

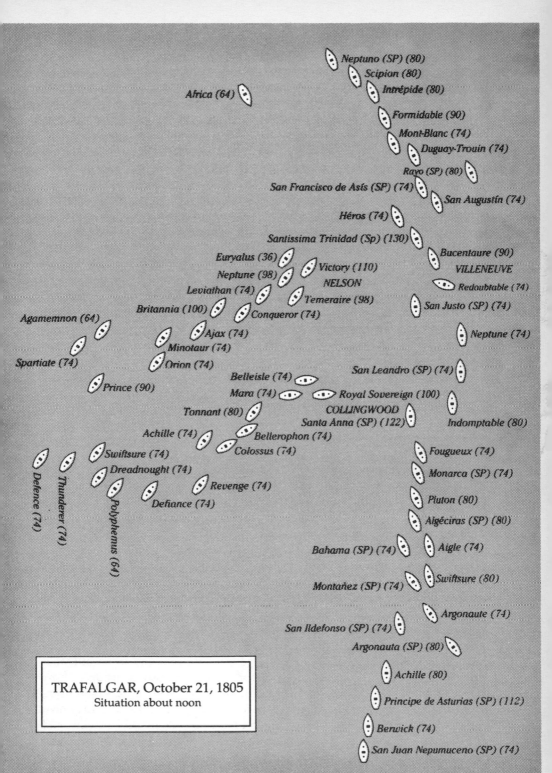

Neptuno (SP) (80)
Scipion (80)
Intrépide (80)
Formidable (90)
Mont-Blanc (74)
Duguay-Trouin (74)
Rayo (SP) (80)
San Augustín (74)
San Francisco de Asís (SP) (74)
Héros (74)
Santissima Trinidad (Sp) (130)
Bucentaure (90)
VILLENEUVE
Africa (64)
Euryalus (36)
Victory (110)
Neptune (98)
NELSON
Redoubtable (74)
Leviathan (74)
Temeraire (98)
San Justo (SP) (74)
Britannia (100)
Conqueror (74)
Ajax (74)
Neptune (74)
Agamemnon (64)
Minotaur (74)
Spartiate (74)
Orion (74)
San Leandro (SP) (74)
Prince (90)
Belleisle (74)
Mara (74)
Royal Sovereign (100)
Tonnant (80)
COLLINGWOOD
Santa Anna (SP) (122)
Indomptable (80)
Achille (74)
Bellerophon (74)
Swiftsure (74)
Colossus (74)
Fougueux (74)
Dreadnought (74)
Monarca (SP) (74)
Revenge (74)
Pluton (80)
Defiance (74)
Algéciras (SP) (80)
Defence (74)
Thunderer (74)
Polyphemus (64)
Bahama (SP) (74)
Aigle (74)
Montañez (SP) (74)
Swiftsure (80)
Argonaute (74)
San Ildefonso (SP) (74)
Argonauta (SP) (80)
Achille (80)
Principe de Asturias (SP) (112)
Berwick (74)
San Juan Nepumuceno (SP) (74)

TRAFALGAR, October 21, 1805
Situation about noon

Barham in Whitehall to the seamen of the fleet they believed that one more battle properly fought ought to finish the naval war. Under Collingwood, a somewhat dour if brave commander, the fleet had not been altogether a happy one; but Nelson had always been a charismatic leader, and the memories of the Nile, Copenhagen, and the swift long chase across the Atlantic naturally enhanced his magnetism. In tribute to him (but without necessarily revealing his position to the enemy), most of his ships had been repainted since his arrival in the style of the Mediterranean squadrons with which he had won his fame, black hulls with a yellow band along each tier of gunports, but with black port-lids to create a checkerboard effect.

Villeneuve knew well enough that Nelson would not attack in the old line-ahead fashion. The British would concentrate on part of his line and try to break it. Villeneuve was sufficiently shrewd to surmise, in fact, that Nelson would probably try to cut off his rear. But the French admiral also knew that his captains and seamen did not have the ability to sail with the British expertly enough to counter Nelson's moves, especially in the light winds of this autumn morning. When he was sure the British fleet would force a battle, he turned his ships back toward Cádiz. Villeneuve had been able to devise no better riposte to Nelson's expected assault toward his rear than to remind his captains to be ready for the standard French signal for any ship not engaged with an enemy to go into action by the quickest possible means, and to remind them also that in the confusion of combat they should not await signals from the admiral but take initiatives themselves. Though defensive, these latter orders were not otherwise so different from Nelson's; it was the quality of the seamen that differed decisively.

Villeneuve's order to turn was given at six in the morning but not completed until about ten. By that time the French and Spanish ships were formed in a straggling line, concave toward the enemy, about five miles (nine kilometers) long, with their ships in some places two or even three more or less abreast. This latter grouping would tend toward their advantage when the British closed in, by permitting the guns of more than one Allied ship to bear on single British vessels as they sought to penetrate the line. Nevertheless, the British converged on them confidently. Nelson when he saw the Allies turn back northward, about 7:00 A.M., had signaled to bear up on them. There has been debate about whether he intended his ships to bear up together, in line abreast, or in succession, in line ahead; but the debate matters little because his own and Collingwood's flagships were swift vessels, and they naturally led the way as two lines took shape sailing north of east. Nelson, to the westward and windward when the maneuver began, sailed to the north or left and windward, while Collingwood, to the right and leeward at the beginning of the maneuver, sailed to the south and leeward. But behind *Victory* and *Royal Sovereign* the British became two sword-thrusts aimed at the Combined Fleet.

Because the southern end of the concave Allied formation bent westward, Collingwood in the *Royal Sovereign* penetrated it first, about noon. Other ships of his division came into action close behind him. Nelson for a time sailed as if aiming for the Allied van, in order to discourage it from turning yet again to assist the others, but then he bore down on the enemy line astern of Villeneuve's flagship, the *Bucentaire,* 100. About 12:30 the *Victory* gave the *Bucentaire* a raking broadside, but Nelson was unable to penetrate the enemy line because the French *Redoubtable,* 74, following behind *Bucentaire,* closed tightly upon the Allied flagship. The *Victory* collided with the *Redoubtable,* and these two ships, grappled together, drifted to leeward, opening a gap in the Allied line through which the British ships that had been following Nelson could pass. Although the *Victory's* cannon were soon tearing apart the *Redoubtable's* hull, the musketry from the French ship almost cleared the *Victory's* upper deck and mortally wounded Lord Nelson. Through a series of pathetic and romantic dialogues with admiring subordinates, he lingered until about 4:30 P.M., when he received the news that his fleet had won the day, and he died.

The battle had become a melee, a result not inconsistent with either Nelson's or Villeneuve's orders, but working to the advantage of the British in spite of the initial grouping of many of the Allies in twos and threes. For in fact it was the British whose skills permitted their ships to work well enough together that they ended up fighting frequently in pairs against enemy vessels now reduced to fighting singly. In the rear, British ships were soon breaking through multiple gaps in the Allied line, while others passed astern of it and engaged from leeward. Of the Allied rear division of nine French and nine Spanish battleships—from the Spaniard *Santa Anna,* 122, southward—six Spanish and five French ships struck their colors, while another Frenchman, *Achille,* 80, did not surrender but had part of its crew rescued by the British after it had become a helpless, sinking wreck. The Allied van had made a tentative gesture toward turning into the action but had then gone on its way to escape to Cádiz. Altogether the Allies lost one ship of the line sunk and seventeen captured, including the *Bucentaire* and the *Santissima Trinidad.* With all his flagship's masts gone, Villeneuve had ordered a boat so he could shift his flag but found there was no boat to be had, and he surrendered about the same time that Nelson died.

In a British fleet already appalled in spite of victory by Nelson's death, the immediate aftermath of Trafalgar was bitter anticlimax. A southwest breeze had come up more and more briskly during the day, and by evening it had swelled into a gale. The British lost their tow on several of their prizes, and aboard the *Bucentaire* and the *Algéçiras,* 80, the French survivors threatened to overwhelm the prize crews, whereupon agreements were reached for British and French seamen together to try to take the ships into Cádiz for mutual safety, with the understanding that the prize crews would not be held as prisoners. The *Algéçiras* reached the roadstead, but the *Bucentaire* was wrecked off Punte San Sebastian at the south end of the harbor; the French ship *Indomptable,* 80, rescued many seamen of both nationalities but was then itself wrecked with heavy casualties among all aboard. Four other captured vessels were beached after their tows were cut off; two others, including the *Santissima Trinidad,* sank; the British destroyed three more; another two, *Santa Anna* and *Neptune,* 80, were recaptured by an Allied sortie two days after the battle, but *Neptune* became yet another victim of the terrible postbattle storm. Thus only four Allied ships were carried as prizes into Gibraltar.

Sixteen ships of the victorious fleet were so badly damaged that they had to be sent home; the British reported 1,690 killed and wounded. With the Royal Navy's foremost admiral among that number, Trafalgar was anything but a cheap or easy triumph. But the Allies must have lost over 5,000, with French casualties not reported but with the Spanish reporting over 2,400; the *Redoubtable* alone lost 491 killed and 81 wounded out of a crew of less than 600. Immediate disappointments aside, Trafalgar was the decisive battle that Barham and Nelson had sought. The climax of so long a series of British naval victories and French defeats, it assured that Napoleon would not revive his invasion project and gave the Royal Navy an undisputed command of the seas that endured through all the rest of the Napoleonic Wars.

Nelson and Command at Sea

The melee of Trafalgar was also the culmination of certain of the main tendencies in the evolution of naval command and thus of professional naval officership in the age of sail. The line ahead as the cynosure of naval battle tactics had been a response both to the limitations of naval officers' military professionalism and the consequent dangers of entrusting them with initiatives, and to the much more specific difficulty of the fleet or squadron commander's retaining control over his ships in the midst of action, when the smoke of battle made communication by signal flags uncertain at best and frequently impossible, even with the stationing of repeating frigates abreast of flagships but far enough removed that they might duplicate signals without being enveloped in smoke. But the line ahead had mitigated problems of command and control at the cost of tactical stalemate, and therefore aggressive admirals had since the middle of the eighteenth century more and more frequently abandoned it, risking a deterioration of command and control over their battle for the sake of restoring decision to battle and thus to naval war. By the time of Trafalgar, both rival commanders took it for granted that there would be no stately processions of opposing ships in line exchanging broadsides with their opposite numbers. Nelson and Villeneuve alike issued orders contemplating a melee.

Yet Nelson had also shown a consistent concern for the problems of command, communication, and control, the C³ of late-twentieth-century military discourse. The occasional spillover of his erratic personal qualities into his naval conduct notwithstanding, he was as professional an officer as eighteenth- and early-nineteenth-century navies could display, self-taught by experience, study, and reflection so that he was far more than a superb seaman: he was a tactician and strategist as well, of attainments that any more systematically educated military officer of a later time could envy. He had as complete a grasp as any theoretically educated naval strategist of the value of the decisive battle, the battle if possible of virtual annihilation of the enemy, not as an end in itself but as an instrument of diplomacy (witness Copenhagen and its effects upon the armed neutrals) and of the struggle to exert economic pressure on the enemy. He was a military professional also in his concern for transmitting his own tactical and strategic conceptions to his principal commissioned subordinates, and most consistently in his wrestling with the issues of command, communication, and control so that his professional judgments could shape the course of battle and of the war.

Initially, and most impressively demonstrated in the campaign of the Nile, Nelson's favored method of controlling battle in spite of the limits of signal communications, and without a reversion to the stereotyped tactics of the line ahead, was to conduct what amounted to seminars with his captains, reviewing with them every contingency at all likely to develop when they engaged the enemy fleet, sounding them out and guiding their thoughts on how best to meet every contingency, and arriving—to use twentieth-century terminology again— at a shared tactical doctrine. At the battle of the Nile the limitations of signal communications did not much matter; Nelson and his captains had amply rehearsed what to do if the French fleet should be discovered to be at anchor, as it was in Aboukir Bay. At the Nile, Nelson relied on the extent to which his seminars and particularly their generating of a shared military doctrine had disseminated his own professionalism among his captains, making it an advantage more than a risk to allow the captains a generous area for judgment and initiative. His trust in his educational system and in his captains was not ill-placed.

But even in the method by which Nelson prepared his captains for the battle of the Nile there lurked implicitly a danger of overcentralization in command and control. A lesser officer than Nelson could readily transform his seminars into devices for imposing fixed judgments on the captains before battle, imposing a new sort of expectation of stereotyped conduct. Even in Nelson's hands, there was the danger of the impossibility of foreseeing every contingency or combination of contingencies. Nelson had experienced too many of the accidents of naval combat to neglect the role of chance in war, and the best of seminars and doctrine could not altogether prepare for the effects of chance and fortune except by bestowing upon suitably professional officers a yet more generous encouragement of individual judgment and initiative than had Nelson at the Nile. It may well be that Nelson's next great battle after the Nile, Copenhagen, encouraged his thinking along these lines, with its reminders of the dangers of overcentralized control in the shape of those well-intentioned but uncomprehending orders sent into the midst of the fray by the nonparticipating Sir Hyde Parker, the orders that Nelson took it upon himself to ignore.

For Trafalgar, in any event, Nelson developed still further the logic of his Nile system of command and control in naval battle. In the slightly more than three weeks between his arrival off Cádiz and the battle, he again instructed his captains in the likely contingencies and his preferred responses to them. Many of the captains were of course already members of the band of brothers who had come into his orbit during earlier campaigns and knew well his habits of thought. But the way in which he chose to fight Villeneuve's Combined Fleet was to break as free as possible from any systematized design of tactical maneuver and deliberately to institute a melee, which is to say deliberately to court confusion. In such a battle the judgments and initiatives of his now reasonably professional senior subordinates would have the widest scope of all—seconded, to be sure, by that consistent trump card, the quality of British seamanship.

Thus Nelson's plan deliberately carried himself in the *Victory* and his second in command, Collingwood, in the *Royal Sovereign* into the forefront of the attack and the forefront of danger. Nelson's death was a not unpredictable outcome. Therefore the criticism can be made that Nelson and Collingwood were inviting the loss of their control over the battle, that for the sake of maintaining command and control they should have remained somewhere behind the van of the two attacks, where they might better have observed the overall shape of the battle and with good luck communicated better with their captains. But "with good luck" is a crucial phrase here; in battle, adequate communication was rare, and amid the smoke of battle so was an adequate overall view on the part of senior commanders no matter where they might position themselves.

The essence of Nelson's final method of coping with the chaos of battle— the proverbial fog of war—was to accept and even enhance the chaos. With a fleet of seamen such as his, commanded by captains who understood his turn of mind, a confused battle could only enhance the advantage over the French and Spanish. It remains significant that Villeneuve's orders on the brink of battle were not much different from Nelson's in their urging of individual initiative upon the captains. Villeneuve also was a veteran of enough sea fights to recognize that the fog of war was nearly impossible to dissipate, so that battle must be conducted in acceptance of it. But Villeneuve was infinitely more cautious than Nelson because he recognized, too, that the fog of war would assist the British while it would injure his Combined Fleet.

The thoughtful evolution of Nelson's methods of command and control, to make the best of primitive communications and to turn difficulties to advantage, in itself stamps him as a professional military man, in the sense of having become a clinical student of war at a time when his brother naval officers remained professional less in the conduct of war than in seamanship alone.

Command of the Sea

Trafalgar and the completion of the collapse of Napoleon's invasion plans ended the active campaigns of rival fleets against each other for the duration of the Napoleonic Wars. Henceforth the Royal Navy exploited the command of the seas of which Trafalgar assured it to regulate nearly all the world's maritime commerce to British advantage and French disadvantage. In the process, the British also gradually gobbled up at least for the duration of the wars control of the overseas colonies of France and the Netherlands. Because Spain soon passed from enemy to ally of the British, the Spanish Empire was dealt with more gently, but Britain did little to discourage the rise of independence movements within this empire.

We must recall again, however, that we are not discussing wars of nearly total economic mobilization in the manner of the twentieth-century World Wars. The British did not interdict all trade with Napoleon's continental empire and its tributaries. Rather, they controlled trade with Napoleonic Europe in such ways as to maximize the immediate and long-term profits of British merchants at the expense of all others. The consequent impediments to European commerce were not enough in themselves to have caused Napoleon's downfall. An empire continental in extent afforded the French the resources to withstand British sea power. The tendency to deny this latter statement is an example of the habit of the strategists of sea power to exaggerate its adverse effects upon continental powers, a habit that has produced in turn an adverse effect on British strategy over the centuries by exaggerating the potential accomplishments of sea power when unaccompanied against continental adversaries by the commitment of sub-stantial forces on land. In the end, to defeat Napoleon Great Britain had to deploy again on the Continent British land forces comparable to those that Marlborough had led.

All this is not to say that British sea power failed to trouble Napoleon greatly; in fact, by indirect means sea power contributed much to his final down-fall, in that its annoying effects pushed him into a series of policy decisions that ultimately proved fatal to him. Meanwhile, Napoleon also sought to trouble the British Navy and British commercial interests in as many retaliatory ways as he could, and to secure his imperial destiny no matter what the contrary policy of the recalcitrant little island nation might be.

14 THE CLIMAX OF NAPOLEONIC WAR: TO AUSTERLITZ AND JENA-AUERSTÄDT

Geeneral Bonaparte's abandonment of himself to his Egyptian pursuit of Oriental grandeur set in motion a series of ill consequences for France—though not, paradoxically, for the errant general—that for a time appeared almost unlimited. In addition to offering up a French army and fleet for destruction by British sea power, Bonaparte by removing the threat of his military genius from the Continent invited France's rivals to reform the just-broken coalition against it. During the autumn of 1798 there rallied around the continuous opposition of the British a Second Coalition including Austria, Russia, the Two Sicilies, Portugal, and both the Papacy and the Ottoman Sultanate. Disillusionment over the history of the First Coalition sufficiently pervaded the Second that the aims were no longer so grandiosely antirepublican as they had been early in the decade. Instead, the partners of the Second Coalition were mostly ready to settle for enough of an undoing of the Treaty of Campo Formio to reestablish a semblance of a European balance of power.

The overture to the War of the Second Coalition proved absurdly incongruous even to such a relatively modest but respectable aim. It was the invasion of the Roman Republic by the Kingdom of the Two Sicilies, an invasion commanded reluctantly and without illusion by the sober General Mack, but also wafted along on the tides of romance associated at the Neapolitan court with the first ardors of the affair between Horatio Nelson and Emma Hamilton. There is no sadder evidence of the besotting influence of the affair upon the admiral than its capacity to win his sponsorship for this enterprise, which by December (Nivôse) the French in central Italy had rebuffed so completely that the court of King Ferdinand (Fernando) I had to flee to Palermo.

But when the overture had faded, the principal movements did not open so well for France. If the hostile coalition had lost its pristine antirepublican zeal, the French themselves had lost much of their republican and nationalist ardor, a decline hastened by the corrupt cynicism of the current government of the Directory; and for the present there was no Bonapartist charisma on hand to take its place. At the beginning of 1799, the Directory nevertheless ordered its armies to take the offensive; but everywhere they were repulsed, and on some fronts worse was in store.

Suvorov in Italy, 1799: The Trebbia and Novi

On the upper Rhine, the Archduke Charles could bring a numerical advantage of some 80,000 to 40,000 as well as his considerable talents in generalship to bear against Jourdan. The Archduke triumphed in the battle of Stokach (Stockach) on March 25 (5 Germinal An VII); fortunately for the French, he was too cautious to employ his excellent and numerous cavalry for that onslaught of the mobile arm which is customarily necessary to transform the margin of victory from a narrow to a possibly decisive one, so that Jourdan's force substantially escaped to fight another day, its losses of about 11 percent being proportionately no worse than the Austrians'. In Switzerland, meanwhile, the bolder generalship of Masséna actually won the French a measure of offensive success in spite of numerical odds similar to those that handicapped Jourdan; but in this central theater harsh geography imposed a predictable stalemate.

In the War of the Second as of the First Coalition, however, the most dramatic events were reserved for the much-fought-over and therefore long-suffering upper reaches of the Italian peninsula. Not only did the coalition plan its principal effort on land for this theater; in addition, an event almost as meteoric as the rise of General Bonaparte, and of at least comparable long-run significance, attended the new campaign: the intervention of Russia in the military history of central Europe.

This intervention was headed, furthermore, by a general not unworthy of comparison with Bonaparte in terms of ability and magnetism, Field Marshal Alexander (Aleksandr) Vasilievitch Count Suvorov-Rimnisky. Now approaching seventy years of age but with more vigor than most commanders a generation younger, Suvorov had developed so formidable a reputation that while initially he led westward only 17,000 Russian troops—more marched not far behind—it was agreed beforehand that he should command a mainly Austrian army that grew to 90,000. His reputation was formidable enough also that the Austrians felt obliged to accept without demur his assigning of Russian officers to improve Austrian troops in the bayonet assaults he favored as the culmination of his aggressive tactics. His reputation was the more formidable because he was known for an aggressive ruthlessness beyond the battlefield. Not for this Muscovite were eighteenth-century Western ideas of enhancing limitations upon the violence of war. His sack of Ismail in Bessarabia on December 11/22, 1790, when he was a general of infantry, reenacted some of the worst horrors of the Thirty Years War in massacre and plunder of a noncombatant population.

The renewed war in northern Italy had gone badly for the French even before the arrival of the menace from the East. The undistinguished Schérer had again commanded his old Army of Italy at the outset of the campaign. He rendered this army little if at all more ready for action than he had in his previous tenure. Schérer's crossing of the Adige in accordance with the Directory's general orders for the offensive resulted in a defeat at the hands of the Austrians—again superior in numbers, by 56,000 to 41,000—at Magnano near Verona on March 5 (15 Ventôse An VII). Again also, however, the Austrians failed to pursue as vigorously as they might have; the explanation this time may have lain less in the tactics of their commander, *Feldmarschall Leutnant* Paul Freiherr Kray von Krajova, another veteran of the Seven Years War and of campaigning against the Turks, than in the policies of the government at Vienna, which was no longer so much interested in destruction of the French Revolutionary armies as in simply shooing them out of Lombardy.

Arriving at the front on April 4 (14 Germinal An VII), Suvorov promised to introduce sterner measures. Before the month was out he had crossed the River Chiese and persuaded the French garrison of Brescia to surrender by offering massacre as the alternative, a threat that there was no reason to doubt he would have fulfilled. Schérer having decided that resignation was the better part of valor, Moreau now prepared the Army of Italy to defend the line of the Adda River—the scene of Bonaparte's capture of the bridge at Lodi in 1796—with strongpoints at the famous bridge and also at Cassano d'Adda and Lecco. On April 26 (7 Floréal) Suvorov attacked all along the line, giving the brunt of the fighting to his Austrian allies, now under *Feldmarschall Leutnant* Michael Friedrich Benoit Melas, who had served in the Habsburg Emperor's army since 1746. Melas was usually a cautious tactician of the mid-eighteenth-century school, but Suvorov's Russian officers had employed fear to instill unwonted recklessness in the Austrian infantry, and Melas complied faithfully with the field marshal's orders to attack repeatedly regardless of losses. Much to the point, furthermore, Moreau retained only about 20,000 men against at least twice that number. Melas broke through at Cassano, suffering 6,000 casualties but taking 7,000 prisoners. The French withdrew in less than impressive order to the Ticino, and on April 29 the city of Milan witnessed Cossack cavalry riding through its streets.

Suvorov now proposed to turn northward to unite with all the major Austrian armies, including that of the Archduke Charles, to form an irresistible mass capable of winning an absolute victory. Vienna was so little accustomed to strategies of annihilation as to suspect that Suvorov's ruthlessness passed the boundaries of sanity. In any event, the Austrian government was unwilling to direct its Italian forces elsewhere until the tricolor had been hauled down from every fortress in North Italy. This resolution was strengthened, furthermore, by news that the French army in the south, the recent conquerors of Naples, now under the able command of Jacques Étienne Joseph Alexandre Macdonald, *général de division*, had responded to the threat of its isolation implicit in Suvorov's success by marching northward to try to link up with Moreau.

The Russian field marshal had been so intent on winning acceptance of his larger design that by the time he turned his attention southward again he found himself with 40,000 active troops—much of his force had had to be disposed in garrisons—at Alessandria, potentially within the jaws of a nutcracker formed by 35,000 of Macdonald's Army of Naples marching north and the remnants of Moreau's Army of Italy, which had continued its retreat as far as the area of Gavi in the Apennines.

Suvorov affected disdain for a generalship that guided its maneuvers by such textbookish concepts as that of interior lines, an inferior force's use of a position in the chord of an arc to disconcert superior forces that had to cooperate across the greater distances of the arc itself. His own and the Russian Army's traditions favored the counsels of impulsive action over such niceties of Western military education. Nevertheless, Suvorov sent out instructions carefully calculated to exploit his interior lines, both to keep Moreau's attention occupied and to maintain sufficient forces in hand to deal with Macdonald whether he moved to Piacenza, his most likely destination whence to reach out to Moreau, or whether instead he continued marching more directly northward to break the siege of Mantua being conducted by Kray, promoted to *Feldzeugmeister*, as part of Vienna's fortress-collecting hobby.

The outcome was that Suvorov with his main body, now 30,000 men, reached the vicinity of Piacenza just in time, not to prevent Macdonald's 35,000 from driving an Austrian garrison out of the place, but to prevent the Army of Naples from capitalizing on this success by means of a prompt reunion with the Army of Italy.

On June 17–19, 1799 (30 Prairial–1 Messidor An VII), Suvorov's and Macdonald's armies squared off in the battle of the Trebbia near Piacenza. The battle was an affair much more to Suvorov's avowed liking than the preliminary maneuvers; it was among the bitterest and most costly struggles of the French Revolutionary Wars. After spending the first day in mutually unsuccessful efforts to divine each other's strength and intentions, both Suvorov and Macdonald attacked. The latter believed that the enemy's main force was not yet present and that prompt action would give the Army of Naples the maximum advantage of numbers. The former believed that he himself was superior in numbers and that anyway Macdonald's force consisted largely of untested Italian recruits; his temperament being what it was, Suvorov would probably have attacked no matter what he believed.

The ensuing slugging match was exactly that, a brutal exchange of assaults and casualties without sophistication. In the theater of war where Bonaparte had scored more than one of his triumphs primarily through moral force rather than tactical skill, however much of that quality he possessed, the weight of sheer inspirational impetus now lay on the opposite side of the lines, thanks to Suvorov. The Austrians and Russians lost about 7,000 casualties, the French about 6,000 in the main fighting but another 9,000 after Suvorov's unstinting determination broke them. That same determination enabled Suvorov to accomplish the much-recommended but rarely achieved desideratum of the aftermath of battle, a devastating pursuit. Macdonald retreated to Parma and Modena and thence across the Apennines and eventually to Genoa. Suvorov turned to finish off Moreau.

Against the apparent accumulation of disasters, the Directory chose to replace that general with a known exemplar of aggressive tactics, one of the heroes of Bonaparte's battle of Lodi and presumably an apt counter to Suvorov, Barthélemy Catherine Joubert, *général de division*. Taking command of some 35,000 troops who had gathered in the hills south of Genoa, Joubert responded by attacking successfully an Austrian force at Acqui on August 13 (26 Thermidor An VII). This feat produced the dubious reward of setting up a confrontation with Suvorov and his main force, now about 45,000, at Novi two days later. Joubert's subordinates were sufficiently cowed by the mad Russian that they urged avoiding battle lest the result be suicidal. Joubert's reputation and his preliminary victory at Acqui served to precipitate a corresponding recommendation against battle from Suvorov's Austrian subordinates. Naturally, the field marshal ignored them.

Almost as naturally, Suvorov seized the initiative, and for sixteen hours his troops mounted assault after assault against fortified positions on high ground. The fighting eventually became enough of a melee, however, that in the end the defenders' losses exceeded the attackers'—11,000 to 8,000; once more, the discrepancy is partially accounted for by the confusion of retreat. Joubert himself was among the French dead. Suvorov's resolution and charisma again go far to explain the outcome.

Moreau came back to lead the Army of Italy, but it was a shattered army now, and even the rapid march of a new Army of the Alps by way of the Mont Cenis Pass into Italy could not reverse the verdict of the Trebbia and Novi. Suvorov quickly overawed the newcomers. Suvorov's Italian campaign of 1799 accomplished nothing less than the undoing of Bonaparte's Italian victories of 1796–1797.

Suvorov and Masséna in Switzerland, 1799

The remainder of Suvorov's campaigning in the West, however, was dramatic in its incidents but anticlimactic in terms of significance. The Austrian government had agreed at length to accept his proposal that he march into Switzerland. Austria, Russia, and Great Britain had further decided that the rugged Alps formed the appropriate arena in which to utilize the hardy Russian soldiery. But Vienna nevertheless undercut the basic premise of Suvorov's original design, that of a concentration of force to produce complete victory, by removing the army of the Archduke Charles from the scene and dispatching it to the Middle Rhine. There remained to combine with Suvorov a lesser Austrian force of 25,000 under *Feldmarschall Leutnant* Johann Conrad Freiherr Hotze and 30,000 Russians under a commander far different from Suvorov—but far more typical of officers in the unprofessional Tsarist service where advancement depended on the vagaries of court favor—Lieutenant General Alexander (Aleksandr) Mikhailovitch Korsakov-Rimski, whose incompetence was matched by his arrogance. These ingredients could not suffice for anything approximating Suvorov's earlier designs.

The field marshal complied with his new orders no less faithfully for all that; if anything, the ineptitude of others strengthened his resolve to triumph. Leaving Melas with 60,000 Austrians to hold Italy, Suvorov with 28,000—his Russians and one Austrian corps—set out via Varese for the St. Gotthard Pass into Switzerland. There Masséna waited with an army of 77,000 drawn up in a huge irregular arc from Basel along the Limmat River, the Züricher See, and the Linth River to Glarus and thence through the St. Gotthard to the Simplon Pass. A small Austrian corps faced the upper part of the arc; Korsakov confronted the center in the Zürich area; Hotze faced the southern curve. Rather than march through Hotze's position along the exterior of the arc to join Korsakov, Suvorov with his usual audacity proposed to strike straight through the St. Gotthard and thence through the valley of the Reuss to Altdorf, Schwyz, and Zürich, driving through Masséna's rear areas.

Masséna reacted in a manner that confirmed his high ranking among the Revolutionary generals. In late September 1799 (Vendémiaire An VIII), while Suvorov was approaching the St. Gotthard, Masséna weakened much of his cordon to concentrate against Korsakov for a knockout blow before Suvorov could effectively intervene. At the second battle of Zürich, September 25–26 (3–4 Vendémiaire), Masséna substantially succeeded in this aim. (Masséna had fought the first battle of Zürich, losing the city but achieving at least a draw strategically against an Austrian force, earlier in 1799, on June 4–7 [16–19 Prairial An VII]). Korsakov lost some 8,000 wounded, 100 guns, and an indeterminate number of prisoners. He had been practically swept off the chessboard.

Meanwhile Suvorov was storming the St. Gotthard Pass, an enterprise almost too daunting even for his tough Russian peasants, except that their stern grandfather of a field marshal was present to urge, cajole, and shame them onward. Twelve hours of fighting were required to break relatively small numbers of defenders, and Swiss geography held greater horrors still in store. French engineers wrecked the Teufelsbrücke—the Devil's Bridge—on the Reuss, yet the French rear guard also fought desperately in defense of the ruins, to delay Suvorov's advance and make it as costly as possible. In the narrow Swiss valleys, the marshal's stubborn resolution was no longer so great a virtue. Able to deploy only on a narrow front, he sent battalion after battalion in futile grasps for the remains of the bridge before the discovery of a ford permitted outflanking the defenders.

Pushing into Altdorf, Suvorov found that the French had removed all the boats from his side of the Vierwald Stätter See (the Lake of the Four Forest Cantons) so that this body of water almost barred his further way toward Zürich. Cliffs rising from the eastern shore made a march along that bank impossible. Suvorov struck off on a northeasterly angle, driving soldiers and horses and pack animals single file through the Kunzig Pass into the Muotta Thal. During three days of climbing and descent, many men and animals went lost over the precipices, while the French had now worked parties around to harry the Russians' rear.

In the Muotta Thal came word that Korsakov's army was destroyed—and thus that the whole arduous march through the Alps had almost certainly been a wild goose chase, because without Korsakov there were not enough Allied soldiers to overcome Masséna in terrain such as this. Suvorov nevertheless pressed on through additional harsh passes and declivities to Ilanz on the Vorder Rhein, which he reached on October 8 (16 Vendémiaire) with only about 15,000 men remaining to him. Thence he was able to make contact with the Archduke Charles, who on learning of Korsakov's defeat had detached a force on a precautionary expedition to cover his own southern flank. The two senior Allied commanders negotiated about opening a combined effort after all, but they could agree neither on a plan nor about who should command. By late October, Suvorov was withdrawing his remnant into winter quarters near Augsburg.

Needless to say, Suvorov's Swiss campaign is much more controversial than its predecessor campaign in Italy. It raises doubts even about the field marshal's larger strategic judgment, because the more ambitious expedition into Switzerland that he had proposed in the summer would have encountered much the same geographic obstacles. It reveals the fragility even of his operational and tactical leadership; he was not an educated professional, and while in his encounters with Macdonald he had displayed for a time practically a professional's finesse in maneuver, his principal reliance was always upon his audacity, resolution, and personal magnetism. In the constricted valleys of Switzerland, where no amount of these qualities could overcome the capacity of small numbers of defenders to hold back his fierce Russians however fervently he inspired them, his very strengths betrayed him into eventual failure. Driving forward his army against the obstacles of men and nature in Switzerland nearly destroyed it.

Even before the Swiss campaign, moreover, Suvorov's dictatorial leadership style was wearing thin with his Austrian allies. His Russian officers helped for a time to instill aggressiveness into the Habsburg troops; but in most matters of technical proficiency the Kaiser's army already excelled the Tsar's—certainly in officer professionalism—and relations between the Austrians and the Russians were growing frayed at every level well before the close of Suvorov's Italian campaign. Suvorov's own zealousness became increasingly hard to swallow, and after he flew into a tantrum over his disagreements with the Archduke Charles his usefulness as an ally was done.

In his finest hour, Suvorov had reversed the verdict of Bonaparte's first Italian campaign—and as a general he was not so different from Bonaparte. The latter approached somewhat closer toward the model of the educated professional soldier and depended considerably less on sheer aggressiveness and élan; Suvorov never matched Bonaparte's tactical and strategic subtleties at their best. Nevertheless, the Corsican like the Russian depended ultimately on charisma and will-power, and in time reliance on those evanescent qualities would betray him even as they betrayed Suvorov. But for Suvorov as well as for Bonaparte, charisma and will brought their shining moments. Tsar Paul I did him no more than adequate honor by creating Suvorov Prince Italijsky—Prince of Italy. For the student of war, it is a disappointment that Suvorov and Bonaparte never confronted each other directly.

Returning home, the Russian field marshal nevertheless soon found himself out of favor, and he died unhappy early in the following year, on May 7/18, 1800. For the time of the collapse of his Swiss campaign was also the time when the

Anglo-Russian invasion of the Netherlands fizzled out. There, too, bad relations between Russian officers and their allies contributed to fiasco. The Tsar, even more volatile than his generals, thereupon broke his alliances first with Austria and then with Britain, to enter upon his flirtation with Bonaparte.

The First Consul's Military Reforms: The Corps System

Meanwhile Suvorov's ejection of the French from Upper Italy had proven not the least ingredient in the brew that bubbled up into the coup of the 18th Brumaire, brought down the Directory, and led to the elevation of Bonaparte as First Consul and soon as virtual dictator of the French Republic. These latter events in turn were bound to lead to a major French effort to reconquer Italy. Bonaparte was not the man to acquiesce in Suvorov's conquests.

The First Consul found French military organization in enough disarray that it seemed fortunate that the reverses of 1799 had not been worse. The source of this good fortune lay largely in the fact that the energies of the Archduke Charles did not match his abilities; a tendency toward nervous exhaustion under stress largely accounted for his doing no more on the Middle Rhine in the autumn of 1799 than to capture Mannheim before Suvorov's Swiss adventures directed his attention southward. In Italy, however, the Austrians had kept up the pressure after Suvorov's departure, driving one remnant of the French armies into Genoa and another into Nice.

French military troubles had their sources partly in recruitment. On September 5, 1798 (18 Fructidor An VII), General Jourdan, acting in a civil capacity as president of the Conseil des Cinq-Cents (the Five Hundred), the lower legislative chamber of the Directory, had pushed into law a Conscription Act often known by his name. This law was intended to follow up the *Réquisition* Law of 1793 by making conscription permanent. It divided all available men into five groups according to age, profession, and marital status, and it envisaged calling up a fixed number of men in annual classes. In 1799, however, the principle of a universal military obligation was diluted by permitting substitution; men about to be drafted were allowed to find volunteer replacements to fill the communal quotas. Much more damaging, the revolutionary enthusiasm of 1793 had fallen so badly that enforcement of conscription lagged in terms of bringing forward recruits and still more in the matter of preventing their desertion en route to the armies. In a draft of 10,250 dispatched to the Army of Italy, for example, only 310 arrived. Unreliable logistics aggravated by an empty treasury did nothing to rekindle zeal. The new First Consul found the muster rolls of the armies impressive in the numbers they contained but the reality one of insufficient numbers and of shabbiness and low morale among those soldiers who did stand by the colors.

Bonaparte tightened the conscription system, in particular assembling the conscripts first in fortresses in the interior of France where they could be kept well under control, and then dispatching them to the field in relatively small drafts that could be not only controlled but more readily assimilated when they reached the armies. While he was engaged in organizational reform, he also took the long overdue step of removing practically all of the last civilian elements that had clung to the artillery as an inheritance from the time when gunnery was a tradesmen's guild. Soldiers replaced civilian drivers; government horses replaced their hired teams.

Another change with lasting implications for the French and eventually other armies was Bonaparte's decision for all field armies to adopt the *corps d'armée* system. This plan of organization was to be further standardized in the French Army by military reforms between 1802 and 1804. The division had already enabled the armies of the French Revolutionary Wars to maneuver with a flexibility beyond the capacities of most armies of the earlier eighteenth century. But a division operating alone was vulnerable because it lacked both the numbers and usually the combination of arms to afford it sustained combat power should it encounter a substantially larger enemy force. More than a division could be, a *corps d'armée* was a miniature army. In fact, the French now abandoned efforts to include all arms in a division, having concluded that on the divisional level the infantry and cavalry worked best separately; operating at its own divisional strength gave the mobile arm an impact it could not otherwise exert. The corps did not acquire a fixed table of organization, but while its strength could be varied according to circumstances, it always comprised varying numbers of infantry divisions, a division or occasionally a brigade of cavalry, at least one battery of 12-pounder guns directly controlled by corps headquarters, and supporting services. Each infantry division would still have its own artillery, and the cavalry would have horse artillery—artillery with all elements mounted. Varying from about 9,000 men to over 21,000, this miniature army, the corps, not only permitted a larger field army to continue to maneuver flexibly, approaching the enemy by a number of roads and fitting superbly into the concept of *la manœuvre sur les derrières*; a corps had the resources and resilience to stand up to a force considerably larger than itself for a considerable time. Because of their lack of a fixed strength, as well as the possibility of creating new ones in mid-campaign, the corps could also confuse enemy intelligence.

A senior general or later a marshal commanded each corps. Each corps and each division received a staff that tended to become an increasingly effective administrative instrument. In general, each corps also had representatives from army headquarters to provide liaison.

The Crossing of the Alps and the Battle of Marengo

On January 25, 1800 (5 Pluviôse An VIII), Bonaparte decreed the assembly of all available forces in the interior into an Army of Reserve. This army was to be a mass of maneuver under the First Consul's personal command; because the law, however, debarred him from such a military post, Louis-Alexandre Berthier, *général de division*, technically was Commander in Chief, but in fact Berthier acted as Bonaparte's chief of staff. Formed around Dijon, thus accessible to both the Army of Italy and the Army of the Rhine, this force was built up from conscripts around depleted divisions from Egypt and Italy. Its nucleus, however, consisted of two and a half infantry divisions and a cavalry brigade from the veteran Army of the West that had suppressed the uprisings in La Vendée, along with a new formation: picked, elite troops of the Consular Guard. Within six weeks, albeit indispensably aided by Berthier, but while also reorganizing and administering the civil government of France and its foreign policy, Bonaparte manufactured nearly from scratch the foundation of what would become his *Grande Armée*.

French possession of Switzerland further assured that the Army of Reserve could reinforce either the Army of the Rhine, on the Upper Rhine and now commanded by Moreau, or the Army of Italy, in command of which Masséna had replaced Moreau. While conducting desultory peace negotiations with Austria and Great Britain—he would have been willing enough to grant France a respite but was hardly overeager—the First Consul laid his plan of campaign. Bonaparte probably intended first to make Germany the major theater of war in 1800, with the strong Austrian army under Kray in the Black Forest, more than 100,000 men, the object of the strongest French army, that of the Rhine, also with more than 100,000. This design would have accorded with Bonaparte's habitual preference for a direct strategy of annihilation aimed at the destruction of the main enemy army through battle. Not least in this preference for striking at the jugular did Bonaparte resemble Suvorov. The design would also have led toward the Imperial capital of Vienna. But Moreau proved an uncooperative subordinate, little concealing his distaste for taking orders from the diminutive Corsican six years junior to him in age.

General Melas, now commanding for the enemy in Italy, also influenced Bonaparte toward changing his plan. Melas used his own force of over 100,000, comparable in strength to Kray's, to seize the initiative by attacking the French force now called the Army of Liguria, led by the resolute Masséna but in spite of reinforcements dangerously low in numbers. With relative ease, on April 8, 1800 (18 Germinal An VIII), the Austrians broke the French detachments covering the Mont Cenis and thus threatened to rupture completely Masséna's communications with his homeland. So tenuous did these connections become that Bonaparte feared they were cut completely. He was not far wrong; Masséna with some 10,000 men was soon confined to Genoa, while a separate left wing detachment of 1,000, commanded by Louis Gabriel Suchet, *général de division*, withdrew behind the Var River and Nice.

Bonaparte therefore ordered Berthier to hasten with 40,000 men from the Dijon concentration through the St. Bernard Pass to the rescue of Masséna. Berthier protested accurately enough that as yet he had only 25,000 actual effectives and that equipment was far from complete, but nevertheless he soon marched with an approximation of the intended force. Because of such conduct, Bonaparte would grow to trust him more and more.

But the Austrians had put Genoa under siege, with the Royal Navy cutting it off from aid by sea. The doughty Masséna repulsed an attack on April 30 (8 Floréal), mounted several sorties of his own successful enough to raise his troops' morale, and got out word to Bonaparte that he could stretch his food supply until late May. Melas meanwhile had left 21,000 troops as an ample force to deal with Masséna's 10,000 and marched with 30,000 toward Suchet and

France. Great Britain had promised 10,000 troops from Minorca as well as the help of the navy for an attack on Toulon and the redemption of the 1793 effort that had inadvertently propelled Buonaparte to fame.

On May 9 (19 Floréal) Bonaparte joined Berthier at Geneva (Genève), to take charge of counterpreparations against Melas and the British. He had informed Masséna that Genoa must hold out until May 30 (10 Prairial) and Suchet that he must stand firm until June 4 (15 Prairial), and he felt confident of the steadiness of these leaders, particularly Masséna. But his main intent now developed not as the relief of the scattered remnants of the Army of Liguria—that would have to wait, however desperate Masséna might become—but rather, and characteristically, the destruction of Melas's army. If Bonaparte marched for Genoa, Melas would probably be able to move back into his line of communications to shield the place. If Bonaparte marched instead against Melas, he might find a means to sever the Austrian's communications, perhaps fatally. Political as well as military considerations impelled the First Consul to choose the latter alternative. The stability of the Consular government was still uncertain; Bonaparte believed he needed a spectacular and complete triumph to assure his place as head of the government of France—a place that his concept of his destiny now told him was rightfully his. Yet it was imperative that should Bonaparte cross the Alps to threaten Melas's rear before the latter could work serious mischief in southern France, Masséna and Suchet must hold their ground to keep Melas occupied.

Already during the preceding winter, even while contemplating a main effort in Germany, Bonaparte had ordered a thorough reconnaissance of the Alpine passes into Italy—the kind of care that helped distinguish him from Suvorov. The best overland route from Geneva lay through the Little St. Bernard Pass, but Bonaparte rejected this avenue because it would require larger supply trains than a passage through the Great St. Bernard Pass, in that Villeneuve near the northern opening of the latter could be supplied across Lake Geneva by boat. The Great St. Bernard therefore became the obvious route from Geneva, in spite of the fact that it was perilously narrow and a section of it appeared impassable to artillery. The Simplon, farther east, led most directly toward Genoa and the relief of Masséna. The St. Gotthard, still farther east, could best accommodate the passage of an entire army. But because Melas's center of gravity was by late April moving westward toward the Var River, the object of striking at Melas confirmed the decision to use the Great St. Bernard in spite of its obstacles.

After joining Berthier at Geneva, Bonaparte experienced several days of frustration awaiting needed supplies; Berthier's early complaint about shortages was destined never to be satisfactorily remedied in the course of this campaign, notwithstanding the First Consul's improvements in French administration military and otherwise and the fact that Carnot had been returned to the War Ministry. Nevertheless, on May 14 (24 Floréal) the I Army Corps of the Army of Reserve, commanded by Jean Lannes, confirmed as *général de division* just four days earlier, a veteran of Egypt and along with Berthier one of Bonaparte's closest personal friends, led off the French offensive. Melas closed up to the Var on the same day.

Additional French forces of 1,000 and 11,500, respectively, began to march through the Simplon and St. Gotthard Passes. They would not expose themselves by descending into the Italian plain before the main army had done so, but meanwhile they might confuse Melas and help discourage intervention by Kray, no matter how uncooperative Moreau might continue to be. To give the latter his due, he had actually crossed the Rhine between April 25 and May 8 (5–18 Floréal) and bested troops of Kray's army in three small engagements.

To try to add to Melas's confusion, yet another 2,400 French soldiers were ordered through the Mont Cenis west of the St. Bernard. Further, a division of 6,500 would use the Little St. Bernard. Both these columns were to converge on Bonaparte's main army, which now threaded its way through the defiles of the Great St. Bernard, still deep in snow, some of the guns carried on sledges riding on rollers, others dragged on tree trunks hollowed out to form troughs, 100 men to a gun. Among the shortages there was a dearth of mules. The local inhabitants fled to avoid forced labor service. The gun carriages were disassembled and carried by the soldiers in pieces, except that the mountings of the 8-pounders were carried on stretchers, ten men to a stretcher. The summit of the pass is 8,120 feet (2,475 meters) above sea level, the distance through the pass from Montigny to Aosta twenty-five miles (forty kilometers). It required two days to drag a gun through. The Army of Reserve, over 50,000 men, climbed in five columns setting out at daily intervals, each soldier carrying nine days' rations and forty cartridges.

On May 19 (29 Floréal) Lannes's vanguard reached the Fort of Bard, which from a perch on a precipitous rock blocked the road on the south side of the pass. An Austrian garrison of 400 grenadiers of the Kinsky Regiment and twenty-six guns proved to be waiting there. It took three days merely to clear the Austrians from the village around the fort, and reducing the fort itself seemed likely to impose a hopelessly extended delay.

Bonaparte himself crossed the pass astride a mule on May 20 and reached Berthier's headquarters six miles (9.6 kilometers) short of Bard that evening. Here there was news, fortunately, that Lannes had discovered a by-way around the fort toward Ivrea, infantrymen following mule tracks and clinging to the side of Monte Alberado. The engineers were unable to improve the trail enough for cavalry or guns to follow, however, and two efforts to drag guns through Bard under the eyes of the fort at night were detected and ended in failure. On the night of May 24 (4 Prairial), however, two 4-pounders and one caisson passed the fort by this method, and the next night two 8-pounders and two howitzers followed. Bonaparte left one division and all the rest of his guns to reduce the fort and hastened forward with the six guns and the bulk of his infantry.

Bard did not surrender until June 2 (13 Prairial), so that its resistance more than merits the overworked adjective gallant. Its 400 men had held up the infantry of the Army of Reserve for four days and most of the artillery for two weeks. But Bonaparte nevertheless won his gamble that without his guns he would still have enough force that the time he bought through bypassing the fort would save his campaign. Suchet had repulsed an attack on the Var on May 22. By that time, Melas had been convinced for three days that the Army of Reserve had become a threat to his rear concentrating in Switzerland. He was as confused as Bonaparte intended him to be, however, about which column in which pass represented the principal French effort. At first Melas moved his main available force toward Turin (Turino), thinking the Mont Cenis column was the principal threat. But on May 24 he heard from Fort Bard that a large French army was moving past it. Supported by gunfire from British frigates, the Austrians made their last futile effort against Suchet on the Var two days later. The same day the attacking troops received an order from Melas to fall back on Genoa, where Masséna still held out. Melas had not only lost the initiative; he knew not where to turn to save himself from indeterminate dangers approaching from the north.

On May 30–31 the French main body led by Joachim Murat, *général de division*, broke the effort of *Feldmarschall Leutnant* Philipp Freiherr Vukassovich, commanding Melas's right, to hold the line of the Ticino. On the morning of June 2 Murat's men entered Milan, and Bonaparte followed that evening. The city had been a major base for Melas and was crammed full of the food and war matériel the French so badly needed. So was Pavia, which was entered by the cavalry of the energetic Lannes the same day.

Bonaparte's decision to focus on Melas was further vindicated by the outcome at Genoa. There on May 7 a Captain Hanceschi who had traveled by rowboat through the British naval blockade and then swam ashore with his sword between his teeth told Masséna that Bonaparte was marching through the Alps. Unsure, however, how close the First Consul might be, Masséna decided with good reason that he had already amply fulfilled his duty. On May 31 he mounted a last sortie to show the enemy that he could still sting, although a diet of horsemeat and sour bread made from bran, straw, oats, and cocoa had left his men barely able to lift their weapons. He then agreed to parley.

But he would not capitulate outright. He threatened instead to try to fight his way out. The Austrians, endangered in their rear, could not be sure he was incapable of it. On June 4, consequently, they agreed to Masséna's terms: The French would be allowed to evacuate Genoa, taking their artillery, and would be free to fight again once they were within their own lines behind the Var. Bonaparte eventually complained that Masséna should have held out longer, but thereby he displayed the petty and jealous side of his character at close to its worst. Masséna had fully served Bonaparte's strategic purpose; if the immediately subsequent troubles might have been prevented, Bonaparte had far stronger means than did Masséna with which to have warded them off.

With his army closing up in the area of Milan, Bonaparte had achieved the first step toward destroying Melas; he had broken the Austrian army's best line of communications and retreat. As rapidly as possible, he moved toward breaking the secondary line also, from Alessandria through the dangerous Stradella defile and thence to Mantua. Without waiting for his artillery to catch up from Bard, and leaving enough detachments behind to continue blocking escape through Milan, Bonaparte pushed his main body forward across the Po River. Murat stormed the Po bridge at Piacenza on June 5 (16 Prairial) and took the city two days later. On the 6th, Lannes crossed the river at San Cipriano. The season

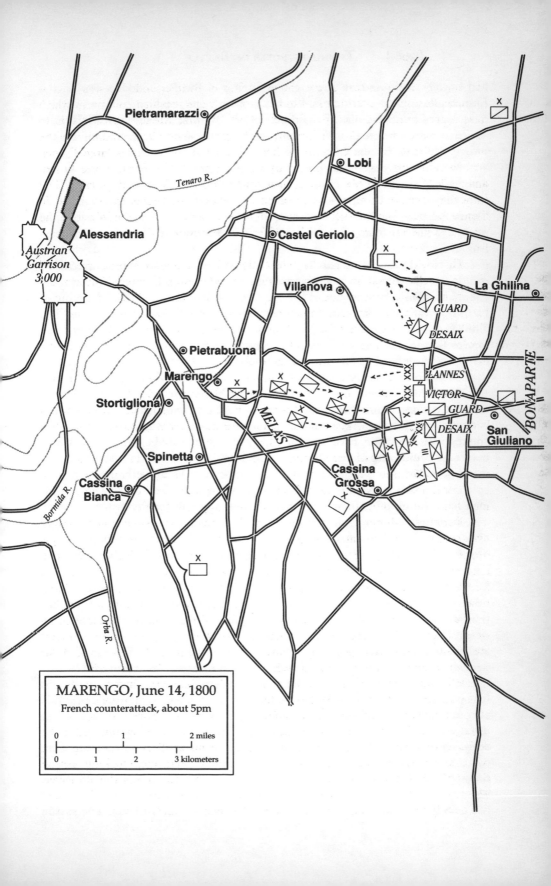

Pietramarazzi ◉

Tenaro R.

Alessandria

Austrian
Garrison
3,000

⊠ X

◉ Lobi

Castel Geriolo ◉

X

La Ghilina ◉

Villanova ◉

⊠ X GUARD

X ⊠ DESAIX

◉ Pietrabuona

Marengo ◉

XXX LANNES

XX

X VICTOR

GUARD

X ⊠ ⊠ ⊠

Stortigliona ◉

X ⊠

⊠

X ⊠ DESAIX

San
Giuliano

BONAPARTE

MELAS

Spinetta ◉

Cassina
Bianca ◉

Cassina
Grossa ◉

Bormida R.

X

X

X

Orba R.

MARENGO, June 14, 1800

French counterattack, about 5pm

0   1   2 miles

0   1   2   3 kilometers

had turned rainy, and on the night of June 7–8 the Po flooded, slowing the French crossings. Nevertheless, Lannes moved on to press an Austrian detachment out of the Stradella. While the French cordon was hardly invulnerable to Austrian efforts to break it at various points, Bonaparte was well along toward forcing Melas to fall back on Genoa and the support of the British Navy.

Melas, however, preferred to accept the risks of battle. In spite of the dangerously scattered condition of his army at the time he perceived the threat from the Army of Reserve—with the Austrians dispersed from near the Var to Turin, Alessandria, Brescia, Verona, and Genoa—and in spite of an enterprising pursuit of the Var force by Suchet that extracted heavy casualties from it, Melas had about 38,000 men concentrated around Alessandria within a few days of the French capture of the Stradella. The Austrian commander felt confident he could fight Bonaparte in this vicinity with at least equal numbers. In fact, the French had only about 28,000 in hand, and Bonaparte underestimated the rapidity of his rival's concentration, believing that only 22,000 Austrians were nearby. Thus Bonaparte's generalship, however admirable in its unswerving determination to destroy the enemy army, had failed to deny Melas a favorable opportunity for a battlefield victory that could undo all the French accomplishments in the campaign thus far. And should Melas lose, he could still fall back on Genoa.

The First Consul demonstrated that he was miscalculating by ordering Lannes westward from the Stradella toward Voghera, assuring him he could deal with any Austrian force he might meet. With no exact knowledge of the enemy's whereabouts, however, Bonaparte promptly felt uneasy about this assurance; but before he could send more cautious orders into Lannes's hands that corps commander, with 8,000 troops, engaged 18,000 troops at Montebello on June 9.

Bonaparte's fabled luck held out. Although one of Lannes's two divisions engaged was new and of uncertain quality, both divisions fought with uncommon determination. Moreover, Claude Victor-Perrin, *général de division*, arrived with 5,000 of his III Army Corps for a timely flank attack. Lannes and Victor not only drove back the enemy but imposed casualties of 2,100 killed and wounded and an equal number of prisoners for only 500 French losses.

This result probably contributed to a triumph of confidence over nervousness during the succeeding few days notwithstanding Bonaparte's experiencing both emotions. On June 13, the French pushed onto the plain of Marengo between Voghera and Alessandria. This plain was reported to be one of the best arenas for the deployment of cavalry in all of North Italy, so the part of Bonaparte that was nervous over ignorance of the enemy felt some surprise in finding it easily taken. But the confident side of Bonaparte—the Bonaparte dazzled by his own destiny—permitted his troops to encamp on the plain in scattered condition without adequate preparations for defense or adequate reconnaissance to discover what might lie just to the west. The corps organization may have tempted Bonaparte to put excessive reliance upon the capacity of scattered miniature armies to stand alone. The American reader will be reminded of Major-General Ulysses S. Grant's careless disposition of his divisions in the woods around Shiloh Church on the night of April 5–6, 1862.

Bonaparte like Grant was about to become a victim of a major assault reinforced by tactical surprise. Fortunately for him, his enemy like Grant's committed gross enough blunders in the execution of the assault to compensate for a good deal of carelessness. To reach the plain of Marengo, the Austrians had to cross the Bormida River, on the east shore of which they had retained only a single bridgehead. Therefore the attacking troops had to file out of Alessandria by a single road and deploy on an excessively narrow front. Their attack was bound to be slow in developing momentum. Furthermore, Melas cut down his attacking force to slightly over 28,000 by failing to include in it the 3,000-men garrison of the citadel of Alessandria and by detaching another 2,300 to look into a report that Suchet's cavalry had reached Acqui some twenty miles (thirty-two kilometers) to the southwest.

The French were fortunate also that despite its reputation as a suitable cavalry battlefield, the plain of Marengo was much broken up by roads, stone farmhouses, fences, garden walls, vineyards, and ditches, all favoring the defense. To get at the French positions, the Austrians had to cross not only the Bromida River but also the Fontanone Creek, usually of little account but swollen by the rains—which continued into the night before the battle—to become a serious obstacle.

Even so, the battle of Marengo might well have proven a severe defeat for France and a disaster for the career of Bonaparte had it not been for the astute leadership of Louis Charles Ardaunt Desaix de Veygoux, *général de division*, just returned from Egypt and given a freshly formed, unnumbered corps.

At eight in the morning of June 14 (25 Prairial), Bonaparte received from Murat's staff a report that the Austrians were advancing in force, but he refused to take the news seriously. Fighting began about nine, and within about half an hour the Austrians were making headway. Melas had issued extra rations and new uniforms for the occasion and had instilled in his junior officers some of the fire of Suvorov, which the officers in turn imparted to the troops through brave personal leadership. Not until about two o'clock, however, did Bonaparte feel sufficient concern to ride to the highest ground available for a survey of the scene. Then he saw his army hard-pressed and in danger of falling back from its positions in and on both sides of the village of Marengo. He called up the slight reserves he had close at hand, with the 900-man infantry of the Consular Guard as the nucleus, and the army corps of General Desaix.

The latter had been ordered southward toward Novi to meet a reported threat from that quarter, an order reiterated by Bonaparte as recently as nine in the morning although cavalry reconnaissance the preceding afternoon had found nothing there. Desaix's march had been necessarily delayed by preparations to cross the Scrivia River, however, and during the first hour of battle Desaix had grown increasingly concerned about the noise of combat to his north. Before ten the corps commander ordered another reconnaissance to Novi, which again found no Austrians there. Desaix promptly decided to march no farther until he had reported his scouts' finding to Bonaparte and received new orders. It was because of this decision that his corps was within striking distance of the battlefield when Bonaparte belatedly recalled it.

Nevertheless, Bonaparte's incaution and the resolution of the ninety-one-year-old Melas to retain the fruits of the campaign he had waged with Suvorov were well on their way to producing the Austrian victory that the insecure government of the Consulate—and Bonaparte's destiny—could not afford. The Consular Guard arrived to form square and repulse several cavalry charges, but it had to fall back in the face of concentrated artillery fire and heavy infantry attacks against two sides of its square, losing 260 men. The whole French line retreated some three miles (about five kilometers) to attempt to form a new front hinged on a place called San Giuliano.

A cavalry assault delivered against the withdrawal might have turned it into a rout, but now Melas's mistakes began to compensate for Bonaparte's. There was no substantial organized body of Austrian horse available, partly because of the diversion of 2,300 to Acqui, partly because of the attrition inflicted by the Consular Guard, partly because of dispersion of the remainder into detachments. Moreover, Melas was strangely indifferent to the need to throw in the mobile instrument of decision. Or perhaps not so strangely; his age and the strain of the past several weeks, culminating in a battle in which two horses were shot under him, probably caught up with him. In mid-afternoon he returned to Alessandria.

Thus deprived of vigorous leadership, the Austrians did not get their follow-up attack out of Marengo under way until almost 4:30 P.M. The respite permitted Bonaparte to organize his San Giuliano line, and most important it allowed Desaix, marching cross country to the sound of the guns, to rejoin, mainly anchoring the French left. The new French position was a strong one, well screened by stone walls, vineyards, and orchards. But Desaix himself—not just his fresh troops—formed the soul of the defense. When the Austrian assault against the San Giuliano line approached what he sensed was its climax, he led one of his divisions in a countercharge. Supported by guns massed at his earlier request, the effort halted the Austrian momentum—at the price of Desaix's life.

With the outcome now finely balanced, French cavalry did what Austrian horse had failed to do. François Étienne Kellermann, *général de brigade* and son of the victor of Valmy, charged his mounted brigade into the right flank of the Austrian advance, broke the final impetus of the enemy infantry, and then turned quickly upon a force of Austrian dragoons before they could intervene. Bonaparte then committed the cavalry of the Consular Guard, and the battle of Marengo was transformed from an Austrian victory into an Austrian rout. The French admitted 5,835 casualties in the course of the action; the Austrians lost about 6,000 dead, 8,000 captured, 40 guns, and 15 colors.

Melas's consequent and understandable condition of shock was another piece of good fortune for Bonaparte, because in spite of the favorable ratio of casualty figures, the nearly lost battle had left the French army in no condition for pursuit. The shock persisted long enough, moreover, so destroying Melas's earlier resolution, that the Austrian commander was induced to agree to the Convention of Alessandria the next day, sealing Bonaparte's victory. The Austrians agreed to withdraw all of their forces to the east side of the Ticino and to surrender their remaining fortresses in Piedmont, Lombardy, and the Milanese. They would cease operations until Vienna replied to an offer of peace dispatched by Bonaparte.

But it had required General Desaix to rescue Bonaparte's destiny. The First Consul's strategic thrust for Melas's jugular had been a model of consistent pursuit of the critical objective that promised to win the war, and it had been a model most especially of operations against the enemy's lines of communications as the operational means to the strategic purpose of a battle that would destroy the enemy army. In tactics, however, Bonaparte's overreliance on improvisation and fortune—the critical limitation of his professionalism—had nearly done him in. His tactical mistakes had also helped frustrate the complete attainment of his strategic objective. Melas's army had been bludgeoned but not destroyed, and the Convention of Alessandria permitted 60,000 Austrian troops with 1,300 guns to form line behind the Mincio.

Nevertheless, the Italian campaign of 1800 in its contrasts with the campaign of 1796 underlines the differences separating the strategic vision of Bonaparte as it had by now matured from the more cautious style of war practiced in both campaigns by the Austrians. In 1796 the French had initially taken the offensive, but after reaching the Po they had become entangled in the siege of Mantua instead of focusing on the destruction of the enemy armies. The Austrian riposte had been to choose the strategic objective of breaking the siege, an effort that the French had repulsed in the battles of Castiglione, Arcola, and Rivoli. Austrian strategy in 1796 remained that of a war for geographic objectives, particularly fortresses, essentially a war of posts. In 1800 it was the Austrians who initially took the offensive. But they continued to aim their strategy at the capture of critical positions—particularly Genoa and the line of the Var. Had Bonaparte's riposte been to seek first the relief of Genoa, his action would have been equivalent to the Austrian effort in 1796 to save Mantua. Instead, he aimed at a battle that would destroy the enemy army, choosing this strategy of annihilation as the most direct and expeditious military means toward his larger political objectives of stabilizing his new government and destroying the Second Coalition. In spite of the partial undermining of his grand strategic vision by faulty tactical execution, he came close enough to achieving his strategic objective that thereafter his political objectives did not much longer elude him.

And he did not count so much on fortune that he would fail to grow as a general.

Moreau at Hohenlinden

The Convention of Alessandria suspended the fighting in Germany as well as in Italy. Moreau, who because of his reluctance to work in harmony with Bonaparte deserved no small part of the blame for the incompleteness of the victory in Italy, had won several minor battles in Germany and thereby pushed the Austrians under Kray back from the Rhine into a well-fortified position at Ulm on the Danube. This campaign, however, not only left Kray's army much more nearly intact than Melas's but also failed to disrupt Austrian communications with northeastern Italy behind the Ticino, assuring Melas of his refuge there.

Bonaparte hoped to capitalize on Marengo enough to extend the Convention of Alessandria into a peace treaty—to anchor his new government upon a reputation for peacemaking. Largely for this reason the suspension of hostilities was prolonged through the entire normal campaigning season of 1800. The Austrians, however, were not ready to concede that they had lost the war, and their treaty of alliance with Great Britain forbade them to negotiate separately from the British, who felt still less reason to come to terms with the obviously ambitious French dictator. Pitt in fact produced a new subsidy treaty to encourage Vienna. The Austrians nevertheless were sufficiently desirous of a breathing spell that they purchased one of the extensions of the armistice by going to the length of surrendering Ulm.

Still, it did not require any of his powers of genius for Bonaparte to perceive that the Austrians were merely buying time. He was able to use the respite to open other negotiations toward stabilizing relations with Prussia and Russia, while French diplomacy also won promises of Spanish support in the naval war and against Great Britain's ally Portugal.

By late autumn the Austrians felt ready for another test of arms. They reopened hostilities on November 22 (1 Frimaire An IX).

The sequel was an extraordinary winter campaign. The First Consul ordered Moreau to resume his offensive on the Danube, with Vienna as his obvious destination and precipitating a decisive battle of annihilation as his larger strategic goal. Subsidiary offensives were to be conducted by a restored Army of Italy, with the Army of Reserve incorporated into it for a total of 95,000 men, commanded by Guillaume Marie Anne Brune, *général de division*, and by a smallish—14,000—Army of the Grisons under Macdonald, the latter to cross the Alps to descend upon the rear of Austria's Italian forces.

Macdonald's march through the Splügen was not least among the features making the campaign extraordinary; it surpassed Suvorov's and Bonaparte's Alpine crossings because it was achieved in the very worst of winter. Leading a maneuver force of 7,000 men, Macdonald took them through Alpine snowstorms and avalanches largely by means of the sheer magnetism of his presence and example. When he reached Lake Como on December 12 (21 Frimaire) and found Austrian fortifications blocking the passes to Trent (It., Trento; Ger., Trient), he executed another mountain crossing if anything more arduous than the first, and captured the city. Unfortunately for the French, Brune meanwhile did nothing to take advantage of this menace to the Austrian rear.

But in this campaign Moreau was no Brune. The First Consul was now firmly in the saddle, and Moreau evidently sensed he was no longer to be trifled with. The 119,000 men of the Army of the Rhine advanced promptly from their winter base around Munich, moving in six scattered columns. The rival Austrian Army of Germany, 136,000 men, had passed from the command of the unspectacular Kray, whose retreats earlier in the year had left Vienna dissatisfied, first to *Feldzeugmeister* Franz Freiherr Lauer, then to the Archduke Johan Baptiste Josef Fabian Sebastian, nephew of Emperor Franz II and son of Leopold, Grand Duke of Tuscany, the future Emperor Leopold II. Lauer was an experienced professional soldier but dour and unpopular. The Archduke John was eighteen years old, modest and uncertain of himself, as well he might be, and with almost no military training; but Vienna expected him to reinspire the troops by bringing the ruling house of Habsburg to their immediate command. Lauer continued as the day-to-day director of the army, but the Archduke felt obliged to contribute his own strategic vision, such as it was.

The Austrians initially thought that their Army of Germany would stand on the defensive, while opportunities might offer themselves for initiatives in the somewhat less unsuitable winter campaigning weather of northern Italy. Macdonald, however, helped prevent Italian opportunities from developing, whereas the Archduke John and Lauer decided that Moreau's dispersed columns invited a surprise attack against the French left as it moved toward the River Inn. While Moreau advanced more slowly than Bonaparte would have been likely to do, the Austrians were slower yet to get their movement under way; the long respite notwithstanding, their front-line troops were short of supplies. Once they marched, furthermore, they were plagued by alternating snow and rain and rapidly deteriorating roads. Their ponderosity permitted Moreau to discern the threat to his left. Exploiting the capacity for more rapid movement that continued to distinguish the French Revolutionary armies from their enemies, Moreau effected a substantial concentration in the forest of Hohenlinden east of Munich, on the main road over which the Austrian column of maneuver was laboriously advancing.

On December 3 (12 Frimaire) battle erupted along the muddy forest paths. It began literally as a meeting engagement, neither side having reconnoitered adequately to locate the enemy until their main forces collided. While Michel Ney and Emmanuel, marquis de Grouchy, both *générals de division*, distinguished themselves in confused fighting whereby their corps contained the Austrians, Moreau sent Antoine Richepans, *général de division*, with a third corps against the left of the Austrian column. This was an excellent example of using the corps organization in the fashion in which it was intended, but the conditions of the forest defiles almost defeated the intent. Richepans blundered into a secondary Austrian column that contrived in turn to cut his corps in two. Nevertheless, Richepans drove forward the head of his column to strike his objective, the Archduke's principal column. He succeeded spectacularly, reaching the enemy's rear and overrunning his baggage train and his artillery park before crashing in behind the troops engaging Ney and Grouchy. The Archduke's army began to come apart at the seams. The rear of Richepans's corps fought its way out of its own difficulties in time to trap thousands of fleeing whitecoats.

Hohenlinden was the decisive victory that had eluded Bonaparte himself in the Marengo campaign. The Austrians lost as many as 20,000 men, about 12,000 of them prisoners, along with ninety guns, and the Army of Germany disintegrated. The Emperor summoned the Archduke Charles from convalescence to take command of the defeated army, and with reluctance that most able Austrian general obeyed; but it was too late. Efforts to form a new line in front of Salzburg had already failed, and it was probably beyond any leader's capacity to fill the void now open between Hohenlinden and Vienna. So hopeless were the circumstances that Austrian militia refused to take the field, while Hungary rigidly retained the right throughout the war to muster its troops on its own terms and did not now see utility in mustering the levy of the Kingdom, the *Insurrectio*. (In any event, the Archduke so distrusted militias that he sent home those who did appear.)

French casualties at Hohenlinden were about 5,000, certainly a moderate toll in proportion to the results. At the time and since, nevertheless, there has been a marked tendency to begrudge Moreau credit for the victory. It is true that Ney, Grouchy, and certainly Richepans made indispensable contributions, while Moreau's initial dispersed advance and his reconnaissance were both decidedly flawed. Still, Bonaparte too could scarcely have won at Marengo without Desaix; and Moreau at Hohenlinden achieved the necessary concentration because he perceived the enemy's intentions before the battle, used the corps system more effectively than had Bonaparte at Marengo, and conceived the flank attack that Richepans executed so magnificently. No doubt critics outside France have been infected somewhat by French nationalists' resentment of Moreau's subsequent career. The general himself was far from grudging in his admiration of his own achievement. Never reconciled to the upstart Corsican's elevation above him, in his infatuation with his own brilliance he now lent himself to royalist plots against the Consulate and after imprisonment was exiled. From late 1804 to 1813 he lived at Morrisville, Pennsylvania, on the Delaware River above Philadelphia. Representatives of Tsar Alexander I then persuaded him to become a military adviser to their sovereign, and as such he took part in the 1813 campaign until the battle of Dresden, where he was mortally wounded on August 27, dying five days later.

The Austrians had to make peace to save their capital. Moreau's troops were already advancing into Upper Austria when an armistice was signed at Steyer (Steyr) on Christmas Day (4 Nivôse An IX). French and Austrian negotiators thereupon resumed their discussions of permanent peace terms at Leoben, while French arms maintained pressure outside the armistice zone by overrunning Tuscany and expelling from the Papal States a Neapolitan army that had returned there during the distractions of the recent campaigns. The Leoben discussions were sure to be more successful now that the Austrians were militarily impotent. They produced the Treaty of Lunéville of February 9, 1801 (20 Pluviôse An IX), in which Bonaparte's continued concern for stability at home impelled him into striking generosity. The main terms merely reaffirmed the settlement of Campo Formio, so that diplomatically Austria had lost nothing by its effort to overturn that arrangement. The First Consul's generosity extended even to restoring the King of the Two Sicilies to his prewar possessions.

The Peace of Amiens

Pitt's Second Coalition had followed the First Coalition into the dustbin, though Great Britain still fought on. Waged as it was under the shadow of Nelson's naval victory at the Nile, the War of the Second Coalition dramatized the limitations of sea power. The Royal Navy's dominance of the seas and of the very coast behind which the Marengo campaign took shape could not prevent Bonaparte from recouping his Egyptian losses and more, establishing himself as master of the prodigious energies of Revolutionary France and reestablishing France as the predominant power of Europe. Not until Great Britain again became a military amphibian as in Marlborough's day, combining with naval power an army capable of continental intervention beyond the scale of the ludicrous Netherlands expedition of 1799, would the stubbornness of British resistance find its reward in the ability to mount an effective offensive strategy. But such were the persistent limits of Pitt's strategic conceptions and those of almost his whole island nation that nearly ten more years of war had to be endured before Britain bestirred itself to deploy a respectable army. And then that army was to find that in land warfare there would be no more immediately decisive battles; rather, the new mass armies were to prove the source of more resilient military strength than ever before, with the search for the single decisive battle on land still more elusive than before—so that the British Army when belatedly enlarged for an appropriate contribution to Allied strategy would be destined to fight for yet more long years before the Wars of the French Revolution and of Bonaparte finally became resolved.

In the meantime, the Nile's display of the comparative decisiveness of naval war notwithstanding, naval power alone could not award the British even the satisfaction of complete success in Egypt. The Pitt Ministry fell on March 14, 1801, its collapse precipitated less by the Treaty of Lunéville and the dissolution of Pitt's coalition than by political quarrels closer to home, most critically King George III's repugnance toward Pitt's policy of Catholic emancipation in Ireland. The dull new ministry of the dull Henry Addington nevertheless had to face up to the implications of Lunéville and of Britain's inability to resist the master of continental warfare in his own element. Anglo-French peace negotiations at Amiens dragged on tediously, but when Bonaparte learned that the remnant of his old Army of the Orient was about to have to surrender, he pushed the negotiations to a conclusion to deny the British a full savoring—and full diplomatic exploitation—of their victory. The last French resistance in Egypt ended with the surrender of Alexandria on September 2, 1801 (14 Fructidor An IX). The news reached Paris a few days before it arrived in London, and before Addington's government heard of it, the possibility of capitalizing on it was foreclosed by the signing of the Preliminaries of Amiens on October 1 (9 Vendémiaire An IX). The Preliminaries became part of the Peace of Amiens of March 25, 1802 (4 Germinal An X). Although this peace of Germinal was concluded even as the seeds of renewed war were germinating, Bonaparte's peacemaker image was sufficiently attained at last to permit his arranging his appointment as Consul for life on August 2, 1802 (4 Thermidor An X).

By the time warm weather returned yet again, France would be mobilizing an Army of England around Boulogne for the cross-Channel invasion project.

Napoleon on the Eve of His Greatest Campaigns

Napoleon Bonaparte was so consistently a land animal, and his strategic judgment so often deteriorated when he confronted the sea, that doubt has arisen about how earnest was his intent to invade England after hostilities resumed on May 16, 1803 (26 Floréal An X). Perhaps the strongest evidence of genuine intent lay, paradoxically, in the shortage of horses and wagons in the army that was assembling at Boulogne and elsewhere along the Channel coast; these means of land transport would have been an encumbrance to a Channel crossing, so that Bonaparte expected to pick them up only after he had landed in England. Meanwhile the shortage of them was sure to be a handicap in a continental campaign. Thus the army on the Channel was evidently not intended for a continental campaign.

The newly crowned Emperor Napoleon continued to focus his preparations on England and to neglect the land transport of his army even as British diplomacy, stimulated by Pitt's return as First Lord of the Treasury and the King's First Minister on May 12, 1804, succeeded in drawing Russia and Austria toward a Third Coalition and thus toward war against the French Empire. The British played skillfully upon Tsar Alexander I's disgruntlement over the disappointment of his ambition, after Austria's defeat, to share with France the ascendancy over central Europe left vacant by Vienna's eclipse. Instead of permitting such sharing, the French had decidedly gone their own way. This course also gave the British material with which to nourish Austrian resentments, because France had drastically refashioned the Holy Roman Empire of the German Nation, reducing its constituent polities from 350 to 39, without the consent of the Holy Roman Emperor himself, and while otherwise riding roughshod over his interests in Germany and Italy. The process of offending Austria reached a climax on May 26, 1805 (6 Prairial An XIII), when Napoleon in the *Duomo* of Milan placed upon his imperial crown the historic Iron Crown of Lombardy to proclaim himself King of Italy; such a unification of Italy with France and exclusion of the Habsburgs from North Italy was altogether unacceptable to Vienna.

Russia became an ally of Great Britain on March 30/April 11, 1805 (21 Germinal An XIII), and Austria on August 3 (21 Fructidor An XIII). Sweden and the Two Sicilies also joined the Third Coalition. From at least the previous autumn Napoleon had been developing plans for a new offensive against Austria, this time with its main thrust aimed directly at Vienna. He waited, however, until August 25 (7 Fructidor), when he learned that Villeneuve had abandoned all efforts to gain naval control of the Channel and sailed south for Cádiz, before finally giving up preparations for the invasion of England to turn eastward instead. This long delay is another indication that Napoleon's invasion preparations were no mere façade.

France and Austria were even now not formally at war, and if the delay in responding to Austrian military preparations had been lengthy, it was by no means unduly dangerous to Napoleon's interests. The Emperor had used the interval of peace and the time at Boulogne further to improve his army and particularly its flexible *corps d'armée* organization—and, as events would demonstrate, to reflect upon his military experiences in such a way as to improve his own generalship. Through self-study and reflection he had made himself a more professional soldier than ever before. The Austrians also had used the interval of peace for further reform of their military organization, also particularly by adopting the essentials of the *corps d'armée* system. But while Napoleon believed that

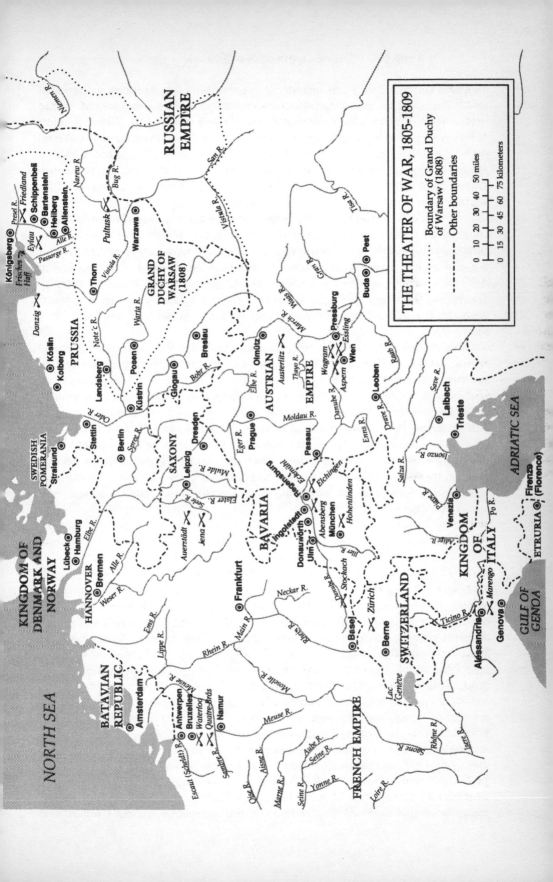

THE THEATER OF WAR, 1805–1809

.... Boundary of Grand Duchy of Warsaw (1808)
—·—·— Other boundaries

0   10   20   30   40   50 miles
0   15   30   45   60   75 kilometers

NORTH SEA

KINGDOM OF DENMARK AND NORWAY

RUSSIAN EMPIRE

SWEDISH POMERANIA

PRUSSIA

GRAND DUCHY OF WARSAW (1808)

BATAVIAN REPUBLIC

HANNOVER

SAXONY

AUSTRIAN EMPIRE

BAVARIA

FRENCH EMPIRE

SWITZERLAND

KINGDOM OF ITALY

ETRURIA

GULF OF GENOA

ADRIATIC SEA

Niemen R.
Königsberg
Friedland
Presl. R.
Eylau
Schippenbeil
Bartenstein
Heilberg
Allenstein
Frisches Haff
Alle R.
Passorge R.
Danzig
Pultusk
Narew R.
Bug R.
Warszawa
Thorn
Vistula R.
San R.
Kösslin
Kolberg
Landsberg
Posen
Warta R.
Note'c R.
Küstrin
Glogau
Oder R.
Breslau
Bobr R.
Olmütz
Stralsund
Stettin
Berlin
Spree R.
Leipzig
Dresden
Eger R.
Prague
Moldau R.
Elbe R.
Austerlitz
Thaya R.
Wagram
March R.
Pressburg
Essling
Wien
Aspern
Leoben
Raab R.
Buda
Pest
Theiss R.
Gran R.
Waag R.
Laibach
Trieste
Save R.
Drave R.
Salza R.
Enns R.
Danube R.
Passau
Eckmühl
Regensburg
Elchingen
Abensberg
Hohenlinden
München
Donauwörth
Ulm
Stockach
Iller R.
Ingolstadt
Lübeck
Hamburg
Bremen
Elbe R.
Aller R.
Weser R.
Ems R.
Lippe R.
Amsterdam
Meuse R.
Antwerpen
Bruxelles
Waterloo
Quatre-Bras
Namur
Escaut (Scheldt) R.
Sambre R.
Aisne R.
Oise R.
Marne R.
Seine R.
Yonne R.
Aube R.
Loire R.
Frankfurt
Main R.
Neckar R.
Rhein R.
Moselle R.
Rhône R.
Saône R.
Isère R.
Basel
Berne
Zürich
Lac Genève
Ticino R.
Alessandria
Marengo
Genova
Venezia
Adige R.
Po R.
Firenze (Florence)
Auerstädt
Jena
Saale R.
Mulde R.
Elster R.
Muldau R.
Isonzo R.
Piave R.

his corps commanders were veterans enough to be entrusted with a considerable—though as we shall emphasize, a nevertheless limited—measure of discretionary responsibility, the Habsburg high command lacked a similar confidence in its senior generals. The Austrians undermined much of the potential value of their adoption of corps by continuing to apply to these miniature armies the same sort of centralized control that had prevailed in the smaller and more unitary field armies of the eighteenth century. Therefore Austrian corps could not maneuver freely, and the difficulties of centralized control in armies of 100,000 made for painfully slow movement. Similarly, the Austrians had also attempted to free their armies from the straitjacket of an eighteenth-century-style logistical system by encouraging commanders to provision their troops from the countryside through requisitions. Consequently many horses from the wagon train were turned over to the artillery, which needed them. But the habits of generations died hard, and again the Austrian Army had trouble liberating itself from the impediments to a mobility and maneuverability comparable to the French.

Napoleon's plans aimed at exploiting these deficiencies. He believed, rightly, that even without a full complement of horses for transport, the cavalry, and the artillery, his army was more than a match for its enemies in mobility as well as on the battlefield. The primary strength of the French Army now resided in its infantry—after so long a contrary history, a dramatic testimony to the effects of the Revolution. About a fourth of the men were veterans who had served since the early Revolutionary Wars; another fourth had served since about the beginning of the Consulate; and while the remaining half were conscripts and volunteers mustered in since 1801, the veteran 50 percent gave the army a steadiness and savvy amply remedying the principal French tactical deficiencies of ten years before.

The Ulm Campaign

Vienna mobilized its main field armies, some 94,000 men under the Archduke Charles and another 22,000 under the Archduke John (Hohenlinden notwithstanding), in the North Italy theater over which the war had largely been precipitated, and which had become through the past decade the habitual center of conflict. Napoleon intended, however, that a French force of 50,000 under Masséna—now like other senior commanders a *maréchal de l'Empire*—should hold these Austrians in check while this time he directed his own efforts toward the Danube.

Nevertheless it was the Austrians who made the first major move in southern Germany, when on September 2 (15 Fructidor An XIII) a whitecoat army of 72,000 marched to occupy Bavaria. The commanding general was Prince-Archduke Ferdinand d'Este, an Italian prince closely related to the Habsburgs; the chief of staff and in large part actual commander was the able Karl Mack von Leiberich, now a *Feldmarschall Leutnant* and a principal author of the recent Austrian military reforms. It was to be Mack's ill fortune to take the field before the reforms had matured and to find himself placed by Vienna's policy and strategy in an almost impossible position. That he had risen from the ranks and was a Protestant would not help his reputation in adversity.

The intent of the move into Bavaria was to appropriate subsistence and other supplies for Austria and to deny them to Napoleon. The Austrians also hoped to add the Bavarian Army of 75,000 to the coalition forces. The Habsburg Emperor called upon the Elector Maximilian-Josef of Bavaria to place his army under Ferdinand's command, but the Elector contrived to prolong negotiations until his army had slipped away northwest to Bamberg. Nevertheless, the Austrians succeeded in denuding Bavaria of subsistence thoroughly enough to cause Napoleon trouble later on.

Meanwhile a Russian army of 100,000 men was on the march to unite with Ferdinand's army near Ulm, where the River Iller meets the Danube. Mack thereupon decided to position Ferdinand's army in an entrenched camp at Ulm, gathering all his hoard of foodstuffs there. He believed that he would thus compel Napoleon to besiege him, with the French handicapped in such an operation by his stripping of the Bavarian countryside. The army in Ulm could become the anvil against which the Russian hammer might destroy the French. Ferdinand was skeptical of the plan—wisely, as events turned out—but Mack was trying to compensate as best he could for Austrian deficiencies in mobility and flexibility, and in that light his plan was not unreasonable. Mack believed that it assured that even if Napoleon defeated him, the French would suffer heavily in the process.

Napoleon had thrown out a cavalry screen along the middle Rhine as early as August 24 (6 Fructidor), and the next day he dispatched Marshal Murat and other agents secretly into Germany to reconnoiter the terrain and Austrian activities in the Ulm area, where, though he was still mainly ignorant of enemy movements, he assumed the Austrians were likely to concentrate. The principal French army—the *Grande Armée* as now at last it was designated—had begun moving eastward and southward on August 27, behind a cloud of deceptive subsidiary movements. On September 13 (26 Fructidor) Napoleon learned from Murat of the invasion of Bavaria, and subsequent communications kept him well informed about the Austrians, though not about the Russian advance.

By September 26 (4 Vendémiaire An XIV), with Franco-Austrian diplomatic relations finally broken off, the Grand Army had crossed the Rhine, made its way through the defiles of the Black Forest north of the Neckar (except for the cavalry, which used passes south of that river), and was deployed beyond the forest and mountains to confront Ulm. Mack's designs were already in part successful, however, because the French were suffering from shortages of almost all kinds of supplies, aggravated by their lack of transport; boots were wearing out, and coats for protection against the cooling weather were in short supply. But Napoleon drove his troops deeper into Bavaria nevertheless, marching his corps along parallel roads toward the Danube between Donauwörth and Ingolstadt with the intention of interposing between the Austrians and the still imprecisely located oncoming Russians, to defeat the two enemy armies in detail. This movement was completed by October 7 (15 Vendémiaire), with the Austrians in the path of the French abandoning the Danube bridges and retreating westward to Ulm.

Unfortunately at least for the immediate prospects for Napoleon's new effort toward the strategic objective of destroying the enemy armies, the weather turned bad the next day. Freezing rain opened a series of foul days that made quagmires of the roads and minimized the French advantage in mobility. The French supply situation went from bad to desperate, with discipline beginning to break down as the men insisted on foraging on their own. At this juncture Mack changed his plans and decided to move out from Ulm. Misinformation, particularly a report of a British landing at Boulogne, led him to underestimate Napoleon's numbers, and rumors of German disaffection over the latest French invasion encouraged him to think that more willing assistance from other German states might now be available. He determined upon a modestly Napoleonic scheme of his own, to march northeast across the French lines of communications.

The principal road on which Mack planned to move was washed into the Danube by downpours on October 11, but the French corps that was supposed to be patrolling against the sort of effort that Mack was now undertaking—Marshal Ney's VI Army Corps—proved to have left only a single division, that of Pierre Antoine Dupont de l'Étang, *général de division*, in any position to interfere. The Austrians mauled Dupont around Albeck and Haslach and might well have destroyed his force had not Mack been wounded in the action, whereupon Austrian coordination vanished. Nevertheless, the Austrians captured orders revealing Ney's dispositions and the openness of the route before them. Mack prepared to hurry on to Regensburg, where according to the latest reports about his allies he might expect to link up with the Russians. Mack was well on his way to frustrating Napoleon's plan of campaign.

But Mack had been an unlucky general since his first major campaign and his fortunes did not change now. *Feldmarschall Leutnant* Franz Freiherr Werneck protested that his corps was too weary to move on to Regensburg at the pace ordered by Mack, and Ferdinand intervened to support Werneck. Movement was delayed; the French seemed to be turning up everywhere to the north, east, and south by the time it was resumed; and now the Austrians were also running short of food and less accustomed to improvising the procurement of it. For three days Mack struggled to get a serious advance under way again, but when he succeeded, in a new and more easterly direction, *Feldmarschall Leutnant* Johann Graf Riesch's corps collided with Ney's corps at the partially ruined Danube bridge at Elchingen.

The battle of Elchingen, October 14 (22 Vendémiaire), was shaped by Ney's reaction to Napoleon's resentment of the negligence that had left the road through Albeck open and nearly wrecked Dupont's division. Determined to redeem himself, Ney ordered an attack across the precarious route provided by the remaining stringers of the bridge. A spearhead of the VI Corps achieved this feat under heavy fire, new planks were quickly laid across the stringers, and a day's hard fighting sent Riesch into retreat toward Ulm.

Ferdinand now announced that rather than give the French the opportunity to capture a Habsburg he must flee the army. *Feldmarschall Leutnant* Karl Philipp Fürst zu Schwarzenburg deserted the corps he had commanded with a similar rationalization. Ferdinand urged Mack to flee as well, but that unlucky officer was determined at least to go down like a soldier and in the process to win whatever advantage might still be attainable, to buy time for others if nothing else. Leading Werneck's corps and some cavalry, Ferdinand found an escape route northward toward Nördlingen. Werneck hit a French rear-area force near Heidenheim; he was pinched off from his heavy artillery and trains, and fighting again so soon exhausted his remaining strength, so that he surrendered his infantry, some 10,000. Ferdinand with some 3,500 cavalry contrived to complete his getaway.

After Elchingen, Mack had little choice but to return to his entrenched camp at Ulm. As early as the day after Elchingen, Napoleon was bringing troops close up to Ulm and demanded that Mack surrender. Although reduced to about 27,000 men, Mack refused. He had little food but plenty of ammunition, and he still counted on the stripping of supplies from the surrounding country to hurt Napoleon. The French indeed were still suffering from hunger pangs and the cold, and such trains as they had were still far behind the Ulm front. But except for the sturdy Mack, the Austrians had sunk into almost total demoralization.

The French opened artillery fire against Ulm on October 16. The next morning mutinous subordinates virtually forced Mack into negotiations. Still hoping for the Russians to arrive, Mack agreed to an armistice with the proviso that he would surrender if relief failed to arrive in twenty-one days. Napoleon nevertheless infiltrated French soldiers into the garrison, and they soon helped provoke rioting among the Austrian rank and file. Napoleon then dispatched armed parties ostensibly to restore order. They overpowered the guards at the gates, and Mack decided that he had to surrender unconditionally. He did so on October 22 (30 Vendémiaire)—the day after Trafalgar.

At Ulm as at Marengo, Napoleon was lucky, this time in the caliber of his opponents except for Mack. Nevertheless, the Ulm campaign deserves more attention than it tends to receive. It was swiftly to be eclipsed by one of Napoleon's two most spectacular victories, the battle of Austerlitz. Austerlitz appeals to most military students more than Ulm because military studies are so little a scientific matter and so much colored by emotions, and Austerlitz offers the emotional appeal of the thunderstroke victory of the battle of annihilation: the battlefield victory so decisive that it effectively destroys an enemy army in a single clash of arms. From his first Italian campaign, Bonaparte so much relied on this kind of swift and climactic battlefield resolution of his strategic objectives, and the spectacular quality of his greatest battlefield victories has appealed so much to the emotions as well as the reason of most commentators on Napoleonic war ever since, that we think of Napoleon as preeminently the general of the battle of annihilation. Ulm supplies a corrective to that overly simple—and because of its inducements to other generals to seek battle continually, that potentially dangerous—view of Napoleon's generalship.

Napoleon did not worship battle. He made battle serve him; he did not seek battle for its own sake, simply for the intoxication to be found in it. As he approached the height of his powers, his strategic objective was with ever-increasing consistency the annihilation of the enemy army. But the Ulm campaign shows him content to secure the virtual annihilation of the enemy by the less bloody expedient of capturing his army. If he could do that, he could achieve his objective with much smaller losses to himself than battle implied, and he surely was not so mesmerized by battle as to accept its casualties when other means might permit him to attain his objective more cheaply. Napoleon could be a strategist of finesse as well as a strategist of overpoweringly forceful blows.

Yet we are apt to forget these things, because so soon after the freezing rains of Ulm there shone the sun of Austerlitz.

The Austerlitz Campaign: Preliminaries

From Ulm, Napoleon hastened eastward to rejoin a group of corps under Jean-Baptiste Jules Bernadotte, *maréchal de l'Empire*, that he had dispatched to watch the Russians. The latter were not far distant, already astride the River Inn; but while Napoleon estimated their strength at 100,000 with 60,000 Austrians soon available to join them, in fact the ravages of bad weather, bad roads, and a deficient supply system had reduced their force to some 36,000 Russians and 22,000 Austrians. Still, there was cause for haste, because Austria in its humiliation was gathering reinforcements, and Prussia was mobilizing.

Napoleon established an advanced base at Augsburg where he gathered such supplies as he could and created workshops and bakeries. But the precaution scarcely caused his troops to skip a beat in their march. The Russian commander, Lieutenant-General Mikhail Ilarionovich (or Hilarionovich) Golenischev-Kutusov (or Kutuzov), learned of Mack's surrender on October 23 (October 11 by the Russian calendar) and promptly withdrew east of the Inn, burning the bridges. In spite of the destruction of the bridges, the French, advancing along the right bank of the Danube, crossed the Inn as early as October 6 (6 Brumaire An XIV). The next day Kutusov abandoned Braunau. Emperor Franz II, though making persistent efforts to open negotiations as the familiar Habsburg method of buying time, also enjoined Kutusov to hold the line of the Ems River as long as possible, regarding its steep banks hopefully as a key to success. The Russian commander replied that the swiftness of the French advance and the depleted condition of his own troops made such a stand impossible, and the retreat continued. Napoleon, who could sense timidity in the enemy when it was much less evident than this, hastened on, no longer to protect Bernadotte but to strike for the Russo-Austrian army or Vienna.

But Kutusov was not altogether without Suvorov's spirit, nor his troops without the sturdiness of Suvorov's men. Crossing to the north bank of the Danube at Krems on November 9, two days later he perceived a chance to trap a division of the provisional corps of Marshal Adolphe Edouard Casimir Joseph Mortier in a narrow defile at Dürrenstein. Though the division managed to fight off assaults in front, flank, and rear, both the Russian soldiers and their commander gave the French renewed cause to respect them. The French casualties of 3,000 amounted to 60 percent of the troops engaged, and the defending force might have been destroyed had not the reliable Dupont arrived at the head of his own division to effect a rescue.

To Kutusov as to Napoleon, the armies were the real prizes of strategy, and the Russian commander had placed himself in position to deliver his riposte against Mortier and, more importantly, to safeguard the line of retreat to his homeland at a heavy price for the Austrians: his crossing of the Danube had uncovered Vienna. Among the causes of the near-disaster at Dürrenstein from the French perspective, in fact, was neglect of march security caused by the infatuation of Murat at the head of the cavalry screen with the possible glory of leading the French Army into the Habsburg capital. The Austrians indeed declared Vienna an open city, and Murat entered unopposed. In the city the French took 500 cannon, 100,000 muskets, great stores of ammunition, and rich quantities of other badly needed supplies.

Napoleon himself also bore a share of the blame for Dürrenstein, since the ease of his recent triumphs had rendered him carelessly forgetful of the isolation of Mortier's corps. Characteristically, the French Emperor seems to have lashed out all the more harshly at Murat for his imperfect screening of Mortier because of his awareness of his own share of the blame—but with fortunate results. After riding through Vienna south of the Danube on November 14 (23 Brumaire), Murat found the capital's main bridge still strongly guarded by an Austrian force ready to demolish it, the open status of the city notwithstanding. Along with Marshal Lannes of the V Army Corps, Murat bluffed his way to capturing the bridge by calmly striding toward the defenders and onto the span, shouting that there was an armistice. The two marshals then kept a parley going until French troops rushed and took the bridge while Murat's and Lannes's sheer presence and magnetism kept the Austrians from responding. Napoleon now had the supplies and the choice of routes from which to threaten Kutusov's line of retreat and the existence of his army all over again. The French main army would strike through Vienna, while Bernadotte with the I Corps crossed the Danube at Melk to pick up Mortier and envelop Kutusov's army.

Yet Napoleon's subordinates could not equal their commander in keeping their eyes fixed on the main objective, the enemy army. Did this failure represent a flaw in the Emperor's system of generalship? Primarily self-educated as a professional soldier himself, he did not press the foundation of military schools as diligently as he might have. This was true notwithstanding the establishment of L'École Spéciale Militaire at Fontainebleau in 1802, moved to Saint-Cyr six years later, for this was a cadet school and not a higher school of professional officership. Nor did Napoleon seek to share an understanding of his principles with his marshals as Nelson did with his captains; instead the Emperor treated his military methods as mysteries lest they be taken up by potential rivals. The most senior of Napoleon's commanders remained in large measure experienced and sometimes gifted military craftsmen, but not quite professionals in terms of education for waging war. Napoleon continued to prescribe campaign plans for them much more explicitly than a Nelson would have, compensating for the uncertainties of war only with the injunction that once battle began, everyone was to march to the sound of the guns. Often that amount of discretionary authority was sufficient for tactical purposes. It was in strategy that the limited professional education of marshals and generals most dangerously crippled their judgment on occasions when Napoleon could not prescribe everything. It was in strategy that Murat had failed by choosing Vienna as his principal objective over the enemy army; it was in strategy that Murat's limited grasp now betrayed him into failing the Emperor again.

Not that Murat alone was at fault. Napoleon's new design for eliminating Kutusov began to go awry when an accumulation of difficulties slowed Berna-dotte's crossing of the Danube by a day, until November 15. But the fatal blow came elsewhere that day, as Murat, leading the advance north from Vienna, struck Kutusov's rear guard but, suspending action, allowed himself to be talked into granting a provisional armistice. This time it was apparently dreams of the prestige of a peacemaker that led Murat astray. Napoleon forthwith reminded him both of the limits of his authority as commander of the advance guard and that the strategic objective remained the destruction of the enemy army. The French Emperor promptly repudiated the armistice, but by that time it was too late to close any traps. Murat's professional education should have come earlier than in Napoleon's disgruntled reactions to his elementary strategic errors.

The Austerlitz Campaign: The Great Battle

In spite of the logistical riches of Vienna, Napoleon's headlong late-autumn march now had to pause, to try to remedy the deterioration of the army into a band of undernourished ragamuffins. In spite of the riches of Vienna, in fact, shoes and overcoats had to be resupplied from France. Napoleon decided to replenish his stores and to regroup in the area of Brünn, some sixty miles (ninety-seven kilometers) north of Vienna. The Russians and Austrians of course used the respite for similar purposes, including the gathering in of enough reinforcements to raise what had been Kutusov's army, encamped around Olmütz, to 86,000 men. It was now the army of Tsar Alexander I, who had taken personal command, with his brother Emperor, Franz II, close at his side. (But the two Emperors were brothers more in appearance than in fact; not only were they mutually jealous, but Kutusov's campaign had not disabused the Russians of a contempt for the Austrians that they had felt at least since Suvorov's time.) The Archduke Charles meanwhile had managed to give Mas-séna the slip and was marching north from Italy with about 80,000; he reached the area of Marburg on the Drave River by late November. Another small Austrian force of 9,000 under Ferdinand d'Este was about to march northward toward Olmütz from Prague.

With this constellation of forces, the Allies would have been well advised to await the arrival of the two latter armies in the area of campaign before doing anything further. But as winter approached they were having trouble feeding themselves unless they were in motion, for they soon stripped the Olmütz district of provisions, and they were hard-pressed to utilize their accustomed eighteenth-century depot system because the Russians had stripped much of the Habsburg Empire of horses. Kutusov therefore wanted to retreat eastward again;

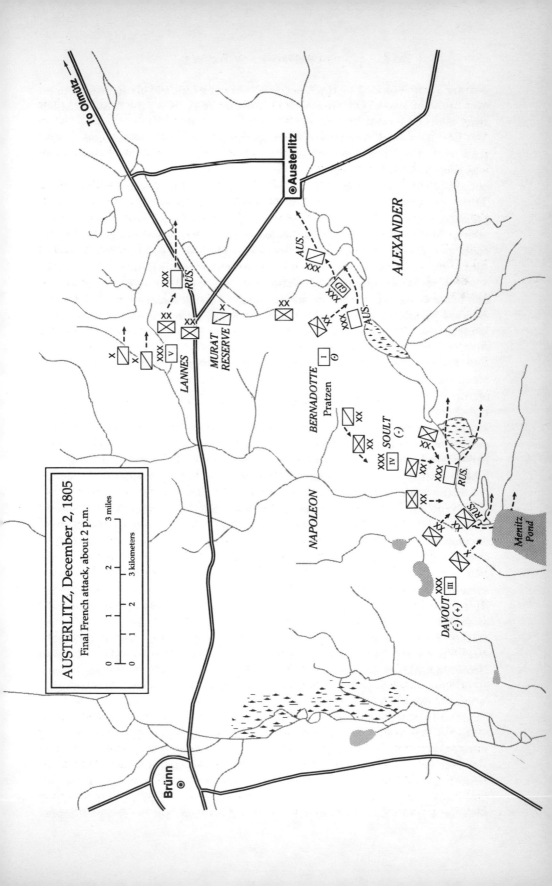

AUSTERLITZ, December 2, 1805

Final French attack, about 2 p.m.

To Olmütz

Austerlitz

Brünn

ALEXANDER

NAPOLEON

BERNADOTTE
Pratzen

SOULT (-)

DAVOUT
(-) (+)

LANNES

MURAT
RESERVE

RUS.

AUS.

AUS.

RUS.

RUS.

RUS.

Menitz
Pond

3 miles

3 kilometers

0   1   2

0   1   2

but the Tsar, seconded by the Austrians, overruled him and chose instead to go over to the offensive. On November 27 (6 Frimaire An XIV) the Austro-Russian army marched toward Brünn.

Both sides had been industriously spying on each other under cover of less than halfhearted negotiations toward another armistice. Napoleon accordingly was soon apprised of his enemies' activities, while they in turn received the benefit of the impressions from the French camp that he wanted to give them. These impressions were of French weakness. Napoleon had cultivated them precisely in order to tempt the enemy into the aggressive action he was now taking. Already near the limits of his logistical tether, Napoleon feared that he could not afford a further pursuit eastward. He also could ill afford allowing Alexander, Charles, and Ferdinand to concentrate against him. Able neither to advance nor stand still, his only solution was to bring about an enemy attack on him and a decisive battle before all the Austro-Russian forces could concentrate. Abetted by his enemies' own logistical problems, he had made his part of the latest armistice negotiations appear so timid and pleading that the Russians and Austrians blandly lent themselves to his design.

The particulars of the design sprang from Napoleon's diligent personal reconnaissance of the Brünn area. About midway between Brünn and the town of Austerlitz (Slavkov in the Czech language of this Moravian section of the Habsburg Empire), which lay fifteen miles (twenty-four kilometers) to the east-southeast, he had found the sort of natural defensive position on which a small portion of his army might conduct an effective resistance against superior numbers while his main force prepared a counterblow. The area was wooded and broken by the low valleys of numerous streams and a group of lakes (the latter in fact being artificial ponds that are no longer to be found).

Napoleon had taken the precaution of readying an alternate line of retreat northward into Bohemia, but he did not expect to use it; events were developing almost altogether to his taste. He deployed the IV Corps of Marshal Nicolas Jean de Dieu Soult and a large part of Murat's cavalry, some 23,600 and 7,400 men respectively, behind—west of—the Goldbach Brook some three miles (five kilometers) east of the town of Austerlitz. The Austro-Russian army could be expected to deploy on the relatively high plateau east of the brook and around the town of Pratzen, 900 to 1,000 feet (275 to 305 meters) above sea level, to strike directly or turn the flank of this deliberately weak French right wing. Napoleon brought up the III Corps of Marshal Louis Nicolas Davout to support Soult and Murat if necessary. But after a forty-eight-hour march covering the ninety miles (145 kilometers) from Vienna by late December 1 (10 Frimaire An XIV), the bulk of the French army lay concealed behind another plateau west of the Goldbach, a somewhat lower elevation than the Pratzen Plateau, called today the Breitesfeld and rising to a summit about 850 feet (260 meters) called the Zurlan.

Napoleon's plan was that at the critical moment, after the enemy had sufficiently exhausted himself against the bait posed by the French right, he would hurl the remainder of his troops, Davout on the right and Lannes and Bernadotte with the V and I Corps on the left, against the enemy's rear. The plan represented a model exploitation of the *corps d'armée* system of organization. It also represented a maturation of perhaps the preeminent Napoleonic tactical maneuver, *la manœuvre sur les derrières*, which, coming at the climax of a battle when the enemy was already on the brink of exhaustion, would unhinge the enemy psychologically, rupture his line of retreat, and impose a sufficiently devastating combination of physical and psychological damage to produce the practical destruction of the enemy army.

Allied attacks on the French across the Goldbach began late on December 1. Anticipating the attack, Napoleon was touring his camps to inspirit the troops, and many of them had ignited bivouac straw into bonfires in his honor. The infatuated Allied high command assumed that these fires were the familiar ruse to conceal a retreat and grew yet more overconfident. Already the young Tsar had insisted against the Habsburg Emperor and Kutusov that there must be a full-scale attack on the morrow; that decision was now assured. The specifics of the Allied plan were developed by *Feldmarschall Leutnant* Franz Ritter von Weyrother, detailed as chief of staff to Kutusov. Weyrother explained his plan on a large-scale map at one in the morning. The Allies would cross the Goldbach in force south of the French right, turn north to envelop the French, and cut the Brünn-Vienna road. A secondary attack would hold the French left in place. The plan divided the Allied army into seven major formations each with a mission of its own. Such complexity was all the more dangerous because the language barrier probably left the design imperfectly understood by some of the Russian leaders. Moreover, some of the generals remained opposed to the whole idea of attacking, and there was enough disgruntlement and sheer indifference that the mood was scarcely electric. Most of the generals evidently paid little attention to Weyrother's map; Kutusov, who was just short of sixty, chose the occasion for a snooze.

The late autumn temperatures had turned just high enough to make the ground muddy and treacherous, especially along the stream banks, though the lakes were still frozen. In the morning hours of December 2 there was a fog that further assured the concealment from the Allies of Napoleon's massing for a counterattack. As the Allied advance developed, its spearhead appeared farther south than Napoleon had anticipated, so he added almost all of Soult's corps to his offensive scheme and left only a small part of the IV Corps in a primarily defensive role; instead, Davout's corps, farther to the right, would play the part earlier assigned to Soult. The uncertainties of battlefield communications before the radio being what they were, Napoleon's latest orders failed to reach Davout; but when Soult's cavalry found itself hard-pressed and sent word to the III Corps commander, Napoleon's standing injunction to march to the sound of the guns came into good use. Davout deployed rapidly; he took upon himself at Austerlitz something of the role of Desaix at Marengo.

Weyrother's plan was not only excessively complicated. Its offensive thrust by the Allied left pulled the main weight of the army, the left flank of Russian troops under the Russian Field Marshal Friedrich Wilhelm, Count of Buxhöwden (or Buxhowden), farther and farther away from the center of the Pratzen Plateau. On the plateau, only the 16,200 men of *Feldzeugmeister* Carl Graf

Kolowrat-Krakowski's formation and the 10,500 of the Allied reserve under the Grand Duke Constantine, brother of the Tsar, would be available to resist a French counterstroke.

Against the French right, the main Allied attack scored at least a measure of the success to which its superior numbers seemed to entitle it. By mid-morning Davout had been pushed back about a mile, but he retained the integrity of his formations and contact with the French center. The fighting on his front continued throughout the day, and all day long a French force that began with some 12,500 men—many of them weary after the march from Vienna—held back more than 40,000 of the enemy.

Napoleon meanwhile did not wait long to launch his counterattack. By about eight in the morning he decided that the Allies were fully enough engaged to warrant his throwing forward the bulk of Soult's corps and Murat's cavalry. As early as about ten the Pratzen Plateau had fallen to Soult. The French were now well along not only toward cutting the line of retreat of the Allied force that was assailing Davout but toward cutting between Kolowrat and Constantine to separate Constantine and the Allied right flank from the main part of the Austro-Russian army.

So the afternoon sun broke through the fog to shine on a French victory; the only remaining question was how great a victory. On the Pratzen it was the counterattacking French who outnumbered the Allies by about two to one, but Kutusov was with Kolowrat's formation, and under fire he did not nap; he quickly changed Kolowrat's front to his right and opened another phase of the battle that lasted through much of the day, this time with the Allies defending stoutly against superior numbers. Some time after midday, however, Napoleon pulled Bernadotte's I Corps out of the action that along with Lannes's V it had been fighting against the secondary Allied attack on the French left, conducted by the formation of Field Marshal Peter (Pyotr) Prince Bagration. Bernadotte charged with a decisive weight into the battle around Pratzen.

Napoleon then ordered the whole French center to incline toward its right for a *manœuvre sur les derrières* against the Allied main force to the south and west. This threat in turn helped precipitate a dramatic countercharge on the Pratzen Plateau by the Russian Imperial Guard from the Grand Duke's reserve formation. But the Russian Guard were too completely paradeground troops, trained less for fighting than for display. They advanced in superbly aligned ranks, but they accelerated into their running charge with the bayonet too early and reached the French line out of breath. Still, they scored a brief triumph, breaking the French first line, but Napoleon opportunely dispatched the cavalry of his own Imperial Guard in a countercharge. The outnumbered Allies around Pratzen broke at last, and by about 2:30 the Allied main force was cut off as Napoleon intended. Buxhöwden ordered half his troops to retreat eastward and the other half to fight their way north along the Goldbach; but it was too late for the first move now that the French were swarming everywhere, and the second was hopeless. Buxhöwden's Russians had to flee southward. Many were captured. Many tried to escape across the frozen lakes, but a French cannonade along with the weight of men, horses, and guns broke the ice, and many fell into the cold waters; how numerous were those who died in this way is uncertain, but it may well have been 2,000.

Marshal Bagration on the opposite flank now decided he must retreat also to preserve his force, which by and large had fought Lannes to a deadlock. As Bagration withdrew, the early dusk of December settled in to end the fighting between 4:30 and 5. The French were too battered and disorganized to pursue Bagration effectively, and he managed to cover about forty miles (sixty-four kilometers) in the next forty hours. It should be noted again that in spite of the standard call of military textbooks for vigorous pursuit, the phenomenon is rare even when the greatest generals have won their greatest victories.

Austerlitz was surely a great Napoleonic victory, destined to be one of the Emperor's two most complete. The Allies lost some 11,000 Russians and 4,000 Austrians killed and wounded and another 12,000 prisoners to the French, along with 180 guns and 45 to 50 colors and standards. French losses were about 2,000 killed, 7,000 wounded, and some 573 captured, a relatively light toll considering the severity of much of the fighting on Davout's front and on the Pratzen Plateau. The ratio between Allied and French casualty figures goes far to explain why Austerlitz came to be regarded as the epitome of the Napoleonic battle. The ratio favored the French so greatly that, if Napoleon's army was too much injured to pursue immediately, that army was nevertheless still a highly effective force, while the Allied army had been substantially destroyed. The combination of shattering numbers of casualties with the psychological damage wrought by the abrupt shift from supreme confidence to devastating defeat, and especially by the virtual entrapment of much of the army through the successful *manœuvre sur les derrières* against Buxhöwden's force, meant that Napoleon had practically annihilated the enemy army as an effective fighting force.

The most able strategists since Gustavus Adolphus had aimed at the destruction of the enemy army as the strategic objective that would most directly and economically resolve the issues of war in their favor. Of all the strategists of modern war until 1805, only Gustavus and Marlborough had approached the completeness of Napoleon's success in attaining the enemy army's annihilation in a single climactic battle. After a certain blurring of strategic purposes during the supposedly limited wars of the eighteenth century, the fury of the French Revolution had restored the strategy of annihilation as the strategic norm. Now at Austerlitz Napoleon had as nearly accomplished the enemy army's battlefield annihilation as any general of modern times. Napoleon and Austerlitz henceforth became cynosures of strategic study in all European armies.

And the high drama of Austerlitz assured its overshadowing in military studies the more complete and less costly, but also less spectacular, method of destroying an enemy army that Napoleon had demonstrated at Ulm. Henceforth the concept of a strategy of annihilation remained inextricably intertwined with the worship of battle among European soldiers as the means to annihilation. The annihilation of the enemy army was emphatically reasserted as the European general's standard strategic goal. The Austerlitz battle, the thunderstroke victory that destroyed the enemy army in a single clash of arms, became almost every general's hoped-for means to the goal.

But not every general was Napoleon, and more than ever before, fighting bloody battles became henceforth almost an object in itself.

The Jena-Auerstädt Campaign: Preliminaries

The Third Coalition failed less spectacularly but scarcely less surely elsewhere than on the field of Austerlitz. The coalition's only glimmer of success occurred with an Anglo-Russian occupation of Naples, which fizzled into a hasty reembarkation of the troops as soon as the news of Austerlitz arrived. Another Anglo-Russian expedition was supposed to entertain Napoleon in northern Europe, but here the Russians accomplished practically nothing, while the British did little more than enlist Hanoverians, to the annoyance of the Prussians, whose army had marched into Hanover when the French withdrew most of their occupying force for concentration elsewhere.

It was not until December 4 that Napoleon got a pursuit under way from the Austerlitz battlefield, and by that time he had received an appeal for an interview from the Emperor Franz. The meeting led to an armistice agreement before the day was out, with the Russians to be included if they returned home. The Tsar and Kutusov in fact hastened to claim to Davout that they had already concluded an armistice, to forestall that hero of Austerlitz from completing the destruction of their army when his pursuit caught up with what remained of it.

The Austrian armistice led to another Habsburg humiliation in the Treaty of Pressburg of December 26 (5 Nivôse An XIV), which confirmed the decisiveness of Austerlitz. So triumphant was Napoleon's strategy of annihilation that Austria virtually abandoned its status as a great power. It ceded its territories in Italy to the Kingdom of Italy and in south Germany to France's allies Bavaria and Württemberg; it recognized Bavaria and Württemberg as independent kingdoms free of all feudal ties to the Holy Roman Empire of the German Nation; the title of Holy Roman Emperor became practically empty. Napoleon rubbed in the latter point by spending part of his energy in the first half of 1806 in wringing still further concessions from Austria, until on July 12 the Holy Roman Empire was formally dissolved and its Emperor Franz II became simply Emperor Franz I of Austria. Thirteen days later there came into being the Confederation of the Rhine, a satellite of the French Empire consisting of Bavaria, Württemberg, Baden, Hesse-Darmstadt, and a number of smaller principalities.

In keeping with other recent vacillations in Russian policy, the Tsar went out of his way after Austerlitz to make public profession of his admiration for Napoleon. The Emperor of the French, susceptible to flattery in spite of his shrewdness, ignored the advice of his Foreign Minister, Charles Maurice de Talleyrand-Périgord, that Austria would make a more reliable pillar of support in the East than Russia. Consequently a preliminary agreement of peace and friendship was negotiated with Russia, only to stall unratified as, true to Talleyrand's suspicions, Tsar Alexander shifted again by supporting the Prussians in their escalating quarrel with France.

That quarrel had been brewing all through the campaigns of 1805. Bernadotte's corps had violated Prussian neutrality by marching through the enclave of

Ansbach during the Ulm campaign, and the Prussians had mobilized. Despite irritations with the British, King Frederick William (Friedrich Wilhelm) III of Prussia had gradually made up his mind that his country ought to be in on what he anticipated would be the Third Coalition's destruction of the power of the upstart Bonaparte. By November 28 Christian August Curt Graf von Haugwitz had arrived at the French Emperor's headquarters to deliver a virtual ultimatum as a prelude to Prussian entry into the war. Napoleon managed to fob Haugwitz off to Talleyrand, who stalled him without delivery of his message until after Austerlitz. Then Haugwitz rightly concluded that his sovereign would not want the message delivered at all. Prussia demobilized.

Nevertheless, in this instance attempted flattery of the victor did not serve to ease tensions. Napoleon was too well aware of the hostile intentions that Prussia had harbored and not nearly so much impressed by Prussian as by Russian power, the memory of Frederick the Great notwithstanding. Whatever lingering respect the Emperor of the French might have held for Frederick II's army was diluted by his contempt for Frederick William III as a callow opportunist, a fair enough estimate. So he treated Prussia with little more tenderness than defeated Austria, forcing Berlin to yield several patches of territory, including the principality of Cleves which he joined with Berg to make a grand duchy for Murat, husband of Napoleon's sister Caroline. Moreover, Napoleon insisted that Prussia agree to join in any economic measures that he might invoke against Great Britain. In return, Napoleon allowed Prussia to retain Hanover, a concession however that injected a poison into Prussian foreign policy be aggravating the estrangement from Britain.

Napoleon wanted Prussian foreign policy poisoned in ways that would enhance Prussia's isolation because the independence of Prussia stood as the most important remaining obstacle to his domination of Germany. He was determined to find pretexts for crushing that independence. After the armistice with Austria, he deployed the *Grande Armée* in south Germany in such a manner that its dispositions presented no obvious threat to Prussia but nevertheless so that its corps could quickly be concentrated on the upper Main for an invasion of Prussia. Here he left it to each of the corps commanders to rest and train his troops and to assimilate recruits in his own way; to that extent as well as to their experienced instinct to march to the sound of the guns he was willing to trust their discretion. Again he busied himself sending spies into the potential enemy's country and digesting their reports as a prelude to war. As conflict became imminent, he informed the corps commanders of his general plan to advance toward Berlin from the Bamberg-Würzburg area. He would thus cover a line of communications reaching from Mainz to Frankfurt am Main, with a secondary line of communications from Bamberg to Augsburg also secured. His brother Louis Bonaparte, crowned King of Holland on May 24, 1806, and an experienced artillerist and cavalryman, headed 30,000 troops deployed to threaten Prussia's flank from the lower Rhine.

To Napoleon, the Prussian Army no longer deserved the aura of greatness it had inherited. Its experience of recent warfare was limited. While the basic military education of its junior officers remained sound, Frederick had never provided much of a schooling in higher command; he had preferred to keep the reins in his own hands (at least as much as did Napoleon himself). When Frederick passed away, exceptional leadership had passed from the Prussian Army with him. This deficiency was aggravated by the new battlefield tactics, corps system, and logistical flexibility of the French Revolutionary armies as improved by Napoleon. The Prussian Army remained wedded to eighteenth-century linear tactics and to a depot system of supply, with twelve miles (nineteen kilometers) regarded as a hard day's march. The high command continued to exercise a centralized control that undercut any approach toward a corps system. Prussian divisions, newly organized, were the all-arms formations that the French had abandoned in 1800.

Prussia continued to maintain an army disproportionate to its population— 254,000 men on paper, including garrison troops and militia. But without the resolve toward preparedness that had characterized Frederick the Great and his immediate predecessors, the system was compromised by furloughing two-thirds of the infantry and half the cavalry from ten to eleven months of the year. Yet this extension of the always debatable furlough system did not have the possibly beneficial effect of uniting civilian and military outlooks. Instead, as the quality of the army declined, civilian resentment of the burdens of maintaining a great-power army in a small country increased apace. When soldiers marched by in overworn uniforms and still carrying the muskets of the Seven Years War, the outcome of Prussia's military exertions no longer seemed worth the sacrifices entailed. Sentiment drifted back toward the antimilitary attitudes that had made Prussia one of the least martial of German states before the Great Elector.

Under Frederick William III, who was no soldier, the senior Prussian command was still exercised by the Duke of Brunswick, now seventy-one years old. The senior military adviser to the King, *Generalfeldmarschall* Richard Joachim Heinrich von Möllendorff (or Mollendorff), was eighty-two. The principal field commanders were in their sixties. Age tied these soldiers more firmly to the remnants of Frederick II's military system and deepened the blindness with which Prussia foolishly took up Napoleon's gauge of battle.

On August 7, 1806, the Prussian government learned that Napoleon was tempting Britain with the return of Hanover as a peace offering. Immediately a war faction gained ascendancy over Frederick William, headed by the zealously patriotic Queen Luise, Princess of Mecklenburg-Strelitz, a considerably stronger personality than her husband, the King. On August 10 Prussia began mobilizing once more. In September its army invaded Saxony to compel that state to join it in war. On September 26 it issued an ultimatum that all French troops withdraw west of the Rhine and that Prussia be free to organize its own league of north German states. The Prussians knew the ultimatum meant war. Including the Saxons, but with much of the Prussian Army cooped up in garrisons, the Prussians could oppose Napoleon with 171,000 men in the field. Two Russian armies totaling 60,000 men were forming around Brest Litovsk, evidently with anti-French intentions despite the courtship between Napoleon and the Tsar, but with their specific intent unclear.

Prussia summoned Napoleon to deliver his answer to the ultimatum by

October 8. He did not in fact receive the demands until the 7th. On September 18 and 19, however, he had drawn up a characteristically detailed plan for the initial movements of the *Grande Armée* should war come. While his plan underwent modifications as new intelligence arrived, his army was ready enough that it began moving the same day the ultimatum arrived and entered Prussian-occupied territory the next day.

The routes of the French led through the Thüringer Wald, a hilly area inhospitable to cavalry, where the checking of a large mounted force might have blocked the advance of the whole army. For this reason and to facilitate surprising the Prussians with the swift onslaught of the French infantry upon them, Napoleon adopted the experiment of holding back his cavalry behind the leading infantry columns, except for a few vedettes. The infantry advanced in a huge battalion square of some 200,000 men, ready to fight in every direction and to overwhelm any outpost they might encounter.

The Prussians had intended to maintain the initiative that they had seized by moving into Saxony, but with their elderly generals overfond of councils of war, they were busy debating the form their offensive should take while their army lay extended in a loose defensive cordon all the way from Mainz to Dresden. Upon this cordon the French pounced as early as October 9. They hastened out of the north slopes of the Thüringer Wald to overcome the Prussians stationed along the upper Saale River. At Saalfeld on the 10th Lannes's V Corps killed Prince Ludwig-Ferdinand (Louis-Ferdinand) of Prussia, commander of the advance guard of the 42,000-man field army of *General der Infanterie* Friedrich Ludwig Fürst von Hohenlohe-Ingelfingen. The next day French light cavalry followed up by capturing Hohenlohe's supply train.

The quick French triumphs left the Saxons of Hohenlohe's army near mutiny and the Prussians dispirited. Hohenlohe retreated to the area of Weimar and Jena to try to pull his army together. It required considerable effort from the sixty-year-old general simply to quell a panic among the soldiers in the streets of Jena on the afternoon of the 10th, when there was a false alarm of a French attack.

On the more open ground beyond the Saale, the French cavalry resumed their accustomed place in the van, but Murat again disappointed his brother-in-law with lackadaisical leadership, and the Emperor grew so disgusted that he authorized Antoine Charles Louis Lassalle, *général de brigade* and commanding the foremost cavalry, to offer up to 6,000 francs' reward for information about the Prussian dispositions. If he could find and pin down the enemy, his immediate aim now was a *manœuvre sur les derrières* to cut the Prussian line of communications with Berlin. Impatient to get on with it—he had already written to Frederick William telling him the outcome was assured and that he ought to make peace—he let the strong battalion square of his original advance break up and allowed Lannes's V Corps and Marshal Pierre François Charles Augereau's VII Corps behind it to reach out toward Weimar and Jena in an isolated probe that could be dangerous should the Prussians offer a riposte.

The Duke of Brunswick with the largest Prussian field army having marched to support Hohenlohe, the Prussians in fact had a concentration of about 100,000 that could have leaped upon Lannes and Augereau by October 13. The *Grande Armée* had already marched so hard, moreover, that the Emperor ordered the 13th to be a day of rest for most of it. Fortunately for Napoleon in the latest of his impetuosities, the Prussian commanders were again preoccupied with debate among themselves. Any spare energies they might have possessed went into placating the Saxons, especially reminding them that their complaints about inadequate supplies could have been just as well voiced by the Prussians themselves, while also seeking urgent help from the Commissary at Weimar, who was none other than Johann Wolfgang von Goethe.

On the afternoon of the 13th Napoleon was on the road from Gera to Jena when he heard from Lannes that the V Corps had occupied the latter place and that there were Prussians not far to the northward. The Emperor hastened forward to meet Lannes about 3:00 P.M. and to reconnoiter from the Landgrafenberg height northwest of the city and beyond another crossing of the winding Saale River. While another, higher summit, the Dornberg, prevented his seeing all of the broken and partly wooded plateau occupied by the Prussian Army, he concluded that most of that force had to be in the vicinity, and he ordered his own army to concentrate toward Jena, if necessary marching all night.

In fact the main body of the Prussian Army had already begun marching northward away from Jena, because the setbacks since October 9 had caused timidity to rise uppermost in the Prussian debates, and because the French center of gravity had moved far enough beyond Lannes and Augereau to begin to achieve Napoleon's aim of a threat to Prussian communications with Berlin. The withdrawal was down the west bank of the Saale through Freiburg and Merseburg; Brunswick commanded it. Hohenlohe remained behind to command a rear guard near Jena, while a smaller rear guard remained around Weimar.

The extent of the Prussian campfires during the night confirmed Napoleon's conviction that the main enemy army still lay in front of the Landgrafenberg at Jena. He therefore ordered an attack from the Landgrafenberg for October 14, while Davout with the III Corps followed by Bernadotte—since June the Prince de Ponte Corvo—with the I were to march up the Saale toward Apolda for the decisive *manœuvre sur les derrières*.

These orders were to lead to an even more complete destruction of the enemy army than Napoleon had achieved at Austerlitz, but not by the method prescribed, because that method was based on the erroneous belief that the Prussian main force still lay in front of the Landgrafenberg.

The Jena-Auerstädt Campaign: The Battles

The battle of Jena began early in the morning of October 14 in a heavy fog. Lannes's men had strained during the night to prepare a practicable road to carry them to the narrow summit of the Landgrafenberg whence to launch their attack, while Augereau's corps on Lannes's left and Marshal Soult's IV Corps on his right marched to attack out of ravines on the flanks of the Landgrafenberg, all to aim at the Dornberg and its plateau. The French had

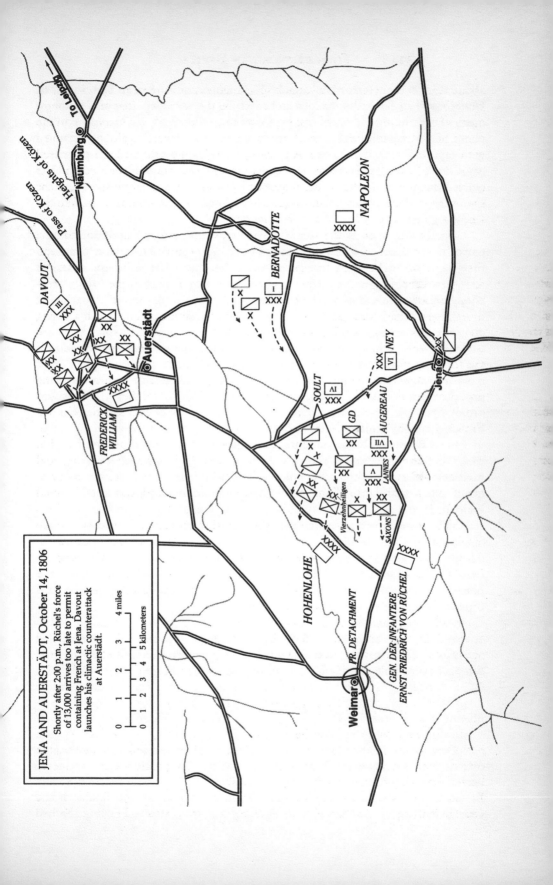

JENA AND AUERSTÄDT, October 14, 1806

Shortly after 2:00 p.m., Rüchel's force of 13,000 arrives too late to permit containing French at Jena. Davout launches his climactic counterattack at Auerstädt.

To Leipzig

Heights of Kösen

Pass of Kösen

Naumburg

DAVOUT

Auerstädt

FREDERICK WILLIAM

BERNADOTTE

NAPOLEON

NEY

SOULT

GD

AUGEREAU

LANNES

Jena

Vierzehnheiligen

SAXONS

HOHENLOHE

PR. DETACHMENT

Weimar

GEN. DER INFANTERE
ERNST FRIEDRICH VON RÜCHEL

0   1   2   3   4 miles
0   1   2   3   4   5 kilometers

about 60,000 men formed to attack, Hohenlohe some 38,000. Nevertheless, Hohenlohe had belatedly decided to recapture the initiative, not realizing how many of the enemy had come up. Had it not been for the fog, Prussian artillery might indeed have inflicted much damage upon the French, because Lannes's men especially would have been exposed as they deployed on the Landgrafenberg. By the time the Prussian advance was well under way, Lannes's corps had crossed the perilously narrow neck of land between the Landgrafenberg and the Dornberg, while Augereau's and Soult's were climbing from the ravines onto the Dornberg plateau.

The Prussians charged the French at first in the best Frederician manner, but as they paused to fire, the French worked up a sufficiently heavy counterfire—largely from behind houses and trees—that the climactic Prussian bayonet attack failed to attain its proper momentum. The French were still loosely enough arrayed that they might have been susceptible to a cavalry attack, but the Prussians had frittered away their squadrons of horse into their all-arms divisions and lacked a sufficient cavalry mass for the purpose.

Altogether, the Prussians mounted three additional infantry assaults beyond the first, but the remnants of Frederician discipline could not accomplish much more than to compel admiration for bravery; they were unable to overcome the superior numbers that the French brought to the field. In artillery, the Prussians actually had the advantage in numbers of guns, by about two to one; but the French gradually outdueled them.

Soon after noon Napoleon ordered his own attack, now a counterstroke. For about an hour the Prussians kept up a stout resistance in spite of losses and weariness, but at last their front broke, and Murat led the French cavalry to exploit their disarray. In classic fashion the mobile arm employed at the correct moment turned retreat into rout. The 13,000 Prussian troops who had remained around Weimar arrived opportunely to prevent the rout from becoming unabated disaster, for a time stemming the French onslaught with a courageous display of Frederician volley fire. Then they too were worn down and fled. The casualty figures at Jena followed the usual pattern of a battle in which the unleashing of cavalry produces decisive results. The French losses were about 5,000, but the Prussians and Saxons lost some 11,000 killed and wounded and 15,000 prisoners, along with 200 cannon and 30 flags.

Well before the battle ended, Napoleon knew that he had miscalculated and was not fighting the main body of the enemy. From far to the northeast came a faint rumble suggesting that to Davout or Bernadotte or both might have fallen that task. In fact it was Davout who, ten or more miles (sixteen or more kilometers) away, north of the town of Auerstädt (Auerstadt or Auerstedt), was playing a still greater role than that of Desaix at Marengo or himself at Austerlitz.

Davout with his III Corps had crossed the Saale at Kösen in the morning to effect the planned *manœuvre sur les derrières* while Napoleon pinned the enemy down near Jena. Instead of being pinned, however, the Prussian main army, with Frederick William himself on the scene, came marching into collision with Davout as the French reached a plateau above the Saale after ascending through the Kösen defile from the river. There were at least 50,000 Prussians to about 26,000 French.

The Prussians, furthermore, had been marching in two columns, while the French emerged from the defile in one, so that the Prussians might have been expected to deploy more rapidly. But the Prussians still moved to the attack at seventy-five paces per minute, while the French deployed at the quick or double, 120 or 150 paces per minute. The result was that they were able to form line rapidly enough to avoid being overwhelmed, and also through a long morning's fighting to shift troops swiftly enough to wavering sections of their line. Davout himself seemed always to be present at the critical points and to initiate the critical reinforcing moves. By midday, nevertheless, the French were nearly exhausted, and the Prussians retained a strong reserve ready for commitment.

At this juncture, however, the de facto Prussian commander, the Duke of Brunswick, fell mortally wounded. The Duke's more than able *Quartiermeister-lieutenant*—his chief of staff—*Oberstlieutenant* Gerhard Johann David von Scharnhorst, happened to be at another part of the field, bolstering the army's left flank. The commander of the reserve, *Generallieutenant* Friedrich Adolf Graf von Kalckreuth (or Kalkreuth), refused to attack without a direct order from the Commander in Chief. Frederick William, however, was off on the Prussian right, participating bravely but to no good purpose in the battle. Apparently neither the King nor Scharnhorst was promptly informed of Brunswick's fate. *General der Kavallerie* Gerhard Leberecht von Blücher, sixty-four years old and thus meeting the Prussian norm for antiquity but decidedly above the norm in his zest for combat, tried to remedy Kalckreuth's diffidence with a cavalry attack, but again the lack of a large enough mass of horsemen defeated the purpose.

The division of Charles Antoine Louis Alexis Morand, *général de brigade*, on Davout's left repelled the last serious Prussian assault. Exhaustion notwithstanding, Morand then advanced pivoting on his right inward against the Prussian right flank. Davout ordered the division of Louis Friant, *général de division*, similarly to pivot against the Prussian left. Caught in the nutcracker, the Prussian front collapsed, despite Kalckreuth's commitment of his reserve along with renewed efforts by Blücher.

The Prussian officers at Auerstädt uniformly credited the French with about twice as many men as they actually had; but Davout had fought his battle alone, Bernadotte through a series of misunderstandings and almost willful obtusity having withdrawn the I Corps to a location about midway between Jena and Auerstädt where he debated with himself about which battle to enter and at last marched to Jena too late to do any good. Alone, Davout had kept control of the shape of the conflict in spite of two-to-one odds against him and completed the defeat of his enemy with a textbook double envelopment. He had lost more than Napoleon at Jena, almost 8,000 men, but he inflicted losses of 12,000 killed and wounded along with 3,000 prisoners and 115 guns on his enemies. Davout's conduct of the battle of Auerstädt is one of the signal achievements of all military history; his ennoblement as duc d'Auerstaedt seems a small enough reward.

So battered and demoralized were the Prussians that in the next four weeks their once-proud army evaporated. The retreat of the main body, reasonably orderly at first, disintegrated during the night of October 15–16 into a flight not much better controlled than that from Jena. As Frederick William and his subordinates gradually regained a measure of discipline over the remnants, they headed for the mouth of the Elbe and Lübeck, hoping to find help from the British or the Russians. The transformation of many soldiers into fugitives continued along the way, however, because the officers persisted in forbidding foraging and confiscations among the populace, which far from contributing willingly to the resupply of the army, or showing a modicum of humanity toward the wounded and the sick, prepared obsequiously to welcome the victorious French (so obsequiously that the subsequent welcomes earned only French contempt).

When Napoleon received Davout's first report of Auerstädt at nine on the morning of October 15, he could scarcely believe it. Until a second, confirmatory report arrived about noon, the Emperor still believed he might have to fight another battle against the Prussians, to deal with the main body that had eluded him at Jena. He ordered Saxon prisoners released as a preliminary to turning Saxony into an ally. A full-fledged pursuit got under way on the 16th, vigorous enough to give another push to the Prussian Army's disintegration. On October 26 Davout entered Berlin, after marching 166 miles (267 kilometers) in twelve days and fighting two rear-guard actions along the way. Bernadotte was following, but his unscarred troops could not keep up with Davout's pace.

Two days later Murat's cavalry overtook Hohenlohe's force near Prenzlau north of Berlin. By claiming that he had 100,000 men when in fact he had no infantry and only tired horsemen with worn-out mounts, Murat bluffed Hohenlohe into surrendering the 16,000 troops remaining to him. That left only Blücher with any semblance of a Prussian field army. Hoping either to escape by sea or to make contact with Swedish forces reported to be near Lübeck, Blücher stormed into the latter neutral free city on November 5. No Swedish army was there. The next day Soult and Bernadotte arrived to assault, overrun, and sack the city. Blücher got away with a small force but was captured on the 7th.

Altogether, at Jena, Auerstädt, and in the pursuit, Napoleon's army took 140,000 prisoners, 800 field guns, and 250 flags. This campaign was destined to remain the greatest triumph of Napoleon's strategy of annihilation. The Prussian Army was almost totally destroyed. Never was a Napoleonic *manœuvre sur les derrières* that unfolded according to plan so successful as Davout's *manœuvre sur les derrières* that ended in unanticipated collision with the main Prussian Army.

Yet it should be a standing caution to strategists of annihilation who tend to heed too little the embittering consequences of total defeat that from the ashes of Jena and Auerstädt the Prussians raised up an even more formidable army than Frederick's had been at its highest glory. And this new Prussian Army was destined not only to contribute mightily to the ultimate defeat of Napoleon, but to become the nucleus of an army that twice more humbled France and in the twentieth century bestrode nearly all Europe and long held most of the world at bay.

THE GRADUAL ECLIPSE OF THE BATTLE OF ANNIHILATION; THE RISE OF THE WAR OF ATTRITION

I n the exhilaration following his destruction of the old Prussian Army, the Emperor felt so sure of the completeness of his domination of the Continent that from Berlin he turned again toward dealing with the pestiferous opposition of the island kingdom across the Channel. On November 21, 1806, he issued the Berlin Decrees, the foundation of what came to be called the Continental System, in which he formalized and extended earlier efforts to counter the economic warfare waged against France by the Royal Navy with a species of blockade raised up in spite of the absence of French sea power. In that absence, Napoleon would exploit instead his domination of the Continent. He declared the British Isles blockaded in that all commerce and correspondence between them and the parts of Europe under French control were forbidden. All British goods already in those parts of Europe were to be confiscated.

Focusing on Great Britain as the principal remaining rival, however, was somewhat premature. Infuriating as Napoleon found the British, issuing the Berlin Decrees may have been to some degree a diversion from thinking about another intractable problem, the unwillingness of Tsar Alexander to incorporate Russia into the Napoleonic system even after the latest demonstration of French military might. Russia's refusal to agree to a definitive peace in fact led Prussia to a similar refusal in spite of the near-destruction of its army. Behind the few Prussian detachments remaining in East Prussia, Poland, and Silesia there moved menacing Russian formations. On November 9 came word that at least 56,000 of the Tsar's soldiers had advanced westward toward the Prussian frontier in late October.

Eylau

Four days earlier Napoleon had already sent Davout eastward to reconnoiter at the head of 2,500 dragoons. The whole *Grande Armée* soon began to follow, as promptly as minimal rest and refitting permitted. But Napoleon reluctantly continued to send out peace overtures. As head of state as well as Commander in Chief of the army he had to concern himself with domestic politics in distant France, where, his military victories notwithstanding, the honeymoon of the early days of the Empire was ending and his counterrevolution was beginning to provoke dissent. As Commander in Chief he was unsure how to cope with the numerous Russians and their country's great distances should they continue to display recalcitrance. Foreseeing a need for more troops and especially for more horsemen, Napoleon reinforced his cavalry from as far away as Italy. He had already begun what was to grow into an addictive habit with an early call-up of the 1806 class of conscripts, which gave him a pool of 80,000 newly trained infantry, the first of whom were already arriving in his camps. He now accelerated also the conscription of the class of 1807. He further stepped up recruiting efforts in the subject and satellite states of Europe.

In Prussia, the French lines of communications were already dangerously extended. The most likely axis of an eastward advance was directly toward the old Polish capital of Warsaw. Not only was the city a major road junction, but also the first French penetrations of Poland were inspiring fierce welcoming outbursts of Polish patriotism, which Napoleon might find it useful to stimulate. Yet a march toward Warsaw would leave a strong Russian concentration on the French left, unconquered Silesia in the rear, and uncertain Austria to the right. Too-hearty encouragement of Polish nationalism might cement solidarity among Russia, Austria, and Prussia and perhaps goad Austria back into the war. Moving still farther eastward beyond the Vistula from Warsaw, furthermore, would involve the French Army in difficult, marshy terrain broken by several rivers. Nevertheless, Napoleon chose the Warsaw route.

The logistical difficulties were about to prove worse than Napoleon seems to have anticipated—or ever would recognize they might be, at least until after 1812. Except for the Egyptian adventure, he was accustomed to campaigning in reasonably rich, well populated countries with moderate distances. The mobility of the French Revolutionary armies was possible largely because they lived off the land through which they marched. So did the Russian armies—their inability to stand still had helped precipitate the battle of Austerlitz—but their accustomed scale of supply was more Spartan than the French. Napoleon was sufficiently aware of the distances and the frequent emptiness of eastern Europe that as he prepared for his next marches, he gathered wagons in numbers that for him were unprecedented, along with horses and ponies, preparing to subsist as much as necessary through a depot system. But as with the Austrians who found it hard to break the opposite habits, the Revolutionary armies were ill prepared to cope with elaborate wagon transport. They lacked the necessary organizational means, and the soldiers, unaccustomed to handling draft animals, used them too hard and broke them down. It did not help that many of the roads were mere tracks.

The Tsar meanwhile had felt uncertain of his own purposes—which was not uncharacteristic of Alexander I. Moreover, the French had contrived distractions by stirring the Ottoman Empire into a renewal of its almost perpetual war with Muscovy and by stimulating anti-Russian activities in Persia. Russian mobilization, always ponderous, was more than usually slow and hesitant. But the provocation of the French march into Poland was such that Alexander gradually steeled himself for another fight.

Murat at the head of the French cavalry screen entered Warsaw on November 28. A Russian force under one of the Tsar's many German officers, the Hanoverian General of Cavalry Levin August Bennigsen, had occupied the city until two days earlier but in the uncertain political circumstances had elected to evacuate rather than fight. As his corps successively entered the Polish capital, Napoleon chose to balance the conflicting elements of the Polish problem by forming the six Polish departments taken from Prussia into a semiautonomous political unit led by seven Polish noblemen; he was careful to do no more than hint at further Polish independence.

As Napoleon had feared, the enemy formed strongly on his left flank to harry his tenuous communications with Berlin. The remaining Prussian field force, about 15,000, was around Thorn, and Russian forces of about 50,000 under Field Marshal Aleksandr Count Kamenskoi (or Kamenski) lay behind the Werra, Narew, and Bug Rivers farther east. Although he had won distinction under Suvorov, Kamenskoi at seventy-five was no longer fit for field command, but he had reasonably able senior subordinates in Bennigsen and Buxhöwden. They performed their mission of behaving as nuisances so well that Napoleon decided he must deal with them to save his army from a miserable winter.

His plan was typical of him, to compel the Russians to concentrate around Pultusk to meet a strong French threat there, and meanwhile to send another strong column across the Narew to turn the Russian left and endanger their own communications and rear. The movement began on December 23. In the cold and with the difficult terrain and poor roads, however, all movements took longer than expected, attempted coordination of timing broke down, and the Russians eluded the trap. On December 25 Bennigsen with 37,000 men fought a rear-guard action against the 20,000 of Lannes's V Corps at Pultusk, in which Bennigsen attempted to envelop Lannes's right but was thwarted by the arrival of 5,000 men of Davout's III Corps. Bennigsen reported that he had defeated 60,000 men under Napoleon himself. But matters were bad enough for the French; as the Emperor moved among his soldiers they openly grumbled that he was driving them too hard. Napoleon in turn announced to the world that he had won a brilliant victory, but he went into winter quarters rather than risk the misery that would accompany the uncertain logistics of a farther advance.

There was misery enough already. To survive at all, it was necessary to disperse the *Grande Armée* over an area some 120 miles (over 190 kilometers) from west to east, from Thorn to Briansk, and 150 miles (over 240 kilometers) from north to south, from the shores of the Frisches Haff not far south of Königsberg to Warsaw. Marshal Ney with his VI Corps around Gilzenburg was in the least productive of all the billeting areas, and trying to mitigate the hunger of his men he pushed his cantonments north and east until he made contact with the outposts of the Russian army, its forces in this area now commanded by Bennigsen. Fearing trouble, Napoleon scolded Ney and called him back. But meanwhile Bennigsen evidently concluded that Napoleon had reopened the campaign and was reaching for Königsberg. The Russian commander concentrated his forces toward his right and began to move across the supposed French axis of advance, heading for Danzig, where a surviving Prussian garrison was under siege. Both Ney and Bernadotte, whose I Corps lay between Ney and the Baltic, withdrew in the face of this probe.

Napoleon decided that Bennigsen was opening a winter offensive and on January 28 issued orders for his counterstroke. Again his plan was to cut off the Russian troops from the Russian border, this time by going around their right rear. Ney and Bernadotte were to contain the enemy along the line Hohenstein-Osteröde; if, however, they had to fall back farther they would serve just as well by drawing the enemy deeper into the proposed trap. The bulk of the *Grand Armée* would march north toward Bischofstein to break Bennigsen's communications with Königsberg and the east. In spite of the winter's hardships, the corps commanders had 80,000 men ready to march on a sixty-mile (ninety-seven-kilometer) front by January 31.

But the characteristically detailed version of the orders for the campaign that Napoleon dispatched to Bernadotte never reached him. Instead, the orders were intercepted by roving Cossacks and delivered to Bennigsen. The latter promptly reversed his course to escape the developing trap. He first tried to concentrate on Allenstein, but Murat's cavalry and Soult's IV Corps arrived there ahead of him. He next prescribed a rendezvous at Joukendorf, where again most of his troops arrived too late; but a detachment held off Soult and Murat long enough to tempt Napoleon into an enveloping maneuver that accomplished nothing except to consume enough time to permit Bennigsen to attain his concentration at last, at Preussich-Eylau. Rapidly though the French had gotten under way and marched to forestall the initial Russian concentrations, the bad roads and now snowdrifts and still colder weather than in the Pultusk campaign continued to disrupt Napoleon's movement schedules. And the exceedingly short winter days aggravated his problems.

At Eylau, Murat and Soult again overtook the enemy late on February 7, and there was skirmishing that evening. With 60,000 men at hand and the 15,000-man Prussian field force expected the next morning, Bennigsen stood to fight. His infantry were bolstered by strong batteries of the exceptionally heavy field artillery with which the Russians customarily fought, including many 18- and 24-pounders (8.163 and 10.844 kilograms; 5.29 and 5.83 inches, or 134.366 and 148.082 mm in their British equivalents).

Napoleon planned a double envelopment. Soult and Augereau were to attack and fix in place the Russian army, with Murat and the Imperial Guard in reserve. Ney and Davout were to follow with attacks against the Russian right and left, respectively. Still once more, however, the season and the terrain frustrated the Emperor. Ney reached the scene too late. He also failed to intercept the Prussian force, which he should have done had he reached his assigned positions on time. The Prussians thereupon arrived at the opportune moment to check Davout when he was on the verge of crushing Bennigsen's left and left rear. Augereau's VII Corps meanwhile carried out its part with a head-on assault in a snowstorm, losing more than 40 percent killed and wounded, with Augereau among the latter; the corps was soon disbanded. As Ney at length approached the field, Bennigsen withdrew, but Napoleon once more felt unable to pursue. Total French killed and wounded numbered between 20,000 and 25,000 along with some 1,200 taken prisoner. The Russians left about 11,000 dead behind them and lost 2,500 prisoners, mainly wounded.

Despite the Russian withdrawal, Eylau was scarcely better than a drawn battle. If Bennigsen had been alert enough to develop some appreciation of the extent of Augereau's losses in the French center and had then counterattacked, Napoleon might have found the outcome much worse. As it was, the Russians were just sufficiently aware of the weakness of the French center after the VII Corps debacle and just sufficiently enterprising in initiating counterefforts that they nearly captured the Emperor. Altogether, Eylau was Napoleon's first major check on the European continent. It sent across Europe a wave of relief at the thought that he was not invincible.

And for good reason. To be sure, the Eylau campaign might not have presented so stark a contrast to the overwhelming success of the immediately preceding Jena-Auerstädt campaign had it not been for the weather and the short hours of daylight. But there were reasons to believe that Napoleon's troubles ran much deeper than those of the season. A grave danger in any military offensive, but especially for a consumingly ambitious conqueror, is overextension. In time the lines of communications are apt to be stretched too thin, the demands upon an army's logistical system become too difficult to master, in pre-motorized armies men and horses are simply marched too far. Frequently the most spectacular offensive victories—like Jena-Auerstädt—represent the maximum inflation of a balloon, with the bursting point just ahead. They express the farthest possible extension of the conqueror's effective power, his last spasm of sustainable energy, and if he presses beyond them he presses too far.

It is significant that Napoleon could find the resources to plunge eastward from Berlin only by ignoring evidence that in the wake of Trafalgar, Spain had been ready to defect from its French alliance had he failed in the campaign of 1806. Dealing with Spain would have to wait until later. Attempting to control all Europe from Iberia to the Oder and now still farther, to the Vistula and the Frisches Haff, he was overextending not only his logistics but his own span of control.

This latter was of special importance. Napoleon tried to keep all the threads of control over his Empire in his own hands, politically as well as militarily. The Empire had grown too big for that; the military extension alone was too great. Even in the most successful Napoleonic campaigns there had almost always been disturbing instances of corps commanders' failing to meet the complex demands of time and position imposed on them; witness Bernadotte's absence from both Jena and Auerstädt. In the Eylau campaign, it was not weather alone that explained why the various corps repeatedly failed to march as they were supposed to do. It was also significant that their commanders were more frequently quarreling with one another than before and more openly jealous of one another. It was significant, too, that while disciplining the rank and file had never been one of Napoleon's strong points—in the armies of Revolutionary France it probably could not have been—the troops now felt free to be loud in the voicing of their discontents, and particularly to protest that they were being asked to endure too much. It was true.

The overextension of the Empire and specifically of Napoleon's span of control was to bring about the Emperor's downfall. The Eylau campaign laid the symptoms bare. But Napoleon, always more the instinctive genius than the professional, continued to prefer to believe that his destiny would not betray him. He pressed forward still more. For a time, he even contrived to paper over the warning symptoms.

Friedland

After Eylau, Napoleon had little choice but to return to winter quarters for a more complete rest, refitting, and recruitment of the ranks. Fortunately for him, the Russians also subsided, into only minor harassment of his communications, and thus he received the necessary leisure. Again the various French corps dispersed across a wide area, from the Frisches Haff to Warsaw, but with Thorn, relatively safe behind the cordon of cantonments, now set up as an advanced base and the nexus of the main line of communications. By early June 1807 the French had over 200,000 men in eastern Europe and ready to take the field.

Napoleon planned to resume operations on June 10, but the enemy anticipated him. Leaving the Prussian field force and Russian reinforcement of it to feint against and contain Bernadotte on Napoleon's northern flank—the Prince of Ponte Corvo reported his outposts under attack on the morning of June 5— Bennigsen drew his main weight southward and on June 3 and 4 began driving Ney back from Altkirch toward Guttstadt. Not until the 5th, the same day that he received Bernadotte's report of renewed action, did Napoleon learn about the events on Ney's front. The Emperor then ordered all his forces to prepare to move on the 6th, and by that day he had focused his mind in a manner that would soon show that those opponents who were encouraged by Eylau should not yet by any means allow their optimism to carry them away. Napoleon promptly perceived the action against Bernadotte as the mere amusement it was and prepared to shift his own weight to the right to envelop the concentration that he accurately discerned Bennigsen had made around Heilsberg. The French would march hard and fast northeast to Königsberg and by capturing the city both deprive Bennigsen of his base and trap him against the sea.

On June 11 Murat opened the standard attack aimed at fixing the enemy in his position, closely followed by Soult with the IV Corps. Napoleon himself was present and ordered a major effort to follow up initial success. The weather of the Eylau campaign, however, had not only handicapped the French; it had prevented the Russians from indulging a habit to which they now reverted to the French Emperor's further discomfiture. At Eylau the frozen ground had debarred the Russians from digging field fortifications; but it was their custom to do so, and Napoleon's major effort at Heilsberg quickly earned a bloody nose against the Russian entrenchments, of which French intelligence ought to have been better aware. Napoleon nevertheless poured more men into the battle of Heilsberg, until it cost him 12,000 killed and wounded with nothing to show for it.

This contretemps did not, however, alter the soundness of Napoleon's principal design. It did cause Bennigsen to retreat to Bertenstein and to turn thence toward Schippenbeil, but Napoleon continued to press his own mass of maneuver toward Friedland on the west bank of the River Alle, where he would be between Bennigsen and Königsberg.

Yet the French proved still to be caught in the toils that had so often frustrated them recently. While Napoleon's strategic judgment remained first rate, the Russians proved capable, in a country where they felt more at ease than their enemies, of outmarching the French. Not only that, but they concealed their own movement toward Friedland so effectively that for the better part of two days Napoleon was apparently in the dark as to their whereabouts. By the evening of June 12 they were taking up positions around Friedland. About one the next morning, the leading brigades of the new Cavalry Reserve Corps under Lannes —largely Saxon in nationality—swept aside the Russian pickets in the western outskirts of Friedland and then encountered sufficient force to have to go over to the defensive. By two o'clock there was enough light for Lannes on a low ridge to see Russians crossing the Alle into Friedland and toward himself in large numbers.

Bennigsen about the same time reached the erroneous conclusion that only a reinforced French infantry division confronted him, and in the next few hours he opened an attack. By full daylight fighting spread across a front of almost three miles (five kilometers) west of Friedland. Bennigsen had 60,000 men at his disposal. Lannes deployed his much smaller force with an excellent eye for tactical position, selecting hills that thoroughly commanded the only two roads by which the Russians could debouch from the streets of the town. His purpose was to take advantage of Bennigsen's evidently aggressive mood to lock the Russians inextricably in combat, knowing that Napoleon hoped to prevent any further Russian withdrawals and to force the showdown battle of annihilation that had eluded him at Eylau.

On several occasions during the morning Lannes was in danger of paying the penalty of seeing his advance guard overrun. Fortunately, Lannes was ably seconded by General Grouchy, commanding his own dragoon division and several miscellaneous detachments, who with stubbornness and tactical skill rivaling Lannes's raced the enemy for high ground on the French left around Heinrichsdorf. Fortunately also, Marshal Mortier arrived with a reorganized VII Corps of Dutch cavalry, French and Polish infantry, and artillery of all three nationalities just in time to keep General Bagration from overwhelming Lan-

nes's right. Altogether, Lannes with never more than 26,000 men held back
Bennigsen's army of more than twice as many for some nine hours, an achievement that helps place him near the top in distinction among Napoleon's
marshalate.

The Emperor arrived about noon, by which time a mutually agreeable lull
was descending upon the battlefield. Napoleon needed time to bring up the
Grand Armée for the desired knockout blow; Bennigsen apparently decided that
his bolt was shot and that he would fight defensively until he could withdraw
under cover of darkness. Napoleon resumed his effort about five in the afternoon, launching his main attack on his right with Ney's VI Corps supported by
parts of the I Corps, now commanded by General Victor. The Russians had their
backs to the Alle, which they could cross by only three bridges. Their army was
divided, furthermore, by the Mühlen Floss (Mill Stream). Ney's attack was
intended to compress and trap their left wing in Friedland on a narrow tongue of
land between the Mühlen Floss and a bend of the Alle.

Ney soon carried the Sortlach Wood, a highly contested landmark in the
morning's battle, and drove part of the Russian left into the river adjacent to the
wood. The Russian infantry in this area began to degenerate into a disorderly mass
that huddled against the river bank, just as Napoleon desired. A Russian cavalry
charge deserving of the word gallant interrupted French progress by stopping
Ney, but an attack by General Dupont's division of Victor's corps straight east
along the more southerly of the two roads from Friedland, along with a counterattack by French cavalry against the Russian horse, made the interruption brief.
Alexandre Antoine Hureau de Sénarmont, *général de brigade*, Victor's Chief of
Artillery and an experienced officer of that arm, now brought up an assemblage of
guns to pour fire into the crowded Russians at close, case-shot range. Napoleon as
an artilleryman himself had consistently made good use of his cannons, especially
in preparation for infantry assaults, the guns often moving out ahead of the main
infantry charge to soften up the defense. But never before Friedland had that
enhancement of artillery mobility which immediately preceded the French Revolution paid off in such sheer destruction rained down on infantry almost helpless
to reply. Nor did the Russians achieve effective counterbattery work, despite the
heavy caliber of many of their guns. Sénarmont's bombardment alone may have
inflicted some 4,000 casualties on the Russians.

Ney and Dupont resumed their attacks, Dupont beating back a countereffort by Bennigsen's final reserve, the Russian Imperial Guard; Sénarmont
greatly aided Dupont by blowing apart the van of the charging Guard cavalry.
Dupont then seized the Russians' temporary bridges across the Mühlen Floss
and crossed the stream to assail the left of the Russian center, about the time
that Mortier and Lannes, hitherto still fighting a holding battle, launched attacks
against the enemy center and right. The town of Friedland had caught fire, and
the bridges over the Alle were burned (the Russians themselves having perhaps
through error or mischance set one or more of them alight).

Bennigsen's whole army was breaking up, though many regiments formed
squares when they found themselves isolated and fought almost to the last man,
still raked by French artillery as well as assailed by French foot and horse from

almost every direction. Most of the Russians could not swim, so many drowned when they were forced into the river. At that juncture many others surrendered. Almost 5,000 on the Russian right were able to escape northward along the west bank of the Alle because Grouchy idly allowed them to do so, ignoring the maxim to advance to the sound of the guns and later pleading that he had no orders to advance.

The French victory was at last cut short about 10:30 in the evening by darkness and by the lack of bridges over which to pursue those of the enemy who had managed to cross the Alle. Nevertheless, Friedland was almost another Austerlitz if not a Jena-Auerstädt in the magnitude of Napoleon's triumph. While the casualty figures are if anything even more uncertain that usual, the French seem to have lost about 12,000 out of 86,000 eventually on the field, of whom some 15,000 were never engaged. The Russians left some 11,000 dead on the field and recorded some 7,000 wounded. How many drowned is guesswork. In any event, Napoleon had for the time being erased the setback of Eylau with another spectacularly successful application of his strategy of annihilation through a thunderstroke of battle. And he had done so in the first battle in which very large portions of his army had not been French—a fact that would prove to be of double-edged significance; it testified in a new way to his mastery of the art of command, but it also foreshadowed increasing problems in finding the requisite manpower to serve the Emperor's ambitions.

The Peace of Tilsit

As usual, triumph in battle so exhausted the victors that the pursuit beloved of military critics scarcely occurred. The French lost contact with Bennigsen's army during the night of June 14–15.

The remaining Prussian field force had moved into Königsberg while Bennigsen was on his way to that city before the battle. Soult had come up to Königsberg and begun to bombard it when the Prussians on the 15th received news of Friedland and despairingly pulled out. The French took Königsberg the next day. The Prussians and Bennigsen's remnants alike now marched hard toward a convergence at Tilsit on the Niemen River, burning bridges as they went. The French several times caught up with Prussian and Russian rear guards, causing several flareups of action, but not with the main bodies. On June 19 Murat was probing toward Tilsit when he met plenipotentiaries dispatched by the Tsar to request an armistice.

Napoleon was more than happy to grant the request, because summer weather and Friedland notwithstanding, eastern European logistics were still a cancer gnawing at his army. The armistice, ratified on June 23, led to the famous meeting two days later of Napoleon and Alexander on a raft moored in the middle of the Niemen, and thus to the Peace of Tilsit. On July 7 the French and Russians signed a peace treaty, various separate articles, and an agreement of defensive alliance. On July 9 the Prussians agreed to a separate treaty, the defeat of the Russians having left the Prussians' situation completely hopeless for the present.

Napoleon was still trying to court Alexander to incorporate Russia into his Continental System for the defeat of Great Britain. Therefore he was generous to the Tsar. Alexander lost no territory except for the Ionian Islands and the Dalmatian coast, which he agreed to cede to France in return for French help against the Ottoman Sultan if that potentate refused to make peace within three months, whereupon Russia was to be compensated with all of Turkey's European possessions except Rumelia. The intransigence of the Turks and the march of other events prevented the complete unfolding of this scheme, though the Ionian Isles and the Dalmatian coast for a time became formally a part of France. Russia was also to be allowed to extend its Asian territories and was to annex Finland. The Tsar undertook to mediate with Great Britain toward a general peace. Failing that effort, Russia would join the Continental System and attempt to bring in Sweden, Denmark, and Portugal.

The presence of the attractive as well as willful Queen Louise at Tilsit and her untiring efforts to bring Napoleon under her spell did not suffice—though the Emperor was charmed—to save Prussia from draconian terms. The terms surely were unwisely harsh, calculated to eliminate Prussia as a great power but serving instead to stimulate the determination of civil and military reformers. East Frisia was confirmed as an addition to Louis Bonaparte's Kingdom of the Netherlands, while certain Westphalian areas went to Murat's Grand Duchy of Berg, Murat having become grand duc de Berg et Clèves on March 15, 1806. Hesse-Cassel and all the remaining Prussian provinces west of the Elbe entered into a new Kingdom of Westphalia for Napoleon's brother Jérôme. Except for the small province of Bialystok, ceded to the Tsar, and Danzig, which became a free city and remained occupied by French troops, Prussian provinces in Poland made up a Grand Duchy of Warsaw to be ruled by the King of Saxony. A separate convention of July 12 provided that Prussia must pay a large indemnity before the French Army would withdraw from its territory.

Nor was Prussia's humiliation yet complete. When Napoleon discerned signs of a potentially dangerous Prussian military revival in spite of Tilsit, he imposed upon Frederick William an additional Convention of Paris in September 1808, limiting the Prussian Army to 42,000 men. The artificial inflation of a minor German state into a great power thus seemed at an end.

Alexander's agreement to help persuade Portugal to join the Continental System was seemingly a lesser element in the Tilsit settlement but harbored vast implications. Not only did it bespeak the extreme porousness of Napoleon's proclaimed blockade of Great Britain, a condition that plagued the French Emperor almost everywhere in Europe, but it was also among the first links in a chain of events that would lead to the battle of Waterloo.

The Iberian Disease

For the sake of completing his work in eastern Europe, Napoleon had so far ignored the restlessness regarding the French alliance that Spain had begun to display after Trafalgar. He felt concern, however, that worse results might come from it than a persisting Iberian leakage in the Continental System.

Trafalgar opened the possibility that the British might land troops in Iberia, and that they might find Spanish and Portuguese support. That possibility as well as economic considerations led Napoleon after Tilsit toward bringing the Iberian countries to heel. He was already considering eliminating the independence of both. Meanwhile, having returned to Paris, in the month after Tilsit he called on Portugal to comply with his Berlin Decrees. At the same time he persuaded King Carlos IV of Spain and his "Principe de la Paz" and Premier Manuel (or Manoel) de Godoy y Álvarez de Faria, Rios Sánchez y Zarzoso, to permit French troops to march through Spain on their way to Portugal. Godoy, the corrupt favorite of the Spanish Queen, Maria Luisa of Parma, had initiated the move toward defection from the alliance, so Napoleon saw himself as damping down his Iberian troubles from several directions.

Portugal, however, was displaying no more responsiveness to Napoleon than to protract negotiations, so he resolved to delay no further in dealing with it while increasingly drawing Spain and particularly Godoy into his net. Under the secret Treaty of Fontainebleau of October 27, 1807, Spanish troops were to assist the French in overrunning Portugal, whereupon the country was to be carved apart, the French remaining in Lisbon, much of the south forming a new Principality of Algarve to be ruled by Godoy. Already, on October 19, a French expeditionary force of 25,000 men had set out for Portugal under Jean Andoche Junot, *général de division*.

The bribery of the Prince of the Peace with his new domain notwithstanding, Spanish troops and supplies mostly failed to appear, and by the time Junot reached the Portuguese border on November 23 this absence of help along with bad weather and roads had cut his force to 6,000. Nevertheless, he raced to Lisbon with a select vanguard of 2,000 and nearly captured the Prince Regent, Prince João (John), and his government, who just two days earlier had taken flight for Brazil on the decks of the Royal Navy.

French reinforcements crossed the Pyrenees to permit Junot to occupy the length of Portugal, while by early 1808 there were as many as 100,000 French troops along his lines of communications in Spain as well. This disproportionately large force reflected a new Napoleonic resolve. Spain's failure to produce the aid promised at Fontainebleau had combined with Napoleon's recollection of its earlier shortcomings and vacillations and with his contempt for inefficiency and weakness—terms almost synonymous with the Spanish government—to seal his gradually maturing decision that under one guise or another he must take practical control over Spain. Though long incubating, this decision was not one to which the Emperor actually gave careful thought. In his harsh treatment of Prussia, he had defied the law of unforeseen consequences with calculation; he knew he was taking risks. With Spain, his invitation to unforeseen consequences was offhanded. It was more a matter of impatience than of rational calculation.

Between February 6 and March 18 a variety of ruses and treachery—Godoy, now secretly on Napoleon's payroll, assisted in them—enabled the French Army to occupy the frontier fortresses of Pamplona, San Sebastian, Barcelona, and Figueras. On March 14 Murat, awarded the regional command as Emperor's

Lieutenant in Spain, entered Madrid. At first the Spanish government and people remained as inert as their recent habits led Napoleon to expect. But heavy
requisitions and behavior by the troops that was rough and arrogant even by the
usual standards of occupying armies—the French soldiers shared the Emperor's
low regard for the Spanish—lit an unanticipated fire.

The heir to the throne, Fernando (Ferdinand), Principe de las Asturias,
whom Napoleon had cultivated and whose ambitions the Emperor had encouraged as a counterweight to the untrustworthy Godoy, took advantage of popular
protests against the French occupation and the government's surrender to
frighten King Carlos into signing an abdication in Fernando's favor. Napoleon
soon discovered, however, that Fernando was hardly the man to control the
Spanish situation (not that the Emperor had entertained serious illusions). On
May 2 a rising of the Madrid populace against the French provoked Napoleon
into forcing the abdication of both Carlos and Fernando. A council of regency
was induced to offer the throne to Napoleon's brother Joseph, who became King
of Spain on June 6. (Since March 31, 1806 he had been King of Naples; Murat,
inordinately ambitious and recently disgruntled because he had not received the
Polish crown, took Joseph's place there.)

In the meantime, Murat had fallen sick and the central French authority in
Spain was temporarily paralyzed. During this interval revolt spread throughout
Spain. Provincial juntas assumed authority in various parts of the country and
appealed to Great Britain for aid. London decided to send an expeditionary
force. Spanish regulars and militia began to coalesce into armies of resistance,
numbering perhaps 100,000 in all, but widely dispersed and without a high
command to coordinate them. The French began to march strong columns hither
and yon across the country, with mixed results. Among many other incidents,
they were repulsed when they stormed Valencia; but on the day after Joseph
Bonaparte's accession to the throne, General Dupont captured and sacked
Córdoba.

As Dupont departed the city burdened with spoils, however, he found himself harassed by the largest single contingent of Spanish soldiers, the 30,000-man
Army of Andalusia. Apparently stunned by the sudden emergence of so strong
and apparently energetic a Spanish force, Dupont retreated across the Tagus
River into the Sierra de Guadarama of central Spain, where it was he and the
French Army who became inert. The Army of Andalusia thereupon broke up
into five columns the better to isolate Dupont. Dupont's passivity allowed the
enemy to capture Bailén (Baylen), which commands the southern passes into
and out of the mountains. Lest he be entrapped, Dupont bestirred himself to try
to retake Bailén, but on July 19 he was defeated in a series of piecemeal attacks
and thereupon trapped indeed.

On July 20, after bickering with the Spanish over just which troops should
be included as part of his command, Dupont surrendered some 17,635 men. This
capitulation was of course far worse than the check Napoleon had suffered at
Eylau; so complete a French defeat at the hands of a ragtag army sent a seismic
tremor all through Europe. When in addition the French failed in enterprises
against Saragossa and Gerona, their hold on Spain and their very communica-

tions with France appeared so insecure that on August 1 King Joseph fled Madrid for northern Spain.

The Spanish insurrection isolated Junot in Portugal. Beginning on the day of Joseph's flight and continuing through the next four days, the British expeditionary force of 14,000 men, commanded by Lieutenant-General Sir Arthur Wellesley pending the arrival of a more senior officer, landed at Mondego Bay north of Lisbon. Wellesley had just returned to England after winning a sterling reputation in India. The British intent was to secure Lisbon and thence, joining with Portuguese and Spanish forces, to advance up the Tagus and Douro (or Duero) Rivers into the Iberian interior. Junot, of sterner stuff than Dupont, did not despair but began to concentrate his garrisons while he dispatched Henri François Delaborde, *général de division*, with 4,400 men to delay the British. Delaborde fought Wellesley almost to a standstill at Roliça (or Roleia or Roriça) on Wellesley's route to Lisbon on August 15, although British and Portuguese numbers—including 1,350 of the latter—finally compelled him to withdraw.

Wellesley advanced another ten miles (sixteen kilometers) northward before halting at Vimiero (or Vimiera, Vimeiro, or Vimeira) to cover the landing of 5,000 British reinforcements. Wellesley would have preferred to go on to turn the defile of Torres Vedras into the interior by way of a road from Vimiero to Maíra, but on the night of August 20 Lieutenant-General Sir Harry Burrard, first Baronet Burrard, his senior in their rank, arrived offshore and forbade it. Then Junot decided to attack the British at Vimiero on August 21 before their intervention could gather further momentum.

Unfortunately for the French, Junot still had only 13,050 troops against Wellesley's force now of 17,000. The causes of French numerical weakness lay partly in Junot's own failure to effect his concentration as rapidly as might have been possible, but to a greater extent in the circumstance that Junot had felt obliged to leave a 6,500-man garrison in Lisbon because the Russian Mediterranean fleet, though in harbor there, caught and blockaded by the British on its way home, refused Junot's request to land troops to take the place of its French allies. Wellesley's position was susceptible to an envelopment of its left flank to cut it off from the sea, which Junot attempted. But with his shortage of troops, the French commander neither made the flanking force strong enough to carry out its mission nor put enough strength into his direct assaults on the British front to fix Wellesley so he could not counter the envelopment effort, let alone to break the front. Vimiero thus became Wellesley's first clear-cut Iberian victory in what was destined to be a long succession of them.

Unfortunately for the British, General Burrard's orders prevented the pursuit that Wellesley desired. Still more unfortunately, the intended commander of the expeditionary force arrived the next day, Lieutenant-General Sir Hew Whitefoord Dalrymple, known as "Dowager." Only fifty-eight years old but with the temperament of a frail septuagenarian, he not only forbade all further advance until reinforcements arrived but gladly accepted Junot's proposal that he ship the latter's force to France in exchange for such part of Portugal as it still controlled—the Convention of Cintra of August 30, 1808. Junot thus got away with weapons and baggage from a predicament that was otherwise hopeless. In a month his troops were back in Spain to fight again. The resulting outcry in Britain over the failure to force Junot into a complete surrender led to the recall not only of Dalrymple but of Burrard and Wellesley also for a court of inquiry, which acquitted all three of them.

Command of the British expeditionary force passed to Lieutenant-General Sir John Moore. Moore was well known as a first-rate trainer of troops—good training was almost always, it will be remembered, a strong point in the British Army—and as something of a tactical reformer. During the invasion danger of 1803, the British had concentrated the army in what were for them large formations in southern England. The Duke of York as Commander-in-Chief had taken the opportunity to appoint Moore, then a major-general, to exercise his training talents on one of the formations, at Shorncliffe Camp in Kent. Moore achieved enough to win his knighthood in 1804 and promotion in 1805.

Part of York's thinking was that British inability to deal with the French Revolutionaries' increased use of skirmishing tactics went far to explain the setbacks that his army had suffered in its recent continental forays. Traditional British eighteenth-century linear tactics permitted the enemy's skirmishers too free a hand in swarming close to the redcoat lines and wearing them down with fire often delivered from behind cover before the climactic assaults and exchanges of volleys began. In consequence, an experimental corps of light troops had been formed in the summer of 1798, training in Essex as a combined-arms force of light infantry, light cavalry, and horse artillery—the latter comprising guns whose crews were entirely mounted. It was York's increased emphasis on light troops departing from the rigidity of the line for skirmishing tactics that Moore especially applied at Shorncliffe Camp. Moore's ideas were by no means original, deriving from York and the Continent; but he possessed an uncommon leadership capacity for winning his subordinates' confidence and bringing out the best in them down to the rear-rank privates, and his beginning of the revivification of the historic excellence of the British Army's rank and file would have a large impact on the outcome of the Napoleonic Wars.

Moore's command in Iberia was reinforced from home until it included 30,000 British soldiers. At this point it was no longer simply an expeditionary force; it was the British Army. After a decade and a half of nearly continuous war waged against the *levée en masse* of Revolutionary France, Great Britain had still stubbornly refused to accept the strain of recruiting an army remotely approaching continental dimensions; the military disdain that mingled with Napoleon's grudging respect for British tenacity, wealth, and naval achievements was not without cause.

More important for the long haul remaining against Napoleon than the Duke of York's and Sir John Moore's tactical reforms, the British War Office had just begun a reluctant reform in recruitment. Full-fledged conscription was anathema in Great Britain, the ancient British tradition of universal-service militia having been clouded by identification of the nation in arms with French radical excess. But the male population of Great Britain between the ages of eighteen and thirty-five was still required to serve in the militia, This institution had come to be divided into the New Militia, which was actually the old, a force of part-time soldiers based on a modicum of universal military training and to be called upon in emergencies, and the Old Militia, in arms for the duration of the war as a home-defense force. (There were also volunteers, privately recruited and paid for by patriotic organizations, and fencibles, new regular regiments but raised only for the duration and for home service.) Upon this crazy quilt the War Office now imposed as much order as was politically possible.

The Old Militia evolved into a feeder force for the regular army. The members of the Old Militia were volunteers too young to be regulars and men balloted, that is chosen by lot, to fill district quotas. The Old Militia now came to be called on in turn to meet quotas for the regular service; and because the members of the Old Militia had to serve through the war anyway, and because pay and bounties were higher for regulars, this system raised most of the men who were wanted. The British regulars increased to 237,000, and from the inception of the reforms to the end of the war about 40 percent of the recruits came from the militia. Britain had moved a halting step toward conscription and a European-scale army, the lack of which had so far undermined the increasingly ambitious continental policies that Pitt was undertaking before his death on January 23, 1806.

The Spanish Campaign of Sir John Moore

To assure effective command of what was for the time being practically the British Army, Sir John Moore would have to join together the approximately 20,000 men he found at Lisbon with another 10,000 shipped to Corunna in the northwest corner of Spain under Major-General Sir David Baird. With Portugal back in Allied hands, the plan was for Moore to move toward Corunna and thence to cooperate with the Spanish to drive the French from Spain as well. Moore chose to make the move by land rather than by sea, lest the approach of winter delay him in the Atlantic storms. His infantry would march north by relatively direct routes; but because the roads of Iberia north of the Tagus River were exceptionally poor even by the Peninsula's standards, Moore's artillery, cavalry, and reserve ammunition column were to follow a decidedly circuitous route by way of Madrid. Baird was to march south to meet Moore, and the combined army would assemble at Valladolid, Burgos, or some other convenient meeting place.

The various newly promising efforts to reverse Britain's record of ineptitude against Napoleon on land were about to run afoul, however, of renewed military activity by the French Emperor himself. Napoleon could scarcely allow recent events in Iberia to go unchallenged. He hastened reinforcements across the Pyrenees until his numbers there exceeded 200,000, and Napoleon himself left Paris on October 30 to take command of them.

There followed a rapid and catastrophic series of Spanish defeats, the French rolling unbroken all across the Spanish North. By the time Moore arrived at Salamanca about November 23, the Spanish troops with whom he was supposed to cooperate were collapsing almost everywhere, and strong French forces had interposed between him and Baird. He was fortunate, and it said much for the marching stamina of British troops, that his artillery column was able to find its way to rejoin him on December 5.

Moore considered withdrawing to Lisbon, but he bravely resolved instead to continue eastward and northward. He know Napoleon was on the verge of recapturing Madrid; in fact the city surrendered on December 4. Hoping that Madrid still held, Moore decided on December 6 to drive for Valladolid and Burgos after all, to get astride Napoleon's main line of communications and perhaps save the Spanish capital. On December 10 he learned that Madrid had fallen. He still persisted toward Valladolid.

The disdain that was part of Napoleon's attitude toward the British may not have been without cause, but nonetheless it misled the Emperor into repeated underestimations of his island foes. He assumed that Moore must have retreated toward Portugal, and preparing Spanish bases, he readied his main army to follow by marching down the Tagus River to Lisbon. He directed Soult (since June 1808 duc de La Dalmatie) with the VIII Corps to cover Burgos and northwest Spain while he did so.

The bold General Moore had in fact learned on December 13, from a capture of typically detailed Napoleonic orders dated the 10th, that Soult was essentially isolated. He decided to fall on the VIII Corps to attempt to destroy it. He ordered his transport vessels from Lisbon to Corunna and Vigo, intending to fall back through Galicia after he had dealt with Soult and to change his base to northwest Spain. On December 19 Napoleon heard from Soult that some of his outposts had been attacked by British cavalry, but the Emperor still believed this action must be a feint to cover Moore's retreat to Lisbon. Nevertheless, he ordered Ney, who with the VI Corps was in the extreme northwest corner of Spain, to close in toward Soult and prepare to join in moving against Moore. If Moore proved serious about approaching Soult, then Napoleon proposed to destroy Moore's army in turn. Further news on December 20 seemed to confirm that the British general was indeed serious.

On December 20 Baird linked up with Moore. On the 23rd, Moore had concentrated the British forces at Sahagun and was poised to attack Soult, when he heard from the Spanish that since December 18 Napoleon had been hurrying toward him with much superior numbers. While the date of the 18th was an exaggeration, the suggestion that Napoleon was hurrying was anything but; so intent was the Emperor on cornering the British and ridding himself of their army that with 50,000 men and 150 guns he traveled 100 miles (160 kilometers) in less than five days through the Escorial Pass, although wintry weather had set in on the 19th and the pass was snow-covered. For Moore to have persisted against Soult would have been less bold than foolhardy, so Moore began retreating northwestward on the morning of the 24th.

While Moore was not the general that Sir Arthur Wellesley was later to prove to be, and while the British nation has over the years attempted to compensate for the customary inadequacies of its land force by applauding well-conducted retreats as if they were victories—witness much of the celebration of Dunkirk—it is by no means excessive to state that Moore's conduct of the retreat to Corunna is evidence of exceptional leadership qualities. The weather remained foul, food supplies inevitably fell short in a desolate countryside rendered more desolate by the snows, discipline was sorely strained, and Napoleon long remained confident that his renowned hard-marching infantry would catch up with the British. But when the Emperor arrived at Astorga on the first day of the New Year and learned that Moore had passed through on the last day of 1808, he gave up the pursuit, took away much of his army, and left it to Soult with 40,000 men to try to finish the job.

Moore arrived at Corunna on January 11, 1809. He deployed his army across the road from Lugo, with his left on the Mero Rover. His transports appeared in the harbor on the 14th. Moore immediately embarked his wounded and sick, his cavalry and guns. He had blown bridges as he retreated, which helps explain why Soult did not show up until the next day. On the 16th, however, the French attacked. Winter marches had severely diminished the effective strength of both armies, and it is possible that Moore by now had superior numbers. More likely, the Duke of Dalmatia had a slight numerical advantage, though not enough to make success likely in an attack—perhaps 16,000 French to 15,000 British, with forty French cannon to the nine light guns Moore had not yet put on shipboard.

In the event, Soult's assaults failed. Moore was organizing the Guards Brigade for a counterattack when at 4:50 P.M. a cannonball struck him and badly wounded his right side and shoulder. Not realizing that the issue of the battle was decided, he frequently ordered his stretcher bearers to halt as they carried him from the field, so he could again face the fighting. A final, practically hopeless French assault was turned back about 5:30. Moore died at his headquarters soon after eight in the evening and was buried in an unmarked grave on the landward ramparts while it was still dark early the next morning. As his body was lowered, his troops were marching down to the ships. In the fighting at Corunna, the British lost some 800 or 900 casualties, the French about twice as many. By the end of January, 27,000 evacuated troops had reached England.

Moore would be a British hero in time. For the moment, however, the national talent for glorifying retreats had not yet done its work, and in spite of his death he was much criticized, both for the abandonment of the Iberian countries and for the half naked condition of his soldiers as they returned home. Nevertheless, the eventual heroic status is well deserved. Napoleon with 300,000 troops had almost completed the reconquest of Spain and the crushing of Spanish resistance when Moore with only about one-tenth that number embarrassed him enough to give the resistance time to rally and sufficient new hope to make rallying possible.

The Emergence of Wellington

Napoleon had returned to France because troubles that he considered more dangerous than those in Spain were brewing elsewhere in Europe. Nevertheless, his armies spread out across the Iberian Peninsula like a gigantic ink blot after Corunna, albeit meeting stubborn clots of Spanish and Portuguese resistance. The Spanish rebels had formed a supreme junta that nominally controlled about 100,000 troops, but there was still no real rebel unity of command.

Soult's mission included proceeding from Galicia to occupy Lisbon, but he never arrived at the Portuguese capital. Instead, Sir Arthur Wellesley returned there on April 22, 1809, to resume command of British forces in Iberia. He was reinforced to some 25,000 British troops, including some German auxiliaries, and he commanded as well the Portuguese regulars, some 16,000, and several thousands of Portuguese militia who were observing and harassing the French. The Portuguese Army was in process of being greatly improved in administration and training by a British veteran of Sir John Moore's campaign, Major-General William Carr Beresford, who held the Portuguese rank of marshal since March 2.

Wellesley moved with what would prove to be characteristic promptness to regain a measure of initiative. Dispatching Beresford and the Portuguese on a flanking march to attack Amarante behind Soult's force on the Douro, Wellesley on May 5 led his British troops north toward that river and a rendezvous with Soult's force of somewhat over 20,000. The Duke of Dalmatia was led to expect that Wellesley would attempt to cross the river with fishing craft collected near its mouth. Instead, on May 12 the British crossed upstream, both just above Oporto and farther east. Thrown off balance, Soult was driven out of Oporto and forced into retreat. Portugal was now returning to rebellion all around him, and his logistics were impossible. His best route of withdrawal lay through Amarante, but he now discovered that this place had fallen to Beresford. He felt obliged to abandon his guns and much of his baggage and fall back through the Sierra Catalina to Orense, a hard march that cost 5,000 men, Wellesley had begun even more successfully on his second tour in Portugal than on his first.

But Sir John Moore's expedition had fallen far short of its loftier goals largely because of the uncertainties of Spanish support, and those uncertainties remained to limit what Wellesley might accomplish. From Soult, Wellesley turned to deal with Victor, now a *maréchal de l'Empire* and duc de Belluno, who with about 25,000 men was covering no less an objective than the Spanish capital, Madrid.

Wellesley left Beresford with 20,000 troops near Ciudad Rodrigo to shield Portugal. He himself with 22,000 joined a major Spanish force, some 40,000 under the sixty-nine-year-old Gregorio García de la Cuesta, Captain-General of Old Castile, together marching up the Tagus toward Madrid. In front of their superior numbers Victor retreated to Talavera, where however King Joseph was able to bring 50,000 French reserves to his aid. Another Spanish force of 25,000, along with 4,000 Portuguese who were commanded by Lieutenant-Colonel Sir Robert Thomas Wilson of the 20th Light Dragoons, were to have helped keep Joseph busy by threatening Madrid from the north; but in spite of Wilson's prodding they had failed to do much. Similarly, Cuesta was to provide a screen, particularly in the pass of Boños, to protect his and Wellesley's left flank from other French forces still to the north, under Ney, now duc d'Elchingen, and Mortier, now duc de Trévise; but he failed to do so. Nor did the Spanish rebels deliver provisions as promised, so that when Wellesley approached Joseph's concentration, not only had the numerical balance turned against him but his army was half starved.

Joseph therefore felt the odds justified his attacking Wellesley and Cuesta, which he did near Talavera on July 27 with the French army organized into two corps under Victor and Jourdan. In a two-day battle, however, Wellesley turned back a series of French attacks, in spite of only the most grudging cooperation from Cuesta, and in spite of a panic among some of the Spanish troops late on the first day. The key to the outcome of Talavera, besides Wellesley's resolution, was the disciplined firepower of the British infantry. While amply shielding their main positions with skirmishers as taught by Sir John Moore, that infantry also poured forth from their traditional linear deployment a volume of continuous fire that melted the heads of the attacking French columns. The armies of Revolutionary France had almost never in their many campaigns confronted anything so devastating as the disciplined volleys of well-trained and well-led British troops. The French suffered over 7,000 casualties, the Allies about 6,500, but of these a measure of respective Spanish and British participation in the hard fighting lay in the 1,200 casualties of the former in contrast to over 5,000 for the latter.

Wellesley was to be elevated to the peerage as Baron Douro and Viscount Wellington for this defensive victory, but the outcome of Talavera did not remedy the precariousness into which the limits of Spanish assistance had thrown his offensive like Sir John Moore's before it. Although barely able to feed his men, Wellesley initially turned to march toward a collision with the threat from the north; but on August 23 he learned that Soult's remaining troops had joined those of Ney and Mortier, all under Soult's command, and that because of Cuesta's neglect this concentrated force had readily traversed the pass of Baños. In the face of this danger Cuesta decamped, and Wellesley soon learned that Soult was between him and the bridge at Almaraz on the Tagus, more than threatening his line of retreat.

Wellesley made haste to withdraw to the south bank of the Tagus. By means of exceedingly rapid marching he reached Almaraz in advance of Soult and destroyed the Tagus bridge there. Thence he was able to make good his escape to Lisbon. He marched in summer's heat rather than winter's cold, but otherwise this campaign was strikingly similar to Moore's. On the positive side, British marching speed and endurance were becoming almost as impressive as the tactical effectiveness of the redcoated infantry. Negatively, both campaigns had been undercut by the effects of Spanish disunity of command and other deficiencies of less-than-regular forces. Moore had had to flee the Peninsula; Wellesley had been in acute danger of entrapment. Nevertheless, Wellesley believed he could discern the foundations of eventual success—but it would be a success of a strategy of erosion, not of a Napoleonic strategy of annihilation on the Austerlitz or the Jena-Auerstädt model.

British persistence in fighting in Iberia and supporting the local nationalisms should in time generate a more consistent and better organized local effort. It might help that for his measure of success so far, Wellesley had been appointed Captain-General by Spain and Marshal-General by Portugal. Secondly, Wellesley perceived that in the often-desolate reaches of the Peninsula, efficient organization of logistics was crucial. While his own army had come too close to starving, French logistics were not highly successful in this environment either; the French still relied on the Revolutionary armies' typical foraging off the country to a greater extent than Iberian geography warranted. If the British could considerably improve their own logistics, with better quartermasters and commissaries and a better system of depots and wagon transport, the French vulnerabilities could be exploited. Wellesley was confident of his own skills and of his ability to make the requisite improvements.

The Military Resurgence of Austria

The troubles that had first recalled Napoleon's direct attention eastward before Sir John Moore's campaign of 1808 and then demanded his swift return to Paris after Moore had been forced into the retreat to Corunna were the by-now familiar ones of overextension of the French Empire. Napoleon had stretched his domains beyond his span of effective control, he was attempting the personal supervision of too much, and when the Corsican cat was away in Spain the mice would play elsewhere—particularly in Austria, where the Imperial court had never intended to accept the 1805 and 1806 settlements permanently, and where the substitution of French for Austrian preponderance in Germany could not but be regarded as contrary to the very order of nature. The French defeat at Bailén and the subsequent flight of King Joseph had so aroused Austrian hopes that there developed a shift of policy toward the renewal of war carrying too much momentum to be reversed by subsequent Napoleonic triumphs in the Peninsula. Because those triumphs depended in part on the French Emperor's personal presence in Spain, they actually gave further stimulus to the Austrian war party, by suggesting that Napoleon's preoccupation with Spain offered the time to strike. Before Sir John Moore's hungry redcoats had dragged themselves onto the decks at Corunna, Austria had decided on renewed war.

Napoleon was well aware of all these developments. He attempted diplomatic conciliation, but his approach failed, because among other, more basic reasons, the Tsar as usual was an inconstant supporter and did not apply the restraining pressure on Vienna that Napoleon desired.

But of course Napoleon also took military precautions, with conspicuous efficiency. After the Peace of Tilsit the French Army had gradually withdrawn from Germany, leaving only about 63,000 men in three commands, under Davout, in Prussia; under Nicolas Charles, comte Oudinot, *général de division*, in west central Germany; and under Marshal François Joseph Lefebvre, duc de Danzig because of his victorious siege of that place, in Bavaria. While he was still chasing Moore, Napoleon sent to his current War Minister, Henri Jacques Guillaume Clarke, *général de division*, orders that brought a rapid but quiet augmentation of those commands. Clarke was to institute an early call for the conscription class of 1810. With these recruits he would have enough men to add fourth and fifth battalions to all the regiments across the Rhine. One of the reasons for keeping garrisons in Germany had been to insist that the members of the Confederation of the Rhine enforce French-style conscription; those member states were now notified that their contingents might soon be needed.

Later, Napoleon withdrew the Imperial Guard from Spain, and a new IV

Corps was organized at Ulm. On returning to Paris, Napoleon proposed detailed march orders to concentrate his main army by April 15 to be ready to maneuver in the area Regensburg-Landshut-Augsburg. Berthier, now prince de Neuchâtel, would command the army in Germany until Napoleon arrived. The Emperor intended to preempt the anticipated Austrian attack. He concluded that the Austrians would not be ready until the end of April.

He miscalculated. The Austrians had resolved to fight again not only because they were encouraged by French setbacks in Spain but also because they felt new confidence in their own army. The best of their commanders, the capable Archduke Charles, had been supervising yet another, and more complete, program of army reform for the past three years. On February 10, 1806 Charles had been appointed *Generalissimus* as prospective commander of all forces in war and in peacetime supervisor and director of the entire Habsburg military organization, including the *Hofkriegsrat*, the war council that traditionally exercised overall control. Charles had still further patterned the Austrian Army on the French Napoleonic model, and he had accomplished much.

Especially, he had increased the size of the forces and Austria's ability to concentrate heavy masses on the battlefield. The numerical growth of the French Revolutionary armies had been nourished by the spirit of the Revolution; conscription of an unprecedented completeness had become possible in France because the people of the Revolutionary Republic had been willing to commit themselves to the defense of a cause and a government that they saw as their own to an extent that they would not have committed themselves to the old monarchy. They could be recruited in larger numbers than before; they could be relied upon not to desert as never before; their armies could subsist off the countries through which they marched by means of widespread foraging, which under the *ancien régime* would have constituted an invitation for multitudes to run away. Napoleon's empire managed to retain enough of the aura of a people's government that it could continue these military practices of the Republic, with the magnetism of the Emperor as a reinforcement. Austria, in contrast, could not invoke the defense of a popular government as the rationale for mass recruitment; Austria still stood for as complete as possible a preservation of the *ancien régime*. But if Vienna could not use republicanism as the foundation of recruitment, it could use a form of nationalism, even in defense of a multinational empire.

By 1809 French domination of Europe had persisted so long and had extended itself so far that all over Europe hatred of the French amounted to a call to arms. In Germany, including the German portions of the Austrian Empire, this hatred translated itself into something more positive, a nascent German nationalism. But even in the other Austrian dominions, where an equivalent nationalism scarcely existed and where Vienna would not have wished to stimulate it if it had, resentment and hatred of the French encouraged a mass recruitment that might well have been impossible for earlier Habsburg governments.

For the renewal of war in 1809, Austria was ready to deploy 300,000 regular troops and 771 guns. In addition, Charles had organized a national militia, the *Landwehr*, in the Austrian dominions, and had directed the revitalization of the historic Hungarian militia, the Hungarian Insurrection. Consequently the Habsburgs had 230,000 second-line troops to back up the regulars, although the organization and training of the militia were far from complete. Charles hoped that before the new campaign had ended he could raise the Austrian strength to 700,000.

He believed that the larger numbers were necessary not only for overall balance against the French but because French Revolutionary tactics, and particularly the use of assault columns, had much increased the density of men per mile of front. With the linear tactics of the eighteenth century, 15,000 men per mile had been ample, but Austria in its recent wars had found that double that number often did not possess enough resiliency to withstand the French. Obviously, by choosing to match mass against mass Charles was rejecting the British solution that was beginning to serve well on the Peninsula, the retention of linear tactics but with more highly trained troops for more rapid and effective volley fire and increased use of screens of light infantry. But when Charles was rebuilding the Austrian Army, the British method had yet to prove itself. Moreover, the British system was a fragile one, in part a resort of necessity born out of Britain's unwillingness to mobilize an army of continental scale. The Austrian Empire possessed the manpower to meet the French on their own numerical terms. The Archduke determined to utilize that manpower as the foundation of Austria's resurgence.

There remained limitations upon the reform of the essentially conservative Austrian Army. For example, while the French deployed from line into battalion column with both flanks of the battalion simultaneously forming upon the center, the Austrians formed from the line upon the right-flank company, a slower process. The Austrians still carried out most evolutions at a pace of ninety steps per minute or at what they considered the maneuver pace, 105 steps per minute; a pace of 120 steps per minute, frequently used by the French, was rarely employed by the Austrians. So Austrian movement remained slower and more cumbersome than French. Furthermore, the Austrians in their regular forces neglected the development of skirmishing and open-order tactics; in particular, they restricted the flexibility of a screen of skirmishers by attempting to control it tightly through orders transmitted by the battalion drums, a prescription for undue rigidity at best and for confusion and misunderstanding amid the rumble of battle.

Undue rigidity still characterized also the higher functions of command and control. The higher officers remained products of the eighteenth-century age of unitary battlefield command, and they were still slow to understand the proper handling of corps to exploit their potential for flexible maneuver. Charles managed to retire twenty-five generals, but the remainder averaged sixty-three years of age. Nor were these officers true professionals. The Habsburg army had yet to develop an adequate system of military education, nor were the officers adequately encouraged by any means other than schools to study and to think.

Charles attempted a partial attack on the deficiencies of the officer corps through the development of a strategic doctrine, the lack of which he believed to have been an important cause of Austria's defeats, and through efforts to stimulate the study of it. Under his name there appeared a manual on the subject: Erzherzog Karl, *Grundsätze der höheren Kriegs-Kunst für die Generale der öster-reichische-Armée (The Fundamentals of the Higher Art of War for the Generals of the Austrian Army)*.[1] The work was written in collaboration with *Feldmarschall Leutnant* Karl Friedrich von Lindeman and substantially revised by *Feldmarschall Leutnant* Anton Freiherr Mayer von Heldenfeld, but it surely reflects for the most part the ideas and experience of Charles rather than of Lindeman or Mayer. Nevertheless, like the reformed Austrian Army, its innovations were strongly straitened by tradition. It urged efforts toward the swift resolution of campaigns, implying a Napoleonic style of rapid movement climaxed by decisive battle; but while it advocated concentrating superior numbers at the decisive point in order to achieve this climactic battle, it also retained the depot system of supply—impeding rapid movement—and warned against any maneuver that would expose one's line of communications. Corps were to move by convergent routes, but their movements should be closely coordinated to guard against unexpected contingencies. Nothing was said about initiative and discretion among senior commanders; tight control from the top was evidently still to be the order of the day.

Notwithstanding Austria's characteristic hesitancy in adopting anything new, however, the reforms of the Archduke Charles were about to prove sufficient to generate the most formidable opposition and the most difficult campaign that Napoleon had yet encountered. The Austrians in the campaign of 1809 tested the French Emperor even more sorely than had the Russians at Eylau.

The Campaign of 1809: Eckmühl and Ebelsberg

Far from being unready to move before the end of April as Napoleon anticipated, the Austrians seized the initiative on April 9. On the evening of April 12 Napoleon learned from the semaphor telegraph system that he had installed for communication across French-controlled Europe that on the 9th the Archduke Charles had led 209,000 Austrian troops into Bavaria.

Napoleon's preparations gave him by now 170,000 troops in southern Germany, 50,000 of them German troops from the Confederation of the Rhine, almost half of the French recent conscripts. One of the Austrian spearheads was advancing from Pilsen (Plezň) toward Regensburg, which city the vanguard of Davout's III Corps was just entering, with most of the corps well behind. Berthier ordered Davout, reinforced by Oudinot's II Corps, to hold Regensburg. This order directly contradicted Napoleon's instructions to Berthier in case the Austrians should contrive to grasp the initiative, and it probably reflected Berthier's fear that he might be blamed nevertheless if a precipitate French withdrawal occurred. Meanwhile another Austrian spearhead drove the vanguard of Lefebvre's VII Corps out of Landshut, and the effect of this development in combination with Berthier's orders was to open a seventy-six-mile (122-kilome-

1. (Wien [Vienna]: Österreichisches Hofkriegsrat, 1806).

ter) gap between the two principal wings of the French army, Davout's and Oudinot's left and Lefebvre's right.

Napoleon left Paris at 4:00 A.M. on the 14th and arrived at Donauwörth about the same hour on the 17th. He had expected to find Berthier present there for a conference and his army well in hand. He found neither. The Prince of Neuchâtel had gone forward to Augsburg, and the Emperor had already learned en route something about the dangerously scattered condition of his troops. Before the morning was out, Napoleon had hurried off orders to Davout and Oudinot to withdraw immediately to Ingolstadt, and to Lefebvre and the Bavarian forces on the right to support this movement.

Thus the Austrian initiative along with failures in French command had begun the campaign of 1809 by placing the Archduke Charles in a position to fall on the separate wings of the French army and destroy it in detail. The Austrians had capitalized well on their aggressiveness and their military reforms. But now the incompleteness of the reforms—the fundamental conservatism of the Austrian Army—once more tripped up the whitecoats on the brink of triumph. A single day's march could have brought the bulk of Charles's forces upon either exposed French wing; but Austrian light cavalry, though diligent in screening the advance of Charles's army, did not operate independently enough for its commanders to perceive the opportunity and report it to higher headquarters. Absence of initiative below the highest levels remained a chief bane of the Habsburg forces. Instead of seizing his opportunity, Charles moved ponderously toward an Austrian convergence on Regensburg. Napoleon soon felt strong enough to begin reaching out with his right in the Landshut area for *manœuvre sur les derrières* against the Archduke's communications.

Thereby he handed the latter another opportunity. Austrian standards in reconnaissance and marching speed were not yet up to those of the French at their best, but in a broken and difficult country French intelligence was not performing at its best. The Austrians effected their own concentration more rapidly than the French perceived and also reacted more promptly then their enemies recognized to the threat to their communications, by means of a bold and admirable decision on Charles's part to strike at the root of the danger by advancing against Napoleon's main army. The effect was that Charles approached Eckmühl (Eggmühl) south of Regensburg on April 22 with four corps well in hand against a French army again dangerously divided, with only 20,000 men of Davout's III Corps facing about 75,000 Austrians under Charles's immediate command. Charles ordered 40,000 troops of two of his corps to fall hard on Davout's left, or north, wing while his other two corps marched farther north around that wing for Abbach on the Danube, to cut in turn Napoleon's line of communications to that river.

The Austrians opened the battle of Eckmühl about midday on the 22nd, gradually gaining momentum in their attack on the III Corps left despite Davout's hastening of reinforcements to the threatened area. But their relative slowness in marching and their inadequate development of the corps system snatched this latest opportunity from their grasp. By the early morning hours of the 22nd Napoleon at Landshut had become convinced that he was pursuing and directly threatening only a small portion of the Austrian army and that Charles with the enemy main body was still to the north and a danger to both his own left wing—Davout—and to his connection with the Danube. Acting promptly on this belated but altogether correct presumption, Napoleon ordered a concentration on Eckmühl and himself rode hard toward the danger. Because during the early hours of April 22 French troops covered seventeen to nineteen miles (twenty-seven to thirty-one kilometers) in a time that the Austrians required to march ten miles (sixteen kilometers), Davout was not threatened by greatly superior numbers for long. In midafternoon Lannes (now duc de Montebello), marching from Landshut, approached the Austrian left with his Provisional Corps of 30,000. Davout thereupon ordered a counterattack to fix the Austrians in place for the consummation of the typically Napoleonic maneuver thus unfolding out of rapid recovery and improvisation.

Lannes struck the Austrian left and left rear and pushed toward Eckmühl from the south and east about 4:30 P.M. About the same time Lefebvre's VII Corps arrived to strike the opposite Austrian flank. Much of the Archduke's force was not yet engaged, but Austrian corps were not yet conditioned to withstand adversity in the assurance that the meaning of the corps system was that other formations would soon reinforce them. Instead of the promise of the uncommitted troops' steadying the threatened Austrian front, the latter not only failed to hold long enough to be reinforced but retreated in disorder and spread the contagion of defeat rearward. The Austrians lost some 7,000 killed and wounded and, because of the nature of the battle's dénouement, some 5,000 prisoners. The French probably suffered about 6,000 total casualties. Napoleon accepted the protestations of several senior commanders that the men were too tired to pursue—given the hard marching that for many had preceded the fighting, an accurate diagnosis, confirmed by subsequent reports—and there was no general follow-through, although the Emperor sent seventy-four squadrons of cavalry to harry the retreat.

The Archduke Charles quickly threw a ponton bridge across the Danube downstream from Regensburg and crossed most of his army to the north bank. For a time he left a substantial force to defend Regensburg, but changing his mind he evacuated all but six battalions, who were to hold the medieval fortress town as long as possible. In the subsequent bombardment, Napoleon suffered the only wound of his career, inflicted by a spent cannonball that struck his right foot. When the walls were breached, a French assault party was able to make its way to the Regensburg bridge and thence to trap the garrison.

The defense of the fortress made little difference. Charles received reinforcements that increased his army to 90,000, but the Austrian troops had been stunned by their inability to make a better showing in battle after all the efforts to reform the army, and morale was exceedingly low. If Napoleon had known how low, he might have pressed on in pursuit of Charles. Napoleon was concerned, however, because another Austrian army, 75,000 men under the Archduke John, was creating serious trouble for his Viceroy of Italy, his stepson, Prince Eugène de Beauharnais, *colonel général* of the Chasseurs of the Guard. The twenty-nine-year-old Eugène, personally commanding the Army of Italy, had begun the campaign with a field force of fewer than 20,000, and while he had up to 50,000 more in scattered garrisons from which to draw reinforcements, the Austrian initiative at first left him unable to do more than station a strong force in Venice and otherwise withdraw behind the River Adige with his main army.

Only sketchy and doubtful news of these events reached the French Emperor, whose feeling for Eugène was reflected in fatherly letters of military advice, sharing his thoughts on strategy and tactics a good deal more freely than he was accustomed to doing with the marshals. In these circumstances, Napoleon desired to insert the *Grande Armée* between the Archdukes Charles and John to minimize the mischief that might be perpetrated by the latter.

He might at the same time maximize his own opportunities, because the best way to interpose between the two archdukes would be to take advantage of Charles's withdrawal to the north of the Danube by striking directly eastward toward Vienna. Such movement toward the Habsburg capital might well induce the Emperor Franz I, who was certainly not a paragon of boldness, to call both archdukes back to defend the city, which would bring both within range for Napoleon to pursue his favorite strategy of annihilation of the enemy army, possibly by dealing with John and Charles separately. Therefore Napoleon left it to Davout to watch the Archduke Charles's retreat while he himself and the main army resumed the marches they had interrupted to turn back to Eckmühl.

The forces Napoleon had earlier been pursuing, originally the left wing of Charles's army under *Feldmarschall Leutnant* Johann Freiherr Hiller, offered a partial redemption of their army's reputation and of the efficacy of Charles's reforms after all, by turning at bay at Ebelsberg (or Ebersberg) on the Train River on May 3. With 40,000 men and seventy guns, Hiller intended to buy time for reconstructing the Austrian forces and organizing Vienna's defenses. Masséna, now duc de Rivoli, commanded the IV Corps in Napoleon's van and rushed a fortified bridge to mount a series of frontal attacks against the town of Ebelsberg and its castle, costing about 4,000 casualties. This toll was unnecessary, because Lannes and the Provisional Corps were moving against Hiller's rear. Although the Austrians lost perhaps 4,000 prisoners when they abandoned the position, in addition to 2,000 or more additional casualties, the fight at Ebelsberg both improved Austrian morale and purchased some of the time desired. (How much credit Hiller deserves is debatable; while the battle raged, he enjoyed a leisurely lunch.) Hiller crossed to the north bank of the Danube, burning bridges and removing all boats from a considerable stretch of the river and heading for a meeting with the Archduke Charles.

The latter was en route to Vienna, as Napoleon had foreseen. Napoleon and Hiller meanwhile also hastened toward the capital, along opposite banks of the Danube. The time bought by Hiller at Ebelsberg proved insufficient to save the city, because Lannes reached the outskirts early on May 10 to find the fortifications strengthened but still inadequate. He seized the suburbs and massed his guns to bombard the inner city, whereupon the defenders moved out on May 2 and a French army entered for the second time in four years. Again the Vienna arsenals were well stocked to ease Napoleon's logistical problems.

Charles and Hiller converged in the neighborhood of Wagram (Deutch-Wagram), some ten miles (sixteen kilometers) southeast of Vienna. Because the fall of the capital had not sufficiently discouraged the Austrians to persuade them to make peace (though they had sent out feelers after Eckmühl), Napoleon now had to attempt again the destruction of either or both of the main Austrian armies. The French Emperor had hoped to cross the Danube within three or four days after capturing the capital and thus to forestall the juncture of Charles and Hiller, but once more the latter's work proved to have served the Austrians well. The French found it so difficult to gather the materials needed to span the many branches of the Danube, some 2,000 yards or meters in width and at this time of year largely in flood, that four days were consumed in collecting bridging supplies. In spite of Napoleon's personal prodding, another four days then went into building a bridge to Lobau Island on the north shore, one of many islands studding this part of the river. The French army began crossing the Danube in force on May 20.

Not until that afternoon did Charles begin to march toward the bridgehead from his camps to the north. His delay in responding to the French bridge construction and failure to resist the crossing (although a heavy hulk sent downstream on the afternoon of the 20th broke the bridge across the main channel of the river and interrupted the crossing) may have reflected in fact the aggravation of his usual caution by his recent setbacks; some of his own generals thought him too cautious on this occasion. Nevertheless, Charles had a simple yet excellent plan to allow as many French to cross as he thought he could beat, and then to strike them. He was about to redeem the previous failures of his military reforms and his own leadership by inflicting on Napoleon his first unquestionable battlefield defeat, in the battle of Aspern-Essling on May 21–22.

The Campaign of 1809: Aspern-Essling

Aspern (Gross-Aspern) and Essling (or Esslingen) were villages a little over a mile apart on the north bank of the Danube just beyond Lobau Island. They punctuated the Marchfeld, an open plain much used by the Austrian Army as a maneuver ground. On the morning of Whitsunday, May 21, Napoleon himself began a reconnaissance of that bank and soon found a screen of Austrian cavalry too strong for his advance guard to pierce. In fact the Archduke Charles was at hand with 95,000 troops and 292 guns, while the French had only 23,000 men and 44 guns across the river. Charles was also uncertain about his enemy's precise numbers, but an observatory on the Bissamberg (or Bisamberg) near Vienna allowed the Austrians to witness all that the French were doing, and of course Charles's army knew the Marchfeld thoroughly. Throughout the crossing operation, Napoleon had been decidedly casual about the difficulties and dangers posed by the wide Danube, and his offhandedness was now not for the first time leading him into trouble. To make matters worse, the Danube bridge broke again toward midmorning of the 21st.

On the other hand, the French could stand their ground in an excellent defensive position. Both villages lay too close to the Danube to be turned, and both offered ready-made strong points, a church and a cemetery in Aspern and a granary in Essling. The Austrians were characteristically slow in getting their attacks started, but they came forward in five columns about 2:30 P.M., three columns concentrating against Aspern to break Napoleon's left flank and destroy the bridge once and for all, the other two to attack Essling. The Austrian cavalry was in the center, to deal with any French cavalry that might attack the heads of the infantry columns. The Austrian artillery commenced a devastating barrage. By this time the French bridge was in service again, but a succession of floating weights continued to make traversing the wide and swift Danube precarious and uncertain.

Masséna with part of his IV Corps defended Aspern, while Lannes leading another part of the corps guarded Essling. Hiller carried the former place in the first Austrian charge, but Masséna soon recaptured it and then throughout the day displayed once more the tenacity with which he had held Genoa in 1800. Seesaw fighting for the village reached a climax late in the day when Charles personally led a heavy and desperate assault, which overran much of Aspern only to recede when Messéna led a counterattack that regained everything except the church and cemetery. The fighting for Essling differed in little except the smaller numbers involved, certainly not in severity. Such French infantry as had deployed between the two villages had to shift to those places as reinforcements. Napoleon attempted a diversion that might remedy the weakness of his center by sending forward his own cavalry in that sector under Jean-Baptiste de Bessières, *maréchal de l'Empire*. Aiming at the enemy's troublesome line of artillery, a first charge failed, but a second drove away many of the guns, rode around supporting infantry squares, and defeated the Austrian cavalry.

When darkness suspended the fighting about 8:00 P.M., the French had been reinforced to 31,500 men and 90 guns, but they were still much outnumbered, and passage of the river remained uncertain. The opposing armies bivouacked where they stood, at some places within pistol shot of each other. Determined not to concede that the oft-defeated Austrians were now able to defeat him, Napoleon continued to draw troops into his bridgehead through the night, until by daylight of May 22 he had doubled the numbers with which he began the day before, with more cavalry, Lannes's II Corps, and the Imperial Guard.

At earliest dawn Messéna attacked at Aspern and cleared the village—only to be driven back in turn. At 5:00 A.M. the Austrians tried again at Essling, only to be driven back also. At seven Napoleon launched a major assault along his center and reaching to his right, three divisions of Lannes's corps led by the indefatigable Lannes himself. They broke through, and Bessières's cavalry was unleashed again to exploit what now seemed about to become a French victory after all.

Once more the Archduke Charles intervened personally, and it was only his direct dispatching of reinforcements from right and left and the magnetism of his courage and presence that held the Austrian center together. But another French blow would surely break it, and Napoleon knew that Davout and the III Corps were coming up.

Before eight o'clock, however, the parade of Austrian battering devices down the Danube against the French bridge came to feature nothing less than a floating mill, which swept away the center section of the bridge. Davout could

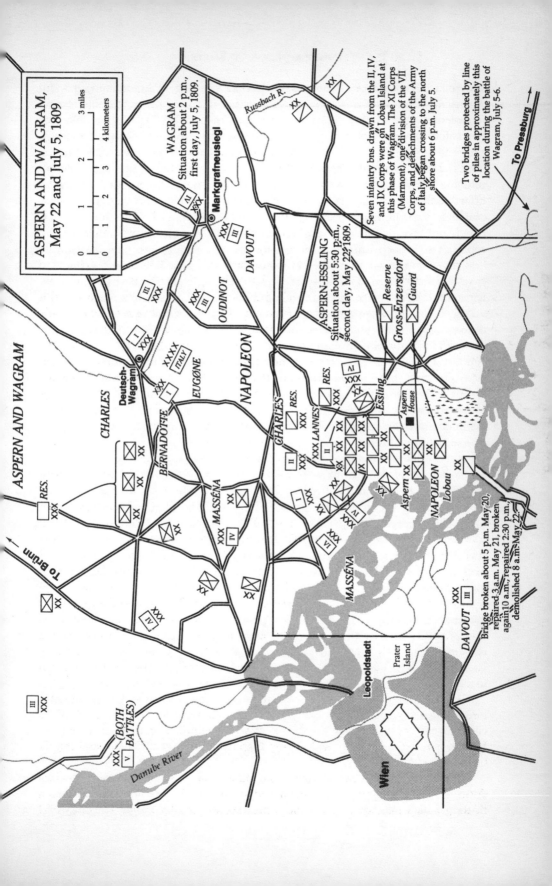

ASPERN AND WAGRAM

ASPERN AND WAGRAM,
May 22 and July 5, 1809.

WAGRAM
Situation about 2 p.m.,
first day, July 5, 1809.

ASPERN-ESSLING
Situation about 5:30 p.m.,
second day, May 22, 1809.

Seven infantry bns. drawn from the II, IV,
and IX Corps were on Lobau Island at
this phase of Wagram. The XI Corps
(Marmont), one division of the VII
Corps, and detachments of the Army
of Italy began crossing to the north
shore about 6 p.m. July 5.

Two bridges protected by line
of piles in approximately this
location during the battle of
Wagram, July 5-6.

To Pressburg

Bridge broken about 5 p.m. May 20,
repaired 3 a.m. May 21, broken
again 10 a.m., repaired 2:30 p.m.,
demolished 8 a.m. May 22.

To Brünn

Russbach R.

Markgrafneusiegl

DAVOUT

OUDINOT

Deutsch-
Wagram

ITALY

EUGÈNE

NAPOLEON

CHARLES

BERNADOTTE

RES.

MASSÉNA

Gross-Enzersdorf

Reserve

Guard

Essling

Aspern
House

LANNES

RES.

RES.

CHARLES

NAPOLEON

Aspern

Lobau

MASSÉNA

DAVOUT

Leopoldstadt

Prater
Island

Wien

Danube River

(BOTH
BATTLES)

0   1   2   3 miles

0   1   2   3   4 kilometers

not come. Napoleon had to suspend Lannes's attack. Thus encouraged, the Austrians with a determination unprecedented in their previous battles against Napoleon resumed their assaults upon Aspern and Essling. Aspern changed hands four times before Masséna regained a strong grip on it. Lannes's ammunition was running low, so Napoleon ordered him back to the line of the villages. The Austrians mounted five unsuccessful assaults on Essling before a sixth got into the village but failed to take the granary. Charles then shifted his main effort back to the center; there, too, the French held, but ammunition was reaching them from the south bank of the Danube only in a trickle, in small boats, and about 2:00 P.M. Napoleon learned that the bridge was beyond quick repair. The French Emperor thereupon ordered a retreat into Lobau Island.

To cover the withdrawal, he also ordered a new assault to clear Essling. The infantry of the Young Guard—just formed in 1809, from the best of the recent conscript classes—with the exception of only two of its battalions delivered the attack, driving through the village yet again. In spite of this diversion, the withdrawal was difficult and costly, with Charles straining himself and his men to make the victory as complete as possible. The French had almost no artillery support. Lannes's courage and leadership may have been the principal ingredients offsetting the similar qualities of the Archduke and preventing a rout; but Lannes fell mortally wounded, the first of Napoleon's marshalate to die of wounds suffered in battle. At the end, the Old Guard stood firm to allow the completion of the withdrawal to the island. Fighting ended by 4:00 P.M. The retreat continued through the night.

The Austrians did not follow up, however, even to the extent that a costly battle permitted. Instead of so much as bombarding Lobau, let alone crossing the Danube to fall on the French rear, the Archduke Charles now spent his energies urging his brother, the Emperor, that the advantageous hour had struck for making peace.

The French lost about 21,000 casualties, the Austrians 23,400. Thus the statistics of losses showed no decisive margin of victory, and in fact Aspern would probably not have been an Austrian victory at all if the French had been able to keep their main bridge open for an hour longer on May 22. But the latter failure was a result of Napoleon's larger carelessness about reconnaissance in general and the nature of the Danube in particular, and these failures plus the vindication of the Austrian military reforms at least in terms of the fighting capacity of the troops together produced a victory clear enough for the Austrians to take considerable satisfaction from it. They *could* defeat Napoleon, after all. His legend of invincibility was fast fading, for he had been checked at Eylau, his subordinates frequently beaten in Spain, and now he himself had directed a lost battle at last.

The Campaign of 1809: Wagram

Of course, Napoleon had no intention of leaving matters at that. Some 100,000 of his soldiers crowded little Lobau Island, many of them wounded, with hospital stores as well as ammunition in desperately short supply.

The Emperor felt constrained to call a council of war, a rarity in a career in which he preferred always to control all the reins of command; but when the marshals counselled retreat from Lobau, Napoleon refused, arguing that ceasing to apply pressure would free Charles to operate against the French line of communications and thus propel the *Grande Armée* all the way back to Strasbourg. Immediately Napoleon summoned reinforcements from almost everywhere in his empire.

These included some 56,000 men of the Army of Italy under Prince Eugène. On learning on April 28 of his stepfather's victory at Eckmühl, Eugène had gone over to the offensive against the Archduke John, who because of the same news was recalled into Hungary. Eugène displayed the benefits of the military education he had received from Napoleon in the skill of his pursuit, of his partial envelopment of the Austrian rear guard and victory at the Piave River on May 8, and of his rupture of the Austrian frontier defenses on May 14–18. His march into Austria was accomplished in the face of cold weather and hunger as he crossed the Styrian Alps, and it was climaxed by a smashing though small-scale triumph over an Austrian detachment under *Feldmarschall Leutnant* Franz Freiherr Jellačić von (or de) Bužem near Leoben on May 25 and a bigger victory over the Archduke John's main army at Raab on June 14. The latter battle featured a well-executed Napoleonic *manœuvre sur les derrières* by Eugène's cavalry, and it was followed by the investment of the fortress of Raab and on June 25 its surrender. Napoleon enjoyed both paternal pride and the gratification of having Eugène and the Army of Italy on hand for the resumption of his main offensive.

The reinforcements in fact brought the *Grande Armée* to 189,000 by the end of June, while, even counting the forces of the Archduke John, Charles could count only on some 148,000, despite the incorporation of 60,000 *Landwehr* into his main force. It required resistance to the wishes of the Emperor Franz to retain that many, because the latter wanted Charles to detach sizable numbers to help the Archduke Ferdinand battle an exasperating Polish uprising led by the Minister of War of the French-sponsored Grand Duchy of Warsaw, a former aide-de-camp to the Emperor Franz, Jósef Antoni Prince Poniatowski. Part of the trouble derived from a perennial Habsburg headache; Hungary did not send forward men in the quantities expected, Napoleon having played upon Hungarian nationalism to stir up a restlessness akin to that of the Poles.

After Aspern, furthermore, the effectiveness of Charles's cavalry and artillery suffered a dramatic decline, as the Austrian administrative machinery somehow failed to produce an adequate supply of replacement horses. In contrast, Napoleon ruthlessly scoured the Austrian domains occupied by his forces to replenish every logistical category. Meanwhile he gradually reached out from Lobau Island to seize a plethora of other small Danubian islands, enlarging his control of the river and permitting him to mystify Charles about the location of his next major crossing, though he also rebuilt the Lobau ponton bridge and created a trestle bridge beside it.

In fact, he decided that there was not much chance to engender further mystification or to achieve any real measure of surprise in crossing his big army, so on the night of July 3–4 he began pulling additional troops into Lobau. On the stormy night of July 5 Masséna's IV Corps floated another ponton bridge and began filing out of Lobau, not directly into the old Aspern bridgehead, where Charles expected the French, but farther east near Gross–Engersdorf.

This small surprise disconcerted Charles, but in any event he had decided with his staff and his corps commanders that the balance of power in cavalry and artillery had swung so drastically in favor of the French that the Austrian army could probably not again contest the Aspern-Essling battleground. The problem was not simply one of horses but of Napoleon's buildup of a huge battery of 150 guns to cover any foray north from Lobau. Yet Charles vacillated; he left an Advance Guard, about a corps in size, along the Danube—not enough to hold the river line, yet too much to be sacrificed. The Austrian main body withdrew to the line Bissamberg–Deutsch-Wagram–Markgrafneushiedl, whence they hoped to maneuver to cut the French off from their bridges; but in his indecision Charles had not entrenched the new line. The Archduke John's force of 12,500 men was still some twenty miles (thirty-two kilometers) to the east at Pressburg but was expected to join in the coming effort.

The *Grande Armée* completed other bridges from Lobau to the north bank and in the early afternoon of July 5 proceeded northward in force to locate and pin down the enemy. The advance took the shape of an opening fan as Napoleon's army claimed space for maneuver. The Austrians contrived only ill-coordinated efforts to slow the advance, any idea of interposing between the French and their bridges soon proving impracticable, and by evening Napoleon held a salient along the north bank some fifteen miles (twenty-four kilometers) wide. His troops were in position to attack the Wagram plateau, the pivot of the Austrian position.

This position was a naturally strong one, shielded from Deutsch-Wagram through Markgrafneushiedl by the Russbach, a stream readily passable by infantry but a severe obstacle to cavalry and artillery because of thickets along its banks. The French deployment had been leisurely by the best French standards, largely because so many men had at first been crowded into the narrow spaces of Lobau and the initial bridgeheads on the north shore. But as usual the Austrian deployment had been still slower, and Napoleon perceived that the enemy was not yet completely in place to take advantage of the strengths of the Wagram position. Although it was already evening, he therefore sent his corps forward in a frontal attack.

The attack took off so hastily that it was necessarily piecemeal, but it became a source of enough danger to the Austrians that again the Archduke Charles plunged into personal peril to lead reserve grenadiers in checking it. At least twice the French penetrated the village of Deutsch-Wagram but were driven out. The last penetration was by Bernadotte, now commanding the IX Saxon Corps; as usual he was late, when a more timely effort on his part might have made French possession of the town stick. As it was, Napoleon's attempt to exploit enemy slowness failed.

Through an unseasonably cold night, the two armies slept fitfully on their arms. Shooting by nervous pickets occasionally touched off brief fire fights.

Encouraged by the repulse of the French on the previous evening as well as by Aspern, the Archduke Charles decided to take the initiative on July 6, to anticipate Napoleon's attack. He would hurl four corps against Masséna's IV corps on the French left, which from its bivouacs on the line Leopoldsau-Süssenbrünn (or Sussenbrunn or Sussenbraun)-Aderklaa threatened to curl around the western end of the Russbach lines. A diversionary attack was to occupy Davout's III Corps on the French right, and when the Archduke John arrived he was to join in this effort. But the doubts and vacillations that had marred Charles's preparations for the new French advance still afflicted him; he did not dispatch his order until well after midnight, which made coordinated attacks impossible. Furthermore, John's march to the scene appears to have been deliberately slow, as if he did not wish to participate.

In spite of the incoherence of the Austrian advances, however, by eleven in the morning Masséna's left had been driven back almost to Aspern, while Bernadotte, immediately east of Masséna, had been frightened into a hasty retreat that uncovered the strong position afforded by the stoutly built village of Aderklaa. The village was lost, and Napoleon at length had had enough of Bernadotte; he banished him from the field. Messéna, though injured on July 2 by a falling horse and commanding from an elegant carriage, fortunately launched this command post forward drawn by four white horses to lead part of his own corps back into Aderklaa. But because the Austrian advance farther to the left was threatening the connection with Lobau Island and the Danube, Napoleon next dispatched Masséna in his chariot to disengage from Aderklaa and to march south with reinforcements to stem the retreat that Bernadotte had touched off. Masséna carried out this difficult operation with his customary skill and then held the whole threatened left with his usual tenacity, aided by the massive battery that Napoleon had planted earlier on Lobau Island.

In spite of Charles's intent, on the opposite, eastern flank it had been Davout and the French who struck first. Through the morning they gradually pushed back the Austrian left. Nevertheless, the course of the battle of Wagram thus far indicated like the battle of Aspern that former margins of combat superiority of the French over the Austrians had almost disappeared. The Austrians might remain inferior in mobility and coordination, but their soldiers fought as stoutly as Napoleon's in the attack or on the defense. In part, Austrian standards had risen, stimulated by those emotions that aided the Habsburgs' recruitment of a mass army. In part, French élan had declined, dissipated by endless war.

Yet Napoleon's feel for the flow of a battle and his sense of his destiny had scarcely declined. While the crisis on his left remained unresolved as Masséna trundled thither, his line of retreat therefore remained threatened, and chaos if not despair infected all the French rear areas except Davout's, the Emperor resolved that perceptions must be as confused and emotions as uncertain among the enemy. Consequently he would attack, building on Davout's success and extending that momentum westward. The key role went to Macdonald's V Corps, which would form up on the right of Masséna's new position and thrust toward Süssenbrünn and neighboring Gerosdorf, threatening to break the Austrians who were attacking Masséna away from Charles's main body.

The reserve cavalry and the Imperial Guard were to support Macdonald's corps. A battery of 104 guns would provide artillery cover. Thirty thousand strong, the V Corps and the cavalry advanced in a huge hollow square; fourteen battalions deployed on a front one battalion wide, the remainder of the infantry deployed in columns on either flank, the cavalry closing up the rear. The purpose of this formation was, while amply protecting the flanks of the assault, to compel every man to persist in moving forward lest he be trampled by men and horses coming from the rear. Nevertheless, many of the men faltered, under a storm of Austrian artillery—additional evidence of the decline of French élan. Perhaps as few as a tenth of the original 30,000 pressed the attack home. But with the massed French guns in turn tearing apart the Austrian line, Macdonald's troops penetrated it, and the cavalry and the Guard came on to exploit the penetration. Charles's army was indeed divided in two, and there was nothing left for the Austrian commander but to withdraw and reconsolidate his forces as best he could.

Less even than usual after one of these grand-scale battles was Napoleon's army in fit condition to pursue. The III Corps, in fact, although it had been successful against the Austrian left almost all day, and although in Davout it possessed one of the steadiest leaders in the army, wavered when about five in the afternoon it discovered the Archduke John's force belatedly arriving and threatening its right flank. This deflation of the last effort of otherwise reliable but now exhausted and horror-stricken soldiers reflected the appalling cost of Wagram. The French lost 39,500 casualties, including even in victory about 7,000 prisoners. The Austrians lost about 40,000.

Yet however narrowly, Napoleon had attained another triumph. In immediate if not in long-range impact, Aspern was reversed—the long–range impact, however, involving the further deterioration of the Napoleonic legend of invincibility, because the reformed Austrian Army had made even victory so costly that Napoleon could not afford many more days like July 6, 1809. Still, for the present the Austrians were ready to make yet another peace. Napoleon felt gratified enough to name Berthier prince de Wagram because he had presided over the essential details of the crossings of the Danube, and to promote Macdonald to the marshalate for his climactic assault.

The Campaign of 1809: Resolution

The Archduke Charles, who like his great adversary seemed to live a charmed life on the battlefield, had nevertheless suffered a slight wound by the time in midafternoon he realized that another fight was lost. He kept his center closely engaged and well under control to cover the retreat, and his reserve eventually checked Macdonald around Jägerhaus. Altogether, the Austrian Army reconfirmed its prowess with a well-conducted and orderly withdrawal.

The direction of the retreat was toward Znaim (or Znaym), where Charles hoped to cross the Thaya River and use it as a temporary shield. Auguste Fréderic Louis Viesse de Marmont, duc de Raguse (Ragusa) and *général de division*, commanding the IX Corps in the van of the French pursuit, anticipated Charles's intentions. Marmont drove his comparatively fresh troops, who had been in reserve at Wagram, to crossings of the Thaya east of Znaim, and then he hurried down the left bank of the river to try to prevent Charles from crossing. In spite of hard marching, however, he found Charles's army mostly across the stream when he reached Znaim on July 10. Nevertheless, he took the risk of opening a battle against a much larger force in the hope of fixing the Austrians until the bulk of the French army came up. Early on the 11th Masséna arrived with the IV Corps, and Marmont appeared to have succeeded.

So Charles believed, and he also believed that his army was too much injured to fight again immediately. Therefore he requested an armistice, to which Napoleon agreed, cutting short the battle of Znaim. The French Emperor also considered his troops too exhausted to make another battle as yet worth the risks.

Months of diplomatic bickering followed before the new peace treaty was concluded. Franz I, often timorous amid full-scale war, now proved truculent when the pressures against him eased. The British were still busy in Iberia, and they also landed 40,000 troops on Walcheren Island at one of the mouths of the Scheldt on August 11 to try to breathe new life into the war in northern Europe. This foray for a time encouraged the party of defiance in Austria. But the British failed to exploit their occupation of Walcheren by advancing on Antwerp, and Bernadotte, dispatched to the scene, partially redeemed himself by sealing them into their beachhead. There they languished under "Walcheren fever," an ailment akin to malaria, until they withdrew on September 30 with 106 killed in action and 4,000 dead of disease. The Netherlands had not been a fortunate place for Britain in the French Revolutionary and Napoleonic Wars.

Meanwhile Austria's internal squabbles had led the Emperor to the folly of dismissing the Archduke Charles from command on July 18, an action that scarcely enhanced Austrian ability to resume the fight. Thus in disarray, the Austrians at length acceded to the Treaty of Schönbrunn, signed by Franz I at the palace on October 14. Napoleon considered his terms generous in light of repeated Austrian provocations, but in fact they were harsh considering the narrow margin of French military success in the latest round of fighting. Austria ceded Salzburg and the Inn-Viertel provinces, which eventually went (briefly, as matters proved) to Bavaria. Austria turned over to France the Frioul, Carniola, and Carinthia, the parts of Croatia and Dalmatia north of the Save River, and the city of Trieste. Large areas of Austrian Poland around Lublin and Krakow went to the Grand Duchy of Warsaw. Austria had to pay France an indemnity amounting to almost 85 million francs, to recognize Joseph as King of Spain, and to reaffirm the exclusion of British troops from her domains. A Prussian-style solution was applied to limit her military power; her army was restricted to 150,000 men. Altogether, the Austrian Emperor lost more than 3 million of his 16 million subjects.

This figure included about 400,000 inhabitants of the Tarnopol area of Galicia ceded to Tsar Alexander. The Tsar had put in his bid for much more. His small gain, a reward for having remained at least neutral, was in fact intended by Napoleon as a rebuke for his lack of support. The ambiguity of the Russian part of the Schönbrunn settlement reflected of course the larger ambiguity of Russia's place in Napoleonic Europe. Rather than forsake Russian participation in the Continental System, Napoleon doled out the Tarnopol concession to the Tsar and rebuffed Polish pleas that he transform the Grand Duchy of Warsaw into a restored Kingdom of Poland. In dubious return, the Tsar soon mounted a campaign to win over Polish sentiment for a Polish kingdom with himself wearing the crown, while he concentrated troops on the eastern frontier of the Grand Duchy to take advantage of a positive response.

Moreover, Napoleon was now forty and still lacked an heir to his empire. The Empress Josephine, born Marie Rose Josephine Tascher de la Pagerie and married in 1774 to Alexandre, vicomte de Beauharnais before her marriage on March 9, 1796 (19 Ventôse An IV), to Bonaparte, had not produced a child in her second marriage. On December 15, 1809, Napoleon divorced her to open the way for his marriage to the eighteen-year-old Maria Louise of Austria, daughter of Franz I. On March 11, 1810, Napoleon was wedded in Vienna with Berthier standing as his proxy, and the new Empress Marie-Louise thereupon traveled to France.

CAMPAIGNS OF EXHAUSTION AND ATTRITION

Beyond the disquietudes of the absence of an heir, the leakage of the Continental System, and the precarious nature of the military victory of 1809, there remained also the Iberian sickness gnawing at the Napoleonic Empire. The outcome of Wagram left Napoleon free, he thought, to dispatch large reinforcements to the Peninsula. Soult as Major-General of the Army in Spain, in effect chief of staff there, was to take three corps, 70,000 men, to suppress resistance in Andalusia. He was to be followed by Masséna, now prince d'Essling, with three corps all part of the Imperial Guard, 120,000 men, to base himself on Salamanca for operations against Portugal. The total French force in Spain would then amount to some 370,000. No one could be sure yet how much its effectiveness would be undercut by Napoleon's failure to encourage his generals to exercise initiative and his insistence on controlling everything himself, in Iberia even at long distance; in the sequel, these aspects of Napoleonic leadership were to produce an operational rigidity that went far to negate French tactical flexibility.

The Lines of Torres Vedras

Soult began well by capturing Seville (Sevilla) on January 31, 1810, and then investing Cádiz, to which the Spanish Supreme Junta had fled from Seville and where it had resigned its powers to a regency of four members. Masséna began his campaign early in June 1810, instructing Soult to cooperate by attacking Badajoz, just on the Spanish side of the Portuguese border, and Elva, just inside Portugal on the southern approach to Lisbon, while Masséna himself moved against Ciudad Rodrigo on the northern approach.

The Walcheren Island fiasco had precipitated a Cabinet crisis in London, and the latest Austrian defection naturally aggravated tendencies toward irresolution. A considerable parliamentary faction favored withdrawal of Viscount Wellington's army from the Peninsula. Wellington had accordingly gone over to a cautious defensive strategy. In October 1809 he had directed the secret construction of the Lines of Torres Vedras, conducted by Lieutenant-Colonel Richard Fletcher, Royal Engineers, and seventeen sapper officers with in time 10,000 local laborers. These lines were to be a triple cordon of forts facing north and protecting Lisbon, stretching for nearly thirty miles (forty-eight kilometers), with their flanks resting on the ocean to the west and the Tagus estuary to the east.

Wellington had about 35,000 British troops, 30,000 Portuguese regulars, and 30,000 Portuguese militia. With these men he stood for the present in advance of the Torres Vedras Lines, watching the roads into Portugal from the east and especially those through Ciudad Rodrigo north of the Tagus and Badajoz south of the river. In the face of Masséna's advance, Wellington's actions remained cautious. He allowed Ciudad Rodrigo to fall on June 10, Almeida to fall after a siege on August 27. One month after that date Wellington chose to offer Masséna battle where, just north of Coimbra, the route of the French crossed the Sierra de Bussaco (Busaco). With about 60,000 French troops against 50,000 Allies, about half of them Portuguese, the aggressive Masséna confidently launched a frontal assault. British linear tactics and musketry did good work again; the Allies repulsed the French and exacted about 5,000 casualties, losing some 1,300 themselves.

The next day, however, Masséna turned the Bussaco position by way of the Boyalva Pass and Sardão, a route that the Portuguese had neglected to fortify. Wellington then retreated via Coimbra to the Torres Vedras Lines, behind which on his urging much of the peasantry had already fled, leaving burned crops behind them. As Wellington's rear guard filed into the lines on October 10, 108 redoubts had been constructed, mounting 447 guns. The lines were still under construction, and a further forty-two redoubts were added later. Some 25,000 men were needed to garrison the redoubts, while Wellington's main army massed around Mafra as a mobile force ready to march toward any threatened sector on specially constructed roads. With these works Wellington sought, barring a contrary political decision that the defenses were also intended to discourage, to maintain a British military presence in support of Portuguese and Spanish resistance until a more favorable day for offensive action might dawn.

Whether that day would come seemed decidedly questionable. The problems of overextension and the recent fissures in the legend of invincibility notwithstanding, the Napoleonic Empire in late 1810 and early 1811 not only bestrode all Europe except for a corner of Portugal and pockets in Spain, but could at last envisage an assured future. The new Empress was pregnant, and on March 20, 1811 she gave birth to the long-awaited heir, Napoléon François Charles Joseph Bonaparte, who was immediately proclaimed Napoleon II, King of Italy.

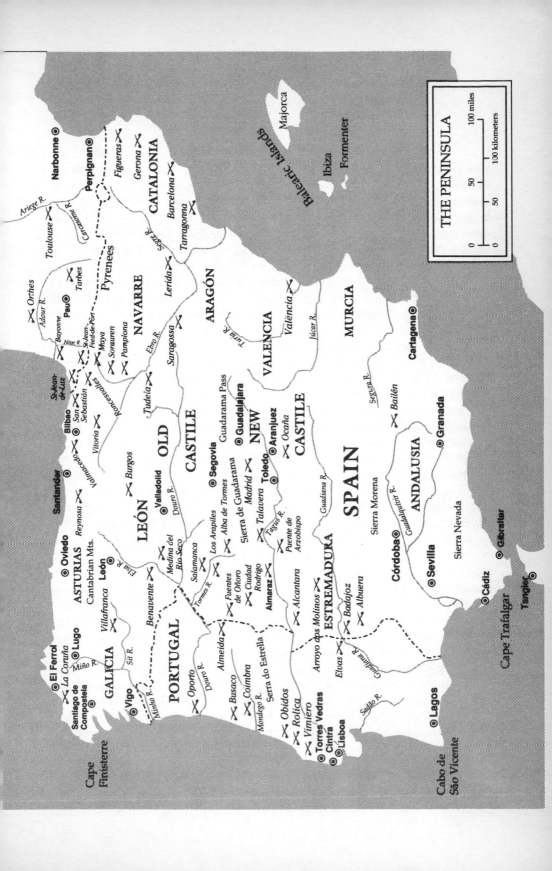

The Iberian Campaign of 1811:
Attrition, Logistics, and Stalemate

At least the Lines of Torres Vedras did their work of halting the latest triumphant French procession through Iberia. Indeed, as Masséna approached the lines, the Portuguese recaptured Coimbra in his rear. With his line of communications thus endangered, the Torres Vedras redoubts apparently too strong to be assailed successfully by his force at hand, and the Anglo-Portuguese armies frustrating his attempts to cross to the south of the Tagus, Masséna asked Napoleon for reinforcements and on November 15 withdrew the short distance to Santarem. Soult had fared no better against Badajoz and Elvas.

In the longer run, the Lines of Torres Vedras did their work so well that the year 1811 saw the balance in the Peninsular War shift a considerable distance back toward the Allies. Napoleon refused Masséna the requested reinforcements. At the same time the British Cabinet similarly failed to resolve on supporting Wellington enough that he might go over to a strong offensive, while the Spanish insurrection simmered but its leaders achieved no clarity of strategic design. Thus 1811 saw no decisive strategic alterations; but the French suffered the year's greater frustrations.

Instead of reinforcing Masséna, Napoleon sent orders to Soult to try harder against Badajoz in the hope of opening an alternative, southern route to Lisbon. Soult dutifully invested Badajoz on January 26, 1811, and captured it from the Spanish on March 10. In the meantime, however, an Anglo-Spanish force distracted him by attempting to break the investment of Cádiz that was being conducted simultaneously by Soult's subordinate Marshal Victor. Victor nonetheless persisted in spite of an Allied tactical victory at the battle of Barrosa on March 5. The strategic effect of all these early 1811 operations in southern Iberia was to cancel each other out; but the British did better in the north.

Denied reinforcements, Masséna had sat staring at the Lines of Torres Vedras all through the winter. Wellington's earlier efforts to have the Portuguese peasants burn their crops before they fled behind the lines had been intended to deny Masséna so much subsistence that he would not be able to remain thus immobile, but obviously the scorched-earth policy had not succeeded as thoroughly as the British general hoped. On the other hand, it worked well enough that Masséna's provisions were never ample, and consequently, on the day of Barrosa the Prince of Essling decided to abandon any thought of outstaring Wellington and to withdraw into Spain. Hunger among his troops was the precipitating cause of the retreat.

The withdrawal became yet another of those nightmare marches through barren hills and mountains that plagued both sides in Iberia and proved that logistics was, as Wellington perceived, the key to ultimate success. Hungry and almost without horses—because the beasts had already starved—when they set out, Masséna's men found no sufficient foodstuffs in the desolate north Portuguese area through which they marched. Therefore they grew progressively weaker, more demoralized, and more inclined to straggle or desert. Wellington emerged from the Torres Vedras Lines to follow, but because of his own uncertain political support he was unwilling to risk losing men in any close harrying of the retreat that might bring on a considerable battle. He settled for harassing actions against the French rear guard, which was ably commanded by Ney, and for directing the Portuguese to remove boats from the Mondego and Douro Rivers and to break up roads north of the Douro. The results were bad enough for the French. By the time Masséna halted his withdrawal at Salamanca in April, he had lost 30,000 men since departing that place the previous year, 6,000 of them in the retreat from Santarem alone.

Masséna left behind him a garrison at Almeida within Portugal as a foothold for an eventual return toward Lisbon. On April 9 Wellington ordered Major-General Sir Brent Spencer, his second in command, to invest Almeida. This effort provoked Masséna, his supplies partially replenished, to stir westward from Salamanca again in a relief attempt. Wellington thereupon took personal charge at Almeida. Nearby, at Fuentes de Oñoro, Masséna's advance guard attacked Wellington on May 3, and two days later the French launched another and more formidable assault. This battle of Fuentes de Oñoro (or Fuentes d'Onor in the French lexicon) was notable at the time and significant for the future because of the performance of Wellington's Light Division, which was a new development out of the reforms in infantry tactics begun by Sir John Moore at Shorncliffe. Two divisions of the French VI Corps well supported by cavalry were about to break the Allied right when the Light Division arrived at the scene. The steadiness of the Light Division and its tactical flexibility under fire changed the course of the second day's battle from French to Allied victory, and this in the face of a French numerical advantage of 45,000 to 33,000 and against no less a battle captain than Masséna. Losing about twice the Allied casualty toll of 1,520, Masséna returned to Salamanca. On May 11, Wellington captured Almeida.

Wellington initially had left Almeida to General Spencer because he himself had intended to join Beresford in the task of recapturing Badajoz and thus removing the southern threat to Lisbon and breaking the strategic standoff in the south. Beresford had proceeded to invest Badajoz without the presence of his superior officer, leading Soult into a countermove with 24,260 men and forty-eight guns against Beresford's 35,000 men—7,000 of them British—and thirty-eight guns. When Soult approached, Beresford suspended his siege of Badajoz and took up a defensive position behind the Albuera (or Albuhera) River. The resulting battle of Albuera of May 16, 1811 unfolded not unlike the battle of Fuentes de Oñoro, and it demonstrated that while the Light Division was destined for particular fame, it was not alone among Wellington's British troops in tactical excellence.

Once more the French attacks concentrated on the Allied right, which was held by Spanish troops. This Allied flank was in fact turned by a Napoleonic *manœuvre sur les derrières*, and the French overran six guns. Successive efforts by Beresford to form a new defensive line met frustration. Then on his own initiative Major-General Galbraith Lowry Cole brought up the 4,000 men of his British 4th Division. The increasingly proverbial British musketry repulsed a

French cavalry charge and a follow-up infantry assault, and then a countercharge routed the French left and decided the battle. The casualties reflected the severity of the fighting: about 8,000 among the French, 6,000 among the Allies.

Such tactical skill notwithstanding, the rise in Allied fortunes in the Peninsular campaign of 1811 though marked was hardly decisive or irreversible. Wellington came south from Almeida to help Beresford resume the siege of Badajoz, but he in turn was followed by Marmont, Masséna's successor as French commander in Iberia, who brought sufficient reinforcements toward Soult that Wellington pulled away and the French kept Badajoz. The British commander then turned his attention to besieging Ciudad Rodrigo, but here too he had to retire in the face of an advance by a superior force under Marmont. The latter harried the Allied retreat closely enough to give the British several more opportunities to display their tactical prowess in rear-guard actions. But here once more there was tactical success without commensurate strategic advantage. The Allies were scoring gains, but by no means decisive or unalterable ones.

Not British resolution to exploit Napoleon's overextension into Spain but Napoleon's willingness to risk still further overextension elsewhere afforded such prospects as there were that the strategic deadlock on the Peninsula might not extend yet another year, through 1812. As the new year opened, it brought with it prospects that Napoleon would again draw troops away from Spain—and this time for the sake of the most vast overextension imaginable: to Russia.

The Invasion of Russia: Preliminaries

The Continental System continued to leak. Great Britain, however uncertain its military strategy, persisted in stubborn resistance to Napoleon and in economic exploitation of the gaps in Napoleon's prohibition of its continental commerce. And the French Emperor, unwilling to confront again the task of finding an invasion route across the English Channel, chose to strike at his troubles not directly against the British source of so many of them but against a secondary source, his own quasi-ally beyond the Vistula.

Relations between Napoleon and Tsar Alexander had deteriorated almost steadily since Tilsit. Before he married Maria Louise of Austria, Napoleon had inquired about marriage to the Grand Duchess Anna Pavlovna, the Tsar's youngest sister; but Alexander himself had orchestrated the response, a maddening show of schoolgirlish coyness. To fortify the Continental System, Napoleon annexed a number of northern European states, including in 1810 the Kingdom of the Netherlands and the north German principality of Oldenburg. Peter Friedrich Ludwig, secular Bishop of Lübeck and heir to Duke Wilhelm of Oldenburg, happened to be the Tsar's brother-in-law, so Alexander protested, and a dispute with Napoleon over compensation erupted. Alexander raised the Russian tariff on French wines while admitting English shipping to Russian ports in the guise of neutral shipping. Rival Napoleonic and Tsarist ambitions in Poland also still rankled. Both the Emperor of the French and the Tsar of All the Russias gradually resolved to go to war.

It was no longer a decision that came so easily for Napoleon. Infatuated

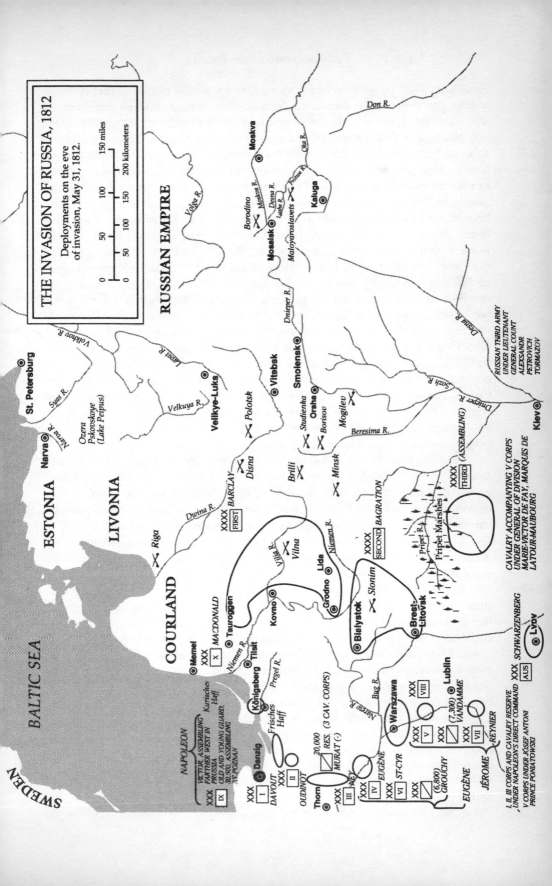

THE INVASION OF RUSSIA, 1812

Deployments on the eve of invasion, May 31, 1812.

though he might be with assurance of his destiny, he was not altogether unaware of the dangers of further overextension of his span of control (even if he failed to moderate the danger by educating and trusting subordinate commanders). He was also aware of the strain of prolonged war upon French fighting morale in particular and upon popular support for his regime in general. His caution led him to seek as much as possible to distribute the burdens of a Russian war among his satellite states and allies. So strenuously did he insist and so thoroughly was he the master of Europe (if only he could have rested content with his mastery) that of the troops mobilized for the invasion of Russia, somewhat more than half were Germans, Austrians, Prussians, Swedes, Dutch, Poles, Italians, Illyrians, and even more unwilling Spanish and Portuguese.

The decision to fight Russia also came uneasily because of logistical concerns. The logistical perils even of a limited foray into eastern Europe had contributed much to the setback at Eylau; to plunge deep into Russia manifestly had to be far worse. Napoleon concluded that he had to revert to the eighteenth-century depot system. Thus huge stores of supplies were accumulated at Warsaw, Thorn, Danzig, and elsewhere in French-dominated eastern Europe. In the spring of 1812 this same region of eastern Europe was combed for food stores to accumulate extra rations. New transportation battalions were formed. The French Navy found a new role in managing coastal and river craft to assist with supply. The principal line of communications was to extend from Königsberg to the Niemen River and up the Niemen to Kovno. The Pregel River from Königsberg to Insterburg would provide another line of support.

Returning to the depot system would reduce the mobility of the French Army. So also would the incorporation into it of so many non-French troops unschooled in French standards of marching. And the war-weariness of the French themselves was destined to display itself in a lack of motivation for hurrying into battle and a consequent further lagging of the rate of march.

The French would operate also under handicaps in intelligence unprecedented in Napoleon's continental campaigns. The Emperor was able to learn little of the dispositions of the Tsar's army. Lieutenant-General Mikhail Bogdanovich Baron Barclay de Tolly, a Livonian of Scots ancestry, was known to command about 40,000 troops in the Vilna area; his mission was to cover both Russian capitals, St. Petersburg and Moscow. Bagration with another 33,000–40,000 was known to be deployed around Volkovich, south of Barclay but north of the Pripet Marshes. A similar force was in process of formation on the Austrian frontier south of the Pripet Marshes. Another 50,000 or so were pinned down far to the south by the perennial war against the Ottoman Turks. Knowing only this much of Russian dispositions, Napoleon knew still less of their plans.

One factor concerning Russia of which he could not be certain nevertheless worked to his advantage. With generally primitive communications and a scattered population, the Tsarist Empire still lacked any ability comparable to France's or even Austria's to transform potential military manpower into actual soldiers. Not even the muster-roll strength of the Russian Army—600,000—existed in reality. The actual total was about 420,000. The Russian plans that Napoleon could not learn were based on exaggerated assumptions about available Russian strength and supplies. Barclay with his First Army of the West, reinforced by June 1812 to a paper strength of 153,000 and an actual strength of 127,000, was expected to retreat gradually to a fortified camp at Drissa on the Dvina River. This camp was then supposed to become the pivot of resistance, but it was badly located with a broad river to its rear and thus might become a trap for its own garrison. When the French attacked it, however, the Russians expected them not only to be weakened by fatigue and failing logistics, but to be assailed by Bagration's Second Army of the West in their right rear. If the Austrians did not invade south of the Pripet Marshes, then the Third Army of the West forming on their border would also move north.

Napoleon commanded ample forces to contend against the numbers that the Russians actually mobilized, but he had perhaps too many for his methods of command. For the invasion of the vast Russian Empire he collected in fact the largest army Europe had seen since the partly mythical armies of the ancients, 614,000 men. This aggregate was far too large for a single commander's span of control, even if that commander was a genius. Yet Napoleon continued to exercise centralized authority and to attempt to prescribe and supervise all administrative and operational arrangements in detail, up to the moment of combat when he recognized there was no alternative to the formula that everyone should march to the sound of the guns. Even had he not insisted on centralized authority, such authority would have had to revert to him anyway, because of one of the fatal flaws of his generalship—his failure to nurture through education and the sharing of responsibility a truly professional officer corps whose members would be schooled and prepared to think for themselves and to exercise initiative. This problem of command and control was aggravated, of course, by the diverse nationalities that made up the invading army.

The 614,000 troops mobilized for the great invasion, about 300,000 of them French, included a first line of some 449,000 that would constitute the main invasion force and a second line of 165,000 intended mainly as a source of replacements. (In addition, Napoleon ordered the registration of all the remaining males in France and their organization for home defense while the regular forces were mostly so far away.) Among the 449,000 troops of the first line, the Emperor would command directly (but not much more personally than he tried to command all formations) a principal army of almost 250,000, deployed around Thorn and to the north, consisting of three *corps d'armée*, the Imperial Guard (itself numbering some 50,000), and two cavalry corps. In an elaboration of the ideas behind the corps system, the corps now varied considerably in numbers, in proportion to Napoleon's estimates of the capacities of their commanders. Davout's I Corps mustered as many as 72,000. Oudinot's (now a *maréchal de l'Empire*) II and Ney's III Corps had about 40,000 each or slightly less. King Joachim of Naples—Murat—commanded the cavalry. The main army consisted primarily of French soldiers.

On the right rear of the main army there would march an auxiliary army of three corps, in total about 80,000 men, mainly Italians and Bavarians, commanded by the Viceroy of Italy, Eugène de Beauharnais. Next on the right, around Warsaw, was a second auxiliary army under Napoleon's brother Jérôme,

King of Westphalia, comprising some 77,000 of Jérôme's own subjects, Saxons, Hessians, and Poles. On the far right, around Lvov, was the Austrian Corps of about 34,000 under *General der Cavallerie* Karl Philipp Fürst zu Schwarzenberg. Far to the north, on the extreme left along the Baltic, was Macdonald's X Corps, some 32,000 Prussians, other Germans, and Poles, like Schwarzenberg's corps not directly attached to any of the armies. The entire force was especially strong in cavalry, about 80,000, Napoleon believing that this arm like a more tightly reorganized supply system was particularly appropriate to the geography of the coming campaign.

In addition to 80,000 cavalry horses, the invading army had 30,000 artillery horses and about 90,000 horses in the supply trains. There were some 25,000 vehicles, including about 4,500 four-animal wagons with a capacity of 3,300 pounds (1,500 kilograms) each, 2,400 heavy wagons carrying 2,200 pounds (1,000 kilograms) each, 2,400 light carts carrying 1,323 pounds (600 kilograms) each, plus ammunition caissons, ambulances, and other vehicles. Some transport companies received draft oxen instead of horses. Great herds of cattle and oxen were to follow the armies to provide fresh meat. Each soldier was to have twenty-four days' rations before the campaign began.

To administer as well as to command and control this huge enterprise, Napoleon relied excessively on himself. It was as though he had undertaken the personal management of nearly all the affairs of a city of more than half a million inhabitants—difficult enough in a city that does not change its location, much more difficult in what amounted to a migrating city, much more difficult still once the inhabitants experienced the stresses and injuries of combat. To assist him, the Emperor not only lacked subordinate commanders adequately prepared to make decisions and exercise initiatives for themselves. He also lacked any organization resembling the staffs that the later developments of professional officership would provide for the commanders of divisions and corps, let alone armies the size of his invasion force. While Berthier, his chief of staff, was much rewarded and praised by the Emperor himself, Napoleon's jealousy of any authority except his own actually relegated the prince de Wagram to the role of a glorified chief clerk. In the disproportion between the scale of the campaign and the span of control of the lone man at its center, Napoleon's invasion of Russia represents overextension of responsibilities and capacities almost to the point of madness.

Because Napoleon could not control everything he pretended to control, the careful logistical arrangements varied a great deal in the extent to which they were put into practice. Davout repaid the confidence Napoleon had shown when he gave him an exceptionally big corps by taking infinite pains with administration and logistics. Davout tried to make every regiment a self-sufficient mobile community. Every needful kind of workman was to be found in every one of his regiments—tailors, shoemakers, gunsmiths, bakers, builders. The corps commander even gave attention to the most efficient method of packing a knapsack, so that every soldier could use his own carrying capacity to the utmost.

But other corps commanders did not match Davout in this sort of meticulousness, and there were also deficiencies throughout the army that not even the most thorough corps commander could remedy. Among the worst was the failure to provide adequate medical supplies. From the beginning, sickness was to plague the invading army, and sickness more than the forces of the Tsar would prove the most terrible adversary of the *Grande Armée*.

The Invasion of Russia: To Borodino

From the beginning, in fact, Napoleon's now megalomaniacal extension of his efforts to do too much caused almost every preparation and plan to go awry. It says much for Napoleon's genius that by June 22, 1812 (June 10 according to the Julian calendar still in use in Russia), he had contrived to mass his armies on the Russian frontier quietly and with relatively few mishaps. Late that night, disguised in a Polish hussar's cloak and forage cap, the Emperor in person selected the bridge sites for the main army's crossing of the Niemen. Two hours before midnight on the 23rd the cavalry vanguard began to cross in boats, and shortly thereafter the pontoniers of the main army began to assemble their bridges. But even as the principal crossings were conducted on June 24 and 25 (June 12 and 13 Julian), torrid heat not untypical of the season and place Napoleon had chosen for the assault began to erode the strength and health of the men, and an insidious degeneration began to take hold of the Emperor's schemes.

Napoleon's strategic and operational plan was by no means unsound. In strategic judgment there is no reason to believe that the Napoleon of 1812 was less masterful than ever. While he never fully communicated his strategic designs—that was part of the fatal leadership flaw—and consequently there can be doubt about what he intended in Russia, the basic intentions seem apparent enough. They embodied a strategy of annihilation aimed at the enemy armies. They looked toward a classic *manœuvre sur les derrières* as the means of accomplishing that strategy. Moreover, the master strategist was the Napoleon of Ulm more than the Napoleon of Austerlitz; the sort of infatuation with the thunderstroke battle that Austerlitz and Jena-Auerstädt were to engender in would-be disciples of Napoleon, to the extent that this malady might at times have infected the Emperor himself, did not detract from the 1812 plans. For that reason alone, the 1812 plans considered as strategy rather than in terms of logistics and administration rank among Napoleon's most impressive.

Napoleon had carefully studied the Russian disasters of Charles XII, and he intended a rapid campaign that would give geography and weather little chance to undo him as they had Charles. He hoped to destroy the principal enemy forces within twenty days. After crossing the Niemen, Napoleon's main army was to press rapidly toward Vilna, pushing back Barclay's Russian army while Eugène's army guarded its exposed right flank. Meanwhile Jérôme and Schwarzenberg would tie down Bagration's army along the Bug River. After about twelve days, however, Jérôme was to begin withdrawing slowly, moving northward along the Narew River toward a junction with Eugène. This withdrawal was designed to lure Bagration's army westward in pursuit. Meanwhile Napoleon's own advance, strongest on its left, would turn to reach toward and around Barclay's right. The effect once Jérôme linked up with Eugène and the main army would be a Napoleonic concentration of 400,000 men on the right and right-rear of both Barclay and Bagration. The Russians would have been maneuvered into a pocket in the area Grodno-Slonim with the Pripet Marshes blocking escape to the south and the French confronting them in the west and north as well as curling around them in the northeast.

If during the development of this plan Bagration pushed Jérôme harder than expected, the Narew and the Vistula and their fortifications would still enable Jérôme to preserve his army from destruction, and the Russians would simply be trapped farther westward than under the principal design. If the out-maneuvered Russians did not surrender, they would have to fight under circumstances of desperation; while Napoleon was not infatuated with Austerlitz-style battles, he certainly recognized that in war even the most skillful maneuvering may not in itself produce victory without hard fighting.

But climate, logistics, and inadequate control of too inflated an army for Napoleonic methods of command crumpled the best of strategic plans. The Tsar responded to the invasion by declaring he would not make peace while a single enemy remained on Russian soil, but in the face of Napoleon's immense juggernaut the Russian field commanders cautiously fell back. They retreated with considerable skill. Tsar Alexander himself had tried to school the senior Russian commanders in the conduct of war, and by now he had witnessed enough campaigning that he was able to do so to good effect. The Russian officer corps in general remained well behind the standards of professionalism attained by the French, but the abilities of army and corps chieftains were respectable.

The withering heat of the days of the crossing of the Niemen persisted, and Napoleon's army immediately began to lose men and horses to sunstroke and dehydration. Beginning on June 29/17,* however, the heat broke under a five-day rainstorm, and then the Russian roads turned to mud. The supply wagons could scarcely move. Troops foraged the countryside ruthlessly, but Napoleon's choice of season meant that crops were still green. Almost nothing could be found for the horses, and colic broke out among them. Ten days after the start of the invasion Napoleon's army had lost a third of its horses.

Twenty days from the start of the invasion the army had penetrated only about 200 miles (or about 325 kilometers), and the strength of the first-line forces had fallen well below 300,000. The strategic plan had disintegrated. Bagration had failed to march into the snare Napoleon had set for him. At one point the Emperor had concluded that the Russian Second Army was at least standing its ground and might be vulnerable on that account, and he ordered Jérôme to hasten toward the upper reaches of the Niemen to fix it in position. But it was only the Russian V Corps, not an entire army, that had attracted Napoleon's attention, and the reason was that withdrawal orders had not reached it. When Jérôme's columns approached menacingly, the flight of the corps was prompt, and the possibility of even a smaller-scale entrapment eluded the French.

*The Julian-calendar date follows the solidus.

Jérôme's movements were distressingly slow, and he was slow also to open lateral communications with the main army once it reached Vilna as Napoleon urged him to do. Partly in consequence of the latter delinquency, staff officers took a long and roundabout route from Jérôme's headquarters to Napoleon's with the news that Russia had made peace with Turkey and that large forces from the south would soon join the Russians facing the French. Napoleon grew disgusted enough to authorize Davout to take command of Jérôme's army, should their forces converge and the good of the service require it. Unknown to Davout, however, the Emperor did not inform Jérôme of this order. When on July 13/1 Davout felt it necessary to invoke his new authority, Jérôme in a huff turned over his command to his chief of staff, Jean Gabriel Marchand, *comte de l'Empire* and *général de division*, who was still more in the dark about Napoleon's intentions. Jérôme resigned to return to Westphalia.

The Russians' sufferings were mild by comparison. The Tsar wanted to stand and fight at the fortified camp at Drissa, but Barclay's persuasions against it and Bagration's failure to follow an appropriate line of retreat convinced Alexander to withdraw farther eastward to Vitebsk. The concomitant Russian bickering led to no important opportunities for the French. Repeatedly, French troops failed to close on their intended victims because the Russians refused to risk large forces to support rear guards or other detachments. The French Army was growing incapable of seizing opportunities, and the Russian Army in any event was foreclosing one opportunity after another.

On July 28/16 Murat learned that with Barclay falling back from Vitebsk as he had earlier abandoned Drissa, the two main Russian armies were intending to converge at Smolensk. The next day Napoleon decided to abandon the pursuit for seven or eight days, allowing the army to close up and rest while twenty days' reserve rations were gathered. Men and animals alike desperately needed the respite. Anyway, Napoleon seems to have calculated that if he allowed Barclay and Bagration to unite he might have a better chance of destroying both of them.

Whatever occurred, however, seemed to turn out well for the Russians and badly for the French. As soon as Bagration's army converged on Barclay's, the former set out to destroy the Tsar's confidence in and the authority of the latter, who was senior. On August 7–8/July 25–26 Barclay tried to open an attack by the combined Russian armies against Napoleon's camps west of Smolensk, but the acrimony between the two Russian generals and the failure of their staffs to coordinate their armies' movements were instrumental in preventing the attack from materializing. For the Russian cause, however, the fizzle was actually fortunate, because an enemy assault was the very thing for which Napoleon had rested his army and was ready and waiting; it would almost certainly have been a Russian disaster, Napoleon's difficulties notwithstanding.

The Russians again refusing to take the bait he offered them, Napoleon decided by August 16 that his army was rested enough to mount its own attack on Smolensk that day. The town was protected by eighteenth-century fortifications featuring a brick wall and outside it a ditch and a glacis. When the French attack began, the Russian commanders apparently concluded that this assault was the fixing-in-place of a Napoleonic *manœuvre sur les derrières*, which would curl south and east of them to break their communications. Consequently Bagration shifted his army about forty miles (sixty-four kilometers) eastward along the road to Moscow, while Barclay remained in Smolensk.

The fighting there progressed from preliminary French assaults on August 16/4 to more serious efforts the next day. Massed French guns failed to break the walls but set afire buildings behind them, and Napoleon had Davout prepare for a climactic assault early on the 18th. An hour before midnight on the 17th, however, Barclay ordered an evacuation under cover of darkness. Evidently Napoleon had intended his assaults on Smolensk as more than a fixing-in-place operation; whatever his purpose, the Russians were not yet ready to risk their principal armies.

They escaped neatly, and in the following days they fought a series of similarly successful rear-guard actions to shield similar well-executed retreats. Thereby they continued the process of eroding the physical strength as well as the morale of Napoleon's army, undercutting much of the recuperation that Napoleon had accomplished before attacking Smolensk. Unfortunately for the Russian Army, nevertheless, Barclay as principal designer of this strategy of erosion had not long to remain as the chief field commander. Alexander had been losing patience with him at least since his refusal to fight at Drissa. Bagration continued to chip away at the foundations of his authority. His own chief subordinates had protested against the evacuation of Smolensk, believing that by turning back the French attacks on August 16 and 17/4 and 5 they had been in process of winning a victory that could have become still greater. And continual retreat rarely improves a general's status with his government, no matter how well advised it may be. Kutusov, now a prince and promoted to field marshal, received the Tsar's commission to assume command of the Russian armies in front of Moscow. It was Kutusov's intention to cease retreating and to fight a full-scale battle in the hope of checking Napoleon's march toward the ancient Russian capital.

Napoleon sensed the approach of battle and halted his advance on September 2 and 3/August 21 and 22 for another brief respite and to close up his forces. On the second day of the halt he called for precise reckonings of available men, horses, ammunition, and medical supplies. The accounting brought fresh evidence of the heavy toll of the invasion so far in spite of the absence of a major battle. The *Grande Armée* had about 128,000 men at hand and 6,000 able to join it within five days.

Kutusov deployed Barclay's and Bagration's armies, about 121,000 men, behind the Kalatsha River where it crossed the New Post Road between Smolensk and Moscow. The Russians held higher ground than the French in a generally open countryside. They hastily fortified their position, but Kutusov's main reliance apparently was upon the stolid toughness of the Russian soldier to stand up in the face of hard fighting. To that end, his pronouncements to his troops played upon the theme of mystic dedication to the Russian motherland.

Napoleon carefully reconnoitered the Russian position on September 6/August 25 but discovered no good opening for his favored movements against the enemy's flank or rear. Kutusov evidently expected the French to try to turn his right, but this part of his line lay immediately behind the Kalatsha, and Napoleon judged the stream banks to be too steep. Davout proposed a deep envelopment of the enemy left, but Napoleon rejected this idea apparently because he wanted to minimize any further strain of marching before he fought. He settled for a massive assault that might break Kutusov's left and thus open the way to rolling up the Russian line.

It was by no means the best of Napoleonic battle plans. The Emperor was suffering from a severe cold, and his performance throughout the battle of Borodino, as the struggle came to be called, seems to have reflected a consequent lethargy. It was to be the first of a series of battles during which the state of Napoleon's health detracted from his performance, and another indictment of a system of command that put too much responsibility upon one man.

The battle that began about six in the morning of September 7/August 26 degenerated accordingly into a brutal slugging match. A diversionary effort by Prince Eugène's Italian troops on Napoleon's left promptly captured the village of Borodino, and there were other local successes, especially where Davout commanded. But the *Grande Armée* achieved no decisive progress. Kutusov had to shift troops in large numbers from his right to the main action on his left and in the center, but the Russians yielded no critical ground. Ney, commanding the III Corps on the French right center, received four wounds. Bagration fell mortally wounded.

Napoleon presided over the battle through the morning hours with seeming alertness, but by afternoon his cold overcame his energy and he lost his grip. He had refused appeals to release the Imperial Guard to exploit an apparent advantage along the Old Post Road on his extreme right before noon, and he never did commit this, his principal reserve. Toward the opposite flank, Eugène captured a tactically important Russian redoubt about three in the afternoon, but again there was no release of reserves for a follow-through. Napoleon's only positive contribution of the afternoon came when Kutusov attempted a late and ill-advised counterattack. The French Emperor's acceding to the use of his reserve artillery led to the smashing of the Russian assault columns before they could begin their work.

By late afternoon, the French had gained the whole of the initial Russian line, but Kutusov's army still stood unbroken on the next ridge. The fighting guttered out in indecision. Kutusov decided to retreat during the night rather than face additional heavy losses after he had suffered some 44,000 casualties. Nevertheless, although the French loss was smaller—about 38,000—the impact of Borodino upon morale favored the Russians. The *Grande Armée* had suffered too many losses already in the course of its exhausting and frustrating marches across the endless Russian plains; its morale was already perilously near the breaking point, and now the once invincible army had been able to fight its way to nothing better than a tactical draw, while the Russians could congratulate themselves on fighting Napoleon to a standstill.

So it was in a mood of unease and foreboding rather than of triumph that Napoleon's army entered Moscow.

Moscow and the Terrible Retreat

Having fought his battle, Kutusov decided to contest the road to this one of the Russian capitals no more. As the French approached the city, the Russian authorities drove most of the population east toward Ryazan. They carried off or crippled the city's fire-fighting equipment—though they left large quantities of weapons, ammunition, and other military stores to be taken by the French. On September 14/2 the commanding officer of the French vanguard, Horace François Bastien de la Porte Sebastiani, *comte de l'Empire* and *général de division*, reached Moscow as the Russians were still in the process of evacuating it. He agreed to a seven-hour armistice rather than risk street fighting that was likely to set wooden buildings on fire and deprive the French of shelter and supplies. Napoleon arrived late in the afternoon and was annoyed to discover that no Russian functionaries remained to surrender the city, which not only deprived him of a triumphant ceremony but under the international law of war threw a question mark across his exploitation of the city's resources. The French Emperor spent the night in a house in the western suburbs and the next morning rode to the Kremlin, where he established his headquarters.

Fires had appeared in Moscow the preceding day. Additional fires flared up on the 15th, and during the following night they broke out of control, to continue burning for seventy-two hours. Deliberate arson, probably planned in part by Kutusov, combined with accidental conflagrations to destroy most of the city, although not the Kremlin. The new devastation where shelter and supplies had been expected gave a crushing blow to the already abysmal morale of Napoleon's army. In fact, considerable supplies were saved, but it required a determined effort by Napoleon to restore discipline to an army on its way to becoming a band of looters.

For a time Murat's reconnaissances inspired optimistic conclusions that Kutusov's army was also disintegrating. But unfortunately for the French, such reports did not continue for long. Instead, Kutusov proved to be hovering around Kaluga, southwest of Moscow, with the army that had been facing the Turks now no longer far away from a junction with the main army.

Napoleon was now 550 miles (885 kilometers) from the Niemen, and Cossacks were harrying his communications. His capture of Russia's religious capital had soured into the worst predicament in which he had ever found himself, worse than Egypt, because all the principal strength of the French Army was in peril. To try to save face, if not much more, on October 4/September 22 Napoleon sent a deputation to Russian headquarters to try to arrange an armistice. Kutusov agreed to a de facto truce but disclaimed authority to yield more, and the Tsar soon made clear his determination to keep his original pledge that there should be no peace until the enemy abandoned Russian soil.

Even should he decide to retreat, Napoleon could not be sure of enough food and forage. The commissary stores found in Moscow would probably carry his men as far as Smolensk, but these stores did not include enough forage for the remaining, suffering animals. The main route between Moscow and Smolensk would provide little along the way, because it had already been stripped bare. Some stocks had been gathered in Smolensk and farther west, but not enough to assure continued nourishment to men and animals between Smolensk and Poland. To make the best of all these circumstances, including the Russian refusal to negotiate, Napoleon in early October contemplated a retreat to Smolensk, going into winter quarters there and around Minsk, and in the spring marching on St. Petersburg. But the problem of sustenance drove him toward choosing not the direct Moscow-Smolensk road but a circuitous southward swing through Kaluga, the center of a fertile area that by report was not yet denuded of provisions.

Kutusov precipitated the Emperor's movement by striking hard on October 18/6 against Murat's patrols around Tarutino and Vinkovo, southwest of Moscow. Kutusov's de facto truce had lulled Murat's vigilance, and Bennigsen was able to capture a defile north of Murat and thus to threaten him with isolation. Murat successfully struck back, but Napoleon now marched most of the *Grande Armée* out of Moscow toward Tarutino to relieve Murat, and on beyond toward the Kaluga region and its hoped-for food and forage.

Yet more rainy weather and muddy roads caused the army to move still more slowly than the pitiable condition of the horses might otherwise have dictated. Late on October 23/11 Prince Eugène, now commanding the IV Corps, was leading the van as the army approached the crossing of the Lugha River at Maloyaroslavets. The banks of the Lugha are steep, and there is badly broken country to the south, so Eugène decided not to risk a major crossing until the next day. He sent two battalions across the Lugha bridge but kept the rest of his force on the north bank. At sunrise the next morning, however, Russian troops hastened by Kutusov to locate and harass the French line of march arrived to drive back Eugène's advanced battalions from the south bank.

The hard-fought battle of Maloyaroslavets thus erupted, pitting Eugène's corps and supporting troops totaling about 15,000 against some 20,000 Russians. The initial Russian attack failed to capture the Lugha bridge, but Eugène's counterattack failed to dislodge the Russians. The Russians then came on in greater strength and took the bridge. That structure changed hands repeatedly in the course of the day, Eugène finally regaining it at the end but losing about 5,000 casualties to 6,000 Russian losses. But the French had not taken a bridgehead across the Lugha.

Napoleon arrived on October 25/13 to reconnoiter while skirmishing continued. He was nearly captured by a Cossack foray, which may have helped seal his decision—uncharacteristically made in consultation with his marshals and accepting their majority opinion—not to accept the losses of a further contest for the Lugha crossing. The *Grande Armée* therefore turned back from the inviting prospects of Kaluga to the now-barren route of its earlier advance to Moscow. The negative decision was one that the Bonaparte of Arcola, of confidence in his destiny, would not have made; it was ominous not only in itself but for what it signaled of the decline of that Napoleonic self-confidence that had so often more than made up for professional flaws.

The turning at Maloyaroslavets was another damaging physical and moral blow to the French Army. Napoleon's terrible retreat from Moscow is a storied event that has come to symbolize his ultimate ruin, but the images of bitter cold that the march summons up are more than a little misleading. The autumn of 1812 was a mild one in Russia. The debilitating heat of summer was gone at last, and after Maloyaroslavets the weather for a considerable time was cool to moderately cold but dry and stimulating. The first frost came on October 27/15, late for Russia, and it was not until November 8/October 27 that even the nights turned sharply cold. Snow, it is true, began falling on November 4/October 23, and thereafter the already hungry horses often could not graze, and guns and wagons were abandoned on icy roads. Yet it was the demoralization of the army more than the weather that made the first phases of the retreat terrible. The *Grande Armée* after Moscow and Maloyaroslavets had already sunk far toward the desperation of every man for himself. Napoleon's inability to command and control the army now reached its disastrous nadir.

Matters might have gone yet worse had Kutusov followed the retreat with vigor, but the Russian commander, now prince of Smolensk for his accomplishments so far, was content to wait for General Winter to do much of his work for him. Raiding Cossacks nevertheless were so troublesome a plague that near the beginning of November Napoleon ordered his army to march in hollow squares. Only the Imperial Guard seems to have retained enough discipline to obey the order, and in the middle of their square, near the head of the army, Napoleon marched westward, abandoning virtually any plan except to escape and nearly abandoning efforts to control the march.

Smolensk was reached on November 9/October 28. There, thanks to Kutusov's lethargy, Napoleon's army was able to rest for five days. On November 16/4, two days after the resumption of the retreat, Russian forces attacked the French column around Krasny, threatening to cut the *Grande Armée* in two. Napoleon roused himself enough to lead an eastward counterattack the next day, which converged with one from Davout coming westward and left most of the remnant of the army intact. Ney with the III Corps, however, acting as rear guard, stayed in Smolensk until the morning of the 17th/5th in the face of warnings from Davout that he might find himself isolated if he did not hurry. The next day Ney collided with much of Kutusov's army, barring his way at Krasny where Napoleon and Davout had kept the road open the day before but whence they had moved on. Refusing a surrender demand, the erratic Ney partially compensated for his slowness by keeping his campfires burning the next night while he found a roundabout escape route; but he had to abandon his guns and baggage, and when he restored contact with the main army he retained only 800 of 6,000 men.

The crossing of the Beresina River was the next great obstacle. The *Grande Armée* now numbered fewer than 50,000 effectives, though perhaps 40,000 stragglers followed behind it. The Krasny episode indicated that Kutusov, now close on Napoleon's heels, might well decide to strike for the kill, while another 34,000 Russians up from the south were marching along the west bank of the Beresina and therefore stood between Napoleon and Poland. The relatively warm autumn here turned into a curse rather than a blessing for the French, furthermore, because the stream was in flood when it usually would have been frozen, and many of the neighboring fields were quagmires. Moreover, Napoleon in his funk had ordered the ponton train to be burned, and the Russians on the west bank destroyed the bridge at Borisov.

Jean-Baptiste, baron Eblé, *général de division* and commander of the bridging train, had taken the first step toward rescuing the French Army by partially disobeying Napoleon's orders. He had saved two field forges, two wagons of charcoal, and six wagons of sapper tools from the burning of the bridging equipment, which meant he could still erect a bridge if enough timber could be found. Next, Jean-Baptiste Juvenal, baron de Corbineau, *général de brigade*, reported that his cavalry of Oudinot's II Corps had discovered a ford over the Beresina near the village of Studienka north of Borisov, a suitable bridging site where the houses could supply the necessary timber. While the central command of the army had almost evaporated and only the constituent parts remained, some of those parts were still in good working order.

Indeed, hearing of the intentions of Eblé and Corbineau brought Napoleon back to life. He issued the requisite orders for a rapid convergence on the Studienka crossing, and he also ordered Oudinot with his II Corps to march on Uchlodi some ten miles (sixteen kilometers) south of Borisov to distract the attention of the enemy force guarding the west bank. Commenced on November 23/11, this ruse worked amazingly well.

Promptly Eblé began constructing two 300-foot (100-meter) bridges at Studienka. Corbineau's cavalry forded the Beresina to cover the construction on the far side. The first of the bridges was completed about 1:00 P.M. on November 26/14, and Oudinot's corps, returned to the scene, hastened over to reinforce Corbineau and secure the bridgehead. The second bridge opened two hours later.

Most of the army had not yet crossed, however, when the Russians who had earlier been decoyed southward arrived nevertheless on the scene to open a battle for the western bridgehead. Meanwhile Russian troops also began pressing Marshal Victor's IX Corps, guarding the crossing operation against attack from the east. Napoleon's headquarters and the Imperial Guard had crossed by the early afternoon, but about 4:00 P.M. one of the bridges broke and panic ensued. Once more it was Eblé who played the part of savior, restoring order, repairing the bridge, and opening a way through a traffic jam of corpses and abandoned vehicles for the crossing to resume.

By evening the fighting formations had crossed except for Victor's rear guard, and the bridges were opened to noncombatants. But most of these insisted on waiting for daylight. The next morning Russian artillery was able to bombard the bridges, and the previously broken one ruptured again under the fire. Nevertheless, almost all of Victor's rear guard passed the river by early evening of November 29/17. Again the stragglers were given their chance, and again they refused to cross by night. But with the Russians closing in, Eblé was ordered to set fire to the bridges at seven in the morning of the 30th/18th. His sense of humanity compelled him to delay until 8:30, to give the stragglers a final chance. Those unfortunates then stampeded onto the crossings, some achieving a frantic escape, as many as 10,000 being cut down by the Cossacks; total casualties among noncombatants at the Beresina were as high as 30,000.

In part the crossing of the Beresina was a flickering of the former glories of the *Grande Armée*, especially in the stout defense of the bridges by Oudinot and Victor. At a cost of 25,000 combatant casualties the French imposed 20,000 casualties on the Russians and saved what remained of their army. But the slaughter of the stragglers marked a most inglorious end to organized operations in the invasion of Russia.

The rest of the retreat was hardly more than a breathless flight. Three days after the crossing the number of effectives in Napoleon's army was down to 8,800. At Smorgoni on December 5/November 23 the Emperor turned over command to Murat and hurried away to Paris to raise a new army. He was in the Tuileries by December 18. After his departure, the winter cold at last set in and the remnant of the army disintegrated still further. Rightly regarding it as impossible to obey Napoleon's order to take up winter quarters at Vilna, Murat continued the flight to Königsberg, which he reached on December 19 with some 400 Guard infantry and 600 dismounted Guard cavalry. Others straggled in for a long time afterward.

Prussia's Reversal of Alliances and the Sixth Coalition

To the south, Schwarzenberg in November reached a verbal understanding with the Russians to withdraw his troops from their country, and on January 30/18 he signed a formal convention neutralizing his force. The Prussian contingent responded more dramatically to the reversal of the European balance of power. On December 30/18 the commander of the Prussian contingent serving with Macdonald's corps, *Generalmajor* Johann David Ludwig Yorck (or York), reached the Convention of Tauroggen with the Russians. Yorck's troops, 17,000 men, had been cut off from the retreating French on December 25/13. German and Italian émigrés in the Russian Army thereupon opened negotiations with Yorck leading to the convention, whereby Yorck's force became neutrals. King Frederick William III felt obliged to repudiate the convention, but the Prussian Army did not fight for Napoleon again, and events had begun to move toward the reversal of the Prussian humiliation of Jena-Auerstädt and Tilsit.

The Russians halted their pursuit—if their leisurely advance from the Beresina can be called that—at the Niemen. The Tsar's armies also were badly depleted in numbers and footsore, hungry, and exhausted.

The Prussian defection nevertheless caused Murat to conclude that he must fall back further from Königsberg to Posen. There on January 10, 1813, he turned over the command to Eugène and started out for Paris. The correctness of Murat's judgment in withdrawing was confirmed by the difficulties that welled up around his successor, for the Viceroy of Italy soon found himself hard-pressed to maintain French garrisons anywhere in Prussia. Frederick William's repudiation of the Convention of Tauroggen had been occasioned by no motive stronger than lingering fear of Napoleon. As the truth of accounts of the ruination of the *Grande Armée* became increasingly evident, the King shifted toward sympathy for the Prussian patriots who set up a growing clamor for the repudiation of all ties to the French and a reassertion of full Prussian sovereignty. Numerous secret societies with influential members pushed in that direction. So above all did the army, eager to break free from the 42,000-man limit. The Tsar, too, added his pressure and that of his nearby armies to the call for Prussian liberation from the shackles of France. Gradually, open hostility assailed Eugène's garrisons in Prussia and hampered at every turn their quest for provisions and other supplies. The 14,000 French soldiers who had gathered around Eugène at Posen withdrew by cautious stages to Magdeburg on the Elbe. Meanwhile Frederick William and his government walked a tightrope between rival claims of allegiance and alliance.

The determination to cut that tightrope and force Prussia's return to his circle of satellites gave the most immediate impetus to Napoleon's labors during the winter of 1812–1813 toward calling forth a new army. It was fortunate for him that the *Grande Armée* that died in Russia had been only about half French. Therefore he found the military resources of his country not yet altogether drained, and once he was back in Paris he also found his personal powers of confidence and decision returning to an approximation of their former vigor.

When he reached the French capital in mid-December, the Emperor found 120,000 partially trained conscripts already available. He also had his third line of 1812, the men left behind for home defense, most of them mustered into a reorganized National Guard. He immediately called 80,000 of these men into full-time service, and he managed to discover another 100,000 who had in one way or another avoided service between 1809 and 1812. He called on retired veterans and the navy for yet more troops; he drew soldiers from the army of nearly 200,000 still in Spain; he called again for levies from the Confederation of the Rhine and Italy, and he proved strong enough still to compel the recipients of the calls to disgorge part of the assigned quotas, in spite of fears that the Rhine states especially had to feel as they looked eastward toward the Russians.

By the end of March 1813, in consequence, Napoleon had more than 200,000 men moving to succor Eugène on the Elbe, and during the first half of April they were concentrated in the angle between the Elbe and the Saale to threaten either Dresden or untrustworthy Berlin. The cavalry of this force lacked sufficient good horses, and many of the troopers were still far from being skilled riders. The artillery was only slowly approaching Napoleon's standard number of guns. But a remarkably high proportion of the officers and NCOs of the *Grande Armée* had escaped from Russia, and thus the training of the recruits could progress with rapidity. Even the Imperial Guard returned to a reasonable facsimile of its former self with a combination of veteran cadres and the selected best of the new conscripts. French public support for Napoleon faltered as awareness of events in Russia spread westward, but not enough to temper military revival to any serious extent.

As the new campaigning season approached, Tsar Alexander dreamed more and more vividly of himself as the liberator of all Europe; but Kutusov was able to dilute his enthusiasms by means of realistic references to the condition of the Russian Army, so that the eastward movement of 200,000 French troops at the end of March confronted no more than equal numbers of hostile forces arrayed in eastern Germany. The Russian penetration of Europe had continued to be hesitant and ponderous. Nevertheless, numerous clouds still shadowed Napoleon's horizons. Bavaria and Württemberg were listening to Austrian pleas that at least they turn neutral. On February 28 Prussia had entered into the secret Convention of Kalisch with Russia, promising to join together in liberating Germany and dividing dominion over the country. Frederick William III tried to keep the lid on the secret until he felt sure he was safely rid of French garrisons, conceding only that in the meantime Prussian forces would follow the Russians' westward marches as far as the Oder River while avoiding open hostilities with the French. On March 15 the French learned of this sequel to Yorck's Convention of Tauroggen, and thereupon Franco-Prussian relations degenerated swiftly to a Prussian declaration of war on March 27.

Marshal Bernadotte had escaped from the disfavor in which Napoleon held him after Wagram by means of his own transfer of loyalties. In 1806 he had shown uncommon courtesy to a Swedish division that surrendered to the French after being caught up in the fall of Lübeck. Remembering this kindness while also seeking a possibly useful dynastic connection, the Swedish States General on October 21, 1810 had elected the prince de Ponte Corvo to be Crown Prince of Sweden as well, and thus heir to King Charles (Carl) XIII. The following month the King had in fact adopted the new Crown Prince, who changed his name to Charles-Jean (Carl Johan). While Napoleon had somewhat reluctantly bestowed his blessing on this process, Bernadotte used his new position to turn against his former and now unappreciative master. Napoleon provided him with a good reason: Bernadotte wished to serve his new country well, but as a prelude to the invasion of Russia, Napoleon had seized Swedish Pomerania in March 1812. In July 1813, Bernadotte led Sweden into the new coalition against France.

From this coalition, the Sixth, Austria for the time being remained ambiguously aloof. Maria Louise did not count for as much of a Habsburg hostage as Napoleon had hoped, but Vienna had been defeated too often and too expensively to feel haste about assuming new risks.

Napoleon took command in the field again at Erfurt on April 25. In adversity his strategy remained offensive, to seek a new battle of annihilation that by ruining the new coalition's field armies would rupture the alliance before it was fully formed. The weakness of his cavalry militated against this strategy, however, and the palpable resentment against France that now filled the German countryside aggravated his difficulties in procuring information. Moving almost blindly, Napoleon nevertheless advanced eastward, toward Merseburg and Leipzig, with about a third of his army comprising a strong vanguard while the rest followed as a mass of maneuver. He hoped to draw the Russians and Prussians southward enough that by proceeding rapidly from Leipzig to Dresden he might cut them off from Berlin.

The Allied high command, however, had grown a good deal too battlewise and astute to be drawn easily into any such snare. Particularly in the Prussian Army, the campaign to redeem and avenge 1806 had by now begun to create a standard of professionalism higher than any previously attained by any modern army, and the effects were about to shape the final phases of the Napoleonic Wars.

THE RESURGENCE OF MILITARY PROFESSIONALISM

For all his brilliance in military command, Frederick the Great had failed to elevate the professional standards of the Prussian officer corps as a whole. In this he resembled Napoleon; his own brilliance helped persuade him that he need not bestir himself unduly to cultivate professional excellence among his subordinates, especially in the higher arts of command, in the reaches of operations and strategy beyond battlefield tactics. Like Napoleon, he thought it safer for his ambitions that in these realms his army should be dependent upon himself. If anything, the effects of Frederick's reign were retrogressive upon Prussian attainments in officer professionalism.

In no small measure, this excessive Frederician reliance on individual genius was the seed that spawned the disasters of 1806. Without Frederick, the Prussian Army carried its disciplined skill in eighteenth-century tactics on into the nineteenth century; but without Frederick and without adequate means or incentive toward professional study of operations and strategy, the Prussian Army could not cope with Napoleon's flexible operational use of improved mobility and the corps system in support of his new emphasis on a strategy of annihilation through battle. Without Frederick, even tactical excellence ossified into a rigid pattern that could not cope with French tactical innovations.

Rigidly disciplined and caste-bound as was the whole Prussian state as well as its army, Jena and Auerstädt and the subsequent additional humiliation of the Peace of Tilsit nevertheless administered so brutal a shock as to jar both state and army into reforming efforts. The campaign of 1806 practically destroyed the Prussian Army. More even than in any other European state, the destruction of the Prussian Army was tantamount to the destruction of the state itself, at least to Prussia as it had existed since the time of the Great Elector. For in a state that remained the least of the great powers in population and resources, it was only the strength and excellence of the army that preserved Prussia from reversion to the mere pawn and plaything of the stronger powers that Brandenburg had been during the Thirty Years War. Tilsit pushed Prussia perilously backward toward that helpless condition. Only the rejuvenation of the army could restore Prussia, and even the conservative advisers of King Frederick William III could not but recognize that rejuvenation adequate to overcome the current calamities meant major changes in state and army, to recapture with new methods the spirit of the best aspects of the Prussian military system from the Great Elector to Frederick II.

The Prussian Military Reforms

The necessities of and the suggestions for methods of thoroughgoing reforms were urged upon the King and his counselors by a circle of able and energetic leaders both civilian and military. It was testimony to the underlying vitality of the Prussian state and Army, in spite of their deficiencies, that the crisis called forth leadership worthy of the hour.

Among civilians ardent for change and capable of defining the form it should take, Heinrich Friederich Karl Freiherr vom und zum Stein was preeminent. Born in the Duchy of Nassau of an old family of knights of the Holy Roman Empire, he had taken service with Prussia in 1780 out of admiration for Frederick the Great. After Tilsit Frederick William III appointed Stein his chief minister with charge over all external and internal affairs, virtual dictator for the restoration of the country. Beyond undertaking the revival of the army, Stein brought about the Edict of Emancipation of October 9, 1807, which abolished serfdom in Prussia as of October 8, 1810, and ended class distinctions as they applied to land tenure and to access to occupations. His further reforming efforts were cut short when Napoleon pressured Frederick William to dismiss him and declared him an enemy of France, whereupon he felt compelled to flee Berlin on January 5, 1809, toward asylum in the Austrian Empire.

Stein's successor as *Staatskanzler* in June 1810 was Karl Augustus Freiherr von Hardenberg. Hardenberg like Stein was an outsider, a Hanoverian, attracted to serving the Prussian King, whose administration he had entered in 1790. He is often linked with Stein as one of the two great Prussian civil reformers of the day, but in fact he was a good deal more conservative than Stein. He slowed the pace of change in a manner that placated Napoleon and accorded much more closely than Stein's zeal with the more limited reforming desires of Frederick William.

As with civil reform, Hardenberg slowed but did not still the reshaping of the Prussian Army. In the army, the principal agency of change had been a Reorganization Commission appointed by the King in July 1807. The dominant figure on the commission had proven to be *Generalmajor* Gerhard Johann David von Scharnhorst, another Hanoverian transplant and *Quartiermeister Leutnant* (Chief of Staff) to the Duke of Brunswick during the 1806 campaign. Stein assured Scharnhorst free access to the King through his appointment as aide-de-camp-general. Scharnhorst was ably and closely assisted by a Saxon transplant and veteran of service in the War of American Independence as a subaltern in the forces of the Markgraf of Baireuth (Bayreuth), *Oberstlieutenant* and Chief of Engineers August Wilhelm Anton Neihardt von Gneisenau, as well as by a native Prussian, *Major* Karl Wilhelm Georg von Grolman (or Grolmann).

Scharnhorst proposed to do nothing less than to carry the professionalization of the Prussian officer corps a giant step farther than military professionalism had proceeded in any army until now, let alone in the hitherto caste-bound Prussian Army where professionalism had been bridled not only by Frederick the Great's preference for relying on himself but also by that King's belief, widely shared among the Prussian governing class, that only the nobility possessed the inherent ability to become good officers.

For Prussia to rise again and redeem itself against Napoleon, Scharnhorst recognized, it surely could not rely on the leadership of an individual military genius comparable to Napoleon. No such genius was available. Frederick II was dead. Scharnhorst himself was a highly capable officer who acknowledged the limits of his own capacity, an introverted, schoolmasterish man who lacked the spark of the great combat commanders. But if Prussia could not counter the individual military genius of Napoleon with a comparable genius of its own, Scharnhorst believed that it could do something better. It could educate its officers more rigorously in the military art than any state had ever done before, and it could then select the most promising graduates of its military educational system and pool their capacities in a collective brain to command the army. The collective intelligence of the best minds of the Prussian Army ought to be able to excel any individual genius in the conduct of war, most especially since such a collective governing body could possess a span of control far exceeding that of the most able individual commander. At least as early as 1807, it will be remembered, it was the limitations of Napoleon's span of control, the overriding reach of his ambitions beyond the abilities of any individual brilliance including his own, that more than any other single factor had begun to undermine his military designs.

The foundation for Scharnhorst's reforms was an order of August 6, 1808, prepared by Grolman:

> A claim to the position of officer shall from now on be warranted, in peacetime by knowledge and education, in time of war by exceptional bravery and qualities of perception. From the whole nation, therefore, all individuals who possess these qualities can lay title to the highest positions of honour in the military establishment. All social preference which has hitherto existed is herewith terminated in the military establishment, and everyone, without regard for his background, has the same duties and the same rights.[1]

1. Quoted in Gordon A. Craig, *The Politics of the Prussian Army, 1640–1945* (New York and Oxford: Oxford University Press, 1958), p. 43, citing Karl Demeter, *Das deutsche Heer und seine Offiziere* (Berlin: Verlag von Reimar Hobbing, 1935), p. 65, and Emil K.G.H.W.A. von Conrady, *Leben und Werken des Generals der Infanterie und kommandieres Generals des V. Armeekorps Carl von Grolman* (3 vols., Berlin: E. S. Mittler, 1894–1896), I, 159–160.

This ringing declaration by no means achieved immediate reality. Indeed it had not yet become altogether a reality when the Kingdom of Prussia perished in 1918. The replacement of Stein by Hardenberg promptly curtailed the promised equality of opportunity to advance, for Scharnhorst's military reforms were altogether in harmony with Stein's conception of civil equality, while neither Hardenberg nor the King shared those conceptions. Nevertheless, Scharnhorst attempted to base officer selection and advancement upon the principles of the order, and his success though far from complete was considerable. In the Prussian Army while Scharnhorst led the reform commission, knowledge and education in peacetime and bravery and skill in war became principal criteria for officer advancement.

Of course these had been principal criteria wherever officership had begun to be a profession, ever since the independence struggle of the Dutch Republic. Scharnhorst and his associates intended to push officer professionalism still further. The reformers created a system of military schools for officer candidates and officers more rigorous than any other, culminating in a revitalized Superior Military Academy *(Oberkriegscollegium)* that was to evolve into the *Kriegsakademie*. A central Office for Military Education supervised these institutions. At the Superior Military Academy in Berlin, selected officers received a three-year course that included mathematics, physics, chemistry, French and German, tactics, strategy, and military geography. Scharnhorst took personal charge of the upper class, or *Selekta*, which became the nucleus of a further innovation, the new-style General Staff.

The reformers consolidated Prussian military administration, formerly divided confusingly among several offices, into a Ministry of War, consisting of a General War Department *(Allgemeine Kriegsdepartement)* and a Military Economy Department *(Militär Ökonomiedepartement)*. The latter branch dealt with finance and supply, the former with all other military matters. As part of his desire to rein in the reformers, the King for the time being refused to appoint a Minister of War; but he named Scharnhorst to head the General War Department and to hold the title of Chief of the General Staff *(Chef der Generalstab)* as well.

The General Staff henceforth became Scharnhorst's proposed collective brain of the Prussian Army, to be pitted against the individual genius of Napoleon. As rapidly as possible, Scharnhorst brought into it the most capable graduates of the military educational system. This institutionalization of educated collective military intelligence was the essence of Scharnhorst's extension of officer professionalism. The institutionalization took practical effect most especially in the efforts of the reformers through the *Oberkriegscollegium* and the General Staff to shape a collective conceptualization of the conduct of war, a common doctrine of war, adherence to whose principles would make for coordinated strategic, operational, and tactical action throughout the army, by means of mutual understanding and thus without excessive centralization of command. When the war against Napoleon resumed in 1813, staff officers were assigned to all army and corps commanders. The army and corps commanders then received increased authority to exercise individual initiative, but their consultation with their staff officers—largely educated in Scharnhorst's conceptions—and the shared doctrine of those officers gave unprecedented assurance of coordination.

Scharnhorst, Gneisenau, and Grolman were liberal nationalists as well as good soldiers, that is, men infected by both the social revolutionary and the nationalist principles of the French Revolution. They believed that Prussia must share in those principles to regain its proper place among the powers. When the Prussian Army had been crushed in 1806 and the state humiliated, the Prussian people had tended to slumber in apathy, taking as little notice as they could, because no vital connection of sentiment had linked the people with the army and the conservative state and monarchy. Beyond enhanced military profession-alism, the military reformers proposed to bind army and people together, under the aegis of a liberalized state that would win the devotion of the people not only out of patriotism but because it would protect them in the exercise of the rights of man.

The reformers proposed to build a new army upon the ruins of the Freder-ician system by reviving the principle of a universal obligation to military service, a principle existing in Prussia at least since the time of Frederick William I but minimized by Frederick II, who preferred to recruit mercenaries and to keep his own people preoccupied with business and agriculture while isolated from all potentially subversive involvement in the state. Scharnhorst and the reformers now substituted a plan in which the Prussian regular army would be reinforced in war by volunteer riflemen, the *Jäger*; by a *Landwehr* of all men aged seven-teen to forty not serving in the regular army or the *Jäger*; and by a home-defense *Landsturm* of the remaining adult male population. The *Jäger* volunteers were largely men of the middle class, a segment of society who also received large numbers of commissions in the *Landwehr*. The militia of the *Landwehr* were to have equality of status with the regular regiments when embodied into the army, and were to constitute the tangible link binding together the army and the nation. The officers of the army were to be active citizens as well as soldiers, and the army school system was to encompass enough of a liberal education to encourage such soldier-citizenship.

The limitation of the Prussian Army to 42,000 men inevitably dampened the reformers' plans for a Prussian nation in arms. In spite of efforts to build a reserve force behind the 42,000-man active army, Prussia returned to war against Napoleon in 1813 with only 65,675 officers and men in both regulars and reserves.

The reformers also had to contend with a decree of September 26, 1810, which, on the insistence of Napoleon, excluded all foreigners from the Prussian service. Scharnhorst continued to be exempted upon direct application to Napo-leon, but when the Prussian Army invaded Russia under Napoleon's orders, he went on an extended leave of absence. As Prussia shifted its alliance, Scharnhorst returned to be Chief of Staff *(Quartiermeisterlieutenant)* to *General der Kavallerie* Gerhard Leberecht von Blücher.

During the War of National Liberation that followed 1813, the reformers were in large part successful in realizing their vision of the nation in arms and in uniting army and nation in patriotic fervor. Building upon the *Jäger* and *Land-*

wehr as well as the regular army, Prussia eventually put some 280,000 men into the field for the 1813 campaign, about 6 percent of its population. The *Landwehr* fought effectively as a citizen-soldier army with its own citizen-soldier leaders. Drawing all categories of troops forward was the professional leadership that the reformers and their staff system provided at the top. Scharnorst, promoted to *Generallieutenant*, died of blood poisoning early in the fighting, on June 8, 1813, from a neglected wound suffered at the battle of Lützen or Gross Görschen; but Gneisenau provided a worthy successor as Chief of Staff to Blücher and, in partnership with Blücher, as an exemplar of Scharnhorst's new staff system and of enhanced military professionalism at their best.

Lützen

Of course the Prussian advances in military professionalism could not immediately revolutionize the whole Allied conduct of war. The Russians remained the predominant partners in the ground forces of the Sixth Coalition during the early stages of the new campaign. Many holdovers from the Frederician system still shaped Prussian operations and tactics. And Napoleon's individual genius remained a formidable force to be overcome, especially when in adversity it recaptured much of its dazzling brilliance.

Tsar Alexander I and his closest advisers were astonished by the rapidity of Napoleon's military reorganization and disconcerted by his prompt advance eastward in the late spring of 1813. More fully professional officers who had made a study of Napoleon or who had long experience against him found his promptness not unexpected. In this category was Kutusov's successor as Russian field commander, Lieutenant General Ludwig Adolf Peter Count Wittgenstein. (Kutusov, in rapidly declining health, had been sent homeward and on March 25/13 died.) Yet more decidedly in this category was the bluff, shrewd General von Blücher, the Prussian field commander, counseled as he was by Scharnhorst.

The Allied commanders weighed two avenues of response to Napoleon's aggressiveness. They might withdraw behind the Elbe, there to recruit their own strength further, perhaps drawing Austria into the new coalition. Or they might try to exploit their four-to-one superiority in cavalry and their nearly two-to-one superiority in numbers of guns to try to strike advantageously against Napoleon's advance, preferably while he was astride the next major river obstacle along his line of march before the Elbe, the Saale, and after much of his army had entered the open country east of that stream favoring mounted operations. To retreat would be to risk deflating the enthusiasm generated by the French disasters in Russia and the rapid forming of the new coalition. In any event, the French already held bridgeheads across the Elbe at Magdeburg and Wittenberg. The more aggressive option therefore was quickly chosen.

On April 30 Napoleon began crossing the Saale through Merseburg. The next day, the French III Corps of Marshal Ney—reputedly the last Frenchman to leave Russia and since March 25 prince de la Moskowa—occupied the town of Lützen, the site of Gustavus Adolphus's battle of that name, about fifteen miles (twenty-four kilometers) by road southeast of Merseburg and some five miles

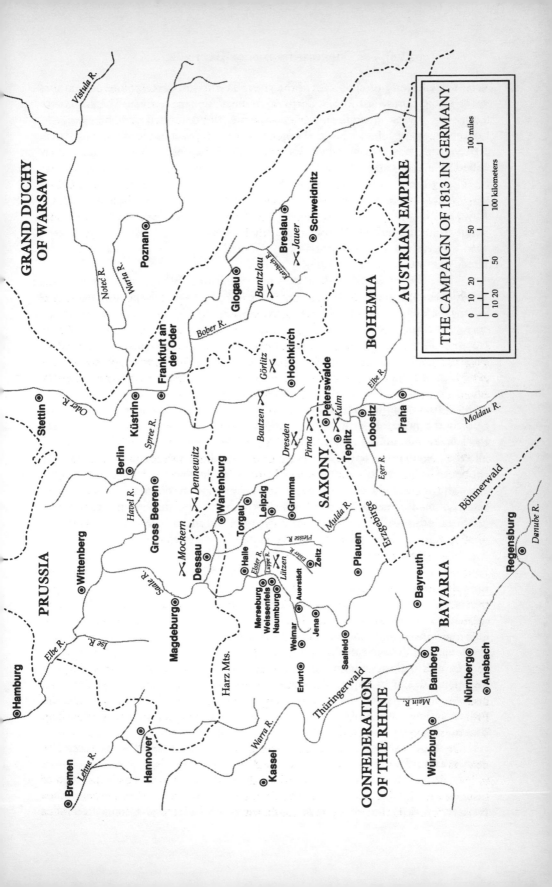

THE CAMPAIGN OF 1813 IN GERMANY

GRAND DUCHY OF WARSAW

PRUSSIA

SAXONY

BOHEMIA

AUSTRIAN EMPIRE

CONFEDERATION OF THE RHINE

BAVARIA

Vistula R.
Notec R.
Warta R.
Oder R.
Spree R.
Havel R.
Ise R.
Saale R.
Elbe R.
Leine R.
Warra R.
Main R.
Bober R.
Katzbach R.
Mulda R.
Pleisse R.
Elster R.
Luppe R.
Elster R.
Eger R.
Moldau R.
Danube R.
Erzgebirge
Böhmerwald
Harz Mts.
Thüringerwald

Hamburg
Bremen
Stettin
Poznan
Hannover
Berlin
Küstrin
Frankfurt an der Oder
Glogau
Bunzlau
Breslau
Jauer
Schweidnitz
Magdeburg
Wittenberg
Gross Beeren
Möckern
Dessau
Wartenburg
Dennewitz
Torgau
Halle
Merseburg
Weissenfels
Naumburg
Lützen
Leipzig
Grimma
Zeitz
Auerstädt
Jena
Weimar
Erfurt
Saalfeld
Kassel
Würzburg
Bamberg
Nürnberg
Ansbach
Regensburg
Bayreuth
Plauen
Görlitz
Hochkirch
Bautzen
Dresden
Pirna
Peterswalde
Kulm
Teplitz
Lobositz
Praha

100 miles
100 kilometers
0 10 20   50   100
0 10 20   50   100

(eight kilometers) directly east of the river. Ten miles (sixteen kilometers) and more to the northward, the V Corps of Jacques Alexandre Bernard Law, comte Lauriston, *général de division*, was approaching the defended city of Leipzig. At another crossing of the Saale, Weissenfels to the southwest, there was brisk fighting that day, during which Jean-Baptiste Bessières, now duc d'Istrie, was killed by a cannonball.

Early the next day Ney began occupying a group of villages south of Lützen. Wittgenstein now decided to attack this force at the village of Kaja (or Kaya) on its right flank. He thought he would hit a weak flank guard, the destruction of which would open the way to capturing the Weissenfels-Lützen road and isolate a large portion of the French army that was imagined to be already closing up on Lauriston.

The Allies attacked at about 11:45 in the morning. Blücher with the Prussian cavalry charged into a larger force than expected between Kaja and Gross Görschen, the entire division of Joseph comte Souham, *général de division*, of Ney's corps. The surprise led Blücher to pause to call up artillery, while Souham's troops took possession of the village of Gross Görschen. Meanwhile the Allied cavalry struck another of Ney's divisions, that of Jean-Baptiste baron Girard, *général de division*, just to the west. Both French divisions consisted largely of raw conscripts, and both were at least as surprised to be hit as their enemies were to find them in so much force. Napoleon himself was near Lauriston, but hearing the noise of battle to the southwest—he was standing at the time near the Lützen monument to Gustavus Adolphus—he sent orders to Ney to hold at all costs. Souham's conscripts nevertheless broke under overpowering artillery fire, but Girard's held firm until the VI Corps of Marshal Marmont arrived in the early afternoon. Girard's stand permitted Ney to gather other troops for a counterattack on the eastern portion of his corps front, and through the early afternoon the advantage tilted now one way, now the other, the battle ebbing and flowing through Klein Görschen and neighboring hamlets.

Napoleon reached the field about 2:30 P.M. Finding Ney's corps at ebb tide, he ordered the Guard cavalry to form a straggler line against retreat, while he himself plunged into the melee to encourage resolution through his magnetic presence, through exhortation, and reputedly through the soles of his boots applied to unwilling posteriors. But despite appeals from both Ney and Marmont he withheld reinforcement by the bulk of the Imperial Guard as it reached the scene and became available.

In mechanical imitation of Napoleon's methods but without his warrior's intuition, Alexander apparently held back the Russian grenadier and Guard infantry—in mechanical imitation, because for the Allies the timely moment passed without commitment of the reserve. Not only did Blücher's troops fight themselves to exhaustion; but Blücher was wounded, Yorck took over in his stead, and both skill and momentum sagged among the Prussians. By about 5:30 there was a lull in the battle.

It was Napoleon's hour. About six o'clock, seventy French guns opened fire, massed southwest of Kaja and close enough to the enemy center to fire varieties of case shot—projectiles exploding at close range to spray a hail of missiles into the enemy. They pulverized the Allies opposite them and wrecked the resolution of already weary Allied infantry. Then Napoleon sent forward the Young Guard, followed by the Old and remarkably well supported by Ney's tired soldiers, into the breach. The enemy collapsed, and out of the ruins of the Russian campaign Napoleon had drawn not only a new army but a victorious one. No battle displays to better advantage than Lützen the value that his genius retained in its patient outfacing of adversity—tactical as well as strategic—and its precise sense of timing to exploit the enemy's physical and psychological vulnerabilities.

Alas for the French, that weakness in cavalry on which the enemy had counted as a reason for risking battle now assured that even less than usual after a costly struggle would there be an effective pursuit. The French had suffered about 20,000 casualties; while Allied losses have been estimated as low as 11,500, more likely they approximated the French. But Napoleon lacked the means to prevent the Allies from drawing off the bulk of their army to safety.

Bautzen

Having weakened their own morale by helping Napoleon recapture some of his image of invulnerability, the Allies were left to beat the retreat that they had rejected in the first place because of its likely injury to their morale, a withdrawal behind the Elbe. Thus their stand near the Saale had inflicted a double misfortune upon them, while Napoleon's agents continued to recruit so successfully that he was now able to organize a second field army under Ney to aggravate their difficulties. Wittgenstein retired from Lützen toward Dresden with some 96,000 men and 450 guns in the main Allied field army, with a secondary force of about 30,000 withdrawing northward to shield Berlin. Napoleon followed with about 115,000 men and 150 guns, while another 85,000 men and 150 guns under Ney prepared to operate vigorously enough in the direction of Berlin that Napoleon hoped the Prussians would depart from the Russians to defend their capital.

This they did not do, in spite of bickering about the question within Allied headquarters. Meanwhile the Russians partially botched their efforts to destroy the crossings of the Elbe at Dresden, blowing up a stone bridge but allowing the French to capture enough pontons that the river did not delay their advance as much as the Allies hoped it might. By May 9 the French had two bridgeheads on the east bank at Dresden. At the same time Napoleon was putting pressure on Saxony to open to him the more northerly crossing at Torgau. King Friedrich Augustus of Saxony (Friedrich Augustus III in his former capacity as Elector of the Holy Roman Empire, Friedrich Augustus I as the first monarch to assume the title King of Saxony) had joined Napoleon's Confederation of the Rhine; but since the Russian disasters he preferred neutrality and was currently in exile under that other sovereign of ambiguous allegiances and confusing numerology, the former Franz II of the Holy Roman Empire who was now Franz I of Austria. Napoleon threatened Friedrich with a declaration of felony unless he behaved as a loyal member of the Confederation of the Rhine, and with such a threat more than credible, on May 10 the King's orders arrived at Torgau for the place and its Saxon defenders to be turned over to Napoleon.

These developments precipitated yet another Allied retreat, this time behind the River Spree, where they took up an exceedingly strong position about seven miles (eleven kilometers) in length, extending northeast to southwest from the village of Glein on the right to about a mile (or about a kilometer and a half) south of the larger and walled town of Bautzen on the left. They held a dominating height called Burk and excellent defensive ground on which the obstacles formed by woods and villages were supplemented with entrenched batteries. The Spree further shielded their left and center and was an obstruction to any approach to their right, where the ground between the river and their front was covered with a complex of ponds and watercourses. Even on their left and center, their front immediately behind the river was an outpost line screening a yet stronger position behind the marshes of a tributary stream, the Blösaer Wasser.

The battle of Lützen having demonstrated again the values of Napoleon's genius, the battle of Bautzen that was about to be fought against the new Allied position proved to demonstrate once more the converse, the weaknesses inherent in Napoleon's failure to develop adequate standards of professional skill among his subordinates because he trusted his genius too much.

Ney's army of five corps had failed to produce the hoped-for effect of drawing the Prussians away from the Russians toward Berlin, but nonetheless Napoleon saw Ney's deployment as opportune for the execution of a classic *manœuvre sur les derrières* against the right rear of the Allies' Bautzen line. Therefore he planned a frontal attack by his main army against that line in spite of its natural strength, the purpose of the frontal attack being not to break through but to fix the enemy in place until Ney could descend on his right flank and rear and thus consummate an Austerlitz or Jena-Auerstädt battle of annihilation.

Turning from his diversionary threat against Berlin, Ney could not be in position to launch the *manœuvre sur les derrières* at Bautzen until May 21. Napoleon spent May 19 in personal reconnaissance of the Allied lines. In order to ensure that the enemy would remain in place, his guns opened fire at noon on the 20th, and his frontal assault got under way three hours later. He focused on the Allied center, leaving the right for Ney and judging the Allied left, where the ground was highest, to be too difficult of access, especially for his artillery. Once more he withheld from the battle a strong reserve force the nucleus of which was the Guard.

Once more the mistakes of the Russian command, particularly the Tsar, assisted the Emperor's purposes. Alexander had developed an *idée fixe* that Napoleon intended to envelop the Allied south flank in order to keep them away from Austria and thus further to assure Austrian neutrality. Therefore the Allied left was especially strengthened, which both rendered the right more vulnerable to Ney's projected maneuver and weakened the center for Napoleon's attack of May 20. In addition, when the French XII Corps of Marshal Oudinot found the hilly country toward the southern part of the battleground unexpectedly conducive to its advance because the heights often screened it from the Russians, and

Oudinot's corps thus played upon Alexander's special fear, the Tsar committed the mistake opposite to his most glaring error at Lützen. There he had held back his reserve and failed to grasp the moment of opportunity; now he threw in his reserve prematurely. The reserve drove Oudinot onto the defensive for a time, but the XII Corps withstood the counterstrokes and ended by forcing the Allies behind the Blösaer Wasser. Farther north, Macdonald's IX Corps captured Bautzen, and Marmont's VI Corps and General of Division and *comte de l'Empire* Henri-Gatien Bertrand's IV captured the high ground of the Burk ridge in spite of stout resistance by Prussians fighting with unwonted ferocity evidently instilled in them by the new patriotism spawned by the humiliation of Jena-Auerstädt and inflamed by the reformers.

Losses on both sides were high, and Marmont and Bertrand had fought their troops close to exhaustion, but Napoleon had attained his object for May 20 merely by keeping the Allies busy. He expected Ney to deliver the decisive blow the next day.

He was expecting too much, events proved, of a brave warrior unskilled in the independent command of troops as numerous as a field army. The fighting resumed as if by nervous impulse soon after dawn, though the French Emperor rested almost until it was time for Ney to act. The Tsar's fear led to a vicious Allied assault upon Oudinot, supervised by Alexander personally, driving the VI Corps from the ground it had taken the day before. But Napoleon cared little for his own right flank; it was better that Alexander's attention should be fixated there. On the all-important French left, Ney initially made such rapid progress against the first opposition to meet him that he reached the town of Preititz, where he was supposed to be by 11:00 A.M., about an hour early.

But there Ney halted. Perhaps he feared that early delivery of the climactic attack would find Napoleon unprepared to cooperate. Perhaps under the unaccustomed strain of independent command of an army he faltered because his rear was drawn out a long distance behind Souham's division in the van. By the time Ney drove forward again, however, as late as 1:00 P.M., the Allies had grown sufficiently aware of the menace shadowing their right-rear that they were moving troops feverishly from their center, and the intended trap was becoming less and less likely to be closed.

Furthermore, Ney compounded his error by giving Souham inadequate support as he tried to push his spearhead beyond Preititz. Prussians shifted from the center and again fighting with their new ferocity drove Souham out of that town and clear back to Glein, over a mile to the north. As Ney belatedly reinforced Souham with the III Corps division of Antoine Guillaume Delmas de la Corte, *général de division,* he allowed Blücher to distract him from the vital business at hand with artillery fire into his right flank. Blücher's action provoked Ney into directing Delmas westward toward the Prussian guns, holding much of his own III Corps in position to support Delmas. This, at least the third major error in generalship committed by Ney since eleven in the morning, practically guaranteed that the Allies would be able to slip past him and that Napoleon's first-rate plan would founder because it depended upon an inadequately prepared subordinate.

Meanwhile the sound of Souham's guns at one o'clock had prompted a by-then impatient Napoleon to hurl forward almost all his resources in the center to complete the immobilizing and thus the destruction of the Allied forces there. The Young Guard joined in, with the support of all the Guard artillery. The Allied center, already depleted to fend off Ney, soon crumpled, and the Tsar and Wittgenstein ordered a general retreat. But victory on the scale of Austerlitz or Jena-Auerstädt again eluded the French. Blücher found his Prussians nearly surrounded in spite of his success in unhinging Ney, but he remained altogether undaunted—his steady resolution was proving to be his strongest asset—and he called back enough of his force from Ney's front to impose just enough of a check upon the French center that most of the Allied army was able to escape.

Again the dearth of French cavalry completed the assurance that there would be no new victory of annihilation. Bautzen was a sore disappointment to the French Emperor, at a time when the need to shake off the shadow of his Russian disasters still made a return to superlative victories seem imperative. The outcome of Bautzen was anything but superlative. Casualties were equally appalling on both sides, some 20,000 for each of the rival armies, and far from gaining an Austerlitz Napoleon was unable even to display symbolic trophies; the Allies escaped with their guns and colors virtually intact, and the French took few prisoners.

In a black mood Napoleon flogged his army eastward from Bautzen in quest of yet another opportunity. He might have felt less dissatisfied had he been able to know fully that the mood in the Allied camps was yet more foul. Wittgenstein felt that with the defeats of Lützen and Bautzen charged to him, he was a scapegoat for his sovereign's amateurish generalship, and he resigned his command. Barclay replaced him and forthwith quarrelled with Blücher, because Barclay believed the Allies must retreat as far as Poland, while Blücher and his new *Quartiermeisterlieutenant—Generalmajor* von Gneisenau—inevitably resisted such an abandonment of the kingdom whose uniform they wore. The bickering Allies compromised on a scheme to fall back on Schweidnitz (or Schwiednitz), short of the Oder and southwest of Breslau, where they could at least shield Silesia and maintain contact with and thus keep up their courtship of Austria.

The interallied squabbling failed, however, to injure substantially the military revival of Prussia or the alertness of Blücher the sword-arm and Gneisenau the brain of its principal field army. Napoleon's choler caused him to drive his advancing columns so hard they they neglected due caution in reconnaissance— the more readily, of course, because of the exasperating weakness in cavalry. On May 26 the Prussians seized one of the resulting opportunities to fall with about twenty squadrons of *Landwehr* cavalry on the exposed XII Corps division of Nicolas Joseph baron Maison, *général de division*, at Haynau some forty miles (sixty-four kilometers) northwest of Schweidnitz. The Prussians mauled the French badly. Oudinot's XII Corps in turn administered a sharp setback to a larger Prussian force at Hoyerswerda two days later, but a failure to exploit the victory until June 6 set up another Prussian success near Luckau that day. By that time hostilities had officially come to a temporary halt, although this news of course took a while to reach all commands. Meanwhile these final events of the Lützen-Bautzen campaign had disproportionate importance in raising the morale of the inexperienced Prussian forces and especially of their second line, the *Landwehr*.

Napoleon's disappointments in the campaign had grown to be aggravated by a well-founded concern for his lengthening lines of communications. Cossacks and other partisans of various descriptions seemed to be swarming all over those lines, and should the Austrians respond to the Allies' blandishments, his logistical condition could well turn disastrous. Already he was dangerously short of ammunition. It is another evidence that, notwithstanding the excellence of his plan at Bautzen, he had passed the height of his powers—and certainly the height of his confidence in his destiny—that these circumstances drove him to accept an Austrian offer of mediation to effect an armistice. The Allies responded to the same offer gladly, as well they might have, because all of Napoleon's problems were offset by worse difficulties on their side, and they had more to gain than to lose by a respite. The pre-1812 Napoleon would almost certainly not have agreed to the thirty-six-hour suspension of hostilities beginning June 2 that led on June 4 to an armistice to last until July 20, pending the result of peace negotiations.

Both sides made gestures toward such negotiations, while both also embarked much more seriously on preparing for the resumption of war. Napoleon brought reinforcements eastward, partially correcting his weakness in cavalry and most particularly getting ammunition wagons to the troops. It is possible that his shortage of ammunition might have become so acute that it alone might justify what appears otherwise to have been a grave error in accepting the armistice. But in other respects the armistice certainly served him badly. Not only did the Russians and Prussians use the time to restore their own troops, the Prussians industriously training new *Landwehr*. In addition, British supplies and money—£2,000,000—poured in liberally. And Austria was at last persuaded to rejoin the struggle. The British promised Austria £500,000 for doing so, and on July 19 the secret Reichenbach Convention promised Austrian military action if Napoleon failed to meet peace terms that he would surely find unacceptable. The armistice meanwhile had been extended to August 17, but on August 12 Austria declared war, and the next day Blücher's Prussians began moving westward from Breslau. The great struggle for control of Europe had resumed.

The Dresden Campaign: A Threat to Berlin

Napoleon's awareness that he was much worse situated than at the beginning of the armistice along with his larger loss of self-confidence led him to a more modest strategic design then had been customary. His purpose became essentially defensive, to hold off a possible Allied military onslaught in a fashion discouraging enough to his enemies that their coalition might rupture politically. To this end his thoughts turned again toward drawing the Prussians northward away from the Russians and Austrians.

On the resumption of hostilities, his main army numbered about 240,000 men grouped around Bautzen and Görlitz, whence they could confront a direct Allied movement westward from Breslau or threaten the flank of a more southerly Allied push from Austria toward Saxony via the valley of the Elbe. Against the latter possibility, Napoleon had also seen to the strong fortification of Dresden, but with orders that reflect his perceptive concern lest a powerful fortress become an immobilizing magnet by means of the fascination it might exert even upon himself. Determined not to lapse into an immobile defensive, he assigned the aggressive role to the 100,000 or so men he had deployed north of his main force. Principally, these troops included 66,000 men in five corps under Oudinot grouped around Luckau on both sides of the Spree and another 16,000 along the Elbe from Torgau to Hamburg.

With much of the Prussian Army in the south, the defense of Berlin was in the hands of the Crown Prince of Sweden, whose adopted country had formally joined the war on July 7, and who commanded somewhat over 100,000 Prussians, Swedes, Russians, and North Germans of various origins. Knowing Bernadotte well, Napoleon considered Oudinot at least a match for him. Oudinot was to stage a concentric advance against Berlin; take it about the fourth or fifth day; then extricate the exposed French garrisons of Küstrin, Stettin, and Danzig; but above all strike at least a moral blow against the Prussian capital that might set the Sixth Coalition to unraveling.

Napoleon's appraisal of Bernadotte was more accurate than his estimate of Oudinot, and it is a curious aspect of his plan that it left the highly capable Davout, who was also in the north, to play a minor role operating out of Hamburg. Nevertheless, Oudinot began reasonably well, albeit cautiously advancing at a more leisurely pace than the Emperor had contemplated. The broken and sometimes marshy terrain of Brandenburg gave him difficulties in maintaining contact among his corps, but he won a series of small victories that nearly frightened Bernadotte into ordering the evacuation of Berlin.

Fortunately for the entire Prussian revival as well as for the Allied coalition, however, *Generallieutenant* Friedrich Wilhelm Freiherr von Bülow was on hand. Something of a dandy and dilettante until the events of 1806 turned him into an exemplar of the professional qualities that Grolman's 1808 declaration said should determine advancement in the Prussian officer corps, Bülow now supplied the backbone lacking in Bernadotte, and Berlin did not fall. Instead, the campaign turned around when Bülow concentrated 30,000 men against one of Oudinot's scattered corps, the VII under Jean Louis Ebénézer Reynier, *général de division*, at Gross-Boeren (or Grossbeeren) on August 23. Bülow's troops overran Reynier's 23,000 French and Saxons, losing about 1,000 casualties but extracting from the enemy some 3,000 along with thirteen guns and sixty wagons.

This reverse need not have had much strategic significance, except that it deflated Oudinot as badly as he had earlier deflated Bernadotte. The French went over to a general retreat, and Napoleon could no longer profit even from a diversion in the north, let alone expect his principal offensive blow to be struck there.

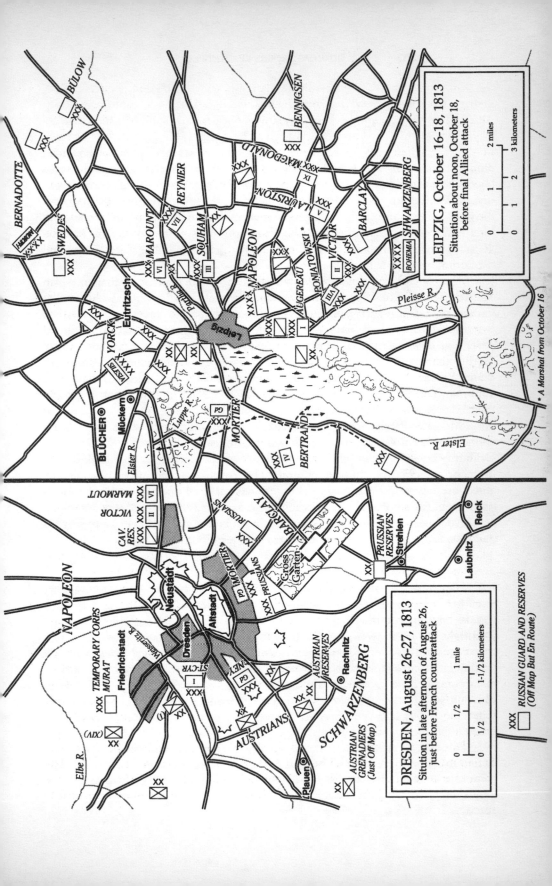

LEIPZIG, October 16-18, 1813
Situation about noon, October 18, before final Allied attack

2 miles
0 1 2 3 kilometers

* A Marshal from October 16

BÜLOW

BERNADOTTE

SWEDES

BENNIGSEN

REYNIER

MARMONT

SOUHAM

NAPOLEON

AUGEREAU

PONIATOWSKI

LAURISTON

MACDONALD

IX

V

VICTOR

II

BARCLAY

SHWARZENBERG

Bohemia

Pleisse R.

YORCK

SILESIA

Eutritzsch

Leipzig

BLÜCHER

Möckern

Elster R.

Luppe R.

Gd

MORTIER

BERTRAND

IV

Elster R.

DRESDEN, August 26-27, 1813
Situation in late afternoon of August 26, just before French counterattack

0 1/2 1 mile
0 1/2 1 1-1/2 kilometers

RUSSIAN GUARD AND RESERVES
(Off Map But En Route)

NAPOLEON

Elbe R.

TEMPORARY CORPS
MURAT

Friedrichstadt

Weisseritz R.

Neustadt

Altstadt

Dresden

ST-CYR

I

NEY

Gd

MORTIER

PRUSSIANS

RUSSIANS

BARCLAY

Gross
Garten

CAV.
RES.

VICTOR

MARMONT

VI

II

PRUSSIAN
RESERVES
Strehlen

Laubnitz

Reick

Räcknitz

AUSTRIAN
RESERVES

SCHWARZENBERG

AUSTRIANS

AUSTRIAN
GRENADIERS
(Just Off Map)

Plauen

The Dresden Campaign:
Dresden, the Katzbach, and Kulm

When they broke the armistice, the Allies had about 95,000 men under Blücher in the Breslau area—the Army of Silesia—and as many as 230,000, mostly Austrians but Russians and Prussians as well, under *Feldmarschall* Prince zu Schwarzenberg in Bohemia—the Army of Bohemia. Schwarzenberg was designated to be generalissimo of all the Allied armies, but this honor meant little, because the Emperors of Russia and Austria and the King of Prussia all took the field with him, bickered among each other, and denied him a free hand.

Austrian caution nevertheless shaped the Allied plan of campaign, which was to operate against Napoleon's flanks and communications but to retreat if he lashed out against either Blücher's or Schwarzenberg's forces, neither Allied army taking the risk of fighting him alone. Had Napoleon adhered to his initial intention of allowing the campaign to hinge on Oudinot's operations toward Berlin, there could have been a series of indecisive maneuvers in the south. But there had always been a touch of the implausible about such a reliance on Oudinot, no matter what he might have accomplished, and it is not surprising that Napoleon soon lost patience with the relatively passive role he had assigned himself. After designating Macdonald to contain Blücher while he himself looked toward Bohemia, the French Emperor decided that because Blücher was evidently behaving more energetically than Schwarzenberg he should deal with Blücher not only first but peremptorily. By August 21, therefore, Blücher was encountering stern French counterattacks east of the Bober River. Even though the overall Allied plan led Blücher to retreat as soon as he learned that Napoleon in person was on the scene, he was hit so hard before he could get away that his raw *Landwehr* units, their morale already undermined because Prussia had not been able to provide them with adequate supplies especially of clothing, suffered severely from desertion.

Napoleon's pursuit of Blücher was abruptly interrupted, however, by news that Schwarzenberg was marching down the valley of the Elbe and thereby threatening his communications. Since Blücher plainly did not intend to stand and fight but rather was acting as though he intended to draw Napoleon into a trap, the French Emperor returned westward and formed new plans while en route. The troops facing Blücher became the Army of the Bober under Macdonald's command, with orders to drive Blücher east of Jauer, a road junction about thirty miles (forty-eight kilometers) west of Breslau, but then to withdraw behind the Bober and remain concentrated in a defensive position. Napoleon's main effort meanwhile would include a feint toward the relief of Dresden against Schwarzenberg's advance, while the principal French forces in fact hastened across the Elbe upriver from Dresden at Königstein to strike the Allied rear. The Emperor believed the pattern of the Allied advance afforded him yet one more opportunity to right his fortunes with a *manœuvre sur les derrières* leading to a decisive battle of annihilation.

For Napoleon's plan to attain full success, however, the fortifications at Dresden had to hold out long enough to fix Schwarzenberg in place to receive the blow against his rear. From the governor of Dresden and commander of the XIV Corps, Laurent Gouvion Saint-Cyr, comte and *maréchal de l'Empire*, Napoleon unhappily received increasingly gloomy indications that he would not be able to hold out long enough. His troops included many Westphalians, who were not reliable, and the civil population was in a panic. Late on August 25 Napoleon's senior orderly officer, the highly trustworthy Colonel Gaspard baron Gourgaud, returned from a personal reconnaissance to Dresden to confirm the most pessimistic judgments from Gouvion Saint-Cyr. The Allies had advanced rapidly enough to throw overwhelming force around the French outer lines as early as the 22nd. Gouvion Saint-Cyr was resisting stoutly, but the enemy could smother him at practically any time they chose.

Furthermore, Napoleon had received sufficient information about Oudinot's retreat in the north to fear for his line of communications from the direction of the lower Elbe. Temporarily shelving the plan for another Austerlitz or Jena-Auerstädt—he hoped to return to it in a day or two—Napoleon swiftly shifted his columns to converge on Dresden, to rescue that city as the indispensable preliminary to any larger scheme. Swiftly the columns marched, because their commanders knew the convergence was urgent. The Imperial Guard covered ninety miles (145 kilometers) in seventy-two hours. Victor's II Corps and Marmont's VI contained many recent conscripts but nevertheless marched 120 miles (153 kilometers) in four days. Meanwhile about 40,000 men in the reinforced I Corps of Dominique Joseph René Vandamme, comte d'Unsebourg and *général de division*, continued to march over the Iser Mountains farther east to approach the Elbe above the Allies and keep the notion of a *manœuvre sur les derrières* alive.

On the morning of August 26 Gouvion Saint-Cyr was awaiting Schwarzenberg's attack on Dresden with 20,000 men, a total that gave him only one man to every ten yards (or meters) on portions of his front. He had bravely purchased some additional time by launching a counterattack on the 25th, but now it was apparent that the overpowering Allied Army of Bohemia was at length resolved to close on him. Partly because of haste in reconstructing the defenses of the city after the French occupation, partly out of Napoleon's deliberate intent to avoid creating a fortress so strong that it would discourage mobile warfare, Dresden's defenses would not have earned an accolade from Vauban. Several of the redoubts were not mutually supporting. Gouvion Saint-Cyr thought it best to begin by defending an outpost line well in advance of the main fortifications.

The Allied attacks commenced about 5:00 A.M. on the 26th. As expected, they gained ground, though the defenders fought at least as stubbornly as anyone could have hoped. By about eleven o'clock the attackers had overrun the outpost line, whereupon they paused to regroup. The Tsar of All the Russias and the King of Prussia watched from the Räcknitz Heights directly south of the city, and despite the morning's progress they were more than troubled, for from the high ground they were able to see dark masses of French reinforcements hastening into the city—Napoleon's main army, including the hard-marching Guard, had arrived. More than troubled is the correct phrase to describe the Allied sovereigns' mood, for in spite of 1812 and since late that year Tsar Alexander had endured so many frustrations in his efforts to complete the destruction of his adversary that he again perceived a magic in Napoleon. When the great conqueror appeared in person almost within shouting distance, his arrival so unnerved Alexander that he was ready to call off the whole attack and withdraw. It was the usually diffident King Frederick William of Prussia who rose to the occasion by observing that one man ought not to cause the whole Allied army to panic. Nevertheless, several hours were wasted by the Allies while the monarchs debated and more French soldiers arrived.

The debate was at length resolved by the Allied soldiers; earlier orders for attacks beyond the French outposts and into the city had never been canceled, and in the late afternoon the troops went forward again in accordance with those orders. While Gouvion Saint-Cyr continued in direct command of a stubborn defense, however, Napoleon was organizing three counterattacking forces, under Murat, Ney, and Morthier. With 300 guns covering their assault, the Allies set fire to Dresden at several places, and they captured all of their immediate objectives including the principal redoubts. But Gouvion Saint-Cyr's outnumbered line never really broke, and when at 5:30 P.M. Napoleon with his still superb intuitive sense of the flow of battle decided the time had come to throw in his counterattacks, the Allies recoiled everywhere. The French streamed back across virtually all the ground they had lost. Napoleon rode in the midst of the counterattacks until he was sure of their success. Then he returned into the city to try to devise a plan for transforming a mere defensive victory into the battle of annihilation he had hoped to fight.

Victor and Marmont arrived during the night, to raise Napoleon's strength to about 120,000. Allied reinforcements came in also, but only enough to increase Schwarzenberg's army from some 150,000 to 170,000, because the Prince felt obliged to divert almost 40,000 to guard against Vandamme's threat to his rear. The Allies nevertheless retained a sufficient numerical edge that, notwithstanding the Tsar's state of mind, Schwarzenberg was able to plan a resumption of his attacks for August 27. He massed 120,000 of his men for a huge onslaught against the French center.

Napoleon's hope of retrieving a decisive victory led him to adopt a plan dovetailing with Schwarzenberg's. He would fight a holding action in the center while attacking on both flanks. Precisely what he intended to accomplish is not clear. It is evident enough that by sending forward Victor's newly arrived infantry along with a cavalry force under Murat on the right, he might crush a portion of the enemy army; because the extreme Allied left, part of the Austrian corps of *Feldmarschall Leutnant* Johann Graf Klenau, was to some degree isolated by the Plauen ravine. Nevertheless, success in that sector would scarcely amount to an Austerlitz. It is also evident enough that the events of the preceding day had given Napoleon ample confirmation that his center could hold against anything the enemy might hurl against it; there Napoleon still had Gouvion Saint-Cyr's men, along with Marmont's corps and, as a general reserve, the Old Guard, about 50,000 of his total. The attack on his left would be led by Ney and Marshal Mortier, their troops including Mortier's Young Guard.

It may be that Napoleon's purpose was more tactical than strategic: that because circumstances had denied him the opportunity to destroy the Allied army through his original design for a *manœuvre sur les derrières*, he intended now simply to beat up both Allied flanks as thoroughly as possible. The attack by his right would hit a partially isolated force; the attack by his left would have no similar advantage but would rain heavy blows upon the principal Russian and Prussian formations of the Army of Bohemia, which stood on the Allied east flank, and would therefore at least undermine the power of those armies if there was no longer an immediate possibility of destroying them. Perhaps, however, Napoleon still clung to a larger strategic objective. His flank attacks might envelop both enemy wings sufficiently to seize the best roads connecting the Allied army with its bases in Bohemia, the Freiberg-Komotau and Pirna-Peterswalde roads. Thereby the Allies could be forced to use inadequate traces through the mountains of the Bohemian border. Moreover, Vandamme's operations from the east might enhance the opportunity to seize the Pirna road.

Whatever his motives, Napoleon was so intent upon staging his flank attacks that he preempted the enemy's attack plan by moving his left wing forward at six in the morning of August 27, his right at 6:30. There had been hard rain during the night, so Napoleon, who might usually attempt to control too much detail but who remained skillful in attending to detail, took pains to modify his effort accordingly. In particular, he saw to the roundup of extra horses from the streets of Dresden to assure his artillery an excess of pulling power to compensate for the mud, and he placed heavy reliance on his recently strengthened cavalry because the enemy infantry would be handicapped by wet firearms and wet ammunition. The mud generally prevented the French cavalry from galloping, but while Allied guns bogged down, French artillery moved effectively enough to blast openings for substantial gains in ground, especially by the cavalry, on both flanks. Murat practically annihilated Klenau's most exposed division west of the Plauen ravine. Ney pushed forward less spectacularly but none the less effectively. The Allies became too distracted to mount a formidable assault in the center, though Napoleon grew impatient when counterefforts by Gouvion Saint-Cyr proved equally futile.

In a somewhat disgruntled frame of mind, Napoleon was riding from the latter's positions to his command post when he noticed a group of evidently senior enemy officers gathered on the Räcknitz Heights and ordered a French battery to fire at them. The group happened to include the Russian and Prussian monarchs as well as Schwarzenberg and a large staff. One of the first French shots at 2,000 yards (or meters) range landed squarely in the headquarters group, mortally wounding the former French Revolutionary hero General Moreau and barely missing Tsar Alexander. Another casualty was the monarchs' remaining enthusiasm for resuming the offensive. They were willing to continue a defensive fight, but Schwarzenberg could see little purpose in doing so with weary troops and an endangered rear. Furthermore, Vandamme was advancing onto the Pirna-Peterswalde road. An Allied council of war decided to retreat.

Had the Allies held their ground, Napoleon planned to attack again on August 28, much along the lines of the second day's battle but with Murat intended to envelop the Allied left. As it was, the battle of Dresden, while far from another Austerlitz, was certainly yet another Napoleonic victory. Fighting with the advantages of the defensive on the first day, and then allowing the artillery to do much of the work on the second, the French imposed about 38,000 casualties on the enemy while losing some 10,000 themselves.

Vandamme's advance condemned the retreat mostly to unsatisfactory mountain trails, but the French did not pursue with enough vigor to take much advantage of this predicament. Napoleon's cavalry was still not what it once had been, and it had tired its horses during the fighting of August 27. The French Emperor failed to give direct supervision to the pursuit but instead returned to Dresden to digest reports of misfortune elsewhere. These reports dealt not only with Oudinot's fiasco but also with a similar failure by Macdonald. Contrary to Napoleon's orders, that marshal had neglected to keep his Army of the Bober well concentrated. Already broken up into three columns, the army clashed with Blücher when its spearhead crossed the Katzbach on August 26. Rains then swept away the bridges over that stream and permitted Blücher to turn around and fight isolated detachments. Rains also did to Macdonald's infantry weapons what they were later to do to the weapons of the Allies on the 27th, and on the Katzbach it was the enemy rather than the French who made superior use of cavalry and artillery. Like the Allies the next day, the French lost practically a whole division of rain-soaked foot soldiers, and the battle along the Katzbach worked wonders in raising the morale of the green and partly naked soldiers of Blücher's Army of Silesia.

Further to sour the already less than plentiful fruits of the French victory at Dresden, near Kulm five miles (eight kilometers) southwest of Peterswalde on August 30 Vandamme's road-blocking operations ran into a strong Allied detachment in close proximity to the headquarters of both Tsar Alexander and King Frederick William. Vandamme staged an admirably energetic assault, but the sovereigns unlike ordinary generals had the ability to order rapid reinforcement without provoking any of the recipients of such orders to waste time with unnecessary questions. There was soon enough Allied strength on hand to outflank Vandamme and threaten his rear, so he had to retire. In the process he himself was captured. The third of the three French efforts apart from the main army's thus ended in a fizzle. The Katzbach and Kulm went a long way toward canceling the psychological effects of Dresden.

The Dresden Campaign:
Futile Maneuvers and the Battle of Dennewitz

To recapture the quickly fading laurels of Dresden, Napoleon considered a march on either Prague or Berlin. He rejected the former alternative, as requiring him to maintain large forces through and across the same Bohemian mountains that had rendered Schwarzenberg's communications uncertain during the recent battle, and this when his lines of communications were already dangerously long and thin. Schwarzenberg would be able to retire deep into Austria if he chose and there to draw out Napoleon's logistics still further. As capital of Bohemia but not of an independent power, Prague was not worth such risks.

As capital of Prussia, Berlin offered the greater opportunities that had prompted Napoleon to elevate Oudinot's role in the campaign. While Oudinot had failed, his and his rivals' armies had not been large enough to consume all the subsistence on the way to and around Berlin, and without the sort of mountain barriers that guarded Prague the road to Berlin therefore had decided logistical advantages. Furthermore, a march on Berlin reopened the old possibility of separating the Prussian forces from their allies by compelling them to turn northward.

Thoughts of Berlin suffered a partial setback when Napoleon learned on September 2 that Oudinot's campaign had been an even worse failure than he had hitherto realized, particularly that Oudinot had retired all the way to Wittenberg. Evidently believing that combative stubbornness was what Oudinot's campaign had lacked, Napoleon sent Ney to take command of the Berlin operations and to right matters there pending the Emperor's own move northward. He urged Ney to advance rapidly from Wittenberg toward Berlin, and he promised to arrive in person with reinforcements to attack the city on September 9 or 10.

Before Napoleon could fulfill this promise with more than the shifting of a few troops, however, news arrived that Macdonald's army was in worse condition and Blücher more aggressive than the bare facts of the action on the Katzbach would have seemed to warrant. Warning Ney of a postponement of help and telling him to call on Davout, Napoleon and the bulk of his army hurried back toward Bautzen to assist Macdonald and squelch Blücher. When he rode into Macdonald's camps, Napoleon discovered matters even yet worse than reports of the Katzbach and its aftermath had led him to expect. Macdonald had allowed his army to descend deep into demoralization and disorder. Napoleon flew into a fury that he vented on troops as well as headquarters, permitting himself so uncontrolled an outburst of temper that some of his officers feared it might prove counterproductive. In fact, the sound and sight of the Emperor so angry shocked Macdonald's men back into soldierly conduct. Unless the outburst was calculated stage-acting, however, it may well have been another sign that the strain of so many years of command responsibility and unsatiated ambition was at length undermining Napoleon's control of himself and therefore of others.

The immediately following events certainly provided new causes for exasperation and further doubts whether his star of destiny still shone. Confronted by Napoleon, Blücher again shifted into reverse, but just as promptly Schwarzenberg took advantage of the movement against Blücher in precisely the manner he had before, by marching against Dresden. Once more, therefore, Napoleon had to turn his attention from Blücher to Schwarzenberg, once more hastening back to Dresden, this time oppressed with ample reason by the sense that all his exertions since the disasters in Russia amounted to little more than walking on a treadmill.

In fact, however, there was a limit upon the ability of events to repeat themselves, because Schwarzenberg had no desire for a reprise of the battle of Dresden, and he retreated rather than risk it. But any comfort that Napoleon might have found in this particular release from the treadmill—and it cannot have been much comfort, for a younger Napoleon probably would have found a way to force Schwarzenberg into another battle—was promptly dashed by word of the latest doings of that brave blunderer Marshal Ney.

On September 6, at Dennewitz forty miles (sixty-four kilometers) south-west of Berlin, Ney plunged his army into a trap set by Bernadotte, or more specifically by General von Bülow. Ney had neglected cavalry reconnaissance, and in effect he was simply ambushed. The tactical flexibility and the persisting élan of the French soldiery almost rescued Ney, but he saw to it that soldierly resourcefulness came to nothing by ordering Oudinot to shift his XII Corps from the left flank to the right just when it was needed on the left. Oudinot was sulking because of his supersession by Ney and obeyed the order even though he knew the effect would be disastrous. Ney's army retreated in disorder, with a loss of 10,000 casualties to the enemy's 7,000. Bülow became Graf von Dennewitz, a fitting reward for the thoroughly professional care with which he had directed all the details of the entrapment and the battle. There could be no more eloquent testimony to Napoleon's disregard for the same quality of officer professionalism than his repeated willingness to reward failure by relying on Marshal Ney. But Ney seemed to display a doglike devotion, and Napoleon valued that more than competence.

The news of Dennewitz along with the elusiveness of Blücher and Schwarzenberg and a further spell of wet weather caused Napoleon to spend much of the rest of September in indecision and inactivity at Dresden. Dennewitz was not so big a battle that defeat in it should inherently have prevented a return to the Berlin strategy of early September; if moving against Berlin had been the appropriate next operation after the battle of Dresden, it remained so still. But the length of the French lines of communications was again making itself felt in equipment shortages and reduced rations, and more importantly, Napoleon was in a funk unprecedented during his years of power.

When he finally made up his mind what to do next, his decision amounted almost to a confession of strategic bankruptcy. He would withdraw west of the Elbe where his logistical difficulties should ease, but he would retain bridge-heads across the river at various places including Dresden, Wittenberg, and Magdeburg while waiting for the enemy's next move. The French retreat began September 24, and it so heartened the Allies that they resumed their quarrels, this time about offensive plans of their own. Albeit with only the loosest of coordination, Bernadotte, Blücher, and Schwarzenberg all began to work their ways toward Napoleon's flanks and rear in a decidedly amorphous but neverthe-less dangerous threat to his already troublesome communications. Out of these somewhat tentative maneuvers, however, was to arise the most decisive battle since Jena-Auerstädt.

Leipzig

During much of the first week of October, Napoleon reverted to—or remained in—his mid-September torpor. Since late September there had been a series of inconclusive actions around the periphery of the French army, in which frustrations continued to pile up in the face of every French initiative, while bickering among the Allied generals simultaneously reduced to at least temporary futility all their gestures toward taking advantage of French discomfiture. The rains continued to pour, unhelpful to all concerned.

By the end of the week the Allies were contriving nevertheless to curl around Napoleon's flanks toward a deployment to the west of the French, astride their lines of communications and retreat. Napoleon, however, was getting his army reasonably well concentrated around Leipzig, where the convergence of the Rivers Elster, Pleisse, Luppe, and Parthe divided the surrounding country into areas separated from each other enough to suggest opportunities that reawakened in the French Emperor some coherent design to deal with his divided enemies one at a time. He counted on Bernadotte to remain relatively passive, so the choice was whether to aim first for a decisive blow against Blücher or Schwarzenberg.

He chose to lash out first against Blücher. If Schwarzenberg in the meantime chose to continue the slow march that was taking him around the south of Leipzig toward Napoleon's westward communications, then perhaps all the better. This same progress should make the Austrian commander vulnerable by the time Napoleon had dealt with Blücher, susceptible to a countermove calculated to turn his attention from French communications to the perilousness of his own line of retreat southward into Bohemia.

Against Blücher, Napoleon marched north with 150,000 troops, expecting to strike the Army of Silesia near Düben on October 9. The march pace did not equal former French standards of celerity, however, and the enemy's scouts gave both Blücher and Bernadotte ample warning before the blow could fall.

These two Allied leaders had been especially conspicuous for the frequency and asperity of their quarrels in a command structure in which squabbles were the norm, and now the Crown Prince of Sweden and the Prussian general had at each other again. Bernadotte wanted to retreat across the Elbe. In the unsubtle mind of Blücher, however, there had formed a resolution to retreat no more. He had retreated too much during his summer maneuvers in the Dresden campaign; retreat was galling to his temperament; he would persist in going forward, west toward the Saale. If Napoleon threatened his communications with Berlin, he still had a sufficient expanse of Prussian territory from which to draw supplies west of Berlin. Napoleon's blow of October 9 struck mostly thin air, because Blücher had continued marching, not to protect his rear as Napoleon had expected, but deeper toward Napoleon's rear—thus turning against Napoleon the very same counteraction and the very kind of psychological pressure that Napoleon had intended to employ next against Schwarzenberg after he had undone Blücher.

This dose of his own medicine sent Napoleon back into indecision. He ordered some of his troops to continue threatening the Allied northern forces, part toward Dessau on the trail of Bernadotte, part toward Wittenberg to elevate the menace to Blücher's Berlin communications and thereby perhaps draw back the stubborn Prussian after all. But Murat, left behind to deal with Schwarzenberg, was dispatching gloomy reports of that commander's possible intentions toward Leipzig, a place that Napoleon did not wish to yield. The northern marches therefore were designed to be reversed quickly if Schwarzenberg's threat to Leipzig should become acute.

During this new bout of indecision Napoleon received the bad news that Bavaria had defected to the Sixth Coalition. He also had to digest an unpleasant consequence of his inability to develop a consistent purposeful strategy when he learned that his desire to retain Dresden as a bridgehead on the Elbe had led to the blockade in that city of two corps, Gouvion Saint-Cyr's XIV and General of Division Georges Mouton, comte de Lobau's I. Moreover, his threat to Blücher's rear was continuing to fail to produce the desired effect. Instead, Blücher set off on a southward march to link up with Schwarzenberg.

This movement left Napoleon with no alternative but to concentrate his own forces on Leipzig, in the hope of marching rapidly enough to defeat Schwarzenberg before Blücher arrived. One possibly redeeming factor and reward for Napoleon's northward foray was that Bernadotte, still bickering with Blücher, had been frightened into declining to march southward immediately with Blücher. But for once Bernadotte's tardiness was to prove of no major consequence. Neither Blücher nor the more affable and eloquent Gneisenau could persuade him to act otherwise.

Early on October 14 Napoleon sent out his orders for all his available corps and divisions to march on Leipzig. He himself arrived at the city in the afternoon, to find Murat defending outposts to the southward against growing belligerence from Schwarzenberg. By the end of the day, all the main French forces had joined the Emperor except for two corps still on their way from the north and the two in Dresden. While Napoleon's purpose remained that of confronting the enemy armies in detail, defeating Schwarzenberg before Blücher could arrive, and while Schwarzenberg's activities so far in the campaign had been leisurely in the extreme, the Austrian marshal now showed enough aggressiveness that Napoleon decided he could afford to go over to the defensive and await Schwarzenberg's attacks. Schwarzenberg after all commanded about 203,000 troops close at hand, a number that French intelligence approximated fairly accurately, while on the night of the 14th–15th Napoleon had only 177,000 immediately available. Leipzig, furthermore, had a city wall that was in disrepair but still useful for defense, and more than that, Napoleon's engineers had been busy creating a defensive line in the suburbs. Marshes between the Elster and Luppe Rivers and between the Elster and the Pleisse meant that the line did not have to extend around the entire circumference.

Napoleon's appreciation of the situation was accurate as far as it went, because Schwarzenberg indeed planned to attack on the morning of October 16. Unfortunately for Napoleon, however, the hard-driving Blücher would also have 54,000 troops of the Army of Silesia in position to attack that morning. It was Blücher's energy and determination that made possible the "Battle of the Nations" in which the Allies would eventually be able to employ 365,000 men with 915 to 1,500 guns against Napoleon's eventual 195,000 with 700 guns. It was altogether fitting that Blücher should be present from the beginning, and he was.

Barclay de Tolly led off for Schwarzenberg, driving 78,000 troops through fog and yet more rain against the southeastern defenses at eight in the morning. Blücher assailed the opposite, northwestern defenses. He assaulted and captured the village of Möchern, which earned him the rank of *Generalfeldmarschall* from this date, and he came within a mile of the Rannstädt Gate to the city. But the Allies made no appreciable impression to the south, and the first day of the battle of Leipzig ended as an indecisive bloodbath.

Having failed to break the French defenses, the Allies sparred more tentatively the next day, October 17. Bernadotte had at length decided to follow Blücher, and the latter was awaiting his arrival, which began during the 17th and ought to be complete for action on the 18th. Schwarzenberg similarly, with the now-cautious Tsar still looking over his shoulder, decided to postpone further major efforts until almost all of his army should arrive.

For the 18th, with the Allied Armies of Bohemia, Silesia, and the North all substantially concentrated, the very size of their assemblage seems to have awed the commanders into thinking of nothing else than more head-on charges such as they had mounted on the first day. So the third day's battle became a repetition of the first, with ill-coordinated Allied blows again piling up casualties on both sides. If anyone earned laurels for skill in the attack that day, it was the rapidly improving and increasingly well-officered Prussians.

Uninspired as the Allied conduct of the battle was, it was not an altogether ineffectual method of compensating for the absence in the Allied high command of a military mind able to meet on equal terms even a Napoleon who was no longer at the summit of his powers. With his ability to draw soldiers from outside France sharply curtailed, and with the French manpower pool eroded by nearly two decades of war and the Emperor's persistently premature calls upon the annual conscript classes, Napoleon could not afford to go on with a battle of attrition on the scale of Leipzig. He was too close to the bottom of his manpower barrel. The allies were employing a variant of Napoleon's own strategy of annihilation, albeit they were destroying his army not by spectacular *manœuvres sur les derrières* but by crudely trading casualties with him when they retained more lives to trade. The result could be even more decisive because the annihilation was in the end more literal—but wars that must be won in this fashion had to be enterprises of highly dubious wisdom to begin with.

Oppressed by intolerable casualties, as early as eleven on the morning of the 18th Napoleon commenced a carefully orchestrated withdrawal through Leipzig and across the Elster. For the retreat, the Leipzig-Lindenau causeway across the swamps and the Elster bridge out of Leipzig toward Lindenau were essential. There was no time to build a parallel, supplementary escape route. The Lindenau bridge, however, had to be prepared so it could be quickly destroyed after the rear guard had crossed it. For the most part the retreat was conducted with skill and success, and the French army might have gotten away with its organization intact. But the inevitable confusion of the final street fighting during the withdrawal through Leipzig, combined with the defection of some Saxon and Baden troops who began firing into the French, generated a panic that led to the premature blowing of the bridge, while it was crowded with

French soldiers and while as many as 20,000 troops were still east of the Elster. These men fought desperately. Some, including Macdonald, escaped by swimming the river, but many were captured or killed.

The Allies suffered perhaps 52,000 casualties, but they could afford the terrible toll better than Napoleon could afford his 38,000 killed and wounded, 15,000 battlefield prisoners, and another 15,000 prisoners taken in the Leipzig hospitals. It was these French casualty figures that made Leipzig the most decisive battle since Jena-Auerstädt. They brought total French casualties for the 1813 campaigns, including fighting in Spain, close to half a million. This price was now beyond France's means to afford. Therefore the battle of Leipzig meant for Napoleon the loss of Germany. The war was returning at last to the frontiers of France, a nation now left with manpower resources only dubiously adequate to its own defense.

18 THE DOWNFALL
OF GENIUS

Napoleon's army marched west from the battlefield of Leipzig with ranks not only thinned but hungry, tattered, and stumblingly weary. The lines of communications had been stretched too long for too many months. The rains would not cease, mud still grasped at tired feet and hooves, and typhus soon broke out.

At least the doomed stand of the 20,000 left east of the Elster pinioned the Allies long enough to ensure against an early pursuit. When the Allies at length broke free from street fighting in Leipzig and sufficiently reorganized their own battered formations, it was predictably Blücher and Gneisenau with the Army of Silesia who tried hardest to exploit the outcome of Leipzig into a yet more fully realized strategy of annihilation. They marched along roads parallel to Napoleon's but north of him, hoping to outrace him, to turn his northern flank, and perhaps even to beat him to the Rhine. But their army was not yet capable of outpacing the proverbially rapid marching of the French.

Bernadotte took his forces out of the pursuit, ostensibly to threaten Holland, in fact to serve exclusively Swedish interests against Denmark. Schwarzenberg adopted a leisurely pace just as predictably as Blücher pushed his troops hard. The Austrian field marshal evidently counted on the recent defection of Bavaria from Napoleon to bring about the interposing of sufficient force across the French path to permit the Army of Bohemia to catch up.

On October 23 Napoleon reached Erfurt, where he had established a depot among whose stores he hoped to rest his army while replenishing it and then perhaps to face eastward again to deal with his scattered opponents one by one.

But at Erfurt he learned that Württemberg, his most loyal German ally, was under irresistible pressure to change sides, its army being with him and therefore unable to help the government at home resist the demands upon it. The loss of Württemberg would make any prospect of further efforts to hold Germany altogether a logistical impossibility.

Therefore on October 24, Napoleon resumed his retreat. The depot at Erfurt had permitted some restoration of the soldiers' strength, but not enough to prevent a constant leakage of stragglers—and occasional falling out of the dying or dead. The rains still persisted; the Württemberg troops marched away homeward because they had no choice; shortening days aggravated the pervasive gloom.

But Napoleon and his army could still fight. Near Hanau 43,000 Bavarians in a strong position guarding both ends of a bridge over the Kinzig River sought to delay the French march to Frankfurt-am-Main until part of the Allied main forces could catch up. The French attacked the Bavarians in front and left flank on October 30, supporting the infantry assault with a heavy cannonade, and brushed them aside.

Two days later Napoleon crossed the Rhine at Mainz. His army followed during the next few days. The French were now reduced to about 80,000, with perhaps 40,000 stragglers eventually able to make their way into France to rejoin them. Another 100,000 of Napoleon's soldiers remained in various garrisons left behind in Germany and Poland, but these included many invalids and foreign troops. If the Allies had been able to follow quickly across the Rhine and into France, they might have scored a swift and final knockout. But they, too, were suffering from the rains, mud, and hunger; it was now the Allies whose communications were overstretched. Furthermore, some of their leaders hoped to make peace without invading France, fearing that invasion would again stir up a hornets' nest as it had long ago in the early 1790s. With their councils divided as usual, the Allies paused near Germany's western frontiers to argue with each other and conduct desultory negotiations with Napoleon.

The latter was willing to play at diplomacy too, even going so far as to sign on December 11 an agreement for Fernando VII to return to the Spanish throne in exchange for Spanish neutrality. The agreement came to little, not least because the Spanish were in no hurry to take back their corrupt former monarch; but it helped buy time, during which the French Emperor attempted to stamp new armies out of the ground. Through this winter and into the spring he either called up or at least alerted for call the astonishing total of 936,000 men. But the supply of horses was no better and probably worse than the year before, so that again the French must endure a weakness in cavalry and transport; while finding competent officers was even harder than the previous year. Most of the 936,000 never saw service. Napoleon relied so much on the officers of the Imperial Guard that he expanded it almost into a separate army, but it was a much diluted Guard that would have to help protect the territory of France herself.

The Spanish Campaign of 1812:
Ciudad Rodrigo, Badajoz, Salamanca, Burgos

By the end of 1813 the danger to the French homeland came from the south as well as the east, for the long war of attrition in the Iberian Peninsula had worsened into an incurable cancer already spreading across the Pyrenees.

The Peninsular War remained the quintessential war of attrition. There were no Austerlitz or Jena-Auerstädt victories for either side. But beyond the cumulative casualties and drain on other resources, the seesaw character of the earlier fighting had since 1809 tipped more and more consistently in favor of the British, Portuguese, and Spanish over the French. The tactical advantage had swung toward the Allies before they enjoyed much apparent strategic gain; in strategy, the deadlock seemed to persist as late as 1811. But by 1812 and 1813 the burden of attrition had so worn down the French that in strategy also the flow was clearly shifting against them.

Logistics wore them down even more evidently than casualties. The French armies, accustomed to living off the countryside, could find no adequate provisions. In addition, the Spanish resistance, though as always plagued by quarrelling leadership, had grown by 1812 into an increasingly effective guerrilla army, more and more able to deny the French freedom of movement except in large units, and therefore more and more capable of aggravating French difficulties in finding enough to eat. Moreover, as the resistance became an effective guerrilla insurgency, able to assert military control of the countryside except where the French were present in large numbers, Wellington skillfully exploited also the classic dilemma of opponents of guerrilla warfare. If the French dispersed their forces over wide areas to deal with the guerrillas and to find subsistence, they lacked adequate concentrations to cope with Wellington's British and Portuguese regulars; if however the French concentrated to face the regulars, then they could not deal with the guerrillas infesting the country and could not find enough subsistence. And in any event, the far-flung geography of the guerrilla resistance almost always kept the French armies divided. In spite of Napoleon's invasion of Russia, those armies still numbered about 230,000 at the beginning of 1812, but Wellington with 45,000 British troops repeatedly beat them in detail.

As the 1812 campaign opened in Iberia, Wellington had also improved his ability to capitalize on the enemy's logistical weakness by rendering his own logistics more secure. Basing his army not only on the sea but on the rivers, in the navigation of which the British had grown adept, he established depots at many places where they could be replenished by ships and boats but where his army was always almost certain to be within relatively easy reach. Thus prepared, Wellington set out on another campaign for possession of the fortified towns that commanded the roads connecting Spain and Portugal, particularly Ciudad Rodrigo and Badajoz. This year he began by staging a feint against the latter, held by part of Soult's army, while he himself with his main force besieged Ciudad Rodrigo.

He opened the siege on January 8, still in the grip of a bitter winter. The French garrison numbered about 2,000; Wellington had a force perhaps ten times as large, in five divisions, but needed to scatter much of it to cover the operation against interference by the 40,000 troops of the French Army of the North or the 50,000 of Marmont's Army of Portugal. It wa precisely in this kind of situation, however, that the necessity to try to control the guerrillas prevented the French from using their numbers to best effect against Wellington.

On the first day of Wellington's siege, a British coup captured high ground overlooking Ciudad Rodrigo. The siege operations then proceeded under the direct supervision of Lieutenant-Colonel Fletcher, the able principal engineer of the Torres Vedras lines. According to the formal practice of siegecraft still in vogue, the British calculated that the siege should require twenty-four days. Word soon arrived, however, that in spite of the guerrillas Marmont was moving northward from the Tagus with his main force to interrupt the siege. Wellington therefore determined to take Ciudad Rodrigo by assault before help could arrive.

Fortunately, his artillery had already blasted two breaches in the French defenses. On the night of January 19 the Allies stormed those breaches. The assault cost 568 casualties, but it carried the town and found among the prizes Marmont's siege train of 150 guns. Wellington now controlled the northern invasion route between Spain and Portugal.

After a feint in which he gestured as if his main force would use this route to plunge deeper into Spain, Wellington hurried south to reinforce the operation against Badajoz. Into a further siege he committed as many as 32,000 men in eight divisions, four of the divisions in the siege lines and four screening the effort, along with a more distant screen. There were about 5,000 defenders, 600 of them sick. Once more the Allies won an early success, investing the town on March 16 and capturing an important outlying post, Fort Picurina, nine days later. Once more, however, Wellington decided he must pass from siege to assault to head off relief; this time Soult with major forces from the Army of the South as well as Marmont took the risks of weakening their campaigns against the guerrillas and their subsistence-gathering to concentrate against Wellington.

The capture of Picurina, however, had enabled the Allies to batter with their siege artillery the weakest part of the fortifications, the southeastern wall, and there three breaches had been opened to afford access for an assault that Wellington scheduled for the night of April 6. So the pattern of the attack against Ciudad Rodrigo repeated itself still further—but not completely. The elite Light Division along with the 4th Division stormed the breaches, but the defenders were prepared for that tactic and repulsed the British. Amid the furor, meanwhile, Lieutenant-General Thomas Picton's 3rd Division assailed the heart of the defenses, el Castillo, the Castle, on the northeast corner. By escalade—a vertical climb—Picton's men contrived to take one of the bastions, which opened the way to overrunning the whole Castle. Shortly afterward Major-General James Leith's 5th Division converted a diversionary assault into a penetration of the northwest corner of the defenses, and the French felt compelled to retreat to Fort San Cristóbal across the Guadiara River. There they surrendered the next day.

Capturing these 5,000 French cost the Allies just short of 5,000 casualties, including 3,350 in the assault; but Wellington now controlled both invasion corridors. The British soldiers vented their anger over the casualties upon the hapless inhabitants of Badajoz, in a frenzy of robbery, rape, and murder that their officers did not bring under control until August 11. There had occurred a foreshadowing of this ugly affair at Ciudad Rodrigo and indeed at many other places in Spain. The habitual xenophobia of the English spilled far less of its contempt upon the French enemy than upon Britain's "dago" allies, despised as a filthy, brutish lot not quite human. Great Britain may often have fought for causes that historians—especially such as speak the English language—have regarded as those of civilization against tyranny, from the wars against Louis XIV through those against Napoleon to the struggle to subdue Hitler; but the fine disdain of the Englishman for any foreigner has never been conducive to strict observance of the principle of noncombatant immunity, a regrettable fact that would reveal itself most devastatingly in British aerial bombing during World War II.

Wellington himself was more readily appalled by the tactical imperfections of his troops than by such indulgences as mayhem directed at civilians. But the ruthless side of the character of this Iron Duke (as he would become known) expressed itself more usefully in the growing maturity of his own version of a strategy of annihilation, that object to be attained, however, not through the thunderstroke of an Austerlitz battle but by the cumulative effects of attrition, by exploiting particularly the logistical weaknesses of the French and their impalement upon the dilemmas of counterguerrilla war to accomplish nothing less than the complete destruction of their armies in Spain. Having opened both major gateways into that country, so that he could strike at either Marmont's Army of Portugal or Soult's Army of the South, he next demonstrated the maturing of his strategic grasp by effectively separating those two enemy armies from each other. In a design superbly executed by Lieutenant-General Sir Rowland Hill, the Allies on May 19 demolished the bridge over the Tagus at Almaraz, which had been the chief means of communication between Marmont and Soult.

In what was becoming his standard strategic *modus operandi*, Wellington then staged an ostentatious show of advancing from Badajoz for further dealings with Soult, only to make a rapid turn north to strike at Marmont instead. He found Marmont's army deployed behind the River Douro, and from mid-June to mid-July the rival armies maneuvered indecisively, sweating under a merciless summer sun, each seeking an advantageous opening that neither found. Wellington laid siege to three strong forts at Salamanca hoping to lure Marmont into a vulnerable position in the course of attempting their relief; but while Wellington captured the forts, Marmont refused the bait. In the middle of July, moreover, Wellington learned that Marmont was about to receive substantial reinforcements, and on July 21 the British commander ordered the evacuation of hospitals and rear-area supplies in preparation for a retreat into Portugal.

Marmont in turn learned of these preparations and decided that Wellington must be vulnerable to a counteroffensive. Not yet reinforced as Wellington anticipated but commanding 50,000 men and seventy-eight guns, the marshal moved to swing around east of Wellington's positions shielding Salamanca and thence to turn back to descend on the Ciudad Rodrigo road, cutting Wellington's line of communications. Wellington had about 46,000 men with sixty guns. Until July 22 he was uncertain whether Marmont's main force was attempting to move around his left or his right, but that morning intelligence pointed correctly to a French maneuver around his right and ultimately toward the Ciudad Rodrigo road.

Before Wellington could forestall him, Marmont that same morning took possession of a commanding height, the Arapiles Mayor or Greater Arapiles, henceforth called by the combatants the French Arapiles, southeast of Salamanca and across the River Tormes. Wellington countered by seizing—barely ahead of a French effort—the Arapiles Menor or Lesser Arapiles, hereafter the English Arapiles, and held the village of Arapiles just west of the French summit and southeast of the English height.

Marmont believed that the English Arapiles and the village constituted the right flank defenses of an Allied position now facing east outside Salamanca. To continue his maneuver toward the Allied line of communications, he instructed his forces to march rapidly westward from the area of the French Arapiles, thus turning Wellington's right and striking for his rear. Wellington, however, now perceived his rival's intentions accurately enough to have anticipated this threat, and with remarkable skill and stealth he conducted a nearly complete change of front, until by noon the Arapiles positions that at the beginning of the day had in fact been his right were essentially his left, with his army facing southward from the English Arapiles for about three miles (five kilometers) to the west southwest. Thus Marmont's intended *manœuvre sur les derrières* would be a march straight across the Allied front, exposing the French right flank to that front. Reverse slopes made it possible for Wellington to conceal this change of front, but it was nevertheless a masterfully conducted maneuver.

Marmont would not only be marching parallel to his enemy's front, but he so conducted his march that his army divided into three segments with considerable gaps between them. The Allies began their assaults upon the exposed French column about 4:45 P.M., when the British 3rd Division struck the leading segment of the French. Meanwhile Portuguese troops assaulted the French Arapiles, which provoked a French counterattack against the English Arapiles and a sharp struggle for control of the heights, ending with each side retaining its original hilltop. Before that resolution, however, the British had broken the van of the French march to the west and sent its fugitives scurrying back into the second segment of the march. While that segment was thus confused, Wellington ordered the 5th Division and a cavalry charge upon it. Its confusion and vulnerability permitted the cavalry to ride on through, breaking several imperfectly formed infantry squares. Marmont himself was among the French casualties, badly wounded.

The battle of Salamanca seemed about to degenerate into a rout of the French then and there, but Bertrand comte Clausel (usually given thus, but more correctly Clauzel), *général de division*, took command in place of Marmont and, though severely wounded also, rallied the Army of Portugal. After assuring that British as well as Portuguese assaults had been safely contained in the Arapiles sector, Clausel sent forward an attack against the British 4th Division, tired out from the Arapiles fighting, and created a virtual rout after all, but in France's favor. He exploited his advantage with a cavalry attack as well executed as the earlier one by the British. Thereby he drove a salient deep into Wellington's position.

But the iron in Wellington's character proved itself especially in adversity. The British general calmly brought up his 6th Division, hitherto lightly engaged, to seal the north shoulder of the salient, while deploying a combination of available Portuguese troops in addition to a concentration of guns against the southern shoulder. Just as calmly, he took care to form a new reserve from the 1st and 7th Divisions, behind the salient. The issue hung briefly in suspense, but Clausel's attackers suffered too many casualties to permit them to sustain their drive, and the French had no more reserves to throw in. The French tide receded.

Salamanca was unquestionably Wellington's greatest victory thus far. His troops inflicted 14,000 casualties in return for 5,214 of their own, and both his change of front in the morning and his cool and decisive response to the crisis of Clausel's attack in the late afternoon bore the marks of possible greatness in generalship. The Allies' trophies included twelve guns, two eagles, and a number of standards. Moreover, the defeat so unnerved King Joseph that he abandoned his capital, and on August 12 Wellington entered Madrid. The French had left a garrison in the Retiro, an inner fortress, and there the Allies captured 1,100 prisoners and an additional 100 guns and two eagles along with a considerable quantity of stores. Wellington turned the prisoners over to Spanish guerrillas as a token of confidence in them but then had to intervene to interrupt a brutal process of killing those who lagged behind on their march to confinement.

The comparative casualty figures and a triumphant entry into Madrid notwithstanding, Salamanca fell short of ranking as an Allied Austerlitz or Jena-Auerstädt. The French army had substantially escaped, and the defeat precipitated a French decision to unite the bulk of their armies in Spain to pose more formidable obstacles before Wellington. Their doing so might ease pressure against the guerrillas, but overall French superiority in numbers of regulars remained so great that a concentration could offer the threat of crushing Wellington through sheer weight, after which the guerrilla resistance would be bereft of its indispensable regular support.

And Wellington's next confrontation with an army commanded by Clausel ended in fact in an Allied setback. His performance at Salamanca won Clausel the command of the Army of the North, which was anchored on the city and castle of Burgos. To forestall the developing French concentration, with large parts of the French Armies of Portugal and the South marching toward Clausel, and also to capture a road junction important to communications between central Spain and France, Wellington laid siege to Burgos beginning September 19. The British commander had grown overconfident, underestimating the strength of fortifications that the French had modernized in 1808, and bringing up an insufficient artillery train and siege equipment. The garrison consisted of 2,000 troops resolutely commanded by Jean Louis Dubreton, *général de brigade*. On the second day the Allies captured one of the most important strongpoints on a height partially dominating the castle itself. But thereafter events turned sour for them. Rain flooded their approach trenches. Four assaults failed. Large French contingents from the Army of Portugal and the Army of the South approached the scene. Wellington attempted a last assault on October 18. Three days later he ordered a retreat, having suffered more than 2,000 casualties to only 623 French losses.

Moreover, the French forces maneuvering in the background were so strong that Wellington felt obliged to abandon not only the siege of Burgos but the possession of Madrid as well. Once more the Spanish capital fell to the French, and Wellington's retreat from Burgos became an episode distressingly reminiscent of Sir John Moore's retreat to Corunna; a prolonged withdrawal across barren terrain eroded discipline and eventually cost 7,000 men who fell out of the ranks.

Wellington spent the winter of 1812–1813 around Ciudad Rodrigo. In spite of the disappointing end of the 1812 campaign, however, it was not the mere standoff that its predecessors had been. The Allies continued to hold Badajoz as well as Ciudad Rodrigo and therefore still controlled the principal invasion routes from Portugal into Spain. The French decision after Salamanca to concentrate much of their force led Soult to abandon Andalusia. The victory of Salamanca prompted the Spanish Cortés to name Wellington to command all the Spanish armies on September 22. Before Salamanca, he was already Earl of Wellington in recognition of Ciudad Rodrigo; Salamanca produced his elevation to Marquess of Wellington on September 11, 1812.

Altogether, Wellington's successes of 1812 were sufficient that the year's campaign has often been considered the opening of the climactic, and for the Allies the victorious, phase of the Peninsular War. The next year, however, afforded the Allies considerably larger offensive opportunities, for the obvious reason that Napoleon's Russian disasters left his Empire lurching into a decidedly uncertain future. To help cope with the Sixth Coalition, the Emperor recalled the Army of Portugal from the Iberian Peninsula. The possibility of numerical odds so greatly favoring the French that they might simply overwhelm the Allies' Peninsular regulars thereby receded almost out of sight.

The Spanish Campaign of 1813: Vitoria

About 137,000 French troops still guarded León and the central provinces of Spain. Of these some 60,000 under the direct command of King Joseph immediately opposed Wellington; they were deployed from Toledo through Madrid behind the River Tormes to the Douro and thence along that stream to the Esla. An additional 63,000 French soldiers occupied Valencia, Aragón, and Catalonia. Reinforcements from the United Kingdom along with additional Portuguese troops had raised Wellington's regular forces to about 75,000. Wellington had also labored during the winter to improve the organization and coordination

of the guerrillas, with some but necessarily uncertain success among their elusive bands. Both sides anticipated that in Iberia, 1813 would be a year of Allied
offensives and French defense.

In June Wellington moved out from Ciudad Rodrigo along the more northerly of the two main invasion routes, to advance across the River Tormes near
Salamanca. This operation was both sufficiently ostentatious and sufficiently
predictable that it occupied most of Joseph's attention, while Lieutenant-
General Sir Thomas Graham with 40,000 men opened another march toward
Burgos. Graham moved north of the Douro through the Trasos Montes, a district
so rugged that Joseph by no means expected trouble from that direction. Consequently this detached force, with Graham leading it energetically through the
mountain passes, was able to turn Joseph's right flank, obliging him as his situation dawned on him to fall back to Burgos. Uncertain of his ability to hold there
as Graham again curled around his right, the King of Spain blew up the castle
that had previously frustrated the Allies and retreated behind the River Ebro.

Thereupon Wellington sent Graham on yet a third turning movement, in
response to which the not-so-enterprising Joseph fell back again, behind the
Zadorra River—except for his extreme right—near the town of Vitoria. In the
process the French abandoned the port of Santander on the north coast, so that
Wellington was able to shift his lines of communications to that place, much
easing his logistics.

Improved logistics facilitated in turn Wellington's assembly of an Allied
army that at last outnumbered the French who confronted it. By the night of
June 20–21 he had brought up to positions across the Zadorra from Joseph's main
body a force of 70,000 men and ninety guns, including 27,500 Portuguese and
nearly 7,000 Spanish regulars. Joseph, seconded by Marshal Jourdan, now commanded only about 50,000 troops, although he had 153 guns and a reasonably
strong defensive position extending from the heights of Puebla on his left
through the Margarita ridge to other heights on the north bank of the Zadorra on
his right. The defensive position would have been stronger, however, had it been
shorter—it stretched for over eight miles (thirteen kilometers); had it been less
close to and less nearly parallel with the Miranda-Vitoria-Bayonne road, the
French line of retreat; and had the French not strangely neglected to destroy the
seven bridges over the Zadorra in their front.

The Allies advanced to the attack on the morning of June 21. There was
nothing especially subtle or ingenious about Wellington's plan for the battle of
Vitoria; the results he was to obtain sprang from the tactical prowess of his army
and the enemy's mistakes, particularly the neglect of the bridges and of the
vulnerability of the road to Bayonne in France. To begin, the Allies simply
moved forward in four columns, Wellington personally commanding two of them
in the center, Graham leading on the left, and Rowland Hill, by now a lieutenant-general and a Knight of the Bath, commanding on the right.

Graham with two Anglo-Portuguese divisions and many of the Spanish had
the most important mission, to cut the Bayonne road, but his deployment was
delayed for various reasons, and it was Hill who attacked first, at dawn. With
some Spanish troops winding around the enemy's extreme left, Hill's spearhead

of British and Portuguese fought their way to the Puebla summit by 8:00 A.M. They pushed on to capture the village of Subijana de Álava, which assured control of the pass over which the Bayonne road crossed the heights, and then held against a series of strong counterattacks.

Wellington's right center column was waiting for Hill to gain further ground that would loosen the French hold in front of it when about noon the bridge at Tres Puentes was discovered to be unguarded, presumably because French artillery could cover it. But French attention was preoccupied elsewhere, by Hill, and Wellington sent troops of the Light Division to rush the bridge. They took it and were quickly reinforced, particularly by the 3rd Division of Lieutenant-General Sir Thomas Picton, who acted on his own initiative when reinforcements who were supposed to precede him were delayed. Picton opened the Puente de Mendoza bridge farther east, as well as using the Tres Puentes crossing.

This right-center British action carried into the flank of two French divisions that had been engaging Hill. The drive reached a strong point, the Knoll of Ariñez. When it halted there, reinforcements came up and Wellington in person led a renewed assault that drove the enemy from the knoll and in retreat toward the town of Vitoria.

These events had a critical impact on the conduct of the French right guarding the Bayonne road. Graham's assault in that sector reached its full momentum only during the afternoon. Honoré Charles Michel Joseph Reille, *comte de l'Empire* and *général de division*, commanding the French right, had been misled into believing that the Spanish contingent that was the first part of Graham's assault to appear consisted of mere guerrillas unfit for stand-up battle. This delusion eased Graham's task in assailing the French-occupied hills north of the Zadorra and overrunning them, to approach the bridges of Gamarra Mayor and Abachuco (or Abechuco), which would carry him to the vital road. The French dug in their heels, however, and for a time clung stubbornly to the bridge approaches—until Hill's attack against the French left in making possible Wellington's rupture of the French center produced the additional domino effect of exposing the rear of the French last stand on the right. Then everything collapsed for Joseph and Jourdan.

In truth, Graham's capture of his heights had already permitted his artillery to make the Bayonne road almost impassable. Now the Allies broke the escape route and obliged the French to resort to a poor back road to Pamplona (Pampeluna) to withdraw from the battlefield. The road was too rough and the adjacent country too rugged to allow Wellington to use his cavalry for much of a pursuit, but it hardly mattered. The French had to leave behind almost all their artillery—the Allies captured 143 guns—along with most of their ammunition, stores, wagons, and baggage, including money equivalent to £1,000,000 and a huge quantity of booty collected over the years in Spain. The trophies included Jourdan's baton, which Wellington sent to the Prince Regent George. One month to the day later, George reciprocated by promoting Wellington to field-marshal.

Allied casualties amounted to some 5,000 against about 7,500 French losses, an uncommonly favorable ratio. More than that, the retreat over an inadequate road so nearly completed the ruin of the French army that Vitoria was almost an Austerlitz or Jena-Auerstädt in reverse, the climactic victory that virtually assured an end to the Peninsular War. But a climax so satisfying to the Allies was the fruit not of one day's battle so much as of the long, bitter struggle of attrition that had weakened Napoleon's forces in Spain to the verge of ruin before the first gun fired at Vitoria.

Through the Pyrenees and into France: Sorauren, the Nivelle, Orthes, Bayonne, Toulouse

The Allied army could now march to the Pyrenees along much of their length, albeit it did so with an indiscipline and yet further indulgence in plunder and rapine of the sort that sadly detract from the luster of Wellington's generalship. He complained about his soldiers' brutality and, with an aristocratic hauteur that was characteristic of him, implied that it was occasioned by their inferior birth; but other generals have exerted much better control of armies no more promising in their raw material.

The French still held the fortresses of San Sebastian and Pamplona short of the Pyrenees. Napoleon reacted to the news of Vitoria by dispatching Marshal Soult back to Spain from the campaign in Germany. Soult abandoned Valencia and on July 11 arrived at Bayonne to try to scrape together there all the forces he could still find for the relief of San Sebastian and Pamplona, which Wellington was trying to reduce. Lacking a sufficient siege train to give adequate attention to both, Wellington merely blockaded Pamplona while commencing a siege of San Sebastian on July 10. Again the approach of a French relief column provoked the Allies into a premature assault on a besieged city, Graham trying to hasten the fall of San Sebastian by mounting an unsuccessful attack on July 25.

Moreover, the approach of Soult's relief columns had taken Wellington by surprise; a tendency toward overconfidence in the wake of victory was another of his weaknesses. Soult sent forces marching from France to break through the Pyrenees by way of the Maya and Roncesvalles Passes. At the former, the French in reinforced corps strength including National Guardsmen, a total of 20,000, attacked a weak British outpost, also on July 25. Even when all British troops within reach had been thrown into the fight, the defenders numbered only about 6,000. A stubborn resistance held off the French for the day, but in the evening the local British commander, Lieutenant-General Sir William Stewart, decided he must retreat. At Roncesvalles on the same day, General Reille led 20,000 French against another numerically inferior force with similar results. The British imposed a day's delay, but Soult's columns were able to push into Spain.

But not far or for long; Wellington might at times be complacent, but he never lacked alertness. He had already collected three divisions, about 24,000 men, with which he marched to Sorauren just north of Pamplona to intercept Soult. The latter was marching at the head of 36,000 to the relief of the blockaded town. Soult attacked on July 28, assailing a strong position on heights south of Sorauren. In spite of slopes so steep that merely climbing them almost destroyed the momentum of the French, the Allies barely held on until reinforcements arrived to hit the French right flank. Repulsed, Soult decided on the next day not to retreat but to shift west to interpose between Wellington and Graham's force near San Sebastian. This decision led to the second battle of Sorauren on July 30, during which the Allies repelled both a French effort to capture Tolosa, the key position between San Sebastian and Pamplona, and a final attempt to take Sorauren under cover of night.

The capable Soult had made about as strong and energetic an effort to regain a measure of initiative against Wellington as dwindling French resources would have permitted anyone to do, but now he decided he must retreat once more across the Pyrenees. His main force did so on August 2. His operations had cost yet another 10,000 casualties, however, to only 7,000 Allied losses. The Allies resumed the siege of San Sebastian, which except for its castle fell to another costly assault on August 31. The castle followed on September 9, and Pamplona on October 31.

By the latter date, Wellington was already carrying the war into France. The French were not completely gone from Spain, Suchet in particular remaining at large in Catalonia; but the British government urged Wellington to leave such forces to wither on the vine while he himself entered Napoleon's homeland. On October 7 the Allies crossed the River Bedassoa in seven columns to penetrate French territory. One of the columns surprised Soult by crossing under the guidance of local fishermen at a place where shifting sands and the width of the estuary at the river mouth had persuaded the French that a passage was impossible. Thereby Wellington turned Soult's right flank and obliged him to retreat.

He fell back to the Nivelle River, toward which Wellington was probing at the time when Napoleon lost the battle of Leipzig. Reinforced to some 60,000 with about a hundred guns, Soult deployed in three entrenched lines along a dangerously extended front, stretching from the Bay of Biscay in front of St-Jean de Luz along high ground south of the river to Amotz and thence along the north bank to Mont Mandarin near St-Jean Pied de Port and the Nive River. The nature of the terrain seemed to compel this lengthy deployment in order properly to anchor the flanks, but it was no doubt a mistake for Soult to concentrate about a third of his force on a narrow portion of the front immediately adjacent to the coast. Wellington, eager to leave the Pyrenees well behind him before winter set in, attacked on November 10, also on an extended front and in five columns. He so directed the columns, however, that a mass of about 50,000 converged on the French center near Amotz. There the Allied concentration was able to rupture the first and second French lines, almost cutting Soult's army in two. The Nivelle was one of the most skillfully conducted of Wellington's battles, though capitalizing on Soult's mismanaged deployment. The French lost seventy of their guns along with 4,450 men to Allied losses of 2,625.

Soult's fallback position was the city of Bayonne at the mouth of the Adour River, to which he withdrew during the night. Wellington promptly closed in on Bayonne, but the weather now turned predictably bad and the Adour and its tributary the Nive unfordable. Moreover, the Spanish and Portuguese governments were neglecting payment and supply of their troops with Wellington, and this carelessness did nothing to obviate the disposition toward plundering that the Spanish especially displayed as soon as they entered France. French conduct toward the guerrillas and the population that sheltered them in Spain had often enough been of a nature to afford the Spanish cause to think that revenge demanded a wide variety of atrocities; such is the character of guerrilla war. Wellington's Spanish soldiery degenerated into so nearly uncontrollable a marauding and murdering rabble that their not overly fastidious British commander decided he must dispatch 25,000 of them back across the Pyrenees. Relations between Wellington and Great Britain on the one hand and Spain on the other grew so strained that the alliance seemed endangered.

In these circumstances military operations had to be virtually suspended, and it was in these circumstances also that Napoleon took up negotiations with Fernando VII, interned at Valençay, leading to the Treaty of Valençay of December 11. Napoleon recognized Fernando as King of Spain and the Indies, subject to sealing a commercial treaty with France and in return for assurance that supporters of King Joseph would be pardoned and that Fernando would help drive the British from Spain. The current Spanish disputes with Wellington were hardly severe enough, however, to persuade the Spanish Regency to accept the Valençay bargain.

Two days before the signing of the Treaty of Valençay, Wellington had resumed active operations. His front facing north against Bayonne extended from the sea to the left bank of the Nive River. To constrict Soult's logistics, Wellington resolved to cross part of his force to the right bank of the Nive to advance against St-Jean Pied de Port, through which much of the French supplies passed. To have shifted the whole Allied force to the Nive, however, would have exposed Wellington's own line of communications. Therefore Wellington dispatched only a portion of his army, under Hill and Sir William Carr Beresford (for Bussaco a Knight of the Bath), down both sides of the Nive toward Villefranque and the French left.

Soult characteristically and promptly grasped the opportunity presented by the division of the Allied army to stage a counterstroke. On December 10, with 60,000 men and forty guns he attacked the Allied left under Major-General John Hope, some 30,000 men and twenty-four guns holding a position on a ridge adjacent to the Bay of Biscay three miles (five kilometers) south of Biarritz. Soult's swift riposte deserved a better reward than it won. Broken ground so much delayed his committing the full weight of his column that Hope was able to hold on until Wellington shifted some of Beresford's troops to the scene. Still undaunted, Soult sparred with the Allies for the next two days, trying to find another area of vulnerability, then on the 13th attacked up the right bank of the Nive against Hill. Once more Soult managed to commit considerably superior numbers, 35,000 to 14,000, but once more the harsh terrain of the approaches to the Pyrenees offset this advantage. Hill clung to high ground in the face of French charges conducted with the desperate zeal of men conscious of a failing cause and an endangered homeland, until Wellington, delayed because a pontoon bridge had been washed away, arrived with reinforcements. The four days' battles around Bayonne cost the French about 7,000 casualties, the Allies about 5,000.

During 1813 Suchet had continued to trade victories and defeats with Allied forces in eastern Spain, but with enemies closing in on French territory from both south and east he withdrew northward of the Pyrenees early in the new year. Wellington scarcely allowed winter to interrupt his activities, resuming operations against Soult as early as February. His first object for 1814 was to pry the latter loose from Bayonne. For this purpose he decided to repeat the maneuver that had carried him across the Bidassoa. The mouth of the Adour below Bayonne, about 5,000 yards (or meters) wide, was so treacherous to navigation, with a dangerous bar and another pattern of shifting sands, that Soult was unlikely to expect a crossing there to turn the French right, or east, flank, notwithstanding the memory of the Bidassoa. Wellington therefore collected in secret a large number of small vessels of the area, called *chasse-marées*, with which to build a bridge without the necessity of accumulating obvious bridging material on the south bank in sight of the French or hauling such material through the sands. To make sure that Soult's attention would mainly focus elsewhere, on February 14 and 15 Wellington began an enveloping maneuver around the opposite French flank, Soult's left.

Soult took the bait, leaving only 10,000 troops to defend Bayonne while moving with the bulk of his remaining 31,000 to Orthes (or Orthez) on the Gave (mountain stream or torrent) Pau to confront Wellington's easterly feint. Wellington in person then hastened back toward the Bay of Biscay to direct the crossing of the Adour.

Bad weather delayed this operation, however, and Wellington decided that he should not leave Soult unwatched by himself for any considerable time. He traveled east again, leaving the Adour crossing to Lieutenant-General John Hope. With the weather improving, Hope conducted several diversionary maneuvers on the Adour above Bayonne and then on February 22 and 23 got some 600 men across in boats at the mouth. The French even then did not take this threat altogether seriously, and a new weapon, the rocket invented by William Congreve of the Royal Laboratory at Woolwich in 1808, helped frighten away such troops as the French did dispatch to the scene; frightening the uninitiated was actually the principal utility of the Congreve rocket, for its destructive power was not great. On the morning of February 24, therefore, Hope was able to complete a bridge of boats, place batteries to protect it, and begin crossing 8,000 troops across the lower Adour. He invested Bayonne on both banks of the river to begin a siege.

The next day Wellington attacked Soult at Orthes, having sent part of his army across the Pau below that place. The Allies advanced eastward toward Soult on both banks of the *gave*. They had 44,000 men and forty-two guns to Soult's 36,000 men and forty-eight guns. The French held a concave ridge extending from Orthes on the Pau northwestward for about three and a half miles (or about five and a half kilometers). Wellington ordered Hill to stage a diversionary attack against Orthes and the French left while Beresford with the 4th and 7th Divisions assailed the right and Picton with the Light, 3rd, and 6th

Divisions struck the center. The intent was that at least the French right and with good fortune the left also would be turned, to cut the enemy's line of retreat as Picton drove in the center.

Beresford initially made good progress, capturing part of the high ground, but then ran into a powerful artillery barrage that checked him and a counterattack led by General Reille that drove him into retreat. The Allied center also was having trouble, when Wellington observed that the pursuit of Beresford's retreat had opened a gap between the enemy's right and center. He quickly sent troops of the Light Division into the gap. He sent Lieutenant-Colonel John Colborne—Sir John Moore's secretary during the Corunna campaign, promoted from major as Moore's dying wish—with the 52nd Regiment of Foot against Reille's rear, while he himself led the 3rd and 6th Foot against Reille's inner flank.

Also about the same time, Hill was using a newly discovered ford to turn the French left. With his battle disintegrating, Soult now faced the prospect that Hill might capture the Sault de Navailles bridge over another mountain stream, the Luy de Béarn, and thus sever his escape route. He had no choice but to cut short the battle and race Hill over the eight miles (thirteen kilometers) separating his army from the bridge. The French narrowly won the race, but the battle of Orthes cost them 2,650 killed and wounded and 1,350 prisoners to slightly over 2,000 Allied casualties. Wellington was now firmly ensconced on French soil, and discouragement visited accelerating desertions upon Soult.

Leaving Bayonne to resist its siege, that marshal turned east at St-Sever to Aire, there to guard roads to Bordeaux and Toulouse. Beresford nevertheless found an alternate road to Bordeaux, which had promised to open its gates to the Allies and did so. Successive Allied blows drove Soult's despairing army from Aire to Tarbes and thence behind the Garonne River to Toulouse. Here Soult tried in vain to raise the countryside against Wellington as a substitute for those soldiers who were running away.

Wellington hoped to cross the Garonne above Toulouse in order to interpose between Soult and Suchet and then attack the city from the south. He found the terrain too difficult, however, and so crossed below Toulouse at Grenade beginning April 3. But after some 19,000 men had crossed, the Allies' pontoon bridge washed away, leaving the force on the right bank isolated from April 5 to 8. Fortunately for the Allies, Soult's army was no longer in any condition to take advantage of this opportunity, the energy of its commander notwithstanding. On the 8th the Allies captured a bridge at Croix d'Orade, and they now closed in on Toulouse. Wellington had some 49,000 troops at hand, Soult about the same number, of whom nearly 10,000 were local National Guards.

Wellington scheduled his attack on Toulouse for Easter Sunday, April 10. His first objective was the ridge of Mont Rave and its Height of Calvinet, commanding the city from the east and studded with earthworks. To reach this objective, Beresford was dispatched with the 4th and 6th Divisions and a flank guard of cavalry to make a two-mile (three-kilometer) flank march north of the city, while other troops busied the French defenders west of Toulouse. Beresford's column was troubled on the way by muddy ground, artillery fire, occasional musketry, and menacing gestures on the part of Soult's cavalry, along with growing evidence that the supporting diversions were encountering much worse problems. Nevertheless, Beresford persisted onto the high ground and after bitter, seesaw fighting managed to take it. Fittingly, the climax of the battle of Toulouse was shaped by the stubbornness and tactical skill of the British infantry.

Fittingly, because Toulouse was the last major battle of the Peninsular War, which had turned so often on those same qualities of the British Army. The loss of Mont Rave and Calvinet forced Soult to withdraw into the inner defenses of the city, but these were untenable against enemy guns firing from the commanding environs. At 9:00 P.M., on April 11 Soult withdrew southward toward Carcasonne. In the contest for Toulouse, the Allies lost about 4,500, the French 3,236.

The Allies entered the city on April 12. That evening they received news that cut short the Peninsular War.

The Peninsular War: An Assessment

It had been a war fought without the displays of strategic genius so often illuminating other Napoleonic campaigns. It also strikes the military critic as approaching closer than most Napoleonic campaigns to some quintessential model of war, in which genius is rare, and in which decision reached as on the Peninsula only through a terrible process of prolonged attrition is more typical than the thunderstrokes of an Austerlitz or a Jena-Auerstädt. Certainly the Peninsular War with its guerrilla actions as well as its campaigns of attrition seems in the late twentieth century more a harbinger of "modern" war than the other Napoleonic struggles; it is a pity that even the British were so transfixed by the glamor of Napoleon that they subsequently tended to study this, their own Napoleonic land campaign, less than the battles in which the Emperor was more frequently present. Their army might have been better prepared for twentieth-century war had it developed a better understanding of the Peninsula.

As for the absence of genius, Wellington was a highly capable general, but he triumphed in the end not because his strategic and operational designs were inspired but because he was resolute, because he was able to turn the logistics of the Iberian Peninsula to his advantage in a war of attrition, because the Spanish guerrilla uprising helped him and particularly did so in the logistical realm, and because in battle he could rely on the long-standing tactical excellence of the British infantry as it had been refurbished since the 1790s especially by Sir John Moore.

Moreover, just as the Peninsular War ended abruptly because of events elsewhere, so its entire shape depended on events beyond Iberia. If Napoleon had not embarked on the Russian expedition of 1812 and thus become caught up in accumulating disasters, he might have found the means to overcome both the Iberian guerrillas and their British patrons. After all, the British aversion to military commitments on land kept Wellington's regular forces limited to a small scale compared with the armies farther north and east. Yet it is also true that while Wellington's success on the Peninsula depended upon events in other theaters of war, the Iberian campaigns made a considerable contribution toward draining French military manpower ultimately beyond recovery.

The limitations of Great Britain's willingness to invest men and resources in its army even during the struggle against Napoleon remain as a salient feature of the Peninsular War—and of course of all the Napoleonic Wars. British sea power could confine Napoleon to the European Continent and injure the economy of his empire, but it could not strangle the economy of an empire of continental extent, and militarily it could not bring Napoleon down. Land power was needed to do that. Given the duration and expense of Britain's struggle against Napoleon, including the expense of subsidizing one anti-French coalition after another only to have most of the coalitions dissolve, the British would probably have invested their resources much more wisely in a larger and more effective army that could have given the island kingdom a larger role in the only direct means of destroying Napoleon's empire, the campaigns on land. Yet the Peninsular War contributed just enough to the downfall of Napoleon that the British drew from it confirmation of the myth that continental adversaries can be overcome principally by sea power and that a professional land force of continental proportions is not a necessary ingredient of British power.

Military professionalism and effectiveness as well as size of forces entered into the limitations of British land power. The officers of Britain's Peninsular army from Wellington down remained professional only to the degree that self-education and experience could make them so, except for artillery and engineering officers who since the mid-eighteenth century could be schooled in these technical specialties at the Royal Military Academy at Woolwich. It is true that for infantry and cavalry officers, the foundations of the Royal Military Academy, Sandhurst of the present day, were laid in the Napoleonic era. The Duke of York sponsored a school for infantry and cavalry officers in 1799, and a small institution opened at High Wycombe. In 1801 this school was divided into junior and senior departments. The former moved to Marlow and then in 1812 to Sandhurst. The latter remained at High Wycombe and in the middle of the nineteenth century was to evolve into the Staff College, Camberley. But very few young officers emerged from these schools in time to participate in the Peninsular War, and the Sandhurst curriculum would long remain unimpressive. Although the demands of war diluted the social qualifications expected of British officers and drastically reduced the proportion of commissions secured by purchase, the commissioned ranks of the British Army remained haphazardly professional, dedication to study of the arts of command remaining largely a matter of individual or at best regimental whim. The personal influence of Wellington tended to be detrimental to professional growth, not because of a Napoleonic conviction that everything should depend on his individual genius, which he was far too commonsensical to imagine he possessed, but because he was altogether anti-intellectual; after the Napoleonic Wars, when his influence on the entire British Army became predominant for a whole generation, the effects of this bias upon British military professionalization would grow more devastating still.

Because military professionalism is so closely related to the technical skills of engineering, it is significant of British limitations (the college at Woolwich notwithstanding) that Wellington's army was never adequately stocked with the tools and skills of military engineering. It never possessed an adequate siege train, so that conducting sieges was always a more troublesome endeavor than it should have been, and it was partly for this reason that premature assaults occurred so often. Nor did the Peninsular army ever possess an adequate corps of sappers and miners to assist in building siege works. Amateurism and penny-pinching together conspired against the effectiveness of the army in its technical branches.

Nor did Wellington's army ever possess an adequate transport train, for the same reasons. Wellington contrived to have better logistical support than the French in spite of rather than because of the workings of the supply departments at home. He exploited the advantages given him by the Royal Navy and sea-based logistics, by guerrilla interference with his enemy's supplies, and by his own careful administration and hoarding of the logistical resources available to him. It was in the administration and maintenance of his army that Wellington himself was most nearly professional. In spite of limited resources, he made logistics a trump card for his own army and a fatal weakness for the enemy. Not so much through military strategy as through the superior exploitation of available logistical resources did Wellington find the means of winning his war of attrition.

Spain's guerrilla rising also was advantageous to him. It would be unprofitable to try to recount in detail the Spanish guerrilla operations against Napoleon. Like all guerrilla wars, this one was resolved by the total effects of countless raids upon supply depots, outposts, and moving trains laden with matériel, each raid in itself a small affair and more likely than not never recorded in any historical detail. But taken together, the Spanish guerrilla operations not only helped give Wellington his logistical advantages but also gave him an additional indispensable strategic asset, the prevention of French concentrations of force that could have overwhelmed Wellington's army, until the final phase of the war when the French had lost their numerical preponderance.

The Spanish guerrillas were so indispensable to British success in the Peninsular War that it is altogether fitting that the very word guerrilla—Spanish for little war—entered the English language mainly out of the Peninsular War. It is significant also that the first major guerrilla rising to be widely studied as such (though of course the phenomenon of the guerrilla was about as old as the history of war) seems to have contributed greatly to a legacy of disorder and brutality in postwar Spain that has lasted almost until the present day. Guerrilla war involves breaking almost all the rules usually limiting the violence of war, particularly the principle of noncombatant immunity, which falls victim to the guerrillas' blurring if not erasing of the distinction between noncombatant and combatant. Guerrilla war therefore inevitably nourishes a contempt for all rules. Disregard for rules in an arena of guerrilla war tends to spread from the rules limiting the violence of war to all the laws safeguarding an ordered society. The contempt for law nourished by guerrilla war almost always ends by rupturing the social compact itself in any country or region that becomes a theater of guerrilla war. Almost every arena of guerrilla war has been wracked by political and social instability for decades thereafter. Not least in its impact upon the subsequent history of Spain did the guerrilla war against Napoleon set the pattern for modern guerrilla warfare. Twentieth-century devotees of the cult of the guerrilla ought to be mindful of this history.

Napoleon's 1814 Campaign of Maneuver: Sparring

While Soult fought his delaying actions near the northern foot of the Pyrenees during the turn of 1813 into 1814, Napoleon labored to reverse the course of the larger war that was approaching France's eastern borders. If he could yet do this, then Wellington and Spain could be dealt with later.

The Emperor of the French had brought only about 80,000 effective soldiers back across the Rhine with him. At the time, more than 100,000 were still confronting Wellington and the Spanish, and another 20,000 were in the southeast of France watching the passes out of the Alps; some of these might be drawn off for the major contest. Another 100,000 or so had been left behind in various fortresses in Germany and Poland, but these were largely invalids, recent conscripts, and foreigners.

The conscription machinery of the Empire was in the process of attempting to call up no less than 936,000 additional soldiers, but the machinery proved to have become rusty in the extreme. The efforts of General Clarke, duc de Feltre, as Minister of War were so bumbling that it is hard to reject the suspicion of disloyalty. The disease of disloyalty was in any event being diligently transmitted throughout France by an Allied propaganda campaign suggesting that the coalition powers had no quarrel with the French people but only with Napoleon, and that it was only the egomania of the Emperor that still prolonged the war that had already strained France for so many years and killed or maimed so many of its sons. At the lowest levels of the conscription effort as well as in the high councils of the Ministry of War this propaganda and the deep, deep weariness on which it preyed acted to sabotage the Emperor's purposes, and Napoleon could never muster more than about 150,000 of his hoped-for 936,000 levies into his ranks.

Predictably, the Allies nevertheless accorded him a respite on the Rhine frontier. The march across Germany in deteriorating autumn weather had strained the Allied armies almost as badly as the French. Typhus and dysentery ravaged the ranks on both sides of the Rhine. Rest, resupply, and reorganization were as essential to further operations by Blücher, Schwarzenberg, and Bernadotte as to Napoleon. Paradoxically, it was also a problem for the Allies that there was a measure of truth in the propaganda claim that their only enemy was Napoleon, not the French nation. As final victory drew almost within reach, they disagreed about what to do with the French Emperor, his country, and his conquests. They conducted diplomatic negotiations with French emissaries based vaguely on demands for the restriction of France to its natural frontiers; in these negotiations Napoleon was grateful to indulge them, because diplomacy might purchase more time while it also aggravated interallied quarrels. Meanwhile, even on the fringes of Napoleon's empire the Allies did not find everything going their way. An Austrian invasion combined with a popular revolt drove the French from Illyria, but in Italy Eugène was able to contain and occasionally defeat the Austrians with an army mostly of raw Italian levies, turning back overtures offering him Italy if he betrayed Napoleon.

Meanwhile the Prussian reformers civil and military, attaching to themselves a nascent party of German nationalists from other states in a movement that offered the first glimmerings of a later Prussian leadership toward a united Germany, pressed for a rapid replenishment of the Allied armies and a prompt resumption of active campaigning. They prevailed sufficiently to deny Napoleon his hope that his enemies might go into winter quarters. On New Year's Day 1814, the seventy-year-old Blücher, the symbolic focus of the German nationalists, set his Army of Silesia to crossing the Rhine between Koblenz and Mannheim.

With about 100,000 men, Blücher intended to strike first for Nancy. Schwarzenberg's Army of Bohemia of about 200,000 soon moved somewhat reluctantly in support. The Allies had leaned on Switzerland hard enough to secure Swiss permission for passage through the Basel area to threaten the flank of French forces attempting to block Blücher's path. Bernadotte with the Army of the North was also supposed to move out, marching with 120,000 men through the Netherlands and Laon; but he was typically slow in getting under way and did not reach Laon until March.

On the New Year's Day when Blücher's movement began, Napoleon showed his desperation by ordering qualified officers back from the frontier to their home districts to organize partisans, that is, guerrillas. But the French population proved far too worn out by war to respond to the call, and most local civil authorities bestirred themselves even less for this purpose than the military authorities had for the draft. The notion that the struggle now belonged only to Napoleon and need not concern the French people was taking hold.

Beyond this forlorn hope, Napoleon's strategy had to emphasize the defense of Paris. The political capital was also his principal arsenal and his communications center. He had to hold as much of France as possible to continue to have as large as possible a recruiting ground, but Paris was indispensable to continuing the war.

Therefore Napoleon would pivot around Paris, hoping that the Allies would grant him opportunities to defeat their armies separately. As much as possible, fortresses were to be garrisoned by the National Guard, by new conscripts, and by limited-service troops; such defenders might in spite of their shortcomings tie down substantial numbers of the invaders in siege operations, while maximum numbers of able-bodied French veterans were to be freed to resist the Allied spearheads. In particular, the fortress system of the Low Countries, supported by the 15,500-man I Corps of Maison, was expected to prevent invasion by that route.

Nevertheless, the sense of desperation implicit in the call for partisan war was well founded. Napoleon's defensive plans and preparations had by no means progressed far enough to stem the Allied tide that proved to rise so early in the

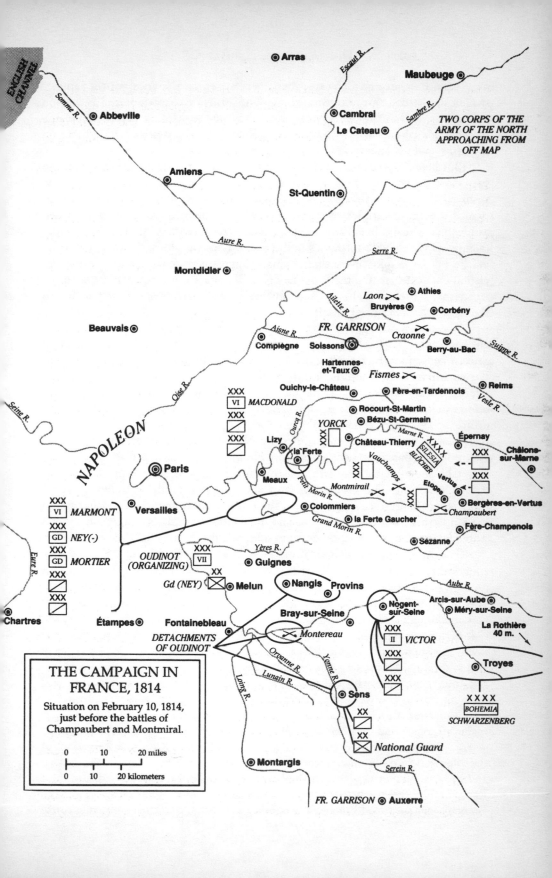

ENGLISH CHANNEL

◉ Arras

Maubeuge ◉

Escaut R.

◉ Cambrai

Le Cateau ◉

Sambre R.

*TWO CORPS OF THE
ARMY OF THE NORTH
APPROACHING FROM
OFF MAP*

Somme R.

◉ Abbeville

◉ Amiens

St-Quentin ◉

Aure R.

Montdidier ◉

Serre R.

Laon ⚔

◉ Athies

Bruyères ◉

◉ Corbény

Beauvais ◉

FR. GARRISON

Ailette R.

Craonne

Suippe R.

Aisne R.

Compiègne ◉

◉ Soissons ◉

Berry-au-Bac ◉

Hartennes-
et-Taux ◉

Fismes ⚔

Vesle R.

◉ Reims

Oise R.

Ouichy-le-Château ◉

◉ Fère-en-Tardennois

XXX
| VI | MACDONALD

◉ Rocourt-St-Martin

XXX
⟋

◉ Bézu-St-Germain

Marne R.

Épernay ◉

Châlons-
sur-Marne

XXX
⟋

Lizy ◉

YORCK
XXX

Château-Thierry ◉

XXXX
SILESIA
BLÜCHER

NAPOLEON

◉ la`Ferte

Ourcq R.

Vauchamps

XXX

Vertus ◉

XXX

◉ Paris

Meaux ◉

Montmirail

Petit Morin R.

Étoges ◉

◉ Bergères-en-Vertus

XXX
⟋

XXX
| VI | MARMONT

◉ Versailles

Colommiers ◉

Grand Morin R.

◉ la Ferte Gaucher

Champaubert

◉ Fère-Champenois

XXX
| GD | NEY(-)

◉ Sézanne

XXX
| GD | MORTIER

OUDINOT
(ORGANIZING)

XXX
| VII |

Yères R.

◉ Guignes

XX

Eure R.

XXX
⟋

Gd (NEY) | XX | ◉ Melun

◉ Nangis

Provins ◉

Aube R.

Arcis-sur-Aube ◉

XXX
⟋

◉ Chartres

◉ Étampes

◉ Fontainebleau

Bray-sur-Seine

Nogent-
sur-Seine ◉

◉ Méry-sur-Seine

*DETACHMENTS
OF OUDINOT*

⚔ *Montereau*

XXX
| II | VICTOR

La Rothière
40 m. →

Orvanne R.

Yonne R.

XXX
⟋

◉ Troyes

Loing R.

Lunain R.

◉ Sens

XXX
⟋

XX

XXXX
BOHEMIA
SCHWARZENBERG

**THE CAMPAIGN IN
FRANCE, 1814**

Situation on February 10, 1814,
just before the battles of
Champaubert and Montmiral.

XX

National Guard

◉ Montargis

Serein R.

0   10   20 miles

0   10   20 kilometers

FR. GARRISON ◉ Auxerre

new year. Blücher and Schwarzenberg overran eastern France with a rapidity that in the latter's case was astonishing. The Army of Silesia entered Nancy on January 25. Advancing quickly up the valley of the Moselle River, Blücher's forces made contact with Schwarzenberg's advance guard near La Rothière on the afternoon of January 28.

But here Napoleon offered his first riposte. He had become aware that the two most dangerous Allied armies were on the point of converging, and he resolved that he must accept the risks of action with inferior numbers against one of the enemy armies to try to prevent the juncture. At least, both Allied armies had already been weakened as Napoleon intended by dropping off detachments to deal with fortresses in their rear. Because Blücher's was the weaker of the enemy armies even though more aggressively commanded, Napoleon lashed out at it first. On the same day that Blücher's van made contact with the Austrians, a French raid surprised Blücher's headquarters and nearly captured the *Generalfeldmarschall* himself.

The next morning, however, Blücher enjoyed the good fortune of receiving an intercepted copy of Napoleon's orders for a counterattack. The Army of Silesia consequently retreated a short distance to cover the exits from the Bar-sur-Aube defile and to await reinforcement from Schwarzenberg. The French harassed the withdrawal but were hampered by snowstorms in their efforts to locate and fix the enemy center of gravity. The Allies suffered similar difficulties in reconnaissance. Blücher had 53,000 men at hand and was soon in firm contact with Schwarzenberg despite Napoleon's intentions, so that he was assured of support from another 60,000. He moved to attack in turn on February 1. But he aimed at La Rothière and thus unwittingly at the strongest sector of Napoleon's front. The French had only about 40,000 available troops, many of them recent conscripts, but they held their ground until nightfall. Blücher won a kind of victory, capturing fifty guns and the contested position, but losses in men were about equal, some 6,000 on each side, and the French disengaged adroitly.

The Allies chose to regard La Rothière as a bigger triumph than it was, congratulating themselves on having beaten Napoleon on French soil. This mood was not conducive to bestirring Schwarzenberg from his customary lethargy, but it inflated Blücher's confidence and impatience and led to his seeking and obtaining his King's permission to resume his advance on February 4, at the risk of relinquishing his contact with Schwarzenberg. Blücher would advance along the south bank of the River Marne toward Paris, while Schwarzenberg swung through Troyes to get astride the Seine toward the same ultimate objective, but meanwhile with only a corps of Cossacks to cover Blücher's left and maintain contact between the Armies of Silesia and Bohemia.

Moreover, Blücher, confident that the French were too weak for a further major response, had by February 6 allowed his army to break into four separate groups. By the night of February 7 Blücher himself was at Sézanne well south of the Marne, while his other three detachments were at Épernay on the Marne and Montmirail and Étages near the River Le Petit Morin between Sézanne and Épernay. Reinforcements were well behind around Vitry. During that night the French again surprised Blücher's headquarters, and to his at least equal surprise the field marshal learned that Napoleon with his main body was on the verge of contriving another riposte after all, to fall on the scattered groups of the Army of Silesia. And the same gloomy night brought tidings that the Cossacks had withdrawn, to leave Blücher's left completely exposed.

As when he digested the evidence of Napoleon's earlier design for a counterstroke and reacted to his own earlier brush with captivity, Blücher was not too proud to pull in his horns, to retreat and seek a reunion with Schwarzenberg. But this time his overconfidence following La Rothière had allowed the Army of Silesia to become too badly strung out. On February 9 Napoleon marched north from Sézanne through rain and mud, many of the inhabitants turning out to help drag his guns now that acquaintance with the Allied soldiers was beginning to overcome their war-weariness. This hard marching permitted the Emperor next day with 30,000 men of Marmont's VI Corps and Ney's corps of the Imperial Guard to descend upon 5,000 Russians near the village of Baye, just north of Étages and Champaubert. In an action that has taken its names from the latter towns, the Russians were not only beaten but subjected to a double envelopment by French cavalry, suffering 4,000 losses to only 200 French casualties, the Russian detachment thus being practically destroyed.

Napoleon immediately marched west along the north bank of Le Petit Morin to catch another Russian detachment of about 18,000 near Montmirail the next day, February 11. First using some 10,500 men mostly of the Old Guard to fix the Russians in place, Napoleon went over to a full attack when Mortier's Guard corps arrived to raise his strength to 20,000. Again the enemy was driven from the field, with losses of about 4,000 that were twice the casualties of the French.

Marmont, left behind at Étages, was unfortunately in the meantime expelled from that place in a counterattack executed by yet another of Blücher's detachments. The Prussian field marshal thus continued to display aggressiveness to the brink of recklessness even in the midst of discomfiture. Since Mortier had been pursuing both the force beaten at Montmirail and a Prussian corps under Yorck that had hovered on the fringe of the Montmirail battle, it was evident that Blücher's threat to Étages could not be overwhelmingly heavy in numbers; the French knew what strength they had been chasing. Therefore, while Marmont conducted a well-ordered retreat, Napoleon countermarched from Montmirail to rejoin him and deal Blücher another direct blow. The Emperor met Marmont near Vauchamps to create a combined force of about 25,000. As Napoleon correctly estimated, Blücher had only about 20,000 of his dispersed army at hand. The French attacked on February 14, quickly driving in an Allied cavalry screen. Before Napoleon could properly deploy his infantry and artillery on wet ground to complete the victory, however, Blücher perceived his peril and drew away. The French harried his retreat so effectively, nevertheless, that his total casualties of Vauchamps swelled to 7,000 men and sixteen guns along with considerable numbers of wagons. The French lost only about 600.

Champaubert, Montmirail, and Vauchamps stirred memories of the young General Bonaparte of the first Italian campaign. Never had Napoleon more skillfully used interior lines and the flexibility of autonomous corps and divisions to strike successive blows against separate opponents than in these actions of the late winter of 1814. Adversity seemingly had reincarnated the general of maneuver warfare who in recent years had lost his place to a Napoleon relying on the strength of numbers to carry him toward inordinately ambitious goals.

And with Blücher for the moment so thoroughly discomfited that no aggressiveness of temperament could immediately return him to the offensive, it was Schwarzenberg's turn to face the rejuvenated Bonaparte. Napoleon in fact hoped initially to continue the pressure against Blücher, to pursue his old favored strategy of annihilation to the destruction of the Army of Silesia, then to be able to assail Schwarzenberg from the rear. The Austrian field marshal, however, though no less leisurely in his generalship than usual, had advanced the foremost elements of the Army of Bohemia as far as Fontainebleau, and consequently he represented too great a danger to Paris to be ignored even briefly. Leaving Marmont and Mortier to harass Blücher, Napoleon hurried his other available forces southward. Some units marched as far as sixty miles (ninety-seven kilometers) in two days.

As early as February 17 French cavalry drove back Schwarzenberg's northwest spearhead from Mormant and Nangis, which precipitated a more general Allied withdrawal throughout the day, briskly harried by the French. Unfortunately for Napoleon, Marshal Victor with the II Corps chose to halt for the night when he found a comfortable château three miles (five kilometers) short of Montereau, where bridges over both the Seine and Yonne Rivers constituted important escape routes for Schwarzenberg's advance elements. Also on the 17th Schwarzenberg tried to fend off Napoleon's pressure by dispatching to the French a prevaricating message that the peace negotiations had led to the signing of a preliminary treaty and that he was accordingly suspending offensive operations; in fact the Allies had broken off negotiations on February 10.

Well enough informed about his own diplomacy that he was not lulled—Schwarzenberg's ploy was little short of preposterous—Napoleon set his sights on the Montereau bridges for the 18th. He replaced Victor with Maurice Étienne Gérard, *général de division, baron de l'Empire*, and commander of the cavalry assault at Mormant. Gérard carefully massed all the artillery he could find and then under an exceedingly heavy barrage launched his attack on Montereau about three in the afternoon, aiming at a ridge that was the bulwark of the Allied position. Napoleon himself led the guns forward to support the infantry attack. With the Allies attempting to disengage, Claude Pierre Pajol, *général de division* and *comte de l'Empire*, led his cavalry division—many of the troopers raw recruits—in a headlong charge across the Seine bridges, through Montereau, and on across the Yonne bridge. Many of the Allies were cut off, and their total casualties amounted to some 6,000 men and twenty-five guns, in contrast to 2,500 French casualties. The use of the artillery and of the mobile arm to assure decision at Montereau was as skillful as in any battle Napoleon had ever commanded.

Napoleon's ability to follow up the success of Montereau was limited by his lack of a bridge train, one of the penalties of his losses during the preceding two years and of the weariness of France. His pursuit had to funnel through Montereau until Macdonald could restore the bridge twenty miles (thirty-two kilometers) up the Seine at Bray. Schwarzenberg used the respite to send the Army of Bohemia into a general retreat from the Troyes area back toward Bar-sur-Aube.

Beyond Napoleon's latest victories, the Austrian commander believed the French Emperor's army to be much bigger than it actually was—as large as 180,000—and imagined that he was seriously menaced in rear by Marshal Augereau, who commanded a French army on the River Rhône but was in fact doing very little. In these circumstances, Schwarzenberg was unwilling to risk committing the Austrian Army even to another Wagram, let alone another Austerlitz, when the political councils of the Habsburg Empire were uncertain whether they wanted to insist on a harder peace than they might already be in a position to get. The intention to make a substantial retreat had to be concealed as much as possible, however, not only from Napoleon but also from the Tsar of Russia and the King of Prussia, until it was a *fait accompli*; yet least of all did Schwarzenberg intend to jeopardize the Austrian Army for the interests of those allies.

Largely to further this purpose of concealment, Schwarzenberg late on February 21 ordered a reconnaissance in force along his front. The reconnaissance collided with the French cavalry screen the next morning. Oudinot with the VII Corps drove Allied forces from a suburb of Méry-sur-Seine lying west of the river and pushed on across the Méry bridge into the town. This action presented Blücher with additional cause for restraint; the van of the Army of Silesia had been hovering north of Méry. Thereupon Napoleon felt satisfied that he could risk a major attack against Schwarzenberg the next day, February 22. Although he had only 70,000 men on hand against Schwarzenberg's 100,000, and although as always in the 1814 campaign many of Napoleon's soldiers were still green and unskillful, the Emperor was confident that he could win the very Wagram or even Austerlitz that Schwarzenberg feared.

And considering the remarkable restoration of Napoleon's military skills now that he was no longer badly overextended, such a victory may well have been ripe for the taking—except that Schwarzenberg quickly followed his reconnaissance of the 21st with a resumption of his retreat, this time in direct defiance of Alexander and Frederick William. He left only one division to hold Troyes until February 24, a task accomplished by threatening to burn the city if Napoleon attacked while promising to evacuate on the morning of the 24th.

Meeting at Bar-sur-Aube the next day, the Russian and Austrian Emperors and the Prussian King agreed after much of the usual squabbling to allow the retreat to continue to Langres. Augereau had commenced just enough activity to lend a touch of credence to Schwarzenberg's fears about him, and the equivalent of two Austrian corps were detached from the main army to reinforce the troops charged with containing him. At the same time, however, the Allied council of war agreed to allow the irrepressible Blücher to resume the offensive, as he had been insisting he must. To that end, they reinforced the Army of Silesia with two corps from Bernadotte's army, the British overcoming the latter's objections by threatening to cut off their subsidies to Sweden. By bringing about this decision, Blücher and the Prussians made all the difference to the 1814 campaign.

Napoleon's 1814 Campaign of Maneuver: Laon, Paris, Fontainebleau

Napoleon had dealt the Prussians so many bloody noses and black eyes in recent days that at first he was loath to believe that they were already returning to the offensive; he was so accustomed to dealing with the Austrians that he had come to expect his other continental opponents to behave like them. Therefore he initiated only limited countermeasures when he learned that Blücher had driven Marmont from La Ferté-Gaucher on February 26. The next day, however, new reports made it evident that Blücher was striking for Paris, so that Napoleon left Macdonald with 40,000 troops to hold the line of the River Aube while the Emperor himself with the bulk of his army turned northward yet again (leaving behind misinformation that Napoleon would soon arrive at Bar-sur-Aube).

Learning nevertheless of Napoleon's countermarch in his direction, and aware of the French shortage of bridging equipment, Blücher was sufficiently cautious that he pulled his whole army north of the Marne River and then north of the Aisne as well, the better to make contact with the reinforcements due from Bernadotte's army. As the Prussian leaders foresaw, Napoleon's logistical limitations again frustrated him, as they had in the pursuit of Schwarzenberg. The French reached the Marne on March 1, in time to gobble up a few wagons and stragglers but not in time to prevent the Army of Silesia from breaking the Marne bridges. It took Napoleon sixteen hours to have the bridge at La Ferte repaired and the march resumed. This delay was critical in affording Blücher time to cross the Aisne, because while part of his army could use a bridge at Berry, the Prussians also had to call on their own bridge train to build a pontoon bridge. And Napoleon's initial delay in responding to Blücher's latest offensive had of course also helped provide time for Allied reinforcements to arrive.

Yet the reinvigorated Napoleon was still driving hard. Blücher had decided to take position on the plateau of Craonne just north of the Aisne, draw Napoleon into an attack, and then turn the tables with a Napoleonic maneuver of his own, an enveloping attack to be executed by the first of the reinforcing corps along with 11,000 cavalry. Napoleon, however, anticipated this design and was prepared to trap the enveloping force should the maneuver develop. Moreover, French bayonets were charging forward on March 7 before Blücher found time to complete his dispositions. With only 37,000 French soldiers against 80,000 Allies—though not all of the latter had finished their march to the field— Napoleon still took the risk of dividing his smaller force to attempt to execute almost a mirror image of Blücher's plan. A French frontal attack fixed the Allied forces on the Craonne plateau while Marshal Ney set forth on an enveloping maneuver. Once more Napoleon seemed to be performing nearly at his old-fashioned best; but once more, as had happened too often, Ney failed him. The marshal attacked prematurely, and the Allies were able both to batter Ney and to fend off Napoleon.

Nevertheless, French casualties at Craonne were only slightly higher than

Allied, 5,400 to 5,000, and Blücher yielded the battlefield to fall back on Laon and a rendezvous with reinforcements that included the corps of the able General von Bülow, Graf Dennewitz. Advancing with a reinforced army of 47,600 against an Army of Silesia now somewhat over 80,000, Napoleon planned characteristically not only to maintain the initiative but to essay yet another *manœuvre sur les derrières*. This time the enveloping maneuver fell to Marmont and the VI Corps. But yet again at Laon on March 9 Napoleon was ill served by his key subordinate—the bane of so many battles for the genius who depended too much on himself and had never developed an adequate professionalism among his lieutenants. Marmont committed the opposite of Ney's recent error, delaying too long before setting his column in motion. The hesitation permitted the enemy to anticipate his move, and General Yorck fell on Marmont with superior force, nearly destroying him. The VI Corps had to retreat through the difficult Festieux Defile. As it approached this narrow escape route, a Prussian column was about to cut it off; but Colonel Étienne Fabvier, discerning the threat and on his own initiative countermarching toward it with his 1,000 men and two guns, struck the Prussians in flank and created enough of a diversion to keep the road open. Just afterward, Prussian cavalry were again on the verge of closing off retreat, when 125 men of the Old Guard, on the scene because they were escorting a convoy, held off an immensely larger force of horsemen.

Napoleon did not learn about all the essentials of Marmont's failure until five the next morning. He then decided to remain for the day in his own position on high ground south of Laon. He knew that a substantial part of Blücher's army had pursued Marmont. If that pursuit had left only a rear guard in front of him, he ought to be able to defeat such a force. If on the other hand the bulk of Blücher's army remained before him, then an aggressive posture should help ease pressure against Marmont. In fact, both scenarios partly developed. Four corps had followed Marmont, so that reconnaissance encouraged Napoleon to launch tentative frontal assaults. Blücher himself was sick, however, and Gneisenau lacked the field marshal's irrepressible daring. In response to Napoleon's activity he called back Marmont's pursuers. Marmont completed his escape, but the Prussians were concentrated again before Napoleon could transform his efforts into anything decisive. At the close of the day, he withdrew after all.

Largely because of Marmont's flirtation with disaster, French losses at Laon numbered 6,000 to the Allies' 4,000. It was these figures rather than any spectacular battlefield dénouement that made Laon a critical action—the statistics, in combination with the fact that Laon was the first major battle of 1814—La Rothière had not merited such a description—that was in any sense a French defeat. Since New Year's Day, Napoleon had kept his empire alive in spite of an exhausted national will and nearly exhausted resources through what amounted almost to a series of conjuring tricks—operational and tactical maneuvers so reminiscent of the days of his highest skill that they offset all manner of weaknesses. Yet French weaknesses were so blatant that only one break in the succession of small triumphs might well destroy forever the illusion that the Napoleonic Empire retained enough strength to survive. Laon was the break in the series; Blücher's unremitting aggressiveness there at length found its reward in an Allied victory just impressive enough to shift the moral balance back from the Napoleon who had so adroitly conjured it into his hands and into the possession of the Allies.

Laon left Napoleon's army psychologically shaken as well as physically tired. Napoleon decided he must rest the troops, which he did first at Soissons and then at Rheims (Reims). For a few days the continuation of Blücher's illness allowed the French a relatively undisturbed repose.

On March 14, however, Schwarzenberg at length began moving again, perhaps stimulated by news from the Pyrenees and the continental Allies' fear that after all Wellington might precede them into Paris. Leaving Mortier and Marmont once more to watch Blücher, Napoleon set off from Rheims toward Schwarzenberg's army on March 17. Even at this late date, however, a French advance remained capable of arousing Schwarzenberg's timidity. The Army of Bohemia turned to retreat, while its commander collapsed with an attack of gout.

Intermittent fighting punctuated Napoleon's pursuit. On March 20 the Allies lashed back at a French detachment that had crossed to the south bank of the Aube around Arcis-sur-Aube. They met two Guard corps commanded by Napoleon in person, and the Emperor coolly beat off numerical odds of two to one, leaving 1,700 casualties to 2,500 Allied losses. On the 24th the French repulsed a similar Allied sortie.

On the 22nd, however, Allied cavalry had intercepted a letter from Napoleon to Marie-Louise setting forth some specifics of his latest design to harry the Army of Bohemia. This discovery proved to aggravate Schwarzenberg's pusillanimity, but not in a manner that assisted Napoleon, as events developed. The Austrian field marshal and the Allied sovereigns decided that Schwarzenberg's larger army should seek refuge by drifting northward to join Blücher's smaller force, so high had Prussian stature risen. On the night of March 23–24 several more French dispatches fell into Allied hands, these being messages from Paris to Napoleon. They revealed that the French capital was nearly defenseless as far as any local garrison and fortifications were concerned, and they prompted Tsar Alexander to assert himself by insisting that Schwarzenberg turn west toward the metropolis. The Allied plan then became a design for the Armies of Bohemia and Silesia to converge on Meaux and march thence to Paris. A diversionary force was to hold Napoleon's attention upon the region of the Aube as long as possible, pretending to be Schwarzenberg's whole army.

One effect of all these shiftings of ground was that when Schwarzenberg turned west, he marched straight into Marmont and Mortier; but with much larger numbers, he drove them back in disorder. On March 26 Napoleon fought the Allied diversionary force near Vitry and routed it, but thereby he learned that both Allied main armies were marching on Paris. It was then too late for his tired soldiers to have a realistic chance of outracing the enemy to the capital. Napoleon's inclination was the bold one of striking farther eastward, away from Paris, to try to throw the Allies into a panic over their lines of communications. But his subordinates expressed dismay and dragged their feet; since Laon, belief in Napoleon's capacity to work magic was much diluted. On March 28 the Emperor acquiesced in a return toward Paris.

Two days later the Allies began attacking the outskirts of the city. Napoleon had left his brother Joseph in charge of the defenses; but having done little to prepare, Joseph now fled the scene. Marmont and Mortier, driven back to the capital, rallied all the troops they could find, centering on the heights of Montmartre. But their numbers were not enough, and at two in the morning of March 31 they retreated southward.

Napoleon had reached Fontainebleau with the remnants of the Guard and a scattering of other troops. He still hoped to harry the Allies' communications. These remained vulnerable, and the inhabitants of Paris proved surprisingly recalcitrant to Allied authority and amenable to an uprising in Napoleon's name. But the marshals and generals had had enough. Ney led a meeting in which Macdonald, Oudinot, and several lesser lights expressed their agreement with Marmont, who was persuaded that he could save France only by betraying the Emperor; he quickly turned his VI Corps over to the Allies.

Napoleon lapsed into lethargy again and allowed Ney and Macdonald to take a leading part in negotiating for an end of the war. After haggling failed to produce a compromise whereby Napoleon might abdicate in favor of his son, on April 6 the Emperor abdicated unconditionally, renouncing for himself and his heirs the thrones of France and of Italy (where Eugène had held off the Allies, including a turncoat Murat, to the last). Final terms reached on April 11 gave Napoleon the island of Elba to rule as Emperor under Allied supervision, while Marie-Louise and his son received the principality of Parma.

On April 20 Napoleon reviewed the Old Guard in the Courtyard of the White Horse at the Palace of Fontainebleau, bidding the nucleus of his most faithful troops an emotional farewell, while selecting 600 who would accompany him as his guard to Elba. At last he embraced the eagle standard of the Old Guard and then set off by coach to board the British frigate *Inconstant*, 36.

The revolt of the marshals had provided a symbolically fitting military end to Napoleon's first empire. In more than this, Napoleon had depended on the marshals and they had failed him. The corps system had burdened the Emperor's principal subordinates with an unprecedented demand for the consistent exercise of professional judgment and of professional tactical, operational, and sometimes even strategic skills. To a degree, the marshals and generals had met this demand remarkably well, considering that many of them had risen from the enlisted ranks and received little professional education, and that Napoleon hoarded his military insights as though they were mysteries to be shared with almost no one. As Napoleon's armies and the geographic boundaries of his conquests grew, however, he had to rely still more on the expertise of his subordinates and particularly on their ability to exercise autonomous command; and too often they lacked the requisite skills.

Militarily, Napoleon's first empire died of overextension beyond the Emperor's span of control. It might have endured longer if the Emperor had not persisted in attempting to hold all power in his own hands, if he had prepared his senior subordinates in the knowledge of professional command and encouraged them in the exercise of that knowledge. Because he did not, the overt failure of the marshals to respond to his wishes in April 1814 was merely the culmination of a deeper and longer-lasting failure. The professional competence of Napoleon's officer corps was inadequate to the requirements that the expansion of the army and the Empire after 1806 placed upon it.

THE END OF AN AGE:

WATERLOO

Of course, the abdication of Fontainebleau did not prove permanent, and Napoleon and his army were to fight one more campaign. But the limitations of the French command system did not change, except that Napoleon himself failed to recover the brilliance with which in 1814 he had seemed so often to recapture his highest individual powers.

Observant of the dissensions that wracked the Allied coalition and restless in his tiny island domain, Napoleon decided to grasp again for higher stakes. On February 26, 1815, he departed from Elba, taking with him in several small boats the 1,100 men to which his guard had grown. The expedition evaded the naval patrols of the restored Bourbon government of King Louis XVIII and landed at Cannes on March 1. To reach Paris, Napoleon chose the difficult route through Grenoble and across the French Alps, believing that his opponents would not expect him by this route and that the terrain would prevent them from concerting efforts against him in time to halt his progress.

That progress became a march of triumph. Every detachment of the Bourbon army that was sent to intercept him switched to his side. The Commander-in-Chief of the Bourbon cavalry, Marshal Ney, conspicuously turned his coat again. By the time Napoleon reached Paris on March 20 the Bourbons had fled, and the restored Emperor completed his takeover of the army and of the machinery of government. He attempted to adapt himself to changed circumstances by accepting limited imperial authority under a constitutional regime.

He also offered peace to the Allies, but his return had precipitated a swift resolution of their principal disagreements and the creation of a Seventh Coalition to which each of the four major Allied powers pledged a field army of

150,000 men. To confront this host Napoleon initially had only the Bourbon army of 224,000, only about 50,000 of them ready for field service; but he bestirred himself and managed to have about 360,000 men under arms by June 1, about half of them available for prompt field service. For the most part they were voluntary enlistees, because Napoleon was wisely cautious concerning a return to conscription, which the Bourbons had abolished in a decidedly popular action. Perhaps never before had Napoleon paid greater attention to logistics, opening new arms manufactories and improving old ones while simplifying weapons designs. Unlike 1814, the Emperor gave personal attention to the fortifications of Paris.

He might also benefit from a few advantages outside the country, in spite of the Allies' hasty reunification. The end of the European war in 1814 and the persistence of the War of 1812 against the United States into 1815 had caused the British to disperse the Royal Navy widely. There was discontent in Germany over the aggrandizement of Prussia, in spite of the Prussians' considerable success in identifying themselves with German nationalism; an extension of Prussian dominion in the Rhineland was provoking reactions against Prussian harshness, and an effort to amalgamate part of the Saxon Army into the Prussian touched off a mutiny that briefly endangered the person of Marshal Blücher. Napoleon began wooing both Great Britain and Austria to pare them from the coalition, and such was the depth of the Allies' disagreements that even the approaches to London did not seem completely chimerical. Interallied quarrels combined with the usual Austrian irresolution to generate real hope of success with Vienna, especially if Napoleon could achieve an early military victory impressive enough to have some moral effect.

The Campaign: Preliminaries

To that end, Napoleon gave thought to a quick march with his immediately available 50,000 against the small Allied force occupying Belgium. He rejected this idea, however, because it would have confirmed the fears of all those who regarded his name as synonymous with war. On the other hand, perhaps he should have attempted it; his forbearance did not detain the preparations of the Allies.

And the military plan on which he settled was a thrust into Belgium after all. In that country lay the nuclei of the Prussian Army under Blücher, since June 3, 1814 Fürst von Wohlstadt (a place on the Katzbach battlefield in Bohemia), and of the British Army under Wellington, since May 1, 1814 a duke. If Napoleon could deal with the Prussians and the British, the Austrians might well take counsel of their fears, and then the Russian forces in western Europe would be far out on a limb. Furthermore, Napoleon could reasonably hope that the differing temperaments of the rash Blücher and the careful Wellington would impede cooperation between his immediate opponents.

Choosing the right subordinate commanders was perhaps a more difficult problem for Napoleon than when and how to wage war, because some of the marshals, such as Marmont and Victor, had remained loyal to the Bourbons;

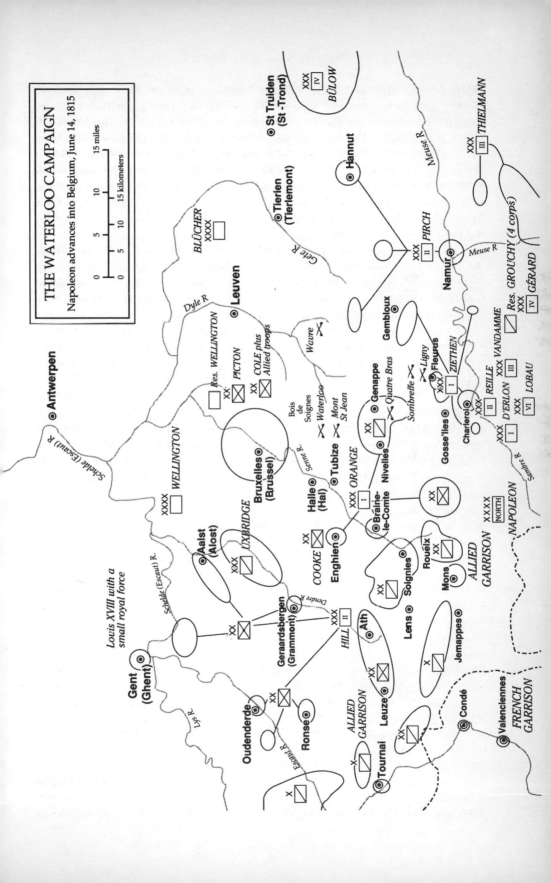

THE WATERLOO CAMPAIGN

Napoleon advances into Belgium, June 14, 1815

0   5   10   15 kilometers
0   5   10   15 miles

while others, such as Macdonald and Masséna, claimed ill health; and still others, such as Jourdan and Mortier, were in fact ill. Ney seemed to have collapsed into utter instability and for a time received only unimportant duties. Thus Napoleon had to draw his principal lieutenants largely from the second rank of his former officers. Jean Rapp, *général de division* and *comte de l'Empire*, for example, received the Army of the Rhine with about 23,000 men and responsibility for holding Schwarzenberg's 225,000 in check along the upper Rhine from Mannheim to Basel. Fortunately, Schwarzenberg had grown no bolder in the past year; the same awareness that had constrained the Archduke Charles, that the Habsburg dynasty depended on his not easily replaceable army, always had to influence Schwarzenberg as well. Another 37,000 French troops in three small armies watched the entire eastern frontier from Basel southward, while 13,000 more guarded the Pyrenees. Needless to say, these forces were of decidedly mixed quality, and their leaders were of decidedly uneven competence in command. Yet another 10,000 troops had to be sent to La Vendée to confront a new insurrection in that old hotbed of counterrevolutionary violence.

The combined effects of these dispositions and of vigorous recruiting left Napoleon by early June with some 128,000 men for his *Armée du Nord* with which he proposed to anticipate any Allied invasion scheme by striking into Belgium to separate and destroy the armies of Wellington and Blücher. At that time Wellington commanded 106,800 Anglo-Dutch troops holding the western half of Belgium from the Brussels-Charleroi road to the Scheldt; he was based on Ostend (Ostende), and his headquarters were at Brussels. Blücher commanded 149,200 Prussians holding eastern Belgium from the Brussels-Charleroi road to the Meuse; he was based on Koblenz, on the Rhine, with headquarters at Namur. Napoleon's plan was to move rapidly and secretly and, achieving sufficient surprise so that the Allies would not be able to complete a concentration against him before he struck at Charleroi, to drive between Wellington's and Blücher's armies. Thus he hoped to compel each of the enemy armies to fall back along its own line of communications, widening the gap between them, so that he could defeat each in turn.

But this plan, though essentially a sound reprise of the strategy of annihilation of Napoleon's best years, depended too much on separating the rival armies and keeping them separated. Unless that could be done, the Army of the North might face numerical odds of two to one. Napoleon in his prime would not have denied so many troops to his main army even if there had been much greater risks than those posed by Schwarzenberg and the other possible opponents south of Belgium. Admirable as his recruiting and administrative efforts had been, Napoleon in his deployment threw away much of the benefit his exertions should have gained.

When Napoleon matured his plan, the Army of the North was still scattered across the wide area bounded by lines from Lille to Metz to Paris. The Allied front in Belgium was ninety miles (145 kilometers) long and about thirty miles (forty-eight kilometers) deep. It would take the Allies three days to close up on their center; but, anticipating Napoleon's design to split them, they believed it impossible that he should be able to concentrate his own dispersed forces stealthily enough that he could fall on them without their receiving adequate warning to permit them to concentrate also.

For the last time, nevertheless, Napoleon accomplished the seemingly impossible. Both sides had numerous spies at work, but Napoleon had contrived to build by far the better intelligence service. He remained well informed about the Allies' dispositions, while they knew little of his. He moved his troops with painstakingly skillful use of irregularities of terrain to screen them from observation. Gérard's IV Corps, with the longest distance to travel, began marching from the Metz area on June 6; other elements soon moved also. Napoleon left Paris on June 11. By June 14 he had achieved a preliminary concentration of his army in three principal groupings, around Solre-sur-Sambre, Beaumont, and Philippeville. His central grouping was thus within ready striking distance—less than a day's march—of Charleroi. And the Allies did not know it and had not begun to move to protect their center.

Wellington's army was in an especially vulnerable deployment. Its commander proposed to concentrate on Gosse'lies, but only a cavalry screen shielded that place, and the screen was not strong enough to buy sufficient time for the projected concentration. Moreover, Wellington's part of Belgium was open country with good roads, inviting a French penetration. Blücher had the advantage of rougher ground with fewer roads, his left protected by the rugged plateau of the Ardennes. All in all, however, Napoleon in his first marches had gone a long way toward compensating for the faulty initial dispositions that had placed too few troops in the Army of the North. He was on the verge of achieving not merely a tactical but a strategic surprise beyond his own most optimistic expectations, and he had set the stage for beating up his enemies piecemeal before they could mass against him.

But the persistent and now aggravated problem of competent subordinates was about to make itself felt again. Furthermore, Berthier, the Emperor's accustomed Chief of Staff, a bureaucrat rather than a major military talent but usually capable within his sphere, had remained with Louis XVIII and escorted his court as it fled to Ghent. He then traveled to Bavaria, where at Bamberg he died mysteriously on June 1 in a fall from a window after watching Allied troops march by. In his absence, Napoleon named Soult as his Chief of Staff—a much better fighting general and a much better independent commander than Berthier, but not the man for the detailed administrative work of the staff. (Again, proper professional education, including the duties of the staff, was a desideratum that Napoleon's army did not meet.)

Napoleon directed Soult to prepare and dispatch orders that would move his formations on June 15 to Charleroi and Marchienne on the Sambre. To General Vandamme, commanding the III Corps, Soult sent the march orders in single copy only and did not follow up to make sure of their delivery. Through mishaps, they were never delivered. Vandamme's corps was to lead the advance to Charleroi in the French center, but having no instructions beyond those to be ready to move at 3:00 A.M., the corps remained stationary on the morning of June 15, while the rest of the army got under way.

This contretemps was all the more unfortunate for the French because, inevitably, accurate information was at last beginning to reach Wellington and Blücher, while time remained essential to Napoleon's purposes. To make matters yet worse, Gérard with the IV Corps farther to the right was also late in starting, because this corps had not been properly concentrated during the night. The two French misfortunes gave badly needed assistance to *Generallieutenant* Hans Ernst Karl Graf von Ziethen (sometimes Zieten), commanding the Prussian I Corps. Ziethen at Charleroi was under instructions to delay the French for twenty-four hours to permit Blücher's army to concentrate behind him; the task would be difficult considering that Ziethen with somewhat over 30,000 men had the bulk of the French army massing before him, that daylight was nearly at its longest of the year, and that Napoleon himself was about to take charge of the effort to break through the I Corps.

Ziethen's outposts conducted a skillful fighting withdrawal from the right bank of the River Sambre during the morning of the 15th. Aided by the self-imposed handicaps of the French, the outposts bought enough time that Napoleon's left and center reached the Sambre bridges at Charleroi and Marchienne only on toward noon. The French cavalry screen found Ziethen's troops holding the bridges too stoutly to be budged until infantry came up. Napoleon hurried forward a portion of the Young Guard, which he personally led against the Charleroi bridge, taking it shortly after noon. General Reille with the French II Corps captured the Marchienne bridge about the same time.

Deprived of the barrier of the Sambre and facing heavy numerical odds, a less able commander than Ziethen would have been likely to mass such force as he had to seek in concentration the best protection he could get. But that would have left open to Napoleon either the road from Marchienne by way of Gosse'lies to Quatre-Bras or the road from Charleroi to Fleurus, and an uncontested advance along either could have permitted Napoleon to achieve his strategic intent of splitting the Allies. Ziethen therefore accepted the risks of a fighting withdrawal along both roads.

Napoleon's personal involvement at Charleroi underscored again his need for competent subordinates. Not trusting his corps commanders, he now reorganized his army by subordinating much of it to two wing commanders, leaving a reserve—initially the Guard—under his own immediate control. The trouble was that he lacked generals of enough operational vision and professional expertise for the wing commands as well. He had called Marshal Ney to the Army of the North after all, and when Ney arrived about three in the afternoon of the 15th the Emperor gave him command of the left wing—Ney, who had so often shown himself unqualified for such responsibility even at his best, and who now seemed far from the peak of his powers. Later Napoleon entrusted the right wing to Grouchy, only promoted to *maréchal de l'Empire* on June 15. Grouchy was more dependable than Ney but short of the demands of his new position in seniority and stature as well as in vision.

Ney and Grouchy took over the advance along the Quatre-Bras and Fleurus roads, respectively. At the outset, Ney performed adequately. He took over just as an attack was about to be launched against the Prussians in Gosse'lies, and he helped drive the enemy from that town. He did not prevent his immediate adversaries from completing a skillful roundabout retreat to Ligny, but he pushed forward energetically enough to the outskirts of Quatre-Bras.

Grouchy, however, acted promptly to confirm that his elevation was questionable. While Napoleon returned to Charleroi to supervise the completion of the crossing of the Sambre, Grouchy advanced about two miles (three kilometers) beyond Charleroi, colliding with Prussians in brigade strength at Gilly. Vandamme having at last arrived at the front, Grouchy paused to confer with him about how to deal with the obstacle. The result was that a small enemy force held up the French advance for at least two hours. Not until Napoleon returned to the vanguard of his army about 5:30 in the afternoon did the advance toward Fleurus resume. Nightfall caused a halt at the latter town.

The combination of Ziethen's admirably executed delaying tactics and French mistakes meant that Blücher had time to bring about the substantial concentration of the Prussian army after all, while the Allies had been sufficiently alerted to Napoleon's purposes that the French Emperor could not feel sure he would succeed in driving an unbreakable wedge between Wellington and Blücher. On the other hand, Napoleon had advanced just far enough that he might yet be able to fight Wellington's and Blücher's armies separately; they remained so divided that one French wing might suffice to hold either in place while the greater part of Napoleon's army, the other wing and the reserve, dealt with the other adversary—crushed that adversary if the Emperor could realize his intent.

Wellington's reactions to the French advance had been less alert and appropriate than those into which Gneisenau and the emerging Prussian professionals helped steer Blücher. It was three in the afternoon before the British commander at Brussels received substantial news that the French had suddenly materialized around Charleroi, and even then the Duke refused to accept that the movement must be Napoleon's main thrust. Rather, Wellington's acute awareness of his maritime umbilical cord had led him to expect that Napoleon would strike at his right and try to cut him off from the English Channel. In this scenario, Napoleon would drive the British into rather than away from Blücher. Therefore Wellington simply put his troops on the alert but at first ordered no riposte to the actions at Marchienne and Charleroi. He thereby enhanced Napoleon's prospects for separating the Allies.

Fortunately for the Allies, the commander of the I Corps of Wellington's Anglo-Dutch army, Prince Willem of Orange, and that officer's immediate subordinates developed a clearer perception of what was going on than did his commanding officer. On their own initiative they saw to the defense of the strategic road junction of Quatre-Bras, and it was the Dutch Prince's defending force that stopped Ney short of Quatre-Bras at the end of the day.

Ney deliberately did not push hard, however, lest he lose contact with Grouchy, of whose delay he was aware. And there was in fact a potential advantage for Napoleon in Allied retention of Quatre-Bras. If the Allies did not retreat separately from each other, they might be tempted into a forward concentration at Quatre-Bras, in which event the French army would be in an excellent position to fall upon whichever Allied army arrived first. In fact, the Allies were embarking on just the moves that would give the French the latter, if lesser, opportunity. On the morning of June 16, Wellington, aware at last of the true general nature of Napoleon's dispositions, had most of his army marching eastward toward Quatre-Bras, except for a reserve that halted at Mont St-Jean some seven miles (eleven kilometers) to the northwest against the possibility of a change in plan. Blücher at the same time intended to take up and hold a position south of the Namur-Nivelles road where he could maintain contact with Wellington and await the only one of his four corps not yet in hand, the IV under Bülow coming from the direction of Gembloux.

Napoleon did not, however, believe on the morning of June 16 that the Allies intended a forward disposition. He still proposed to continue his own advance calculated to strike one or the other main enemy force in detail. He planned to press an advance guard of Grouchy's wing as far as Gembloux to find and hold back Blücher. The reserve would initially march in support of Grouchy. But once Grouchy was firmly established at Sombreffe four miles (six and a half kilometers) southwest of Gembloux and evidently able to hold Blücher in check, the reserve would shift west to join Ney. By the time it reinforced him, Ney should have captured Quatre-Bras, and the main force of Napoleon's attack would then fall on Wellington. Napoleon hoped to throw the Anglo-Dutch army back sufficiently to open the way for a night march to Brussels that would assure splitting Wellington away from Blücher.

He was not yet sure enough of his enemies' dispositions and intentions, however, to depart personally from Charleroi. There he remained during the early morning of June 16, awaiting news from Grouchy and Ney and keeping with him the VI Corps of Marshal Lobau, to keep it fresh for the desired push to Brussels.

Napoleon had conducted the campaign admirably so far. In spite of Ziethen's success in shielding a Prussian concentration, the Emperor had created opportunities for a greater or lesser solution, the splitting apart of the enemy armies and their piecemeal defeat or their defeat, also in detail, during a forward concentration; either way, the ground was readied for a notable Napoleonic triumph. Nevertheless, Napoleon's indecision on the morning of the 16th was another sign of the loss of the mastery that had once been his. The Napoleon of 1805 or 1806 would not have hesitated so much nor left so much to be decided by how his enemies chose to move.

Worse, Napoleon now compounded indecision by proceeding in mid-morning to join Grouchy and to begin turning his main effort toward Blücher after earlier intending a principal thrust against Wellington and giving his commanders the impression that such was his design. It did nothing to clarify matters that he continued to hold the VI Corps behind at Charleroi rather than moving it up to a position whence it might more readily assist either wing. The consequent doubt about his purposes among his principal subordinates proved to make June 16 a considerably worse day for the French than the 15th; Ziethen's delaying action on the 15th had injured French prospects, but not fatally, while on the 16th Napoleon's own indecision was to help snatch defeat from the jaws of incipient victory.

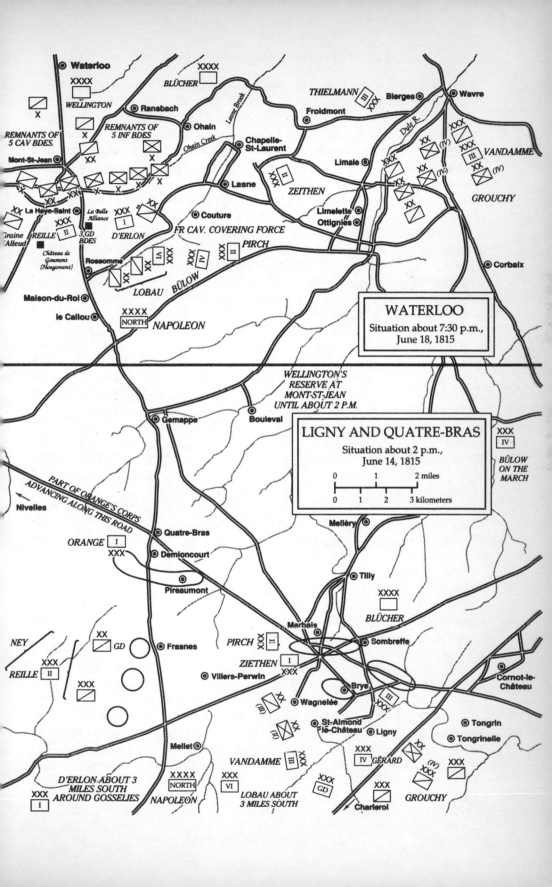

WATERLOO

Situation about 7:30 p.m.,
June 18, 1815

LIGNY AND QUATRE-BRAS

Situation about 2 p.m.,
June 14, 1815

0   1   2 miles

0   1   2   3 kilometers

Waterloo

XXXX
WELLINGTON

XXXX
BLÜCHER

XXXX
THIELMANN III

Bierges

Wavre

X

X
REMNANTS OF
5 CAV BDES.

Ransbach

REMNANTS OF
5 INF BDES

X

Ohain

Froidmont

Dyle R.

XXX
VANDAMME

Mont-St-Jean

XX

X

Ohain Creek

Chapelle-
St-Laurent

Limale

XX (IV)
XXX
XX (IV)

III
XX (IV)

GROUCHY

X

Lasne

XXX II
ZEITHEN

Lasne Brook

Couture

La Haye-Sainte

XXX I

Limelette
Ottignies

XX

XXX
D'ERLON

La Belle
Alliance

FR CAV. COVERING FORCE

XXX

Graine
d'Alleud

REILLE
XXX
II
3 GD
BDES

Rossomme

XX VI
XXX IV
XXX II
PIRCH

Corbaix

Château de
Goumont
(Hougoumont)

LOBAU   BÜLOW

Maison-du-Roi

le Caillou

XXXX
NORTH
NAPOLEON

WELLINGTON'S
RESERVE AT
MONT-ST-JEAN
UNTIL ABOUT 2 P.M.

XXX
IV

BÜLOW
ON THE
MARCH

Gemappe

Bouleval

Mellèry

PART OF ORANGE'S CORPS
ADVANCING ALONG THIS ROAD

Nivelles

Quatre-Bras

ORANGE I
XXX

Demioncourt

Tilly

Pireaumont

XXXX
BLÜCHER

Marbais

NEY

XX GD
REILLE
XXX
II

Frasnes

PIRCH XXX II

Sombreffe

XXX

ZIETHEN I
XXX

Cornot-le-
Château

Villers-Perwin

Brye

III
XXX

St-Almond-
le-Château

Ligny

XX
Wagnelée

Tongrin

Tongrinelle

Mellet

VANDAMME III
XXX

XXX IV GÉRARD

D'ERLON ABOUT 3
MILES SOUTH
AROUND GOSSELIES

XXXX
NORTH
NAPOLEON

XXX VI

LOBAU ABOUT
3 MILES SOUTH

XXX GD

Charleroi

XXX (IV)
XXX
GROUCHY

XXX I

The Campaign: Quatre-Bras and Ligny

Napoleon joined Grouchy about eleven in the morning at Fleurus, still about five miles (eight kilometers) short of Sombreffe. He had been brought thither in part by a report from Grouchy that considerable Prussian forces were massing in front of him. These forces were strong enough to prevent Grouchy's making much progress beyond Fleurus. Furthermore, when he surveyed the scene in person Napoleon thought it significant that the Prussians were deploying parallel to the Namur-Nivelles road rather than at a right angle to it; this alignment implied that their intention was to stand and fight and not merely to cover a retreat. The lesser instead of the greater opportunity was therefore the one presenting itself, to strike and crush a forward deployment rather than to separate the Allies irrevocably from each other. But Napoleon now became confirmed in his recent intention to hit hardest against Blücher after all, and he prepared the orders that led to the materialization of this purpose later in the day in the form of the battle of Ligny, a town about midway between Fleurus and Sombreffe.

Meanwhile developments were in train to produce another major action on the same day on Napoleon's left wing, the battle of Quatre-Bras. Ney had been justified in not attacking hard to secure Quatre-Bras on the evening of June 15, because at the time his connection with Grouchy was uncertain. It was not so justifiable for him to spend the morning of the 16th doing no more than further reconnoitering toward the road junction. As Ney's patrols informed him, Wellington was sending reinforcements to the area; but throughout the morning Ney with two corps directly at hand could almost certainly have captured Quatre-Bras with relative ease. Before 10:00 A.M. he informed Napoleon that large forces were concentrating in his front, to which the Emperor at once replied that they must still be a small enough portion of Wellington's army that Ney should attack and crush them.

On the opposite side of the hill, Wellington himself arrived at Quatre-Bras during the morning but, finding no evidence that a serious threat to him was imminent, arranged for a face-to-face meeting with Blücher at Brye to attempt to make sure that Napoleon would not separate their armies. At the meeting Wellington gave a conditional promise that if not attacked himself he would bring his army to Blücher's aid at Ligny.

Returning to Quatre-Bras, Wellington found, however, that the French had already mounted a much greater threat there than he had anticipated; so far in this campaign his appraisals of the enemy's intentions had not been good. By early afternoon Ney had finally bestirred himself to attack. His two corps, closely concentrated, fell initially on only 7,500 troops of the Prince of Orange's I Corps. The Prince, however, had taken the risk of a wide enough deployment to cover Ney's entire front, and he made good use of a wood and farm buildings as pre-existing defenses. By about 3:00 P.M. his force was beginning to give way to superior numbers, but at that juncture reinforcements began to filter into the battle and Wellington returned to take command. Both sides piled on additional reinforcements—a final division of Reille's corps joined Ney—and the battle seesawed.

About five in the afternoon Ney decided that he could not take Quatre-Bras without the I Corps of Marshal Jean-Baptiste Drouet, comte d'Erlon. This corps had been assigned to Ney's left wing, but after deciding that he needed it, Ney soon after discovered that without his knowledge it had shifted eastward to take part in the fighting at Ligny. In fact Napoleon's headquarters had sent an order detaching the I Corps from the left wing, but in the second major miscarriage of the campaign the order had not been delivered. Ney still believed that Napoleon intended his to be the primary effort of the day. He had received the Emperor's order to crush the Anglo-Dutch forces in front of him, which seemed to confirm this intention. About 5:30 he received yet another imperial order, instructing him to seize Quatre-Bras and then to proceed to Ligny, but emphatically to capture Quatre-Bras first. Ney decided that in the circumstances he ought to call upon d'Erlon's assistance.

The question of Napoleon's intentions aside, however, Ney possessed information that should have made it clear to him that d'Erlon had already progressed too far eastward to be able to intervene effectively in the Quatre-Bras battle. The attempt to call back the I Corps was futile. Mere common sense, let alone professional skill, should have deterred Ney from trying. Furthermore, Ney soon received an oral message from Napoleon saying he must not recall d'Erlon, because the Emperor himself needed the I Corps at Ligny. Infuriated nevertheless because d'Erlon's corps had been taken from him without notice, and still unaware of its formal detachment, Ney flatly told the orderly who bore the message that he refused to obey it. When the orderly remonstrated, Ney terminated the discussion by plunging into the battle.

D'Erlon likewise had never learned of his corps's detachment from the left wing, and so he obeyed Ney's order to turn back westward. By the time that order reached him, he had already reached the edge of the Ligny battlefield, late in the day, and it was nine in the evening before he rejoined Ney. By then the battle of Quatre-Bras had been decided, as sound judgment should have assured Ney it was bound to be.

The climax had come about 7:00 P.M., when Major-General George Cooke arrived on the field with the British Guards Division. This increment raised Wellington's total to about 33,000 against Ney's 22,000. Sensing some such superiority, Wellington opened a general counterattack, and as darkness approached the Allies had driven Ney from Quatre-Bras and back to his starting position of the morning. The day's losses around Quatre-Bras were about 4,000 on the French side and 4,500 for the Allies.

Once more the professional deficiencies of Napoleon's subordinates were largely to blame. If Ney had not frittered the morning away, he should have captured the road junction with possibly serious implications for Wellington's ability to keep his army concentrated. Ney always seemed to move either too late or too early. But Napoleon's indecision about his own intentions was also partly to blame. If Ney had been able to commit d'Erlon's corps as soon as he decided to call on it and when the momentum of the battle still favored him, he might yet have dealt Wellington's army a hard blow.

By the same token, d'Erlon might have contributed decisively at Ligny had his corps not been busy with marching and countermarching. But the fault behind this waste also lay with Napoleon as well as with Ney; the Emperor's order summoning d'Erlon to the east did not make clear either the reduction of Ney's battle from the main effort to a diversion or the urgency of Napoleon's need for d'Erlon.

The Emperor's survey of the scene in front of Grouchy during the morning of June 16 had ended his indecision and convinced him that he could fight against Blücher that day an action that might decide the whole campaign in his favor. With Lobau's corps he would have about 80,000 men on the scene. The Prussians could not have too many more; in fact they numbered about 84,000. Covering the Namur-Nivelles road, the Prussians occupied a series of low ridges with bare slopes, such that much of their army was in plain sight to Napoleon at Fleurus. Their first line held the villages of Brye, St-Amand, and Ligny. Napoleon's plans aimed at a battle of annihilation in his favorite style, featuring a *manœuvre sur les derrières*, though the design was far more complex than his best schemes, not least in its dependence on d'Erlon's arrival from Quatre-Bras. While cavalry and a few infantry pinned down the Prussian left, Vandamme's III Corps and Gérard's IV would assail Blücher's center and right. With that assault fixing and weakening the Prussians, d'Erlon's I Corps would arrive to envelop the Prussian right. Napoleon would then unleash the Guard and other reserves to destroy the Prussian right and center in a vise formed by his own assaults and d'Erlon's.

The design began to unfold about 2:30, when the sound of heavy firing from Quatre-Bras informed Napoleon that Ney was keeping Wellington occupied and that the time to hit Blücher had arrived. A bitter fight flared up around the villages south of the Namur road, about as bitter indeed as any in Napoleon's career, with Vandamme and Gérard gradually gaining ground and, by compelling Blücher to commit more and more reserves, gradually chewing up the Prussian army. After the battle more than 4,000 bodies were to be found on only about 4,000 square yards (or square meters) of this cauldron of conflict. Just as Napoleon prepared to commit the Guard, however, a mass of men were seen advancing toward the French left rear. The time was between 5:30 and 6:00 P.M. The afternoon's vicious fighting had nearly worn out Vandamme's troops, and when they saw this new menace bearing down on them panic began to break out. French artillery had to be turned on fugitives of Napoleon's own army to restore control.

The threatening columns were in fact not enemy reinforcements but d'Erlon's corps, compounding its tragicomedy of errors by marching along the wrong roads for its proposed envelopment of Blücher's right. In these circumstances, Napoleon himself was slow to discern the true identity of the new arrivals. Once he did, about 6:30, he also learned almost immediately afterward that d'Erlon had countermarched.

At this hour of French distress, Blücher adroitly launched a counterattack. He had massed every force available to him, and he led the charge in person—a characteristic gesture by the bellicose old marshal, though a foolish one. Nevertheless, the Prussians scored no advantage, but fell back in some disorder when Napoleon sent forward the chasseurs of the Guard in a counterattack of his own.

The loss of d'Erlon's corps deprived Napoleon of his hope for a battle of annihilation, but he determined still to wound the Prussian army as sorely as possible. He massed the artillery of the Guard to prepare the way for a climactic assault. A thunderstorm delayed the opening of the effort, but about 7:45 the artillery signaled the advance of the Guard in combination with a renewed assault by Gérard's corps. If Napoleon had brought Lobau up close enough to join in fully, he might yet have grasped almost as decisive a victory as he had desired. As it was, the Guard and Gérard broke the battered Prussian center. Blücher personally led another countercharge, but this time his unwisdom was confirmed when his horse was shot from under him and he had to be carried semi-conscious from the field. The countercharge failed, and by 9:00 P.M. the French were driving away the Prussians all along the line.

So the most critical day thus far in the campaign ended with French success after all. The battle of Ligny was a success scarcely unalloyed, but it was certainly a French victory. The Prussians had suffered 25,000 casualties and inflicted only about 11,000. Beaten up as Blücher's army was, Napoleon could still hope it might retreat toward Namur and thus away from the Anglo-Dutch army, enabling him either to finish the job against Blücher or to turn upon Wellington alone.

The Campaign: The Eve of Battle

Had the Emperor been able to visit Prussian headquarters, he would have found considerable encouragement for his hopes. Blücher's Chief of Staff, Gneisenau—Graf von Gneisenau since the time of Blücher's elevation to prince and as a reward for his part in the 1813–1814 triumphs—could not find the army commander. More than a little unnerved by this circumstance, Gneisenau had sunk into a mood of suspicion and distrust directed against Wellington, not understanding why the British field-marshal had failed to keep his promise (more accurately, his qualified promise) to come to the Prussians' assistance. Also, the more Gneisenau learned about the condition of his army, the more discouraged he became. Many of the units were in dismaying disorder; many were almost out of ammunition, and the next day the staff could not locate the ammunition train.

With Gneisenau brooding morosely, it was almost fortuitous that by morning he directed the retreat northward toward Wavre rather than toward Namur as Napoleon expected and hoped. The consequence was that the Prussians were able to remain in contact with the Anglo-Dutch army; the fortuitous element was that Gneisenau in his depression had grown indifferent to this aspect of the situation, and he chose the northward route merely because he thought that it best assured the Prussians' own line of communications.

At that, Gneisenau failed to inform Wellington's headquarters of his army's movements, and the Prussian retreat from Ligny left the Anglo-Dutch left flank dangerously exposed. (Just before his fall from his horse, Blücher had dispatched a message to Wellington warning of the likelihood of a Prussian retreat that would uncover Wellington's left, but the courier had been shot and the message went undelivered.)

Thus in spite of the northward rather than eastward direction of the Prussian retreat, Napoleon would still have an opportunity to defeat and even destroy Wellington alone if the French army acted swiftly. With d'Erlon's corps again at his disposal, a fresh formation as far as the toll of combat was concerned, Ney retained ample strength to pin down the Anglo-Dutch army at Quatre-Bras on June 17. If he did so, Napoleon should be able to envelop Wellington's exposed left.

Unfortunately for the French, the nervous strain of Napoleon's recognition that June 16 had been the critical day so far in the campaign left the aging Emperor unwell by the morning of the 17th. (By the calendar, Napoleon was only forty-six, but the accumulated strain of his years of ambition and responsibility had left him with the deteriorated constitution of a much older man.) With the Emperor relinquishing his grip, neither Soult nor Ney perceived the opportunity at Quatre-Bras clearly enough to capitalize on it. Instead they afforded Wellington leisure to escape. Napoleon's headquarters indeed ordered Ney about 8:00 A.M. to take Quatre-Bras if he could, and if he could not to report accordingly so that Napoleon might assist him. But Ney did nothing. In both the quality of its staff work and the ability of its senior officers to exercise professional discretion, Napoleon's army was running all too true to form.

The Anglo-Dutch army had practically completed its concentration at Quatre-Bras only on the morning of the 17th, when to concentrate there was to court danger, not opportunity. Early that morning Wellington sent a well-armed mission to find the Prussians. On its return the Duke learned that Blücher's army was withdrawing to Wavre. A little later, about nine in the morning, a mission from Gneisenau at last reported to Wellington the Prussians' version of their movements and intentions. Wellington showed himself a better ally than Gneisenau by responding with a message that he would fall back from his present untenable position to Mont St-Jean and would accept battle there provided he was assured of support by one of Blücher's corps. His detailed statement of his intentions received no better reward, however, than a Prussian reply as late as two the next morning. Well before that, nevertheless, Blücher had resumed command; and coming from the sturdy *Generalfeldmarschall* himself, the reply was that Blücher would support Wellington with not one but two and possibly four corps. This earnest of Prussian cooperation, however tardy, became a foundation of the battle and victory of Waterloo.

Meanwhile, about 10:00 A.M. on the 17th Wellington began his withdrawal to Mont St-Jean. This was in sufficient time to circumvent the reanimation of the French army by Napoleon's recovery. Once he was up and about, the Emperor went first to the Ligny battlefield to look after the pursuit of the Prussians. The visit to Ligny expressed a mistaken view of current priorities and a return to

Napoleon's indecision of the preceding day. Not until about 11:00 A.M. did Napoleon reach Ligny, and then it was almost noon before he wrote to Ney to urge once more a renewal of the attacks against Quatre-Bras. Yet again Ney failed to respond. At length, in the early afternoon Napoleon personally led reinforcements to Ney, but only to find that except for a cavalry screen and some artillery Wellington's army had departed from Quatre-Bras.

Until this juncture, the soundness of Napoleon's strategic aim of defeating the two enemy armies separately, by one means or another, had overridden through its soundness all operational and tactical vicissitudes and setbacks. But the supreme opportunity to destroy Wellington that this strategy had by June 17 created did not survive the inaction of the French army throughout that morning, an inaction brought about by Napoleon's excessive centralization of authority, his disability that morning, and the inadequate professional qualities of his senior subordinates and staff.

Napoleon berated Ney and gathered up his own energies for a pursuit, but it was too late. Wellington had already traveled too far for the French to stir up even a rear-guard action, and another thunderstorm retarded everybody's movements but in the circumstances penalized the French more than the Allies.

At dusk Napoleon reached high ground around Rossomme from which he could see that Wellington was deploying his army in defensive array astride the Nivelles-Brussels and Charleroi-Brussels roads that met at Mont St-Jean. The evening was too far gone to permit further battle on the 17th, but the Emperor immediately began formulating a renewed plan to separate Wellington from Blücher, by curling around the left of the new Anglo-Dutch position.

When earlier in the day Napoleon had left Grouchy to join Ney, he instructed the former to resume his march to Gembloux, where French cavalry was in contact with retreating Prussian infantry. Grouchy proceeded to obey the order altogether literally. Marching his wing in one badly organized column along a single road, he reached Gembloux only late in the day and halted there for the night. Consequently the French right wing did not continue applying any serious pressure against the Prussians and in fact allowed contact to fade away. The Prussians, forming up around Wavre, used the respite to achieve a much more rapid recuperation from the effects of Ligny than Napoleon had thought possible.

Waterloo

The climactic battle of the 1815 campaign, fought the next day, June 18, takes its name from the village of Waterloo, where Wellington made his headquarters a mile behind the Mont St-Jean position.

Wellington's main line ran along the low ridge of Mont St-Jean, his troops mostly concealed on the reverse slope with very few of them in front of the crest. There were three advanced outposts: in the Château of Hougoumont (or Goumont) in front of the right or west flank; in the farm and gravel pit of La Haie–Sainte in his center and on the Charleroi-Brussels road; and in the farms and hamlets of Papelotte and La Haie in front of his east flank, adjoining the

Bois de Paris. Wellington had 67,600 troops, of whom 29,800 were British or members of the King's German Legion, the successor to the Hanoverian forces that formerly served the British King. Of 156 guns, 78 were British. Many troops of the Anglo-Dutch army were either recent recruits or recent allies of Napoleon.

Troops of Wellington's two principal corps, the I under the Prince of Orange and the II under Lieutenant-General Sir Rowland Baron Hill, were intermixed along and behind the Mont St-Jean ridge. Wellington wanted veteran troops thoroughly interspersed among those comparatively new to war. One Belgian-Dutch brigade was mistakenly posted in the open on the forward slope near the Mont St-Jean crossroads. Most of the cavalry, under Lieutenant-General Henry William Paget, second Earl of Uxbridge, was in reserve behind the center. It was an anomaly of Wellington's dispositions that they were weighted to the right. Just as at the beginning of the campaign the Duke had been more concerned about the safety of his line of communications to the Channel than with Napoleon's real intent to sever him from Blücher's army, so now still he failed to recognize that it was his connection with the Prussians, and therefore his left, that most tempted Napoleon's attentions. Wellington stationed 17,000 troops at Hal and Tubize eight miles (thirteen kilometers) to his right, to guard against an envelopment there and to serve as a rallying point for his right if his center should be broken. The Château de Hougoumont was occupied in considerably greater force than La Haye–Sainte. And the right flank in general was more strongly held than the left.

To be sure, Wellington expected help from the Prussians on his left. He had Blücher's promise of 2:00 A.M., and Blücher had provided him with an able liaison officer in the person of *Generalmajor* Carl Freiherr von Müffling, to help coordinate the movements of the two Allied armies. The Allied plan as it developed through communications between the two army commanders was that Wellington's army would receive the expected French attack, while Blücher with 89,000 men and ninety-two guns would assail Napoleon's exposed right. Grouchy with 33,000 men and about eighty guns was still about ten miles (sixteen kilometers) east of the prospective Waterloo battlefield; Blücher's resolution to keep his promise of support to Wellington—in spite of his Chief of Staff's doubts about Wellington's loyalty in turn—was attested by his leaving only 17,000 men and forty-four guns along the River Dyle under the III Corps headquarters of *Generallieutenant* Johann Adolf Freiherr von Thielmann (sometimes Thielemann). Unfortunately for the Allies, in spite of the professional improvement of the Prussian officer corps, staff work was not commensurate in quality with Blücher's loyal resolve. The Prussians did not begin their march in support of the Anglo-Dutch army until the morning of June 18 was well advanced. Then faulty planning slowed the march by ordering the rearmost corps—Bülow's IV— to lead it. A fire in Wavre caused further delay.

On the evening of June 17 Napoleon had hoped to attack Wellington at six the next morning, advancing early the better to defeat the Anglo-Dutch army before the Prussians could intervene decisively. But he left his bivouacs too scattered to facilitate an early attack, and to make matters worse there was heavy rain during the night, leaving the ground—largely fields of grain—too sodden for rapid movement, especially by the cavalry and artillery. So the assault was postponed first to 9:00 A.M., then until 11:30, not a good omen for a venture that depended so much on dealing with Wellington's army separately.

Grouchy had written to Napoleon from Gembloux on the night of the 17th to say that he would continue following up the Prussian retreat to make sure that Blücher did not join Wellington. But Napoleon must have known that this purpose was beyond the right wing's capacity, because its geographic position outside the Prussian left flank was such that any action by it would tend to push the Prussians into rather than away from the Anglo-Dutch army. Not until ten in the morning of the 18th did Napoleon answer Grouchy. Then he instructed that marshal to move toward Wavre, whereby the right wing would have approached the French main body and the scene of the approaching battle. The Emperor's implicit intention was to shift Grouchy's axis of maneuver so that he would approach and threaten not the Prussian left but the Prussian right flank. But Napoleon did not say so explicitly, and thus, predictably, Grouchy misunderstood him. He marched directly to Wavre.

Napoleon drew up his army in an imposing mass within full view of the Anglo-Dutch forces and then rode past his lines to the cheers of his men. His plan for June 18 was as simple as that for the 16th had been complex; but as the earlier plan had been too complex, the new one was excessively simple. It was by no means a Napoleonic plan of the first order. Although it retained an element of the idea of the *manœuvre sur les derrières*, its essence was too much that of head-on fighting.

Reille's II Corps and d'Erlon's I formed the first line, drawn up along a low ridge parallel to Wellington's through the inn of La Belle Alliance on the Charleroi road. Adjacent to the inn was Napoleon's command post. Part of Reille's corps was to launch a diversionary attack against Hougoumont, while d'Erlon with four divisions mounted the principal attack, intended to pierce Wellington's left center. Massed cavalry in rear of each flank and Lobau's VI Corps in the center comprised a second line, while the Imperial Guard with more cavalry formed a third. These reserves were to be unleashed at the proper moments to exploit whatever rupture d'Erlon achieved and to press forward to Brussels, driving the fragments of the defeated Anglo-Dutch army and assuring its continued separation from the Prussians. In spite of all that had gone before, Ney was to direct the execution of the plan, under the Emperor's overall supervision.

At some time before 11:30, Napoleon opened a preparatory artillery barrage, which because of Wellington's deployment on the reverse slope did little damage except to the exposed Belgian-Dutch brigade.

At about 11:30 Reille launched his diversionary attack against Hougoumont. Notwithstanding Wellington's previous preoccupation with his right wing, the attack failed in its purpose of convincing the British field-marshal that it was the main effort. By 1:00 P.M. two and a half French divisions were committed to the action, and for a time the French broke into the central courtyard of the château. But Wellington fed in only minimal reinforcements, and though French artillery fire set the buildings ablaze in midafternoon, the British clung stoutly to the position.

Just before d'Erlon launched the main French attack, the capture of a Prussian courier revealed to the French that the mass of men seen emerging from woods to the northeast was Bülow's Prussian IV Corps. Napoleon quickly added a postscript to his latest instructions to Grouchy, telling him that the battle with Wellington had opened, that Bülow's corps had been discovered marching to Wellington's aid, and that Grouchy should hasten westward to deal with Bülow. By the time Grouchy received this belated clear order, however, he was pinned down in a fight with Thielmann and could not obey it.

Meanwhile Napoleon decided he must shift Lobau with the VI Corps and part of the cavalry to deal with Bülow. Lobau chose his consequent position too close to the initial French right flank to shield it as securely as would have been desirable, but otherwise he conducted a skillful defense, and his corps fought well. Nevertheless, the arrival of Bülow had unhinged Napoleon's plan before the battle was fairly commenced. It would probably have been wise for the Emperor to proceed no further with his offensive design for the present but to attempt to resume maneuver for a better opportunity later. He might have done so had he felt a higher respect for Wellington and his army. But Soult and others who had fought in Spain were unable to convey to Napoleon their misgivings about frontal assaults upon the British; if it had been otherwise, his plan would not have depended so much on such assaults in the first place.

Ney thus launched d'Erlon's corps in the primary French effort. Yet again, Ney blundered. Because of unclear and misconceived orders from Ney's headquarters, two of d'Erlon's divisions were formed into unwieldy columns of battalions. Crossing the waterlogged ground through fields of tall grass, these columns broke down into amorphous mobs. The Belgian-Dutch brigade already bludgeoned by French artillery was sent fleeing in disorder, but beyond that the French accomplished little. They were unable to press home the attack on La Haye–Sainte. The rest of their assault struck a veteran British division, the 5th, under Lieutenant-General Sir Thomas Picton. A veteran British division implied superb musketry, and Picton's men aimed their fire from behind a hedgerow on the crest of the Mont St-Jean ridge. The assailants staggered under British volleys but then held their own ground during a vicious fire fight in which Picton was killed.

Choosing his moment shrewdly, Lord Uxbridge hurled his cavalry at d'Erlon's infantry, and the mobile arm soon seemed about to achieve the decisiveness that distinguishes its proper use. British horsemen drove the French off the ridge and across the valley south of it, inflicting 3,000 casualties, capturing two eagle standards, and overrunning two batteries of artillery. But Uxbridge failed keep the charge under control, and it overextended itself, whereupon a French cavalry counterattack ordered by Napoleon himself drove it back in disorder. In the charge and retreat Wellington lost about a third of his cavalry.

Napoleon ordered Ney to try again to take La Haye–Sainte. Another artillery barrage preceded the assault, and during it the Anglo-Dutch line withdrew a short distance to find better cover. Ney mistook this movement for a major withdrawal and decided the time had come to unleash his cavalry. Forty-three squadrons advanced not only against La Haye–Sainte but toward the whole Allied right center—another blunder on Ney's part, because he was assailing the least damaged part of Wellington's front, and in all ways the most strongly held.

The Anglo-Dutch infantry formed squares and repulsed the French horse, who then retreated before an Allied cavalry countercharge. The French committed thirty-seven fresh squadrons, including the heavy cavalry of the Guard, whereupon the horsemen of the earlier French charge rallied and went forward again. If Napoleon had advanced infantry and artillery to bolster the cavalry he might have broken the Anglo-Dutch center despite all the adverse odds. But the Emperor had lapsed into another of his increasingly frequent bouts of lethargy, and nothing of the sort was done. The French cavalry penetrated some of the Allied infantry squares but at length wavered and fell back. About 5:30 P.M. the French staged a last, small-scale charge simply to rescue survivors. With this, the most dramatic part of the battle of Waterloo ended, the grand French attack against the Allied right center. It is significant that this theatrical climax was an assault against the wrong place.

Napoleon was not yet willing to give up, for now he had almost fully engaged his army in a battle on the largest scale, and at this stage of his career the loss of such a battle meant the loss of everything. The Emperor ordered Ney to capture La Haye-Sainte no matter what the cost. Ney advanced the remains of d'Erlon's corps soon after 6:00 P.M. Just at this juncture the defending garrison, the King's German Legion, largely ran out of ammunition. Napoleon's cavalry was therefore able to seize the farm and its outbuildings.

But this small French triumph, like the opening of the battle, came too late. In spite of the delays en route, the faithful Blücher had by now brought two more Prussian corps to the scene. The II Corps under *Generalmajor* Georg Dubislaw Ludwig Pirch reinforced Bülow and made enough headway against Lobau that instead of exploiting Ney's success at La Haye–Sainte, Napoleon had to send two battalions of the Old Guard to the right flank, where their bayonet charge regained the critical lost ground. By the time the emergency on the French right was attended to, however, Ziethen's Prussian I Corps was arriving on the left of Wellington's main position; it had gone astray on the march, but Baron Müffling had found it and redirected it. Wellington then felt free to shift two fresh cavalry brigades from his left to the support of his weary and threatened center.

The brigades were needed, because in the center Napoleon made what proved his last throw of the dice. From La Haye–Sainte, Ney was now bombarding part of the Allied center virtually at point-blank range. It was apparent to both sides that the center was wavering. Ney appealed to Napoleon for a charge of the Imperial Guard.

Because the attention of the Guard had just been directed eastward, it took time to organize even that part of the Guard not committed to the French right for an attack in the center. Not until about 7:00 P.M. did Napoleon himself lead forward almost a dozen battalions of the Guard and turn them over to Ney, for the latter to lead them personally in the assault.

And for the last time Ney displayed both his bravery and his professional ineptitude. Again veering westward from La Haye–Sainte, he led the charge toward the rightward part of Wellington's center—the part that was strongest to begin with and least shaken. There British and Dutch infantry including much of the British Guards rose up out of the standing grain to deliver devastating volleys, and well-placed artillery joined in. The Imperial Guard recoiled at about 8:00 P.M.

As Ziethen's Prussians approached, Napoleon had tried unwisely to offset their moral effect by spreading the rumor that they were Grouchy's men coming to reinforce his army. Just as the Imperial Guard was retreating, however, Ziethen's troops came into action and soon tore into the northeast corner of the French line. This unexpected threat touched off cries of treason among Napoleon's men, and on the heels of the long day's battle and the retreat of the Guard, the very thought could induce panic. Where little over an hour before it had been Wellington's center that seemed about to break, now it was the French army that began disintegrating.

Where in fact was Grouchy? During the morning of the battle he had persisted in his misguided intention to push against the Prussian left, compounding the error by continuing to march ponderously in a single column along the right bank of the River Dyle, failing even to pose a serious threat to the left flank of the Prussians' Wavre position because it was on the left bank. Moreover, he did not bestir himself or his men for an early start, and he paused along the way for a leisurely breakfast. The belated cannonade that opened the battle of Waterloo reached his ears just after he finished this repast. Some of his generals, notably Gérard, now urged him to follow the one maxim that Napoleon had always substituted in a combat emergency for his usual obsession with centralized control: to march to the sound of the guns. But Grouchy required the most centralized of control to keep him from straying from operational good sense; he refused to march to the sound of the Waterloo guns.

Instead, he persisted in his march upon Wavre, where he found Thielmann's III Corps barring the crossings of the Dyle. About 4:00 P.M. Grouchy opened an attack against the crossings, but he dispersed his effort along a considerable stretch of the marshy banks of the river and made little progress. About 5:00 P.M. Grouchy received the Emperor's message that Bülow was arriving at the Waterloo battlefield, but the commander of the right wing was too deeply entangled in his futile struggle and faulty tactics to do much about it. Not until almost dark did a charge by hussars carry the Limale bridge to permit Grouchy's wing to begin crossing the Dyle in force. Then Grouchy's numbers at last overcame Thielmann, and about 11:00 P.M. the Prussians retreated. Each side lost about 2,400 casualties in this action at Wavre, but the crucial fact was that Grouchy had spent all of June 18 making no material contribution to what was happening at Waterloo a short distance away.

Grouchy could not help Napoleon when Wellington sent his whole line forward with a cheer to crush the French as the Imperial Guard recoiled from its failed assault. Three battalions of Napoleon's Guard alone stood up for a time against the Allied charge. In the end, it was only two battalions of the 1st Grenadiers of the Imperial Guard that would not break as the whole of the *Armée du Nord* disintegrated around them.

Lobau's corps was the last large formation to go, holding on against Bülow and Pirch long enough to keep the road back to Charleroi open for the flight of most of Napoleon's army, preventing the disaster from being utterly completed by an Allied envelopment.

Wellington and Blücher met each other shortly before nine o'clock at the inn appropriately called La Belle Alliance. There they agreed that the Anglo-Dutch army had been used so hard that pursuit should be left to the Prussians. Blücher's men accordingly pressed on through the night, driving the French successively from seven would-be bivouacs and at last across the Sambre. Napoleon narrowly escaped capture by Prussian hussars at Genappe.

The Allies lost 22,000 casualties at Waterloo, but the French lost 41,000 and in their retreat left behind almost all their artillery. It was far too costly and complete a defeat to be sustained by the brittle prestige of Napoleon's recently restored Empire. Grouchy, to give him his due, responded to the first news of the disaster by swiftly extricating his wing from Wavre and marching toward Namur, the one good route to Paris open to him. With skill and bravery he evaded Blücher's clutches. On June 20 his rear guard turned about, short of Namur, to drive off the vanguard of Pirch and Thielmann. The next day another rear-guard action held back Pirch while most of Grouchy's men marched through Namur. But it was too late to save Napoleon.

Grouchy notwithstanding, the Allies advanced too rapidly on Paris to permit the adequate completion of the defenses. Davout was there with a paper strength of over 100,000 but only 15,000 reliable troops. The legislative Chambers panicked and turned against Napoleon. The Emperor arrived at the capital at eight in the morning of June 21, leaving Soult to attempt to rally the Army of the North at Juvigny. On June 22, unable to regain the confidence of the Chambers, Napoleon abdicated for a second time.

In the Waterloo campaign, the professional improvements of the Prussian officer corps were still a long way from the standards that would distinguish the Prussian Army by the time of the Austro-Prussian War of 1866 and the Franco-Prussian War of 1870–1871. In the very aftermath of the victory, Grouchy escaped in part because Gneisenau so far forgot himself as to join in the pursuit like an ordinary cavalryman instead of attending to his duties as Chief of Staff, so that Pirch did not receive the proper orders for the pursuit. Nevertheless, by 1815 the Prussians had achieved a level of professional performance in command and staff work that readily excelled both the erratic generalship of the failing French Emperor and the vagaries of subordinate French staff and line officers for whom Napoleon had never seen fit to provide an appropriate military education. The Prussian Army with its superior professional accomplishments and, as a corollary, its steadfast performance of its duty made contributions to the victory of Waterloo indispensable enough that the battle may be termed a triumph of military professionalism over the less-than-professional command standards of Napoleon's army.

None of this comment is intended to detract from the Duke of Wellington's stature as a hero of Waterloo. The calmness of the Iron Duke during the climactic phase of the battle was also invaluable in shaping the outcome, holding the Anglo-Dutch army to its stubborn resistance against the desperate onslaughts of the French. But in the course of the campaign Wellington's strategic judgments had been consistently dubious in quality, disposed as he was from the beginning almost to the end to believe that Napoleon would threaten his right flank and his line of retreat to the Channel rather than his left and the connection between his army and Blücher's. Napoleon outgeneraled Wellington—and Blücher as well—from the opening of the campaign until June 16. On that morning the French army was on the verge of being able to complete either one or the other of Napoleon's strategic designs, either the separation of the two Allied armies from each other or at least their defeat in detail by striking first one and then the other in the course of their forward deployment. The disappointment of Napoleon's strategic hopes on the 16th, the day of Quatre-Bras and Ligny, sprang neither from inherent flaws in Napoleon's strategy nor from achievements of generalship on Wellington's part, but mainly from inadequate professional standards of leadership in the French Army under Napoleon, and of course particularly from the blunderings of Ney (and secondarily from the similar professional flaws of French staff work and from Napoleon's failure, partly because of those flaws, to make his intentions for the day clear). But as far as Wellington's generalship is concerned, his slow concentration at Quatre-Bras gave Napoleon more than ample opportunity not only to defeat the Anglo-Dutch army while the Prussians were elsewhere but to overpower Wellington's own force in detail, as its component parts arrived in slow succession at the crossroads. As late as June 17, it was Ney's lack of skill rather than Wellington's generalship that saved the Anglo-Dutch army from a separate defeat in isolation from the Prussians.

Even in the battle of Waterloo itself, Wellington's generalship was less important to the successful Anglo-Dutch defense than French mistakes and the fighting quality of Wellington's troops, particularly his British troops and the British-trained King's German Legion. Waterloo was the latest of many occasions dating back over the century since the retirement of Marlborough when the limitations of the British officer corps were compensated for by the excellent tactical performance of the British soldiery. The devastating British musket-fire of Waterloo echoed the musketry of Québec and Minden.

But it was the Prussians who, despite the newness, the consequent severe limitations, and sometimes therefore the faltering of their professionalizing system, performed best in the Waterloo campaign. The Prussian commanders of army and corps more consistently made and acted on correct judgments than any other leaders in the campaign save possibly Napoleon himself. Blücher, with Gneisenau at his side (and in spite of the occasional lapses of the Chief of Staff), excelled as an army commander beyond previous expectations for this unsubtle old warrior. More consistently than Wellington, he kept in view the necessity to maintain contact between the two Allied armies as the *sine qua non* of the campaign. In the climax at Waterloo, Blücher's consistent adherence to this perception paid off to make the Prussian army in effect the grand reserve of the Anglo-Dutch army. More than any other element in the battle, it was Wellington's ability to count on Blücher and the Prussians that determined the outcome.

Our narrative of two hundred years of war ends as it began, with the grand though grim spectacle of a climactic battle. Gustavus Adolphus at Breitenfeld had opened the age of battles as an epoch in the history of war. In medieval war, large-scale battles had sometimes occurred, but they were a rarity. Gustavus Adolphus placed a new emphasis on the waging of battle to impose a new decisiveness upon warfare. War in the Middle Ages had tended toward prolonged indecision, but the Swedish King wished to push it toward prompt, emphatic resolution, so that it might better serve his purpose of enhancing the power of his emerging nation-state without undermining its very object by disastrously draining the resources of the state—decidedly limited resources in the case of Gustavus Adolphus's Sweden. In a successful battle, the enemy army might be drastically depleted or even effectively destroyed in a single day, and the enemy might thus be rendered nearly or completely helpless to prolong the war. From Gustavus Adolphus to Napoleon, military strategy tended to be a quest for the destruction of the enemy army with the battle as the means to the rapid and efficacious accomplishment of that destruction.

Notwithstanding the grandeur of climactic battle as a spectacle riveting the emotions—and notwithstanding also its agonies and horror—this strategy of annihilation of the enemy through battle was a rational response to the difficulties of achieving the objects of policy through war. In its rationality, it united the strategy of the era to the rise of officer professionalism. The quest for decisive battle was the educated soldier's rationalist effort to make war cost-effective, the promptness of the decision through battle promising to prevent an inordinate drain upon the resources of the state.

The battle persisted as the centerpiece of war from Breitenfeld through Waterloo even though in the late seventeenth and the eighteenth centuries the objects of war often became less grandiose than those of the struggle for mastery in Central Europe during Gustavus Adolphus's time, when rival political and military ambitions were intensified by the claims of Roman Catholic versus Protestant Christianity. While European statesmen and soldiers from 1648 to 1792 in some measure moderated their rival claims to territorial and dynastic advantage lest excessive ambitions redound against everyone, including their authors, by destabilizing the entire European political system, nevertheless even deliberately moderated claims would be denied fulfillment if wars became merely inconclusive. Therefore, sooner or later the generals of this interval usually described as one of limited war sought battle after all as the means of decision and resolution. The so-called period of limited war reverberates with a roll call of battles by land and by sea—Fontenoy, Minden, Québec, Quiberon Bay, the Saints.

Moreover, the wars of the 1648–1792 interval were not all so limited in purpose as we have sometimes persuaded ourselves, not all so different from the struggles of Gustavus Adolphus or the later, democratically and nationalistically driven Wars of the French Revolution and Napoleon. The wars of Louis XIV were contests for French hegemony in Europe that can hardly be said to have differed in kind from the similar contests of Napoleon, even allowing that democratic nationalism was a factor in the latter but not in the former. The Seven Years War was aimed at the destruction of Prussia as a great power, an object not readily reconciled with bland generalizations about the eighteenth-century interval of limited wars. Given the objectives involved, it is not remarkable that the wars of Louis XIV and Frederick the Great rose up into frequent thunderstrokes of battle comparable to Breitenfeld and Lützen, Austerlitz and Waterloo—Blenheim, Oudenarde, Ramillies, and Malplaquet; Rossbach, Leuthen, Zorndorf, and Kunersdorf.

The Recalcitrant Indecisiveness of War

Yet the prevalence throughout the age of the climactic battle as the hallmark of war and the hoped-for means of decisiveness has tended to obscure another unifying theme in the history of war from Gustavus Adolphus to Napoleon: the persisting, recalcitrant indecisiveness of war, in spite of the strategists' search for decision through destructive battle. The indecisiveness of the Thirty Years War, notwithstanding the ambitions and strategy of Gustavus Adolphus, has been evident enough; the very name given to the struggle implies prolonged stalemate and prepares us to acknowledge that the contest for Catholic versus Protestant, Habsburg versus Bourbon, and south German versus north German supremacy ended in clear-cut triumph for none of these contending parties and causes. But subsequent wars from 1648 to 1815 have often been regarded as contrastingly decisive. Napoleon in particular was hailed in his time and after as the discoverer or rediscoverer of the battle so decisive in its annihilation of the enemy army in a single afternoon that the Napoleonic victories of Austerlitz and

Jena-Auerstädt are regarded as the classic fulfillments of a strategy of annihilation through decisive battle.

Obviously, nevertheless, Napoleon's great victorious battles were decisive only in the short run. They destroyed enemy armies effectively enough that Napoleon was able to impose upon his adversaries peace treaties favorable to himself and unfavorable to them. But the treaties did not last. Against great powers possessing large populations and resources and a measure of political resiliency, the destruction of one army did not preclude their raising another army to fight Napoleon again. Year after year, in seemingly climactic battle after battle, Napoleon pushed his enemies down—but they refused to stay down. Altogether, then, the Napoleonic Wars resembled the Thirty Years War in their prolonged indecision.

The resemblance is all the greater when we remember that the Napoleonic Wars were merely the concluding phase of the Wars of the French Revolution, and that those wars in turn were the concluding phase of a Second Hundred Years War—lasting in fact from 1688 to 1815 and thus more or less continuously for over a century—between France and Great Britain. Viewed in this perspective, Waterloo was surely less a battle decisive in itself than the culmination of a process in which the contending nations had long lurched toward exhaustion, Waterloo proving that France had plunged further down that pit than her rivals.

This perspective regarding Waterloo as merely the culmination of exhaustion and attrition holds true also in terms of a shorter run. In particular, the Peninsular War as the penultimate phase of the Hundred Years War set the scene for the final Franco-British confrontation at Waterloo, and the Peninsular War was a contest not of climactic battles but of attrition; it signaled the imminent eclipse of the age of battles. Before the close of the next great war—the American Civil War—rival military chieftains would have abandoned the quest for rapid strategic decision through the climactic battle to adopt instead a strategy much like Wellington's in Iberia, relying on superior management of resources, both manpower and matériel, to wear down the enemy and outlast him in a prolonged contest of attrition. The age of battles gave way to exchanges of casualties and resources in sustained combat on the pattern of the late campaigns of the American Civil War and, preeminently, of the First World War. In Wellington's reliance on logistical superiority, the Peninsular War even foreshadowed at least dimly the Second World War as a contest of rival economies. In Wellington's dependence on the Spanish national rising, it also foreshadowed the coming age of the guerrilla, as the ultimate departure from the grand, romantic, climactic battle as the essence of strategy.

Because the Second Hundred Years War became a contest of mutual exhaustion, it ended with the power relationship between Great Britain and France not fundamentally altered in spite of the exertions of the war, certainly not in proportion to the costs of the war. To be sure, Great Britain secured an overseas imperial ascendancy; but geography combined with the nature of the early modern commercial economy had always made that result probable, regardless of the war; England was already on the path toward imperial ascendancy before the Second Hundred Years War began. If France meanwhile had been humbled through exhaustion in land warfare, its inherent strength was promptly to rees-tablish it as the preeminent European land power following 1815 even though Louis XIV and Napoleon were gone.

The recalcitrant indecisiveness of war throughout the age of battles made war consistently dubious as a means through the employment of which to secure the political ends of the state. The kind of decisiveness that Gustavus Adolphus and his successors as the leading strategists of the age sought through the pursuit of climactic, victorious battle was the decisiveness that would permit the warring state to achieve its political purposes more rapidly and economically through war than by any other available means, and certainly not at a cost in lives and resources that would be disproportionately high in relation to the purposes achieved. In fact, the chronic indecisiveness of war from the seventeenth through the early nineteenth centuries, war's chronic inability to attain the ends desired when nation-states chose to invoke it except at an inordinately high cost if at all, made warfare not a worthy instrument of policy but an expression of the bank-ruptcy of policy.

This is not to say that the statesmen of the age were always wrong when they chose war. It may well be that the threat of French hegemony in Europe under either Louis XIV or Napoleon imperiled the vital interests of all the other European states enough to justify the use of war to escape that threat. More clearly, the governing elite of the Prussian state (though scarcely the inhabitants of that state in general) gained more than they lost by their resort to war rather than allowing the hostile great powers to destroy Prussia as a major power. More clearly still, the people of France in the first phase of the French Revolutionary Wars had enough to lose if the hostile monarchies should overthrow their revolu-tion that their recourse to force to save it may seem warranted. War sometimes served to defend at not altogether an exorbitant cost institutions and movements that still seem worth defending. But as a positive instrument of policy, as a weapon with which to win positive gains for the national interest at a cost not disproportionate to the gains, war in the age of battles was consistently a disap-pointment and a failure.

In that light, the state serving its interests best was the state that counted least on war as an instrument of policy. This consideration sheds a more favor-able light than do narrower considerations of effective military strategies—in-cluding those expressed in this book—upon Great Britain's persistent efforts to avoid large expenditures of lives and resources in war by refusing to build large armies even in wartime, preferring to emphasize sea power instead. By this means, Great Britain in effect opted out of the use of large-scale war in the continental fashion as an instrument of policy. The Royal Navy gave it just enough leverage in war and diplomacy to permit it to remain one of the most influential of the great powers. This leverage never had so decisive an effect on continental warfare and strategy as Great Britain would have liked or as some admirers of British policy have imagined since. In the terms of military strategy, Britain had to wage unduly lengthy wars because it did not have a large enough and efficient enough army to campaign on land against Louis XIV, Napoleon, or any rival sovereign in the interval between those two, except with the expenditure of long years of time and in continual danger of setbacks; meanwhile sea power could not produce against major continental adversaries sufficiently decisive strategic effects to compensate for the inadequacy of British land power. Great Britain never accorded its soldiers from Marlborough through Wellington the resources that they needed for the efficient pursuit of military victory. On the other hand, none of the greatest continental armies achieved quick victories either.

Thus, viewed from the perspective of long-range national interests rather than of immediately efficacious military strategy, Great Britain's neglect of its army in favor of its navy has much to be said for it after all. By this method Great Britain avoided the heaviest expenses of war as an instrument of policy without altogether eschewing war and thereby abrogating its great-power status. It escaped the worst costs of the inherent indecisiveness of war, and its prosperity and its imperial interests progressed steadily forward.

Battle and the Profession of Officership

For those states that unlike Great Britain chose to make war a central instrument of the pursuit of their goals in national policy, the nurturing of the profession of military officership was a corollary of their utilization of war. The Dutch in their struggle to secure national independence—one of the most persuasive examples in this era of the occasional utility of war in defending national values in spite of war's tendency toward costly indecision—had invented the modern profession of officership, substituting men educated in the military art for the knightly warriors whom the United Provinces in large part lacked. Gustavus Adolphus then seized upon the concept of the educated officer corps—of officership as a profession—for purposes different from those of the Dutch, for a war of national aggrandizement rather than the defense of national independence. Gustavus Adolphus did so because he needed to wage war decisively, to attain his objects quickly before Sweden's limited resources were played out.

He therefore pursued the decisive battle. But to destroy enemy armies through decisive battles of annihilation, Gustavus could not rely on slipshod, fortuitously successful battlefield command. He had to educate his officers to a degree of professional skill sufficient to permit them to march an army to the battlefield with enough administrative competence that the army did not disintegrate or lose its means of logistical sustenance along the way, and then sufficient that the tactical handling of the troops in combat would be skillful enough to make a decisive margin of victory in terms of numbers and cohesion retained versus numbers and cohesiveness stripped from the enemy a realistic goal.

Gustavus Adolphus appeared to succeed well enough in his purposes that his methods came to be emulated. While he failed ultimately to establish Sweden as a great power, that failure could readily be explained away either by his premature death or by reference to the dearth of Swedish resources rather than in terms of inherent flaws in his policy and strategy. Accordingly, Louis XIV took up and applied the same military methods, including the professionalization of the officer corps, for much the same purposes. He used an enlarged army and an increasingly professional band of officers to seek to wage war efficiently enough, and therefore with decisive enough results, to make war a suitable instrument for the attainment of French mastery in Europe. And Louis succeeded for a long enough time and to a sufficient degree in approaching that mastery—it required a combination of almost all the other states of Europe in prolonged wars to stop him—so that henceforth an educated, professional officer corps became the norm in all major European armies. Without professional skills, armies could no longer be supplied, maneuvered, and fought effectively enough to serve the military purposes of great or even medium-sized powers.

In spite of occasional retrogressions, including Frederick the Great's and Napoleon's relative neglect of the values of a professional officer corps because they relied so exclusively on themselves, there occurred no substantial deviation from a growing acceptance through the seventeenth and eighteenth centuries of the necessity for military professionalism in land armies throughout Europe. The gradual differentiation of military officership from statesmanship because of the growth of military professionalism found an expression in the decreasing frequency throughout this period of the appearance of monarchs as battlefield commanders. The performances of the Russian and Austrian Emperors and the Prussian King when they took to the field during the climactic phases of the Napoleonic Wars were humbling ones for reasons not to be found only in the mental capacities and the characters of those particular sovereigns. Effective military command had come to require an expertise that monarchs not extensively educated in the art of war could no longer possess.

The rise of professional qualifications for leadership in land armies had also come to differentiate army from naval command. In the navies, the lag of officer education in military professionalism brought about by concentration on the difficult art of seamanship encouraged tactical inflexibility that in turn limited potentialities for operational and strategic achievement. In the navies, tactical, operational, and strategic study and thought all stagnated except under the occasional impetus of an infrequent genius—meaning of course Nelson above all others.

In the absence of a strong tradition of naval officer professionalism it is all the more remarkable that Nelson, unlike Napoleon, shared with his subordinates the perceptions springing from his own genius to transform them into competent professionals by means of education—his shipboard seminars for his captains. Anyone challenged to establish effective military institutions and somehow given the choice of Nelson or Napoleon to create them for him ought to select Nelson. Almost singlehandedly, the victory of the Nile and Trafalgar began to carry naval officership into the era of professionalization.

Officer Professionalism and the Violence of War

The initial effect of the emergence and gradual rise of officer professionalism upon the violence and brutality of war appears to have been to encourage restraint. Officer professionalism was probably one of many elements fostering the transition from the often unrestrained depredations against civilian lives and property in the Thirty Years War to the relative confinement of violence to the battlefield and the relative immunity of civilians from harm to their persons and property in the wars of the late seventeenth and the eighteenth centuries. While limiting the objectives of war helped limit the violence of the means whereby wars were fought, the notion that post–1648 wars were limited in aim can, as we have seen, readily be exaggerated. The tendency to limit the violence of the means sprang also from better disciplining of armies by increasingly professional officers, the superior logistical systems installed by improved military administration, and the recognition by officers possessing a strategic education and insight that indiscriminate violence was likely to prove strategically counterproductive.

It is consistent with this conclusion that early officer professionalism helped curb the violence of war, particularly violence directed against noncombatants. When after 1792 the Wars of the French Revolution and Napoleon began to break free from some of the limitations that had been imposed since 1648, the source of such a return toward indiscriminate violence as occurred, for example, in the guerrilla struggles in Spain, lay not so much in the quality of officership as in nationalism's reinjection into war of mass emotions akin to those of the religious hostilities that had done much to generate the atrocities of the Thirty Years War.

On the other hand, in the increasing differentiation of military officership from civilian statesmanship there lay the danger that in time officers might lose sight of the political purposes of war and elevate military means above political ends. Such a process might in turn obscure the possible strategic counterproductivity of indiscriminate violence, because political and strategic vision ought to be closely conjoined, and their separation can impair both. The divorcement of military means from considerations of political objectives might encourage rather than discourage unrestrained violence. In 1815, however, that potential for professional officership to move toward rather than away from indiscriminately violent war remained a possibility only.

It was a possibility that the newly enhanced variety of officer professionalism developed by the Prussian reformers might conceivably encourage. The greater the separation of military expertise from civilian statesmanship, the greater the chance that military means might take on a life of their own separate from and even undercutting political ends. Down the road of enhanced military autonomy lay the claim that military necessity might demand such means as unrestricted submarine warfare or the aerial bombing of cities. But so far, up to 1815, military professionalism had helped restrain rather than escalate the violence of war, and particularly had helped to restrict that violence to enemy combatants while protecting civilian lives and property.

The gravest threat to the limitations upon the violence of war lay neither in the autonomy of professional officers nor in the return of popular emotionalism to war, with democracy and nationalism supplying after 1792 the enthusiasms and hatreds that in the sixteenth and early seventeenth centuries had erupted out of religious rivalries. The gravest threat to restraints upon the violence of war resided rather in the persistent, intractable tendency of war toward indecisiveness. From Gustavus Adolphus to Napoleon, policymakers continually failed to capture in war the goals for which they resorted to war, except at costs that sorely undercut if they did not altogether nullify the value of the goals. From Gustavus Adolphus to Napoleon, soldiers in spite of growing professional skills failed to instill into war the capacity to achieve objectives at reasonable cost— the capacity for decisiveness—in pursuit of which sovereigns and statesmen cultivated officer professionalism in the first place.

And because war by remaining indecisive remained an unsatisfactory instrument for the pursuit of political ends, war continually nourished a frustration among its authors, threatening to break out in the more and more unlimited application of violence. To accept war was to accept violence as a permissible instrument for the attainment of political objectives. Once violence was deemed acceptable, then if limited violence failed to secure the desired ends, there was always a temptation to try unlimited violence.

The plunder and rapine that made the army of Gustavus Adolphus not the Christian host of his aspirations but a byword for cruelty from the Baltic to Bohemia, the rape of the Rhenish Palatinate by the forces of Louis XIV amidst the supposed period of limited war, the repeated degeneration of the Spanish war of liberation against Napoleon into bouts of thievery and murder by all concerned, conspicuously including Wellington's British soldiers— all these descents into visions of Hell owed much to the frustrations of the belligerents from kings and generals down to the lowliest soldiery, over prolonged campaigning and prolonged fatigue, hunger, and misery that seemingly accomplished no purpose at all.

The larger the objectives of war, the more acute the frustration of indecision. When sometimes in the late seventeenth and the eighteenth centuries wars were in fact as limited in their objectives as the stereotyped version of the period would suggest, disappointment spawned by indecision could be contained, and the rigors imposed upon the soldiers might also be limited and moderate enough to prevent their inclination toward brutality from rising up in demoniacal fury. But when the chronic indecisiveness of war disappointed the fulfillment of expectations as large as those of hegemony in Europe or national liberation from hated oppressors, then frustration almost inevitably generated both the calculated and the spontaneous resort to deeper and baser cruelties, to the sack of cities and the ravishing of countrysides both in search of revenge and in the usually vain hope that larger cruelties will break the enemy's spirit.

War in the age of battles was not an effective extension of policy by other means. With partial exceptions encompassing those powers that like Great Britain could sometimes remain on war's periphery and even fight it by proxy, war was not the extension of policy but the bankruptcy of policy.

BIBLIOGRAPHICAL
NOTES

Any historical study of the military art and particularly of strategy in the early modern and modern eras must begin with Edward Mead Earle, ed., with the collaboration of Gordon A. Craig and Felix Gilbert, *Makers of Modern Strategy from* [Niccolò] *Machiavelli to Hitler* (Princeton, New Jersey: Princeton University Press, 1943), and with its much revised and updated counterpart, Peter Paret, ed., with the collaboration of Gordon A. Craig and Felix Gilbert, *Makers of Modern Strategy: Military Thought from Machiavelli to the Nuclear Age* (Princeton, New Jersey: Princeton University Press, 1986).

A magisterial examination of the conduct of European war from the earliest times, encompassing tactics, strategy, and logistics, is Archer Jones, *The Art of War in the Western World* (Urbana and Chicago: University of Illinois Press, 1987). The now-classic survey of war in the modern era, beginning at about the same point as the present book, is Theodore Ropp, *War in the Modern World*, New, Revised Edition (New York, N.Y.: Collier Books, 1962).

Emphasizing the late nineteenth and the twentieth centuries but indispensable to studying the art of command in the early modern era as well, an art crucial to the quest for decision in battle, is Martin van Creveld, *Command in War* (Cambridge, Massachusetts and London, England: Harvard University Press, 1985).

Thoroughly impressive in scholarship and in interpretive grasp, but perhaps underrating the degree of autonomy that military power can achieve in relation to the general economic well-being of a state, is Paul Kennedy, *The Rise and Fall of the Great Powers: Economic Change and Military Conflict from 1500 to 2000* (New York: Random House, 1988).

Indispensable on the evolution of the technology of war, and regarding technology not simply as military hardware but as the embodiment of systems of ideas, is Martin van Creveld, *Technology and War: From 2000 B.C. to the Present* (New York: The Free Press, A Division of Macmillan, Inc.; London: Collier Macmillan Publishers, 1989). A collection of essays on military technology similarly relating the hardware to larger dimensions of warfare, and particularly to the evolution of military organization, is John A. Lynn, ed., *Tools of War: Instruments, Ideas, and Institutions of Warfare, 1445–1871* (Urbana and London: University of Illinois Press, 1990).

A comprehensive history of weaponry that is especially useful on early modern armament is William Reid, *Arms through the Ages* (New York, Hagerstown, San Francisco, London: Harper & Row, Publishers, 1976).

On the profession of military officership the pioneering and most stimulating observations are those of Samuel P. Huntington, *The Soldier and the State: The Theory and Politics of Civil-Military Relations* (Cambridge, Massachusetts: The Belknap Press of Harvard University Press, 1957). Huntington dates the origin of the profession of officership considerably later than does the present author, from the Prussian military reforms of the Napoleonic era and from still later in other states. His analysis of the nature of the profession nevertheless remains the best available. There is also much about officership as a profession, with judgments concerning the time of its origin more nearly corresponding to those in this book, in Jacques [Jacobus Adrianus Antonicus] van Doorn, *The Soldier and Social Change: Comparative Studies in the History and Sociology of the Military* (Beverly Hills, London: SAGE Publications, 1975). For further similar views see Gerke Teitler, *The Genesis of the Professional Officers' Corps,* tr. Cristina N. Ter Heide-Lopy, Inter-University Seminar on Armed Forces and Society (Beverly Hills/London: SAGE Publications, 1977); original edition, *De wordung von het professionele officierscorps* (Rotterdam: Universitaire Pres Rotterdam, 1974).

On the institutional aspects of military forces more generally in the early part of the age of battles, see André Corvisier, *Armies and Societies in Europe, 1494–1789,* tr. Abigail Thomas Siddall (Bloomington and London: Indiana University Press, 1979); original edition, *Armées et sociétés en Europe de 1494 à 1789* (Paris: Presses Universitaires de France, 1976).

The battles of the age are recounted, with brief transitional narratives linking each battle to the next, in John Frederick Charles Fuller, *A Military History of the Western World,* 3 vols. (New York: Funk & Wagnalls Company, 1953–1957), II, *From the Defeat of the Spanish Armada, 1588 to the Battle of Waterloo, 1815* (1955).

Without a superior as an interpretative and critical study of a particular army is Corelli Barnett, *Britain and Her Army 1509–1970: A Military, Political and Social Survey* (New York: William Morrow & Company, 1970). For a tactical focus, see Frederick Myatt, *The British Infantry 1660–1945: The Evolution of a Fighting Force* (Poole, Dorset: Blandford Press, 1983).

CHAPTERS ONE, THE RETURN OF THE LEGIONS, AND TWO, THE LIMITS OF THE NEW LEGIONS

A much-needed summing up on the fathers of modern warfare has appeared recently: Gunther E. Rothenberg, ch. 2, "Maurice of Nassau, Gustavus Adolphus, Raimondo Montecuccoli, and the 'Military Revolution' of the Seventeenth Century," in Peter Paret, ed., with the collaboration of Gordon A. Craig and Felix Gilbert, *Makers of Modern Strategy: Military Thought from Machiavelli to the Nuclear Age* (Princeton, New Jersey: Princeton University Press, 1986), pp. 32–63, especially pp. 37–45 on Maurice and pp. 45–55 on Gustavus. Rothenberg writes with awareness of an earlier, seminal work on the transition to modern war, Michael Roberts, *The Military Revolution, 1560–1660: An Inaugural Lecture Delivered before the Queen's University of Belfast* (Belfast: M. Bond, 1956). Roberts has also superbly delineated the contributions of Gustavus II Adolphus to modern war in his *Gustavus Adolphus: A History of Sweden,* 2 vols. (London, New York: Longmans, Green and Co., 1953–1958). See further Roberts's essay, "The Military Revolution, 1560–1660," in his *Essays in Swedish History* (London: Weidenfeld & Nicholson, 1967), pp. 195–225. Sir George Norman Clark has written a comprehensive survey of *War and Society in the Seventeenth Century* (Cambridge: Cambridge University Press, 1958). Appearing too late to be digested fully for the present work but indispensable henceforth to the student of early modern war is Geoffrey Parker, *The Military Revolution: Military Innovation and the Rise of the West, 1500–1800* (Cambridge, New York, Port Chester, Melbourne, Sydney: Cambridge University Press, 1958).

Stimulating thoughts on the birth of modern war as well as on a host of topics military and otherwise are to be found in William H. McNeil's erudite *The Pursuit of Power: Technology, Armed Forces, and Society since A.D. 1000* (Chicago: University of Chicago Press, 1982), especially in ch. 3, "The Business of War in Europe, 1000–1600," pp. 63–116, and ch. 4, "Advances in Europe's Art of War, 1600–1750," pp. 117–143. McNeil offers a particularly good concise consideration of the Dutch contributions on pp. 122–123, 126–134. Also on the Dutch see Maury G. Feld, "Middle-Class Society and the Rise of Military Professionalism: The Dutch Army 1589–1609," *Armed Forces and Society: An Interdisciplinary Journal on Military Institutions, Civil-Military Relations, Arms Control and Peacekeeping, and Conflict Management,* I (Summer 1975): 419–442.

The best recent histories of the Dutch struggle for independence are Pieter Geyl, *The Revolt of the Netherlands, 1555–1609*, Second Edition (London: Ernest Benn Limited; New York: Barnes & Noble Books [A Division of Harper & Row Publishers Inc.], 1958), and Geoffrey Parker, *The Dutch Revolt* (Ithaca, New York: Cornell University Press, 1977). On the Spanish Army in the Netherlands an already-classic work is Geoffrey Parker, *The Army of Flanders and the Spanish Road, 1567–1659: The Logistics of Spanish Victory and Defeat in the Low Countries War* (Cambridge: Cambridge University Press, 1972).

The current standard history of the Thirty Years War is Geoffrey Parker, Simon Adams, Gerhard Benecke, Richard Bonney, John H. Elliott, Robert John Weston Evans, Christopher R. Friedrichs, Bodo Nischan, Eric Ladewig Petersen (index under Ladewig Petersen), Michael Roberts; Research assistants, Andre W. Carus, Sheilagh C. Ogilvie, *The Thirty Years' War*, Revised Edition (London: Routledge & Kegan Paul Ltd., 1987). Still not to be missed because of its literary craftsmanship as well as its historical insight is Cicely Veronica Wedgwood, *The Thirty Years War* (London: Jonathan Cape Ltd., 1938). On the more directly military history of this and related wars, see David Maland, *Europe at War, 1600–1650* (Totowa, New Jersey: Rowman and Littlefield, 1980). See also Josef V. Polišenský, with the collaboration of Frederick Snider, *War and Society in Europe, 1618–1648* (Cambridge, London, New York, Melbourne: Cambridge University Press, 1978).

On Wallenstein see Francis Watson, *Wallenstein: Soldier Under Saturn: A Biography* (London: Chatto & Windus, 1938), and for the conduct of his military activities, Fritz Redlich, *The German Military Enterpriser and His Work Force: A Study in European Economic and Social History*, 2 vols. (Wiesbaden: Franz Steiner, 1964–1965).

CHAPTER THREE, UNDER THE LILY BANNERS

The works already cited as offering comprehensive overviews of the Thirty Years War of course apply here. There is an excellent brief account of "Rocroi, 1643," by Cyril Falls, in Cyril Falls, ed., *Great Military Battles* (New York: The Macmillan Company, 1964), pp. 16–29.

CHAPTER FOUR, THE ARMY OF THE SUN KING

On the army of Louis XIV see Pierre Goubert, *Louis XIV and Twenty Million Frenchmen*, tr. Anne Carter (New York: Pantheon Books, 1970); original edition, *Louis XIV et vingt millions de Français* (Paris: Fayard, 1966); John Baptist Wolf, *Louis XIV* (New York: W. W. Norton & Company, 1968); Warren Hamilton Lewis, *The Splendid Century: Life in the France of Louis XIV* (Garden City, New York: Doubleday Anchor Books, Doubleday & Company, Inc., 1957), with a concise treatment in ch. 5, "The Army," pp. 125–143. On administration of the military, there is Louis André, *Michel Le Tellier et Louvois* (Paris: A. Colin, 1945).

On the fortress and siegecraft warfare that Vauban symbolized and brought to its apogee, an excellent introduction—and a work readily understandable though its subject can be obfuscated by technicalities—is Christopher Duffy, *Fire and Stone: The Science of Fortress Warfare 1660–1860* (New York: Hippocrene Books, 1975). For an excellent introduction see Henri Guerlac, ch. 2, "Vauban: The Impact of Science on War," in Edward Mead Earle, ed., with the collaboration of Gordon A. Craig and Felix Gilbert, *Makers of Modern Strategy: Military Thought from Machiavelli to Hitler* (Princeton, New Jersey: Princeton University Press, 1943), pp. 26–48; reprinted as ch. 3 in Peter Paret, ed., with the collaboration of Gordon A. Craig and Felix Gilbert, *Makers of Modern Strategy from Machiavelli to the Nuclear Age* (Princeton, New Jersey: Princeton University Press, 1986), pp. 64–90.

The themes of this chapter are well developed for the various European armies in

Martin Duffy, ed., *The Military Revolution and the State 1500–1800*, Exeter Studies in History, Number 1 (Exeter: University of Exeter Press, 1980).

The English Army of the middle to late seventeenth century was of less importance to military history than the French but has been well served by the historians. A standard work is Sir Charles Harding Firth, *Cromwell's Army: A History of the English Soldier during the Civil Wars, the Commonwealth and the Protectorate*, 4th ed. (London: Methuen; New York: Barnes & Noble, 1962). Mark A. Kishlansky, *The Rise of the New Model Army* (Cambridge: Cambridge University Press, 1979) is useful on the development of organization. A recent overview is Philip J. Haythornthwaite, *The English Civil War, 1642–1651* (Poole, Dorset: Blandford Press, 1983). There is a good brief introduction in ch. 1, "The Age of Cromwell, 1625–1685," in Lord Michael Carver, *The Seven Ages of the British Army* (New York: Beaufort Books, 1984), pp. 1–37. On the English Army under Charles I and James II, see John Charles Roger Childs, *The Army of Charles II* (London: Routledge & Kegan Paul; Toronto: University of Toronto Press, 1976), and the same author's *The Army, James II, and the Glorious Revolution* (New York: St. Martin's Press, 1980).

CHAPTER FIVE, MARLBOROUGH'S BATTLES

Still indispensable as well as a sheer joy to read is Winston S. Churchill, *Marlborough: His Life and Times* (6 vols., New York: Charles Scribner's Sons, 1933–1938). This monument should be supplemented, however, by David Chandler, *Marlborough as Military Commander* (New York: Charles Scribner's Sons, 1973). On military organization and tactics, see the same author's *The Art of Warfare in the Age of Marlborough* (New York: Hippocrene Books, Inc., 1976). On the latter topics see also Richard E. Scouller, *The Armies of Queen Anne* (Oxford: The Clarendon Press, 1966) and Hugh Cuthbert Bosset Rogers, *The British Army of the Eighteenth Century* (New York: Hippocrene Books, Inc., 1977). For a concise introduction, see ch. 2, "The Age of Marlborough, 1685–1763," in Lord Michael Carver, *The Seven Ages of the British Army* (New York: Beaufort Books, Inc., 1984), pp. 38–72.

For Marlborough's great coadjutor there is Nicholas Henderson, *Prince Eugen of Savoy* (New York: Frederick A. Praeger, Publisher, 1965).

On the role of the Netherlands, see Alice Clare Carter, *Neutrality or Commitment: The Evolution of Dutch Foreign Policy 1667–1795* (London: Edward Arnold, 1975).

CHAPTER SIX, THE EMERGENCE OF THE GREAT POWERS OF EASTERN EUROPE

On Charles XII of Sweden and his army see Frans G. Bengtsson, *The Life of Charles XII, King of Sweden, 1697–1718*, tr. Naomi Walford, With an Introduction by Eric Linklater (London: Macmillan; New York: St. Martin's Press, 1960); original edition, *Karl XII: A Levnad* (Stockholm: Nostedt, 1959); also Ragnhild M. Hatton, *Charles XII of Sweden* (New York: Weybright and Talley, 1969).

On Peter the Great, see Vasili Osipovich Klyuchevsky (library cataloguing under Kliuchevskii), *Peter the Great*, tr. Liliana Archibald (New York: St. Martin's Press, 1958). The beginnings of the modern Russian Army are studied in Christopher Duffy, *Russia's Military Way to the West: Origins and Nature of Russian Military Power 1700–1800* (London, Boston: Routledge & Kegan Paul, 1981).

A useful introduction to the Habsburg army of the early modern era can be found in Thomas M. Barker, *The Military Intellectual and Battle: Raimondo Montecuccoli and the Thirty Years War* (Albany, New York: State University of New York Press, 1974). On the *Grenzer*, but with incidental information about much else in Habsburg military history, see Gunther E. Rothenberg, *The Austrian Military Border in Croatia, 1522–1747*, Illinois Studies in the Social Sciences (Urbana: University of Illinois Press, 1960), and the same author's *The Military Border in Croatia, 1740–1881: A Study of an Imperial Institution* (Chicago: University of Chicago Press, 1966). On the Habsburgs' military problems to the east in the eighteenth century there is Karl A. Roider, *Austria's Eastern Question, 1700–1790* (Princeton, New Jersey: Princeton University Press, 1982).

On the siege of Vienna by the Turks, see Thomas M. Barker, *Double Eagle and Crescent: Vienna's Second Turkish Siege and Its Historical Setting* (Albany: State University of New York Press, 1967), and John Walter Stoye, *The Siege of Vienna* (New York: Holt, Rinehart and Winston, 1965).

The subsequent military preeminence of Prussia and Germany accounts for the existence of an uncommonly rich literature on the origins of the Prussian Army. Within this literature there stands out Gordon A. Craig, *The Politics of the Prussian Army, 1640–1945* (New York and Oxford: Oxford University Press, 1956). Other studies of note include Karl Demeter, *Das Deutsche Offizierskorps*, Revidierte Auflage (Frankfurt am Main: Bernard & Graefe Verlag für Wehrwesen, 1962); English language edition, *The German Officer-Corps in Society and State, 1650–1945*, tr. Angus Malcolm, Introduction by Michael Howard (New York, Washington: Frederick A. Praeger, Publishers, 1965); Walter Goerlitz, *Das Deutsche Generalstab* (Frankfurt am Main: Verlag der Frankfurter Hefte, 1952; English language edition, *History of the German General Staff, 1657–1945*, tr. Brian Battershaw, Introduction by Walter Millis (New York: Praeger, 1953); Martin Kitchen, *A Military History of Germany from the Eighteenth Century to the Present Day* (Bloomington/London: Indiana University Press, 1975).

CHAPTER SEVEN, THE RISE OF NAVAL POWER

Indispensable not only on the Royal Navy but on the entire development of modern naval war is Geoffrey J. Marcus, *A Naval History of England*, 2 vols. to date, I, *The Formative Centuries* (Boston, Toronto: An Atlantic Monthly Press Book, Little, Brown and Company, 1962); II, *The Age of Nelson, The Royal Navy 1793–1815* (New York: The Viking Press, 1971). Also essential is Paul M. Kennedy, *The Rise and Fall of British Naval Mastery* (New York: Charles Scribner's Sons, 1976).

Still decidedly worth pondering is the seminal work on naval strategy, Alfred Thayer Mahan, *The Influence of Sea Power upon History, 1660–1783* (Boston: Little, Brown and Company, 1890). For a more recent overview, see Clark G. Reynolds, *Command of the Sea: The History and Strategy of Maritime Empires* (New York: William Morrow, 1974).

On English naval officership an excellent work, without parallel for any army in the early modern period, is Michael Lewis, *England's Sea-Officers: The Story of the Naval Profession* (London: G. Allen & Unwin Ltd., 1939).

For the early modern English Navy see Julian S. Corbett, *Drake and the Tudor Navy* (London: Longmans, Green, 1898). For a wider perspective than that of the English on sea power and early European expansionism there is Carlo M. Cipolla, *Guns, Sails, and Empires: Technological Innovation and the Early Phase of European Expansion, 1400–1700* (New York: Pantheon Books, 1966).

On the Armada, the reader should not miss the breadth and eloquence of Garrett Mattingly, *The Armada* (Boston: Houghton Mifflin Company, Cambridge: The Riverside Press, 1959). For a new view of the rival naval armaments, see Geoffrey Parker, "Why the Armada Failed," *History Today*, XXXVIII (May 1988): 26–33; reprinted in *MHQ: The Quarterly Journal of Military History*, I (Autumn 1988): 18–27.

For the navy of the English Commonwealth and Protectorate see Hans-Christoph Junge, *Flottenpolitik und Revolution: Die Entstehung der englischen Seemacht während der Herrschaft Cromwells* (Stuttgart: Klett-Cotta, 1980).

On English and British naval administration, the best introduction is Norman A. M. Rodger, *The Admiralty* (Lavenham, England: T. Dalton, 1979).

For the eventual and long-lasting great rival of the English Navy, the standard traditional history is Charles Germain Marie Baird de La Roncière (catalogued under La Ronciere), *Histoire de la marine française* . . . , 6 vols. (Paris: Plon-Nourret c^ie^, 1899–1932).

An excellent recent work is Ernest H. Jenkins, *A History of the French Navy: From Its Beginnings to the Present Day* (Annapolis: Naval Institute Press, 1973). For specifics on the period of this chapter, see Geoffrey Symcox, *The Crisis of French Sea Power, 1689–1697: From the Guerre d'Escadre to the Guerre de Course* (The Hague: M. Nijhoff, 1974).

For the evolution of naval tactics and particularly of the doctrine of the line ahead, see Julian Stafford Corbett, ed., *Fighting Instructions, 1530–1816,* Ed. with Elucidations from Contemporary Authorities (London: Printed for the Navy Records Society, 1905).

Indispensable for its background discussion of the age of sail as well as for its title topic is an early work by one of the greatest of American military critics and historians, Bernard Brodie, *Sea Power in the Machine Age* (Princeton: Princeton University Press; London: Humphrey Milford, Oxford University Press, 1941).

CHAPTER EIGHT, THE BATTLES OF FREDERICK THE GREAT

The best introduction to Frederick the Great and indeed to European warfare in his time remains Gerhard Ritter, *Friedrich der Grosse: Ein historisches Profil* (Heidelberg: Quelle & Meyer, 1954; English language edition, *Frederick the Great: A Historical Profile,* tr. with an intro. by Peter Paret [Berkeley and Los Angeles: University of California Press, 1968). Christopher Duffy has contributed an up-to-date military biography, *The Military Life of Frederick the Great* (New York: Atheneum, 1986). A sophisticated recent biography dealing with the multiple facets of Frederick's complex character is Robert B. Asprey, *Frederick the Great: The Magnificent Enigma* (New York: Ticknor & Fields, 1986). See also Robert R. Palmer, ch. 3, "Frederick the Great, Guibert, [Dietrich von] Bülow: From Dynastic to National War," in Edward Mead Earle, ed., with the collaboration of Gordon A. Craig and Felix Gilbert, *Makers of Modern Strategy: Military Thought from Machiavelli to Hitler* (Princeton, New Jersey: Princeton University Press, 1943), pp. 49–74, especially pp. 49–62; reprinted as ch. 4 in Peter Paret, ed., with the collaboration of Gordon A. Craig and Felix Gilbert, *Makers of Modern Strategy from Machiavelli to the Nuclear Age* (Princeton, New Jersey: Princeton University Press, 1986), pp. 91–119, especially pp. 91–105.

On European armies and warfare in the Frederician era more generally, there is an admirable, new, concise work by Christopher Duffy, *The Military Experience in the Age of Reason* (New York: Atheneum, 1988). The same prolific author has written books dealing specifically with Frederick's army and with two of the armies opposing Frederick: Christopher Duffy, *The Army of Frederick the Great,* Historic Armies and Navies (New York: Hippocrene Books, 1974); idem, *The Army of Maria Theresa,* Historic Armies and Navies (New York: Hippocrene Books, 1977); idem, *Russia's Military Road to the West: Origins and Nature of Russian Military Power, 1700–1800* (London: Routledge & Kegan Paul, 1981).

A first-rate study of the French Army, with information beyond the specific period of its title, is Lee Kennett, *The French Armies in the Seven Years' War: A Study in Military Organization and Administration* (Durham, N.C.: Duke University Press, 1967).

Also of wider scope than its title might suggest is Alice Clare Carter, *The Dutch Republic in Europe in the Seven Years War* (Coral Gables, Florida: University of Miami Press, 1971).

On the British Army, attention should again be called to Corelli Barnett, *Britain and Her Army 1508–1970: A Military, Political and Social Survey* (New York: William Morrow Company, 1970) and Hugh Cuthbert Bosset Rogers, *The British Army of the Eighteenth Century* (New York, N.Y.: Hippocrene Books, 1977). An excellent work deserving of more recognition is John A. Houlding, *Fit for Service: The Training of the British Army, 1715–1795* (Oxford: Clarendon Press; New York: Oxford University Press, 1981). For the Continental intervention in alliance with Frederick the Great, see Reginald Savory, *His Britannic Majesty's Army in Germany During the Seven Years' War* (Oxford: Clarendon Press, 1966).

A monumental work that deals mainly with later periods of German military history but that ought to be consulted on the era of Frederick the Great is Gerhard Ritter,

Staatskunst und Kriegshandwerk: Das Problem des «Militarismus» in Deutschland, 4 vols. (Munich: Verlag R. Oldenbourg, 1954–1968; English language edition, *The Sword and the Scepter: The Problem of Militarism in Germany*, tr. Heinz Norden, 4 vols. [Coral Gables, Florida: University of Miami Press, 1969–1973]).

CHAPTER NINE, THE FRENCH AND BRITISH ARMED FORCES FROM THE RHINE TO THE ST. LAWRENCE

On the British Navy, see again Geoffrey J. Marcus, *A Naval History of England*, 2 vols. to date, I, *The Formative Centuries* (Boston, Toronto: An Atlantic Monthly Press Book, Little, Brown and Company, 1962); II, *The Age of Nelson, The Royal Navy 1793–1815* (New York: Viking Press, 1971); and Paul M. Kennedy, *The Rise and Fall of British Naval Mastery* (New York: Charles Scribner's Sons, 1976). On the French Navy, see again Ernest H. Jenkins, *A History of the French Navy: From Its Beginnings to the Present Day* (Annapolis: Naval Institute Press, 1973). On the British Army, see again Corelli Barnett, *Britain and Her Army 1508–1970: A Military, Political and Social Survey* (New York: William Morrow & Company, 1970); John A. Houlding, *Fit for Service: The Training of the British Army, 1715–1795* (Oxford: Clarendon Press; New York: Oxford University Press, 1981); Hugh Cuthbert Bosset Rogers, *The British Army of the Eighteenth Century* (New York, N.Y.: Hippocrene Books, Inc., 1977); Reginald Savory, *His Britannic Majesty's Army in Germany during the Seven Years' War* (Oxford: Clarendon Press, 1966). On the French Army, see again Lee Kennett, *The French Armies in the Seven Years' War: A study in military organization and administration* (Durham, N.C.: Duke University Press, 1967).

On "the Forty-Five" and Culloden, standard works include John Prebble, *Culloden* (New York: Atheneum, 1962), which inserts much about the general nature of the Jacobite rising and the rival forces into an eloquent history of the immediate Culloden campaign, and Katherine Tomasson and Francis Buist, *Battles of the '45* British Battles Series, (New York: The Macmillan Company, 1962). There is a recent work focusing on William Augustus, Duke of Cumberland: William A. Speck, *The Butcher: The Duke of Cumberland and the Suppression of the 45* (Oxford: Basil Blackwell, 1981).

On the French Army under Louis XV see in addition to Kennett, op. cit., John Manchip White, *Marshal of France: The Life and Times of Maurice, Comte de Saxe /1696–1750/* (Chicago, New York, San Francisco: Rand McNally & Company, 1961); see particularly ch. 10, "Fontenoy, 1745," pp. 145–166. There is also a useful account of "Fontenoy, 1745," by Jacques Boudet in Cyril Falls, ed., *Great Military Battles* (New York: The Macmillan Company, 1964), pp. 50–57.

On the British versus French imperial struggle for America there is Gerald S. Graham, *Empire of the North Atlantic: The Maritime Struggle for North America*, Second Edition (Toronto: University of Toronto Press, 1958). The best account of the battle of Québec is Charles P. Stacey, *Quebec, 1759: The Siege and the Battle* (New York: St. Martin's Press, 1959). For a brief overview of the battle, see Christopher Hibbert, "Quebec, 1759," in Falls, ed., op. cit., pp. 66–77.

A superb account of the battle of Quiberon Bay is Geoffrey Marcus, *Quiberon Bay: The Campaign in Home Waters, 1759* (Barre, Massachusetts: Barre Publishing Company, 1966).

CHAPTER TEN, TOWARD WARS OF NATIONS

The best overview of the War for American Independence as a global contest is a work surveying it from the British perspective, Piers Mackesy, *The War for America, 1775–1783* (Cambridge, Massachusetts: Harvard University Press, 1965). This book is excellent on strategy and also offers an exceptionally detailed and insightfully critical analysis of British military and naval administration in the late eighteenth century.

The most comprehensive recent account of the war from the American perspective is Don Higginbotham, *The War of American Independence: Military Attitudes, Policies, and Practice, 1763–1789*, Louis Morton, general editor, The Wars of the United States (New York, New York: The Macmillan Company; London: Collier-Macmillan Ltd., 1971). The book aims so much for comprehensiveness in dealing with politics, economics, society, and thought, however, that it somewhat belies its subtitle with less military coverage than might be expected. Thus the best detailed account of the campaigns, with good material also on military organization, remains Christopher Ward, *The War of the Revolution*, ed. John Richard Alden, 2 vols. (New York: The Macmillan Company, 1952). Worthy of its title in its remarkably encyclopedic coverage is Mark Mayo Boatner III, *Encyclopedia of the American Revolution* Bicentennial Edition (New York: David McKay Company, Inc., 1974).

For American Revolutionary military institutions in their political, social, and intellectual context, see Don Higginbotham, *War and Society in Revolutionary America: The Wider Dimensions of Conflict* (Columbia: University of South Carolina Press, 1988); John Shy, *A People Numerous and Armed: Reflections on the Military Struggle for American Independence* (New York: Oxford University Press, 1976); James Kirby Martin and Mark Edward Lender, *A Respectable Army: The Military Origins of the Republic, 1763–1788* (Arlington Heights, Ill.: Harlan Davidson, 1982); and Charles Royster, *A Revolutionary People at War: The Continental Army and American Character, 1775–1783* (Chapel Hill, North Carolina: Published for the Institute of Early American History and Culture, Williamsburg, Virginia, by The University of North Carolina Press, 1979). The two former works consist largely of republications of essays and articles published by their authors elsewhere. More specifically directed to Revolutionary military organization is Robert K. Wright, Jr., *The Continental Army*, Army Lineage Series (Washington, D.C.: Center of Military History United States Army, 1983).

On American strategy, and particularly that of General George Washington, see Dave Richard Palmer, *The Way of the Fox: American Strategy in the War for America 1775–1783*, Contributions in Military History Number 8 (Westport, Connecticut: London, England: Greenwood Press, 1975).

On the climactic campaign including the battle of the Capes of the Chesapeake there is Burke Davis, *The Campaign That Won America: The Story of Yorktown* (New York: Dial Press, 1970).

For the Royal Navy in the American Revolution, see Sir William Milburne James, *The British Navy in Adversity: A Study of the War of American Independence* (London: Longmans, Green and Co., Ltd., 1926). More a diplomatic history than the naval study suggested by its title is Jonathan R. Dull, *The French Navy and American Independence: A Study of Arms and Diplomacy, 1774–1787* (Princeton, New Jersey: Princeton University Press, 1975). For the French effort to invade England there is Alfred Temple Patterson, *The Other Armada: The Franco-Spanish Attempt to Invade Britain in 1779* (Manchester: Manchester University Press, 1960).

CHAPTER ELEVEN,
PRELUDE TO REVOLUTION

Lee Kennett, *The French Armies in the Seven Years' War: A Study in Military Organization and Administration* (Durham, N.C.: Duke University Press, 1967), is invaluable. See particularly p. 57 for the statistics on French noble officers in Germany in 1758, p. 66 for officers' pay scales in Germany, p. 67 for British lieutenant-generals' and their French equivalents' ration allowances, p. 66 for relative numbers of officers in the French and Prussian armies. An excellent recent account of the French military reforms, especially tactical, just before and into the early years of the French Revolutionary Wars is John A. Lynn, *The Bayonets of the Republic: Motivation and Tactics in the Army of Revolutionary France, 1791–94* (Urbana: University of Illinois Press, 1984). See also David Bien, "The Army in the French Enlightenment: Reform, Reaction, and Revolution," *Past and*

Present: A Journal of Historical Studies, No. 85 (1979): 68–98. On contemporary tactical reforms elsewhere in Europe, focusing on Prussia but setting developments there into a wider context, see Peter Paret, *Yorck and the Era of Prussian Reform, 1807–1815* (Princeton, New Jersey: Princeton University Press, 1966).

On Guibert, see Robert R. Palmer, ch. 3, "Frederick the Great, Guibert, [Dietrich von] Bülow: From Dynastic to National War," in Edward Mead Earle, ed., with the collaboration of Gordon A. Craig and Felix Gilbert, *Makers of Modern Strategy: Military Thought from Machiavelli to Hitler* (Princeton, New Jersey: Princeton University Press, 1943), pp. 49–74, especially pp. 62–68; reprinted as ch. 4 in Peter Paret, ed., with the collaboration of Gordon A. Craig and Felix Gilbert, *Makers of Modern Strategy from Machiavelli to the Nuclear Age* (Princeton, New Jersey: Princeton University Press, 1986), pp. 71–119, especially pp. 105–113.

There are excellent background chapters on the French Army on the eve of the Revolution in: ch. 1, "All the King's Horses and the King's Men: The Royal Army," pp. 5–26, in John R. Elting, *Swords Around a Throne: Napoleon's Grande Armée* (New York: Free Press, A Division of Macmillan, Inc.; London: Collier Macmillan Publishers, 1988); ch. 2, "Armies and Warfare during the Last Years of the *Ancien Regime*," pp. 11–30, in Gunther E. Rothenberg, *The Art of Warfare in the Age of Napoleon* (Bloomington: Indiana University Press, 1978).

CHAPTER TWELVE,
THE FRENCH REVOLUTION

On the armies and campaigns of the early phases of the French Revolutionary Wars, see John A. Lynn, *The Bayonets of the Republic: Motivation and Tactics in the Army of Revolutionary France, 1791–94* (Urbana and Chicago: University of Illinois Press, 1984); Steven T. Ross, *Quest for Victory: French Military Strategy 1792–1799* (South Brunswick and New York: A. S. Barnes and Company; London: Thomas Yoseloff Ltd, 1973); ch. 2, " 'Liberté, Egalité, Fraternité': The Armies of the Revolution," in John R. Elting, *Swords around a Throne: Napoleon's Grande Armée* (New York: The Free Press, A Division of Macmillan Inc.; London: Collier Macmillan, 1988), pp. 27–54; Ramsay Weston Phipps, *The Armies of the First French Republic and the Rise of the Marshals of Napoleon I . . . ,* 5 vols. (London: Oxford University Press, 1926–1939); Gunther E. Rothenberg, *The Art of Warfare in the Age of Napoleon* (Bloomington and London: Indiana University Press, 1978), pp. 31–41; Spencer Wilkinson, *The French Army before Napoleon: Lectures delivered before the University of Oxford in Michaelmas Term, 1914* (Oxford: Clarendon Press, 1915).

On Carnot there is Marcel Reinhard, *Le Grand Carnot,* 2 vols. (Paris: Hachette, 1950–1952).

On the rise of Napoleone Buonaparte, see first Jean Alphonse Lambert Colin, *L'education militaire de Napoléon* (Paris: R. Chapelot et Cᵉ, 1900), and then for his emergence as General Bonaparte, the same author's *Études sur la campagne de 1796–97 en Italie par J. C.* (Paris: L. Baudoin, 1898); Guglielmo Ferrero, *The Gamble: Bonaparte in Italy, 1796–97,* tr. Bertha Pritchard and Lily C. Freeman (New York: Walker, 1961). See also the finest study of Napoleon as a military commander, David G. Chandler, *The Campaigns of Napoleon* (New York: The Macmillan Company, 1966).

Except for Arthur Maxime Chuquet, *Dumouriez* (Paris: Hachette & Cⁱᵉ, 1914), there are no really satisfying full-length biographies of the early generals of the French Revolution. See, however, Georges Six, *Dictionnaire biographique des généraux & admiraux français de la Révolution et de l'Empire,* Préface par le commandant André Lasseray, 2 vols. (Paris: Librairie historique et nobiliaire Georges Saffroy, 1934), and the same author's *Les généraux de la Révolution et de l'Empire* (Paris: Bordes, 1948).

For the military opponents of Revolutionary France, see especially the predictably excellent work by Gunther E. Rothenberg, *Napoleon's Great Adversaries: The Archduke Charles and the Austrian Army, 1792–1814* (Bloomington: Indiana University Press, 1982).

Indispensable to a military survey of the French Revolutionary and Napoleonic Wars is Vincent J. Esposito and John Robert Elting, *A Military History and Atlas of the Napoleonic Wars* (Compiled for the Department of Military Art and Engineering, The United States Military Academy, West Point, N.Y.; New York, Washington: Frederick A. Praeger, 1964). After a brief summary of "The Early Wars of the Revolution, 1792–94," Map 1 and facing page, it begins in detail with "The Italian Campaign," Maps 2–31 and facing pages. An equally indispensable reference work is David G. Chandler, *Dictionary of the Napoleonic Wars* (New York: Macmillan Publishing Co., Inc., 1979).

CHAPTER THIRTEEN,
SEA POWER AND EMPIRE

On the Royal Navy in the age of the French Revolution and Empire, see again Geoffrey J. Marcus, *A Naval History of England*, II, *The Age of Nelson, The Royal Navy 1793–1815* (New York: Viking Press, 1971). On the French Navy, see in addition to Ernest H. Jenkins, *A History of the French Navy: From Its Beginnings to the Present Day* (Annapolis: Naval Institute Press, 1973), ch. 15, "Matters Nautical: *La Marine*," in John R. Elting, *Swords Around a Throne: Napoleon's Grande Armée* (New York: The Free Press, A Division of Macmillan, Inc.; London: Collier Macmillan Publishers, 1988), pp. 297–312.

Oliver Warner narrates the story of *The Glorious First of June* (New York: The Macmillan Company, 1961).

On William Pitt and British strategy see John Holland Rose, *William Pitt and National Revival* (London: G. Bell and Sons, Ltd., 1911) and the same author's *William Pitt and the Great War* (London: G. Bell and Sons, Ltd., 1911). Piers Mackesy writes with his customary authority in *Statesmen at War: The Strategy of Overthrow, 1798–1799* (London, New York: Longmans, 1974) and *The War in the Mediterranean, 1803–1810* (Cambridge: Harvard University Press, 1957).

My views on Nelson's method of command have been much influenced by conversations with my former student Michael A. Palmer, historian at the U.S. Navy History Center, Washington Navy Yard, Washington, D.C.; for a brief exposition see Michael A. Palmer, "Lord Nelson: Master of Command," *Naval War College Review*, XLI, Number 1/ Sequence 321 (Winter 1988): 105–116. The best modern biography is David Walder's *Nelson: A Biography* (New York: The Dial Press/James Wade, 1978). On Nelson and his captains there is also Ludovic Kennedy, *Nelson's Captains* (New York: W. W. Norton & Company, 1951).

On the Egyptian campaign see James Christopher Herold, *Bonaparte in Egypt* (New York: Harper & Row, 1962), and Clement Étienne Marie de Taffenel, marquis de La Jonquière, *L'expedition d'Egypt, 1798–1801*, 5 vols. (Paris: H. Charles Lavauzelle, 1889–1902).

Two of the naval battles of the era are detailed in Christopher Lloyd, *St. Vincent & Camperdown* (New York: Macmillan Company, 1963). Still a sound account of Trafalgar is Sir Julian Stafford Corbett, *The Campaign of Trafalgar* (New Edition, 2 vols. (London, New York: Longmans, Green and Co., 1919). A good recent summary is ch. 1, "Trafalgar," in John Keegan, *The Price of Admiralty: The Evolution of Naval Warfare* (New York: Viking, 1989), pp. 9–95. On the naval war in the English Channel see John Leyland, ed., *Dispatches and Letters Relating to the Blockade of Brest, 1803–1805*, 2 vols. (London, New York: Longmans, 1974).

CHAPTER FOURTEEN,
THE CLIMAX OF NAPOLEONIC WAR

On the neglected Suvorov there is Philip Longworth, *The Art of Victory: The Life and Achievements of Field-Marshal Suvorov* (New York: Holt, Rinehart and Winston, 1966). On the Russian Army there is Marcel Gayda and Andre Krijitsky, *L'armée russe sous le Tsar Alexandre I, de 1805 à 1815* (Paris: Le Sabretache, 1960). On the Austrians, see again Gunther E. Rothenberg, *Napoleon's Great Adversaries: The Archduke Charles and the Austrian Army, 1792-1814* (Bloomington: Indiana University Press, 1982). On the Prussian Army, see William Oswald Shanahan, *Prussian Military Reforms, 1786-1813* (New York: Columbia University Press, 1945). For the opponents of Napoleonic France in general, a work emphasizing regiments and uniforms but also more widely informative is Richard Warner, ed., *Napoleon's Enemies* (London: Osprey Publishing, 1977).

For Napoleon's conduct of war in this period, David G. Chandler, *The Campaigns of Napoleon* (New York: The Macmillan Company, 1966), is unsurpassed; see especially part 3, "Napoleon's Art of War: A study of Napoleon's philosophy of war, an analysis of his strategic and battle methods—and the sources of his ideas," pp. 131-201; part 5, "Toward the Summit: The Conspirator and the Peacemaker: The *coup d'état* of *Brumaire* and the Italian Campaign of 1800," pp. 251-304; part 6, "The Works of Peace and the Road to War: Napoleon's Reconstruction of France and the renewed struggle with England to the formation of the Third Coalition; The creation of *La Grande Armée*," pp. 305-378; part 7, "From the Rhine to the Danube: Napoleon's Destruction of the Third Coalition," pp. 379-439; part 8, "Rossbach Avenged: The Campaign of 1806 against Prussia," pp. 441-506.

For the reorganization of Napoleon's army see again John R. Elting, *Swords Around a Throne: Napoleon's Grande Armée* (New York: The Free Press, A Division of Macmillan, Inc.; London: Collier Macmillan Publishers, 1988), especially ch. 3, "Enter la Grande Armée," pp. 55-66.

For a superb collection of essays synthesizing the most recent scholarship on *les maréchaux de l'Empire*, see David G. Chandler, ed., *Napoleon's Marshals* (New York: Macmillan Publishing Company, 1986). Also useful is Peter Young, *Napoleon's Marshals* (New York: Hippocrene Books, 1973).

Among the surprisingly few satisfactory biographies of the marshals individually are James Handyside Marshall-Cornwall, *Marshal Massena* (London, New York: Oxford University Press, 1965); Daniel Reichel, *Davout et l'art de la guerre: Recherches sur la formation, l'action pendant la Révolution et les commandements du maréchal Davout, duc d'Auerstaedt, prince d'Eckmühl, 1770-1823*, Préface de André Corvisier (Lausanne: Centre d'histoire et prospective militaire; Neuchâtel, Paris: Delachaux et Niestlé, 1975); Raymond Horricks, *Marshal Ney: The Romance and the Real* (Tunbridge Wells: Midas Books; New York: Hippocrene Books, 1982); [Guillaume Auguste Balthazar Eugène] Henri Bonnal, *La vie militaire du maréchal Ney, duc d'Elchingen, prince de la Moskowa . . .* , 3 vols. (Paris: Librairie militaire R. Chapelot et Cie, 1910-1914); Victor B. Derrecegaix, *L'maréchal Berthier, prince de Wagram & de Neufchâtel*, 2 vols. (Paris: R. Chapelot et Cie, 1904-1905).

Notable works on particular battles and campaigns include Frederick N. Maude, *The Ulm Campaign, 1905* (London: G. Allen & Company, Ltd.; New York: The Macmillan Company, 1912); Christopher Duffy, *Austerlitz 1805* (Hamden, Connecticut: Archon Books, 1977); Henry Lachouque, *Napoléon à Austerlitz*, Préface de madame la comtesse de Witt, née princesse Marie Clotilde Napoléon (Paris: G. Victor, 1961); Claude Manceron, *Austerlitz, 2 decembre 1805* (Paris: R. Laffont, 1960); English language edition, *Austerlitz: The Story of a Battle*, tr. Georg Umoi (New York: W. W. Norton & Company, Inc., 1966); [Guillaume Auguste Balthazar Eugène] Henri Bonnal, *La manœuvre de Iéna: Étude sur la stratégie de Napoléon et sa psychologie du 5 septembre au 14 octobre 1806* (Paris: R. Chapelot et Ce, 1904); Henry Lachouque, *Iéna*, Préface de S.A. le prince Achille Murat (Besançon: G. Victor, 1961); Frederick N. Maude, *The Jena Campaign, 1806* (London: S. Sonnenschein & Co. Lim.; New York: The Macmillan Company, 1909).

CHAPTER FIFTEEN, THE GRADUAL ECLIPSE
OF THE BATTLE OF ANNIHILATION; THE
RISE OF THE WAR OF ATTRITION

The campaigns of 1807-1809 lack the glamour of the Austerlitz, Jena-Auerstädt, and Waterloo campaigns; but largely because of their signaling the resurgence of resistance to Napoleon, particularly in Austria, they have generated a considerable literature.

See again David G. Chandler, *The Campaigns of Napoleon* (New York: The Macmillan Company, 1966), especially part 9, "Winter War: Napoleon's Campaigns in East Prussia and Poland, October 1806 to February 1807," pp. 507–555; part 10, "Spring Recovery: The renewed Campaign against Russia, culminating in the Battle of Friedland and the Treaty of Tilsit," pp. 557–590; part 11, "Peninsular Intrigues: The Campaigns in Poland and Spain, 1807–1809," pp. 591–660; part 12, "Hapsburgs Resurgent: The Last Success: The Danube Campaign of 1809, Culminating in the Battle of Wagram and the Peace of Schön-brunn," pp. 661–736. For the Austrians, see Gunther E. Rothenberg, *Napoleon's Great Adversaries: The Archduke Charles and the Austrian Army, 1792–1814* (Bloomington: Indiana University Press, 1982), ch. 6, "Archduke Charles and the Second Reform Period, 1806–9," pp. 103–122; ch. 7, "Archduke Charles and the War of 1809: the Ratisbon Phase," pp. 123–146; ch. 8, "The War of 1809: Aspern-Essling and Wagram," pp. 147–171.

On the opening events of the chapter, see Francis Loraine Petre, *Napoleon's Campaign in Poland, 1806–7: A Military History of Napoleon's First War with Russia, Verified from Unpublished Official Documents,* Third Edition (London: J. Lane; New York: J. Lane Company, 1901; repr., Introduction by David Chandler, New York: Hippocrene Books, 1975).

For the background to the British Army's campaigns in the Peninsula there is the excellent Richard Gilchrist Glover, *Peninsular Preparation: The Reform of the British Army 1795–1809* (Cambridge: Cambridge University Press, 1963).

A good recent history of the Napoleonic Wars in Spain and Portugal is David Gates, *The Spanish Ulcer: A History of the Peninsular War* (New York, London: W. W. Norton, 1986). Established as a standard is Michael Glover, *The Peninsular War, 1807–1814: A Concise Military History* (Newton Abbot: David & Charles; Hamden, Connecticut: Archon Books, 1974). On Sir John Moore's campaign there is David William Davies, *Sir John Moore's Peninsular Campaign, 1808–1809* (The Hague: Martinus Nijhoff, 1974).

The current standard biography of Wellington is Elizabeth [Harman Pakenham, seventh Countess of] Longford, *Wellington,* 2 vols., I, *The Years of the Sword* (New York: and Evanston: Harper & Row, Publishers, 1969; II, *Pillar of State* (New York: Evanston, San Francisco, London: Harper & Row, Publishers, 1972). See also Godfrey Davies, *Wellington and His Army* (Oxford: Blackwell, 1954).

The Peninsular War emerges as a war of attrition in Raymond Rudorff, *War to the Death: The Sieges of Saragossa, 1808–09* (New York: Macmillan Publishing Co., Inc., 1974).

On French leadership in Spain see Richard Humble, *Napoleon's Peninsular Marshals* (New York: Taplinger Publishing Company, 1973).

The standard biography of the Archduke Charles is Oskar Criste, *Erzherzog Carl von Österreich: Ein Lebensbild im Auftrage seiner Enkel, der Herren Erzherzoge Friedrich und Eugen,* 3 vols. (Vienna and Leipzig: W. Braumüller, 1912). A more critical recent work is Manfried Rauchensteiner, *Kaiser Franz und Erzherzog Carl: Dynastie und Heerwesen in Österreich, 1796–1809* (Vienna: Verlag für Geschichte und Politik, 1972). For recent reflections on the generalship and strategic thought of Archduke Charles, see Joszef Zacher, "Die Frage des Verteidigungskrieges im Gebirgsland in den Schriften Erzherzog Carls," and Manfried Rauchensteiner, "Erzherzog Carl und der Begrenzte Krieg," in Manfried Rauchensteiner, ed., *Clausewitz, Jomini, Erzherzog Carl: Eine geistige Trilogie des 19. Jahrhunderts und ihre Bedeutung für die Gegenwart: Johann Christoph Allmayer-Beck zum 70. Geburtstag* (Vienna: Österreichischer Bundesverlag, 1988), pp. 129–148, 149–167.

Because of the implications for Austrian military revival and French decline there is a considerable literature on the campaign of Aspern and Wagram. See especially Robert M. Epstein, *Prince Eugene at War: 1809: A Study of the Role of Prince Eugene de Beauharnais in the Franco-Austrian War of 1809* (Arlington, Texas: Empire Games Press, 1984); August Menge, *Die Schlacht von Aspern am 21. und 22. Mai 1809: Eine Erläuterung der Kriegführung Napoleons I und des Erzherzogs Carl von Österreich* (Berlin: G. Stilke, 1900); Francis Loraine Petre, *Napoleon and the Archduke Charles: A History of the Franco-Austrian Campaign in the Danube Valley in 1809* (London: J. Lane; New York: J. Lane Company, 1909 [1908];

reprinted London: Arms and Armour Press; New York: Hippocrene Books, 1976); Manfried Rauchensteiner, *Die Schlacht von Aspern am 21. und 22. Mai 1809*, Militärhistorische Schriftenreihe Heft 11 (Vienna: Österreichischer Bundesverlag, 1969), and the same author's *Die Schlacht bei Deutsch Wagram am 5. und 6. Juli 1809*, Militärhistorische Schriftenreihe Heft 36 (Vienna: Österreichischer Bundesverlag, 1977).

CHAPTER SIXTEEN, CAMPAIGNS OF EXHAUSTION AND ATTRITION

On the Iberian Campaign, see again David Gates, *The Spanish Ulcer: A History of the Peninsular War* (New York: London: W. W. Norton & Company, 1986), and Michael Glover, *The Peninsular War, 1807-1814: A Concise Military History* (Newton Abbot: David & Charles; Hamden, Conn.: Archon Books, 1974).

For the invasion of Russia, see David G. Chandler, *The Campaigns of Napoleon* (New York: The Macmillan Company, 1966), parts 13 and 14, "The Road to Moscow: The first part of Napoleon's Russian Campaign, June 22 to September 15, 1812," and "Retreat: The second part of Napoleon's Russian Campaign, September 16, 1812 to January 1813," pp. 737–810, 811–861. Standard accounts include Reginald George Burton, *Napoleon's Invasion of Russia* (London: G. Allen & Company, Ltd.; New York: The Macmillan Company, 1914); Daria Olivier, *L'incendie de Moscou (15 septembre 1812)* (Paris: R. Laffont, 1964); English language edition, *The Burning of Moscow, 1812*, tr. Michael Heron (New York: Thomas Y. Crowell, 1967); Alan Warwick Palmer, *Napoleon in Russia* (New York: Simon and Schuster, 1967). On the most spectacular battle of the invasion there is Christopher Duffy, *Borodino and the War of 1812* (New York: Charles Scribner's Sons, 1973).

For Prussia's reversal of alliances see Peter Paret, *Yorck and the Era of Prussian Reform, 1807-1815* (Princeton, New Jersey: Princeton University Press, 1966), pp. 192–195.

CHAPTER SEVENTEEN, THE RESURGENCE OF MILITARY PROFESSIONALISM

On the Prussian military reforms after 1806, Gordon A. Craig, *The Politics of the Prussian Army, 1640-1945* (New York and Oxford: Oxford University Press, 1956), pp. 37–52, is superb, as is Peter Paret, *Yorck and the Era of Prussian Reform, 1807-1815* (Princeton, New Jersey: Princeton University Press, 1966). For Austrian military reform and preparations, see Gunther E. Rothenberg, *Napoleon's Great Adversaries: The Archduke Charles and the Austrian Army, 1792-1814* (Bloomington: Indiana University Press, 1982), pp. 172–178.

On the formation of the new alliance against Napoleon, see Gordon A. Craig, *Problems of Coalition Warfare: The Military Alliance against Napoleon, 1813-1815* [Lieutenant General Hubert Reilly] Harmon Memorial Lectures in Military History, Number Seven, (Colorado: United States Air Force Academy, 1965); repr. in Gordon A. Craig, *War, Politics, and Diplomacy: Selected Essays* (New York: Frederick A. Praeger, Publisher, 1966), pp. 22–45, and in Harry R. Borowski, ed., *The Harmon Memorial Lectures in Military History, 1959-1987: A Collection of the First Thirty Harmon Lectures Given at the United States Air Force Academy*, Special Studies (Washington, D.C.: Office of Air Force History United States Air Force, 1988), pp. 325–346.

Again see David G. Chandler, *The Campaigns of Napoleon* (New York: The Macmillan Company, 1966), particularly part 15, "Twilight: The Struggle of the Nations: Napoleon's attempts to hold Germany and destroy the Allies, culminating in the heavy defeat sustained at the Battle of Leipzig," pp. 863–941, and part 16, " 'La Patrie en Danger': The Campaign of 1814, culminating in Napoleon's abdication," pp. 943–1004.

Another excellent work by Francis Loraine Petre covers *Napoleon's Last Campaign in Germany, 1813* (London: John Lane; New York: John Lane Company, 1912; repr., London: Arms & Armour Press; New York: Hippocrene Books, 1974). See also James Philip Lawford, *Napoleon: The Last Campaigns, 1813-15* (New York: Crown Publishers, 1977).

The literature on the battle of Leipzig is less extensive than might be expected. See *Europe against Napoleon: The Leipzig Campaign, 1813, From Eyewitness Accounts,* ed. and tr. Antony Brett-Jones (London: Macmillan, Ltd., 1970).

CHAPTER EIGHTEEN,
THE DOWNFALL OF GENIUS

See again David Gates, *The Spanish Ulcer: A History of the Peninsular War* (New York, London: W. W. Norton Company, 1986); Michael Glover, *The Peninsular War, 1807–1814: A Concise Military History* (Newton Abbot: David & Charles; Hamden, Connecticut: Archon Books, 1974); Elizabeth [Harman Pakenham, seventh Countess of] Longford, *Wellington,* 2 vols., I, *The Years of the Sword* (New York and Evanston: Harper & Row, Publishers, 1969); II, *Pillar of State* (New York, Evanston, San Francisco, London: Harper & Row, Publishers, 1972).

On Salamanca in particular, see Peter Young and James Philip Lawford, *Wellington's Masterpiece: The Battle and Campaign of Salamanca* (London: Allen and Unwin, 1972).

On the conclusion of the Peninsular War there is Paul Marie Joseph Vidal de la Blache (usually catalogued under Vidal), *L'évacuation de l'Espagne et l'invasion dans le Midi (juin 1813–avril 1814),* 2 vols. (Paris: Berger-Levrault, 1914).

As the finale of the Age of Battles and of Napoleonic war, and as an event particularly important in the military history of Great Britain, the campaign and battle of Waterloo have nourished an exceptionally rich literature, especially in English. For Waterloo as the British soldier experienced it, John Keegan, *The Face of Battle* (New York: Viking Press, 1976), ch. 3, "Waterloo, June 18th, 1815," pp. 117–203, is not to be missed. An opulently illustrated volume is Henry Lachouque, *Waterloo, 1815,* Conception et présentation, Juan Carlos Carmigniani; Préface, Jean François Chiappe; Illustrations, baron Louis de Beaufort; Cartes de Jean-Claude Quennevat (Paris: Stock, 1972); English language edition, *Waterloo,* Visual conception by Juan Carlos Carmigniani, Uniform plates by Baron Louis de Beaufort, Maps by Jean-Claude Quennevat, Introduction by David G. Chandler (London: Arms and Armour Press, 1975).

For an emphasis more specifically on command, see David G. Chandler, *The Campaigns of Napoleon* (New York: The Macmillan Company, 1966), part 17, "The Campaign of the Hundred Days: Napoleon's return from exile and the Events leading to his final abdication," pp. 1005–1095, and Elizabeth [Harman Pakenham, seventh Countess of] Longford, *Wellington,* 2 vols., I, *The Years of the Sword* (New York and Evanston: Harper & Row, Publishers, 1969); II, *Pillar of State* (New York, Evanston, San Francisco, London: Harper & Row, Publishers, 1972), I, part 3, pp. 391–491.

See also *The Hundred Days, Napoleon's Last Campaign from Eyewitness Accounts,* Compiled, Edited, and Translated by Antony Brett-Jones (New York: St. Martin's Press, 1964); David Armine Howarth, *Waterloo: Day of Battle* (New York: Atheneum, 1968); Jac Weller, *Wellington at Waterloo* (New York: Thomas Y. Crowell, 1967); Archibald Frank Becke, *Napoleon and Waterloo: The Emperor's Campaign with the Armée du Nord, 1815,* Revised Edition, Mainly Re-written (London: K. Paul, Trench, Trübner & Co., Ltd., 1936); John Naylor, *Waterloo* (New York: The Macmillan Company, 1960).

INDEX